TRUMAN

TRUMAN

THE RISE TO POWER

Richard Lawrence Miller

McGRAW-HILL BOOK COMPANY

New York   St. Louis   San Francisco   Bogotá
Guatemala   Hamburg   Lisbon   Madrid
Panama   Paris
Tokyo   Toronto

Appreciation is expressed for permission to quote from the following sources: Elizabeth Paxton Forsling, "Remembering Delaware Street," *Jackson County Historical Society Journal,* May 1962 and November 1963, reprinted by permission of the Jackson County Historical Society; Harry S. Truman, *Year of Decisions* (New York: Doubleday & Co., 1955), reprinted by permission of Margaret Truman Daniel.

123456789DOCDOC8765

ISBN 0-07-042185-4

LIBRARY OF CONGRESS CATALOGING-IN-PUBLICATION DATA

Miller, Richard Lawrence.
  Truman: the Missouri heritage.

  Bibliography: p.
  Includes index.
  1. Truman, Harry S., 1884–1972. 2. Presidents—United States—Biography. – I. Title.
  E814.M55 1986   973.918′092′4 [B]   85-12842
  ISBN 0-07-042185-4

Book design by Beth Tondreau

To
Liz Safly

Contents

Preface

At the start of this research project I shared the popular perception of Truman as a down-home sort of character with a refreshing honesty that seems absent from politics today. After going into the matter thoroughly I now view him as a professional big-city machine politician, involved in shady personal and political dealings. Yet he was different from many of his corrupt colleagues, not only in that he avoided prison or assassination, but in his sense of the future—a direction in which he felt his county, state, and nation should go. Truman was politically ambitious, but it wasn't blind ambition. He had a social conscience and exercised his power not only on behalf of sordid cronies but for the good (as he perceived it) of all citizens.

In researching this book I discovered that there is a "Truman Establishment" that is very uneasy about investigations into his role with the Pendergast machine. These self-appointed keepers of Truman's reputation do both him and the nation a disservice. They do Truman a disservice by portraying him as an almost saccharine figure, a portrayal that trivializes his painful struggles to balance his duties as a machine politician with the obligations he felt toward citizens. They harm the nation by leading citizens to believe we should reject out-of-hand the services of persons with questionable business and political associates.

Acknowledgments

The Harry S. Truman Library Institute, after initially refusing to provide any support at all, finally granted $500 to finance the research and writing of this book. Major funding came instead from Patricia J. Schneider and Mary Jeanne O'Halloran, who grew up in Kansas City and believed the true story of Harry Truman should be told.

Bess, why am I an enigma? I try to be just what I am and tell the truth about as much as the average person.

—Harry S. Truman, November 1913

TRUMAN

Chapter 1

MOVING TOWARD INDEPENDENCE

Harry Truman was born into a world in which humankind knew it was governed by nature, not man. Rural people worked hard and played gently. They read newspapers with claims of alarums in the land, but saw no evidence of them in their lives. Life was hard but calm. Time flowed like a broad river.

Gone was the Missouri frontier, and gone were its pioneers. Yes, there were old folks who remembered, but they were now former pioneers. The pioneer era was locked inside them, and could be seen no more. Their children were the men and women of the 1880s whose task was not to conquer a world, but to hold onto one.

Such was the work of John Anderson Truman and Martha Ellen Young ("Mattie") when their son Harry was born. It was the second pregnancy and first child of a marriage not yet three years old, yet the parents were not young and inexperienced. Both were in their thirties.

Many are the paths to happiness, and Harry's beloved "mamma" found hers. "If you get married, you ought to stay home and take care of your babies and the home," she said. Such a life is not for every woman, nor even for every mother, but no complaints are recorded from Mattie. She knew of alternatives—her career-minded sister-in-law Mary Martha Truman was a living example. Mattie herself had possessed sufficient intellectual curiosity and family wealth to attend the Ladies Baptist College of Lexington, Missouri. "One of the best teachers I ever had was Mrs. A. J. Warren, a Yankee, but she was good and she was smart. I took drawing lessons from her sister, Miss Babcock. I liked going to parties and horseback riding." There were monthly dances at the college. Mattie laughingly described herself as a lightfoot Baptist. "If anything makes me angry, it is the statement that I am overly religious," she said later. After her college years there were dances three nights a week in the parlors of neighboring farmers. Mattie would arrive on horseback from across the unfenced fields. "Of course I rode sidesaddle!" "I'm strictly opposed to women wearing trousers. Girls look just . . . terrible in trousers." Friends remembered her as feisty from antebellum childhood until her old age in the atomic era. She lived as a homemaker, and preferred it that way.[1]

Many men might have been overpowered by intimate contact with the surging personality of Martha Ellen Young. She chose the indomitable John Anderson Truman, who had been born into comfortable financial circumstances. One of his sisters remarked that "there were no common people" among their neighbors. The young bucks held jousts, using lances. Harry's cousin Ethel Noland related:

> The Southern people liked Sir Walter Scott, and they all knew their Scott, better perhaps than Shakespeare. An annual social event of the neighborhood was a tournament on May Day, in which the young men rode pell-mell, as you do in tournaments, armed with spears, by means of which they tried to take rings off an overhanging arm that stuck out over the race course. . . . The knights were named after their favorite characters in Scott's poems and novels, such as The Knight of Snowdon, James Fitz-James, Ivanhoe, and so on. If a young man didn't have a good horse, it would be like a young man not having a car in this day and age, and they all had good horses, Kentucky stock, because they all had come from Kentucky.

This was rural Missouri, but not the dirt farmer crowd. The Trumans had slaves for dirty work. A family member later reported that Anderson Shipp Truman, John's father, had five slaves, but they were women, and not good for much work. Some of these females married slaves belonging to other households, but the children were owned by Truman.[2]

By the time of John's marriage to Mattie, his energy could no longer be confined by the sky and the prairie and the seasons. He wanted to engage in trade, and make his fortune. He started as a horse and mule trader, an occupation with the same reputation that used car selling would have a century later. The choice of careers surprised John's father, who noted that no one believed a horse trader even when he told the truth.[3]

A few months after his marriage, it was said that John "sold out" in Jackson County, and moved far south to Lamar, Missouri. Whether "sold out" refers to farming or animal trading is unclear. Nor do we know why John chose the tiny, distant town of Lamar. What is clear is that when he and Mattie first stepped from a carriage (lent by her wealthy father) onto the streets of Lamar, they arrived with a grubstake that John had already earned, or had perhaps received from his father, who moved to Lamar with them. John's sister Mary Martha arrived in town a few months later, having been invited by her father and brother when they first arrived.[4]

The grubstake money allowed the Trumans to acquire a newly built house of their own in November 1882, a feat few newlyweds could accomplish even a century later. East end of town, on a street with no name, four rooms downstairs, two "headstooping" bedrooms upstairs, white clapboard, 20 x 28 feet, $685. No closets, attic, or basement. Well, smokehouse, and toilet all outside.

Harry Truman greeted the world from his mother's bedroom at 4:00 P.M., May 8, 1884. Mattie did the work, and the attending physician, W. L. Griffin, socked the father with a $15.00 fee. In celebration of the birth John nailed a mule shoe over the door of the house, and planted a pine seedling that grew straight and tall in the yard. The parents were less prompt about recording the birth with the state government—they did it on June 5 (and no one got around to adding that the white male's name was Harry until 1942). The oft-told story is that the future president was named for his uncle Harrison; the shortened version "Harry" was adopted as a family compromise. Likewise the middle letter "S" was a compromise to mollify the two grandfathers, Solomon Young and Anderson Shipp Truman. Seemingly small points, but persons caught in such controversies know otherwise.[5]

Two days after the big event the Baptist circuit rider Rev. Washington Pease came to visit. Harry was entrusted to the arms of the preacher, who took him outside as far as the gate, where he lifted the infant upward toward the sun and pronounced him fit.[6]

In March 1883 John spent $200 acquiring the lot diagonally across the street for a horse and mule business. In the sale barn John was becoming known as one of the slickest mule traders Lamar had ever seen, with operations extending to Springfield, Joplin, and St. Louis. Trade was adequate, with dozens of animals passing through the Truman sale barn every week. John was called "the kind of a man who never passed a cow but what he stopped and tried to buy her." A sharp deal might take half a day, with neither John nor his customers hesitating to do some skinning.

Dickering over prices accompanied dickering about Democrat politics. The atmosphere was one of masculine gossip. Women could not vote. The $75.00 bet John won on the presidential election in November 1884 had less to do with savvy than with the party loyalty of a red-hot Democrat. The loser in the bet, Republican lawyer Sam Van Poll, paid off in promissory notes. Years later Van Poll recalled that John received little, if any, of the cash, which no doubt reinforced John's estimation of Republicans. It's doubtful that Sam Van Poll ever chuckled about this to the quick-tempered Truman's face. Townsfolk described John as a sport who would knock your hat off as a prank, and knock your head off if you crossed him. One of Harry's friends remembered John as "tough. That's where that hickory comes from, you know, that's the old man. . . . If he wanted to do something, he would do it, and he'd just as soon take you out in the middle of the street and prove it to you."[7]

In late March 1885 John sold his house for $1,600, and moved his business, himself, Harry, his wife Big Mat, his sister Little Matt, and his father to Harrisonville, Missouri. The move has been glibly blamed on the failure of the Lamar mule-trading business. In reality the trading operation was yielding a fair, if unremarkable, living for the Truman family. There are any number of reasons for relocating a business, particularly this type of business. Perhaps John was feeling restless, or perhaps his travels buying and driving stock had suggested that Harrisonville would be more profitable, or perhaps his wife wanted to be closer to her parents. At any rate, he didn't leave Lamar as a penniless, busted tradesman. He arrived in Harrisonville with enough capital to reestablish himself in the very same business.[8]

On arriving in Harrisonville the Truman clan immediately took sick with colds. John and Harry worsened, and the two Truman women wore themselves out in frantic nursing. "Baby is real sick now, he is so cross we can't do anything," said Little Matt. The nursing, kind neighbors, "the cutest Dr.," an "awful nice" druggist, hop bitters, and time effected cures. The father had been "*very* sick for almost three weeks."[9]

The stay in Harrisonville was brief, and this time the mule and horse business really may have failed. John moved northward again, still closer to the old Truman and Young homesteads, and began raising corn. The family lived on the Dye farm, about five miles southeast of Belton, near Peculiar, Missouri. Isaac P. Dye had gone prospecting, and he rented his seventy-one acres to the Trumans. Little Matt was no longer with them, but another family member arrived in April 1886, Harry's younger brother John Vivian. The house was on a hilltop, facing south, with two stories and nine rooms.[10]

Harry's maternal grandmother Harriet Louisa Young watched with glee one day as he chased a frog around the backyard. Supposedly she cautioned the boy against hurting the frog. He slapped his knees and laughed loudly each time the frog hopped. This small incident is noteworthy because it was Harry's first conscious memory, and because Grandmother Young viewed it as displaying a remarkable sense of humor in a two-year-old who had a reputation for gravity and seriousness. Another time he was poking a stick at toads, and then he followed a dog out of the yard and down a corn row. His mother was not alarmed that the toddler would be lost in the cornfield, saying the dog would come back and lead someone to Harry. She knew the sturdiness of small boys. Her favorite brother, Harrison, came to visit his new nephew Vivian, and wanted Harry to see something going on outside the house. Harry remembered his mother dropping him from an upstairs window into his uncle's arms. The distance was probably less dramatic than the memory.[11]

Harrison Young was a bear, taller than six feet and weighing over two hundred pounds—"strong as a wrestler." A handsome, lifelong bachelor, a master storyteller, and "genius at games of chance," Harry recalled. Harrison's two nephews often visited the Young farm at Grandview, Missouri, where the uncle had a box of jew's harps that Harry's mother passed out to area children as treats. Harrison was fond of both nephews, particularly his namesake Harry, teaching him checkers, seven up, and cooncan. Any occasion might prompt a story from the uncle about his life in the West and in old Jackson County. Sitting under an old pine, the uncle asked Harry why he was headed into the field of white corn. Harry explained he was after ears for roasting and corn pudding, a specialty of the cook. Harrison asked the boy

> if I knew what was the record number of ears of corn a man had eaten at one sitting. Of course I didn't and he proceeded to tell me about a pal of his who had made the record on a bet by eating 13 roasting ears. Then this pal cultivated a severe stomach ache and had to send for the doctor. The doctor worked over him most of the night and then told him he'd better send for the preacher and do a little praying because medical aid was at an end.
>
> Well, the man was in such pain he finally sent for the parson and the good man prayed for him; he was very earnestly told that he'd have to pray for himself. He told the preacher that he was not a praying man and didn't think he could do it. However the extremity was so great that he finally decided to make the attempt.
>
> So he got down on his knees in the old-fashioned revival manner and this was his petition to the Almighty:
>
> "Oh Lord, I am in great pain and misery. I have eaten 13 roasting ears and I don't seem to be able to take care of them. I am praying to you for help, and Lord I'm not like the damned howling church members in the amen corner; if you'll relieve me of seven of these damned ears of corn I'll try to wrastle around the other six."[12]

This was the genial old uncle Harry loved. But Harrison also had a dark side, a brutal temper that could become deadly. He once tried to kill his brother Will in a saloon fight at Grandview. Will fled to their aunt Mary's place to convalesce from the gunshot wounds.[13]

Harrison liked to divide his time between the family farm in Grandview and the bright lights of Kansas City. His father Solomon was too old to manage the farm by himself, and found Harrison's help too uncertain. So he asked his son-in-law John to manage the property. John agreed, and in March 1887 moved his family to the

Grandview farm. Moving in with the in-laws is often considered a sign of bad luck, but in this case it turned out well.

Solomon Young was not the wealthiest man in Missouri, but at a certain point additional money has no effect on one's lifestyle. Solomon had already made, lost, and regained several fortunes. The supplies he sold to his Masonic brother and his distant relative Brigham Young helped the Mormons open the West. Solomon owned between 40,000 and 120,000 acres near Sacramento before the Civil War, and drove cattle from Missouri into the West. Grandview children were frightened of these animals with normal bodies but long horns.

Solomon wanted to settle on his veritable kingdom in California, but his Kentucky-born wife Louisa said Missouri was wild enough for her. So they built their mansion on the five thousand acres they owned in Jackson County. No photos survive, but a granddaughter who lived there said the wooden house was like Tara in *Gone With the Wind*. From the spacious veranda on the north side a visitor stepped through the front door into a wide central hall with a large room on either side. A piano graced the parlor. From that hall a grand staircase ascended to the upper floor that contained bedrooms. Each room had a fireplace. The dining room was at the back of the house, and a covered walkway led to the separate kitchen and smokehouse. Additional small buildings were quarters for the couple dozen or so slaves. They strung catgut across their open windows, and the haunting tones of aeolian harps provided background music for life in the mansion.

At Louisa Young's insistence the entire antebellum family gathered promptly for meals. A slave waved a fan to keep insects from the dining table. Afterward Louisa supervised cleanup by the slaves, who put the washed dishes on long wooden racks to dry in the sun. The Young daughters (including Harry's mother) sewed and mended, and the boys worked the fields and cared for livestock. A slave wet nurse cared for the Young babies.

Solomon ruled his family, with son Harrison sharing power as he grew older. They disapproved daughter Ada's choice for a husband in 1872, forcibly removing her from the man she loved by sending her to her aunt (presumably Hettie Powell) in St. Louis. But in 1878 no effort was made to stop Ada's marriage to bank president Joseph Van Cloostere of Murphysboro, Illinois.[14]

By the time John moved his family to Grandview in March 1887, the Young slaves had been replaced by hired help, and the property had been reduced from thousands of acres to hundreds. Still, from this high ground John could see Lawrence, Kansas, forty miles to the west, Lee's Summit to the east, Belton to the south, and Kansas City to the north. Standing in front of the mansion, scanning the vistas before him, he could hardly have felt like a terrible failure as he took over his in-laws' domain.

As a business proposition, the main Young farm was 440 acres on one side of the road, and 160 acres on the other. Four miles away was another Young farm of nine hundred to one thousand acres, also supervised by John. Wheat, corn, oats, and clover were the crops; cattle, mules, hogs, and sheep were the commercial animals. Young Harry began to learn farming: "I became familiar with every sort of animal on the farm and watched the wheat harvest, the threshing and the corn shucking, mowing and stacking hay, and every evening at suppertime heard my father tell a dozen farm hands what to do and how to do it."[15]

Solomon was quite taken by Harry, continually telling folks that there was something remarkable about his grandson. One day the patriarch was sick. Harry cautiously drew near the bed, and asked his grandfather how he felt. Solomon "transfixed him with those bold pioneer eyes of his and said sternly, 'How are *you* feeling? You're the one I'm worried about.' " Actually, the old man's question was sensible enough without implying that he foresaw any destiny of greatness for Harry. At the Young farm the boy managed to break his collarbone by falling off a chair while combing his hair! In the very same room Harry nearly died while eating a peach. He swallowed the pit, which caught partway down and cut off the opening to his windpipe. His mother jammed the pit down his gullet with her finger, and saved his life.[16]

Solomon was famed as a breeder of riding and buggy horses. He took good care of these animals, and they were known to live past a quarter century. Solomon took Harry for "countless" buggy rides behind the high-steppers. What they talked about is largely unrecorded, but Harry jotted down one fragment decades later: "My old Grandpa Young told me that a scrub never outgrew his parentage and the white trash would remain just that no matter how much money and education they obtained. I used to doubt it, but I fear the old man was more nearly right than I." Solomon was considered a great judge of horseflesh, and in this capacity was called to the county fair in Belton. He took Harry with him, in a big two-wheeled cart with high wheels, pulled by a strawberry roan. For six days straight Harry sat in the judges' stand with Grandpa when the races were called, ate striped candy and peanuts, and (Harry wrote much later) had "the best time a kid ever had."[17]

Solomon's attentions included his other grandson, Vivian, who, Harry recalled, "had lovely long curls. Grandpa and I cut off his curls one day by putting him in a highchair out on the south porch. Mamma was angry enough to spank us both, but she had such respect for her father that she only frowned at him." Nor were Solomon's attentions limited to the boys. He let his granddaughter Suda sit on his lap and comb his flowing beard. Yet it was with Harry that this big man, strong as a mule team, shared something special.[18]

His other grandfather, who also doted on him, Harry seems to have known less well. This was partly because the mild-mannered Anderson Shipp Truman died when Harry was only three, while Solomon lived another six years. Harry remembered Grandfather Truman as "a dignified, pleasant man." When the Truman clan moved to the Young spread, Anderson sold his nearby farm and moved into the Young residence. "He had a bedroom upstairs," Harry recalled. "He spent a lot of his time there. Believe me, you didn't go into it without an invitation." In early summer Grandfather Truman came down with dysentery, which worsened rapidly. His children were summoned to the dying man's bedside. Harry's Aunt Emma came from her farm about four miles northeast. Aunt Ella came from Independence. Aunt Matt was there, too. (Harry fondly remembered each of her happier visits as "an event, sure enough. She taught us all sorts of outdoor games.") Grandfather Truman was sick only four days before he died. Harry later wrote, "I . . . was very curious about what was happening." After the last moments Harry heard one of his aunts say, "He's gone." Harry ran to the bed and yanked the beard of the corpse, trying to awaken it. The burial was the next day, July 4. Harry later wrote, "Grandpa Truman was a grand man and petted me a great deal. He was a strong Baptist and violently anti-Catholic."[19]

Toward the end of his own life Harry Truman reflected on his grandfathers. "To be honest, I didn't like either of the old men very much at the time. But when I looked back as an adult, my respect and affection for them grew with every passing year. Half of everything I became I owe to them."[20]

His grandmother Mary Jane Truman died before his parents married. His grandmother Harriet Louisa Young, however, lived with them on the Grandview farm. The small, wrinkled old woman would sit by the stove, a shawl around her shoulders, and her grandchildren fought over the honor of lighting her pipe. Harry remembered her wonderful cookies. She must have been warm-hearted; she adopted homeless children into her household. Several lived there with Harry.[21]

Harry and Vivian had the run of the six hundred acres surrounding the mansion, and they often went past the maple grove to the beautiful bluegrass meadow of the south pasture. The boys were followed everywhere by Tandy, the black-and-tan dog, and Bob, the Maltese gray cat. Harry remembered: "The old cat was named Bob, because one day when he was asleep in front of the big fireplace in the dining room a coal of fire popped out, lit on the end of his tail, and burned off about an inch of it. I can well remember his yowls, and I can see him yet as he ran up the corner of the room all the way to the ceiling." Tandy was hardly bigger than Bob, and Harry enjoyed watching them comically chase field mice.[22]

Solomon was partial to maples. The maple grove "was row on row of beautiful maple trees, a quarter of a mile long and six rows wide," Harry wrote. Harry and Vivian received a red wagon, and with their pal John Chancellor (or Chandler) took turns pulling one another in the wagon through the grove. "We discovered a mud hole at the end of the grove, and I pulled the wagon with the two boys in it into the hole and upset it. It seemed a good thing to do, and it was repeated several times, taking turn about. When my mother found us, we were plastered with mud and dirty water from head to foot." Harry's role as ringleader was discovered: "What a spanking I received. I can feel it yet! Every stitch of clothes on all three of us had to be changed, scrubbed and dried, and so did we!"[23]

Mattie Truman kept a slipper or switch handy; but John, despite a quick temper, apparently never struck his children. Harry claimed that his father's verbal scoldings "hurt worse than a good spanking." An example: "My father bought me a beautiful black Shetland pony and the grandest saddle to ride him with I ever saw." Harry rode all over the farm on this pony, beside John's big horse. "He'd lead my pony and I felt perfectly safe—but one day coming down the north road toward the house I fell off the pony." John refused to slow down, and left his son to walk a half mile back home, crying. The father said Harry ought to stay on foot if he couldn't stay on the pony at a walk. "I learned a lesson," Harry later wrote.[24]

Solomon's half-sister Hettie (or Hetty) Powell visited every year from St. Louis. She took Harry and Vivian on a journey to the back pasture, which young Harry thought was something of an expedition (it was really only half a mile). There "we would hunt birds' nests in the tall prairie grass and gather daisies, prairie wildflowers, and wild strawberries. When we returned to the house we'd require a good scrubbing and a long nap."[25]

Uncle Harrison occasionally came from the seemingly distant Kansas City. Harry later wrote, "He would bring Vivian and me the most wonderful things to play with and all kinds of candy, nuts, and fruit. When he came it was just like Christmas."[26]

Harry also remembered the passing seasons:

In the fall, when the apples and peaches were ripe, they were picked, the peaches dried and the apples buried in the ground with straw and boards above them. In midwinter the apples would be dug up, and were they good! My mother and grandmother dried a lot of peaches and apples, and what fine pies they would make in the winter. There were peach butter, apple butter, grape butter, jellies and preserves, all made in the kitchen by Mama, Grandma, and the German hired girl. All were good cooks. [Actually Harry's mother and grandmother left most of the cooking to servants.]

Later, after the fall freeze, came hog-killing time, with sausages, souse, pickled pigs' feet, and the rendering of lard in a big iron kettle in the smokehouse.[27] . . . My mother and grandmother worked over the sausage and the rendering of the lard. They had a recipe for rendering lard that caused it to become just as white as snow and to keep forever. They stored it in large tin cans and fixed some of the sausage . . . in jars . . . , and then they would put the rest of it in sacks and smoke it with the hams and bacon.[28]

The Trumans weren't trapped on the farm by any means. They visited relatives in Independence, such as John's sister Margaret Ellen Noland and her family. Ethel Noland recounted one visit:

> I remember Harry's mother playing the piano for us and she played some things that were for the benefit of the older members of the family—for us she played things she thought we would like, and one . . . I can recall, was "Little Brown Jug" and she not only played it, but she sang it to our delight. . . . Harry and Vivian were there and Vivian must have been very tiny—not even two, but Harry must have been four, and I was four and a half. But I remember Vivian scratched his fingernail on something and Harry said "Oh, Vivian, don't, you make me stingy!"
>
> The grown people laughed and I didn't know what made them laugh but I afterwards knew that he meant "scringe."[29]

The summer of 1889 saw two notable events in Harry Truman's life. In July the family went to an Independence Day observance in Grandview. That night Harry jumped as each rocket whooshed aloft, but paid no attention to the colorful fireworks display overhead. He couldn't see it. Mattie was already concerned that her older son couldn't make out an approaching buggy or a cow across the pasture. The fireworks incident made her resolve to take Harry to a doctor immediately, without waiting for her husband to return from a business trip. The family physician was Dr. Charlie Lester (son of the Civil War–era family physician). He apparently advised Mattie to take Harry to an eye doctor in Kansas City, one Dr. Thompson, Lester's brother-in-law. Mother and son rode off to Kansas City in a farm wagon.

Harry's impaired vision has been described both as nearsightedness and farsightedness, but the symptoms certainly suggest nearsightedness. The doctor prescribed very thick spectacles, a prescription that Harry said remained almost the same throughout his life. That suggests the affliction wasn't ordinary nearsightedness. The doctor warned the five-year-old boy against physical sports that might endanger his very expensive glasses, a warning Harry took to heart. "I was afraid my eyes would get knocked out if there was too much of a rough and tumble play." Yet he felt that his world expanded rather than diminished—he could see things he had never seen before. For instance, he discovered that the family Bible (which he had begun to read with his mother's help at age four) had fine print in addition to the large. Despite the corrected vision, "I've been 'fine printed' many a time since," Harry later said ruefully.[30]

The other notable event occurred in August when Harry and Vivian heard animallike cries from upstairs in the grand house. They believed they had a new pet, but their father explained they actually had a new sister, Mary Jane.

Harry was now nearing school age, and his mother (who had attended college) was concerned that her children receive a good education. She wanted them to attend the city schools. This was a major family decision, as city schooling meant that John would have to leave his job as manager of his in-laws' property. No family rancor is recorded about this, and the move itself indicates that John put family ahead of job. The partnership between him and Solomon Young was dissolved, and in 1890 the Trumans moved to Independence, Missouri.[31]

Chapter 2
SCHOOL DAYS

Independence, Missouri, was already aquainted with the Truman clan. Among the assorted relatives left behind at the Young farm was a first cousin of Harry, Solomon Chiles. In Harry's sunny memories of his childhood on the farm, this teenager "really made life pleasant for us." Others remembered Sol Chiles's mean temper and how after an outburst he would break down and weep. In this the son was but a faint shadow of his father James.[1]

A hardy man who "could ride like a cowpuncher," Harry's uncle James J. Chiles appreciated fine horseflesh, and cut a fine figure astride a black thoroughbred sauntering through Independence. After the Civil War Chiles retained his slaves Jane, Ira, and John as servants. When Martha Ellen Young wanted to go dancing despite her father Solomon's opposition, she simply traveled to Independence to visit her brother-in-law James and her sister Sallie. A relative wrote, "Sallie even loaned Mattie one of her more sophisticated dresses to wear." Not only was James J. Chiles son-in-law to the wealthy Solomon Young, Chiles was kin to such influential men as John Franklin Chiles (once owner of forty slaves) and former Jackson County presiding judge Richard B. Chiles. If family connections meant anything, James J. Chiles was a man the town could respect.[2]

Despite these connections, Harry's uncle Jim was not a man the townspeople admired. Quite the contrary. He was short tempered by nature, and the fuse disappeared completely when he was liquored up. In this state he became a fiend, imagining insults to his honor, and punishing offenders with a blacksnake whip and a pair of cap-and-ball dragoon pistols. Now, as long as Jim confined himself to blowing holes through black citizens and rounding them up at gunpoint for forced labor, the good townspeople of Independence could tolerate his obnoxious behavior. His "coon hunting" helped maintain his nickname, "Jim Crow" Chiles. Trouble arose when other toughs in town began to rally around him. They rode together shooting out windows. White folks minding their own business behind these windows began turning up injured and dead. The good townspeople decided they had had enough of Jim, and dealt with him the way Missouri towns were dealing with such folks over a century later.[3]

Jim Crow was used to citizens trying to keep out of his way. So he may not have felt there was an unusually large "free fire" zone around him on that September Sunday. He may have been too drunk to notice; he was definitely too drunk to care. He received word that Marshal Peacock was going to arrest him for creating a public disturbance, a distinct insult to his honor. Chiles went after Peacock like an enraged bull. When the gunfire stopped on the northwest corner of the town square, a group of black citizens cautiously approached Chiles's corpse. The dead man's eyes were wide open. A gray-haired former slave asked, "Is he dead, sir?" On hearing that Harry's uncle was indeed dead, the citizen fell to his knees and cried upward to the heavens, "Lord, Lord, thank you, Lord! No more niggers going to get killed now, Lord! Hallelujah!" Celebration was general in the black community; the white folks made Peacock mayor.

Memories were long and kinship ties close in Jackson County. When years later John Anderson Truman married a sister of Jim Crow's widow, the incident became a concern to the Trumans as well as to the Youngs. Years later Harry still referred to it. A sore point may have been the death of Harry's "half blind, half crazy" cousin Elijah ("Lige") who was "his father's shadow" and was cut down as Peacock threw lead at Jim.*

About the time the Trumans moved to Independence William G. Chiles was eastern judge of Jackson County. C. C. (Neal) Chiles

---

*Jim Crow's son Willie was killed in an accident in 1882. His widow Sallie, who married Belton contractor E. T. Dunsmore in 1886, died a slow and terrible death after her dress caught fire in 1909.

was organizing the Bank of Independence. He was the father-in-law of former Jackson County prosecutor William H. Wallace, long-time partner of former Jackson County presiding judge George W. Gates (whose son George P. Gates was a wealthy miller helping Neal Chiles set up the Bank of Independence). Wallace was kin to former Missouri attorney general John A. Hockaday, and was law partner in the firm of Comings & Slover with Gates's son Edward Payson Gates, who was soon to be county circuit judge. Partner James H. Slover had already been a circuit judge, and would hold that post again. Independence school board president Hinton H. Noland was also kin. Livestock man Benjamin Holmes (nephew of John Truman's mother) was soon to become mayor of Kansas City. Truman kinsman Isaac McCoy was a founder of Kansas City, and Harry's maternal grandmother was a close friend of wealthy Kansas Citian John Wornall. The maternal grandparents rented Dr. Lykens's farm, and Lykens' widow married George Caleb Bingham. The list could go on, but the point is made. John wasn't moving into a vacuum where no one knew him. Indeed, his kin were among the town's elite. He himself had been in the delegation welcoming President Cleveland to Kansas City in 1887.[4]

John Truman established himself with little fuss as an Independence businessman, resuming his old trade of livestock dealer. In December 1890 he bought several adjoining lots on Crysler Street from a Jewish couple, Sam and Clara Blitz. Sam Blitz was a wealthy merchant. The price was $4,000, of which John paid $1,000 down and financed $3,000 with a mortgage. A few months later he sold this property to his brother-in-law Harrison for $4,300. That same day, March 12, 1891, Harrison sold the property to his sister Mattie for $4,400. Thus the Young family money not only cleared all debt from this property but also protected it from any future creditors of John, since he no longer owned it. In mid-1892 he bought two more lots on Railroad Avenue for $600.[5]

Inside a wire fence that John strung around the back of the Crysler Street property were the horses, mules, cattle, hogs, sheep, and goats of his trade. Up to five hundred goats at a time were kept here. To Harry the property seemed to encompass acres. "With our barns, chicken house, and a grand yard in which to play, all the boys and girls in the neighborhood for blocks around congregated at our house. We always had ponies and horses to ride, goats to hitch to our little wagon, which was made like a big one." Vivian had a pair of red goats, and harness maker (later county eastern judge) Henry Rummel made a miniature set of double harness so the boys could use the goats to pull the wagon for walnut hunting. "We always had dogs and cats, pigeons and pet pigs," Harry said. "My goat was bald with a black face."[6]

John also had a household garden with a memorable strawberry bed and vegetables that relatives still talked about a half century later, particularly his yellow "peach" tomatoes. Despite the farmyard atmosphere and proximity to the MoPac tracks, the property was in a desirable end of town. Community leaders such as the Woodsons, the Proctors (who would later become Truman kin), and the Wilsons lived in fine homes across the street. The Trumans' white-frame house in front of the livestock yard was crowned at the northwest corner with cupola and gilded rooster weather vane. The Trumans had servants, a black family. "Old Letch" Simpson was the gardener. His wife "Aunty" Caroline Simpson was the cook and washerwoman. The Trumans always called her Hunter rather than Simpson, probably a social custom that had nothing to do with feminism. Their crippled daughter Delsie lived with the Trumans, as did their sons Claude, Horace, and "Fat" Sam. They had an older daughter Amy whom Harry never saw.[7]

As was customary in Southern towns of that era, the Truman children played freely with the servants' children, and with the son and daughter of a black family that was friendly with Caroline Simpson. "What a grand time we had," Harry recalled. "No color line was drawn. Nearly every family had a negro cook and a yard man, who was a negro. The cook was a good one and the yard man kept the wood for the kitchen stove sawed, mowed the yard, trimmed the trees and the bushes." The genial race relations young Harry remembered were true only for children. As adolescence approached, Southern towns drew a distinct color line between childhood friends. Even in childhood the line was visible to those with an eye to see— Harry's schoolmates were all white. Harry was also wrong about almost every family having servants. This may have been true for his neighborhood, but not for all.[8]

In addition to the livestock business in town, John ran a rented farm southeast of Independence with the help of Old Letch Simpson. John also began to diversify into other mercantile pursuits. Together

with Oscar Mindrup he had a flourishing real estate business. All
such enterprises have their tales of big ones that got away. John's
was forty acres he refused to buy, farmland near the spot where his
wife was born. He felt he would never turn a profit on this rural
property. When it later became urbanized (centered near 39th and
Troost in Kansas City) the profits would have been high indeed.
Another opportunity lost (or, more accurately, stolen) was John's
invention of an automatic railroad switch in an era when all switches
were hand thrown. While he dickered over royalties with Chicago
& Alton and Missouri Pacific, MoPac pirated his invention, and he
got nothing.[9]

When the Trumans arrived in town the minister at First Presbyterian, Rev. Addison Madeira, gave the children a special welcome. Because of this the parents decided that the family would
attend the church even though they were Baptists. Another factor
was that the town divided into social cliques based on church attendance, and the Presbyterians were the top of this hierarchy. The
Trumans attended every Sunday until they moved from Independence over a decade later. Here in Sunday School kindergarten Harry
first met Elizabeth Wallace. At that first meeting he probably knew
nothing of her family's wealth and social standing. Though he later
spoke of her golden hair and blue eyes, the boy didn't seem so
precocious as to have been swayed by that, either. Yet somehow he
knew that Bess Wallace was important to his life. The lifelong romance that developed has been justly celebrated, but its origins and
depths will surely always remain a mystery to outsiders.[10]

Children normally started grammar school at age six, but for some
reason Harry's parents delayed his entry until autumn 1892 when
he was eight-and-a-half. He attended Noland School wearing a white
cap with a sign above the visor, "Grover Cleveland for President
and Adlai Stevenson for Vice President." The triumphant Democrats
had a torchlight parade through Independence. Dave Wallace, Bess's
father, traditionally led all parades astride his big black horse. Harry
remembered his own father in the parade that night, riding a gray.
They marched right past the Wallace home at 610 North Delaware,
and next-door playmate Elizabeth Paxton remembered her own mother
waking her to look over the window sill—she was just tall enough
to watch the men and torches. Harry's red-hot Democrat father
climbed the roof of their house, up to the cupola, where he tied

bunting and a forty-four-star flag to the weather vane, and proclaimed that the flag would remain there as long as Democrats ran the government.[11]

In this grand year for Democracy Harry Truman was a first grader in Southside (later named Noland) School. His teacher was the "very methodical and exacting" Miss Myra Ewin, and Harry claimed he became a favorite of hers. His younger first-grade seatmate Mize Peters later described the schoolroom. "Two children sat together in an old bench with a dividing board that ran down the center. Possibly six or eight benches were fastened together with a child on either side of each bench." Mize recalled that he and Harry had a "desk attached to the back of the seat in front with a shelf underneath for books." Mize said the children loved Miss Ewin, and Harry also remembered first grade as a happy time. He learned how to add and subtract. His mother had already taught him to read, and he enjoyed the New Franklin *First Reader* and other books from the series. His second-grade teacher at Southside was Miss Minnie Ward. She taught the left-handed Harry to write with his right hand.[12]

In January 1894 diphtheria struck the Truman household. Harry and Vivian fell seriously ill. In hopes of saving their sister Mary Jane from the disease, the parents had Letch Simpson rush her to the Young farm in Grandview. This was nearly an all-day trip in the big farm wagon, and the family didn't learn of her safe arrival for almost two days. Mary Jane escaped the diphtheria, but Harry and Vivian needed the best medical care Independence could provide. Dr. Tom Twyman and Dr. Charlie Lester gave them ipecac and whiskey. "I've hated the smell of both ever since," Harry said later. Dr. Twyman also recommended that Harry eat ice. Mattie opened the window, scooped up a handful of snow, and fed it to Harry. This treatment cleared the mucus from his throat. Both brothers seemed to be recovering when Harry's throat closed in diphtheric paralysis while he was drinking a glass of milk. He lost his power of speech, and his arms and legs were rapidly paralyzed. Nearly ten years old, Harry had to be wheeled around in a baby carriage for months. He was older than most of his classmates, already ridiculed by them for his glasses, and this experience cannot have improved his standing in the harsh evaluations of children. A woman called Grandma Vaile was summoned as a practical nurse, and Harry was put on her porch to take in the sunlight. Vivian recovered promptly, but Harry's affliction lingered. Only gradually did he begin to talk again, followed by regaining control of his hands, then his limbs. School was out of the question, and Harry dropped out.[13]

This was on top of two other family tragedies. In January 1892 Solomon Young died unexpectedly, though he had been sick for weeks with pneumonia. Then, in 1893, as Vivian later described it, "a nigger wench was filling a lamp from [a] coal oil can and lit a match to see." The Young family mansion went up in flames. Plans to construct another grand mansion were forever postponed for lack of money, and the quickly erected "temporary" house still stood nearly a century later (a matter of humiliation for some family members).[14]

During the six months it took Harry to shake off the paralysis, his parents had to decide how to proceed with his schooling. Should he resume second grade in the fall? He was ten years old and of normal intelligence. (In later years his teachers unanimously remembered Harry as a top student, but this age difference may have given him an edge over the early competition. This may also have been a reason he had so much time to read—most ten-year-olds could probably do second-grade work in a snap. The age gap may also have reduced ridicule about his glasses or anything else.) Harry received lessons from Miss Jennie Clements in the summer of 1894, in the hope that he could catch up. Catch up he did, and was even allowed to skip third grade (a relatively common practice at that time). So he was now closer in age to his classmates in Miss Mamie Dunne's fourth grade at the newly constructed Westside or Columbian School, named for the recent World's Fair. His lowest mark that year was 80 in arithmetic, but he raised that to 100 in the third term. He generally made 90's in the other subjects: spelling, reading, writing, language—and deportment (Harry always wore a clean shirt and tie to school, never overalls). The Columbian School was next door to Grandma Vaile's house where Harry had convalesced.[15]

Another physical problem arose. Harry's big toe got in the way as he slammed the cellar door at the South Crysler Street house, slicing off the end of the toe. Harry recalled, "Mamma held it in place until Dr. Tom Twyman . . . put some iodoform on it and it stayed put and got well!" Someone once asked Vivian if his mother was frightened by Harry's physical misadventures. Vivian smiled and replied, "She didn't scare easy." Harry did better with dentists.

He went to old man Gaines in Independence, who possessed a curly goatee and a sense of mischief. As he worked on Harry the dentist began "reminiscing," culminating with a horror story of an excruciatingly painful tooth extraction. Thereupon Gaines brandished the very tooth, indeed a gigantic one, which Harry recognized as coming from a cow, not a man. Gaines assured Harry that none of his teeth needed to come out.[16]

About the time Harry was in fourth grade his father was drilling a well behind their house so the livestock could drink. Sulphur water came in at 140 feet, a taste too terrible for cattle. So the bit bored deeper, piercing two deposits of gas and one of oil. Although Independence, Missouri, could hardly be viewed as oil country, the strike meant that the Trumans could view the utility trusts with disdain. The house was piped for gas, and the Trumans furnished free gas to four or five neighbors. Harry's playmate Mize Peters remembered visiting the Truman house, and "A lot of people older than I was thought it was a very wonderful thing to have a natural gas well right there in town." Vivian had to clean out the gas well. A large bucket with attached rope was dropped down the shaft. Vivian then pulled it out by riding a horse about a block down the street, the horse doing the grunt work instead of him. Then the process would start over again, as many times as necessary thoroughly to clean the well. Harry later recalled that "oil choked off the gas," ending "an ideal setup." The end was messier than Harry recounted, and is worth considering in detail for what it says about John's business sense and his standing in the community.[17]

On February 6, 1895 John hired F. M. Burkett to deepen the well hole. John agreed to pay $1.25 a foot and to supply casing, promising to pay cash for half of each week's work. The balance was to come at job's end. W. H. Wintersteen, a thirty-year-old teamster, was on the drill crew, and remembered what happened when they reached $359\frac{1}{2}$ feet. "I was drilling and we struck the gas and I stopped as ordered by Mr. Burkett." Wintersteen continued, "Truman came home in the afternoon. We tested for gas, and lighting it, the gas burned. A piece of gunny sack fell into the well while we were smothering the fire and we afterwards got it out. . . . Truman said to Burkett, 'The well is all right; you need go no further; you had better stop here. I will accept the well. Put in the casing.' " Wintersteen said the well was in good shape when he left.

John had a different story. He claimed that the February 6 contract was replaced by a copartnership formed five days later. Truman and Burkett, along with J. W. Mercer, J. A. Gwin, J. J. Randall, J. M. Callahan, J. F. Buchanan, and T. C. Caldwell—some of the town's leading citizens—supposedly chipped in $25.00 each to drill the well, no deeper than three hundred feet. John's close friend Joseph W. Mercer was a one-armed Confederate veteran in the Kansas City wholesale grocery firm of Berkham (or Beckham), Mercer & Co. Vice-president of the Independence First National Bank, Mercer was active in city politics (Independence city counsel and mayor), county politics (Jackson County treasurer), and state politics (Missouri treasurer). Harry once noted how in the latter office Mercer had become wealthy "by lending out state money and putting the interest in his pocket. My grandfather introduced me to him when I was a boy. Old Mercer was running for county judge then, and my grandfather suggested that if the people of the state ever found out what he'd done with their money he might have a hard time getting elected. But the old man just smiled and said he was sure nobody could prove anything against him." John A. Gwin ran a Main Street saloon on the town square. Such establishments were headquarters for political intrigue. J. M. Callahan was a prominent lawyer for years, politically active, and a Pendergast leader in Independence. J. F. Buchanan was the future father-in-law of John Truman's real estate partner Oscar Mindrup, and did abstracts, loans, and real estate work on the west side of the square. Former mayor Thomas C. Caldwell was a real estate agent. On March 30, in the midst of this gas enterprise, Caldwell and Callahan witnessed the fateful will of John Truman's mother-in-law, Harriet Louisa Young.

If gas "in paying quantities" was found, the partners were to pay John $2,000 for half-interest in the well and gas. John claimed that after "gas in large quantities" was discovered, Burkett maliciously tried to destroy the well, plugging it "by forcing to the bottom of said well, gunny sacks and other substances, so as to prevent the flow of gas," and that Burkett "abandoned the work without first having been notified so to do." John declared that the well was left in such condition that he and the remaining partners had to expend much "money, time and labor" to get it in shape again.

The bottom line was money. In April 1895 Burkett and his lawyer,

A. F. Evans, hauled John into court, saying he still owed $130.87½ on the February 6 contract. John and his attorney, J. M. Callahan, said that John owed nothing, that no work had been done under the abandoned February 6 contract. Moreover, John countersued for $300 in damages because of the alleged sabotage, and called on Justice of the Peace J. H. Hawthorne to make Burkett "give security for the payment of costs in the cause for the reason that said plaintiff is irresponsible and unable to pay said costs, and the same cannot be made off him by law." John called J. R. Johnson, Fred Studer, and Claud Simpson as witnesses to back his story. Regardless of John's veracity, the law saw a hole in his position. He had earlier paid about half of the tab required by the February 6 contract, thus admitting the contract's validity. Justice of the Peace Hawthorne ruled in Burkett's favor, ordering John to pay $130 and costs plus 6 percent annual interest. The hearing and decision took less than a day.

A week later John filed bond for appeal, and the case went to Jackson County Circuit Court. In that bond John, William Tobenes, William Baruch, Joseph J. Randall, J. F. Buchanan, and city treasurer E. M. Arnold guaranteed payment of $260 to Burkett if John lost the appeal. Some of these men, of course, were part of the alleged February 11 copartnership. Their willingness to back John with their own money gives weight to John's story. On October 28, before the appeal came up, John requested a change of venue because he had discovered within the last twenty-four hours that the judge was "prejudiced against this defendant and for the reason that the plaintiff and his attorney has an undue influence over the mind of the Judge." On December 12 the Circuit Court upheld the $130 judgment. Apparently Burkett didn't expect John to let the matter drop. On January 4, 1896 Burkett got circuit clerk Michael J. Pendergast (brother of the man later known as Boss Tom) to order a deposition taken from W. H. Wintersteen in Fort Dodge, Iowa. The deposition began the same day! No further records appear; John apparently paid the judgment.[18]

Feelings ran high in this case, and it may have been this case or a similar one in Judge James H. Slover's court that prompted a violent outburst from John. During cross-examination the opposing lawyer responded to an answer by leaning toward John's face and shouting, "Now, John, you know that's a damn lie!" Five-foot-six-inch John sprang at the lawyer from the witness chair, and the two-hundred-pound lawyer tore out of the courthouse ahead of him. John walked back in alone a few minutes later.

"Did you get him, John?" Judge Slover asked.

"No, he got away. He ran inside a building across the street."

"Too bad," the judge replied. "That fellow really had a good beating coming to him."

This tells something not only about courtroom decorum and John Anderson Truman's character, but about his relationship with Judge Slover.[19]

Harry was quoted as saying that his father would "fight like a buzzsaw" if John's honor were impugned. Reportedly he "limped home bruised and bloodied" from fistfights with political opponents. John was one of the town's staunchest supporters of Christian Ott for county judge, and beat up one of Ott's critics. And Harry remembered John almost always being in a fight on election day. Mize Peters described John as "very quick-tempered and he didn't mind a good, honest fight." He gave as good as he got, sometimes better. Peters described the results of one fracas:

> It was when my father had his livery stable. My father was a stockman, and he had a sales barn right across from the county jail in an old rock and frame building. . . . Harry's father was a stockman, and he rode a horse and carried a stub of a buggy whip with him. One day Rube Shrout, a high-tempered, high-strung fellow came in to the barn to get his horse and buggy. He had a knot bleeding on his face and he was about to cry. My father asked him, "Rube, what's the matter?"
>
> He said, "I got in an argument with John Truman uptown and he hit me with a whip."[20]

Although he never struck his children, "if anybody jumped on his kids, they were in for it," Harry remembered.

This family protectiveness also extended from Harry to his parents, sister, and brother. Forty years after John's death Harry wouldn't tolerate even kindly criticism of his father. Harry's protectiveness toward his mother became well known. Less known was his childhood fretting over Vivian's mischief and over sister Mary Jane. In childhood Harry did his sister's hair and rocked her to sleep, singing.

As president he wrote, "Yesterday was Mary Jane's birthday. She is 60 years old. Seems impossible. I always remember her as a little girl I had to rock to sleep every afternoon, and who always wanted to follow me everywhere I went. She was surely good to mamma, and she still thinks pretty well of her older brother." He elaborated on the family's closeness:

> My father and mother were sentimentalists. My father had been raised by a religious man, Grandfather Truman, who set the women of his family on a pedestal and kept them there. No one could make remarks about my aunts or my mother in my father's presence without getting into serious trouble.
>
> My sister Mary Jane, named for his mother, was my father's favorite, and he made my brother and me look after her to see that she was properly protected in play and at school. We were a closely knit family and exceedingly fond of each other.[21]

Harry's piano lessons began about this time. He sat at the Kimball upright with his mother, who showed him what the keys and pedals did. Harry understood readily. He played with the great wooden box rather than fighting it as most small boys do. Animal trading, housework, music—Harry's parents viewed all these pursuits as important parts of life; if their older son showed a particular talent he should be helped to develop it. To do otherwise would be to reject a gift from God. Both parents sang hymns with their hearts, not their throats, and surely knew that to play music was to praise the Lord. "Do you remember how Father loved to sing?" Harry's sister asked. "You'd always have some idea where he was during the day, out in the barn or in the field, because you'd hear him singing." The Trumans' new next-door neighbor, Florence Burrus, taught piano, and Harry began to study under her. She used a simple method of replacing notes with numbers, to make practicing easier at first. Then she showed him how the notes and staff fit together. The first composition Harry played was "The Return of Spring," which he had heard his mother play. Next was Mendelssohn's "Songs without Words," followed by works by Chopin, Weber, Jackson, and Newland. Harry's high-school piano recitals would be praised highly, and the company that marketed the "shorthand" music teaching used by Florence Burrus would advertise Harry's skill as proof of the system's usefulness: "He will play at sight on the piano any piece set before him, seemingly as well as if he had been drilled for the occasion. . . . He will instantly improvise any style of music desired and change off to other styles as fast as they are suggested." Though he later staunchly denied it, in high school Harry was credited with composing a piano tone poem evoking the chariot race in *Ben Hur*. A decade or so later Harry listened to his sister "practicing on a Mozart sonata that has the most beautiful melody I know of. It makes you think of Greek and Roman fairy stories. Did you ever sit and listen to an orchestra play a fine overture and imagine that things were as they ought to be and not as they are? Music that I can understand always makes me feel that way. I think some of the old masters must have been in communication with a fairy goddess of some sort. That is, Mozart, Chopin, and Verdi were. Wagner and Bach evidently were in cahoots with Pluto."[22]

The Trumans were now living in a new neighborhood. They had sold the Crysler Street property to Flora Taylor in November 1895 for $10,000; a lien of $1,900 payable to John Anderson Truman on or before March 14, 1896 was part of the deal. The Taylors in turn sold Martha Ellen Truman the house and lot at 909 West Waldo for $4,000. Once again John's creditors could not seize his house, since he didn't own it.[23]

Elizabeth Paxton, a neighborhood girl of the era, remembered that the houses "were mostly Victorian, with large comfortable rooms, high ceilings, and windows with wooden shutters closed in the summer against the blazing sun. No matter how hot a day would be, the rooms were cool and shadowy. The houses were surrounded with expansive lawns, trees, shrubbery, and at the back vegetable and flower gardens were often found. Also, there were barns and carriage houses, sometimes a wash house and a wood shed. Most people had their own horses and a cow or two. This was the time before the automobile." She went on:

I remember most the summers when the children played out of doors, and only went into the houses to eat. . . .

Later, when dusk came, we became quite free again, we would run about the lawn. We would run about the garden and catch lightning bugs and put them in glass bottles. . . .

After the evening had turned into night, then all the children of the neighborhood . . . might appear, and we would choose up sides for Run Sheep Run. We could have as many as 15 children on a side . . . and we always had our favorite captain who called out the signals. We would hide all over the neighborhood in old carriage houses, under porches, down dark cellar stairways, at the back of a latticed porch, sometimes even on the tops of roofs. When the cry came "Run Sheep Run" what wild running there was. I can assure you that no longer did little girls have that starched scrubbed look. The dresses had wilted and the sashes were trailing on the ground, spider webs might cover the curls. But everyone was happy and tired, and about ready for bed.

On the porches of the houses, the mothers and fathers, and perhaps guests, would be sitting, fighting June bugs. The sounds of their voices could be heard and mingled with the happy voices of the children at play. Older boys and girls might be walking arm in arm under the deep shade of the maple trees. . . . Voices were a part of the evening. Friendly voices of good will between neighbors, an intimate connection of the life of the street.

Children's games spilled into the street. "People driving in horse-drawn conveyances knew the children well. They did not expect them to stop play; they would merely detour any game that was going on, and sometimes might pull off to the side and catch a ball or two."[24]

Harry became part of the Waldo Avenue Gang, "gang" then being a term of gentle connotations. Technically the Wallace family was on Delaware, but their children Bess, Frank, and George were part of the Waldo Avenue Gang, as were the Paxton children who lived next door to them. Mr. Paxton was a lawyer who served several years as city counselor. Waldo Avenue Gang member Henry Chiles noted that the Paxton boys and the Wallace boys "were about equal in number, and they would get in a big row, . . . then they'd send Bess in there to settle it. They were all afraid of her; she didn't fool around. . . . She was a pretty good fighter." Little Elsie Lee Southern of the local newspaper family lived on the other side of the Paxtons. Woodland College (a girls' school run by Professor Bryant where Mrs. Paxton taught English) was across the street from the Trumans. The Bryant family lived in the next block east, and was kin to the politically powerful Ott banking family and the Bundschu merchant family. The Sawyer banking family and the good-humored post-master Bostian lived at the end of Waldo Avenue. Also nearby were the Gates milling family, Harry's Noland cousins, banker C. C. Chiles, county judge R. D. Mize, and the immensely wealthy Swope family, kin to the Chrismans.[25]

The Trumans were already or would become relatives to many of these influential neighbors—the Allens, Bryants, Otts, Gateses, Wallaces, Southerns, Bostians, Sawyers, Chileses, Bundschus. Whether they were distantly or closely related, these folks looked on one another as kin, a powerful attachment in a small Southern town.

"We had wonderful times in that neighborhood," Harry recalled fondly. "Like us, Jim Wright and the McCarrolls were interested in raising pigeons. We had fantails, pouters, and many kinds of common everyday pigeons. We carried on quite a trading business in pigeons, chickens, cats, and pups. My mother was very patient with us and our pals and always came to our defense when we went a little too far and the various fathers decided to take a hand."[26]

Henry Chiles told how the kids would play cowboy or shinny in the alley behind the Truman house, "rougher than the games they play now." Harry "took an almost daily music lesson and he came by with a great big leather music folio or portfolio, or whatever you call it, under his arm. He would come by and watch us and maybe he would hit a lick or two in the shinny or try to throw a rope." Henry Bundschu (whose grandfather had been a business partner of Bess Wallace's great uncle) added this story:

I first remember him [Harry] as a quiet boy in short pants wearing heavy spectacles. He usually had a music roll in one hand and a lot of books under the other arm. He attended to his own business, and seemed to do whatever his mother told him. He practiced on the piano and studied his lessons, and didn't take part in the games and rough play of the other boys. However, I have a distinct recollection of one Saturday afternoon. We wanted to play ball in Bryant's pasture across the street from the Truman house on West Waldo, but didn't have enough boys to make up a game. Finally, Vivian said, "I'll get Harry to play with us." My reaction, like a lot of the others, was to the effect that in the first place Harry wouldn't be interested, and in the second place a ball game would be a little too rough for him. To make a long story short, Harry quit his practicing on the piano and joined us on the lot.

Harry also recalled that Saturday afternoon he was shanghaied as umpire and later shifted to enthusiastic player. Bundschu continued: "He took his place at first base and it wasn't but a few minutes before we found out that he could holler louder, throw the ball harder and play just as rough as any kid on the lot. If there was anybody there that harbored the idea that because Harry Truman played the piano he couldn't play baseball, it vanished in the sunlight of an open unequivocal demonstration."[27]

Although Harry was teased about his glasses and piano lessons and book reading, he wasn't regarded as a sissy mama's boy. Henry Chiles admitted that boys "wanted to call him sissy, but they just didn't do it because they had a lot of respect for him. I remember one time we were playing, I think, another game that we played, Jesse James or robbers, and we were the Dalton brothers out in Kansas—that's about the time they got killed—and we were arguing about them. Harry came in—we got the history mixed up ourselves—but Harry came in and straightened it out, just who were the Dalton brothers and how many got killed. Things like that the boys had a lot of respect for." And there were plenty of ways to demonstrate physical stamina without resorting to sports that endangered eyeglasses. Harry noted: "In the 1880's and early 1900's young people had great times in the country districts of the middle west. There were unpolluted streams, ponds, small lakes and beautiful pastures adjoining small centers of population where boys could enjoy games, swimming, ball games, tag and long adventurous walks. Walks which might take them to small creeks and perhaps to great rivers." Though he felt lonely, Harry was no outcast; he was an active participant in neighborhood play even though he avoided the roughest games.[28]

Of his father's livestock business, Harry wrote:

Our back yard was surrounded by a high board fence to keep the stock safely off the street. Usually there were goats, calves, two or three cows, my pony, and my father's horses to be taken care of. The cows had to be milked and the horses curried, watered, and fed every morning and evening. In the summertime the cows had to be taken to pasture a mile or so away after morning milking and returned the same evening. The goats and calves had to be taken to the big public spring at Blue Avenue and River, two blocks south of our house, for water.[29]

Henry Chiles remembered that Harry's father

had a lot on the corner of Waldo that run back to the alley. Oh, it covered several lots wide and had a barn and he kept one to a dozen cattle in there all the time. He'd slick them up and if necessary he'd drive them to Kansas City and sell them to the stockyard. . . . The only way to get them there was to ship them on the train or drive them. So people within 50 miles of the stockyard didn't ever do anything but drive them. . . . It would take more time to get them on the train car and off the car than it would to drive through, so they just drove them through.

Though Harry might ride all night in the saddle next to his father, taking livestock to Kansas City, he seems otherwise to have been little involved in his father's animal trade business. John, however, made Vivian a partner in the stock business when he was twelve years old, letting him handle money through a checking account.[30]

Decades later Harry wrote the epitaph of all such childhoods: "After a while we began to grow up. The gang scattered here and there, and shortly the serious business of education, jobs, and girls began to take all our time."[31]

The Truman family's move from Crysler Street to Waldo Avenue put Harry in the Ott School. Bess Wallace's aunt Nanny was his fifth-grade teacher: "a wonder of a teacher," Harry later said, "who had been at it for 30 years and knew her job." Miss Entrekin gave him sixth-grade lessons. The Waldo Avenue Gang and the Delaware Kids had two favorite paths to school. One was called the "Neck," and went under the Air Line trestle, skirting the black community. The other was "Race Hill," also known as Farmer Street. The nickname came from its hilly nature, the kids racing up and down the slopes to school. It was a favorite sledding spot in winter. Students walked home for noon meals.[32]

For seventh grade Harry returned to the Columbian School where he was taught by principal Caroline Stoll and Miss Ardelia Hardin. Miss Stoll reported that Harry "was never involved in any boyish pranks and took his school work seriously." Mize Peters agreed: "He was always smart but he didn't try to impress people with his smartness. He enjoyed studying and learning." Cousin Ethel Noland also remembered, "He was a very fine little boy, a very good little boy, I must say, really quite the best little boy in the whole family connection and possibly the best one in his room wherever he went to school."[33]

Harry worked hard to cultivate such opinions.

> I used to watch my father and mother closely to learn what I could do to please them, just as I did with my schoolteachers and playmates. Because of my efforts to get along with my associates I usually was able to get what I wanted. It was successful on the farm, in school, in the Army, and particularly in the Senate.
>
> Whenever I entered a new schoolroom I would watch the teacher and her attitude toward the pupils, study hard, and try to know my lesson better than anyone else.[34]

Already Harry was developing a plan. Although he could fit into neighborhood play when he wanted to, he often preferred to read a book. Adults commented that he seemed "old." He had few toys, and lacked a bicycle. Harry doesn't seem to have complained. He seems rather to have been an intellectual from an early age, finding amusements with his mind. Yet he was no introvert. On the contrary, he was well liked and in demand for settling schoolyard disputes via skilled mediation rather than fists.[35]

The boy read and read and read. He claimed to have read the entire Bible twice by age eleven, and twice more by the time he finished grade school. He also claimed to have read all the books in the Independence public library either by the time he started or finished high school—all of them: encyclopedias, histories, Abbott's *Lives*, George Eliot, Sir Walter Scott. Someone calculated that Harry had to have read more than a book a day for his claim to have been true, but it was true enough. "I can remember going through and many times I would see Harry in there reading," his teacher Miss Ardelia Hardin remembered. "It was after school principally." Henry Chiles agreed. "I saw Harry go home many a time with two or three

books on weekends, and I guess by Monday he had them all read."
Ethel Noland said, "That boy read—I don't know anybody in the
world that ever read as much or as constantly as he did." Schoolmate
Paul Rider (who would one day marry Madeline Bostian of the
Waldo Avenue Gang) recalled Harry's roaring through historical
novels by James Fenimore Cooper, Muhlbach's *At the Court of Frederick the Great*, novels by Polish author Henryk Sienkiewicz, and Mark
Twain. "Before I was 12 years old, I had read everything Mark
Twain had published up to that time," Harry declared. The Truman
family owned the so-called complete set put out by Harper & Brothers. Harry's parents filled their home with books. He read half a
dozen simultaneously, switching back and forth as he tired momen-
tarily of one or another. At home he and his father read together
from the family copy of Plutarch's *Lives*. Harry said he read "every
word" in the family's forty-volume set of Shakespeare. Gibbon's
Rome, Greene's England, Dickens's London, Hugo's Paris—Harry
inhaled them all.[36]

His favorite of all, though, was a four-volume set of biographies,
Great Men and Famous Women edited by Charles Francis Horne. This
magnificently illustrated set was published in 1894, so the family
must have purchased it soon afterward. Harry's mother gave the set
to him. (The biographical sketches were themselves written by great
men—"Winfield Scott," for example, was written by Hon. Theodore
Roosevelt, U.S. Civil Service Commission.) These are heroes, men
who overcame human limitations, who cast aside mortal frailties and
battled with other gods, in victory magnanimous, in defeat sublime.
Harry loved these mythological accounts, refreshing the souls of
readers. Mythology is not untrue—quite the contrary. But mythology distorts reality to make it fit psychic needs. In Horne's books
the distortion is that as heroes become more than men, they become
less than human. Thus the accounts demean their subjects' accomplishments, despite the laudatory style. The style is literate, not at
all juvenile. Yet the purpose is not enlightenment, but inspiration.
Years later Harry could still reel off names of the men he read about
day after day in Horne's books: Richelieu, Cyrus, Alexander, Han-
nibal, Charlemagne, Hermann, Constantine the Great and Small,
Mahomet the Prophet and Conqueror, Saladin, Charles Martel,
Richard the Lion Hearted and III, Gustavus Adolphus the Lion of
the North, King Henry IV, Edward the Black Prince and his father,

Napoleon, Charles V, Sir Francis Drake, Captain Kidd, Robert E. Lee, Stonewall Jackson, Andrew Jackson, George Washington, Thomas Jefferson, Ben Franklin. Harry remembered the military leaders, but rarely mentioned the others. Although he later said the Bible was the most influential book he read, Horne's biographies were his favorite youthful reading. "Reading history, to me, was far more than a romantic adventure. It was solid instruction and wise teaching which I somehow felt that I wanted and needed."[37]

Harry didn't merely memorize bits of trivia. He organized all this information into an organic whole and carried it in his head. In later years knowledgeable men marveled at the president's grasp of history. Secretary of State Dean Acheson was awed as President Truman outlined the rise of Central Asia, covering centuries of rulers without reference to any notes, and, moreover, showing his listeners how this heritage was affecting current events they had just been discussing. "You could see," Acheson said, "why these people were moving around, what the pressures were, what was pushing them. You could see the sort of seething of human life over this vast area." Harry had an amazing grasp of the knowledge he was acquiring. Even in grade school there was a purpose to all this reading. It was part of his plan:[38]

> A man cannot make his plans for his personal future until he finds out definitely what he proposes to do with himself. I can remember when I was very young—in the fifth, sixth, and seventh grade at school, wondering what my own future would be. I was an avid reader of history and particularly the lives of great men and famous women. I found that some were born to greatness, some attained it by accident, and some worked for it.
>
> Most of Plutarch's and Abbott's greats were great by inheritance and position. But there were many who came from nothing to the top. Some were honorable and decent, some were unscrupulous and personally no good.
>
> In the picture of the great in the United States, most were honorable, hardworking men who were ready when opportunity knocked. Most had training on the farm, in finance, or in the military.

He also found that "There are three things that get a man. No. 1 is power. . . . No. 2 is ambition for high social recognition. That is all tinsel and fake. No. 3 is appetite or inability to exercise physical restraint [i.e., drunkenness and sexual lust]."[39]

This was Harry Truman's plan for his life. He would learn farming, finance, and the military. He would avoid love of power, disdain the opinions of plutocrats, and not yield to drunkenness and sexual temptation. This plan was apparently congealing as he entered high school, and he would follow it strictly all his life. That in itself is remarkable. More impressive, the plan was developed from study of biographies, that is, based on an analysis of what actually happened in the real world rather than on any abstract principles. This demonstrated a sophisticated mind at work, one that intuitively grasped the power of the scientific method (analyzing results of conduct in other lives) over authority (parents, teachers, preachers). As noted, Harry knew how to ingratiate himself to authority without submitting to it. "When growing up it occurred to me to watch the people around me to find out what they thought and what pleased them most," he said. He would use authority, not fight it.[40]

The brilliance of this life plan was its adaptability. Rather than narrowly limit himself to planning for a particular career, Harry planned a way of living. He knew (not hoped, but *knew*) that this way of life would present him with career opportunities. They wouldn't be ends in themselves, but rather manifestations of his way of life, so he could grab and let go of them without concern. What outsiders would see as career setbacks, Harry would see as experiments that had served their purpose. He would on occasion become discouraged, but he would never abandon his life's plan. He knew the plan would present him with more opportunities. "Make no little plans. Make the biggest one you can think of, and spend the rest of your life carrying it out."[41]

And so Harry entered high school making the biggest plan he could think of. Fourteen years old, with thoughts as bold as thoughts can be.

The Spanish-American War broke out in the last weeks of Harry's grammar-school career. Admiral Dewey and General Shafter became heroes to Harry, particularly Shafter, who overcame a physical handicap. Now, however, there was a chance Harry could go to war for real. Boys his age had fought in the War Between the States, and

Harry knew that military experience was important in the careers of great men. Demonstrating his organizational ability, he formed a rifle company (.22 cal.), the Independence Junior Militia. The dozen or so boys elected a captain, and drilled weekly around the neighborhood. The drills sometimes included shooting a neighbor's chicken, which would then be cooked over a hidden fire in the woods a couple of blocks north of Waldo Avenue. The boys sometimes headed off to the Little Blue River or even the Missouri. While the other boys fished, Harry "lounged on the bank and read, offering advice or reading favorite paragraphs, often to the disgust of his carefree companions." Older Independence boys were already at Camp Alger near Washington, D.C., and Harry's cousin Ralph Truman would serve in Cuba and the Philippines. Independence high-school teachers Ardelia Hardin and W. L. C. Palmer even traveled to Washington to offer more support to their former pupils who were about to engage in combat (this trip encouraged the two teachers to become engaged thus spiking Miss Hardin's career in a town that normally didn't permit married women to teach). The war ended before Harry began high school that autumn.[42]

In this era Independence grammar school had seven grades, and high school had three. Harry began attending high-school classes at the Ott School, which also housed elementary pupils. Harry and Charlie Ross, one of his Junior Militia fellows, campaigned for the bond issue that permitted a new high school to be built, later named Bryant School in honor of Harry's neighbor, Professor Bryant (of the now defunct Woodland College). Harry's high-school class finished its senior year at the new building. Math teacher Sallie Brown doubled as librarian at Ott, although Carrie Wallace (cousin of Bess, and daughter of fifth-grade teacher Nannie Wallace) was the main librarian at Ott and then at Bryant.[43]

Harry took the standard three-year course of required subjects and electives: history and geography from Miss Maggie Phelps, English and literature from Miss Matilda (Tillie) Brown, algebra and geometry from Miss Sallie Brown and Miss McDonald, science from Professor Palmer, and math and Latin from Miss Ardelia Hardin (who, like Harry, was a former student of Miss Ewin). Professors Patrick, Baldwin, and Bryant also taught Harry. Miss Hardin thought Harry probably received his third year of Latin (Cicero) from Miss Berta Entrekin (his sixth-grade teacher), and someone else thought

Miss Tillie Brown (kin to Jefferson Davis) gave Harry history instruction. Harry recalled that his high-school curriculum also included astronomy, music, logic, and rhetoric. He was a debate team
captain. Squaring his shoulders, he spoke in the affirmative on "Tariff for Revenue Only" (he maintained the affirmative stance on that
issue throughout his adult career).[44]

"A little bit shy and not the aggressive type. I know his teachers
all admired him," Miss Hardin said of Harry, praising his "stead-
fastness in always having his lessons and his proclivity for reading
and particularly reading history in the library." She remembered
Harry's interest in Gettysburg:

> He would want me to tell the whole story about father having
> been wounded three times in Pickett's Charge and left on the field
> as dead; and how three days afterwards, he was found by Catholic
> sisters going over the battlefield looking for wounded soldiers and
> was taken to Baltimore to be nursed back to health; and how after
> his recovery, and on crutches, the United States Government asked
> for his allegiance, which he wouldn't give; and how he was kept
> in prison from then until the end of the war. Harry always wanted
> to know all about that.
>
> Father was . . . in General Lee's Army of Northern Vir-
> ginia. . . . Several times my father was asked to come to the high
> school in those days and talk to Miss Margaret Phelps' history
> class about his experiences in the War Between the States. I can
> remember that Harry would tell me how he considered General
> Robert E. Lee a great hero.[45]

In his first year of high school Harry's classroom routine was
thrown awry by his part-time job at Jim Clinton's drugstore on the
town square. This wasn't Harry's first paying job. Earlier he had
been a newsboy. "I didn't sell very many," he recalled. "I bought
them for one cent, sold them for two and spent the profits on ice
cream sodas." Now Harry made the sodas. He also opened the store
at 6:30 each morning, swept the sidewalk, mopped the floor, and
threw out the trash. The main thing he remembered, however, was
bottles—hundreds, maybe a thousand, seemingly millions. He had
to dust and wipe them all, in addition to all the shelves and patent
medicine cases. Clinton's Magical Oil for all Pains and Aches went
for 50¢ a bottle. Clinton's Rose Cream for all Roughness on Hands

and Face was two bits. Clinton's One Hour Cough Cure for All Coughs and Colds and Clinton's Golden Eye Water for Inflamed and Sore Eyes were also two-bit remedies. Clinton's Hair Renewer softened the scalp and (Clinton said) renewed the Growth of Hair. After cleaning all those bottles Harry had to dust the prescription ones. Decades later he still moaned about "interminable rows and rows of bottles with those Latin abbreviations on them." He was never able to get them all cleaned before heading off to school, and the next morning he had to resume (having worked the soda fountain the previous afternoon—"it was the bane of my existence to . . . turn the ice cream freezer for the day's output of ice cream"). He also had to wash the store windows each week and change the displays. He worked all day Saturday and Sunday. He had to do it every morning. Jim Clinton was described as "a businessman who was all business." For all this labor Harry earned three silver dollars a week. (The store operated on the cash system.) He called his first week's wages "the biggest thing that had happened to me, and my father told me to save it for myself when I tried to give it to him on coming home that Saturday night." Although a hard worker, Harry developed the habit of goldbricking: "I spent most of my odd moments and many that belonged to my employer reading the life of Napoleon—always hoping that in the end he'd win the Battle of Waterloo." After a year of this regimen, his father mercifully suggested that he quit the job in order to study harder at school. Harry said he accepted his father's suggestion, seeming to rationalize that he left the job in obedience to his father rather than because he was unable to keep up the pace.[46]

Harry later wrote of one important lesson he learned at Clinton's:

In a little closet under the prescription case, which faced the front and shut off the view of the back end of the store, was an assortment of whiskey bottles. Early in the morning, sometimes before Mr. Clinton arrived, the good church members and Anti-Saloon Leaguers would come in for their early-morning drink behind the prescription case at ten cents an ounce. They would wipe their mouths, peep through the observation hole in the front of the case, and depart. This procedure gave a fourteen-year-old boy quite a viewpoint on the public front of leading citizens and "amen-corner-praying" churchmen.

There were saloons aplenty around the square in Independence, and many leading men in town made no bones about going into them and buying a drink. I learned to think more highly of them than I did of the prescription-counter drinkers.[47]

Nearly a century later that story has a quaint sound, but Harry knew he wasn't looking at weakness and clay feet. He was looking at demagogues, men who were disrupting the community over issues they didn't care about. Thus he learned early the cynical contempt that some leaders had for their community, and that such men were influenced by naked power rather than discussion of issues. But this didn't destroy his own idealism. What he saw at Clinton's instead helped him to understand this one aspect of politics. The world Harry Truman saw was far more complex than that perceived by some of his fellow citizens of Independence.

Freed of his drugstore job, Harry plunged into his last two years of high school with gusto. His industriousness in Latin went beyond verb drills. Henry Bundschu remembered Harry, Charlie Ross, Elmer Twyman (son of the physician Tom who saved Harry's sliced-off toe), and Tasker Taylor as "playful but serious fellow students. . . . When they were studying Caesar's Gallic Wars, they took it so seriously that they gathered at Elmer Twyman's house and actually built a replica of Caesar's bridge across the Rhine. They would argue, experiment and work until they finally produced a splendid miniature model of the bridge itself. I was younger, and marvelled at their intelligence and their achievements."[48]

Harry studied Caesar and Cicero intently. Indeed, students of Latin classics saw clear influence of Cicero in Truman's presidential writing style. In high school, he read all of Cicero's orations, and translated them with Charlie Ross. Cousin Nellie Noland also helped Harry with translations, and twice a week Harry studied Caesar and Cicero at his aunt Ella Noland's house, along with Ethel and Nellie and his classmate Bess Wallace. Harry said he and Bess would never have gotten through Latin satisfactorily without these sessions. Harry sometimes brought over two fencing foils, and although none of the four Latin students knew anything about fencing they nonetheless swashbuckled across the porch or in a playroom.[49]

Harry and Bess had attended school together since fifth grade, and lived only two blocks apart all that time. They knew each other well and were definitely friends. Harry's statements of romantic interest are clear enough. In school "she sat behind me. I could not keep my mind on lessons or anything else. I read *sweet* stories. Always she was the heroine and I the hero." Also, "If I succeeded in carrying her books to school or back home for her I had a big day." These are the comments of a shy admirer from afar. Harry once admitted that he never spoke a word to Bess for five years after he met her in Sunday school kindergarten. We find no accounts of Harry and Bess dating in the twentieth-century sense. Quite possibly Harry was too shy to suggest purely social outings. "I was always afraid of the girls my age and older," he said. When he went to parties cousin Ethel, not Bess, was at his side. Did the shy and sensitive boy feel uncomfortable about his awakening sexuality?[50]

In an essay he titled "Early 1900's and Late 1890's" an elderly Harry Truman wrote: "Boys and girls alike have a natural curiosity about nature and life generally. If they are not properly informed by parents or teachers they will find out about things one way or another. There should be some proper way to instruct both boys and girls in their early teen age years in what reproduction means and how it takes place. If that isn't done knowledge comes to them in the wrong way. That should not happen." This is a rare, perhaps unique, statement on the topic from Truman's pen. Did the normal urgings of a male adolescent conflict with Truman's lifelong belief that women were otherworldly creatures to be set on pedestals and protected from danger? Did he think that women had to be protected from his feelings? Such thoughts would not ease his social awkwardness.[51]

What were Bess's feelings? Was Harry's love reciprocated? Bess was a vigorous and personable girl, unafraid to defeat boys at sports, unafraid to express her opinions bluntly, a feisty live wire with a brilliant social life. She was a dominating (not domineering) sort. She was much like Harry's mother.

Among the various accounts of Bess's social life at this time we find no mention of Harry. Years later mutual friends reported that no romance was evident, and none had been confided. Despite his later writings that suggested he might have followed Bess around like a puppy, Harry's infatuation was unknown to anyone. Of her feelings during this period Bess never gave a verbal clue to history. Even if Harry failed to confide his admiration to her, she was surely smart enough to perceive that he was smitten. Though Harry would later refer to Bess as his childhood sweetheart, he secretly admitted, "She never noticed me. I went all the way to graduation in high school with her and still she never paid me any attention except on occasion to let me carry her books home sometimes." Nothing in Bess's actions nor in Harry's writings reveals a special relationship between them then.[52]

Harry continued to have a special relationship with pianos. "I distinctly recall, when we were together in high school, seeing the President on the street with his music roll," Charlie Ross said. "Mothers held him up as a model, so he took a lot of kidding. It required a lot of courage for a kid to take music lessons in a town like Independence." Harry didn't mind. "I never had to be driven to practice," he said. "Practicing was pleasure and not work and I wish I could have found more time for it." During high school he got up at 5:00 A.M. for two hours of such pleasure before classes. Beginning his last year of grammar school he rode the streetcar into Kansas City twice a week for lessons under Mrs. Edwin C. White. She was Theodor Leschetizky's pupil in Vienna and studied also under Madame Fannie Bloomfield Zeisler, whom Harry called the greatest woman pianist of her time. Harry would walk into Mrs. White's great brick house at 27th and Brooklyn, sit erect before the Steinway, wrists rigid, fingers bony and sure. "Mozart," Mrs. White would command, or Chopin, Bach, Beethoven, Liszt. And Harry would bring forth the melodies. He learned not to look at the keyboard, and seemed transported by the sounds. She gave Harry the showy, brilliant pieces for recitals. The Czerny drills, Clementi's "Gradus ad Parnassum," Scarlatti's "Pastorale," Mendelssohn's "Scherzo Brillante," Mozart's "Ninth Sonata," Beethoven's "Sonata Pathétique," MacDowell's "Woodland Sketches"—Harry mastered them.

He had difficulty, however, making the turn in Paderewski's "Minuet in G." Like Mrs. White, Paderewski had been a student under Leschetizky, and when Paderewski came to Kansas City's Shubert Hall Harry and Mrs. White were there. She took Harry backstage afterward and told Paderewski that her pupil had trouble with the minuet. "Sit down there, son," Paderewski said, and showed the frightened thirteen-year-old how to make the turn. Kansas City hosted Paderewski, Moriz Rosenthal, and Joseph Lhévinne in less than one month's time. Harry attended each concert, and heard all three pianists play Chopin's A-flat major waltz (Opus 42) and the "Blue Danube." Harry decided Lhévinne was best, and thereafter always tried to attend his concerts.[53]

Another extracurricular interest was politics. Harry's father was now an associate of Democrat National Committeeman William T. Kemper, head of the Kemper Grain Co. and president of the Kansas City Board of Trade. The latter position made Kemper one of the most powerful men in the Midwest, as the Board controlled grain prices. Kemper allied himself with the political faction headed by James Pendergast, and was a key figure in getting Pendergast's candidate James Reed elected mayor of Kansas City in 1900. Reed's election as county prosecutor two years earlier moved Pendergast toward political dominance in the county. Reed's election as mayor would do the same for Pendergast in Kansas City. This was a grudge match, as the Republican mayor had beat up Reed two years earlier, pounding him unconscious. In terms of political strategy Jackson County was divided into two districts—western (Kansas City) and eastern (every place else, including Independence).

John Anderson Truman was becoming wealthy with his speculations on wheat futures at the Board of Trade, and had business and family connections with the elite of Independence. He was a man of influence in Jackson County's eastern district, had been in the official delegation that had welcomed President Cleveland to Kansas City some years earlier, and in 1900 attended the national Democratic convention in Kansas City as Kemper's guest. While John sat in Kemper's personal box at convention hall, Harry circulated as a convention page—probably his first spoils appointment. "I'm afraid as a page I was a dud. But I ran many errands for Mr. Kemper."

"I can remember sitting high up just like a peanut in the peanut gallery," Harry said, "listening to William Jennings Bryan fill that hall with his voice until every rafter shook and every beam trembled." No microphones amplified Bryan's voice. Toward the end of the twentieth century Bryan was remembered mainly through the fictional drama *Inherit the Wind,* based on his final actions when he was a sick and embittered old man. That was not the Bryan who in his prime captivated the nation, who came within twenty thousand votes of the White House in 1896, and who received more votes in 1908 than Wilson received in 1912. In the New Deal era Boss Tom Pendergast would call Bryan the only "sincere reformer." Harry described himself and his father as "rabid" Bryan men in 1900—Harry's uncle Harrison was the "gold" Democrat.[54]

Harry was also involved with his high-school yearbook. He and his classmates took literature instruction under Miss Tillie Brown. "They thrilled to the knights and adventures," she said, "those boys and girls loved 'Merlin and the Gleam'" by Tennyson. In a burst of adolescent enthusiasm they decided to publish a yearbook with Professor Palmer's help, and they called it *The Gleam*. This was the first yearbook produced at Independence High School, and it differed from typical high-school yearbooks of the latter twentieth century by appearing in a magazine format and emphasizing essays. Harry claimed that he, Charlie Ross, Tasker Taylor, and Howard Morrison were the editors; *The Gleam* itself credited Charlie Ross, Mary Taylor, Laura Kingsbury, Faith Schlicter, and Mary Womack. Miss Hardin, however, affirmed that "Harry did have a good deal to do with it . . . although his name is not in there as one of the editors." Business manager Tasker Taylor did the artwork. The yearbook's cover, Miss Tillie recalled, "showed Lynette riding into the distance, but following was Gareth, the knight, youngest of King Arthur's nephews." On the inside was a drawing of a sailing vessel departing shore, with lines from Tennyson:

> Not of the sunlight,
> Not of the moonlight;
> Not of the starlight!
> O young Mariner,
> Down to the haven,
> Call your companions,
> Launch your vessel
> And crowd your canvas,
> And, ere it vanishes
> Over the margin,
> After it, follow it,
> Follow the Gleam.

The class of 1901 posed on the school steps. Above them, over the front doors, was the Latin motto *"Juventus Spes Mundi,"* Youth the Hope of the World. The class was excited about the new century that had begun just a few months earlier, and Elmer Twyman told his school chums that "invention, reform, and improvement is every-where. . . . We lack nothing but the air-ship and the philosopher's stone, or, perhaps, the 'fountain of youth.' " Yet Twyman was con-cerned that a civil war was approaching between rich and poor, capital and labor. He warned his classmates, "Already the first light-ning flashes rip the sky." The Independence High School class of 1901 felt it was graduating into a troubled nation.

On Thursday, May 30 came the final minutes of Harry's high-school days. Eleven boys in black and thirty girls in white waited for their cue. Miss Entrekin played their music, and they marched into the auditorium. All around them, filling every seat and spilling into the aisles, were the class of 1901's families, friends, neighbors. Reaching the stage they formed themselves in three semicircles. Rev-erend Norfleet offered the opening invocation. Following brief re-marks by Professor Palmer the class took over the program. Erle Louise Devin gave an instrumental solo, William Lloyd Garrett read his prize essay "The Poet's Mission," Celeste Gertrude Dixon pre-sented her vocal solo, Laura Kingsbury read her essay about the class motto, "Follow the Gleam." Then came Josephine Robinson's instrumental solo, and the oration "William Shakespeare" delivered by the top honor-roll student Charles Griffith Ross. An instrumental duet by Agnes L. Roberts and Julia Maude Rice preceded Mary C. Taylor's valedictory address. School board president Sea then pre-sented medals and diplomas, and Harry Truman's childhood ended.

The young men and women crowded around their beloved Tillie Brown to say good-bye. When Charlie Ross came up she put her arms around her prize pupil and kissed him. The other boys asked her to pass that kiss around, but Miss Tillie demurred. She promised, however, that when the rest of the boys did something worthwhile they'd get their reward, too. She added that she hoped yet to kiss a president of the United States.

Harry slipped a poem into his wallet, a poem he carried with him after graduation and into the White House. His choice was eerie—Tennyson's "Locksley Hall."

For I dipt into the future, far as human eye could see,
Saw the Vision of the world, and all the wonder that would be;

Saw the heavens fill with commerce, argosies of magic sails,
Pilots of the purple twilight, dropping down with costly bales;

Heard the heavens fill with shouting, there rain'd a ghastly dew
From the nations' airy navies grappling in the central blue;

Far along the world-wide whisper of the south-wind rushing warm,
With the standards of the peoples plunging thro' the thunder-storm;

Till the war-drum throbb'd no longer, and the battle-flags were furl'd
In the Parliament of Man, the Federation of the World.

There the common sense of most shall hold a fretful realm in awe,
And the kindly earth shall slumber, lapt in universal law.[55]

Chapter 3

CITY LIGHTS

When he graduated from high school Harry Truman was in the midst of a quixotic project exhibiting an unusual lack of foresight. He and Fielding Houchens had been taking special history and geography lessons from Miss Phelps two nights a week, in hopes of gaining appointments to West Point or Annapolis. At some moment after graduation, Harry realized that U.S. military officers had to meet certain physical standards. The bespectacled Truman later recalled a somewhat uncertain visit to the U.S. Army recruiting station in Kansas City. After the eye test he abandoned his military academy plans. While he may not have felt those two nights a week had been wasted, he might have felt exasperation.[1]

Harry still planned to pursue academic studies in law and finance, and enrolled that summer in Spalding's Commercial College at the east wing of the New York Life Building in Kansas City. "Thirty-four Years in Business is a guarantee of honest methods, and a record unequaled by any other Western Business College," the ads said. "Practical Courses of Study . . . esteem and confidence of the Business Public in this City and throughout the West. . . . Over 17,000 Graduates and former students. . . . Free Employment Bureau." Harry began to learn bookkeeping, Pittman shorthand, typing, and clerical skills. On the days Harry went to Spalding he also took piano lessons from Mrs. White. Harry's Spalding enrollment continued into early 1902, with time off for an occasional out-of-town excursion.[2]

In summer 1901 Harry spent a month visiting his aunt Ada in Murphysboro, Illinois (the aunt who had been forcibly separated from her true love and sent to St. Louis many years before). Aunt Sallie's (Jim Crow's widow) daughter Suda (whose ears were boxed by Harry's mother) and her four children lived near Ada. These cousins had worn Harry's hand-me-downs, including his black high-button baby shoes, and Harry now met these cousins for the first time. Joe and Ed took Harry swimming and fishing. Emma admired Harry's skill as he played piano duets with Lulu. Since Harry had never learned to dance, Lulu took him to ballroom dancing lessons. Harry said he had "a grand time" with these four cousins. Harry then traveled from the Egypt district of Illinois to St. Louis, and visited his great aunt Hettie, the half-sister of Solomon Young. Hettie's son John took Harry and three other lads to the St. Louis horse races. Seventeen can be a daring age, and Harry had eighteen silver dollars. The five men put down a joint bet of $5.00 on the 25-to-1 nag Claude as a rainstorm began. Claude, a mud horse, came in first, and the silver pulled at Harry's pockets, but not at his soul. "I never had so much money in my life," Harry said, and he never bet on another horse. The excitement was unfinished when Harry returned to Independence, for a young woman he met in Murphysboro had been much taken by him and began to send romantic letters. Her feelings were unreciprocated, and Harry was too inexperienced to deal with the situation unaided. He enlisted Aunt Ada's help in getting the letters stopped.[3]

Back in Independence Harry hooked up with his first cousin Ralph E. Truman, fresh out of the U.S. Army after years in Cuba and the Philippines. In September 1901 the two men traveled to Texas to visit Ralph's father and sister. Harry was at Ralph's father's farm in Lone Oak when they learned that President McKinley had been shot. Afterward the cousins journeyed fifty miles southwest to Wilmer where Ralph's sister Grace lived. The two Truman men and Grace's husband went off to Dallas for some fun. Years later Harry wrote a letter to Ralph, which contained some tantalizing lines: "You remember what a big time you and he [Grace's husband] had with me at Dallas? I was a damn fool about that time. If it had been a year or two later I'd had as good a time as you did. It don't take a fellow long to learn in the National Guard." Back to Lone Oak again and Ralph decided to stay on the farm a while. Harry returned to Independence alone.[4]

John Truman's finances were declining. For a time he had run with the big dogs at the Kansas City Board of Trade, but now they turned on him. In 1901, apparently in just one grain transaction, John lost around $40,000, possibly more. Engulfed by this disaster, which would soon pull him down further, John had to cut expenses drastically. Spalding business college was out, as was any other academic work for Harry. "I never got a university education. You can feel the lack of it when you sit here [at the president's desk]. It is a shortcoming." Cut off, too, were Harry's beloved piano lessons. He would later say he quit at this time because he wasn't master pianist material, and that piano playing was sissy stuff anyway; but these were surely rationalizations to hide the real reason and reduce the hurt.[5]

Somehow John had picked up forty acres in Oregon County, and he now took Harry on an inspection trip to see what the land was worth, probably in hopes of selling it. Apparently they ticketed themselves on the Kansas City, Ft. Scott, and Memphis railroad, and went to Thayer, about as far south as you can get in Missouri. They now needed to backtrack about twenty miles to Thomasville, which had a population of about fifty and so hadn't attracted railroad service. The Truman men hired a buggy and horses in Thayer, and set off. Oregon County is the home of Eleven Point River, a meandering watercourse then at flood stage. The Trumans discovered this the first time they forded it and the water reached the buggy's bed. They discovered this again the second time they forded it, and again the third time. In eight miles they bulled their vehicle and horses through the Eleven Point thirteen times. There was also the matter of the Ozark mountains. Indeed when the Trumans finally reached their destination they discovered that the land was "more perpendicular than horizontal. It ran straight up the side of a mountain." Harry estimated that his father could generate something under five cents cash by selling the parcel. Nonetheless, Harry claimed, "We had a grand trip, however, and returned home very much more familiar with southern Missouri land than when we left."[6]

Harry now had to find a job to help his family survive. In August 1902 he got a job wrapping singles at the *Kansas City Star* mailroom.

Truman wrapped "until he dreamed newspapers, was haunted by newspapers, and could see only the words *Kansas City Star* when he went to bed at night." The first week he made $7.00; the next $5.40. That second week he reached the limits of his endurance, and quit.[7]

Harry next found employment as timekeeper with L. J. Smith Construction Co., a job that used some of his clerical training. The Atchison, Topeka, and Santa Fe railroad was double-tracking its main line from Chicago to Kansas City, and the Smith company was doing the grading near Independence. Harry had loved to watch the MoPac trains go by the Crysler Street house, and now he was a railroad man of sorts himself. Harry pumped a three-wheel handcar to the construction camps six days a week, visiting all three camps twice a day (they were spaced about five miles apart along the track). He had to monitor the time put in by teams and wagons and drivers (30¢ to 35¢ an hour), blacksmiths, cooks, specialists (each 17½¢ an hour), and common laborers (15¢ an hour). Harry's pay was about 13¢ an hour, in theory around $30.00 a month—everyone worked ten-hour days. "In theory" because if Truman made a mistake in a worker's favor, that money was deducted from Truman's pay, a strong incentive for accuracy, although Harry's say was regarded as final if the mistake went the other way—the boss never paid short-changed workers. Harry did get one break: His job included free board; the other workers had $3.50 a week deducted for board. After deductions for errors, Harry's pay averaged about $3.60 a week. "That is where I learned about minimum wages!" he said. He had made almost the same money dusting bottles at Jim Clinton's drugstore. Every other Saturday night Harry went to a saloon in Independence or nearby Sheffield to sign paychecks for men who wanted to be paid then. A few men, mostly farmers with wagons and teams, took their pay less often. Most workers, however, were hobos. They were paid in the saloon in hopes they would drink up their wages and return to the railroad job Monday in order to get fed. Harry observed that this strategy succeeded. About four hundred hobos worked on the construction project—Saturday nights in the saloon must have lacked decorum. Harry commented dryly only that he "saw what alcohol could do to men." He lived in their camps along the Missouri River for the duration of this job. "I became very familiar with hobos and their viewpoints," he said. "They taught me many many things that had been a closed book to me up to this time." He added, "I received a very down-to-earth education in the handling of men." Harry also said that at this job he learned "all the cuss words in the English language—not by ear but by note." Harry held his own in this environment. Foreman Ed Smith (L.J.'s brother) said Harry was "all right from his asshole out in every direction." The construction contract ended in February 1903.[8]

That Harry stuck with such a foul-paying job for so long indicates the severity of his family's financial crisis. In September John and Martha had to sell the Waldo Avenue house to Malinda Yingling for $3,500. This was $500 less than the Trumans had paid in 1895, an even greater loss because U.S. currency had inflated in the intervening years (the buying power of the dollar in 1902 was approximately 82 percent of its 1895 value). John was a shrewd trader, and his willingness to accept such a loss shows how desperately he needed to generate cash. He bought a house in the 900 block of North Liberty Street in Independence. John pursued the livestock trade in Kansas City, and paid $2,000 down and assumed a $1,500 mortgage for a comfortable house there at 2108 Park Avenue. In early April 1903 the family moved to Kansas City, and Harry's grandmother Louisa Young lived there with them for a while.[9]

Harry went to work in the basement of the National Bank of Commerce at Tenth and Walnut in Kansas City. John's old associate William T. Kemper was a director of the bank. Harry applied for work on April 24. The bank had certain standards and asked if Truman used tobacco or liquor, gambled, was in debt, or had "tastes or habits extravagant in proportion to your means." Harry said no to all, and added that he had always lived within his income. In what forms of recreation or amusement do you find pleasure? "Theaters and reading." Where and how do you spend your evenings and Sundays? "At home." Are your eyes weak or imperfect? No response. State what qualifications or talents you possess, if any, which you think especially fit you for the work of a bank clerk. No response, although earlier Harry stated he was "fair" at figures. Bank of Independence cashier M. G. Wood gave a good reference, as did Dr. G. T. Twyman of the Independence medico family: "I have known Harry Truman since his infancy. He is a model young man and worthy all confidence being strictly truthful sober and industrious. The only employment I know of his having was as timekeeper in R.R. construction work where he gave eminent satisfaction." R. E.

Booth, bookkeeper of Sparks Bros. Mule & Horse Co., Kansas City Stock Yards, added: "I have known him for long time; I know his parents—he comes of a good family. He is an honest straightforward steady boy and unquestionably would make you a good clerk. I don't think he has had a great deal of experience."

Harry got the clerk job, promising "obedience to my superiors, and cheerful compliance with all established rules and regulations. I also promise to devote my entire time, energy and ability to the exclusive service of the Bank." The man with power to hire and fire was vice-president Charles H. Moore. "His job was to do the official bawling out," Harry said. "He was an artist at it. He could have humiliated the nerviest man in the world. Anyway, all the boys in the Commerce Zoo were afraid of him, as were all the tellers and bookkeepers. He was never so happy as when he could call some poor inoffensive little clerk up before him in the grand lobby of the biggest bank west of the Mississippi and tell him how dumb and inefficient he was. . . . Raises were hard to get and if a man got an additional five dollars on his monthly pay he was a go-getter, because he'd out-talked the bawler-out and had taken something from the tightest-wad bank president on record."

Harry began going and getting. The National Bank of Commerce had over twelve hundred correspondent banks clearing their checks through the basement vault. Harry had to list the checks, and debit and credit the proper accounts. His work was noticed. "Flintom," C. H. Moore would bark. "Report to me on H. S. Truman. What he is doing, how he is doing it and all about him." Flintom would reply that Harry Truman "is an exceptionally bright young man and is keeping the work up in the vault better than it has ever been kept. He is a willing worker, almost always here and tries hard to please everybody. We never had a boy in the vault like him before. He watches everything very closely and by his watchfulness, detects many errors which a careless boy would let slip through. His appearance is good and his habits and character are of the best."

Harry became personal filing clerk to the cashier, and for Commerce president Dr. W. S. Woods. A. D. Flintom reported Harry "always at his post of duty and his work is always up. He is very accurate in the filing of letters and the boy is very ambitious and tries hard to please everybody he comes in contact with. I do not know of a better young man in the bank." Praise is good, but money is tangible. Harry's services were valued. Bank records show Harry started at $20.00 a month and eventually made double that.

Harry's brother Vivian also hired on at Commerce, in July 1903. His references were R. E. Booth (Sparks Bros. bookkeeper), Jackson County Deputy Clerk John L. Lobb, and J. M. Callahan, John's gas well partner. Callahan wrote, "For a number of years his father and family resided about One block from me. I have known him for Seven or Eight years. I have never heard of him drinking, rowdying or anything that would be detrimental to the boy. The family stood well here and not a breath of suspicion has ever been cast upon any member of the family to my knowledge. Vivian is a grandson of Solomon Young. You doubtless have heard of him, or knew him in his lifetime. Vivian has never been in my employ, but I have for a number of years acted as attorney for his mother and father, and know the boy personally as a bright, intelligent and industrious boy." A decade after Solomon Young's death his name still had influence in business circles.

Callahan's endorsement reveals an important fact when contrasted with Flintom's reports to C. H. Moore. Vivian "will never amount to much as a bank clerk. He is a very different boy from his brother who runs our filing vault," Flintom said. Vivian "writes a miserable hand. . . . He appears to be without ambition. He stands in his own light in a measure, on account of his peculiar disposition. At times he is anxious to work and will do everything willingly and work hard and at other times he will sulk when asked to do things." Flintom's critical reports actually reveal that Vivian didn't like being ordered around by incompetent people and couldn't help showing it occasionally. Indeed, the final report on Vivian admitted that he was "good," and "honest and reliable." Harry's writings show that he and the other clerks regarded their superiors with contempt, but Harry stifled his resentments and pretended a bright-faced enthusiasm. This made a tremendous impression. Harry "is kind and obliging," Flintom told Moore. Harry's life plan was working: "Because of my efforts to get along with my associates I usually was able to get what I wanted. It was successful on the farm, in school, in the Army, and particularly in the Senate. . . . I followed a similar program in my bank jobs."[10]

While Harry worked at Commerce his family's circumstances continued to change. When the Trumans moved from Independence to

Kansas City they were at last out of debt. John had lost a house, 160 acres inherited by Mattie from Solomon Young, and $30,000 to $40,000 in cash, securities, and other property. The lost house on Waldo Avenue had been owned by Mattie, so it could have been retained if John had been less fastidious about paying his debts.

In April 1903 John was once again in the livestock business, but this seems to have fared poorly. The next year he was a watchman for Missouri Elevator, a grain facility near the Missouri River in the east bottoms. This was clearly a job of desperation, yet the family's circumstances weren't desperate. Harry and his father still read Plutarch's *Lives* together, and the two men tossed dimes into an old trunk until they had enough to buy Booklover's Edition of Shakespeare's plays. And there was time for friends and fun. Harry wrote the following to his Noland cousins:

My Dear Cousins:—I'll meet you at EBT&Co's Walnut st entrance on Sat. Feb 6 '04 at 2:15 P.M. and will have *him* along if possible (That's for Nellie.) If not *he'll* come to the theater *Later.*

I shall expect you all to go home with me and stay till Sunday anyway if you can do so write me at home 2108 Park. I think if you will go home with me to supper Mr H will too.

I understand that Mr Beresford is exceedingly good so don't fail to come. I've *all ready* got the seats so if you fail I'll have to take some hobos and I don't want to do that.

Write immediately if you'll stay till Sunday

to Horatio.

Horatio was Harry's current nickname among his cousins, from their common interest in Shakespeare. The warm-hearted letter was on three fragments of bank stationery with the words "CAPITAL $1,000,000.00," which Harry had underlined on the last sheet, inserting the word "My" before CAPITAL, with an added note: "The naughts are on the wrong side." Ethel Noland remembered the many happy outings with her sister, Harry, Henderson ("Mr H"), and other bank employees, and with old Waldo Avenue Gang member Jim Wright. They would go to the theater, have picnics, and play cards. Life wasn't grim for Harry, and thus probably wasn't for his family either.[11]

In May 1903 President Theodore Roosevelt came to town. Harry ran several blocks from the bank to where Roosevelt was making a speech. "I was disappointed to find that he was no giant, but a little man in a long Prince Albert coat to make him look taller." Yet Harry had to admit, "I will never forget the thrill I got at seeing the man who represented the Government of the United States, in person." Harry termed the president's speech "excellent." Roosevelt called on capital and labor to treat each other fairly: "We can work out a really successful result only if those interested will get together and make an honest effort each to understand his neighbor's viewpoint and then an honest effort each, while working for his own interests, to avoid working to the detriment of his neighbor." An unsigned editorial in *The Gleam* expressed similar sentiments: "Sympathy, the art of putting one's self into the other's place, and looking at matters as he looks at them—sympathy, is what we so sadly need in our relations with our fellows."[12]

In February 1905 John sold the Park Avenue house for $3,000 cash (with the buyer assuming the $1,500 mortgage). This was a $1,000 profit. He then obtained eighty acres in Henry County, south toward Lewis, Missouri. Commerce bank records state that both Harry and Vivian quit their jobs in March "on account of their parents removing from Kansas City." The Trumans lived about five miles southwest of the farm, around 508 Bodine Avenue next to Dr. Klutz, in Clinton, Missouri. Vivian probably went to business college in Clinton, but Harry was back in Kansas City after three weeks.[13]

Harry's quick return to Kansas City was no surprise to Commerce bank officials, whose records of March 16, 1905 stated, "it is possible that H. S. Truman . . . will return to Kansas City later on. In case he does, and should want a position, he has handled the filing of our mail better than anyone who has ever had charge of it." Perhaps the return was also no surprise to his folks, as his application for reemployment at Commerce said that his family was "depending on me to help meet expenses" and that he had quit three weeks earlier "to assist in moving and for a rest." His references this time included Kansas City tailor M. R. Wright, father of Harry's Waldo Avenue Gang friend Jim. Harry went through the list of questions about his personal life again. In what forms of recreation and amusement do you find pleasure? "Good plays and gatherings of young people of my own standing." Where and how do you spend your evenings and Sundays? "As above stated and at Church." He resumed his old job.[14]

Harry wasn't kidding about how he spent his free time. Theater-going was a major activity, partly because for a while he worked Saturday afternoons as an usher at the Grand and thus got to see many shows for free. Not that he was unwilling to pay. "Between the time I was about 16 to 20," he said, "I used to go to every vaudeville show that came to Kansas City at the old Orpheum and at the Grand Theater." He also patronized the Gillis, "a blood and thunder show house—they didn't have anything but melodrama at the Gillis—'Arizona,' 'Way Down East,' and plays of that sort," Harry said. The class acts went to the Grand at 7th and Walnut, where Harry saw the Four Cohans, Primrose & Dockstader, Williams & Walker, Chauncey Alcott, "East Lynne." At the 9th Street Orpheum Harry took in Marguerite Sylva, Sarah Bernhardt, Eddie Foy, Chic Sale, John Drew, and many others. The Willis Wood hall was built at this time, and pulled some acts from the Grand, though the Grand still retained its dominance in popular musical comedies. At the Willis Wood Harry saw *Othello, Richard III, Julius Caesar, Hamlet, The Merchant of Venice* with Sir Henry Irving and Ellen Terry, and the impressive performance of Richard Mansfield in *Dr. Jekyll and Mr. Hyde*—"I was afraid to go home after seeing it," he said. Then the Shubert was built, where Harry saw Robert Mantell in *Richelieu,* Paderewski, Moriz Rosenthal, Augusta Cotlow, and Vladimir de Pachmann. He watched the Woodward Stock Company do *Hamlet, Romeo and Juliet,* and *A Midsummer Night's Dream* at the Auditorium. Harry saw "the great Weber and Fields appearance in Convention Hall with Lillian Russell at her best, Nat Wills and all the other great of burlesque." At Convention Hall Harry also took in Joseph Lhévinne and the Metropolitan Opera performances of *Parsifal, Lohengrin, Cavalleria Rusticana, Pagliacci,* and *Les Huguenots.* Decades later he could still tick off the shows he went to at various halls: "I was at an age when things of that sort make an impression," he said. "I've often wondered why there couldn't be a revival of some of those great musical shows of the early 1900's."[15]

Nor was Harry kidding about attending gatherings of young people. On returning to Kansas City he first lived at his paternal aunt

Emma Colgan's place, 2650 East 29th. This was a big house, with National Bank of Commerce clerk Edwin Green and two Union National Bank clerks also rooming there. Harry's cousins Ethel and Nellie Noland would come over for parties and picnics and practical jokes. Ethel remembered one picnic by the Missouri River. "Fred Colgan and the Green boy said what fun it would be to put a message in a bottle, . . . so they did. They wrote their names and their addresses and corked up the bottle and set it afloat." Harry and some others decided it would be great fun to fabricate a reply from two imaginary girls near Mississippi. The pranksters even found a way to mail the fake letter from a Mississippi address. Colgan and Green were much excited. If the joke had been revealed then, much good-natured mirth might have been shared. Harry and his cohorts, however, decided to continue the prank, receiving letters Colgan and Green mailed and concocting replies. According to Ethel portraits were "exchanged" and a serious "romance" evolved. The joke became cruel, yet it was continued. Fred Colgan's mother discovered the truth and demanded that the prank cease. Harry and his cohorts confessed. Ethel recalled genteelly, "The boys didn't take it well at all, and it put kind of a damper on the warm friendship that had existed between the Colgan young people and these young fellows."[16]

Harry moved out of the Colgan residence, perhaps because of the prank, perhaps just to be closer to work. Vivian came up from Clinton to work at First National Bank, and the two brothers lived with other bank boys at Mrs. Trow's boarding house at 1314 Troost. One boarder was Commerce bank messenger Arthur Eisenhower. Harry chuckled that Arthur asked Mrs. Trow for a coal oil lamp, being so fresh from the Kansas prairie that he didn't understand gas jets. Arthur's brother Edgar said, "I mistakenly regarded Arthur as somewhat of a sissy, because he didn't show a great deal of interest in sports. He was always reading a book, or was busy at the piano." One suspects Harry got on well with the brother of his White House successor. Arthur later said, "Harry and I only had a dollar a week left over for riotous living." Harry added, "We lived two in a room and paid five dollars a week for room, breakfast and dinner. For lunch we paid ten cents to a box lunch place on East Eighth Street." Harry remembered he "spent the noon hour eating it in a five-cent picture show." He also had a tribute for his landlady. "We stayed in good condition physically too. Mrs. Trow was a cook you read of but seldom see, and the box lunch was a balanced ration before vitamins were ever heard of."[17]

Harry entertained Casby (or Cosby) Bailey and Ida Trow with his piano playing at this time. What relationship he had with them is unrecorded and probably casual, although he retained a fond regard for Miss Bailey for many years. There was a woman who interested him more seriously, and she wasn't Bess Wallace. According to Ethel Noland, who now lived across the street from Bess, Bess and Harry hadn't seen each other since high school (and they would have no contact for several more years). Ethel did, however, remember Harry's interest in an unnamed Kansas City woman at this time, a young woman older than Harry.[18]

Management at Commerce remained harsh. Just two months after rejoining the bank, Harry accepted a job offer from Union National Bank for the same work and more money. According to bank records his departing salary at Commerce was $40 a month, and Harry claimed his starting salary at Union National was $60 or $75. This was soon raised to $100, Harry said, "a magnificent salary in Kansas City in 1905." A bonus was the friendly and helpful attitude of his Union National superiors, a splendid change from Commerce.[19]

In the spring of 1905 Harry and his associates at Union National were abuzz with talk about the National Guard unit being organized in Kansas City. For people attracted to military service, peacetime duty is a lark. And like banking, the military was then a male preserve, a place away from womenfolk where men could indulge themselves in the pleasures of masculine interaction. Moreover, the National Guard unit's organizer was George R. Collins, whose active role in the Pendergast organization's Kansas City operations added a political element.* Politics was another masculine endeavor in that era, and the Truman family was aligned with Pendergast politics. All these things combined to make this National Guard unit a dream ticket for Harry Truman to receive the military training that was part of his life plan.[20]

---

*The Pendergast brothers had been active in Kansas City politics for two decades, and now had a following large enough to affect state elections. Their Democrat faction allied itself with others, and eventually became an organization fabled as the corrupt Pendergast "machine."

"Truman applied for enlistment. He was a stranger, but being a fine appearing young fellow and a Missourian, he was enlisted," said Collins. Lt. Col. George Halley immediately performed the medical exam. "Couldn't see very well," Harry admitted, "but they needed recruits and took me." He also credited Union National's paying teller (slated to be a sergeant in the Battery) with greasing his path. The whole enlistment process was transacted on June 14, 1905, the day of the new National Guard unit's first muster. Harry was now a private in Light Artillery Battery B, First Brigade.[21]

Harry was proud of his new full-dress uniform, which he described as "beautiful blue with red stripes down the trouser legs and red piping on the cuffs and a red fourragère over the shoulder." He was so excited he went to the Grandview farm one weekend to show off his military duds to grandma Louisa Young. When he walked into the house, and Grandma Young looked at him, Harry knew something was very wrong.[22]

That blue uniform brought back memories to Grandma Young. In May 1861 Gen. Jim Lane (soon to be U.S. senator from Kansas) and his men stopped at the farm and took fifteen of Solomon Young's mules and thirteen horses, shot four hundred Hampshire hogs, killed the hens, set the hay and stock barns ablaze, snatched the family silver from its cache in the well (after threatening to kill an elderly slave unless she revealed the hiding spot), and at gunpoint forced Louisa to make biscuits for the raiders until her fingers blistered, while Martha Ellen cringed under the table. In September 1861 General Sturgess confiscated 150 head of cattle, and in September 1862 Colonel Burris grabbed sixty-five tons of hay, five hundred bushels of corn, forty-four hogs, two horses, a bridle and saddle, and the family featherbeds. October 1862: Colonel Burris returned for thirty thousand nails, seven wagons, twelve hundred pounds of bacon, and took over the house itself for a while as a guardhouse. Later the Federals refused to believe that her son Harrison was indeed her son, and hanged him as a spy. They rode off in time for her and a slave to cut him down alive. Another time Federals jumped their horses over Martha Ellen's head, nearly scalping her with the hooves. Summer 1863: Colonel Nugent relieved Solomon Young of $20,000 in gold while Solomon was returning from a California and Salt Lake City freighting expedition. August 1863: while Solomon was still away, the Jayhawkers came to enforce General Ewing's Order No.

11 expelling civilians from rural Jackson County (despite the loyalty oath Solomon earlier signed in Kansas City), forcing the Youngs to leave the homestead, allowing them only a single cart of family goods as they fled north to Kansas City with their neighbors, the Meadors, the Greens, the Wallaces, the Holmeses. September 1864: Captain Axaline came to the vacated farm and helped himself to thirteen thousand nails, six thousand rations, and one thousand bushels of corn. In one moment Louisa remembered all this, plus the decades of fighting federal bureaucrats, trying to get some monetary compensation. She unloaded her anger on Harry, and told him never to bring the blue uniform back. Abashed at the only scolding his grandmother ever gave him, Harry obeyed.[23]

On some weekends Harry might travel to the Young farm to visit Louisa and Harrison. On other weekends Harry traveled to see his parents in Clinton. Harrison was having trouble getting cooks and farmhands, and he wanted to move back to Kansas City. Harrison explained to Harry that the Truman family could all be reunited on the Grandview farm if the Trumans wanted to manage the property while renting out the Clinton acreage. The deal sounded good to Harry, and he urged his parents to accept the arrangement. Doubtless John needed little encouragement. He had already lost his corn crop when the Grand River flooded, and his previous stint as manager of the Young farm had been bright. In October 1905 the Trumans moved back to the Grandview farm, all except Harry.[24]

Harry freely agreed to move back to the Grandview farm, but he kept his Union Bank job for several more months to pay for a piano and a team of horses. He also used this time to cultivate his banking associates. "Once in a while I would take the chief clerk of the Union National Bank, the head bookkeeper, and the paying teller to the farm for a chicken dinner. My mother was great on fried chicken, baked ham, hot biscuits, and custard pie. We would have a grand time, walk over the farm, look at the livestock, take horseback rides, and then go back to town for more work at the bank." Since the paying teller was also Harry's sergeant in Battery B, this deliberate goodwill was intended to aid his military career as well.[25]

In addition to his continued skillful cultivation of persons in authority, Harry's life plan was on track. He had planned to learn finance, the military, and farming since he knew these were what great men had learned. "From 18 to 22, I spent my time in big banks in Kansas City, and I got some idea of how they run, what finance meant, how they collect, how they keep books." His military experience was just beginning, but it would be unaffected by moving (at least for now) to the Young farm. Uninterested in a banking career, and satisfied with his knowledge of the profession, Harry willingly "cut loose" his job as assistant teller and bookkeeper at Union National Bank to accomplish the third and final element of training that great men had received.[26]

Chapter 4

ANGLES OF
ASCENT

Tradition holds that Harry Truman spent his next decade on the Young farm in Grandview. In truth he did much more than that, so much more that neighbors wondered how he had time for serious farming. These extra activities made Harry a community leader with connections throughout the business and political circles of western Missouri. To appreciate the energy, drive, and ambition such work required, we must first appreciate the work the Young farm required.[1]

The farm was one of Missouri's biggest, six hundred acres, and one reason Harrison asked the Trumans to manage the property was the difficulty of hiring farmhands who were being sucked into Kansas City's ever-growing maw for labor. That alone guaranteed a subtantial workload. In addition, Harry regarded agriculture as an element in the training of great men. So he took on the burden of learning all he could about raising plants and animals, from the wisdom of the ancients (Cato's *De Agri Cultura*) to the latest scientific advances reported in agricultural college bulletins of Missouri and Iowa. He also began keeping careful records of the farm's activities. The records were simple, entered in blank National Bank of Commerce savings account books, but they were more than most farmers bothered with, and the entries demonstrated the large size of the operation, as did the Trumans' use of labor-saving machinery that smaller farms couldn't support. The Trumans also printed up stationery for correspondence, "J.A. Truman & Son, Farmers, Kansas City Home Phone—Hickman 6"—a touch of class that most farmers felt unnecessary.[2]

When Harry arrived on the farm his father was using the land to raise and pasture stock. Harry took keen interest in this. He developed an uncanny ability to predict when a particular animal would give birth, an ability perhaps aided by his careful record keeping of when each cow, sow, and mare was bred. Harry dabbled in thoroughbred horse breeding, apparently renting a stud, but was serious enough about his cattle herd to purchase breeding stock. He registered several with the American Short-Horn Breeders' Association. Harry also worked to develop the Hampshire hogs; reportedly they were his "real love in livestock." Mary Jane said that the habits and appearance of Hampshires appealed to her brother. Mattie agreed, "Yes, he always said they had an equal amount of lean and fat." George Arrington recalled, "I used to try and rile him up by telling him that my breed was better than his, but he'd just smile and change the subject. He finally shut me up one day when I was kidding him about his Hamps by saying, 'All right, George, you raise the lard and I'll raise the meat.' "[3]

Raising and caring for animals was hard work. Harry went at it gamely. He did routine chores such as milking, a task he hated, especially the tails slapping him with manure as they searched out the black flies. He midwifed animals, castrated pigs, stuck cows for bloat. Unlike his neighbors who waited for cholera outbreaks, Harry routinely had his pigs vaccinated. Yet even the best of care was sometimes inadequate. "We buried nearly a hundred steers once that died of something the vet didn't know what," he said. Routine work could be dangerous. Harry carried lifelong scars on his legs from sows that attacked him. In April 1911 a horse or mule kicked his left leg, and Harry went down. Despite the pain, he got up and continued to work, putting in fence posts for the garden. Later that day, he recalled, a "calf threw me when I was trying to take him to his pen from his breakfast. . . . Gluttons are alike be they cats, pigs, or men." Harry landed on the ground with his left leg broken about four inches below the knee. The break was bad, and Harry was bedridden for the entire spring season. He took to crutches, and then used a cane for months.[4]

Crop production showed the most dramatic evidence of Harry's influence. The farm layout made a forty-acre area stick out over a mile from the main fields, costing much time to cultivate since equipment had to be transported that extra distance. He decided to grow hay in that area, thereby improving the farm's efficiency. Neighbor John Slaughter noted, "Harry did something else that nobody had ever thought of in this neighborhood. After he had stacked the first cutting of clover, he covered it with boards for protection against the weather. When the second cutting was ready, he simply removed the covering and put that hay on top of the first cutting. The result was less weather damaged hay." Harry Arrington remembered how Harry reduced soil erosion by dumping bales of spoiled straw into gullies, throwing in timothy seed as soon as dirt had washed over the straw. "Harry Truman had the first sodded waterways I ever saw," Arrington said. The Grandview hardware man, Dave Clements, recalled another innovation: "Farmers around here never thought much about crop rotation until Harry started doing it regular." Harry described the system with pride:

We'd plant corn after clover. Starting with wheat we'd sow clover on the wheat field in the spring and usually get a crop of clover hay that fall. The next year we'd spread all the manure from the farm and the little town adjoining it on the clover field. Nearly every family in the little town of 300 people had a cow or two and a horse. My father and I bought a manure spreader and kept it busy all the time when we were not doing other necessary things. We'd break the clover field up in the fall and plant corn the next spring, sow oats in the corn stubble the next spring and wheat after oats. It would take five years to make the complete rotation but it worked most successfully. We increased the wheat yield from 13 to 19 bushels—the oats from 8 to 50 bushels and the corn from 35 to 70 bushels to the acre. Besides these increased yields in the grain crops we always had two excellent hay crops and at least one seed crop from the clover.

Harry wrote affectionately of his neighbors' agricultural knowledge: "Everyone knew about blackberry winter; they knew that potatoes should be planted on or near St. Patrick's Day in March and that they should be planted in the dark of the moon with the eyes up, that oats should be sowed in the light of the moon in February

and that turnips should be sown on the 26th of July, wet or dry."
His scientific approach must have been striking indeed.[5]

Harry was meticulous with his fieldwork, starting with the choice
of seed. "He taught me the value of testing both seed wheat and
corn way back in 1912," one neighbor said. "He was the only fellow
I ever worked for," said a farmhand, "who had me take all the
buckles off the harness before oiling so the oil would be sure and get
under the buckles." Another hand remembered, "He sure loved to
drive X and Jane, his favorite team, to a corn planter. I never knew
anybody who could hold a candle to him when it came to driving a
planter, a wheat drill, or a binder." Neighbors' memories supported
Harry's own bragging: "It was always my job to plant the corn, sow
the wheat and run the binder to cut the wheat and oats. I usually
pitched hay up to my father on the stack also. My father hated a
crooked corn row or a skipped place in a wheat field." The veterinarian who did hog cholera vaccinations for Harry reported, "He
was always bustling around getting things done. I remember once
when the Trumans were putting out a big corn crop, of seeing three
corn planters running. A few days later I went by and was surprised
to see the same three teams cultivating the corn before it was up.
That was something new to me but it worked, as it gave Harry a
head start on the weeds." Grandview hardware man Dave Clements
agreed. "He was one of the weed fightinest guys I ever knew. If he
came in and bought additional hoes, that meant he had rounded up
some extra help to cut cockleburrs and thistles."[6]

The farm required hired help. Harry said the hands' "usual wage
was 10 cents an hour, $1.20 a day for a 12-hour day. My father and
brother and I always increased their wages when they worked for
us—giving them $1.50 to $2.00 a day and their meals. These were
hard-working, upright, good citizens." Most were, anyway. Truman
farmworker Brownie Huber related that "one afternoon, while they
were cultivating corn, X and Jane came running to the barn with
the cultivator. Harry was scared that in the runaway the team had
injured or perhaps killed the hand so he rushed out to the field only
to find him asleep under a tree. Though he wasn't angry, Harry
fired that fellow right on the spot because he couldn't trust him."[7]

In harvest season L. C. Hall's wheat-threshing machine chewed
up the roads as it lumbered from one farm to another. Grandview
area farmers all came when Hall's rig summoned them with three

long blasts of the steam whistle. These neighbors simply traded work
back and forth at harvest time. With everyone assembling, Hall
would move his arm in a circle, signaling the engineer to engage the
machine. The drive belt would slap together once it started to travel,
and John Strode remembered "you could hear those old belts a
squealing and a squawling until it got up momentum. . . . If you
would happen to get a bunch of wet bundles that hadn't cured right
or they weren't capped right and they got wet in the bundle, . . . those
belts would get to squealing, the old thresher would kick in, and the
smoke would just fly from the engine to build up extra power." The
machine didn't tire, and the men serving it were slaves to its merciless
pace. As B. F. Ervin grew too tired to pitch in wheat bundles, he
saw that Harry Truman "was climbing up over the rear end of my
load and smilingly reaching for my pitchfork. . . . He needed room
for action . . . , with seemingly little effort, maintaining a fast flow
of bundles into the feeder. Every bundle was going into the flying
band-cutting knives in the required 'heads first' position. . . . Soon
he had disposed of the last bundles of wheat on my hay frame. . . . He
quickly drove his load in and resumed his fast forking of bundles."[8]

Dinnertime was noon, and when threshing was at the Truman
place the men would come to the farmhouse. The house was painted
with fancy color accents on the trim, in addition to intricate exterior
stenciling. The residents clearly appreciated beauty, and a Grandview woman recalled the house was "always scrupulously clean and
neat." Harry may have been in the field or in town arranging for
railroad cars to haul the harvest (sometimes bribing the railroad
men with a bottle of whiskey, a technique perhaps learned from his
own railroad days). He would, however, always be at the house in
time to help his sister Mary serve noon dinner, sometimes even
helping to cook it. Mattie refrained from such chores. A neighbor
remembered, "If he had a little time prior to the serving of the meal,
instead of coming out and associating with us men, who were waiting
for a short time before we ate, he played the piano. It was very
noticeable." Considering Harry's normal conviviality and love of
masculine companionship, this behavior was striking indeed.[9]

Folks generally found Harry's company pleasant. Gil Strode came
by Harry on a road. "He didn't know me then, but he stopped and
passed the time of day with me anyway. That's just the way he
was—friendly and interested in other people." Another person re-

membered, "To the people in town [Grandview], he was just the man among men . . . very intelligent and extremely friendly; he was very nice and considerate of everyone." Still another person recalled that farmer Harry Truman "was a very, very genteel and polite human being. He was the type of person that you just felt so at ease when you met him; he was so down-to-earth, and yet he was something else, too, even then."[10]

Harry's popularity and production agriculture skills made him a leader in farming circles. In 1913 he paid his dollar to join Jackson County's new Farm Bureau, and the next year he was elected president of the Washington Township unit of the bureau. Robert Mize, uncle of Harry's grade-school benchmate Mize Peters, was then county eastern judge. His favoritism to the Trumans in county patronage was well known, and was one reason Harry was elected to the Farm Bureau post. The three-member county court funded the bureau, and Harry's prominent position was expected to do no harm when the court discussed the bureau's budget. Harry also promoted the annual township fair and helped establish the township's first 4-H club. Harry allowed himself to be drafted into the Grandview town band. "I have a clarinet here on the desk. It looks like a Chinese puzzle to me." His hitch may have been brief: "I can stand Lodges, militia, and most anything, but I guess a band is going too far." He limited his involvement with Modern Woodmen of America, a fraternal insurance society providing fellowship for members. "I'm not . . . learning any Woodmen foolishness. My head's nearly bursting open from the strain that's been put on it by the Masons, and that's a plenty for one rube." He was also a member of Royal Neighbors of America fraternal insurance society, the Grandview Commercial Club, and the Kansas City Athletic Club.[11]

Harry Truman and his father were both politically active. John was a delegate to the state Democratic convention in 1908. Harry was Democratic clerk for every election in Grandview precinct, tabulating the votes with Republican clerk L. C. Hall, the threshing rig owner. Everyone knew everyone else's politics. When Harry and Hall counted two Socialist votes in one election, Hall joked, "Harry, it looks like old man Green has voted twice." (Both clerks knew that Green's son had also voted this time.) Harry's interest in politics became more than casual. When the Pendergast faction asked him to run for Washington Township committeeman, he felt obliged to enter the race. "I got licked," he reminisced, "but I learned how the situation was worked out, and profited by it." Harry's appointment as Grandview postmaster in December 1914 was an example of the spoils system at its best. He owed the appointment to Congressman William Borland, but had to pass a Post Office Department exam before getting the job—a blend of civil service competence and political accountability that produced an efficiency in government unknown to some later generations. Although Harry was responsible for post office operations, he turned the work—and the $503 annual salary—over to a struggling widow in the L. C. Hall family, Ella. "A lot of money in those days," he said. "It would have paid two farmhands." Harry said Ella had been running the operation before he became postmaster anyway. "I was never in the office at all." He resigned in April 1915, effective at the end of August when his successor (Ella's brother Cecil C. Hall) took over. A Post Office Department audit showed that Harry was 38¢ short in his inventory of postage material. He was ordered to deposit 38¢ immediately, and to notify the Treasury Department when he made good the shortage. Official records show that the United States of America received 38¢ from Harry Truman on September 15, 1915.[12]

Harry's job as a county road overseer was a more formidable appointment. The Trumans were related by blood and marriage to many voters in their part of the country. In the heated eastern judge election of 1912 the Trumans apparently threw their support and influence to Robert Mize. Mize won, and rewarded John Truman with the job of road overseer for district 30 in the Grandview area. Of all county officials, road overseers had the greatest impact on the daily lives of rural residents. In America of the latter twentieth century good roads were routine. In the early part of the century, however, country roads were miracles providing ties to civilization and breaking profound isolation. Only through continual maintenance could the narrow lines scraped across Jackson County be preserved as passable all-weather thoroughfares. This was the job of the county road overseer. In addition, the overseer had political duties. He collected the poll tax, and thus canvassed every voter in the district. (By law people had to pay $3.00 or else work one to three days on the roads.) One could also satisfy the county school tax with road work. The overseer hired men and teams, and thus could reward political allies with county money. In turn, the quality of road maintenance could influence votes in the next county judge election. John Truman's appointment as road overseer indicated his standing in the eyes of Judge Mize and the county court. John struggled to keep the dirt roads open, supervising crews repairing potholes, culverts, and bridges. On one bridge job he "rode up there over the hill, and he could see that the men were trying to take it a bit too easy, and he canned the whole bunch," a Grandview area man recalled. Harry remembered that his father's road workers would "beef about it on the job [but] they'd go home and brag about how old man Truman gave the taxpayers a fair break. I was taught that the expenditure of public money is a public trust."[13]

Eastern judge R. D. Mize of the Pendergast faction appointed Harry to succeed his father as road overseer on the elder Truman's death in November 1914. This was an election year, and although Mize remained eastern judge, the new presiding judge Miles Bulger decided to bolt from the Pendergast organization, which had backed him in the election, and set up a competing political organization. Thus Bulger wanted to cause grief among Pendergast men and began clashing with Harry. Harry's suggestions for road work seem to have been approved routinely at first. Then on July 31, 1915 county highway engineer and Pendergast opponent Allen Southern (a future circuit judge and a future Truman kinsman who, like Harry, had been taught by Nannie Wallace) forwarded opinions from county counselor Armwell Cooper, apparently alleging that Harry was charging the county too much for work performed. This raised Harry's ire, no doubt particularly because he knew of road overseers who collected money for doing nothing. He penned a sputtering reply. "You have a little too much law and not much common sense mixed in these questions. . . . I'll venture to say that neither you nor [former state] Senator Cooper ever fed a team for 30 days." Harry asked "if you could find a man outside a circus parade or motion picture outfit who can drive three teams, one ahead of the other and make each team pull its share." He gave a detailed explanation of how he arrived at the figures he submitted to the county, and then he cranked up his peroration.

When for the sake of good roads I am willing to put in my good teams and my time that I can spend more advantageously else where, the County surely ought not to object to a reasonable compensation. . . . When a man drives my team on county work he works for me and the team works for the County at team prices. It's none of the County's business what I pay him. . . .

Now Judge my father and I have always given Jackson County a better day's work with our teams and ourselves than we'd ask for ourselves and the pay has been little enough, but when it comes to working at the figures you give and in the manner you suggest I can't see my way clear to do it.

I have endeavored to give you a practical man's point of view on the questions involved and I hope you'll accept it in the spirit in which it is given.

This letter was left unmailed. Perhaps a more temperate version went out. Harry continued to serve as road overseer the rest of the year. Judge Mize died, and Harry lost the patronage job by February 1916. "The presiding judge Bulger became dissatisfied because I gave the county too much for the money," Harry huffed.[14]

In 1915 Harry's became a familiar face at Mike Pendergast's 10th Ward Democratic Club while Harry was postmaster and road overseer (a state and federal officer simultaneously). He was appointed to another public office in July 1916, the Hickman Mills Consolidated District One school board. Harry replaced Urial R. Holmes who had been a western cattleman associate of Harry's grandfather Solomon Young. Harry's other grandfather, Anderson Truman, had himself been a school director. Harry attended meetings that decided such issues as adding a room to the high school for $2,000 or less, approving the contractor's workmanship on a new school building, and setting salaries for teachers and janitors. His attendance at meetings slackened as his involvement with a Kansas City business enterprise grew, and his attendance ceased altogether when he left to fight in World War I. His standing in the community was so high, however, that possibly he was retained on the school board even while he was an army officer in France.[15]

To tell of Harry Truman's rise to power we must tell of Freemasonry. He immersed himself in the ritual, symbolism, and philosophy of this brotherhood, which he joined during these Grandview "farm years."

Consider first the secular influence Freemasonry had on Truman's career. The institution had been all-powerful in some nineteenth-century communities of America—in Navoo, Illinois, the civil, religious, and Masonic leaderships were indistinguishable. In Truman's day the situation wasn't so blatant, but community leaders still tended to belong to Masonic lodges, a fact that attracted ambitious young men hoping to lubricate business and political careers through lodge fellowship. Although one might not dare to discuss business matters with the banker or judge at a Masonic gathering, one might have less trouble getting past secretaries and clerks the next day. One might never get invited to the local aristocrat's gala party, but continual contact at the lodge could be just as valuable. In addition, applicants for membership had to be approved unanimously by the lodge. Thus membership certified that one was considered "a regular fellow," the kind of man you could do business with. Membership also allowed one to attend other lodges, and meet community leaders anywhere in the nation. Harry happened to be a Freemason who was deeply interested in the order's spiritual aspects, but the secular aspects did his public career no harm.

In December 1908 a cousin of Harry's mother came over to inspect livestock on the Truman farm. Harry noticed that the man was wearing a pin in the form of a square and compass surrounding the letter "G." Harry had been considering joining a Masonic lodge, and discussed the matter with his kinsman. Just before Christmas the relative returned and handed Harry a petition for initiation into Belton Lodge No. 450. The $20.00 initiation fee was big money in those days, but only $10.00 was required with the application. "I signed up and gave my second cousin a check for $10.00." The petition was received January 2 and held for the standard month of investigation into the candidate's character and motives. Frank Blair took particular interest in the investigation. He was cashier at the Truman family's bank in Belton, and thus in an excellent position to know intimate details of Harry's life. Blair was a state Masonic officer, and Bank of Belton assistant cashier Billy Garrison was Master of Belton Lodge No. 450. The lodge brethren elected Harry to their midst on January 30, 1909, and he received his apprentice's degree on February 9. Over the next weeks, under the guidance of

Blair and Garrison, Harry went through the sorrows and joys of the initiation ceremonies until in March he received his third degree and became a Master Mason. A month or so later Missouri Grand Lecturer James R. McLachlan arrived to hold a three-day lodge of instruction.

Although many Masons are content to learn no more than necessary for the third degree, Harry eagerly grasped this opportunity to receive more Masonic knowledge, and even traveled with McLachlan to Holden and St. Joseph. McLachlan "taught me to be letter perfect in the candidate's lectures. He also made a senior deacon and junior deacon out of me and let me open and close the Lodge of Instruction until I could do it without a bobble." Via this cram course Harry said he also became "almost letter perfect in the ritual" of the first three degrees. "That spring and summer I spent teaching the plow horses all the Masonic lectures." Frank Blair took Harry along on trips to the nine or ten lodges of that Masonic district, and in December 1909 Harry was chosen junior warden of Belton Lodge No. 450. Vivian was chosen senior steward.

"I decided to organize a lodge in Grandview about this time," Harry said. "Some of us went to work on it and in the summer of 1910 succeeded in obtaining enough signers [twenty] to start out a lodge under dispensation." The petition went to the Grand Master who authorized the formation of a lodge at Grandview under dispensation with Harry as Master. Harry went to the September Grand Lodge meeting in St. Louis, where the charter for Grandview Lodge No. 618 was issued. Harry continued as Master under dispensation until the December election when the local lodge elected him Master in his own right. He seems to have possessed only the basic three beginning degrees of Masonry at this time. After 1911 he served one or more terms as secretary, and was elected Master again in 1916. This time he was on at least one route to higher degrees; he received the first fourteen degrees of the Scottish Rite in January 1912. Curiously, he delayed acquisition of the fifteenth through thirty-second degrees until March 1917 when he was serving again as Master of Grandview Lodge. By then he was also a York Rite Knight Templar of Palestine Commandery No. 17, which had once been headed by Bess Wallace's father. These positions in Scottish and York Rite Masonry allowed Harry to be created a Noble of the Mystic Shrine in Ararat Temple situated in the Oasis of Kansas City, Desert of

Missouri. This was in early April 1917, and one of the Nobles recommending him for membership was Leon Thalman, who as Deputy Grand Master of Missouri had been instrumental in getting Grandview Lodge No. 618 into full operation in 1911. Harry was also active in another appendant organization. In 1911 he helped organize Grandview Chapter No. 365 of Eastern Star, and became first worthy patron on July 12. Masonic lodges allowed only males as members, but Eastern Star permitted both sexes. Harry's sister Mary Jane was also a charter member of the Grandview chapter.[16]

Even to a Freemason the recital of Harry's early Masonic record tells nothing of his spiritual journey in the brotherhood. The record shows that he was well thought of by fellow Masons and that he was circulating in high Missouri Masonic circles. Yet one's rank in organizations on this plane of existence tells little about spiritual consciousness. To the non-Mason the titles and mannerisms can seem ludicrous: Most Excellent Master, Super Excellent Master, Knights Kadosh, Royal Jester, Mystic Order Veiled Prophets of Enchanted Realm.

It [Freemasonry] has to be seen in a certain way, under certain conditions. Some people never see it at all. You must understand, this is no dead pile of stones and unmeaning timber. It is a LIVING thing.

When you enter it you hear a sound—a sound as of some mighty poem chanted. Listen long enough, and you will learn that it is made up of the beating of human hearts, of the nameless music of men's souls—that is, if you have ears to hear. If you have eyes, you will presently see the church itself—a looming mystery of many shapes and shadows, leaping sheer from floor to dome. The work of no ordinary builder!

The pillars of it go up like the brawny trunks of heroes; the sweet flesh of men and women is molded about its bulwarks, strong, impregnable; the faces of little children laugh out from every corner stone; the terrible spans and arches of it are the joined hands of comrades; and up in the heights and spaces are inscribed the numberless musings of all the dreamers of the world. It is yet building—building and built upon.

Sometimes the work goes on in deep darkness; sometimes in blinding light; now under the burden of unutterable anguish; now to the tune of great laughter and heroic shoutings like the cry of thunder. Sometimes, in the silence of the night-time, one may hear the tiny hammerings of the comrades at work up in the dome—the comrades that have climbed ahead.[17]

Although Freemasonry is famed as a secret organization, its spiritual secrets aren't imposed by men but by the nature of the knowledge. Only those equipped to understand can understand, and they can discover the truths whether or not they are Freemasons (see Matthew 7:6–8). There is no small group of sages who have the key to all knowledge, and who jealously guard it. The greatest spiritual insights are available to all with an ear to hear. As one Freemason wrote, "Apart from its rites, there is no mystery in Masonry, save the mystery of all great and simple things."[18]

A German handbook, current when Harry became a Mason, said, "Masonry is the activity of closely united men who, employing symbolical forms borrowed principally from the mason's trade and from architecture, work for the welfare of mankind, striving morally to ennoble themselves and others, and thereby to bring about a universal league of mankind, which they aspire to exhibit even now on a small scale." This is no mere rhetoric. For instance, American Freemasonry, unlike many religious denominations, didn't split in the Civil War. Indeed, one night during the Battle of Gettysburg, USA and CSA soldiers reportedly met in cordial fellowship at the Gettysburg lodge.[19]

Freemasonry isn't a religion; it is a socially acceptable means by which interested persons can seek mystical experience. The hard-headed businessman may be interested in spiritual growth and mystical experience. In America few Protestant denominations offer that sort of thing, but it is available through the Masonic lodge attended by all those other "regular fellows" of the community. Perhaps rather few lodge brothers seek much spiritual enlightenment, but some do. Harry Truman was such a man.

Harry's spiritual knowledge guided his conduct. He commonly spoke of his beliefs, but these references have been ignored as the pious mouthings of a politician. On the contrary, these statements are consistent with his public policies—so consistent that the sum of those beliefs must have been the basis of his public policies.

At one time Harry considered himself a Presbyterian, but at the age of eighteen he joined the Benton Boulevard Baptist Church at

Kansas City. Later he changed his membership to Grandview Baptist. There he was active in Baptist Young People's Union. "I'm a Baptist because I think that sect gives the common man the shortest and most direct approach to God."[20]

"My mother owned a big deckle-edged Bible published in 1881, which contained the first revised version of the New Testament parallel to the King James version. I was raised on that book." Even in childhood Harry knew that there were different versions of the word of God. Before leaving grade school he had read the book at least twice, and he continued to read it as part of his Masonic studies. "There is no reading as interesting as the Old and New Testaments, especially those parts referred to in every Masonic Degree from 1 to 33 in the Scottish Rite and through Chapter and Commandery in the York Rite." Harry referred to certain biblical passages again and again. They were the foundations of his public policies.[21]

Although Truman was a Baptist, he didn't feel that belief in the divinity of Jesus was important for salvation. Indeed, he gave high praise to Thomas Jefferson's *The Life and Morals of Jesus of Nazareth* (commonly called Jefferson's Bible), a book that omits any suggestion that Jesus was divine, and presents only His ethical teachings. Even as a young man, Harry said, "I wasn't particularly interested in the religious thing but in the codes that make people behave. That's all." His interest in Freemasonry's spiritual teachings was related to rules of conduct. The particular appeal of Freemasonry was its transcendence not only of Christian denominations but of Christianity itself. In his view the ethical beliefs of Masons were consistent with all great religions. To him the differences among the faiths were petty, and as he rose in public service Truman developed a fantastic desire to unite all adherents of these religions (just as all Freemasons were united) in opposition to societies that in his view had no moral code. Using his power as president of the United States, Truman ecumenically tried to unite all who worshipped the one God. "I have been trying to bring a number of the great religious leaders of the world together in a common affirmation of faith. And that common affirmation . . . is in the 20th chapter of Exodus [Ten Commandments], and in the 5th, 6th, and 7th chapters of the Gospel according to St. Matthew [Sermon on the Mount]." Much to his disgust, the various religious leaders didn't share his opinion that their differences were petty: "They just couldn't see the whole picture." Truman saw this as a failure to unite "their strength against the hosts of irreligion and danger in the world, and that will be the cause of world catastrophe."[22]

To Truman, religion dealt less with humankind's relations with God and more with good works.

> If we really believed in the Brotherhood of Man, it would not be necessary to pass a Fair Employment Practices Act.

> If certain interests were not so greedy for gold, there would be less pressure and lobbying to induce the Congress to allow the Price Control Act to expire, or to keep down minimum wages, or to permit further concentration of economic power.

> A truly religious fervor among our people would go a long way toward obtaining a national health program, a national housing program, a national education program, and an extended and improved social security program. . . .

> Reduce your abundance so that others may have a crust of bread. In short, prove yourselves worthy of the liberty and dignity which you have preserved on this earth.

> A religious heritage such as ours, is not a comfortable thing to live with. It does not mean that we are more virtuous than other people. Instead, it means that we have less excuse for doing the wrong thing—because we are taught right from wrong. . . .

> It means first of all that we must constantly strive for social justice in the life of the Republic. It means we must fight against special privilege, against injustice to those of low income, and against the denial of opportunity, against discrimination based upon race, creed, or national origin.

> Religious heritage also means that we must struggle to maintain our civil liberties. No nation which hopes to live by the law of God can afford to suppress dissent and criticism. You may remember that Israel persecuted the prophets. . . . The kings and priests of Israel tried to deny them freedom of speech. But the prophets were right, and Israel was punished as the prophets had said it would be. . . .

> We must remember that the test of our religious principles lies not just in what we say, not only in our prayers, not even in living blameless personal lives—but in what we do for others.[23]

While Harry was a farmer he lost his father, and found Bess Wallace.

Harry wasn't the only Truman farmer; Vivian and John also worked the land. In 1911 Vivian married and moved off the family farm. John and Harry then ran the farm themselves, with the father clearly the boss. "J.A. Truman & Son, Farmers," the printed stationery said. John's health seems to have begun failing around 1912. He switched from doctor to doctor without cure. By autumn 1913 he was definitely having what was loosely described as "stomach trouble," treating himself with herbal medicine (specifically, dried fruit) from a Chinese doctor in Kansas City. In mid-1914 John fatally injured himself when, as road overseer, he tried to move a boulder. Apparently he strained himself and developed a severe hernia that gradually caused intestinal blockage. The physicians said the condition had been coming on for a decade or more. The pain in his side distracted him, and as the weeks went by weight dropped from his bones. He doggedly held out against radical medical intervention until he could resist no longer. The surgeon at Swedish Hospital said that John would have died without the operation. With it, he lingered five more weeks. Farmhand Brownie Huber recounted, "Harry and I often got up real early and very quietly so as not to awaken his mother and sister. He would make biscuits, cook oatmeal and fry eggs. That is the way it was the morning his father died. I was eating breakfast while Harry went in to stay with the old gentleman, when he appeared at the door and said, 'Dad just passed away.' "[24]

"An Upright Citizen Whose Death Will Be a Blow to His Community," the *Independence Examiner* said. "My father was a very energetic person. He worked from daylight to dark, all the time. And his code was honesty and integrity. His word was good. When he told us that something was a fact, . . . that was just what it was: it was the truth. And he raised my brother and myself to put honor above profit. He was quite a man, my dad was. . . . He was not a talker. He was an acter. He lived what he believed, and taught the rest of us to do the same thing."[25]

Another great event affected Harry in these years. His fantasies about Bess began their move toward reality during one of his common visits to Ethel Noland, who lived across the street from Bess. Ethel recalled that

Mrs. Wallace was very neighborly and she loved to send things. Oh, we did back and forth, you know. She would send over a nice dessert or something, just to share it and here was a plate. Well, we hadn't taken it back and I said, "Why don't you take that plate home, it's been around here a few days."

"Well," he said, "I certainly will."

And Bess came to the door, and of course nothing could have made a bigger occasion than that, to see her again and talk to her.

This apparently was the first time Harry and Bess had seen each other since high school.[26]

A lot had gone on since then. A couple of years after Bess graduated from high school her father committed suicide. The blow was compounded by sneers against her mother, innuendos from townspeople and others that her mother's inflated self-esteem drove Dave Wallace to desperation. There was also gossip that Dave Wallace had worried excessively about money. Why else would one of the most popular men in the county take to drink? Why else would this county politician kill himself just as he was being mentioned for state office? Why else indeed. Years later a relative suggested that throat cancer had something to do with it, running up medical bills, every drop of saliva burning all day long, with Dave's vocal cords squeezed tighter and tighter by the growth. A contemporary account blamed the death on "the insidious disease against which he battled for years, . . . slowly creeping upward toward the brain," but this seems a veiled reference to Dave's alcoholism. Madge Wallace and her children then moved from their house at 610 North Delaware to the home of Madge's parents at 219 North Delaware, across from Ethel Noland, a house later known as the Summer White House.[27]

This is the house where Madge grew up as the daughter of George Gates, one of the wealthier men in Independence. As befitted a young woman of high social rank, Bess was now sent as a commuter to Barstow School—which also removed her from Independence while gossip about her parents diminished. Mary Louise Barstow and Ada Braun ran a finishing school in Kansas City for young ladies of the metropolitan social elite. Although classroom work was held, the school's emphasis was on physical fitness. The school property at

Main and Westport Road had ample space for outdoor athletics, in which Bess excelled.[28]

Back in Independence Bess lived the life expected of a woman of her social standing. "Miss Bessie Wallace entertained her whist club at her home on North Delaware street yesterday afternoon. There were 16 guests. Miss Helen Ross made the high score for the guests and Miss Mattie McCoy for the club members." "Miss Agnes Owens entertained Friday night at her home, 404 North Spring street. Dancing and cards were the amusements of the evening. Prizes were awarded to Miss May Stewart and Mr. John Wood." It was a protected, hothouse life. One could hardly be surprised if the free-spirited Bess Wallace awaited a rescuer.[29]

Bess's friends the Swopes were big money. They were not thrilled when their daughter Frances decided to marry Dr. B. C. Hyde, a William Jewell College graduate who freely admitted having ruined two women, though he denied bilking them of their fortunes while pursuing his carnal pleasures.

In 1909 members of the Swope household who stood between Hyde and his wife's fortune began to sicken and die under Hyde's professional care. Hyde pushed Dr. G. T. Twyman (who had ministered to the diphtheric Harry Truman) and his son Dr. Elmer Twyman (who moved in Bess's social circle) out of the case, but not before they had noticed unusual aspects of Dr. Hyde's medical technique. For instance, he diagnosed one person as suffering from bad blood, and proceeded to drain off a half gallon. The man died. This death could have put Hyde in position to become executor of the Swope fortune, except the patriarch, Col. Thomas Swope, had his heart set on J. H. Hawthorne, the first judge in John Anderson Truman's gas well case. Then Colonel Swope himself died. Then Bess's friend Chrisman Swope. Then Bess's friends Margaret, Lucy Lee, Sarah, and Stella Swope began to take sick, as did others in the house. Bing, bing, bing. Hyde was indicted for murder. His lawyer was Jim Aylward's partner, Frank Walsh. The special prosecutor was Jim Reed. Reed's nearly perfect record as a prosecutor had been spoiled some years earlier by Walsh's successful defense of Jesse James, Jr. So the Hyde case was something of a grudge match, with feelings heightened by politics. This was 1910, an election year, and the outcome of this highly publicized trial could be crucial in the primary election for U.S. Senate because Reed was the foremost spokesman for the Pendergast faction and was a candidate for the Senate. His campaign operated from the office of George R. Collins, who was Harry's captain in the National Guard. By happenstance perhaps too strong for coincidence, Frank Walsh was the chief operative for the Shannon Democrat faction, which then provided the main opposition to Pendergast and therefore to Reed's Senate campaign. Pendergast man Reed won the trial and the primary, and was elected to the Senate by the Missouri legislature. Although Hyde's conviction was reversed, some still believed him guilty. Among them were Bess Wallace and Harry Truman.[30]

According to local gossip, Bess's mother disapproved of Harry, but the gossip may have been wrong to a degree. Ethel Noland knew all the principals from the start, and declared, "There's one myth that I would like to nail. And that is that Mrs. Wallace didn't approve of that match." Ethel continued, "She always liked him, and she favored the match from the very start. In fact, we weren't sure whether she liked him better than Bess did or not." Although Bess moved in high society, this was Independence high society. The Trumans knew the same people, and were among the town's "good families." Harry and Bess grew up only three or four blocks apart, went to the same schools, and had the same circle of friends until the Trumans left town. Much has been made of Bess's grandfather's wealth, but Harry's grandfather had even more money. The social backgrounds of Harry and Bess were similar. There was no reason for Madge Wallace to disapprove of Harry any more than Bess's other callers. Quite the contrary, Ethel Noland said, Mrs. Wallace "approved of him, because she knew that he had qualities that any girl could bank on in the long run." Nonetheless, Harry has been portrayed as a man harried by a vicious mother-in-law who lived with him, making home life an ordeal, draining energy from his work. Part of this was true. Harry bubbled with warm anecdotes about relatives, but had nothing to say about his mother-in-law. Jonathan Daniels's "authorized biography" of Harry omitted mention of her. This silence suggests something strange about that relationship. In a private memorandum Harry probably implied criticism of Madge Wallace when he complained of "my drunken brother-in-law, whom I'd had to employ on the [county patronage] job to keep peace in the family." Margaret Truman has written of frequent bickering between Harry and Madge. So that much of the gossip was true. A White House servant recorded a revealing story about the home atmosphere, an incident when General MacArthur was relieved of command: "When Mrs. Wallace persisted, and asked from her sickbed, 'Bess, why did Harry fire that nice man?', Mrs. 'T' refused to discuss it. Instead, she threw back her shoulders . . . and marched out of the room." Bess disliked "to hear her mother criticize the President in private."[31]

Except for its length, Harry's courtship of Bess was no different from thousands of other courtships. At first he took the Frisco train ("Old Leaky Roof") up to Sheffield where he hopped the streetcar to Independence. Ethel Noland's house was filled with children at this time, and they would come running when he cranked the doorbell three times—the special ring that announced Cousin Harry. He always had time for the children, and they loved him—he might even plop one of them on the piano bench for a "Chopsticks" duet. After freshening up he'd go across the street to Bess's house. The couple might then head for the Willis Wood theater in Kansas City to see a Shakespeare play or a thriller, or hear pianist Vladimir de Pachmann in concert. After the date, Harry often spent the night at Ethel's, since the train back to Grandview was often unavailable at that hour. He made two or three trips a week from Grandview to Independence, and they were a tremendous expenditure of time. Harry pined for an automobile, and his acquisition of a black Stafford in 1914 freed him from the train schedule. Autos were uncommon enough to attract notice, and this was the first one in the Truman family. Harry liked to race other cars (much to the fright of his passengers), and decades later he still fondly recalled "Lizzie's" four-cylinder "improved overhead cam, valve-in-the-head motor. . . . It would go 60 miles an hour—a touring car with high brass windshield and Prest-O-Lite lamps." He bought it secondhand for $600, and repainted it red. In addition to easing the Grandview-Independence trip, the car widened the social activities available to Harry and Bess, with other couples accompanying them on dates.[32]

In between outings Harry carried on a voluminous correspondence with Bess. He wrote often of farm life and country ways.

We have about 400 shocks left yet to shuck before we are done. It is a job invented by Satan himself. Dante sure left something from the tenth circle when he failed to say that the inhabitants of that dire place shucked shock corn. I am sure they do.

I went to a party at Grandview a few days ago, and they tried to teach me the "hoe down" or country dance. I sure had a circus learning. There is a widow up there who particularly adores Vivian, and he of course abominates her. Well when he isn't around she takes her spite out on me. Well, when they started the dance she of course took it upon herself to teach me. Did you ever hear them call a "hoe down"? It goes something like this: "Swing the girl with the pretty brown hair and now the one with the face so fair. Swing the gal with a lantern jaw and now the one from Arkansas. Balance and turn and left and right and all promenade." Then you do it over. You can get most gloriously dizzy and it's a lot cheaper than booze.

You know a pumpkin-vine phone is a 10-party line. When you want to use it you have to take down the receiver and listen while some good sister tells some other good sister who is not so wise how to make butter or how to raise chickens or when it is the right time in the moon to plant onion sets or something else equally important. About the time you think the world is coming to an end or some other direful calamity will certainly overtake you if you don't get to express your feelings into that phone, the good sister will quit, and then if you are quick and have a good, strong voice you can have your say; but you know confidently that everyone in the neighborhood has heard you. If someone would invent a contraption to shut out the other nine when a person wanted to use the tenth, he would be richer and more famous than Edison. But he'd be forever unpopular with us farmers for we'd never know each other's business.

It is the custom of the creeks and hollows to have one of those barbarous things [charivari] whenever anyone gets married. I guess everyone in south Jackson County will come to this one. I went to one once and got a good enamel dishpan belonging to the man's mother and simply beat it to death. She is the third cousin of mine by marriage, and I had to buy a new one. It is the right thing to have shotguns, cowbells, circular saws, tin pans, and every other known noisemaker. The racket has to be kept up until the gentle-man and his bride show themselves. He must pass cigars, and she hands around candy or cake. Everyone is satisfied then, a good social time is had, and we all wonder who'll be next. Woe be unto the man who fails to show up and set up. He'll be visited night after night with noise and finally branded a snob and a cheap screw.

It is an ornery custom, but it has to be stood for out here. Everyone goes, girls and all. We always have a good time and generally land a very fair feed.[33]

The courtship's length caused comment. Late marriages were nothing unusual in the Truman family. Harry probably would have married Bess sooner, but her interest in him as a mate was slow to develop. Bess was in no hurry to marry anyone, and Harry was not interested in anyone else. So that made for a lengthy courtship. Simple enough, though much head scratching has occurred over it.[34]

Harry and Bess apparently renewed their childhood acquaintance in late 1910. Harry's broken leg in April 1911 stopped their visits, but they continued a friendly correspondence that had started shortly after Christmas in 1910. In June 1911 Harry sent Bess a proposal. He probably suspected he was premature and perhaps even too forward, closing the epistle somewhat fearfully with, "Say, Bessie, you'll at least let me keep on being good friends, won't you?" He asked for a prompt reply, as he would be in suspense waiting. The days stretched to a week, and then some. No letter, no phone call, nothing. Harry sent a second letter, and a week later a third. The correspondence showed a pathetic longing that is painful for an outsider to read. One suspects that Bess was stumped by how to reject Harry's proposal without crushing him. At last the expected turndown arrived, much to Harry's relief and disappointment. "What makes me feel real good is that you were good enough to answer me seriously and not make fun of me anyway. . . . You see I never had any desire to say such things to anyone else. All my girl friends think I am a cheerful idiot and a confirmed old bach. They really don't know the reason nor ever will. I have been so afraid you were not even going to let me be your good friend. . . . I guess I am something of a freak myself. I really never had any desire to make love to a girl just for the fun of it, and you have always been the reason." A few days later Harry and Bess got together for the first time in three months, and they continued to see each other as before.[35]

Their visits became more frequent, though Harry wasn't always certain that his invitation would be accepted. When Bess failed to come to his Labor Day party in 1911 after Harry had constructed a tennis court for her to enjoy that day, his anguish is apparent: "I really worked all day Sunday getting that court ready for you. We also had a supply of watermelons on hand. But you can make it some Saturday, and Mamma says you must come to dinner next time." Eventually Bess gave Harry a standing invitation for Sundays, and he finally found enough courage to advise her about what clothes she should wear. She valued his companionship more and more; and as Bess grew to know Harry better, she found him more than a little mysterious despite his ostensible openness. She apparently saw or suspected things in him that even he was unaware of. In November 1913 they gave each other a pledge, which became a formal engagement.[36]

Money may have been one reason for Bess's hesitation. She had to be curious about how Harry would finance married life. Harry was curious, too, and was humiliated that he couldn't afford to buy an engagement ring for Bess. This financial uncertainty delayed their marriage, and World War I delayed it some more. In all, they would wait five and a half years until they both realized enough was enough. Another factor was that Bess loathed farm life. This had to be plain enough to Harry, who must have realized that he could never marry Bess as long as he remained a farmer. This must have influenced his shift away from farming in 1916. The shift also had to be related to the special financial circumstances that developed on the Grandview farm about the time Harry started courting Bess.[37]

The farm was financially successful until Harry's grandmother Harriet Louisa Young died in 1909. She had lived on the farm all these years, but had slipped into senility; her influence was scarcely felt toward the end of her life. When Solomon Young died without a will there was little trouble, as his property simply went to Louisa. Her death, however, could leave quite a few relatives with claims to the $150,000 estate. She made a will in 1895 to avoid such messiness, dividing the estate among her children as follows: $5.00 to Susan Bartleson, $5.00 to Will Young, $5.00 to Sarah Ann Dunsmore, $5.00 to Laura Everhart, $5.00 to Ada Van Cloostere, $74,987.50 (approximately) to Harrison Young, and $74,987.50 (approximately) to Martha Ellen Truman. The Trumans felt that this was an equitable division. After all, they and Harrison Young had kept up the Grandview farm, while the other Young offspring had abandoned the property. The other kinfolk saw things differently. Will remembered how Harrison had run him off the property with only gunshot wounds as a souvenir. Sallie remembered how Solomon cursed her return after her husband Jim Crow had been shot to death, how her daughter had been struck by Mattie for making noise on the stairs, how Mattie burned Sallie's treasured portrait of her husband, and how all this brutality eventually forced Sallie to flee the farm. Ada remembered how Solomon and Harrison forcibly ejected her from the homestead, shipping her off to St. Louis. No, the kinfolk didn't quite see it the way Mattie and Harrison did. Far from avoiding messiness, Louisa Young's will loosed rage that had festered for decades.[38]

The lawyers went to work, and the Trumans lost everything Louisa Young had left them. They retained the land itself, but to buy off all the claimants they had to put the farm under a heavy mortgage—perhaps $30,000. This may have been arranged by Harry's close Masonic associate Frank Blair, cashier at Bank of Belton. In good years the farm might make $15,000, but the bankers reaped that profit. This inability to retain the fruits of his labors must have been yet another factor in Harry's growing disenchantment with farming by 1916. "We never did catch up the debts," he said. "We always owed the bank something, sometimes more, sometimes less, but we always owed the bank." From a business standpoint owing money to a bank is routine; expressing concern about it suggests financial strain.[39]

At first Harry tried to help the farm escape the noose by seeking unencumbered farmland to provide additional income. He did this by joining the last groups of white settlers and speculators in Indian land grabs. In October 1911 Harry and two friends traveled to Gregory, South Dakota, where he registered in a drawing to distribute Indian land. As he prepared for the trip he mused:

I bet there'll be more bohunks and "Rooshans" up there than white men. I think it is a disgrace to the country for those fellows to be in it. If they had only stopped immigration about 20 or 30 years ago, the good Americans could all have had plenty of land and we'd have been an agricultural country forever. You know as long as a country is one of that kind, people are more independent and make better citizens. When it is made up of factories and large cities it soon becomes depressed and makes classes among people. Every farmer thinks he's as good as the President or perhaps a little bit better. When a man works for a boss, he is soon impressed with how small he is and how great the boss is until he actually believes it is so and that money makes the world go round. It does I guess in very large cities.

(A few months earlier Harry had written, "I think one man is just as good as another so long as he's honest and decent and not a nigger or a Chinaman. Uncle Will says that the Lord made a white man from dust, a nigger from mud, then threw up what was left and it came down a Chinaman. He does hate Chinese and Japs. So do I. It is race prejudice I guess. But I am strongly of the opinion that negroes ought to be in Africa, yellow men in Asia, and white men in Europe and America.")

The trains up to South Dakota and back were packed with other fortune seekers. "At nearly every station, we met trains coming back. People on them would yell Sucker! Sucker! at us." Arriving in Gregory around 10:30 P.M. Harry joined the throngs registering for the drawing. "There were about 20 notaries inside of a hollow square. I bet there was more swearing going on there than there ever will be in one place again. I really don't know what a Quaker would have done. They didn't ask you to swear, but just filled out the papers—and you were sworn before you knew what was happening." Harry spent the night on a cot and left early the next morning. "I was so sleepy when I got in the train coming from Omaha to Kansas City that I thought nothing could keep me awake. But there was an old woman and her daughter had the berth opposite me. The old lady had asthma or some wheezy complaint. When she wasn't wheezing or snoring she was quarreling with her daughter." Truman didn't win a claim. "I never could draw anything," he told Bess. "I am born under Neptune or some other far distant and unlucky star."

In September 1913 Harry organized an expedition of his father, brother Vivian, L. C. Hall and his sons William and Stanley, Gaylon Babcock, and Edward Young (a veterinarian; no kin to Solomon) to Harve, Montana, for another try at Indian lands. All eight registered for a chance to win some land, and Harry registered a ninth name, a Spanish-American War veteran who in return paid half of Harry's travel expenses. The trip up, via Minneapolis and St. Paul, took four or five days. From Minneapolis Harry wrote to Bess, "It is cold as an iceberg up here. They say it's been hot at one time, but I don't believe it." Babcock, Young, and one of the Halls got into an automobile the morning they all arrived in Harve and set out to examine the Indian land. "The land was unquestionably good soil, but we were dubious about the rainfall and about the winters and about the crops," Babcock said. "The corn that we saw . . . was very short corn and very different from the type crop that we were used to. And, had I drawn a claim, I'm not sure that I would have tried to have proven up on it." The drawing was the same day, and one of the Halls won a claim. Babcock's father lent them money to prove up the claim (they had to ship livestock and machinery to Harve), but after a couple years the homestead failed. On the day of the drawing, however, the project was bright with hope. The Grandview men all boarded the train home that same day. The Trumans had no land to show for the trip, but John did return with seeds from sumptuous peaches he had bought in Minneapolis.[40]

Harry also attempted to acquire unencumbered land through convoluted litigation that began in 1911 and continued until after he entered the army in World War I. The files of the case, which went to the Missouri Supreme Court, have disappeared. The full story may never be known. In 1896 John's gas well associate J. F. Buchanan prepared an abstract of title for some acreage down south in Shannon County. The next year Frank C. Gallagher acquired the property, and it passed around his family before returning to him in 1906. In 1907 a family named McIntyre sued Gallagher, George E. Schaeffer, and Harry to confirm that the McIntyres owned the property. According to later testimony of Harry, Peter McIntyre and wife had deeded the land to Sabina McNamara who in turn gave interest in 120 acres to Harry. In 1908 Shannon County circuit court decreed that the McIntyres were the true owners. They turned over a one-fourth interest in the land to their lawyer Ed J. Shuck, apparently as a fee for handling the case. Shuck then sued both his client Mary McIntyre and Frank Gallagher to gain actual possession of the property—a confusing move since the circuit court had already stripped Gallagher of any interest in the property. The result of this was a sheriff's sale at which Anna Davis bought the land and then sold a half-interest to J. William Chilton, lawyer, newspaper publisher, and big Ozarks real estate operator. These new owners then sued some of the McIntyres, Gallagher, Harry, and others to strip the defendants of any interest in the land. In effect this was the third time the Shannon County circuit court was asked to decide the issue, and once again, in September 1910, the court ruled that Harry had no interest.

Sometime after all this occurred Harry found out about it and was miffed that he had never been personally served with the petition as to any of these lawsuits that relieved him of 120 acres. (Not being notified by personal service, he had not appeared in court. In routine technical lawsuits such as these his nonappearance would result in a default judgment against him. Unscrupulous litigants could therefore rig a case by an oath that the defendant's whereabouts was unknown and that service was made by publication in the county newspaper where the land was located.) Harry and Gallagher appealed the proceedings in November 1911, arguing that none of the plaintiffs who had sued them had ever had any interest whatsoever in the land, and that moreover the plaintiffs had perpetrated a fraud on the court by never having the Jackson County sheriff personally serve Harry with notice of the litigation. The Shannon County circuit court agreed that fraud had occurred, and decreed that Harry and Gallagher owned the land. The case now went to the Missouri Supreme Court, where Chilton claimed he had attempted to have the Jackson County sheriff serve notice on Harry, but Chilton implied that the sheriff didn't know how to find Harry. The Missouri Supreme Court ruled in February 1917 that even if a fraud had been perpetrated on the Shannon County circuit by persons who had no interest in the land, the court's decree based on that fraud had to stand. In July the Missouri Supreme Court ruled that Harry had never had any interest in the land (even though people seeking the land had repeatedly admitted via their lawsuits that Harry had an arguable interest), and therefore there could be no fraud in failing to serve him with notice that a lawsuit had been instituted to take away from him land he didn't own. Harry's reaction to losing the land is unrecorded. Nor do we know his reaction to being juridically branded a liar.

The litigation had several strange aspects suggesting skulduggery. One witness said he was prepared to bid $300 at the sheriff's sale but allowed Anna Davis to buy the land for $30 because he "did not want to bid against a woman." Chilton couldn't produce the letter in which he implied that the Jackson County sheriff said Harry couldn't be found. Harry couldn't produce the deed from Peter McIntyre and wife to Sabina McNamara, although this deed appeared in J. F. Buchanan's abstract of the land ownership. Chilton's side objected to J. F. Buchanan presenting this history of the land's ownership. Harry claimed that McNamara had in turn given him title to the property. We don't know why McNamara did this, but the people who coveted the acreage obviously thought Harry had some right to it or they wouldn't have brought lawsuits to extinguish that interest. The Supreme Court ruled in effect that neither side had any right to the land, and then awarded it to Chilton. Much about this case remains mysterious, and the documents that might enlighten history are missing from court archives.[41]

As these fruitless attempts to acquire unencumbered land went on, the court battles over Louisa Young's will ground along. "My duty was to help the lawyers defend it," Harry said about the will. He and lawyer friend Fred Boxley had to travel to Estancia, New Mexico, to track down a witness to the will and get a deposition. Harry remembered "That deposition was taken in the office of Frank Jennings. He and his brother Al were the bandits of the 1880's. Al afterwards ran for governor of Oklahoma but was defeated. Frank Jennings was a fine man, and he and Boxley and some other men organized a poker game the night we were in Estancia, but I did not know enough about the game then to get into it."[42]

Even losses that the Young farm suffered during the Civil War became enmeshed in the will controversy. In 1864 Congress created the Southern Claims Commission to deal with claims that loyal citizens of loyal states made for property lawfully seized by the U.S. Army. The procedure for investigating and reimbursing these claims changed over the years. Eventually the U.S. Court of Claims received responsibility for investigations, with Congress having the option of paying or not paying compensation. On June 7, 1890 the Committee on War Claims of the U.S. House of Representatives referred Solomon Young's case to the U.S. Court of Claims. Over twelve years later the court ruled that Solomon Young had been a loyal citizen and was entitled to make a claim. This news made no difference to Solomon Young, who had been dead for a decade, but his widow took up the case. On May 7, 1906 the case finally came before the court. Through her attorney G. W. Hott, Louisa said the United States of America owed her $21,442 for 15 mules, 15 horses, 150 cattle, 44 hogs, 1,200 pounds of bacon, 65 tons hay, 1,500 bushels corn, 6,000 rations, 7 wagons, 43,000 nails, 1 bed, 1 bridle, 1 saddle, and temporary use of 1 house. On May 21 the court ruled that the Yankees had indeed taken each and every thing that Louisa Young alleged, "which was reasonably worth at the time the sum of three thousand eight hundred dollars ($3,800), for which no payment seems to have been made." The court was rather flinty in its recommended compensation, but Louisa Young was $3,800 better off than before. Or so she may have thought. Congress then took up the matter of whether to pay. The Young claim was combined with hundreds of others into the Omnibus Claims Bill. All were carefully dissected in acrimonious debate that refought the Civil War, and the Young claim reappeared unscathed at the end of the process. Congress approved the Omnibus Claims Bill, and President Wilson signed it. This approval was March 4, 1915, almost nine years after the U.S. Court of Claims ruled in favor of Louisa Young. She had died in the meantime, and the terms of her will provided that the $3,800 be split between Martha Ellen Truman and Harrison Young. We know what the relatives thought of that—on March 23 Martha and Harrison had to promise all the money to Susan Bartleson, Will Young, Laura Everhart, Solomon Chiles (Jim Crow's son), Elizabeth Maskome, Susan Wells, and perhaps Joseph Van Cloostere. The Young estate attorney Theoph. L. Carns explained that the U.S. Treasury Department had yet to produce the $3,800. Mattie may have sued the United States for the money, but that aspect remains mysterious, as do elements of the Civil War claims. The files are missing from court archives.[43]

"I've spent my life trying to have all the family get along and love each other," Harry said. This included personal visits and letters. "I have always had correspondence with the family ever since I can remember. Always had. In fact, I was always the clearing house for all the family, even when they weren't speaking to each other. They were speaking to me. Got them all to the point eventually where there was no ill-feeling between us. That's a job with a Kentucky outfit."[44]

Harry seems to have regarded his farm years as difficult. "I put in 10 of the best years of my life running a 600-acre farm. It was a bad time for farmers." He explained, "I tried to dig a living and a surplus out of the ground. My father was most energetic and we all worked faithfully, but if it wasn't the panic of 1907 it was drouth or too much rain or hog cholera or some peculiar sickness among the cattle." Or a killing mortgage. From his banking experience Harry had to know the burden the farm assumed in the wake of Louisa Young's fateful will. (Indeed, he thought selling the farm might be the most prudent action, but feared the blow would be too hard on his mother.) Unexpected expenses arose, such as the medical bills for Harry's father, including $500 for the operation. Harry said that he had to borrow that money on top of everything else, and his sister Mary Jane remembered that in the end the farm's entire Black Angus herd had to be sold to cover the bills from the physician and from elsewhere. Harry's words and actions show a man gradually becoming disenchanted with the soil, spending more and more time on other things as the years passed. When addressing agricultural audiences Truman was upbeat about his farm experience, and this wasn't dissembling. Life is hard for most farmers, yet they honestly point to happy moments. Still, Harry eventually rejected farming, leaving his mother and sister to manage the property as best they could. As president he would talk about returning to the farm, and he could easily have lived an elegant life as a country gentleman in the fashion of George Washington. Yet Harry chose city life when he retired from the White House.[45]

"All sorts of wagers were made that I wouldn't stay [on the farm] over ten days—two weeks—a month—a year at the outside. I stayed ten years. I thought of Cincinnatus and a lot of other farm boys who had made good and I thought maybe by cussing mules and plowing corn I could perhaps overcome my shyness and amount to something."[46]

Harry had now received training in the three basic areas that he felt great men had to know—finance, agriculture, and the military. The woman he loved rejected production agriculture, and so did Harry after his father died. Now he returned to the metropolitan business world of Kansas City with a plan to make his fortune. For the first time Harry's spiritual ideals would be tested in the crucible of capitalist materialism, and he would learn much about fellow men and about his own soul.[47]

Chapter 5
A PURITAN IN BABYLON

There's no one wants to win half so badly as I do.
—Harry S. Truman, 1916[1]

In spring 1915 Harry was depressed about his financial situation. "I'm $12,500 worse off than nothing." Such were the debts caused by the litigation over Louisa's will. Harry's role in that dispute, however, had attracted favorable attention from his uncle, who was a propertied man. Truman hoped this would result in aid from Harrison, either an appointment as business agent for his uncle (much as Solomon Young had done for John Anderson Truman) or else seed money for schemes Harry had devised to make his fortune so he could finally marry Bess Wallace.[2]

His first idea along that line involved Texas real estate, earning commissions by selling land. Both Harrison and L. C. Hall seem to have been involved with this project. From occasional trips to Texas Harry bragged about his salesmanship, and broke off a letter in this vein to Bess because "I think there's a gink watching me do this— as he's my intended victim (can't spell it) I'll have to stop." Harry eventually sold himself on the lands he peddled. "It is now the hard part to convince that uncle of mine that he should give me a boost. If he only would, I know as well as I'm alive that I could make $25,000 in three years and have a farm that would bring $150 an acre." A couple of weeks later that hope had receded: "I doubt very much if he [Harrison] allows me to do anything down here. If he doesn't, I'm going to try and make him loosen up at home."[3]

That opportunity arose in early 1916. Vivian had ridiculed the Texas real estate idea, and had noted that his father-in-law and two associates had bought a mine near Joplin, Missouri, for $30,000 and sold it for $105,000. According to Vivian his father-in-law had another mine that paid him $1,000 a week. Harry now hooked up with Jerry Culbertson. A darling of Kansas City high society, Culbertson had known the Truman family for years, and was well wired with area politicos, as were the Trumans. Culbertson first operated in Cass County, just below Jackson County. When Harry was in high school, Culbertson was Cass County prosecutor, and talked Sheriff Thomas R. Hughes into some gold mine ventures, which failed as such ventures normally do. As the years passed Hughes became a neighbor to the Truman farm. As road supervisor Harry would hire Hughes to work the roads. Neighbor Hughes introduced Harry to Culbertson in 1915, Harry recalled, and in early 1916 the three Masonic brethren along with Harrison Young decided to seek lead and zinc—less exotic than gold, but valuable in quantity.[4]

In January 1916 Culbertson got an option to buy the Eureka Mine & Mill near Commerce, Oklahoma, on the tri-state border by Joplin, Missouri. The selling price if Culbertson exercised the option was $13,500. Around March 4, scarcely two weeks after Harry wrote off the Texas land peddling as impractical, he and Tom Hughes jointly put up $5,000 or $5,500 to become Culbertson's partners. Harry's share must have come from Harrison. On March 5 Harry wrote from Joplin, "My money is in now, and I am feeling better over it every minute. After next week the money will begin to return. When *our* mill is properly repaired we can grind enough ore to make $1,000 a day (half profit). . . . I have been prowling around trying to find someone who thinks the Eureka mine is a fake, but I can't. They all says it's all right, only it needs about $3,000 spent on it. We are doing that. . . . Jerry says the 'hinges of destiny' are greased for our door of opportunity to open."[5]

On March 22 Culbertson, Harry, and Lou Edwards (of Commerce, Oklahoma) signed the articles of incorporation and became the three directors of T-C-H Mining Company. In this document Culbertson and Truman said they were citizens of Oklahoma. The men issued eight thousand shares of stock with a par value of $10.00

each. The par value and the market value of a stock are unrelated. A person who pays a company par value for a share may be unable to resell that share to someone else for the same price on the open market. That was the case with T-C-H. There is some evidence that shares were sold on the installment plan to perhaps twenty-five persons. Harry may not have been entirely joking when he remarked that someone had mistook him for a preacher: "If I can only retain that holy look, I can sell the mine by the blue-sky route and get rich anyway." On April 14 he, Culbertson, and Hughes signed a secret agreement providing that the $5,500 Truman and Hughes had put into the company, and all other money the partners expended on the project, would be a debt the company had to repay to the partners before any dividends were paid to stockholders, even though this debt "is not mentioned in the organization of said corporation." Mrs. Emily Tufts of Kansas City had 250 shares; director Lou Edwards had one share. Most of the rest were held by Truman, Culbertson, and president Tom Hughes. Culbertson apparently promised but never delivered a one-eighth nonassessable interest in the project to two of the men from whom he got the Eureka mine.[6]

Harry didn't think much of Commerce. "This place down here is certainly one beyond the limit. They have smallpox in town. The pest house is just a half a mile from us here at the mill. When it rains there is water six inches deep over everything. When it's dry the dust is as deep over everything. Mr. Hughes and I board across the street with a poor woman who has eight children. . . . She used a bottle for syrup and a glass for a cream pitcher today. She's good and means well so I guess we can put up with it." Harry soon became uneasy about money going into the mine, and none coming out. "I have gotten real penurious and am now staying at the plant nights. . . . I was paying 50 cents a night for someplace to sleep." Harry "expected all sorts of haunts and things to bother me, but if they came around I never saw them." He did have one uneasy experience. "The wind blew so hard here the other night that I expected one of our old tin smokestacks to fall across my bed. If it had, I'd not be writing now because the thing weighs some tons or more. I was all wrought up about it." He felt no such concern about inspecting progress underground. The elevator bucket "is iron and about three feet across and four deep. It goes round and round as it goes down. When I get to the bottom I can't tell north from straight up. We carry little carbide lamps that give about a penny's worth of light. That's plenty though in a place of total darkness."[7]

When operating at its peak the mine had twenty or twenty-five workers. They weren't all full time, but the total payroll for March and April was well over $2,000. Some of the men were dishonest, some unruly, and all were protected by Oklahoma law requiring compulsory arbitration of labor disputes. To the labor expense was added purchase of supplies and repairs of equipment. Covetous-seeming neighbors cut off water needed to refine ore, a move Harry gladly battled because it perhaps indicated that other persons thought the property worth stealing. He whistled in the graveyard to Bess: "I'm not worried. Things couldn't get this close to a win and then drop."[8]

None of the three partners was a full-time supervisor. Culbertson showed up rarely. Hughes was distracted by his farming, and a barn fire pretty much terminated his trips to Commerce. Harry kept up a grueling commute via railroad and automobile, trying to run both the mine and the Grandview farm. This sporadic supervision took its toll on mine production, another problem on top of all the others.[9]

In mid-May Harry's optimism ended. He thought the mine project was doomed, and operations virtually shut down. "It is a setback from which I don't suppose I shall very soon recover. If I don't lose all the livestock I have, it will only be because I shall turn it over to Mamma. I shall join the class who can't sign checks of their own I suppose. It is a hard nut to crack, but it has to be done. There was never one of our name who had sense enough to make money. I am no exception. I shall endeavor to make the farm go as usual, but I'll have to stay on it. My finances are completely exhausted." Harry mournfully told Bess, "You would do better perhaps if you pitch me into the ash heap and pick someone with more sense and ability and not such a soft head."[10]

A sleepless week after that glum assessment Harry was back in Commerce and hoping that his investment might yet be recouped. "We put too much confidence in Jerry's ability to raise money or we'd never have been in this condition." Three days later he blamed the mine superintendent as "the whole cause of our trouble." Harry's close Masonic associate, banker Frank Blair, came through with a loan to attempt a bailout. The local banker in Commerce also helped. By late June the operation was cranked up again. "If we blow up this time," Harry warned, "it sure will scatter the remains far and wide."[11]

Harry kept hoping that something would turn up: "Nothing equals this business for making Micawbers of men." The mine gasped, and in September 1916 it died. "I can't leave until I've satisfied everyone I owe down here that I'm not trying to beat anyone out of his money. I am getting gray-headed doing it but having pretty good success." When Harry left, $1,300 was still owed to creditors. They continued to remind T-C-H Mining Co. of these obligations as the weeks passed, but Truman seems to have regarded these as corporate debts for which he had no liability. Years later at least one creditor proved Truman wrong on that point.[12]

Evidently $13,600 had gone into the project, including a $6,900 payroll. "I have only gone in the hole on this hole about $11,000," Harry wrote on August 5. Perhaps mindful of the source of some of this money, he added, "Uncle Harry will probably cut me off his will, but that can't be helped." Two days later Harrison Young died. At the end of the month, after throwing more good money after bad, Harry wrote, "I'll simply have to suffer from a grand chorus of 'I told you so.' That wouldn't bother me so very badly if I'd only not gone and lost so much money. I'd sure have been right if I'd stayed at home and worked the farm this time. But how did I know Uncle Harry wouldn't live 20 years? And that he'd lease us what he had when he did die. I'd done given up hope in that direction. The unexpected happened, and now I'm all balled up and have gotten Mamma in the same fix. I am going to find a way out though if it takes the hide off both my hands to do it." Harry eventually figured his net loss at $7,500—the other $6,100 apparently came from Hughes and hapless creditors (Culbertson probably put little, if any, of his money into the project). Not only had Harry lost $7,500, he had made no progress on paying off the $12,500 he owed as a result of the Louisa Young will litigation.[13]

"I can't possibly lose forever," Harry cried. "If I just knew which god or goddess had it in for me, I'd try and appease him somehow."[14]

Harrison Young and Martha Truman had divided the heavily mortgaged Solomon Young property between them, and Harry had run both farms after John's death. Harrison willed his farm to Martha and her children as tenants in common, and Harry immediately signed over to his mother all his interest in Harrison's estate. Harry initially misinterpreted the legalese term "tenants" as meaning that the inheritors were leasing the property from the dead man, but in fact they owned it outright. By signing over his share to his mother, Harry compensated her for part of the mining loss. This compensation, however, generated no cash.[15]

About this time Jerry Culbertson placed a newspaper ad calling for cheap Oklahoma land, land that he could promote as "possibly" containing oil. Culbertson planned to organize an oil syndicate, using investments in one property to finance acquisition of a second property, and investments in the second to acquire a third, and on and on across the midcontinent of America. Attorney David H. Morgan of Tulsa heard Culbertson's call. Morgan had spent half a decade leasing and buying likely oil lands from Indians and Freedmen of the Five Civilized Tribes. He knew how to find oil. Culbertson knew how to find money. They made their pact at the Orear-Leslie Building in Kansas City, Missouri. While Morgan was poring over his geological surveys, and Culbertson was glad-handing his investors, someone had to tie the whole thing together. The partners needed someone who could keep track of the money, the stock, the leases, the corporation records. They needed an administrator. Culbertson said he knew just the man.[16]

Culbertson invited Harry to join Atlas-Okla Oil Lands Syndicate via a one-third interest in Morgan & Company Oil Investments Corporation, the investments arm of the syndicate. (Morgan & Company would buy and sell land, leases, and stock certificates.) Harry was already furious with Culbertson over the mining deal, going so far as virtually to blame Culbertson for the project's demise. Harry's banker friend Frank Blair, who had tried to bail him out of the mine, had by now explicitly warned Harry that Culbertson was unreliable. Yet Harry decided to trust his fate to this man once again. To become an oilman all Harry had to do was give Culbertson $5,000, but for that he needed backing from his mother. Harry explained the proposition to her. His mother believed in her son, mortgaged the old Harrison Young farm, and endorsed five $1,000 notes. A neighbor said that Vivian watched and seethed. He watched glib Harry convince their beloved Mamma to put family farmland behind another Jerry Culbertson city-slicker scheme. Vivian could feel Harry's influence over her. A neighbor said that Vivian drank deeply of these feelings, so deeply that the bitter taste stayed with him all his life.[17]

Harry signed the contract on September 25, 1916, turning over the five $1,000 notes (due in ten months) to Morgan & Company. Culbertson now used these notes as collateral for a bank loan to lubricate his investment plans. He had already talked partner David Morgan into trading fifteen hundred acres of eastern Oklahoma for fifteen hundred shares in the oil syndicate. If the business failed, Culbertson would lose nothing since he had put nothing into it. If the business succeeded, Culbertson would get one-third of the profits without sharing any of the risk. Yes, Culbertson understood the oil business.[18]

Unlike investors in many other firms, Harry could see his money working. Culbertson used it to buy advertisements in oil trade journals and Kansas City newspapers. "The success of these companies is the talk of the Mid-Continent field today," proclaimed the editor of Kansas City's journal of high society, "and to those who know, universal credit for the success of these companies is given to Mr. Culbertson. By his aggressive advertising 'Oil Talks' now famous throughout the Mid-Continent fields, these firms have grown by leaps and bounds and bid fair to be one of the greatest successes during the year of 1917." As Atlas-Okla Oil Lands Syndicate became known to the public, Culbertson developed a grander idea. In December 1916 Morgan & Company Oil Investments Corporation was officially set up to sell oil stock. In March 1917 Culbertson replaced Atlas-Okla with Morgan Oil & Refining Co. Atlas-Okla shareholders, who had been able to buy on an installment plan administered by Morgan & Company, now had their Atlas-Okla shares replaced by Morgan Oil shares.[19]

Morgan Oil & Refining Company was a common law trust, offering sixty thousand shares of no par value. The trust document expressly denied "strangers to the Trust" the right to know how money was used or to overturn any action of the trustees, and denied shareholders any right to "an accounting." Since the shareholders in Atlas-Okla had to vote to give up all these rights to the trustees of the new Morgan Oil, this suggests that plans were afoot to do things that could disturb stockholders outside an inner circle. In theory these provisions could be changed if "the holders of at least two-thirds of the shares then outstanding of record" insisted, but only if such "proposed amendment or alteration shall have been given in the call for the meeting"—two nearly impossible conditions.

The trust was crafted with cunning. Forget about stockholder meetings. Forget about state corporation commissioners. All Morgan Oil had to do was to sell stock. The Morgan Oil trust, like so many other Missouri oil company trusts of that time, was designed to be accountable to no one. Thinking *himself* accountable to no one, Jerry Culbertson proceeded with gusto.[20]

Culbertson's stock sales campaign seemed pitched to the unsophisticated investor. Why else would the ads be filled with bombastic language that one oil field *near* Morgan property "is a real gusher," and the sly declaration that Morgan property in "relatively proven" oil fields "is reported" to be "probable Oil and Gas producing territory"? Why else would Culbertson hire salesmen to peddle stock certificates for a dollar apiece? Did salesmen clearly state that John Pierpont had nothing to do with the Morgan & Co. oil "trust"? One salesman described oil as "the business where the small or medium size investor has the greatest chance to win a fortune or a competency, with a less hazard of loss of principal than any other line where their money can be placed. . . . We urge you to make your investment and get your share of the easy money and the big profits that come from a good oil investment. Do not hesitate, but buy today." A critic later said that dozens of men at the Armour packing plant bought, that one woman plunked down $5.00 for each of her 104 shares, and that a widow bought 10½ shares at $25.00 each. The price was whatever you would pay, and you could buy on the installment plan.[21]

Although Harry surely talked up his company among friends, he claimed to have avoided actually selling shares. (Because of this claim one wonders how Bess Wallace acquired her stock.) Harry functioned as treasurer of both Morgan Oil & Refining Co. and its stock-selling arm Morgan & Co. Oil Investments, and he kept the accounts. At most, only twelve thousand shares were sold, but they brought in $200,000. Of this amount Harry received nothing, although Culbertson apparently attached Harry's name to letters soliciting stock purchases. Dave Morgan realized only $250 a month as salary as geological expert. Culbertson made not only $250 a month as salary, but also received a percentage of stock sales. Morgan and Truman decided that Culbertson's percentage was too large, and also decided they "did not entirely approve of Mr. Culbertson's methods of promotion." Even though the Morgan Oil trust agreement may have left the company accountable to neither investors nor the state, the document left Culbertson accountable to both Morgan and Truman.[22]

Truman and Morgan believed that the oil operation should make profits by producing oil. Culbertson felt that financial wizardry provided a surer approach. Many years later Dave Morgan admitted, "We perhaps were a bit dilatory in waking up to the sort of promotion that he [Culbertson] was carrying out . . . perhaps we were a bit negligent." Morgan said also, "We were honestly mistaken in the sterling qualities which were presumed to be possessed by Mr. Culbertson." Harry agreed, "Perhaps Morgan and I were honestly mistaken in the executive qualities which we thought we saw in Culbertson, and too much engrossed in our own responsibilities and duties to see that the sort of promotion he was carrying on was too ambitious and too extravagant for the size of our operations." Once Truman spoke of Culbertson and zinc mine partner Tom Hughes in the same breath, pointedly describing Hughes as "a good man" and omitting any such appellation for Culbertson. Did the partners have a confrontation, with Culbertson arguing that Morgan and Truman were fools to throw away easy money? Truman later grumbled about this oil business: "I always did let ethics beat me out of money and I suppose I always will."[23]

Morgan recalled genteelly that he and Truman "suggested that he [Culbertson] dispose of his stock and interests to Mr. J. Sylvester Mullen." Culbertson dropped out of the operation in March 1917, just after reorganizing it to permit the kind of stock-selling scheme he envisioned (the price of each share had boomed to $25.00 as he left). Although Culbertson might have shaken his head in bewilderment over his partners' sense of ethics, he came out ahead in the deal. When he sold his interest to Joseph Sylvester Mullen of Ardmore, Oklahoma, it was clear profit since he had never put a penny into the operation. Truman and Morgan had no complaints about Mullen. Said Morgan, "I always liked him personally."[24]

Undistracted by partner squabbles after Culbertson's departure, Harry could concentrate on oil. Young Joseph K. Brelsford came from Pueblo, Colorado, as a company auditor, and eventually became treasurer of the investment operation. He recalled that Kansas City was "very much interested in oil. Harry S. Truman was surrounded with people, people, people. Salesmen, lease men, lease owners, scouts, and what have you. Morgan had his duties, but he shoved quite a burden of seeing people over to Truman." Dave Morgan later wrote Harry in fond reminiscence, "Those were the good old days, care-free, no worries and at that time you were kept busy going to the Bank."[25]

During Truman's White House years a critic described Morgan Refining as little more than a printing press issuing stock certificates for Morgan Investments to peddle. Such accusations were unfounded. Truman and Morgan really wanted to find oil. They took the money that Culbertson had raised with stock sales, and spent it exploring and leasing lands in Kansas, Oklahoma, Texas, and Louisiana, plus a skimming plant in Rollin, Kansas. Truman's trip to Oklahoma just before Christmas 1916 may have been oil-related. Morgan Oil joined with Ten Strike Oil Syndicate of Minneapolis to explore for oil, but found only a dry hole. The same resulted when Morgan Oil cooperated with Snell Drilling Co. of Shreveport. The Morgan well near Plaindealing, Louisiana, brought in a gusher of salt water. On the Alice M. Cowan land in Texas, Morgan Oil stopped five hundred feet short of discovering the K-M-A Oil Field. "There was always something present which seemed to stand in the way of final accomplishment of our plans and hopes," Dave Morgan mused.[26]

The company had leased 144,000 acres in western Kansas when World War I broke out. The field man for this operation was Pete Allen, who would become captain of F Battery, 129th Field Artillery, 35th Division while Truman would become captain of D Battery— the men would work together in war as in peace. Morgan Oil became inactive during the war, and allowed the leases to lapse on the 144,000 acres. The major oil corporations then moved into the same area and brought in wells that produced three thousand barrels a day. Morgan Oil also gave up its lease on part of what became the Hugo Gas Field; Harry computed that his share in that discovery alone would have been $7 million. The war's drain on key personnel (such as Harry and Pete Allen) halted a southeastern Kansas test drilling, and those leases were abandoned. The next people to drill there promptly discovered the Teter Pool, and made millions of dollars. Harry later reflected to Dave Morgan, "Well, Dave, if we had carried that well on down and opened up the Teter Field with all that oil, it's a cinch I would not be President today and it's quite probable that you might not even be alive today to enjoy what little you have." These two opportunities, lost because of the war, were ironic—Culbertson's stock promotion scheme had claimed that U.S. involvement in World War I would mean boom times for Morgan Oil.[27]

Over the years Harry and Dave would talk wistfully about how they missed a fortune, but (as we shall later see) at least they made some money from Morgan Oil. The Armour & Co. meatpackers, the widow, and everyone else who heeded Morgan Oil advertisements and salesmen—each and every one of them lost whatever he or she had invested. Some felt cheated. Not true, Dave Morgan insisted. Yet true enough. "Every single individual had a run for their money," Morgan declared. Yes, the money was legitimately spent in the search for oil. But did the meatpackers, the widow, and all the rest make an informed investment?[28]

Harry seems to have been uneasy and defensive about his oil career. He said, "I tried diligently, as a young man just beginning in business, to fill my office as treasurer with promptness and efficiency. It was my duty to deliver such stock certificates as were issued, to collect the money due the company, to sign all checks and to supervise the general financial operation. In my capacity, I was not in a position to decide the company's policies, and had nothing to do with the promotion and sale of stock." Harry wasn't as helpless as all that. As partners he and Morgan had the power to drive Culbertson from the company.[29]

The operation's "hazard" (Harry's term) had attracted him to it, and he clearly felt a twinge of conscience that his company's salesmen promoted it as a conservative investment. Harry's pains four decades later to dissociate himself from his company's policies indicate that he may have felt he failed the first test of his morals against Capitalist materialism. Not that he acquiesced in shady policies or that he failed to act when he realized what was happening. We have seen the contrary. Harry seems to have felt guilty because he was in a position to know, and he failed to keep informed. Far from being an excuse, his ignorance was felt to be a sin.[30]

In all his business interests Harry attempted to make money by providing a product or service. He flatly rejected accumulation of wealth via financial manipulations. The wealth had to be incidental to the product or service, not an end in itself. This was a deliberate decision. Harry wrote, "The American idea of amounting to something in those days was to accumulate money—the man with money no matter how he got it was successful. Well I'd studied the Sermon on the Mount very carefully and the money accumulators and that great document do not agree."[31]

Harry abandoned his oilman career to fight in World War I, an experience that left him a far different man. An experience, too, that would eventually earn him a slot on a Pendergast slate of county office candidates.[32]

Chapter 6

BLOOD BROTHERS

My whole political career is based upon my war service
and war associates.

—Harry S. Truman[1]

Although he admitted to being
"afraid of a gun and would rather run than fight," Harry decided
that military experience was crucial if a man were ever to become
great. It was part of his plan. "So when a National Guard battery
was organized in Kansas City about the time I was 21 I joined it."[2]

Harry could have joined a National Guard unit in Independence,
but he must have felt stronger ties to Kansas City than to Independence—with no need to strengthen or renew association with the
men there. His age may have been a factor. He joined the Guard
scarcely a month after his twenty-first birthday. By law he could
have joined earlier without parental consent, but Harry implied that
he had to wait until twenty-one, for some reason. Harry might naturally want to join the new Kansas City unit coincidentally being
organized at the time he turned twenty-one because his fellow clerks
from Union National Bank and other downtown businesses were
also signing up. Membership in this outfit might give him good
"contacts."[3]

Harry and eighty-nine other men applied for membership in Light
Battery B, an artillery unit. On June 14, 1905 sixty of them received

medical examinations, and fifty-seven were accepted. Lt. Valentine
Porter of Light Battery A (St. Louis) mustered the new unit that
same night at the Coates House hotel, where officers were elected:
Capt. George R. Collins, Sr.; 1st Lt. Fred A. Boxley, Jr.; 1st Lt.
Thomas H. Velle (or Velie); and 1st Lt. and Surgeon Dr. J. Thomas
Pittam. Harry credited his sergeant with getting him into the Guard
despite his need for eyeglasses. Harry carefully cultivated this man,
inviting him to special home-cooked dinners at the Grandview farm.
Harry became especially close to Lieutenant Boxley, a Kansas City
lawyer who later handled the litigation over Louisa Young's will for
the Truman family, and who advised the Morgan oil companies.
Captain Collins was president of the National Benevolent Society (a
fraternal insurance society operating among unsophisticated members of the black community), and was a Pendergast faction operative. Following the Guard unit's first muster the *Kansas City Star*
editorialized, "The new battery organized last night should be a
strong addition to the Third Regiment. At a glance its personnel
seems to be superior, and it is well officered."[4]

The federal government promised six artillery pieces for Battery
B, but these weren't expected in time for the annual Guard encampment at St. Joseph on July 9. Battery A of St. Louis agreed to
share its equipment at the gathering. Surprisingly, Harry seems to
have missed that encampment, but that was just as well. Rain,
meager fresh water, and professional military incompetence made
the event a disaster. In 1906 Harry left his Kansas City bank clerk
job for the Grandview farm. He no longer attended Guard meetings
faithfully, and his family begrudged whatever time he gave to the
militia. In March Captain Collins promoted Harry to corporal—
"the proudest day I ever spent in the military," he said. "I thought
I was the biggest man in the army."[5]

Harry attended his first camp that summer. "Quite an experience.
We went to St. Louis in a day coach on the Missouri Pacific and
then by steamboat down the Mississippi. I learned a lot about public
relations and private ones, too." The trip was a lark. Everyone finally
arrived at Camp DeArmand near Cape Girardeau, Missouri. As at
St. Joseph, problems with rain, water, and military incompetence
abounded. Speaking of the camp as a whole, not of Battery B, the
state adjutant general reported, "Discipline was not of the best, and
the relative difference between a commissioned officer and enlisted

man was not always perceptible." The long-promised three-inch breech-loading rifles still hadn't arrived from the Federals so, Harry recalled, Battery B (Kansas City) doubled up with Battery A (St. Louis) for "target practice and learned to ride horses and caissons across potato rows the wrong way. They also acted as gunners and Numbers 1, 2, and 3 in firing the pieces into the Mississippi River from a bluff." Harry remembered that "when you fired the old thing it rolled back 20 yards, and one of the orders in training was 'cannoneers on the wheels' to roll it back into position." He went on, "A salute was fired for the Governor, and when the outfit returned to Kansas City they were real veterans."[6]

When time came for summer camp in 1907 the federal artillery had finally arrived at Battery B, and the men had been able to drill with the guns. Harry had no small experience handling horses on the farm, and he became a swing driver. This was a job and a half, as a driver had to control his mount and the horse next to him, which were both helping to pull artillery equipment. Harry got a real workout in this task when the battery marched from Kansas City to the July camp in St. Joseph, a good fifty miles. The outfit had to borrow horses from Lemon Brothers Circus, as animals used for routine drill in Kansas City weren't sturdy enough for such a march. The rains that had inundated encampments the past two years reoccurred. Harry recalled, "The principal diversion during that wet week was to dig holes in front of tents where the water was a foot deep over all, and let unsuspecting sergeants and second lieutenants fall into them." He sent Nellie Noland a picture postcard of downtown St. Joseph, and wrote gaily, "We are eating this town up." When Captain Collins needed assistance removing his boots one night, he asked Harry for aid, and the corporal felt proud to be noticed by an officer of such august rank. The fun ended the day after Harry mailed his postcard, when a terrible lightning storm hit the camp. A bolt struck an electric wire leading to the headquarters tent, killing Sgt. Maj. Frank Miller of St. Louis. An official report stated that Miller's "remains were escorted to the train with military honors, and every officer and man in the command was present at the ceremony." Truman remembered that "Battery B felt that some real war had been experienced." The men were in bad shape to ride the horses back home, hampered by saddle sores. Mercifully, the outfit returned by rail.[7]

Toward the end of his first National Guard camp trip Harry sent a picture postcard of the Battery A armory to Ethel Noland, saying "We'll have one someday." At that time Battery A in St. Louis was the only Guard unit in the state with its own armory. All the others rented their quarters. To help pay rent at the Warwick Club dance-hall each member of Battery B had to plunk down two bits whenever he came to drill. Captain Collins was able to generate enough public enthusiasm to get private funding for construction of an armory at 17th and Highland. This was completed in 1908, with title to the structure retained by Parade Real Estate & Building Co. of Kansas City, Missouri. The structure was "well designed and commodious" with an excellent location next to a park, which could be used for mounted drill. On militia nights battery clerk Corporal Truman normally stayed upstairs sorting out the paperwork while the men drilled downstairs. An inspector praised the well-kept records. One evening in 1908 a man presented himself to the battery clerk and asked to enlist. Harry noticed the man's foreign accent and asked how long he had been in the United States. Ted Marks answered, "About six months, sir." Harry replied, "You speak pretty good English for the time you've been here." Marks, a native of Britain, wondered what he was getting into, but joined up.[8]

Federal inspectors the next year rated Battery B quite highly in comparison to other Missouri units. "Physical appearance, character of men, etc., etc., all excellent. Apparently well developed and set up, and men of select character. . . . Average age of all enlisted men about 24 or 25 years. Esprit de corps excellent. . . . One hundred percent of strength may be relied upon if called out." Another regular army inspector found that "the spirit that animates this organization is excellent and worthy of the highest commendation, as evidenced by the fact that an armory costing 50,000 dollars has been erected by the efforts of the members of the organization without any assis-tance from the state. . . . The equipment was generally in good con-dition and well cared for. . . . The inspection was made at night, and consequently little opportunity was afforded the inspector to deter-mine the exact condition of officers and men in regard to instruction. The officers were examined in the various methods of fire and the men in the service of the piece, setting sights and quadrants, re-moving the recoil springs and filling cylinders. The result showed a condition that was to be expected of an organization made up of

men anxious to learn, but handicappped by the lack of proper instructors and by the fact that such drill and training as is possible
under these circumstances can be given only at night." Nonetheless,
the overall rating of Battery B was approximately as good as Battery A.[9]

In August 1908 Battery B went to Joint Maneuver Camp with
federal troops at Ft. Riley, Kansas. Corporal Truman said he "had
a great time and didn't do much work or learn a lot of military
duties." The next outing was a march to Lexington. Several battery
members tried to skip this march, but Captain Collins had them
arrested and forced them to attend. "The action of the battery commander seemed to have an excellent effect," noted a regular army
inspector who went along. On good days the battery made about
nineteen miles; on bad days about seven miles. The horses suffered;
one died. No veterinarian accompanied the march, and no veterinary
supplies were brought along.[10]

Harry was now spending more and more time at the farm. He
lamented that "wheat cutting time interfered with . . . chances to go
to camp." He had reenlisted for another three years in 1908, but
eventually the burden of farm work required him to drop out of the
militia. His captain recalled that Harry "presented a letter from his
mother asking that he be discharged so that he could come home as
his help was needed on the farm, and his discharge was granted by
the Adjutant General." Such a letter may have been written, but it
would only have been an explanation of why Truman wasn't reen-
listing. Harry confided another reason to Bess at the time—he feared
a cannon might maim or kill him. He served out the full hitch, and
was discharged June 13, 1911. Vivian married in October, and left
the farm, leaving its operation to Harry and their father and squelch-
ing any hope that Harry may have had about rejoining the militia.
He wanted to go with his old battery to the Mexican border campaign
in 1916, but felt that his first responsibility was to the farm. This
disappointment may have added to his disenchantment with farming.[11]

On April 1, 1917 Morgan Oil & Refining Co. had a big Kansas City
newspaper ad soliciting investors, but Harry lost enthusiasm in this
enterprise the next day when President Wilson called for war with

Germany. "I was stirred in heart and soul by the war messages of Woodrow Wilson," he said. The Mexican border action had been glorified maneuvers, but now a real war had come. With ties to the farm already loosened Truman felt nothing holding him back. Moreover, his militia service was hardly the kind of military experience a great man needed. Now that a shooting war had come, the training program of his life plan was incomplete. Patriotism aside, a great man would have to join this adventure. "I went to war as all great men had."[12]

Harry's first war service was as an organizer of the 129th Field Artillery regiment.* Six batteries were being formed in Kansas City. On this job Harry worked with Eddie McKim. The organizers "would go down to the Board of Election Commissioners," McKim recalled. "We'd take the [draft age] names out of the election records . . . and try to talk the men into enlisting rather than waiting for the draft." "Kindness, courtesy, and respect for their fellow beings is the motto of everyone in the regiment," potential recruits were told. "The artillery regiment is more like a big family with everyone on the best of terms. No one slacks his work. No one grumbles. The last thought of the officers is to 'bully' the men." Pup Leigh remembered that he and Cue Ball Whitney and Emmet LeMaster just happened to be "walking down Grand Avenue in Kansas City one day; and in front of the Kansas City Gas Company was a sign saying 'Join the Artillery and Ride,' and this appealed to us." Floyd "Skinny" Ricketts grew up with about fifteen other fellows around 22nd and Prospect, and they all joined Battery D together. J. E. Moore talked with his fellow townsmen in Urich, Missouri, and eight of them came to Kansas City and enlisted. This was an era of hometown companies, when the menfolk of a burg would go off to war together, cementing lifelong friendships.[13]

Harry made the most of his old militia connections, and spent a lot of time with the National Guard officers. He enlisted June 22, 1917, the day Battery F was mustered into service, and much to his surprise and delight that same day the men elected him a first lieutenant. Capt. John L. Miles evaluated Harry and approved him as

---

*The outfit names changed as the various units formed, assimilated into the Missouri National Guard, and then transferred to the U.S. Army. From here on, unless otherwise noted, units are called by their eventual U.S. Army designation.

officer material. How Harry passed the vision test is unclear. One version says that the examiner whispered the answers to him. Another says that he had memorized the eye chart. In any case, Harry was dealing with friends—the examiner, Major Pittam, was the old Battery B physician, and recruiting officer Lt. Harry B. "Pete" Allen who signed Harry's papers was a field man for his oil company.[14]

On August 5, 1917 the National Guard artillery regiment in Kansas City was mobilized as the 129th Field Artillery regiment, U.S. Army. The men were now full-time instead of part-time soldiers, and training became more intense. Harry was an instructor. "There are five paragraphs that you learn as a military student: you set out what your plans are; you set out what the enemy's plans are so far as you know; you set out what you are going to do; decide how you are going to do it; then let everybody know where you are going to be and where your supplies are coming from." Harry added, "That's all there is to it." Eddie Jacobson, attending NCO school in Kansas City, remembered Harry's definition of "discipline": "Discipline is the instant obedience of a command—emphasis on the word 'instant.' "[15]

Word arrived that the Kansas City batteries and the rest of the 35th Division (the combined Missouri and Kansas National Guards) would be sent to Camp Doniphan at Ft. Sill in Oklahoma for training. The camp was named for Missouri's Mexican War hero Alexander Doniphan who commanded the longest overland march in military history in 1846. "He made Xenophon's march of the 10,000 look like 30 cents with the 3 rubbed out!" Truman declared. (Doniphan was a relative of President Tyler, to whom Harry claimed unproven kinship.) Some knowledgeable persons were appalled by the Army's choice of Camp Doniphan, and tried to shift the Division to the State Rifle Range at Nevada, Missouri, claiming that the physical environment and weather there were superior to Ft. Sill's. Unfortunately, the suggestion came from the Missouri National Guard. There was a strong intraservice rivalry, and the Army didn't like suggestions from the National Guard. The hostility was reciprocated. The 35th Division went to Camp Doniphan, and found the "climate" hostile indeed.[16]

Things got off to a terrible start when Battery A arrived in late August as the advance detail of the 129th Regiment (which included all the Kansas City artillery units). A day or two after Battery A arrived a soldier roaming the reservation found a shrapnel shell and brought it into camp. Some officer put the shell into the kitchen and soldiers decided to use it as an insulator between a wood partition and the stove. When sufficient temperature was reached, boom. Two cooks and one other Battery A man were killed, three others were injured. The accident cannot have enhanced the Army's regard for National Guard competence. Indeed, a month later Colonel Klemm had to order Kansas City men of the 129th to refrain from touching explosives with which they were unfamiliar, "because of the large number of accidents." Blame for the stove incident was charged to Lt. Jim Pendergast (nephew of Boss Tom and son of Mike). Jim had been having a hard time in the military. Although elected an officer, his commission was stalled. He started in Battery E, switched to Battery D, and then was transferred to Battery A. After being shifted around three batteries in about as many months, with his officer's commission held up, Jim Pendergast was now being charged with the death and injury of men under his care in a ridiculous accident that brought the competence of the whole Missouri National Guard into question. Board of Inquiry member Lieutenant Truman defended Pendergast so ably that he was exonerated. He eventually went to 35th Division Officers Training School where he received his first lieutenant's commission, along with Vic Housholder and Harry Vaughan. Pendergast transferred to the big guns of the 130th Field Artillery regiment, and commanded Battery A there. This was a Topeka, Kansas, unit. One observer wrote that "when the war was ended the men of that battery gave him a beautiful watch, and if he lived in Topeka they'd long ago have elected him mayor." Although in different regiments, Jim and Harry stayed in the same 60th Artillery Brigade in France and, Harry said, "became close personal friends." In a very tangible way Pendergast owed his successful military career to Truman.[17]

When Harry and the rest of the 129th arrived at Camp Doniphan in September they found many of the Missouri Guard's fears about the physical environment justified. Water was inadequate and olive drab in color. The new water lines hadn't been flushed, Tommy Murphy of Battery D noted, and "were full of pipe dope. Everybody had heartburn for a couple of weeks." Almost daily sandstorms limited vision to fifty feet, a disadvantage for artillery training. A dozen or more men were shoehorned into tents designed for maybe five or fewer. Even when eventually supplemented with wood sides four feet high, the tents did little to keep out autumn and winter chill. Tents had Sibley stoves. "We kept that thing going red hot all night long," Skinny Ricketts recalled. The Army didn't get around to supplying enough underwear and winter clothes until December, so the men depended on the Red Cross for handouts. The Army required rain-proof slickers to be turned in for "raincoats" that let the water through. Fatal epidemics of measles and pneumonia swept the camp, along with more isolated but deadly cases of meningitis, diphtheria, and typhoid fever. Scarlet fever and smallpox also appeared. All this for "30 bucks and beans."[18]

These privations surely encouraged the establishment of regimental canteens, and Colonel Klemm ordered Harry to run the 129th's canteen on top of his regular duties. Perhaps Harry was picked because of his banking experience. His oil business experience was also known among the Kansas City officers such as Klemm. In addition, Harry had been organizing social activities to cultivate friendships among fellow officers. Another factor in getting the canteen job may have been a financially successful regimental dance organized under Harry's auspices in Kansas City. Harry knew who the brains of that enterprise had been, and got his old oil associate Capt. Pete Allen to lend Sgt. Eddie Jacobson. Truman and Jacobson had known each other since Harry's bank clerk days, and Truman wanted to draw on Jacobson's civilian experience as a merchandiser. When he first saw the canteen operation Jacobson was appalled that the proceeds were kept in cigar boxes accessible to eighteen clerks. Truman and Jacobson immediately spent $700 for cash registers to provide accountability for the clerks. "Eddie and I sewed up their pockets," Truman metaphorically explained, and the lieutenant deposited the daily take. Among other things the store sold stationery, cigarettes, and food. A "godsend for us to go and get something different than the usual mess hall meals," Skinny Ricketts said. Frank Spina gave two-bit haircuts and dime shaves for a 40 percent commission, and a tailor custom fit uniforms for a price. The canteen became a social spot, and even men from other regiments patronized it. This was a telling comment on the operation's popularity, since the money went into the regimental mess fund. Outsiders were penalizing their own mess funds by shunning their canteens. A well-planned stock of goods, cash registers, daily deposits, and monthly audits made the Truman-Jacobson canteen a financial success. Harry had said that the canteen's goal was to provide conveniences for the men, not make a huge profit. The profit was huge anyway. Truman and Jacobson started out with $2,200 capital taken from the regiment's mess funds, and returned about $17,200 to the funds. Division headquarters cited the canteen as best in the division. "That Jewish boy and I really thought we were businessmen," Harry said.[19]

Friends and relatives visited Harry at Camp Doniphan. Oil partner Dave Morgan stopped by, as did Harry's sister and mother. Mattie "never shed a tear," Harry said proudly. She "smiled at me all the time and told me to do my best for the country." Yet in the bitter cold of the trip back home she wept. Bess Wallace mailed Harry her picture, and on the reverse of a calling card accompanying it she inked, "You didn't expect me in Ft. Sill so soon—did you? I'm depending on this to take you to France and back—all safe and sound. Bess." At last they were betrothed. "When the World War came," Harry related, "we were ready to get married, but since I had to go I didn't think it was right to get married and maybe come home a cripple and have the most beautiful and sweetest girl in the world tied down." He went on, "I'll never forget how my love cried on my shoulder when I told her I was going. That was worth a lifetime on this earth."[20]

Harry had the time and money to make a return visit to Independence the first week of January 1918. He, Pete Allen, Roger Sermon, and C. C. Bundschu got five-day furloughs. Harry could fund his trip home partly because he was then the highest paid officer in Battery F, getting about $265 for January.[21]

The 35th Division's training at Camp Doniphan was thorough. Harry taught at regimental schools, passing along information he had learned only a short time earlier. The men went on forty-eight-hour exercises, excavated elaborate trench systems, blasted them apart with artillery, and rebuilt them. Watchful eyes could see ominous portents. One analyst reported, "The artillery with the exception of three batteries was without equipment; the machine gun battalions had no machine guns; and there was a general shortage of supplies." Another analysis reported poor tactical training and lack of discipline. Questions arose about competence of officers. Artillery commander Brig. Gen. Lucien G. Berry, an analyst reported, felt that "at least one colonel, three other field grade officers, and

12 battery officers were incompetent." A wartime Army investigation questioned Berry's own competence.[22]

General Berry personally examined Harry when he came up for promotion to captain in February. Berry "was six feet tall," Harry said, "wore a handlebar mustache and hated National Guard lieutenants. The old man was fond of privates and corporals but took much pleasure in chewing up young officers with his false teeth and spitting them out in small bits." One time Berry came into the Truman and Jacobson canteen and ordered Jacobson to summon Truman. Harry was busy at the stables preparing for maneuvers. He ran to the canteen and saluted. Berry flipped two bits on the counter, ordered Harry to hand over two packs of cigarettes, and left. This outraged Harry: this was one of Berry's notorious insults against National Guard officers, and Harry's supervision at the stables was important to the maneuvers—horses were the artillery's motive power. Berry was willing to hamper training maneuvers in order to insult a National Guard officer. For ninety minutes before the promotion examination, he said, "I had to stay out in the cold (it was about zero or five above) and wait." Inside at last "the general and his three colonels took me over the jumps for about an hour, and I came out very sure I'd never be promoted."[23]

Nonetheless, Harry's record at Camp Doniphan got him a slot in the advance detail going to France ahead of the rest of the regiment. This was an envied assignment that went to only ten officers and one hundred enlisted men. The train stopped near Kansas City in the predawn hours of March 21. Harry asked a switchman for use of a telephone to call Bess and Mattie. "The switchman was a patriot, too. He said, 'Son, call hell and heaven if you want to, and charge it to the Company.' "

As their train traveled eastward and crossed the Delaware River, Harry's easygoing friend Lt. Jack Hatfield exclaimed, "Oh hell, is that all Washington had to cross?" Harry admitted being disappointed himself, "We thought we'd see something at least as wide as the Mississippi at St. Louis." New York City was an even bigger disappointment:

My Dear Cousins:
I am in the most touted town on earth and it is a vast disappointment. I have stopped at the M. Alpin Hotel, been to the Winter

Garden, walked down Broadway and 42nd Street at night, up 5th Avenue in the daytime, been on top of the Woolworth Building, crossed Brooklyn Bridge, been to a Chinese Chop Suey joint, rode the subway from the Battery to 130th Street, the elevated, and in fact I've done everything I can think of trying to see something to turn my admiration bump into enthusiastic clamor but I feel like Mark [Twain] did when he went to Italy. I want to ask the New Yokers if they ever saw the United States, and when they showed me Grant's Tomb I involuntarily asked, 'Is he dead.' They (the said N' Yokers) stand and expect you to fall dead every time they pull one of these best press agent stunts on you and if you don't they are dead sure you are lacking somewhere.

The Waldorf and the M. Alpin are no better than the Muleback on Baltimore. Broadway is not half as bright as 12th Street on any night and besides it's all torn up and half its length it looks as shoddy as an abandoned fair ground in winter. I'll admit that 5th Avenue looks almost as well as Armour Boulevard on some of its length but not half so well on the rest. Twenty six Broadway is an old time office building like the Shiedley Building in K.C. only taller, and Wall Street is an alley. The view from the Woolworth Building is grand and manifique though you can see old lady Liberty holding up her torch to the incoming wops on one side, Jersey City, Hoboken, Wiehauken, Long Island City, Brooklyn, and Canada, Connecticut if you can look that far on the other. It is 792 feet and 1 inch above the sidewalk. I don't know how the carpenters came to run in that inch but that's what the book says the height is, and I don't think it's any lower than that if as low. Some of Jersey City burned up today while we were on top of the Building. It was a fine sight even if some Hun ought to be shot for doing it.

This town they say has 8000000 people 7500000 of em are of Israelitish extraction 400000 are wops and the rest are white people. Kansas City can produce more good looking girls than two New Yorks. The show Sunday night at the Winter Garden couldn't appear at the Globe and get by. . . . I am sorry I haven't written sooner, but I worked so hard when I went back [from the January furlough] that Bess had to wire me to see why I didn't write and the Home people thought I was dead. Please forgive me.

Sincerely,
Harry[24]

At midnight on Good Friday the advance detail sailed from New York. Writing in the third person, Harry said that he and Lt. Newell Paterson "stood on the deck that night and watched the skyline of the great city disappear, and they both had some very solemn thoughts. There were submarines to be avoided by the great liner, and then there were shells and rifle balls and gas and minewoerfers and pneumonia and a lot of things ahead. They thought of all of them and discussed the situation very thoroughly. They then went below deck and played poker all the rest of the night."[25]

The advance detail arrived at Brest, France, a couple weeks later. Harry stayed at the Continental Hotel where, he said, "six very pleasant days were spent, learning how to drink French wine and what to eat." Harry marveled at his hotel room. "The floor was slick as glass; there was a marble wash stand a couple of meters long by about one inch deep with a couple of bowls and pitchers big enough to take a bath in and a *cut glass* water bottle. The bed was about six feet above the floor, and they use pillows for cover. I had to orient myself every time I came in. There was a mahogany wardrobe with a full length mirror in which I could admire myself in my Sam Brown belt."[26]

After a week of this Harry took a train to artillery school. "They have little bitsy engines like we used to wind up when we were kids," he said, "with a peanut roaster whistle." His enthusiasm was irrepressible. "You'll never know how to appreciate Mark [Twain] really and truly until you read his *Innocents Abroad* and *Tramp Abroad* and then get to come over on a government boat with all expenses paid and an almost really truly salary in the bargain." On arriving at the school Harry billeted in

a real Chateau with a park, a moat and a cute little picture book village out in front. There are marble stairs hand carved wood work and everything like you read about—and I'd give a lot for a baseburner or some steam heat. There's a shower bath that has water right out of the Arctic Ocean in it. Of course the place was built back in 1550 by Catherine de Medici or the Duc de Guies or Henry III, IV, or Cardinal Richiliue or somebody. . . . I suspect that Henry of Navaire maybe or some of his three musketeers were all around here. There's the cutest little branch that runs down through rows of trees. It is about a foot deep and 10 wide, and the French call it a river. It is sure a pretty little stream. I took a walk through an adjoining chateau park the other day and there was a swan and some green and white ducks floating on the river, and it sure looked like a picture. There are old mills all over the country both water and the wind kind like Holland pictures show. You'd never think that war is raging in this same land, it is so peaceable and quiet and pretty.[27]

From the end of April to the start of June Harry lived in elegance, and learned how to destroy it with engines of war. Col. Dick Burleson (whose cousin Albert was in President Wilson's cabinet) ran the artillery school. Harry already had practical experience via the militia and the Ft. Sill School of Fire, but Burleson taught the fine points of French .75-mm pieces. Pvt. Pup Leigh recalled the .75's fondly: "A great piece of artillery, and we loved the gun; it would do tricks. They used to say you could knock a sparrow off a telephone wire at eight or nine thousand yards with the 75." This kind of accuracy required complicated mathematical formulas. Moreover, computations for an aiming point changed continually with the weather. Wind direction and velocity were factors; just as important were temperature, barometric pressure, and even altitude of the gun above sea level. These latter factors affected the force of the explosion propelling the shell, and also the speed of the time train in the projectile's fuse. (Many shells had fuses that were set to detonate in the air without striking an object. Because of all the changing factors the gun crew had to set each fuse just before firing.) Harry had been good at math in high school, but that was the extent of his training. He now crammed higher math. He did well enough at the laborious manual computations of firing data that he was made an artillery instructor. "It seemed to be the policy of all high-ranking artillery officers (and I mean from majors up, by high-ranking) to make a deep dark mystery out of the firing of a battery. They taught us logarithms, square root, trigonometry, navigation and logistics but never did tell us that all they wanted to do was to make the projectile hit the target. . . . Afterwards when they made me a firing instructor in France, I told the boys right off what we were trying to do and explained at some length that all the trimmings were for was to make the first shot more accurate—after that it was just like any other shooting."[28]

Harry's regiment reached France in early June. From the start the men expected an experience far different from Harry's idyll. "I was leaning against the smokestack sleeping," Lt. Edgar Hinde remembered, "and looked up when we got to the dock, and there was a great big hospital there, and I never saw as many wooden-legged and one-armed men in my life. . . . I thought this is a fine welcome to France."[29]

Harry now rejoined his regiment near Angers, and learned from *The New York Times* that he had been a captain almost from the day he arrived in France. Unaware of the appointment he had failed to accept his commission immediately, and thereby lost several months of captain's pay. Captain Truman now became adjutant of his regiment's second battalion (the regiment had two battalions). In essence he was secretary to battalion commander Maj. Marvin Gates. Harry made friends among the officers there, "a bully young chap," Capt. John Thacher called him. "A most pleasant month," Harry said.[30]

The string of cushy assignments ended July 10 when regimental commander Col. Karl Klemm summoned Harry. "I went over everything I'd done for the last 10 days to see if I could find out what I was to be bawled out for, but could think of nothing. I waited around in his office until he'd dressed down a second lieutenant or two and then my time came. He suddenly said to me, 'Harry, how would you like to command a battery?' 'Well, sir,' I said, 'I hope to be able to do that someday.' 'All right, you'll take command of D Battery in the morning.' I saluted, about-faced and walked out."[31]

Battery D's unruliness has been credited with causing the chewing up of three commanders before Harry, but this wasn't quite the case. The first commander, Capt. Charlie Allen, was popular with the men. He was a football coach at Rockhurst College in Kansas City: "I played under him there," Pvt. Eddie McKim recalled. Pvt. Pup Leigh described Allen as a "very likeable guy and easy come, easy go." Lt. Edgar Hinde said Allen just couldn't handle the battery, but McKim claimed that the main problem that led to the captain's removal was mismanagement of the Battery D mess fund. The next captain was Rollin Ritter. First Sgt. Fred Bowman praised him. "A marvelous man; but . . . knowing [Lieutenant Colonel Elliott] and the fellows above, I could understand how they would have the needle in this guy all the time." Especially since Ritter's ignorance of basic commands nearly killed a Battery D man in a routine drill. Both Allen and Ritter were relieved before Battery D left Ft. Sill. The new captain was John Thacher, partner in a big Kansas City corporate law firm and a man with powerful friends (Princeton 1895 *and* a Harvard classmate of the immensely wealthy William Woodward). "Thacher knew what he was doing," McKim said. Thacher was a man with a heart, horrified that a brief argument with Sgt. Walter Menefee had made Menefee reluctant to seek an extension for a pass to visit his dying wife. Thacher took Battery D across the Atlantic. A man whose consumption of liquor fit in well with the battery, Thacher "was very well respected—the men liked Capt. Thacher very much," remembered Cpl. Harry Murphy. When Truman took over the battery Thacher became adjutant of First Battalion and was promoted to major. His superiors must have viewed him as a good officer.[32]

The superiors viewed the men of Battery D as dregs of the earth, and the feeling was reciprocated. Colonel Klemm "was the Prussian type of officer," Pup Leigh thought, "and we didn't like him." Cpl. Harry Murphy agreed, "Very strict—very high headed, arrogant." Eddie McKim summarized the Battery D feelings about Klemm, "My overall impression was that he was a crazy man." In officer elections back at Kansas City Harry had staunchly supported Klemm, the Kansas City candidate for colonel, against the Independence candidate E. M. Stayton. Klemm's father-in-law was a director of Southwest National Bank of Commerce, where Charles H. Moore, Harry's old nemesis from bank clerk days, and W. T. Kemper, a Pendergast ally and friend of Harry's father, were major figures. Klemm's wealthy in-laws were oldtime Pendergast allies. "We elected Klemm and then were sorry we had," Harry admitted. Harry said that Klemm hated the Battery D men because they "couldn't see where a pair of eagles on his shoulders made him any better than they." Lieutenant Colonel Elliott was particularly despised by First Sgt. Fred Bowman. He "wasn't in my opinion a very ethical man, never had been," Bowman said. "Elliott was a big hog. He ate himself to death." Harry also remembered Elliott from prewar days, describing him as "a large fat individual whose military ability was shown by his adroitness in escaping duty of any nature." The men of Battery D were famed for hijinks that might have been crimes in peacetime—selling battery horses to buy cognac, stealing sixteen hundred pounds of cocoa from a YMCA canteen, drilling holes in railway tank cars loaded with wine. These high spirits have been genially attributed to the preponderance of Irish-Americans in the outfit, and indeed there were quite a few. A less publicized contingent was from the Bowery in New York City, tough scabs shipped into Kansas City to break a streetcar strike. On arrival they were unable to detrain because of staunch resistance by union men. So the street-car owners gave the scabs to Kansas City battery recruiters. Lt. Arthur Wilson described the scabs as "several very tough characters." Such were the men Harry was to command into battle. He wrote home that he was not sure he could do it.[33]

Battery D was loaded for bear the morning Harry took command. A couple of nights earlier the men had been celebrating payday when Capt. Pete Allen of Battery F told them to cool the ruckus. Sergeant Bowman recalled that they "just formed a big circle around Pete Allen and said, 'Hurray for Pistol Pete!' And the next thing we know we were under arrest in quarters." The men watched Captain Thacher weep a few tears as he relinquished command. "He was an emotional type guy," Pup Leigh explained, but tears probably didn't instill respect among the Bowery scabs. Pup said, "Truman stood there and he was kind of a rather short fellow, compact, serious face, wearing glasses." Skinny Ricketts said that Harry "gave the impression of a professor more than he did an artillery officer. He had those thick glasses." Harry gave a little speech about what he expected of the men and what they should expect from him: "You boys stick with me, and I'll bring you all back." On paper his words might have communicated manly resolve, but the effect was spoiled by his demeanor. "His knees were knocking together," Eddie McKim remembered, "you could see that he was scared to death." Pup Leigh told how Truman "turned the battery over to the First Sergeant and the First Sergeant told us to fall out, and then we gave Capt. Truman the Bronx cheer, that's a fact."[34]

Harry would go through a lot in the coming months, but he freely admitted that standing in front of Battery D that morning was the most frightening experience of his life. "He could feel the battery sizing him up and wondering how much they could put over on him." Later that day the men arranged a fake runaway with the horses spilling equipment as they pounded into the distance. The intention was to get the little professor excited over nothing. The men didn't know that Harry had years of experience handling horses on the farm and in his militia battery. He just sat on his mount grinning, enjoying the show. When the excitement was over and the men were spent, he ordered the mess cleaned up, and left.[35]

The next morning Harry met the noncoms. For some time Colonel Klemm and Lieutenant Colonel Elliott had been prepared to break up the battery, sending the members to other units and reforming the battery from scratch. Harry told his sergeants and corporals, "I didn't come over here to get along with you. You've got to get along with me. And if there are any of you who can't, speak up right now and I'll bust you back right now." He thereupon delegated battery discipline to the sergeants and corporals, putting their rank under threat if they were unable to handle the privates under them. "When Truman called that meeting of the noncommissioned officers and practically turned the battery over to the noncommissioned officers, that was the key to his success," Cpl. Harry Murphy said. "Gave us to understand that he was going to back us up to the hilt for anything that we did. All we had to do was do our duty and he was going to back us up, and he did." Harry's action was a simple management technique, and it was a masterstroke. Noncoms may have cared less about the fate of their captains, but retaining corporal and sergeant stripes meant a lot. Privates may have felt contempt for officers, but they respected noncom fists. The little professor had given everyone in the battery a practical incentive to behave.[36]

About the time Harry took over Battery D the regiment had moved from the Angers vicinity to Camp Coetquidan in Brittany. For decades the French had used this camp to train artillerymen, and here Battery D's entire brigade honed its skills. Pup Leigh remembered that "after we had had him [Truman] for a week or 10 days we knew who was running it and that he was capable, and he was. On firing problems you began to hit the target." "The battery fired every day all day long," Harry noted, and "made a firing record before they left the camp." In one firing problem

I shot away some 611 rounds of ammunition. Enough to make some dozens of stenographer girls buy Liberty Bonds for the next year. And the best part of it was the projectiles hit the target. The Major remarked when I came up that D Battery is all right. I had the swell head all day—haven't quite got over it yet. If I can make a successful battery commander I shall think I've really done some good in this war. Talk about your infantryman, why he can only shoot one little old bullet at a time at the Hun. I can give one command to *my* battery and send 862 on the way at one round and as many every three seconds until I say stop.

Someone else recounted that Battery D learned "to break loose four guns, ammunition carriages, wagons, field kitchens and huts, and be on the move in 14 minutes, something of a record." This mobility was demonstrated in mid-August when the regiment was ordered east to combat. The day before it departed Harry assembled the entire battery for a detailed check of every item. The next day the battery clattered onto the long railroad platform, with the unit strung out waiting for its train, which had to be made up in the right order: flatcars for materiel and wagon equipment, boxcars for horses, boxcars for men, and that sort of thing. (The boxcars were marked "40 Hommes 8 Chevaux" and were thus interchangeable, much to the disgust of the Hommes.) The stationmaster and artillery commanders had to coordinate everything in advance so that the train would pull up with the correct cars in front of the correct part of each battery. For combat movements time is crucial. The stationmaster started a stopwatch, and Harry ordered Battery D to entrain. The process took forty-eight minutes, best time of any unit.[37]

Two or three days later Battery D detrained at Saulxures in the Vosges Mountains. "Good beer was found here," Harry wrote. For the first time the battery had to park guns and wagons under trees to hide from enemy aerial reconnaissance. "We were suddenly startled by a big thunder-like boom and rumble, repeated several times, and we realized that we were hearing the fire of the big cannons at *the front*," Lt. Vic Housholder wrote, "a strange and indescribable feeling and realization." The battery had arrived in town at night. After sunrise, Lt. Jay M. Lee wrote, "over the hills to the east, perhaps five or six miles away, though they looked much closer, we saw first a puff of white smoke high in air; then another, and another, till 25 or 30 were floating at once lightly and gracefully in the lazy zephyrs of the sky. Then we saw that an aeroplane was the cause of it all; and these were the smoke of anti-aircraft shrapnel." This was a new world to the men of Battery D; they crossed it at night and hid in it by day to make their presence harder to detect. After a couple days in Saulxures Battery D marched in darkness to Kruth. There they dug into position on a mountain in a primeval forest. Great pains were taken with camouflage to avoid being spotted from the air. Housholder ran wires among trees, marking the paths men had to take to firing positions, latrine, and mess hall so the beaten-down path couldn't be spotted from the air. A tree in the way of firing was cut down at night and lashed to the sixteen-foot stump— shortening the tree enough for firing but revealing no change from the air.[38]

And yet how distant the war still seemed. One day Harry and four other men scouted a position in the forest. Around 5:00 P.M. they had a picnic. Supplementing Army rations with a mess kit of huge wild raspberries picked on the spot, the men cracked some champagne and dined under the gaze of a distant castle.[39]

For several days little happened. Sgt. Fred Bowman noted, "The Vosges Mountains came down kind of a V-shaped affair. The Germans on the one side, and the Americans were on the other. You could shoot all day over there and never hurt anything. . . . You couldn't advance anywhere, no place to go." Bowman added, "It was just a quiet sector." A bit too quiet for some tastes. "The Division Commander," Harry said, "decided that things ought to be livened up a little, and he directed the batteries of the 129th to fire 3000 rounds of gas at the Germans, just for practice."[40] Thus started the Battle of Who Run, a jocular name that Battery D used for a confusing incident. There are as many accounts as witnesses; they can't all be accurate. The version that follows is likely.

All the regiment's batteries used auxiliary positions for this exercise. The horses were hitched, and they hauled the guns and other equipment four or five miles along steep and muddy terrain. After about eight hours Battery D finally arrived in the new position, and set up for business. The horses were sent back to a location where they wouldn't be panicked by the noise, a routine precaution. Captain Truman ordered Sergeant Wooldridge to return the animals at a specified time so the battery could move out before the Germans returned fire. At 20:00 hours on August 28 Battery D's four guns began lobbing five hundred rounds of chlorine into Boche land. "We were firing away and having a hell of a good time doing it," Pup Leigh remembered. The job finished, the men waited for Wooldridge and the horses. And waited. And waited. Hiding the muzzle flash of artillery is very hard at nightfall, and every second of delay was giving Jerry time to compute target data for precise return fire. The horses finally appeared a full half hour later, and Harry was none too pleased with Wooldridge. He mounted, and began to direct the departure. In the murky, rainy blackness Harry promptly rode his steed into a large hole. As the animal tumbled, Harry's yellow rain slicker snagged on the saddlehorn and pulled him down also. His assistant in shouting commands for the battery's removal was Lieutenant Housholder, who Harry credited with "the best carrying voice in D Battery." Housholder dismounted and ran to the captain's aid. Harry had "only his upper chest and head sticking out from under his horse. He was gasping like a catfish out of water; all the breath had been 'squashed' out of his lungs so he couldn't utter a sound." Housholder continued, "I tried to pull him out by the arms from under the horse, but I couldn't do it. So I moved around and got the horse by the tail. The horse was kicking his hind legs and carrying on something awful. I managed in that mud to slide the horse off the captain. . . . I set him up against my knee. He was so near gone that his head just flopped over on his chest." Harry soon recovered; but with both the battery commander and his executive officer occupied by this accident, two of the guns got away from their crews and rolled part way downhill. The soggy ground stopped them, mired axle deep in muck. With the other two guns safely on their way Harry ordered the dozen remaining horses hitched to No. 3 piece. "No. 4 was in so deep it looked as if it never would come out," Harry said.[41]

While Battery D struggled to harness twelve horses, incoming German fire began to arrive. "They had 77's, very accurate guns," Pup Leigh recalled. A standard artillery technique for zeroing in on a target is "bracketing"—one or two shells are deliberately fired short, and another deliberately long. An observer watches the explosions ahead and behind the target, and by figuring the difference the precise range can be found to obliterate the target. The horses were terrified by the first explosions, and started to become unmanageable. Already exasperated with Wooldridge for bringing the battery under fire (by tardiness with the animals), Harry suddenly heard Wooldridge yell, "Run, fellers, run! They've got a bracket on us!" Wooldridge was standing near Harry, and the men thought this was an order. "I led the parade," Walter Menefee admitted. "We *all* run." Harry was furious, "Hey! Get back here! Help me hook up these horses and get this battery out of here!" He screamed profanities at the fleeing men—language the battery seldom heard from him before emerged in this moment of rage and urgency. "It took the skin off the ears of those boys," said their chaplain Father Curtis Tiernan. "It turned those boys right around."

Of Harry's moderate use of salty language, one battery member recalled, "We had a story going around about the way he bawled out two soldiers who went AWOL. 'You, you!' he shouted. 'You spoiled our record, you nasty things, you!' " Thus Harry's curses at the Battle of Who Run had a shock value that communicated the urgency of the situation. The effect wasn't so much from what was said, as it was from *Harry* saying it. Not all the battery's members had run off—only some of those trying to get the No. 3 gun unstuck. (Other men with duties nearby were unaware of the incident.) Perhaps a half dozen or more soldiers had stayed with Harry. Their efforts and those of the returnees failed to prevent a stampede by the unhitched horses, leaving half the battery's guns immobile. Harry had to be exasperated as he directed camouflage of the trapped weapons. Yet Pup Leigh noted his outward calm, "You'd have thought that he was sitting in the kitchen of his own home with his feet on a chair and about as much worried. . . . I don't think he'd ever been under fire before either, and it didn't bother him a damned bit."[42]

The trudge back was miserable. While Harry had been dealing with the No. 3 gun, the men waiting with Nos. 1 and 2 were dealing with a gas alarm. Pvt. Johnny Higinbotham, who stood all of four feet eight, struggled to get gas masks on the horses. He and Skinny Ricketts gave up after the second one. Fortunately the masks were unneeded. At last the battery moved out. The trip down the mountain was treacherous. A member of Battery C on this march wrote, "No lights could be used. The night we returned to our old position was the darkest on record, with a constant downpour of rain; winding around strange mountain roads, not knowing at what minute we would veer too far to the right or left and be dashed to the bottom of a precipice. . . . One of our horses, becoming unmanageable, plunged off a precipice to a ravine below."[43]

The darkness, rain, and unsure footing were spooky enough without the added burden of a possibly hostile civilian population. This area became German territory after the Franco-Prussian War in

1871, and now the French had taken it back. The Yanks soon perceived that something was queer. Civilians in the area, including children, had German gas masks. In daylight the Americans "could see the women and children, with masks at alert position, driving the cattle to shelter; then every living thing would disappear and absolute calm would reign. In a few minutes Fritz would break loose with gas, shrapnel, and high explosives." As the batteries slithered down the mountain the men had no way of knowing if unseen eyes were spying. Suddenly a civilian materialized in the road, swinging a lantern that seemed like the sun to Battery C. Was he trying to reveal the Americans to German artillery? A man on the scene said no one waited to ask. "The healthy swing of a 'hob-nail' attached to one of the boys soon had it extinguished."[44]

Harry was in a foul mood as Battery D squished through the mud. He was sopping wet in the night chill, and ached from the horse that fell on him. His first combat mission was designed as almost a book exercise, and he had to explain to Colonel Klemm the loss of two guns and twelve horses. He also had to explain why men under his leadership ran from enemy fire. He felt disgraced. This gloomy reverie was suddenly blasted when "all at once to our left a French battery of 75's opened up. We didn't know they were there or anywhere near, and we didn't know what had happened. That was quite a show, those guns going off almost right in your face." So said Skinny Ricketts of that unnerving incident.[45]

The return trip was quite an experience. For Harry the nadir was when he walked into regimental headquarters and reported. Fortunately Harry and Colonel Klemm got along well. The colonel told him just to go back the next day for the guns (a mission successfully accomplished). Harry learned that plenty of other units panicked when under fire the first time, and that this was no reflection on him. Maj. Marvin Gates urged Truman to court-martial Sergeant Wooldridge, but Truman settled for busting him to private and transferring him to Battery B.[46]

After a few days the regiment headed north. Harry was commander of Battery D's railroad train, next best to being engineer. They pulled out around midnight and leisurely clacked along for thirty-five miles, arriving at Bayon about 4:00 A.M. Harry received an urgent summons and rushed to the station. There stood the regulating officer of the entire 35th Division, Lt. Col. Bennett Clark.

Clark's daddy Champ was Speaker of the U.S. House of Representatives and had challenged Woodrow Wilson for the presidential nomination six years earlier. "In 1912," Harry wrote, "I was engineer for a binder with four mules and horses to make it run. The Convention was in Baltimore. A telegraph station was a quarter of a mile from the southwest corner of the wheat field where my two mules and two horses were glad to have a short breathing spell" while he periodically checked for the latest convention news. "When Bryan made his attack on August Belmont and the Champ Clark forces I was ecstatic but my father wasn't. He was Champ Clark come hell or high water." Now Harry received his orders from Champ's son. Clark said that the area was under enemy observation and being routinely shelled—two dead horses on the platform were grim evidence. Clark ordered Truman to get Battery D off the train in a half hour. This order left Harry "nearly paralyzed" with fear. Forty-eight minutes was the record for getting on a train; getting off was no faster. "It was quite a job," Lt. Art Wilson said, "to load and unload eight stallions and mares into these boxcars and get 'em going and to pull together the guns and the caissons," which also had to be unloaded. This was a superb opportunity for the Germans to wipe out Harry's battery, and the men knew it. With this strong motivation they somehow detrained in a half hour and got under cover in a wooded pasture. Clark's order had been a practical joke; the Germans hadn't touched the place, and the dead horses had been shot by a veterinarian. No harm was done other than to Harry's pride—he later said only two experiences had been more frightening, taking command of Battery D and giving a speech before the D.A.R. congress in Washington. Harry decided the joke was pretty good, and tried it on his old prewar Kansas City artillery associate Lieutenant Colonel Elliott when his Supply Co. train arrived. The gag didn't work as well this time. Elliott made Truman move his unit to a less comfortable spot so the Supply Co. could take cover in Battery D's wooded pasture.[47]

The regiment marched another ten miles north, and halted for a few days in two small French towns. En route they caught up with the 3rd Infantry Brigade resting off the road. The infantry lieutenant colonel told Harry to go ahead and not wait to follow the foot soldiers. So Battery D plodded happily along until the infantry brigade adjutant noticed them three or four miles from their destination. The adjutant, a major, ordered Harry to pull Battery D off the road and wait for the infantry as he was supposed to. Harry fumed but had no choice. This was 9:00 P.M. Battery D could have billeted in town by 10:00 but had to wait for all the infantry they had just passed to go by them. While wasting their time the men watched the Germans pull air raids on two nearby villages. Harry fretted that a stray bomb or some shrapnel from French antiaircraft guns would hit the battery. Finally at 3:30 A.M. the artillerymen were allowed to proceed. They arrived at their destination, and collapsed from exhaustion. Harry was dumbfounded that an Army officer was willing to incapacitate an artillery battery by insisting on a meaningless order of march.[48]

Batteries C and D billeted in Coyviller. Harry wrote, "The village seemed to have more manure than anything else; piled it in front of every house down the one street, and since Manuretown was easier to say than the French name, that's what the outfit called it" (Harry probably gave a euphemism for the real nickname). Yet Lt. Jay Lee claimed that Batteries C and D lucked out with Coyviller. The rest of the regiment stayed in Ville-en-Vermois, nicknamed Stinkville. "It was a dirty, untidy, unattractive place," Lee wrote, "in which the barnyard element strongly asserted itself. In even greater degree than usual, the French farmer-villager here indulged his craving to have his belongings all about him; and living rooms, hay-loft, officers' and enlisted men's billets, and horses, all reposed under one roof." Lee added with disgust that the Americans had to live in a "frankly social" way with the livestock.[49]

Here the regimental band gave up its instruments, much to the relief of the older men. "Our band played every morning to wake us up at 4:30 a.m.," Art Wilson said. "It was a National Guard band, and I think they could only play one tune. It was entitled, 'It Takes a Long, Brown, Dark-skinned Gal to Make a Preacher Lay his Bible Down.' "[50]

A forced march to the front began after dark on September 10. Harry outfoxed himself with what seemed a smart plan. Because the hills out of Manuretown were so steep, he decided to use all the horses to pull half the battery out, then take the horses back for the other half. Unfortunately, the second half got trapped behind Ted Marks's Battery C, which had stalled on the steep climb (since Battery C's horses weren't doubled up). This fouled the order of march, and Major Gates became livid. Things never did get straightened out although everyone reached the proper rendezvous point. "The Colonel had some rather sarcastic remarks to make about Captains of batteries who got lost," Harry said, "but nothing else came of the incident." The next night the regiment marched through Nancy, a dark and eerie town, with "caissons and horses' hoofs rattling and re-echoing on the cobble-stones." Only a dim red light in an occasional doorway showed, and the city seemed deserted except for a solitary sentry. Almost continual rain descended. "The wind swept man and horses," John Thacher wrote, "and made both shake and shiver until our teeth rattled." Each man carried nearly half his weight in equipment. "Sixty to 80 pounds, depending on the number of souvenirs in each pack." Harry noted that "the Germans fought for territory, the English fought to control the seas, the French fought for defense and security, but the Americans fought for souvenirs." Lt. Jay Lee described that night's long, wet, fitful march:

Hardly would the movement get well under way, when down the line would come the command, "Ha-a-a-l-t!" And a moment later, "Dismoun-n-t!" With the necessity of each driver standing by his horses, and the fact of there being nothing to sit on anyway but a muddy road or the rain-soaked weeds and grass beside it, such stops are very trying. Presently, perhaps after what seems an interminable wait, in the far distance forward are heard hopeful sounds, which as they are taken up towards the rear, become distinguishable as the rattling and rumbling of artillery carriages; and above them, at last, from our own commanders, "Moun-n-t!" and "Forwar-r-r-d Mar-r-ch!" The drivers spring to position and "gather" their horses; the foot-soldiers straighten into column; the tired and dozing horses, with a startled shiver, lean into their breast straps, the traces tighten, and the column of carriages rumbles heavily into motion. As often as otherwise this is a "fluke," and after advancing only a few rods, again comes the inevitable "Ha-a-l-t!" and the experience is repeated.

Literally hours were spent at halt that night, due to obstructions or difficulties ahead that we could tell nothing of. An artillery brigade in column occupied at best three or four miles of road space, and with muddy, slippery, crowded roads the opportunities for delay were manifold. To add to the discomfort of the trip, heavy showers came up through the night; and not the least of the annoyances, as any driver will testify, was the fact that to resume the march after a halt and dismount in the rain, meant doing so on a wet saddle. And even when riding, the short, skimpy raincoats which had been substituted at Camp Doniphan for the really effectual "slickers" first issued, were no protection whatever for the knees and thighs. . . .

So slow was our progress that after six hours we had only advanced three or four miles, and were standing at a halt in the dark, mysterious streets of Nancy, when precisely at 1 a.m. of September 12th the whole front to our north broke out in flame, and a tremendous, continuous and awe-inspiring roar of artillery began; while huge searchlights, interspersed with many-starred signal rockets, shot their shafts like the Northern Lights constantly across the sky. We had heard or seen nothing in our experience like it; and though we had had no warning of it, we realized with a sombre enthusiasm that an event big with importance, in which we might well be called upon to participate, was taking place.[51]

For three days and nights Harry and his men halted at Forêt de Haye, waiting to go into action, but they were instead ordered to head toward Forêt d'Argonne. The nightly forced marches through the rain became frantic, covering maybe twenty miles before daybreak. Eddie Jacobson scribbled in his book of Scriptures, "Sept. 21, 1918 Raining, cold—Hope I never see another Yom Kippur like this. Hiked all night wet through and through." On that night, Jay Lee said, "Men moved along in a daze, actually finding themselves napping and wobbling from side to side of the road as they walked."[52]

"After about a week or 10 days most of us were pretty well exhausted, and that also went for the horses," Skinny Ricketts said. "The horses were in bad shape. Every night it seemed we would lose one or two horses. They would just drop by the road exhausted and would have to be destroyed." Eddie McKim noted, "We had to use the culls of four years of warfare in Europe for our stock." Harry Murphy added, "I didn't want to have to care for them, be responsible for them, because they had such a hard life. They were— we were not able to have adequate feed. They got so weak and in such bad condition they practically died in the harness." "There was an order out," Skinny Ricketts remembered, "that we cannoneers who were walking and following the guns were not to hold on to any part of the gun or the caissons so as not to put any more burden on the horses. But walking along almost dead on your feet, you could hardly resist grabbing hold of the caisson to help you along." Harry said when a horse on one of his artillery pieces collapsed he needed "two hours of the hardest work to get that gun back into line where it belonged. Every soldier and every train in France (American) were trying to get to the line by the same road, it seemed, and if a gun or a man became separated from his outfit it was just too bad. The gun finally caught up."[53]

Colonel Klemm knew more about the grand strategy than did his men, and he frantically pushed the regiment to reach its position in time. His behavior seemed inexplicable to those ignorant of the time pressures. Private McKim told of mutinous murmurs. "He double-timed us up Toul Hill from midnight until about four in the morning. I think that somebody might have shot him in the back but they were afraid to shoot because Father Tiernan had the same color slicker." Even officers grew restive, McKim recalled. "That morning we had to doubletime up Toul Hill, Truman took us off the road; and we laid down and slept for awhile, right in the ditch at the side of the road. Then we got up and Klemm came back looking for us, and he said, 'Captain, where have you been?' And Truman said, 'Carrying out orders, sir.'" "From then," Sgt. Squatty Meisburger said, "Battery D would've let him [Truman] walk over them. They adored him." Harry and his fellow officers had decided long before that Klemm was "either drunk or crazy" riding up and down the line of march, throwing overseas caps off the heads of privates, and going berserk when he discovered anyone riding a caisson or limber. Harry declined Klemm's suggestions to punish infractions of rules by doubletiming the exhausted men. Supply Sgt. Jim Doherty, whose industrious scavenging was much admired by Harry, remembered when a member of the battery suffered a painful ankle injury. Colonel Klemm saw the man on Harry's horse, and ordered him off. Harry confronted Klemm, "You can take these bars off my shoulders, but as long as I'm in charge of this battery the man's going to stay on that horse." Klemm let the issue pass, and rode off angrily. To the men he appeared a pompous ass miffed by an injured enlisted man exercising an officer's prerogative to ride instead of walk. More likely Klemm was angry because someone was on Harry's horse while the captain walked, as the animals had to carry minimal burdens to survive the forced march; in the past officers had been ordered to walk. When the regiment arrived at its assigned position Klemm underwent a change, becoming far more reasonable. Yet there remained something strange. He proved fearless under fire, but disregard for one's life is far different from bravery. Harry wrote, "The Colonel was a West Pointer class of 1907 who had left the Army when he was still a second lieutenant of cavalry and married a rich brewer's daughter. When the war came on he helped organize the 2nd Missouri Field Artillery and was elected its Colonel. He had German ideas about discipline and a superiority complex because of his education and his wife's money. He'd never associated with volunteer troops and didn't understand . . . them."[54]

The night of September 22–23 Harry struggled to drag his battery across muddy fields to the terminus of the forced march. At last, he wrote, the destination came into view through the rain, "some small timber clumps about a couple of hundred yards from Hill 290 in the French map. The guns were put into position by putting 12 horses on each one and having every available man push." The job done, an exhausted Harry walked into a woods and flopped in the mud for a brief nap. Arising in the predawn gloom he trudged back to the battery just in time to see German artillery blasting the spot where he had been asleep. Harry wrote that his oil associate Pete Allen had the same experience that morning, "only the shell hit his bed just as he left it and tore it up for him. D Battery set up a kitchen a short distance from the battery position. About 9:00 an enemy shell burst in the neighborhood and blew up the food on the field range, knocked a hole in the stove pipe, and almost ruined the nerves of an excellent cook."[55]

Colonel Klemm told his officers about the Argonne offensive approximately twelve hours before it began. "He then remarked very casually that one of the batteries would be the Infantry Battery and would march up with the infantry, go over the top as close as it possibly could to the infantry, and fire on targets designed by the infantry commander, after it had fired the usual barrage that all the rest had to fire. All the battery commanders simply held their breath waiting to see who would get killed first. Finally Battery C was designated, and the battery commander [Capt. Ted Marks] was heartily congratulated by all the others because of the honor, and a feeling of great relief was felt by the other five battery commanders."[56]

Harry hurried off to prepare his battery for what became a near disaster. A wartime Army investigation concluded that Harry's 35th Division was unfit for battle, was not well disciplined, its men and officers were not well trained, the division staff was inefficient and poorly organized, with changes in staff and commanders hampering efficiency. The investigation criticized lack of liaison, noting that commanders failed to keep in touch with one another and with higher ups. Furthermore, "failure of all commanders to keep a headquarters established where communications could be received was inexcusable," adding confusion to the battle and causing commanders to send units too far ahead without coordination with other units. The investigation particularly questioned the decision of "both the Division Commander and the Chief of Staff to leave their headquarters at the same time." The division commander was criticized for ordering poor tactical formations, and Artillery Commander Brigadier General Berry (who harassed the National Guard officers of Harry's regiment) was one of only two officers in the whole division to be criticized by name. The report noted a general lack of leadership, and found that by the third day of the Argonne drive, Harry's division had ceased to exist as a unit. None of this was Harry's fault, and none of it was known to him before it happened. Yet he suffered the consequences from the very start when he received battle orders only twelve hours before H-Hour, a preparation time that the later Army investigation termed inadequate.[57]

Captain Truman and Lieutenant Housholder planned Battery D's barrage all night by candlelight, continuing computations up to the last moment. Battery D was ordered to fire a thousand rounds an hour, work that had to rotate among three guns much of the time because the fourth had to be out of action ten minutes every hour for cooling. The first hour was easy enough to figure, simply firing to destroy enemy barbed wire. The second and third hours were a trickier rolling barrage. Harry had to shoot just ahead of the American infantry, advancing the range as the troops advanced. A small mistake in Harry's math or by the firing crews could drop shells on the Yanks.[58]

Harry "gathered us around and made a little talk," Pvt. Ed Condon remembered. "It wasn't what you could call a speech, just a quiet talk like an older brother sometimes has with a younger boy. A few things that Harry Truman said that night still stick in my mind: 'I want to tell you this, too, fellows. Right tonight I'm where I want to be—in command of this battery. I'd rather be right here than be President of the United States. You boys are my kind. Now let's go in!' "[59]

At Gun No. 4 Sgt. Squatty Meisburger held his stopwatch, and waited to fire Battery D's first shot in the Argonne offensive. Instead of stationing themselves at observation posts, Harry and the other captains stood with their batteries. At 4:20 A.M., September 26, 1918, God roared and lit the Earth in stroboscopic frenzy. A half-century later Cpl. Harry Murphy still stammered in awe. "That gun squad worked just like clockwork. It was just—it was a sight, they just were perfect. They just got off those rounds so fast that—unbeliev- able." Battery D used four hundred gallons of water to wet the gunnysacks thrown over the barrels ten minutes in every hour. "Steam would arise just as if an engine were underneath letting off surplus driving vapor," Harry said. The only recorded unplanned interrup- tion was near the start when Squatty Meisburger frantically searched for his missing firing data sheet and found it stuffed in Ricketts's ears, where Ricketts had put it to protect against the noise. Chief gun mechanic McKinley Wooden smiled and told Lt. George Ar- rowsmith, "Sir, this is what I've been looking forward to all these years." Major Thacher agreed, "Just the thing we had lived for, and dreamed about." "I felt," Harry wrote, "that I was a Galahad after the Grail." When the barrage ended "everything became as quiet as a church," he said, except for "the typewriter staccato of machine guns further up front." The barrage finished, Harry "then went forward for more trouble than I was ever in before."[60]

26 Sept. 08:15. Adj. 129 F.A. Regiment to Operations Officer 60 F.A. Brigade. "Our mission completed. All ready limber up move. Wait orders." N. T. Paterson.[61]

26 Sept. 08:35. C.O. 60 F.A. Brigade to HQ 35th Div. "I have ordered forward one regiment of 75's." Brig. Gen. L. G. Berry.[62]

Battery D was the first "75 unit" of the regiment to move up. "As we marched on a road under an embankment, a French 155mm. battery fired over my head, and I still have trouble hearing what goes on when there is a noise. I went back and told the French captain what I thought of him, but he couldn't understand me—so it made no difference." Harry proceeded ahead of his battery into the former no-man's-land that had been his target. Near the ruins of Boureuilles he met Colonel Klemm, who asked if Battery D was ready to resume action. Harry replied, "Yes, sir!" even though, as he admitted years later, he "only had one gun and two caissons. The others were in the mud somewhere but were slowly coming up." Klemm assigned Harry's unit as an advance battery to aid infantry and tanks as they reported targets. No reports were coming in, so Klemm told Truman and Major Gates to scout some targets. The colonel mentioned something about machine guns up ahead as the two men left, accompanied by battery executive officer Lt. Gordon Jordan.

They walked up what had once been a good road, the Route Nationale, to the Aire River where the bridge was out. They waded the river (which Harry called a creek). After crossing Hun machine guns pinned them down. Harry thought a swarm of bees was going over his head, then suddenly realized he was hearing bullets. This was the first and only target the recon mission would find, despite consultation with a tank lieutenant and infantry brigadier general on the road. Harry and the others extricated themselves, and returned to their starting point around 3:30 P.M. Klemm and his staff had departed, leaving orders for Battery D to rejoin the rest of the regiment. Thus they were unable to set up and fire at the machine-gun nest. This experience soured Klemm on the tactical concept of advance batteries, as Harry's unit had been wasted waiting for target information when they could have been useful elsewhere. The fault, of course, lay with lack of communications in the 35th Division, not with lack of targets.[63]

26 Sept. "Report front line advancing but give no location. No later information from Hamilton." (Marked Haviland, decoded with Mohawk.)

26 Sept. 14:38. "Left Regt. exact position unknown. . . . Regts. became disorganized in fog resulting in loss of touch. . . . When I know definitely just where our advanced troops are will call for artillery barrage." Peter E. Traub, Cmdr., 35th Div.

26 Sept. 20:20. Liaison Officer 130 F.A. Regt. to Cmdr. 130 F.A. Regt. "Send location of our Post of Command. . . . Need large map of this area, orders and location of batteries."

Battery D was under occasional German artillery fire for almost twelve hours while traveling just one and a half miles to rejoin the regiment. A German dud landed smack between the legs of Pvt. Emil Jeserich, leaving him noticeably disquieted. "It was nothing but a bog," Harry wrote, "mud, mud, mud. The mud was worse than the guns and cannon firing at . . . the battery. Men went to sleep standing up trying to get the pieces across the shell holes and over the ditches." Harry's experience wasn't unique. Because the bridge was out over the Aire the entire regiment had to follow tank tracks across country, using picks and shovels to build an emergency road, devastating the horses. Road building was supposed to be the engineering detachment job, and the entire artillery regiment was jammed up by the wrecked bridge.[64]

26 Sept. 18:15. Chief of Staff First Corps to Cmdr. 35th Division. "Get a competent officer to the place where the artillery is jammed, that it can be taken across by swinging around through the woods and fording. Division Engineer is just returned from there. . . . The Engineers are loafing on the job, . . . put them to work if they have to work all night on that job." Gen. Craig.

26 Sept. To Cmdr. 35th Div. "General Craig . . . directs that we push forward to army objective at all costs, and that artillery must be pushed forward. . . . Am now going to confer with General Berry. . . . 129th Field Artillery reported to have left Boureuilles." W. V. Gallagher, G-3.

The situation began to disintegrate the night of September 26–27 with contradictory orders. Gen. Peter Traub, commander of the 35th Division, left division headquarters to observe the fighting in person. In his absence Chief of Staff Col. Hamilton Hawkins met with an infantry major and with Colonel Klemm (commander of only Truman's regiment) rather than with General Berry (commander of the entire 60th Field Artillery Brigade) to plan the next day's action for the division. Two colonels and a major decided that the 35th Division would renew its attack at 8:30 A.M. September 27, and orders to that effect were sent to all units. When General Traub returned he was aghast, as he had received orders from First Army Corps to resume the attack at 5:30. Traub countermanded the 8:30 attack, and set H-Hour as 5:30. At 1:00 A.M. he went back into the field to deliver these new orders to each brigade and regiment commander, a time-consuming process. He didn't reach some units until after 4:00 A.M. Deciding this was cutting it too close, he sent out a third set of orders, delaying the attack until 6:30. So the second day of the Argonne offensive began in confusion for the 35th Division. The situation would get worse.[65]

At 3:00 A.M. Harry finally got the last gun pulled across the bog, and crawled under a bush to sleep. One or two hours later Captain Paterson awakened him with the news that Battery D had to lay a barrage in ten minutes. Harry told him to go to hell, and arose sleepily to start computing the firing data. Both men knew the order was impossible to carry out, and Battery D wasn't ready until 7:00 A.M., a half hour after the attack had begun. Poor liaison with infantry meant the artillery couldn't locate the front line. Therefore, the barrage range had to be extra long to ensure that friendly fire wouldn't hit American troops. The range was so long that the battery couldn't achieve it, so not a shot was fired. "Battery E," Harry wrote, "put the trail of one gun in a shell hole and fired several rounds at the extreme elevation in the general direction of Germany. That Battery got credit for firing the barrage! The others caught hell for not being able to fire."[66]

27 Sept. 11:15. Chief of Staff 35th Div. to First Corps. By telephone. "At 9:15 139th reports its line held up just south of Charpentry . . . by machine gun fire. . . . The regimental commander reports that he cannot advance until he has more artillery support. The regimental commander of the 140th Infantry reports himself also held up by machine gun fire. . . . On the right half of our sector moving two regiments of 75's up as fast as possible to support the infantry. Only one battalion of 75's has yet been able to do any firing. . . . Expect to have several battalions of 75's in action at noon." Col. Hamilton Hawkins.

After an 11:00 breakfast Battery D moved out to pursue the front line. "Just outside Cheppy," Harry wrote, "the battery came to the fork in the road that went to Varennes. A couple of trees were at this road junction and a pile of American soldiers in all sorts of ghastly positions. Shot by enemy machine gunners. There were 17 of them and nearly a dozen more lying head to heel down the road shot in the back after they'd gone by. The battery had been chattering and carrying on as they usually did when on a road march, and when they saw this spectacle everything became as quiet as a church." Squatty Meisburger watched as a battery member "walked over to a poor fellow who had been split wide open and looked at his identification tag. It bore the name of a major. 'Well, if it can happen to him this quick, no use for us to worry,' remarked the soldier as he returned to the ranks."[67]

27 Sept. 16:45. Chief of Staff 35th Div. to First Corps. "Our lines have been held up all day general along corps objective by machine gun fire from our front and from our left flank, by machine gun nests passed by 28th Div. also by lack of artillery support. Artillery support now partially reestablished and a second attack will be launched late this afternoon."

Early that afternoon Battery D went into position in an orchard just west of Cheppy. Cutting some trees for a free field of fire left the unit clearly visible to any Huns looking in that direction. Leaving his gas mask and .45 behind lest they influence his targeting compass, Harry moved ahead of his artillery to establish an observation post so he could watch explosions from his battery's shells and telephone aiming corrections back to the guns. He found an ideal location on a hill. American lines were shifting back and forth rapidly, and Harry was startled when an infantry sergeant came over to warn him that he was no longer in American-held territory, but two hundred yards into no-man's-land. Harry dropped back promptly. From his new position he directed eighty-two shells onto Charpentry. His land line to the battery went out intermittently, cut by German fire or American hobnails. One interruption came from German airplanes strafing and bombing the battery. The communications officer barely had time to say that the son-of-a-bitch German was dropping something, when the potato masher exploded, ripping the headphones from his skull but leaving him uninjured. "Here comes a German plane flying at about 300 feet," Pup Leigh recalled. "One guy was flying the plane, and the other guy is just firing away cool as hell." A battery horseshoer grabbed a machine gun and pressed the trigger. In his excitement he forgot to aim. "He was just firing it flat," Leigh said, "if you stood to your full height you were a dead man. We never let him forget it, and he never got to handle that machine gun again." The only casualties in the incident were two dead horses—credited to the Germans, not to the Battery D machine gunner.[68]

27 Sept. 17:15. Roadrunner to unnamed recipient. "The enemy seems to be making a stand."

One minute later Harry's regiment was ordered to lay a barrage in support of a renewed attack. Fortunately some, if not all, of the regiment's guns were already aimed near the target, so the order could be obeyed on short notice (they were told they had about fifteen minutes). About half an hour after this operation began, Harry's attention was caught by a flare dropped from a U.S. airplane. Caught under the garish illumination was a German artillery battery going into position. The unit was close, just across the Aire. "A battery seen is a battery lost," Eddie McKim noted. Pup Leigh remembered "Truman didn't panic, he let them take their horses away from the guns. . . . If it had been me I would have probably hollered for D Battery to start firing as soon as I saw them. He didn't do that; he let them get into position, get all set to fire, with their horses by this time a couple miles away. Then he had his firing data exact. It's no good to have a man up there if he don't know what the hell he's doing." In this case Harry knew he was violating orders. The German unit was in a sector reserved for fire from 28th Division artillery, which was not Harry's command. He followed common sense. McKim remembered that "Truman sent back the data . . . and he said, 'Fire at will; fire as fast as you can,' and we just poured them in there." Forty-nine rounds landed on the German guns in two minutes, one round almost every two seconds. The enemy unit was eliminated. Klemm phoned ten minutes later to chew out Truman, heatedly threatening a court martial for firing out of sector. "Go ahead!" he replied. "I'll never pass up a chance like that. We plastered 'em." No order for court martial ever arrived.[69]

Under cover of darkness Harry moved Battery D out of the orchard, as per orders, since German airplanes had spotted the Americans that afternoon. "We got up the road probably a hundred yards," Eddie McKim said, "and where we had just left, boy, the shells were just raining in there." The men were worn out. Cpl. Harry Murphy fell asleep on the ground and awoke to find a boiled potato in his hand. His buddy Sgt. Verne Chaney had been unable to awaken him for chow call. Conditions would worsen.[70]

28 Sept. 12:10. C.O. 3rd Bn. 140th Inf. to Cmding. Gen. 35th Div. "140th Inf. being cut all to pieces by German artillery half or more of first and third battalion casualties, no contact with second battalion or on our right or left, we are in severe straits and Boche are attacking, artillery from two sides. . . . Disaster will result unless we have assistance, barrage and counter barrage."

28 Sept. 12:30. Co. D 137th Inf. to HQ 35th Div. "Being shelled from both flanks and front. Will be impossible to hold without artillery support. Almost out of ammunition. Must have at once." Lt. Verne Breese.

28 Sept. 13:15. From C.O. 3rd Bn. 138th Inf. "Our front line is very thin, our men are pushing ahead but dropping like flies. . . . The German artillery is playing hell with our ranks. I am sending this as I do not know what liaison you have with the front. It is so hard to locate the different headquarters of our division and I am unable to learn from division on our left. The one on our right is having the same trouble. . . . I have just learned that our artillery is unable to give much support, for the reason of being unable to locate our front line. I think our advance should be located for them if it would even have to be stopped for a few hours." Capt. F. A. Bottger.

28 Sept. 13:30. Maj. Loy to Lt. Col. Hay. "Unable to get any information from our brigade headquarters, can't find them, still pushing ahead but am getting heavy artillery fire from hills on our left causing heavy losses trying to get you by phone but cannot."

28 Sept. 15:30. From R.I.O. 138th Inf. "Word just received from our first battalion that they are in front line with various groups of 140th Inf. Subject to terrific cross artillery fire and aerial bombing and machine gun. Only two officers left in our first battalion. Several companies are without officers. We are not in liaison with second or third battalion but are sending to locate them."

28 Sept. 18:45. C.O. 140th Inf. to HQ 35th Div. "Have been separated from my regiment. . . . Have been shelled from east and west by high explosives and gas. . . . No information."

At 9:30 the next morning Harry sent sixty-four shells into a German observation post he had spotted, putting it out of service. An hour and a half later he saw an enemy artillery battery leaving its position, and sent them fifty-six shells in two minutes—one shell every two seconds. Much later a 28th Division colonel told Harry, "You got 'em all right; for when we later came up that way there were six abandoned guns beside the road." When this battery and others in similar positions fired at American infantry, the shells came from the south. Thus American troops thought they were being hit by friendly fire, demoralizing men already in the most difficult of circumstances. Reports of U.S. artillery hitting American troops were immediately checked, and German batteries were always shown to be the source of shells. Harry wrote, "A general of infantry who was watching [a] German counterattack told our Artillery General that the German counterattack was a whiz but *their artillery barrage fell short* and busted them up. *It was our barrage* falling long and where we wanted it to fall. That goes to show you what an infantryman knows of his supporting arm." He added, "I know that my battery shot where it was told to because I observed a great deal of my fire . . . I have reason to believe that every other battery did as well or better than mine." *Kansas City Star* criticisms of the 129th Field Artillery's performance—criticisms fueled in part by his cousin Ralph— enraged Harry. He wrote that the *Star* could "besmirch our reputation and I guess they're happy. But there's a day of reckoning coming." Thus Harry nursed a grudge against the *Star* long before he reentered county politics.[71]

September 28 was a better day for Battery D; they stayed put for a change. The battalion operations report said, "Men rested and horses in fair condition. Late in evening ranges began to increase until enemy lines almost receded to a point out of range from present positions."[72]

29 Sept. 02:00. HQ 35th Div. to HQ 60th Field Artillery Brigade. "It is directed imperatively, that you get as many 75's as you can furnish with ammunition forward to support the infantry. Colonel Ristine has been in the Boche line near territory where our artillery fire fell, and claims it was not effective. The Commanding General directs that you take the necessary steps to make your fire more effective and that the closer it is to the infantry the more effective it will be."

29 Sept. 03:30. HQ 60th Field Artillery Brigade to HQ 35th Div.

"1. Direct hits on one hostile battery were observed, caisson was seen to blow up. It is believed that in all cases the artillery fire was as accurate as could be expected. Constant effort is made to improve the accuracy of the artillery and assist the infantry. The present condition of Col. Ristine's command makes me unwilling to accept him as a military critic. 2. The orders of the Division Commander will be carefully studied by me and thoroughly complied with." Brig. Gen. L. G. Berry.

29 Sept. 08:15. HQ First Corps to HQ 35th Div. "The Corps Commander wants to know if our artillery is all up and supporting the infantry. If not, why not?"

29 Sept. 08:40. HQ First Corps to HQ 35th Div. "If your artillery Brigade Commander is not giving full support and is not to you a satisfactory and loyal commander you are authorized to relieve him."

Even as Battery D fired a protective barrage for the infantry around 8:00 A.M., communications traffic showed growing questions about Harry's brigade and its commander L. G. Berry. Division commander General Peter Traub was already dissatisfied with the rate of fire. He had to order Berry to cooperate with the air corps in target spotting, even though Berry admitted that some enemy batteries couldn't be located without aerial observation. Berry called observation balloons and planes "no damn good," and failed to call for their aid until September 29. The next day he was griping about lack of airplanes.[73]

29 Sept. 09:00. From R.I.O. 138th Inf. "Men in very poor condition. In some cases companies average 30 men. Morale is low."

29 Sept. 10:40. "Have 100 bearers of mule ambulance and two wagons and one Ford out collecting in wounded and there seems to be no end to them. There must be 500 yet to come. They are in all directions from me. Collecting is difficult as snipers and machine gunners are sweeping the field, also aeroplanes. Our artillery fire is feeble. Signed: Gist."

29 Sept. 11:15. C.O. 35th Div. to C.O. First Corps. "Regret to report that this Division cannot advance beyond crest south of Exermont. It is thoroughly disorganized, through loss of officers and many casualties, for which cannot give estimate, owing to intermingling of units. Recommend it be withdrawn for reorganization and

be replaced promptly by other troops in order that the advance may be continued." Peter E. Traub.

The artillerymen didn't need cable traffic to know something was wrong. Stragglers heading toward the rear began passing through the batteries, disorganized soldiers separated from their units and bearing tales of annihilation. Capt. Keith Dancy of Battery A said, "Our infantry claimed every third Boche was armed with a machine gun." Harry's regiment began firing in a frenzy to hold off the Germans. Six rounds a minute was "the book" maximum for the .75's; faster could overheat the guns. The rules were abandoned, and Dancy claimed that guns in his battery reached twenty-one rounds per minute. Even continual cooling by wet blankets failed to keep the barrels below oven temperature. Firing continued as German artillery found the range. When a hostile shell explosion lifted one side of a Battery A gun, Pvt. Stewart Perry reportedly "grinned as he ejected his own cartridge case from the breech and yelled, 'Shove in another one!' " Sergeant Poe claimed that Pvt. Arthur Bloomer's "Jew Luck" saved the squad. Battery C's luck ran out. One German shell hit a caisson and detonated a dozen rounds of ammunition. Another made a direct hit on a gun, killing Cpl. Ralph Kyle and Pvt. John Gersic. Tirey Ford's legs were shattered by a shell that hit in front of his gun, and he later died from head wounds. Pvt. Frank Fraas died a few days later, but Pvt. Arthur Bell survived seventeen wounds. Pvt. Selmo Fulton rushed over from another squad and though wounded continued to fire that gun single-handed. Such was the job of the cannoneer that afternoon—to protect the infantry at any cost. Maj. John Thacher admitted, "I think every man of us had a private understanding with himself that those were to be his last minutes on Earth, and that if he ever got out alive he'd do some noble act of self sacrifice and devotion, like saving his drowning landlord."[74]

29 Sept. 12:00. 130th Field Artillery to HQ 60th Field Artillery Brigade. "Shells which were falling on our troops and which were reported to be from our guns were enemy 77's. I could not see any of our shells falling short."

29 Sept. 12:30. From Command Post 2nd Cavalry. "Troops of the 139th are badly disorganized, stupified, terrified, and inactive."

29 Sept. 15:00. From officer on behalf of Commander 35th Div. By telephone. "70th Brigade is falling back almost to Baulny. The Germans are rushing them back. . . . General [Traub] now leaving Baulny. Germans are coming right on us."

29 Sept. 15:00. "About 200 men left, rush troops at once." Capt. Ralph Truman [cousin of Harry], 140th Inf.

29 Sept. 15:45. "Soldiers are retreating down the ravine in total disorder. The few remaining officers are endeavoring to rally the men. There are no front lines here in the ravine."

Disorganized American troops came past Harry's regiment in ever-growing numbers. French batteries cooperating with his regiment now withdrew, going right by Batteries A, B, and C. An excited French officer shouted for Battery D to retreat. Pvt. James Casey promptly handed the Frenchman a knuckle sandwich. Maj. John Miles ordered preparation for direct fire, perhaps the most chilling command an artilleryman can hear. "The book" specifies this as the final order before the enemy overruns the position. But the enemy never came. Unknown to Harry's regiment, the 110th Engineers had abandoned their tools and gone into action as infantrymen. They saved the situation. Their commander was the man Colonel Klemm had defeated in the National Guard elections back at Kansas City, Maj. E. M. Stayton.[75]

30 Sept. 07:50. To Col. Ristine, C.O. 139th Inf. "We have just received information that the Boche is infiltrating north of the woods about the same as yesterday. We are putting down a barrage north of the woods. Get everybody on the alert. Get ready for anything which may happen."

30 Sept. 09:00. HQ 35th Div. to HQ First Corps. "Every available officer including the Commanding General himself has gone forward to steady the troops. Last reports indicate less than one officer per hundred men. Reserves seem imperative."

30 Sept. 10:00. C.O. Company A 128th Machine Gun Bn. to HQ 35th Div. "Our best men have already been killed. If the sacrifice is necessary we do not complain, but is it necessary." Capt. Schrank.

30 Sept. 12:55. Capt. Vallee to HQ 35th Div. "Unable to locate the General to secure his O.K. or disapproval of plan to advance at 2 o'clock. Have, however, seen Col. Hawkins [chief of staff, 35th

Division] who states advance to be a physical impossibility as men are in the last stages of exhaustion and can do nothing more than hold on until relief comes, which should come soon."

On September 30 Harry's battery lobbed more shells than any day since the Argonne battle began. A messenger recounted the scene.

> I set out on the run, jumping into shell holes when I heard one with my name on it, or crashing myself against outcroppings when those big ones shrieked, "Where are you Corporal Sergeant Shaffer?" . . . I reached the battery in nothing flat, as muddy as an alligator, all the skin off my nose. Captain Harry S. Truman was standing there, his tin hat pushed on the back of his head, directing salvos into some spot toward the northeast. He was a banty officer in spectacles, and when he read my message he started runnin' and cussin' all at the same time, shouting for the guns to turn northwest. He ran about a hundred yards to a little knoll, and what he saw didn't need binoculars. I never heard a man cuss so well or so intelligently, and I'd shoed a million mules. He was shouting back ranges and giving bearings.
>
> The battery didn't say a word. They must have figured the cap'n could do the cussin' for the whole outfit. It was a great sight, like the center ring in Barnum and Bailey at the close of the show, everything clockwork, setting fuses, cutting fuses, slapping shells into breeches and jerking lanyards before the man hardly had time to bolt the door. Shell cases were flipping back like a juggler's act, clanging on tin hats of the ammunition passers, the guns just spitting fire—spit-spit-spit-spit.
>
> Then Captain Truman ran down the knoll and cussed 'em to fire even faster. . . . I finally made out what he saw. There were groups of Germans at the edge of the woods, stooping low and coming on slowly with machine guns on their hips, held by shoulder straps. He shouted some cusswords filled with figures down to the battery, and shells started breaking into the enemy clumps. Whole legs were soon flying through the air. He really broke up that counter-attack. He was still there being shot at when I came to my senses and got off the knoll.

Other batteries continued to receive casualties, but Harry's men were spared. In the whole war only one Battery D man died from wounds.

"There's such a thing as sticking your battery in a spot where they shouldn't be," Pup Leigh said later, "and Truman didn't make those mistakes." His regiment remained in place as the First Division relieved the 35th on October 1. Finally at 11:30 P.M. on October 2 Harry's battalion began pulling out from its position near Cheppy. The march was uneventful, unharassed by enemy shells. For Harry and Battery D the Argonne was over.[76]

The war continued, of course, and Battery D was part of it; but the remaining experience was nothing like the Argonne. After a couple of weeks' rest Harry's unit moved to Verdun, and fired barrages in support of infantry (this was long after the famous battle there). On November 1 Harry wrote home to Ethel and Nellie Noland. "I am now in front of the most famous, and hardest fought for city in France. They say that some 800000 French and 1000000 Huns lost their lives here. It sure looks like it, too. There are Frenchmen buried in my front yard and Dutchmen buried in my back yard and gobs of both scattered over the whole landscape, which by the way is the most dreary outlook I've ever seen. There's one field over west of me here a short distance where every time a shell lights it plows up a piece of someone." He enclosed one of two poppies he found growing through the rocks where vicious fighting had occurred. He sent the other flower to Bess Wallace.[77]

At breakfast on November 11 Squatty Meisburger received orders to report to Harry's dugout. Harry had a "wide grin on his face, and he was stretched out on the ground eating a blueberry pie. Where he got the blueberry pie I don't know. . . . His face was all smeared with blueberries. He handed me a piece of flimsy and said between bites, 'Sergeant, you will take this back and read it to the members of the battery.' " Thus did the men learn the war would end in a couple of hours. The battery completed its barrage commitments at 10:45. Fifteen minutes later hostilities ceased.[78]

"You know that the continual and promiscuous dropping of shells around you will eventually get on your nerves considerably, and mine were pretty tightly strung by 11:00," Harry said. Harry Haven of Battery C wrote "a deep silence seemed to fall over the entire line. There were no wild demonstrations; no cheers." He continued, "By noon, the clouds had broken away. The sun began to shine for the first time in weeks." The men of Battery D drank the sun up, and they drank the moon down. "I don't know what they did in other outfits," Sgt. Sox Werner said, but in Battery D "the vin rougers went rouging, and the cognacers went cognacing." "There were drinks that made you climb mountains," Pvt. Smack Evans wrote, "drinks that made you climb trees in imitation of arboreal ancestors." This behavior was nothing unusual. ("You could turn Battery D loose in the middle of the Sahara, and in an hour they'd all be drunk," Harry said.) This night the French artillerymen behind Battery D joined in. "The French battery became intoxicated as a result of a load of wine which came up on the ammunition narrow gauge. Every single one of them had to march by my bed and salute and yell, 'Vive President Wilson, Vive le capitaine d'artillerie américaine!' No sleep all night, the infantry fired Very pistols, sent up all the flares they could lay their hands on, fired rifles, pistols and whatever else would make noise, all night long." Capt. Ted Marks added, "It looked more like a Fourth of July celebration instead of the front lines."[79]

In early December Harry and some fellow officers got leave and vacationed through France. Harry saw the sights of Paris, including the Folies Bergères ("disgusting," he said, "about what you'd expect at the Gayety only more so") and the Grand Opera ("the building was worth the price of admission"). Having lunch at the Casino de Paris, they were excited when the Princess of Monaco came in. Lieutenant Colonel Elliott noted with disgust that she ordered beer. "It gave all of us common people a letdown," Harry said. "We stopped 24 hours in Marseilles and I saw Gaby Dely, in her own theater the Casino de Marseilles, in a perfectly gorgeous show and she threw me a bunch of violets—I got 'em anyway whether they were intended for me or not. Marseilles is just about as gay as Paris, and Paris is as wild as any place I ever saw. Nice is an ideal place for a vacation. The Blue Mediterranean on one side and the Alps on the other and sunshine and expense until you are completely satisfied and busted. I went to Monte Carlo and saw the finest gambling hell in the world but they wouldn't let me play because I had on uniform." Harry and Marvin Gates then got a car and motored into Italy and back again through the foothills of the Alps.[80]

As a Christmas surprise Battery D's homefolks in Kansas City sent $500 to buy a holiday dinner. Harry located a quarter-ton porker for the meal. "The pig was the most costly animal of his kind that

I ever had a part in buying. He cost us about $235, but the men decided it was money well spent." Major Thacher wrote home:

> You ought to have seen that Mess Hall. We had a Christmas tree with decorations of stars made out of old tin cans and tin foil off of cigarette packages and a chocolate bar for each man, and a khaki handkerchief and cigarettes and cigars. And a genius of a cook made cherry cobblers from some canned cherries we bought down at Bar-le-Duc. Picture it for yourself. A dingy little shack, tacked over with tarpaper to keep out the snow—an island in a sea of mud—but inside! Christmas greens, mistletoe, a piano snitched out from Lord knows what French billets. And crammed with singing and cheering American boys, thinly disguised as soldier-men—all smoking when they weren't stoking and Tommy Murphy singing in his melodious tenor, "Oh, how I hate to get up in the morning" and the tables loaded with roast pig and ham and beans and, at the supreme moment of climax—pie! One of the boys from Headquarters had borrowed a violin from some poilus and made it sob in melodies of home and wives and sweethearts and kids and all the rest until the Battery D quartette had to step in with "Keep your head down Allemand" in order to restore the morale to the occasion. It was a real Christmas and nobody thought of suggesting that we were a long way from the firesides that—well, nobody SPOKE, of them anyhow.[81]

The weeks dragged, and Battery D passed time with busywork, drinking, knuckle drills, and gambling. Long before he made another trip to Paris in March and glimpsed President Wilson, Harry was impatient to leave Europe. "I am very anxious that Woodie cease his gallivantin' around and send us home at once and quickly. As far as we're concerned most of us don't give a whoop (to put it mildly) whether Russia has a Red Government or no Government and if the King of the Lollypops wants to slaughter his subjects or his Prime Minister it's all the same to us. The Hun is whipped and is fast killing and murdering himself so why should we be kept over here to browbeat a Peace Conference that'll skin us anyway."[82]

A couple of weeks after that last visit to Paris, Harry and his regiment sailed for home. Skinny Ricketts remembered, "About all we did on the ship . . . was just lay around and eat and play poker."

And craps. Somehow the idea developed in Battery D that Captain Truman should get a gift from the men, and the gift was financed with dice. "If you want to shoot a dollar," Fred Bowman recalled, "you put a dollar five down there, and the nickel went into the pot" for the present. "We wanted to get him a trophy," Eddie McKim said, "and our idea of a trophy was a big one. We got him a great, big loving cup and the thing must have stood three or four feet high. We had it inscribed to him." McKim added, "I don't think any other captain in the AEF got one of those." Tommy Murphy added, "The fellows looked on him as a dad---I mean that. Everyone called him Capt. Harry. It wasn't exactly army regulations, but that's the way it was."[83]

Harry arrived in the United States on Easter Sunday 1919, having departed on Good Friday a year earlier. Several officers—Harry, Edgar Hinde, Roger Sermon, Harry Jobes, Father Tiernan, and others—did New York City together one night. "Went up to the roof garden in the old Amsterdam Hotel," Hinde said. "We ran into a commander in the Navy that some of them knew, and this guy ordered 10 or 12 drinks and set them down on the table."[84]

The trains carrying Harry's regiment arrived in Kansas City at dawn on May 3. One newspaper reporter wrote, "In the east end of the terminal yards, where the red and green switch lights were yet twinkling through a mist of fog and rain, the first gleam of a headlight pierced the early morning gloom. No sun was ever brighter, no moonbeams ever sweeter." The crowd overcame the guards and swarmed over the soldiers for two hours. Then the 129th formed into ranks and marched through Kansas City amid laughing, crying, and cheering crowds. At Convention Hall the men fell out for a chicken lunch with friends and relatives waiting inside. Then to Camp Funston in Kansas, and then to civilian life on May 6.[85]

Chapter 7

VETERAN BUSINESSMAN

Some way I seem to have an ability for getting myself
into things by my overzealous conduct or anxiety to see
them a success and do not seem to see the consequences
to myself or others until the conclusion comes.

—Harry S. Truman[1]

Harry Truman's marriage to Bess
Wallace began while he was preparing to open a Kansas City haberdashery. She had accepted an engagement ring before the war. The war didn't prompt the engagement, but it delayed the wedding. Harry wanted Bess free if he returned horribly maimed in body or soul. He promised that he "wouldn't look at the French mademoiselles," and he returned to his sweetheart "reasonably pure," he said, and "as clean" as she was.[2]

From France Harry wrote home that the marriage was set for June 28, 1919. The day was hot enough to wilt flowers and guests, but Harry was radiant. After the ceremony at Trinity Episcopal and the reception on the Gates-Wallace lawn, the newlyweds headed for Kansas City's Union Station for their honeymoon in Detroit (for a day or two where they visited Harry's cousin Mary Colgan) and Chicago. Best man Ted Marks, and family attorney Fred Boxley went along to Union Station, leaving behind in Independence a contingent of Harry's other military associates. Decades later Marks still remembered the scene at the train depot. Harry's mother "had me by the arm," he said, "and she was a small woman, and I said to her, 'Well, now, Mrs. Truman, you've lost Harry.' And she looked up at me with those little blue eyes and said, 'Indeed I haven't.' "[3]

Harry had established himself as a Kansas City businessman with the Morgan oil operation, and had kept tabs on it during the war, but the war changed many things. Dave Morgan apparently recognized that the operation would never thrive without Harry's conciliatory presence smoothing disputes among participants. So he sold the two-thirds interest he and Harry held in Morgan Oil & Refining Co. to the same J. Sylvester Mullen who had earlier purchased Culbertson's one-third interest. Morgan did this without consulting Harry, but he probably expected no objection. In this transaction Morgan and Truman became sole owner of Morgan & Co. Oil Investments, which traded in oil properties throughout Louisiana, Texas, Oklahoma, and Kansas. In 1918 the company advertised itself as "The oldest exclusive OIL INVESTMENT Firm in Kansas City" and claimed "fifteen years in the mid-continent oil fields" although it was barely two years old.

A Morgan oil investor sent Harry this plaintive inquiry:

Well, Harry, how is the oil biz? I wrote Mr. Morgan nearly a year ago asking him to see what my stock would be worth. He said the price had "been allowed to sag" but he'd watch and if it came back as he thought it would in 30 or 60 days he'd let me know. It must have "sagged" out of sight—I never heard from him again. Then in Nov. Lizzie wrote Mary Jane [Truman] and has never heard from her. Lynn sent out notices for a meeting of stockholders December 28 - 18. This was followed with a statement a few weeks later that "owing to etc." there had been no meeting but they'd have it April 5 - 19, and that was the last of that—and him, and I'd like just a little to know where I'm at before certain conditions I have to meet come out to meet *me*. Are they, or have they done a d-m- thing since you left, and is the stock worth a whooperee if so how many. I could have turned the money invested a dozen times over out here since I bought in, but as long as you were there I felt it was all to the good, and if you are there now I shall "keep the Faith" but really if it's ever to do any business it's time it started, and if not it's time I started. Understand please there is no reflection on *you* meant, for I have no friend I prize more highly, but as circumstances none of us could foresee called you away, I think it only fair that I should know what is going on, I guess this is enough of this.

Harry's reply contained so many inaccuracies that one can scarcely believe his sincerity:

I am looking into their affairs now. I expect Mr. Mullen in town today or tomorrow when we are going to give things a thorough going over, and I will write you again. It seems that the Morgan Oil & Refining Company has drilled about three dry holes while I was in Europe, and a great deal of their capital, of course, is tied up in these holes, which are of no value whatsoever; but they have a refining process, which, in my opinion, will bring them out all right, although it will take some time to do it. I will be glad to keep you informed as to the prospect, both present and future, whenever developments take place. It is taking me some time to get my hand in on things, as there have been a great many changes while I was away. Mr. Morgan is no longer connected with the Morgan Oil & Refining Co., although he and I are endeavoring to run an oil investment business. Mr. Lynn and Mr. Mullen have complete charge of the Morgan Oil & Refining Co. As I said before, I am going into their affairs pretty thoroughly today and tomorrow. I still have all my holdings in the Morgan Oil & Refining Co. that I had when I started out, and when I get ready to let loose of them I expect to let my friends know about it. I believe if the refining process is carried to a successful conclusion, they will yet make us a great deal of money. I have a great deal of confidence in both Mr. Lynn and Mr. Mullen.

Since W. H. Lynn was one of Culbertson's top stock salesmen, Harry must have felt some uneasiness about him. He knew the "refining process" was a sham that Culbertson concocted to bring in suckers. Truman and Morgan both agreed that Harry had no holdings in Morgan Oil when he wrote the letter. One suspects that Harry spent more time dealing with plans for his wedding two days later than in dealing with a thorough examination of oil company affairs.

A month later Harry wrote another extraordinary letter, this time to Dave Morgan. It was a "cover your ass memo" apparently intended for anyone who asked why Harry left the oil game. He asserted that the family farm was a "several hundred thousand dollars" business that he now had to manage, and therefore he had to leave Morgan & Co. All this was untrue. "I am confident that your estimation of the value of the holdings of this firm is more than $200,000." This didn't mean Harry felt the holdings had that worth; he only agreed that Morgan claimed such valuation. Harry referred to "the very small investment originally made by me in this company" and "the large amount of money which I have drawn, amounting to several times the amount of my original investment." Of the three original partners Harry was the only one who invested any cash— $5,000. Harry's statement indicates that he made at least a $10,000 profit, perhaps far more. Was this true, or just puffery for Morgan to show potential investors? The two men agreed that Harry received no salary while Culbertson was involved, but this says nothing about the return on Harry's investment. Truman and Morgan agreed they both made a small profit from the sale of Morgan Oil & Refining Co., but again that says nothing about their income before the sale. Years later Harry said he had $15,000 or $20,000 cash when he returned from the war, but he didn't explain the source. This may have been oil business profits, or his memory may have compressed events (described shortly) that led to his receiving a $15,000 profit from the Grandview farm. Finally in his letter to Morgan, Harry said he was yielding his interest in Morgan & Co. in exchange for $10,000 cash, all the Morgan Oil & Refining Co. stock owned by Morgan & Co., and a half dozen oil leases. Apparently instead of getting the cash, however, he settled for a mortgaged house Dave Morgan and his wife Lenore owned in Kansas City at 3404 Karnes Blvd. Harry and Bess never lived there, so they must have rented out the property or left it vacant.

Dave Morgan strongly implied that he had sold all of his and Harry's oil interests by early 1919, but Morgan was still president of Morgan & Co. Oil Investments in December 1919 when capital stock was increased from $3,000 to $100,000. This doesn't mean the company received that much money. Indeed, Morgan acquired 97,000 shares at a par value of $1.00 apiece by turning over to the company leases supposedly worth $97,000. This made him owner of about 98 percent of the company.[4]

The sale of Harry's interests in the two Morgan companies allowed him to retire the notes that his mother had endorsed to start the oil business, the notes to which she had pledged family farm property. The farm was safe for now, but Vivian watched with sullen countenance—perhaps wondering how Harry's next appeal to "Mamma" would be clothed. Dave Morgan also made a profit when he sold out of the operation.[5]

Harry was discharged from the military on May 6. He said he checked various commercial possibilities, decided on gents' furnishings, and signed the lease for a store on May 27. Three weeks seem like scarcely enough time to make an informed choice among commercial possibilities, particularly since a substantial part of that time must have been spent with his family in Grandview and with Bess in Independence. A more credible chronology has Eddie Jacobson suggesting the haberdashery to Harry while they were still in Europe. Surely a major factor in his decision was that a haberdashery is a masculine enterprise, generating the convivial male socialization that he loved. Such a business would cater to high-class gents, the live wires who moved the downtown Kansas City business community. Such contacts might be valuable.[6]

Harry's self-confidence was brash. He said the idea for the store came from Eddie Jacobson. The two of them had run the outrageously prosperous regimental canteen, and planned to duplicate the success of that low capital/high return enterprise. As his haberdashery began, Harry was bright with hope.[7]

Harry and Eddie combined their capital to open the business. To generate his portion Harry turned once again to the family farmland. "Harry wanted me to go on running the farm," Mary Jane said, "but I told him if he wasn't going to be at home to help, I would rather give it up. I'd run it two years all alone." The farm had prospered in Harry's absence, and he now reaped the profits. After the summer growing season ended he auctioned off all the equipment, horses, mules, and livestock. He got $4,000 for the 234 hogs—which had increased from 16 prewar animals under Mary Jane's careful management. Harry said he *netted* $15,000 from this sale. All this money went to Harry for the haberdashery—not to Mary Jane, not to Vivian, not to their mother. Vivian's friends reported that he and Mary Jane were none too pleased about ending the farm operations, but Harry's decision to leave the farm forced the sale. Vivian was also said to be unhappy with sending the money into another city-slicker scheme. In addition, Harry now attempted to sell 160 acres plus another 40 to an anonymous "wealthy oilman" for $75,000. Nothing happened. From now on the farmland itself would be rented out. This would reduce the income that Harry's mother received from the land, making it harder to keep up payments on the mortgage that had been required to buy off relatives contesting Louisa Young's will. Harry held no lawful interest in part of this land—he had signed away all his rights to his uncle's portion before getting his mother's $5,000 loan for the Morgan oil business in 1916. The mortgage was refinanced in 1917 as one $5,000 and two $10,000 five-year notes held by T. P. Green and by Harry's Masonic associate Frank Blair. In 1919 Harry gave Vivian, Mary Jane, and his mother a quitclaim deed for all his remaining interests in the farm, and his mother mortgaged still more land for $6,200. This money surely helped finance the haberdashery either as a direct contribution, or indirectly as $6,200 that wasn't taken from the farm sale proceeds. Once again Vivian watched in helpless exasperation as his mother put family farmland behind his brother's city business.[8]

On May 27, a month before Harry's wedding, he and Eddie signed an extravagant store lease with Louis Oppenstein. Oppenstein was a big Kansas City real estate operator in the process of buying a building, and the lease suggests that Oppenstein needed to show financial backers that he could fill the building with tenants. To get Harry and Eddie, Oppenstein agreed to tile five hundred square feet of the store to their order, provide ten electrical outlets, a washbowl, a stairway to the basement, and put in a steel ceiling. Such promises from a landlord may create feelings of goodwill and trust in unwary tenants, and the lease was actually disadvantageous to Harry and Eddie. In the first place they had to pay three months' rent up front when the lease was signed. This $1,050 should have easily covered the renovations, so Oppenstein had to dig nothing from his pocket to do the work. The tragic clause, however, prohibited the tenants from assigning the lease or subletting without the landlord's written consent. That looked innocuous enough standing alone, but was deadly when combined with the provision holding Harry and Eddie personally responsible for the rent for five years even if the business failed. If the business folded, Harry and Eddie might be prohibited from subletting the store so that they could afford to keep paying Oppenstein. At the same time Oppenstein could rent out the store to a new tenant, enjoying that income on top of whatever he could wring from Harry and Eddie.[9]

The store's location was choice, 104 West 12th Street, across from the Muehlebach Hotel. This was Kansas City's top hotel of the era, attracting a free-spending clientele from across the state and the nation. Two gambling halls operated on the corner. The locale was also the heart of Kansas City's business district, filled with Babbits who dressed for success. "Twelfth Street was in its heyday," Eddie said. "The boys wore silk underwear and silk shorts. We sold men's silk shirts at $16." The store also handled hats, hose, collars, ties, handkerchiefs, cuff links, and other jewelry. A patron described the establishment as "right up to snuff. It was a sharp place. It was well run, and it was a beautiful layout." The store opened in the last week of November 1919, and grossed $70,000 in its first year, with a good net. Store hours were 8:00 A.M. to 9:00 P.M. six days a week. Ted Marks remembered Truman "never stayed in the store all day— he would get out and go to lunches and mix with people, you know. He was very well known in that way." Indeed, Truman paid $225 to join the Kansas City Club in the summer of 1919 so he could circulate in the upper-level business community. The Kansas City Club provided an atmosphere of sexism, racism, and anti-Semitism that the town's ruling elite found congenial for important business and civic discussions.[10]

Harry's loving cup from Battery D was prominently displayed at the store, and the haberdashery became a gathering spot for the town's veterans. "I used to go there every time I was downtown; it was sort of a headquarters. You went in there to find out what was going on," ex-Cpl. Harry Murphy said. "Battery D men all went there to get the latest news." Ex-Pvt. Vere Leigh added, "If we needed a shirt or tie, or underwear or something, that's where we bought it." Veterans showed up "especially in the evenings," ex-Capt. Ted Marks remembered. "We'd sit around and gas about the war or something like that. What we should have done and what we shouldn't do." "Every night," ex-Sgt. Eddie Meisburger said, "there would be 20 or 30 of the boys sitting around. There wasn't any room for customers. But Harry seemed glad to have us." The information exchange brought news of jobs for veterans needing work; and the store even served as a study hall for ex-Pvt. Al Ridge who pored over his books, intent on becoming a lawyer. Harry urged Ridge to expand his studies beyond law, saying a lawyer needed to know the Bible, Shakespeare, Plutarch's *Lives*, Plato, and Benjamin Franklin's *Autobiography*. Eddie remembered that Harry "was always ready to advance money for an operation or to pay for the birth of a baby, and once he gave away our entire stock of pajamas to the wounded soldiers in the Kansas City vets' hospital. It got so that I could always tell when a man came in to make a touch. If he addressed my business partner as 'Captain Truman' he was a cash customer. But if he said 'Captain Harry,' that meant credit." Eddie continued, "It is not true . . . that our eventual business troubles were caused by his generosity. Practically all of the loans he made and the credit he advanced were repaid."[11]

Harry also kept up contacts with war associates outside the haberdashery, and made new military connections as well. He had his teeth ground by ex-Lt. George Arrowsmith, and his hair trimmed by ex-Pvt. Frank Spina. Battery D held annual reunions in Kansas City on St. Patrick's Day. These stag gatherings tended toward raunchiness. Ex-Cpl. Murphy remembered one banquet at the elegant Coates House hotel. "In the lobby they had a trash can a good deal like what we used at Ft. Sill, and you were required to urinate in that before you could get into the dining room." Ex-Sgt. Menefee added, "We had some awful reunions. Awful times! . . . I wouldn't want to tell them all." Exactly what happened at the notorious 1921 reunion is unclear. A supply of illegal liquor loosened the veterans' tenuous ties to Western Civilization, and police responded to a riot call. They found a scene rivaling the Marx Brothers, with men prancing on the banquet table as crockery flew through the air and food slid along the floor. The veterans immediately disarmed and disrobed one law officer as the remaining police watched in glee. The only consequences were a tab of $17.80 that Harry had to pay personally for broken dishes, and an invitation from the Elks Club for Battery D to take its business elsewhere next year. The Elks Club reunion paled when the November 1921 American Legion national convention hit town. Women's negligees floated from Muehlebach Hotel windows to the trolley wires in front of the haberdashery, and across the street a stockyard steer ran from an elevator on a upper floor of the Baltimore Hotel. Harry was an active Legionnaire and saw much of the craziness, though no one remembered him participating. He did participate in the main public event during the convention—the dedication of Kansas City's World War monument site where the Liberty Memorial was erected. Harry was not only at the dedication, but presented flags to the five Allied commanders.[12]

A serious military involvement was the Reserve Officers Association. Harry became a major in the Field Artillery Officers Reserve Corps in January 1920. He called a meeting later that year at Morton's restaurant on Baltimore Avenue, which was attended by several dozen reserve officers from all the services. Truman said that they set up the nation's first Reserve Officers Association, from which grew the organized reserve system. Harry claimed to have started a major branch of the U.S. military. Early important members in Kansas City included Col. E. M. Stayton and Commerce Trust Co. vice-president Maj. Jo Zach Miller III, son of a Federal Reserve Bank governor. John Anderson Truman was associated with the Kemper family, which now ran the Commerce banks in Kansas City. W. T. Kemper and the Commerce banks were allies of the Pendergast faction.

The Reserve Officers Association was a means for these men to meet socially and cooperate in honing professional military skills. Meetings generally occurred one night a month, and typically included lectures and practice on weapons simulators. The lecturer would often come from the Ft. Leavenworth Command and General Staff Corps. Before World War II, only officers were in the reserves. Thus, this Kansas City organization was a meeting place for high-class persons. It united community leaders in a selective brotherhood, and Harry was the organization's president.[13]

Harry's military cronies began to make themselves felt in politics. His old major, Marvin Gates, was elected alderman on the Republican ticket in the April 1920 city election. Gates managed large real estate holdings in Kansas City. One of Mrs. Gates's grandfathers was Missouri Lt. Governor George Smith, and her other grandfather was the first president of the University of Missouri. Marvin Gates himself graduated from Yale with fellows like Alfred Gwyne Vanderbilt and Russell C. Leffingwell (President Wilson's assistant treasury secretary). Marvin Gates was a man with powerful connections. In 1920 John Miles, the major in the other battalion of Harry's regiment, won the Jackson County marshal election (a job once held by Boss Tom Pendergast). This election was particularly interesting because Miles was a Republican, and Harry openly supported him. This was a time when county Democrat factions, of which the Pendergast organization was only one, were known to cut deals with the GOP—backing a Republican candidate in return for the GOP supporting the rest of the DEM ticket. In the case of John Miles, however, Harry's support was motivated strictly by friendship. This was an early example of veterans' solidarity in Jackson County elections. Harry and the men around him were making themselves a force in Jackson County politics in 1920. Kansas City elections were a tough business. During the general election of 1920, gunmen kept voters from the polls in some parts of town, and thugs beat up persons in some precincts.[14]

The haberdashery prospered in that election year despite losses from an embezzlement. Exactly how much clerk Oliver M. Solinger stole is undocumented. He was with them from the start. On March 26, 1920 private detectives watched Solinger ring up a $4.04 sale as $3.04 on the cash register, and pocket the dollar difference. They saw him ring up an $8.80 sale as $3.80. This was in a half-hour period, and not every sale was monitored; Solinger could have been stealing a substantial percentage of the store's gross. The owners' initial leniency with Solinger suggests that the dollar loss was modest, but subsequent furious correspondence suggests otherwise. Solinger signed a confession and literally wept on his knees for mercy. Sol emphasized how his mother would be devastated if she learned of this, an appeal sure to affect Harry. Harry convinced Eddie not to press charges, and Eddie even lent Sol money to look for work in another town. In April Harry wrote to Sol, "We shall expect to hear from you in the not far distant future that you are so situated that you can pay all these outstanding debts, and when you have done that we will feel much more friendly to you than we do now." After several months of stalling by Sol, Eddie wrote,

> Here is a chap who was entrusted with the business activity of an institution created by two young fellows who staked practically everything. This chap was treated more like a blood relation or a dear old honest pal. He miscarried the trust and honor placed in him by misappropriating the funds which were vital to the life of the business. When apprehended and caught in the very act of

theft, his pals listened to his whole hearted pleas and gave him his liberty on the promise to make good the funds stolen and mostly to defend the mother's love which this chap grossly abused. For several months no response has this fellow made to the good faith of his friends.

I now ask you, are there thoughts rotten enough to characterize him? Did his friends do the right thing to society to let him loose?

Sol, your obligation to us is a deep one. The mere payment of the money is about the least thing you could do. If you have any manhood left in you come clean. This is a small world, and Harry Truman and I are getting a little bigger each day. Don't be an ungrateful pup like you have almost made me believe you are; you need us. God only knows how much more than we need you.

There is only one answer.

C O M E   C L E A N.

After more stalling, Eddie wrote again: "You have no more manhood about you than the dirty gutter rats that infest 12th and live off the earnings of the women on the street. . . . Must hear from you with a remittance by the 25th day of January or else—I will mail a copy of this letter and copy of your confession to your mother. I will swear out a warrant for your arrest and bring you back to face the music. This is my final letter to you." There the matter apparently ended, with neither compensation for the haberdashery nor a trial for the crook.[15]

Even as the store prospered Harry and Eddie were in hock to bankers. In order to open the store Harry had to establish a line of credit on top of the partners' personal investment. This meant that the banks lent money to the store, and that the business was therefore in debt. Debt is viewed with disapproval by many Americans, but is a necessity in modern commercial practices. Evidently the haberdashery's merchandise served as collateral for the bank loans. This was splendid, because in a crisis the merchandise could be sold to cover the debt. The partners risked nothing, and the debt was no burden. This was important because in law the store was an unlimited liability partnership, which meant Harry and Eddie were personally obligated for any bills the store's revenue couldn't cover. This also meant that in a crunch either partner could be forced to pay all the bills if the other partner ran out of money.[16]

Although the business was doing well enough in October 1920 to get a $5,000 loan from Security State Bank apparently without any collateral other than the merchandise, by February 1921 the store needed more money than banks would lend without additional collateral. To raise capital Harry and Eddie changed the business from a partnership to a corporation. This allowed them to sell stock, and Truman said they raised about $12,000. Harry affectionately noted, "Those were our real friends who went in with us." The corporation had three directors: Truman, Jacobson, and Harry Jobes. Jobes had been captain of the 129th Field Artillery's supply company, outfitting the men in wartime as Truman and Jacobson did in peacetime. Jobes worked for Security State Bank when he returned from the war, and was therefore probably involved with getting that institution to lend money to the haberdashery. Jobes then became a broker with his father Charles S. Jobes, president of Business Men's Assurance Co. This was a prosperous firm organized by W. T. Grant, and its directors would soon include Kansas City leaders such as mayor A. I. Beach, realtor J. C. Nichols, and banker R. C. Kemper. Jobes personally invested at least $1,000 in the haberdashery when it incorporated. Harry's brother-in-law Frank Wallace also put money into the store, probably at this time. Harry's old National Guard buddy Fred Boxley (one-time president of the 4th Ward Democratic Club) did the paperwork for the incorporation. Boxley had handled the Truman family's interests in the Louisa Young will litigation, advised the Morgan Oil companies, and eventually became treasurer of Morgan & Co. Oil Investments. For Harry, Boxley was yet another tie to the Kansas City power structure, since Boxley's law partner was Albert Reeves. One of the town's leading Republicans, Reeves was a friend of Sen. Warren G. Harding. From the White House Harding now dispensed favors to friends, and Reeves would soon become a federal judge holding court in Kansas City.[17]

Soon after Harry incorporated the haberdashery he had to pay an Oklahoma court judgment of about $600 for an unpaid T-C-H Mining Co. debt. Harry's lawyer A. Scott Thompson had managed to tie up the matter so the creditor, Qupaw Supply Co., had to wait nearly five years for satisfaction. In November 1920, however, this debt had been adjudged a personal obligation of Truman, Culbertson, and Hughes, rather than a corporate debt. Although the judgment was against all three associates, Harry probably had to pay the entire amount himself. "I don't remember that I have ever received any fee for this matter," attorney Thompson wrote Harry, "and if you will kindly send me a check for $35 the matter will be closed."[18]

In April 1921 Harry and Bess traded their Karnes Boulevard house for one owned by Westport High School teacher Samuel C. See and his wife Ruth at 3932 Bell. The Karnes Boulevard house apparently had a "whites only" restrictive covenant clause and an $8,500 mortgage when the Trumans acquired it. The latter obligation, at least, was transferred to the Sees. The house on Bell had three mortgages totaling $17,000 when the Sees unloaded it on Harry. In July Harry and Bess paid Felix Gay (or Gray) and wife Clara $5,000 for a 160-acre farm in Johnson County, Kansas. (Johnson County was just across the state line from Kansas City, Missouri. The money for this deal evidently came from sale of the house on Bell. The Johnson County farm had two mortgages totaling $8,800. Harry then formed a partnership with Ed Beach who was to live on the farm, fix it up, and split the crops with Harry. The men agreed that as soon as Beach was able to "brighten every corner, and make the place look home-like in every respect," Harry would sell the property. Harry had purchased a rundown property, planning to rehabilitate it for resale at a profit.[19]

In June 1922 banker Frank Blair was pressing Harry and his mother to pay past-due notes on the Grandview homestead. Earlier that year they began selling off residential lots from the farm to generate cash. Fred Boxley acted as trustee for Mattie in these deals, requiring buyers to covenant for twenty-five years that "No person of African or Asiatic descent, except servants, shall occupy said premises and not to convey said land to such persons, or to any corporation owned or controlled by such persons."[20]

A postwar depression made the haberdashery's finances shaky despite sales of corporation stock. In 1920 creditors had been paid without undue delay, though not instantly. For merchandise purchased in the spring of 1921 payments were sporadic. Few creditors received their money for May shipments, fewer still for June shipments, and only two creditors were paid for July goods. No supplier was paid for merchandise obtained in August and September; one creditor was reimbursed for October shipments, and one for November. When the haberdashery corporation was formed in February

1921 it had only $655 in cash resources. Assuming that the capital from stock sales went for outstanding debts, the haberdashery had to have a vigorous walk-in trade to pay wholesalers for new merchandise shipments as seasons and styles changed. The depression weakened that walk-in trade, so creditors went unpaid. This had nothing to do with the business abilities of Harry or Eddie, and they could do nothing about it. They were trapped, and after a few months of bad cash flow the corporation directors had to close the business. This was a big problem because the depression had shrunk the market value of the store's inventory; selling the inventory would not generate enough money to cover the purchase price of the goods. So all Harry and Eddie could do was cut their losses; they would still owe money.[21]

The loss was big. Harry said the January 1921 inventory had cost $35,000, but now in January 1922 had a market value under $10,000. Truman's January 1921 figure was incorrect. The $35,000 was the gross value of the partnership's property, only $25,000 of it was inventory. In January 1921 the haberdashery apparently owed $9,450 to merchants and $10,000 to banks. It's doubtful that either of these figures dramatically declined. An unexpected debt arose from the lease. This had been carried on the haberdashery's books as an asset of $7,500 on the assumption that the partners could sell the lease. When the business folded, however, Louis Oppenstein exercised the right he reserved in the fine print of the lease and refused to let Harry and Eddie sell it. The "asset" of $7,500 suddenly became a debt of $3,200 (the dollar difference involves time that the lease had run before the store closed). The bottom line is that after closing in 1922 the haberdashery was, according to Harry, about $35,000 in debt.[22]

Harry and Eddie were legally obligated to pay this debt. Although they incorporated in 1921, this didn't affect liabilities they incurred earlier as partners. Incorporation protects investors from a corporation's debts—normally the most an investor can lose is the money paid for stock. (And, indeed, purchasers of stock in Truman & Jacobson, Inc. lost all their money, just as investors in Truman's oil business had lost everything.) Harry and Eddie didn't have this protection, however, since they had signed personally for the merchandise orders, the bank loans, and the lease. Neither man had enough money to pay off, so they consulted lawyer Phineas Rosenberg. He told them to pay the banks in full but to cut a deal with the wholesalers. Every merchant agreed to a percentage settlement, but the partners continued to pay over and above the settlement until each merchant was paid in full. Although most merchandisers were paid in full within four years, the entire process of settling all the haberdashery debts took about fifteen years.[23]

Harry blamed the Republican Party generally and Treasury Secretary Andrew Mellon personally for the economic conditions that ruined the haberdashery. "Lost all I had and all I could borrow," he said of the store. "This was a hard experience for me."[24]

Chapter 8

JOURNEYMAN JUDGE

I learned a lot about government as she is executed in
those two years. They were invaluable in my education.
—Harry S. Truman[1]

For thirty-eight years Harry Truman had sought his right work. This is a long time to search for anything, and we might properly spend a few minutes getting acquainted with the political world he was about to join.

The bottom line of politics in Jackson County—and most other places—was money. The money might be yours or another guy's, and the fight might be over how to acquire more or how to spend it, but money was the issue. For some politicians all this was merely the chips in the game, but players were generally attracted by the convertibility of the chips into cash. Naturally, players were interested in improving the odds of winning. There were two theories on how to do this. One was to develop a system; the other was to rig the game. In Jackson County these theories weren't incompatible.

The system theory required an organization to deliver votes. Several such organizations existed in Jackson County—the Pendergast faction, the Shannon faction, the Bulger faction, the Welch faction, and others. The philosophical differences among them were arcane to outsiders, perhaps even to insiders. Long before the 1920s, however, any serious political candidate belonged to one faction or another. A loner had no impact on a battle fought by professional armies. From time to time some of these armies would ally with one another. These alliances were tenuous, lasting only as long as mutually convenient. Today's friend could be tomorrow's deadly foe, and one's own allies might be treacherous. A person who mastered Jackson County politics coincidentally learned much that was relevant to international diplomacy.

Typically, we hear about how a faction boss would send a bucket of coal to a widow or toss dimes to panhandlers to get their votes. Allegiance to a faction was usually more complex than that. Geography played a role. Boss Welch concentrated his efforts in one particular area of Kansas City. He was a power there, and those votes made him a man other bosses had to deal with. Yet Welch didn't care at all about road conditions in Grandview, and demonstrated little interest in expanding his operation, so few people in rural Jackson County considered joining his faction. Friends and relatives played a role in allegiance. If your best pal or your father was with a faction, then you would probably view it with favor. Jobs played a role. They could be government jobs or jobs with a private contractor doing government work such as road repair, or jobs with a company that allied itself with a political faction. This latter class of employment was particularly important, because those jobs continued regardless of how elections turned out. In Truman's time major employers such as the streetcar company, Commerce banks, Kansas City Gas Co., Kansas City Power and Light Co., and Kansas City Terminal Railroad Co. (which involved all railroads passing through downtown) were considered Pendergast faction allies.[2]

Favors were a major reason great corporations allied with a political faction. The electric company could obtain tax breaks; the railroad could get a street or alley vacated; the bank could handle government funds. None of this was illegal. In return, company officers contributed large sums to their political faction—sums perhaps cleverly diverted from company revenue so the tab was actually carried by customers. Employees might be expected to contribute votes. The Pendergast faction's power came by gradually acquiring support from the great mercantile enterprises of Kansas City. Indeed, when these businessmen ultimately decided the Pendergast organization was no longer useful to them, the machine collapsed.[3]

Elections could be rigged by choice of candidates and by faking the ballot count. Sometimes—particularly as the Pendergast organization changed from a mere faction into a controlling machine—bosses would agree on a slate of candidates. Thus a voter could only ratify a choice already made by an oligarchy, much as voters in the Soviet Union did. Opposition candidates faced a double problem. First, they had to get votes, and second, they had to get those votes counted. Most observers, even Pendergast men, marveled at the lopsided totals the machine produced. Outsiders tended to view this as overkill, but there were strategic reasons for such obvious frauds. At the precinct level the workers were judged by the reported ballot count. So if your precinct reported 300 votes for the machine and 100 against, and neighboring precincts reported 390 to 10, questions arose about your competence if you were in charge—particularly since everyone knew the totals were faked anyway. Precinct workers were zealous, and the counts were lopsided. On the city level, the Pendergast machine's electoral strength resided in what was then the north side of town, the so-called river wards. The machine wasn't nearly as strong in the southwest part of Kansas City, the silk stocking wards. The count had to be lopsided where Pendergast had absolute control in order to offset the count in other areas of town. On the county level, Kansas City totals had to overwhelm any opposition from elsewhere in the county. On the state level, Jackson County totals had to overwhelm not only the rural outstate vote but also the St. Louis machine that rigged the count there. Those totals of 390 to 10 in some precincts weren't examples of Pendergast arrogance, but a logical response to political realities.[4]

Truman and other Pendergast machine leaders derided opponents, ascribing their motives to jealousy or ingratitude. Such an attitude showed little regard for the human spirit. If a person cooperated with the Pendergast machine life was no harder than normal. But the Pendergast machine, because of its ties to large corporations and the underworld, had year-round requirements that could make life hard for many people. A construction company that failed to use Pendergast subcontractors could find its work halted indefinitely by city inspectors. This affected all laid-off workers. An employee of the government or of a Pendergast-allied corporation might be responsible not only for his own vote but for those of his family. Since ballot secrecy was a joke, the machine could determine if the family voted as instructed. You could fear that your brother-in-law's vote might endanger your job even if you worked in private industry. If you complained you might suddenly have trouble with city water or might find your house or factory reassessed and taxes doubled. If a small business could no longer afford to pay bribes it could lose its city license or be wrecked by thugs. Eventually the Pendergast machine bossed the everyday lives of ordinary citizens. Voices raised in protest were silenced by anonymous threats. Some Jackson County politicians were kidnapped and murdered. Yet no one coerced the cheers at Pendergast rallies. Beneficiaries of a dictatorship enthusiastically support it and feel unoppressed. Only the victims experience the terror. In the 1980s some Kansas City residents still feared retribution for revealing their knowledge of what the Pendergast machine had done fifty years earlier.[5]

Truman played a key role in maintaining the Pendergast control of life in Jackson County after 1926. He not only knew of the machine's illegalities but participated in some of them. Although Truman would later be remembered as a champion of civil liberties, this reputation came mostly from his support of civil rights for blacks. That action was motivated by his Masonic belief in the brotherhood of man, not from any dedication to freedom. Truman loved politics, but he held democracy in contempt. Yet as a county politician Truman's desires were far different from those of many of his colleagues. To achieve those desires he had to remain in office, and to win elections he had to be part of the Pendergast machine. Truman was a practical man and used the machine to get what he wanted. His private memoranda of that era show a troubled conscience praying that the ends would justify the means. His compassion and concern for ordinary citizens would be amply demonstrated in the White House, but Truman would always act insensitive about terrors committed by his political allies in Jackson County. Was Truman really indifferent, or could he just not bear to think about his role and responsibility?

In 1921 the Pendergast faction was planning grief for the Bulger faction in the next year's county election. This was a grudge match. In 1914 Miles Bulger got the Pendergasts to help elect him presiding judge of the county. Bulger soon developed inflated ideas of his destiny, and decided he was powerful enough to give the shaft to Pendergast. As presiding judge, Bulger was in an excellent position to do this. One of his victims was District 30 Road Overseer Harry Truman.

Missouri had several kinds of courts. Circuit courts were the judicial operation. County courts were holdovers from early Colonial courts that ran the first British settlements in America. They weren't judicial at all, but were the executive branch of government. Missouri county courts were accountable for everything the county did. They could set the budgets and number of employees in all departments (sheriff, treasurer, highway engineer, and the rest), let contracts, alter tax assessment bills. Even in the 1920s the Jackson County government was a multi-million-dollar operation. The county court controlled patronage through government jobs and work assigned to private contractors and was also in a position to help businesses with tax assessments, county deposits in banks, and the like. The county court was a big deal.

The county court was a three-man body. Miles Bulger was the presiding judge, a lucky break for his ambitions because he was elected at-large by the entire county. The Pendergast river wards weren't necessarily decisive, particularly at this time. Bulger's term was four years—twice as long as that of his colleagues on the court, so he didn't have to win against Pendergast as often. Bulger had been having a merry old time since taking office in 1915, but custom required him to give up the job after the second term. He would move into a state legislature seat gerrymandered to his needs, but he intended to put his man into the county court. The other two judges were elected by separate districts in the county rather than at-large. Only Kansas City residents could vote for the western judge. The eastern judge was elected by the rest of the county, a much smaller rural vote that had as much representation on the court as the large Kansas City vote—one judge for the teeming city, one for the sparser countryside.

Since the Pendergast faction's power in Kansas City was growing, the organization's choice for western judge had a strong edge in the election. Mindful of the need to establish close links with the business elite, the Pendergast organization turned to the J. C. Nichols real estate operation for a candidate. Neither Nichols nor Pendergast was yet the power he would become in his respective sphere, but both would become Kansas City legends. For western judge the Pendergast organization chose one of the toughest and most trusted men around Nichols, Henry McElroy. A few years earlier when the city decided to buy land for the Liberty Memorial—a colossus to remind citizens of the war—a goodly portion of the site was discovered to be the property of a J. C. Nichols group, which was only too happy to sell it to the city. The price was considered fair, and it wasn't a shady deal. The man who maneuvered to acquire the property for Nichols from the many holders of small lots, without anyone discovering what was happening, was Henry McElroy. After the Bulger fiasco the Pendergasts wanted to back a candidate whose factional loyalty could be trusted. "Loyal" would become scarcely adequate to describe McElroy. Even "fanatic" doesn't quite capture his devotion to the Pendergast organization.[6]

Choosing a candidate for eastern judge was trickier. In general, the factional identity of a candidate was the crucial factor. Voters in Jackson County voted for the faction, just as Britishers voted for the party. In Kansas City this gave Pendergast a growing edge. At this time, however, the situation in eastern Jackson County was mixed, so the Pendergast organization needed a candidate who could build a following of his own in addition to faction loyalists, the very thing that had backfired with Bulger. The Pendergast organization needed a man with a track record of loyalty. Ideally, the candidate should have good connections in Independence, the biggest town in the district, which could carry the election. If the candidate also had any ties to one of the farming areas, so much the better. A dream candidate would also have a following among veterans. This bloc had already demonstrated fanatical solidarity transcending factions and parties, electing Marvin Gates and John Miles as Republican officials in overwhelmingly Democrat areas. And as long as the Pendergasts were dreaming, the candidate ought to be essentially a Kansas City man circulating among the business elite whose support the Pendergasts needed to consolidate their power.

The various conflicting accounts of Truman's decision to run for eastern judge all agree that he responded to a call. Savings and loan man Arthur Elliott (second in command of Truman's war regiment), banker E. M. Stayton (who led the 110th Engineers in desperate action that saved Truman's division in the Argonne), railroad promoter George Collins (Truman's old prewar National Guard captain), and several other veteran officers were gabbing one day when the talk turned to the subject of Harry S. Truman. The men agreed that Truman had been "a splendid officer." Stayton went further, saying Truman was "too valuable a man to be allowed to simply settle down" in private life. Stayton proposed that Truman be made eastern judge of Jackson County. Stayton was from Independence, and went to work booming Truman. Truman's relative William Southern was an early recruit. Brother of circuit judge Allen Southern, who as county highway engineer had criticized road overseer Harry Truman, and editor of the *Independence Examiner*, William Southern was a man of no small influence who urged Truman's candidacy on the Pendergast faction. The Pendergasts must have needed little urging. Indeed, Southern's endorsement was engineered by Pendergast lieutenant Nick Phelps, to increase the appearance of Truman's independent strength. Boss Tom Pendergast's brother Mike was in charge of the faction's eastern district operations. Truman knew Mike before the war, and Mike's son Jim was the officer whose career Truman had saved at Camp Doniphan. After the war Jim was a customer at the Truman & Jacobson haberdashery, and was a featured speaker at the notorious Elks Club reunion of Battery D. Around July or August 1921 Jim and Mike asked Truman to be the Pendergast faction candidate for eastern judge next year. Truman agreed. Truman didn't turn to politics in desperation after the haberdashery failed. While in France he had considered becoming a politician on his return. Truman wasn't a supplicant seeking Pendergast faction backing to further his political ambitions. The Pendergasts sought him.[7]

In January 1922 Truman's name began appearing in *Independence Examiner* stories as an "independent candidate" for eastern judge. Technically this was true as Truman had not received formal endorsement from any Pendergast political club. Astute observers knew, however, that Truman had always been with the Pendergasts, and *Examiner* editor William Southern had urged the Pendergasts to support Truman. The portrayal of Truman as "independent" was a trick, surely designed to influence readers who had no strong factional ties. Since *Examiner* stories were reprinted by the rural weeklies, this deceit spread widely. At the same time, readers with factional ties knew of Truman's real loyalty, and would see through the stories.[8]

In March the opening rally of Truman's campaign was disguised as a veterans meeting, with friends welcome. Held in the town of Lee's Summit, the shebang was a major social event including athletics, songs, speeches, and free smokes. About six hundred persons heard E. M. Stayton call for the election of Truman. Truman came unprepared to speak, and when asked to respond he became confused and managed to say only that he was willing to run. This was good enough, and the meeting voted to endorse him. He was thereupon dubbed the American Legion candidate for eastern judge, a controversial title that helped publicize his campaign.[9]

At a meeting of Pendergast leaders the next month in Independence, Mike Pendergast endorsed Truman for eastern judge, according to ex-Lt. Edgar Hinde who was there. The *Independence Examiner* reported that no decisions on candidates were made at the meeting, which was literally true since Mike Pendergast merely reported a decision made *before* the meeting. Thus the fiction of Truman as an independent candidate was maintained for politically unsophisticated readers.[10]

At the end of May 1922 Truman formally filed for eastern judge, and his memory was that Mike Pendergast endorsed him around June at the 10th Ward Democratic Club. This official announcement that Truman was the Pendergast candidate ended the charade that he was unaffiliated.[11]

There were five candidates for the Democrat nomination, one each from the Pendergast, Shannon, and Bulger factions, and two independent snowflakes. "It was a hot affair," Truman said later. He traveled throughout the eastern district making full use of his many relatives and war colleagues. "The soldier stuff and the soldier boys," he said, "won for me." "We all got out and worked for him," Edgar Hinde recalled. "That old bunch of Army boys, they went out and they hustled." Decades later Vere Leigh could still remember how his Battery D cohorts Tommy Murphy and Harry Whitney "knocked on doors out in the country," and how Battery A commander Keith Dancy worked Independence. Truman's childhood friendships still held strong. Mize Peters came to Truman's aid, as did their old teacher Ardelia Hardin. "Independence was a conservative old town," she said. "They kind of looked down on women who wanted to vote, but Mrs. John Paxton, who came out here from Virginia, and was very conservative, too . . . said to me, 'Well, let's ring some door bells—even though they will think it's awful of us—and get out the women's vote.' We did."[12]

The typical public campaign event was a picnic. A Truman associate recalled how years earlier Harry and Vivian and John "on picnic days . . . would hitch two big mules to a spring wagon, and the whole family would set out before dawn" for the gatherings. There young Harry "caught the excitement of politics, something he never has ceased to relish." Now Harry himself was one of the featured attractions. He got Eddie McKim to arrange for him to arrive at one mammoth picnic by airplane after first dropping leaflets on the crowd. ("My Platform: Good Roads, A Budgeted Road Fund, Economy, A Day's Work for a Day's Pay, Fewer Automobiles and More Work for County Employees. Harry S. Truman.") Truman was prone to airsickness. This time he vomited just as he got out of the plane to greet the crowd. He gamely proceeded into the throng, and later made a speech. He had a rough oratorical style. "About the poorest effort of a speech I ever heard," Edgar Hinde said of one attempt. "I suffered for him." Ted Marks agreed: "We were all sitting at the top of the hill when Captain Harry started to talk. By the time he finished, we had slid all the way to the bottom."[13]

Truman briefly sought support from the Ku Klux Klan in this election. "It seemed a fairly harmless patriotic organization," Margaret Truman later explained. Not everyone shared this view. Kansas City newspapers of the era were filled with reports of KKK violence and struggle against the menace. Even Thomas Dixon, author of *The Clansman* (which inspired D. W. Griffith's *The Birth of a Nation*), now condemned the organization. Truman was well aware of the Klan's depredations. Indeed, the previous year he had assisted a Masonic effort to put down the KKK in St. Louis. The Klan represented enough votes in Jackson County, however, for Truman to swallow his scruples and fork over $10 to join. Since this was a political deal Truman met a Klan spokesman at the Hotel Baltimore in Kansas City to agree on what the Klan and Truman intended to do for each other. It turned out that the KKK had an unusual patronage requirement. Most factions would want county jobs, but the Klan instead seemed more concerned about preventing Roman Catholics from getting any county jobs. Truman said nuts to that— he intended to hire any qualified war buddies who needed work, and a lot of them were Roman Catholic. So the deal was off, and

Truman never officially joined the white knights. In an uncharacteristic show of decency the Klan refunded Truman's $10.[14]

Truman did pick up one interesting endorsement, from the Triangle Club. This was a Kansas City businessmen's club he belonged to, similar to Rotary. The endorsement was interesting not so much for its effect on the election (none of Kansas City could vote in the eastern district race) but for its testimony to Truman's standing in Kansas City business circles despite the Independence residency that qualified him to be an eastern district candidate.[15]

On the August primary day smart money was betting on either Truman or the Shannon faction man E. E. Montgomery. Although Truman was the only Independence resident among the candidates, and Independence had almost half the eastern district precincts, the contest looked close. Since the Pendergast western judge candidate Henry McElroy and the Shannon presiding judge candidate Elihu Hayes were about to win, the eastern judge would be the swing vote on patronage and other county government factional matters. Feelings were high. Joe Shannon decided that the Pendergast faction was stealing the election in a precinct on the Kansas City border, and dispatched a raiding party to seize that ballot box and steal the election for Montgomery. Having sensitive ears, the Pendergast faction quickly detected Shannon's plans. Truman asked his war buddy Marshal John Miles to protect the ballot box. Miles sent two deputies, his brother George and 129th Field Artillery veteran John Gibson, to the polls. Brown Harris and banker Albert Ott drove them over. (Ott was a Truman relative and son of Christian Ott whose county judge candidacy John Anderson Truman promoted with his fists.) The polling place was a house in timbered country. As the men arrived Harris saw Jackson County Clerk Pete Kelly (a Shannon man) run "down into the woods as if his life depended on it. And to our utter astonishment, when we got up on this little porch, there stood Joe Shannon in the shadows." Too late, Shannon had dispatched Kelly to stop the raiding party lest they clash with the deputy marshals. Three or four taxicabs shortly pulled up and emptied about twenty brutish gentlemen, four of whom whipped out guns. The mob knocked down Deputy Miles and headed for Deputy Gibson. Gibson pressed his pistol to Shannon's stomach and said, "Your gang may get Miles, but I will get you." Harris recalled, "Shannon then threw up his hands in great terror and yelled to the gang, 'Go away, boys, go away. Everything is all right here.' " Calm was soon restored outside the polling place, and inside the election judges and clerks were left to wrangle undisturbed.[16]

Truman won by about 280 votes out of 12,000. "I made the contest by myself," he claimed. "The organization ran out on me." This is quite possible, as the Pendergast faction had traditionally agreed that the Shannon faction could have the eastern district judgeship. Truman's energetic campaign and victory may have surprised the Pendergasts as much as the events angered the Shannon men. Thus Truman should have felt he owed the Pendergasts nothing. "I won the dirtiest and hardest fought campaign eastern Jackson County has ever seen without money or promises," Truman wrote. He listed his expenditures as $524. Shannon's candidate Montgomery listed even less, but Truman reported that Montgomery "spent somewhere near $15,000 it is said, and his gang made me every kind of a S.O.B. . . but I beat him anyway with a clean campaign." Truman still had to face a Republican opponent in the general election; but since this year Jackson County Democrat factions were united against the GOP, the November contest was a romp.[17]

"I shall endeavor to serve as county judge that no man or woman will be ashamed of having voted for me and to give a square deal to everybody and to keep the only promises that I have made which were made in my speeches to the public." In those speeches Truman promised to bring the county a business administration, eliminate unnecessary jobs, establish a budget, and bring order to county finances. "I want it to be made a felony to spend money the county hasn't on hand." He also outlined his attitude toward roads, which were one of the main responsibilities of the county court. He wanted traffic to determine which roads were hard-surfaced and which were left as oiled dirt. "Properly cared for dirt roads will stand up as well as a Kansas City boulevard." Truman took care to rip into county highway engineer Leo Koehler's handling of the road system and work crews. Koehler was a Republican and would demonstrate the kind of memory attributed to his party's symbol.[18]

Another Republican who would give Truman trouble was Kansas City police commissioner Louis Oppenstein, the haberdashery's landlord. Any partisan pleasure Oppenstein enjoyed from his cruel lease was short lived. Democrat Truman could now escape all haberdashery creditors because a county judge's salary was immune to garnishee proceedings. He didn't even own the house he lived in (his mother-in-law did), and had no personal property worth attaching. As long as Truman took care to keep any bank balances low he was free from creditors while he remained a county judge. (In later years Truman would be praised for not taking bankruptcy to clear his haberdashery debts, but there was nothing courageous or steadfast about this. He avoided bankruptcy because creditors couldn't hound him into it as they did his private-citizen partner Eddie Jacobson. Truman would later use his immunity to evade court judgments won by creditors. Truman had very strong ideas about which debts were just, regardless of whether they were lawful.)[19]

During the 1922 election campaign Truman worked steadily at paying off a $2,500 loan he and Jacobson took out in January from George Buecking's Twelfth Street Bank. (Buecking's son-in-law Ilus Davis would become one of Kansas City's most powerful men, both in politics and banking.) In August Truman voluntarily provided the bank with security—a $1,000 first mortgage of Claude Huckleberry and $1,700 first mortgage of A. L. Mitchell. (The loan no longer had the haberdashery's merchandise backing it.) By November Truman had the debt down to $2,300. In October he once again gave his Johnson County, Kansas, farm (the one he hoped to rehabilitate and sell at a profit) as security for $6,800 owed to Security State Bank. The farm had an $8,800 mortgage, but Truman had a $5,000 equity in the property. As long as real estate values held this was good security. By now, however, Truman had experienced difficulty keeping up the mortgage payments and had been warned that foreclosure was imminent. He was attempting to sell the farm for $20,000 in September, claiming "the only reason I am selling it at that price is because I have so many things to look after I can't give it the attention it ought to have." Soon after taking office Truman again received word that a mortgage holder was going to foreclose, and thus Security State Bank would lose this collateral. Truman held off foreclosure by alleging "I will pay . . . as soon as I can close a deal I am on now," referring to his attempts to sell the farm, efforts that had progressed nowhere near to a closing. The farm remained in Truman's hands, and Ed Beach remained as tenant; but in 1924 Beach's rent payments went directly to Commerce Trust Co. (which had acquired the Truman loan from Security State Bank) to reduce Truman's debt to the bank.[20]

In September 1922 Truman declared, "If a man devotes his time to the office of county judge he will have all the business he can look after without having his own private affairs taking up the time the public pays for. That has been the trouble in the past." Therefore, he announced, in the interest of good government he would close out his haberdashery business. Thus he attempted to disguise his business failure as a civic sacrifice.[21]

The new county court took office on January 1, 1923 amid roses sent by Judge McElroy's friends in Kansas City's Italian community. The three judges planned only routine business until Arthur Young & Co. audited the county. The local press approved: "The three judges are businessmen and in this they expect to follow the line businessmen would follow when taking over a new business, to find out just where they stand before they make a move."[22]

Their first move was to give county highway engineer Leo Koehler damnable problems during several court sessions. Truman had declared in the election campaign, "Our present $8,000 highway engineer seems to have but one ambition and that is to spend the county's money for high-powered automobiles that his henchmen may joyride at the county's expense." Koehler was a Republican, and the judges were now all Democrats. Koehler had also been a close ally of the traitorous Miles Bulger whom the Pendergast faction intended to destroy. The fun started when the judges began musing about the need for the county to slash expenses until the audit was done. They officially ascertained from Koehler that little roadwork was then underway (it being hard to deal with dirt roads when the ground was frozen). McElroy ominously addressed Koehler, "Then we had better begin to retrench by laying off such men in your department as are not needed. What salary do you get, Mr. Koehler?" Koehler said he got $8,000. Truman declared that was too much, and the court lopped two grand from Koehler's income. The court also ordered Koehler to turn in all his department's cars to the county garage so they could be sold. He protested that the law gave him control of the vehicles, but McElroy interrupted with, "That's a matter that can be settled later." "What we want," Truman said, "is to stop these cars from being used for private purposes." Koehler demanded that Truman produce any evidence of such abuse. McElroy angrily declared, "Let us sell these cars and buy a road scraper." He continued, "We can do more work with that than with touring cars. We'll give your men Ford runabouts if they need them." Koehler later snorted that Fords weren't sturdy enough to travel county roads. (Truman's Dodge could barely handle them. "I kept two bags of cement in the back of it so it would not throw me through the windshield while driving on our terrible county roads.") "Visibly moved" by the salary reduction, Koehler accused Truman of being out to get him. Truman replied, "All we ask is that you cooperate with the court." Then, in case anyone had missed the message, the court hired Truman's friend L. R. "Jack" Toliver as a $2,400-a-year superintendent of road repairs to watchdog Koehler. This more than canceled the savings generated by the $2,000 "retrenchment" of Koehler's salary. Koehler accused the court of economizing for Republicans but not for Democrats. McElroy responded, "I think it is in bad taste for you to come in here and tell us how to spend the county's money." McElroy added, "You are a damn poor adviser. You are not competent to advise anybody, and we don't want any of your advice at all." An observer reported, "Judge Truman smiled and seemed to be enjoying himself."[23]

This encounter demonstrated several things. One was a new malevolence in Truman. The happy Harry of Grandview farm days disappeared in World War I. That Harry would never have enjoyed summarily reducing a man's livelihood by $2,000, grinning while the victim squirmed. The Koehler episode showed that Truman was serious about campaign promises, as he had made Koehler's salary and automobile fleet an issue. The incident also affirmed that Truman would be a professional politician in the Pendergast organization, coolly spending $2,400 to hire a patronage man after citing economic necessity for cutting Koehler's salary by $2,000. The incident foreshadowed Judge Henry McElroy's later reign as the meanest bully ever to hold high political office in Kansas City.

Koehler was a courthouse battle veteran and mounted a swift counterattack against the rookie judges. First he got an injunction from "boss Republican" circuit judge Nelson Johnson prohibiting the county court from appointing highway department employees (i.e., Toliver) and from selling highway department cars. The county court sidestepped the first issue by announcing that Jack Toliver had completed his work and was no longer a county employee. The second issue, however, had to be met directly. If Koehler could prevent the sale of county cars, other department heads could defy the county court in other matters. This was bad for sound management but even worse for patronage politics. If Koehler and other department heads could dodge county court orders, the Pendergast faction control of the court would be for nought. Instead of running county government via two of the county judges, the Pendergast organization would have to win every elective office in the county. The Pendergasts were still a few years away from that kind of ability. So the sale of highway department cars started as a Truman campaign promise but wound up as a do-or-die proposition threatening the entire Pendergast county operation. The injunction died on a technicality, and the county court moved swiftly to sell the cars before Koehler regrouped. He was unable to stop the sale but did get another injunction on Friday, March 16, in time to prevent delivery of the autos to the buyers. At least Koehler thought it was in time. Judges McElroy and Hayes were served with notice of the writ, but somehow Truman was missed. The injunction was general knowledge, reported in the Saturday morning newspaper. Truman admitted he knew of the writ on Friday night (and probably knew earlier through talk at the courthouse). He nonetheless scrambled to the county garage Saturday morning with several Pendergast henchmen, at least one of whom had a revolver. Koehler's man at the garage quoted Truman as saying, "We are entitled to the possession of those cars, and I am going to take them, even if I have to go to jail for it." Truman told his men to break the locks chaining the cars, and the vehicles went to the buyers. Koehler got a contempt of court citation slapped on all three county judges. Truman lamely maintained over the weekend, "I do not know anything officially about Mr. Koehler's application for a writ" banning delivery of the autos.

At the contempt hearing Monday afternoon Truman denied the quotation Koehler's garage man attributed to him. Apparently Truman wasn't asked about what he told a newspaper Saturday night, "We had a right to deliver them, writ or no writ." Nor evidently did McElroy account for his Saturday night statement that he would have gladly violated the injunction even though notice *had* been served on him: "I approve of what Judge Truman did. It was absolutely right. Had I been there I would have helped." The contempt citation was dismissed because the sheriff had failed to serve Truman with notice of the writ until Monday, and because the notice served on McElroy and Hayes didn't reveal the contents of the writ. Hayes, who was in the Shannon faction, wondered aloud why a county judge would involve himself in such a minor routine matter as delivery of automobiles, a verbal barb understood by everyone who knew that Truman's action was a desperate move to protect the Pendergast county operation. A couple of months later the circuit court ruled that the county judges had full authority to sell county highway department autos but couldn't hire workers in the highway department. On the surface this looked like a decision conceding one issue to the county judges and one to Koehler. Actually, Koehler won nothing. The county court had many other ways to give out patronage jobs, and Koehler's hirings had to be approved by the county court in order to get paid. Despite Koehler's attack, the authority of the county judges (and thereby Pendergast) over county departments remained unchanged.[24]

Koehler also attacked Truman and McElroy through the legislature. There were two kinds of county road employees—the highway department men answerable to Koehler, and the road overseers answerable directly to the county court. The traitorous Miles Bulger, whom the Pendergasts now intended to destroy, and Koehler were political allies. Bulger was no longer a county judge, instead serving in the Missouri legislature where he represented a midtown Kansas City district even though he lived in Crestwood (a suburban J. C. Nichols real estate development restricted to wealthy white folks). Representative Bulger got a senator ally to introduce a bill rescinding the county court's power to appoint road overseers. Instead Koehler would get to draw up six districts, each headed by a district engineer with an unlimited number of deputies. The bill also took the county special road and bridge fund from the county court and gave it to Koehler. Cynics said that Bulger introduced the bill after Koehler guaranteed him half the patronage. The road overseer system had been the basis of Bulger's political organization as county judge. (The attentive reader may remember that Bulger fired Pendergast road overseer Harry Truman in 1915 or 1916.) This bill was a way for Bulger to recover some of that patronage at the expense of the Pendergasts.

Rumors predicted the Shannon faction would support the bill because the Pendergasts were apparently welshing on the "50-50" agreement. This was an old deal between Tom Pendergast and Joe

Shannon that they would divide patronage evenly no matter how many offices either faction won in elections. This worked fine except when Tom or Joe decided he was strong enough to eliminate the other. The aggressor would hog all the jobs, and the victim would ally with the Republicans in the next election and replace the Democrats with the GOP. Then Tom and Joe would make up and defeat the Republicans next time. Such factional strife was the main way Republicans could win in Jackson County, and Republican Koehler surely realized that Bulger's road overseer bill would feed bitterness that Truman was causing with his appointments of road overseers. Soon after the election Truman began redrawing the road overseer districts, ostensibly to improve efficiency although he was also receiving information on how to gerrymander the lines for best political effect. The eastern judge always had a lot of influence regarding overseers since they operated solely in the eastern district. So Truman's activity was uncontroversial until he announced the appointments. The Shannon man on the court, Judge Hayes, exploded when Truman and McElroy wouldn't allow him to name the road overseers he wanted: "If I can't name the nine I want, I might as well not name any." Hayes told Truman, "Take the whole list if you want it." When the court voted on the list of overseers Hayes said, "I vote 'no' on the whole thing." Some observers saw the heavy hand of Mike Pendergast in Truman's actions. Mike never thought much of the 50-50 deal—it was hard to fire up the troops when the battle didn't affect the spoils.

Orations on the nature of good government ascended through the hot air while the Jefferson City solons debated Bulger's bill. The keen rhetoric soon identified the bill's effect on three crucial principles basic to the future of the republic: the kind of pie, the size of pieces, and who shall be the servers thereof. For some reason many rural legislators thought of Bulger as antiboss, and he had a lot of influence in the House of Representatives where he was chairman of the Democrat caucus. Hard feelings and fists of fury notwithstanding, the bill zipped through both the Senate and House and went to Governor Hyde's desk. A Republican swept into office with Harding, Hyde was considered pig enough to sign the bill. The howls from Jackson County were awesome. Truman and McElroy vowed if the bill became law, to vote against any tax levy for the special road and bridge fund, and Koehler predicted a mandamus suit to force the county court to pass a special road and bridge fund levy. Old Judge William H. Wallace, a self-styled defender of taxpayers and a Truman relative who had been a law partner of Bess Truman's great-grandfather, called an indignation meeting that voted that Koehler couldn't be trusted to control the special road and bridge fund. Even the Cass County Court asked Hyde to veto the bill. The governor gratified Jackson County Democrats with a veto. Mike Pendergast praised Hyde, saying the Pendergast organization "should remember Governor Hyde for this . . . especially remembering the Democratic traitors who made the veto necessary." Mike said Hyde should be forgiven for any past acts, that the veto wiped the slate clean. (Hyde would dirty it again by joining President Hoover's cabinet.)[25]

Bulger reportedly credited McElroy with instigating a grand jury probe of Bulger's handling of county affairs. This was going on while the Koehler controversy raged. During the grand jury investigation McElroy and Truman voted to sell the county car Judge Hayes was using, and fire his chauffeur, a Bulger man named Fred Snyder. This left Hayes sputtering, and had the gratifying effect of offending both the Shannon and Bulger camps. This petty act was probably far from McElroy's thoughts as he walked along one day, hands in pockets. Suddenly he felt great pain as fists pummeled his body. Peering from his torn and bloodied face he saw Miles Bulger and Fred Snyder rushing away. The ambush was a tactical success (McElroy hadn't returned a single punch) but a strategic disaster. McElroy now had a very personal reason to crush Bulger. McElroy pressed no charges; this was an affair of honor. The mind behind McElroy's bandaged and disfigured face began to devise sophisticated revenge.[26]

The statute of limitations allowed Bulger to escape indictment. The grand jury nonetheless had a lot to say about Bulger's administration of the county. So did the Arthur Young & Co. audit that McElroy and Truman commissioned. The audit was supposed to be for 1922, but for some reason it went back to Bulger's first year as presiding judge. When Bulger came in the county had a $117 deficit. When he left (replaced by Hayes) the county had a $1,208,000 deficit. Of this, $786,000 accumulated in 1922 alone, mostly from the special road and bridge fund that Bulger tried to turn over to Koehler. Since Koehler had approved all expenditures from this fund under Bulger, the audit generated much of the outcry against turning the money completely over to Koehler, who was now branded as an irresponsible highway engineer. The audit and grand jury report worked up the populace against Bulger. Rev. L. M. Birkhead of All Souls Unitarian Church in Kansas City preached a sermon demanding jail for county grafters, telling his congregation, "What we need is a new political deal."[27]

The grand jury paid particular attention to the "Miles Bulger Industrial Home for Negro Boys." This was intended to house juvenile delinquents and the innocent homeless, but the new county court had yet to accept the building, which had cost $165,000. "I want this building investigated," McElroy said, noting that his son's school could accommodate one thousand pupils, and cost $150,000. The Bulger Home could accommodate sixty youths. The grand jury found the unoccupied building "magnificent," adding that an adequate one could have been constructed at half the price. "Apparently no expense has been spared," the grand jury said, also noting that the facility would be expensive to operate. Shortly after the report the county judges addressed a luncheon meeting of the Triangle Club at Kansas City's Muehlebach Hotel. The new Triangle president that year, Ruby Garrett, would later become one of the most important Pendergast men in Kansas City. This businessmen's community service club had endorsed Truman in the election, and at this luncheon he was introduced as "one of the most honored members of the Triangle Club." All three judges received cheers and applause for their speeches, followed by a standing ovation. McElroy condemned spending $75,000 to $100,000 on county cars in 1922, telling the businessmen "that money was being paid out while old men at the Jackson County home were sleeping in their work clothes and without blankets. The county paid for the upkeep of those cars and failed to provide proper clothing and bedding for the inmates of its institutions." McElroy declared he wasn't intimidated by Bulger's ambush. He called on the club to investigate the Bulger Home, which it immediately agreed to do. The club had already been helping a county juvenile facility—the McCune Home for white boys—so the club investigators were familiar with such institutions and could make a quick report. The committee found wainscoting of "highly polished marble" and steam radiators "encased in marble with brass gratings." The main hall was of "highly polished marble and mahoganized woodwork, a magnificent drinking fountain and marble settees. . . . All stairways are either marble or terrazzo." The building compared favorably with "Kansas City's most exclusive clubs" and "may more properly be designated as a monument such as a grateful people might erect or dedicate to the memory of a Lincoln." Hardly fit for juveniles, especially blacks, the committee said. Although a certain element of the population alway fears that the poor have life too easy, Bulger did seem to spend tax money on too lavish a scale for this juvenile home. Upkeep was estimated at $100 per month per child—building upkeep, not food or clothing. McElroy declared, "The building is not adapted for anything but the spending of money." McElroy and Truman responded to a petition by twenty-nine blacks to change the name from "Miles Bulger" Home to "Jackson County Industrial Home for Negro Boys," and ordered all references to Bulger chiseled from the building. Judge Hayes voted against this.[28]

With Bulger discredited in the eyes of any thinking voter, McElroy and Truman now moved against him in the courts. The two judges, with Hayes abstaining, first appointed L. R. Ash and former county highway engineer E. M. Stayton as a road planning commission. A prominent member of the Kansas City Chamber of Commerce, Stayton's military and political associations with Truman have been noted. Ash's previous examination of a shoddy road built under Bulger had resulted in the contractor being ordered to refund $20,000 to the county. Stayton and Ash now quickly found that the resurfacing of the Hickman Mills road in 1922 was worthless. The contractor applied a half-inch of surface although the contract called for one and a half inches, yet Bulger's cohort Koehler certified the work as up to specifications. On receiving this report the county court formally charged Bulger, Koehler, former eastern judge Gilday, and the contractor Southwest Company Engineers and Contractors with corruption and fraud, and filed suit to recover $60,000 from their personal pockets. The county court also sued Bulger, Gilday, and three petroleum suppliers for $68,000, charging that the price the companies had charged the county for oil was so high that corruption was obvious. Earlier McElroy had sought to recover $11,000 of the $16,500 vehicle insurance premiums the Bulger court had paid for 1922. McElroy objected to the lack of deductible clauses, adding nearly $7,000 to the cost. He also complained that the insurance companies had included personal liability coverage even though the companies knew the county was exempt from such suits. The county court eventually sued Bulger, Thomas McGee & Sons, Fidelity & Guarantee Insurance Companies, and National Fire Insurance Company to recover $3,600 in premiums. R. B. Jones & Sons refunded $176 before suit was filed. On April 20, 1923 McElroy announced that he had received a death threat warning him to lay off Bulger. A month later Truman announced a $19,000 suit against Bulger, Gilday, Koehler, and Jackson County Crusher company to recover money paid for rock that was never delivered.[29]

While Truman and McElroy were going after Bulger and the Republicans, they were also busy alienating the Shannon Democrats by hogging the patronage. Votes on court matters became routinely two-to-one, McElroy and Truman winning over Hayes. Matters turned ugly in April 1923 when McElroy and Truman asked the Missouri attorney general to dismiss a Shannon man holding a job that the county court didn't even control. War came June 1. The previous night Mike Pendergast promised followers that the fourteen Pendergast men at the county garage whom Koehler had fired just that afternoon "will be cared for and will be back on their jobs very soon." Mike indicated that Shannon Democrats were behind the firings, and angrily predicted trouble for the Shannon faction. At the same meeting Truman announced that he and McElroy would commence hostilities. The rumor and gossip that operate in a county courthouse packed the courtroom with Pendergast and Shannon supporters the next day. Truman proposed that the court replace county purchasing agent Eugene Jarboe, a Shannon man who had refused what he termed "sideline" instructions from Truman and McElroy requesting him to buy supplies from particular individuals, with county license inspector William Kirby, a Pendergast alderman in Kansas City who had been getting generous consideration in salary and number of deputies over the objection of Judge Hayes. Truman also proposed that Jack Toliver, a central figure in the fight with Koehler, then get the county license inspector job. McElroy and Truman voted for each motion; Hayes voted no. The deeds were done. Jarboe was in the courtroom and asked why he had been fired. McElroy replied, "I haven't time to discuss it." Jarboe thought McElroy had to be a small man to say that, mighty small. "Red with rage and trembling" Jarboe told "Judge McElroy in a loud, insolent, and threatening voice and in open Court and in the hearing of divers persons assembled in the Courtroom where said Court was in session the following obscene and insolent and approbrious language to-wit: 'I don't give a damn for you politically or any other way. My opinion of you personally is that you can stand flat-footed and kiss a gnat's ass.' "

Truman leaped up and demanded an apology from Jarboe. After repeated urgings from Truman and Hayes, Jarboe did so and left the room. "This man was my only appointee," Hayes declared. "He was the only one I was permitted to name. He should not have been discharged." McElroy and Truman ordered Jarboe jailed for two days to teach him some respect. Unlike a circuit court, a county court's authority to jail someone for contempt was a hoary prerogative almost never exercised. (Indeed, because Truman and McElroy in their excitement failed to follow the arcane requirements, Jarboe would never sit inside the Independence Bastille.) Hayes could scarcely believe what was happening, and the courtroom was in an uproar with angry Pendergast and Shannon faction members ready for action. White-faced, Hayes emotionally proposed that assorted Pendergast men be fired, calling McElroy and Truman worse than Bulger. McElroy replied in kind, and the Pendergast judges defeated the proposal. Truman and McElroy ordered Koehler to close and lock the garage, and intimated all future county road work would be under private contract, thus stripping Koehler of all power. (McElroy would later call the garage a liability to the county and suggest that the garage be sold.) Capping the day's work, over Hayes's protests Truman and McElroy appointed George Shaw, one of Truman's opponents on the 1922 primary election ballot, to a patronage plum. Shaw was a Shannon man turned traitor, and the Pendergasts' public reward for this conduct was an insult to the Shannon faction.[30]

Having guaranteed reelection opposition from the Republicans, Bulger Democrats, and Shannon Democrats, Truman next proceeded to alienate a powerful Pendergast river ward leader.

Truman had close ties with his Kansas City cousin Ralph "Snapper" Truman. They had occasionally seen each other in France while fighting in the 35th Division. Snapper had proven his credentials as a Pendergast man before the war by harassing Kansas City mayor Henry Jost, a Pendergast opponent, with a lawsuit that went to the Missouri Supreme Court. During the war Charlie Ross served under

Captain Snapper. Charlie was the son of Mike Ross, a Pendergast river ward chieftain who had remarkable success in gaining local government contracts for street paving. Father and son were both tough characters, and during the war Charlie refused to obey Snapper's orders. Snapper threw Charlie in the guardhouse for an extended period. Had he known Snapper better Charlie might have been grateful for such leniency (Snapper once personally and summarily shot and wounded a slacker on the battlefield), but instead Charlie's daddy Mike Ross vowed to get Snapper Truman someday. After the war Snapper rejoined the Kansas City police force as a detective. He ran down a tip about stolen property in a river ward hotel. Mike Ross got the hotel manager to swear falsely that using "coercion and intimidation" Snapper had extorted $300 from the manager. Without questioning Snapper, a grand jury indicted him in June 1920. Snapper told Judge Ralph Latshaw that the charge was a frame-up instigated by Mike Ross. The hotel manager confessed his perjury, and Snapper was free. And angry. He suggested to cousin Harry in January 1923, "You might be able to take a rap at my friend, Mike Ross," and advised, "Get one of the other judges to cooperate with you . . . to take him to a genuine cleaning." Harry answered, "Don't worry about our mutual friend Mike. If I can put a crimp in him it won't take me long to do it. I think his case will come up later. He is no friend of mine, and I know how you love him. What was that good for nothing boy's first name?"[31]

Truman saw his chance to crimp Ross when the new Jackson County park system started. The county judges appointed commissioners—including Truman's war associate Harry Jobes whose father was president of the Kansas City board of public works—to establish small roadside parks with benches and campsites. The idea was to advertise scenic beauty, attract tourists, and provide easy rural recreation for city dwellers. Judge McElroy announced that Willie Ross (son of Mike) had generously donated a $19,000 county warrant to fund the project. A county warrant was a document authorizing the county treasurer to pay the specified amount to the bearer. Since the Ross outfit had never been noted for civic generosity, this donation came under immediate and harsh scrutiny. Cynics suggested that the donation was intended to affect the county court's upcoming vote on awarding $230,000 in road contracts. Koehler had recommended that the Ross company be rejected as an irresponsible bidder due to poor past performance. Old ex-judge William H. Wallace agreed, saying property owners along the roads wouldn't even try to watchdog Ross because he was too tricky. The donated warrant had an interesting history of its own. The Ross company had been ordered to refund to the county $20,000 for unsatisfactory road work. This $19,000 warrant had been issued for the very project Ross was supposed to repay. The old county court had tried to cancel the warrant in December 1922, but was told Ross could only be asked to surrender the document. Now in September 1923 Ross was finally turning in this warrant, and trying to make the surrender look like a charitable donation.

Court observers were taken aback when Truman allied himself with Hayes against McElroy in rejecting the Ross bids. McElroy interrupted former county judge Kimball when he tried to tell the history of the $19,000 warrant, but Truman and Hayes overruled McElroy and let Kimball explain how Ross had overcharged $59,000 for county roadwork. Old William Wallace heatedly condemned the proposal to use the warrant for parks, whereupon McElroy asked, "Are you a lawyer?"—a cheeky insult to one of the best-known attorneys in the region. "I have been a lawyer and judge here for 40 years, and you are the first person to question my standing," Wallace replied. McElroy rejoined, "I believe we have heard as much of your argument as will be of benefit to us." Wallace (who himself was no amateur at intimidation) pounded the table and shouted, "You can't stop me! You can't bulldoze me as you did Judge Kimball . . . ! I'll talk until I've finished what I have to say!" When Wallace was done Truman and Hayes voted to cancel the warrant, an action that would automatically increase the county treasury by $19,000. Truman waited for Ralph Latshaw to hand over the warrant to be stamped "canceled." Latshaw said he had already given it to McElroy. McElroy baldly stated that he rejected the court order and would return the warrant—still valid because it hadn't been stamped "canceled"—to Ross. And this is exactly what McElroy did. Truman watched helplessly and could only vent frustration at Latshaw, telling him he should never have delivered the warrant to McElroy. Truman added, "Let Ross go into the circuit court to collect it and see how far he gets."[32]

Truman's scheme to get even with Ross cost the county potentially $19,000. The episode also showed McElroy that he could administer government by defying the law. It is a lesson McElroy took to heart.

Truman had broken with McElroy to settle an old score with Ross, but the two judges began to split on other matters as well. For instance, there was McElroy's investigation of whether physicians were abusing county permits to write prescriptions for ethyl alcohol. McElroy said, "Alcohol must be a mighty effective remedy for many of the diseases now going around in Kansas City." McElroy particularly questioned why physicians charged more for these prescriptions than for others. The next day a medico stopped McElroy in the hall and tried to explain how the paperwork for ethyl alcohol prescriptions justified an extra charge. Ever the bully, McElroy told the doctor to step into the courtroom and watch his permit get revoked. Truman was in the hall, and protested, "This is Dr. Stephen Ragan, a widely known physician." McElroy insisted, and the county court convened to hear his motion. Judge Hayes said, "I've known Dr. Ragan many years and know he is a high class physician. I vote no." Truman: "The doctor and I have been friends some time. I don't believe he would charge too high. I vote no." Ragan left with his permit intact and a lesson about the hazards of trying to confuse Henry McElroy with the facts. McElroy made another mistake a month later when he bullied pool hall operator L. E. Harvey, haughtily demanding that Harvey be denied a county license for his business, and refusing to let the incapacitated 129th Field Artillery veteran defend himself. Truman broke in: "I vote for his license." Hayes also voted yes, and the license was granted.[33]

The war had to have been on Truman's mind during that court session, as the 35th Division reunion was underway in Excelsior Springs some miles north of Kansas City. There the veterans elected Truman, and Jacob "Tuck" Milligan of Richmond, Missouri, to the 35th Division Association's executive committee. As president of the association Truman had, a few months before, introduced speakers at a Coates House hotel reunion dinner in Kansas City. Milligan had been a prominent guest at that gathering. Tuck and his brother Maurice would later demonstrate an intense and unfriendly interest in Truman's career. The county court adjourned for two weeks in July 1923, and Truman used that time to attend a military training camp. His letters to Bess are full of boyish high spirits, "You should see my eyebrow on my upper lip, or toothbrush as someone called it." They had "a badger fight which was a scream. The boys who were sold on it were really scared to death before it came off, and when the badger was pulled out one of them jump[ed] over the table and nearly broke his neck." In the midst of this activity Truman also kept informed about politics: "I see that the *Journal* is still laying a pick at the county court. If Mr. Dickey had gotten his streets accepted he'd have been pleased with the operation of the court." Walter S. Dickey was a robber baron capitalist frustrated by the overhunting of victims in Kansas City, and desiring new prey elsewhere. He had a suburban real estate subdivision, and tried to convince the county court to make the streets into county roads, thus relieving him of construction and maintenance costs. This sort of favor was not unheard of, but Dickey was the prominent Republican newspaper publisher of the *Kansas City Journal,* and thus got a frigid reception from Truman and McElroy. An old saying in politics warns against picking fights with newspapers, but summer camp made Truman feisty: "I'll be able to lick all the rabbits [Shannon Democrats] and the *Kansas City Journal,* too, when I get home."[34]

Back home Truman participated in two more projects alienating considerable numbers of Jackson County voters. One was suppression of so-called "chicken-dinner farms." "Complaints Pour in About Jangling Music and Loud Laughter at Roadhouses Where Bacchus, Not Volstead, Reigns." For many years residents of Kansas City had, for a sum, been able to purchase the most sordid entertainments. The advent of the automobile and the entrepreneurship of rural property owners had now made these same entertainments available in pastoral settings. Judge McElroy took particular interest in helping Truman's war buddy John Miles (the county marshal) suppress these chicken-dinner farms. The ostensible reason was criminal activity associated with the places. Since liquor was illegal, except when consumed on order of a physician, plenty of this particular criminal activity could be proven. Crimes of passion or stupidity under the influence of alcohol could also be proven. Cynics might wonder if McElroy's concern about chicken-dinner farms, as opposed to the hundreds of similar operations in Kansas City, had something to do with Pendergast organization rake-offs (or lack thereof) from the less easily monitored rural establishments. Headlines soon revealed the results of the McElroy-Truman effort. "Gloom at Chicken Farms." "Raucous Discord of Jazz Bands Is Stilled and Revel Is Fled."

Truman's reputation as a killjoy increased with his support of the "spooning squad"—six deputy marshals to help rural Jackson County residents and visitors resist sexual temptation. Critics could scarcely believe county money was being spent on this. "Don't you men know life is too short to bother about spooning? What do you expect them to do after a hard day's work? Go out and eat worms?" Truman and Marshal Miles took this crusade seriously. The *Kansas City Star* reported "dog days for the 'snuggle puppy.' " Some years later Truman said privately, "American finishing schools are usually the finish of any girl that goes to them. They learn birth control, to smoke, drink, and new movements in carnal intercourse. If the country goes to hell as Babylon, Ninevah, Rome, and Russia did it will owe a large part of its failure to the higher educational institutions for women." Truman added, "Someday we'll awake, have a reformation of the heart, teach our kids honor, and kill a few sex psychologists, put boys in high schools to themselves with *men* teachers (not sissies), close all the girls finishing schools, shoot all the efficiency experts, and become a nation of God's people once more."[35]

Protestant fundamentalism was rampant in the Kansas City area. William Jewell College had just attracted national notoriety by dismissing Bible Department chairman Arthur Wakefield Slaten, whose distinguished scholarship raised questions too disturbing for faith to hear. This incident was a hot topic at the May 1923 meeting of the Southern Baptist Convention in Kansas City. William Jennings Bryan was the featured speaker. Truman laughed with the rest of the friendly crowd as his old hero heaped ridicule upon modernists. "Evolution is merely a guess," Bryan said, "and I disapprove of allowing atheists to puff their guesses in the faces of children in school. If they want to teach their theories as truth, let them build their own colleges."[36]

Having alienated drinkers, sexers, Republicans, Bulger Democrats, Shannon Democrats, and even some river ward Pendergast Democrats, McElroy and Truman managed to offend yet another group—judges of the circuit court and their patronage employees. The trouble broke out when the county prosecutor asked the county court for more deputies to clear the backlog of criminal cases. McElroy replied that the fault was not in the prosecutor's office but in the circuit judges who were too lazy to do an honest day's work. This statement did not escape judicial notice. The arrows whizzed back and forth between the county and circuit courts. McElroy had solid evidence to back his assertion—numbers of circuit court holidays, case loads, and so forth. The circuit judges responded with indignation but never quite denied McElroy's numbers. This bickering worsened the feelings in a more serious dispute over county welfare activities.[37]

Jackson County had several welfare activities. The county provided doles, medical care for the indigent, and institutional homes for the poor. Truman, McElroy, and Hayes personally had to consider each case. This procedure made sense in nineteenth-century rural Missouri where judges probably knew the applicants. In twentieth-century Jackson County, which included Kansas City, the case load grew staggering. Even with investigators doing legwork to determine the needs of each applicant, county judges still had to consider the merits of each case and keep tabs on conditions at various county welfare institutions. This activity was probably good for the soul but nonetheless an impediment to efficient administration of county government.

A few years earlier the state legislature had passed a law turning supervision of Jackson County juvenile homes over to the circuit court—the judges who presided over trials. This created a two-headed monster. The circuit court hired and fired and ran up bills, and the county court had to fund the operation. The circuit judges had the authority; the county judges had the accountability. This also added political inefficiency to administrative inefficiency. If a faction wanted the juvenile homes patronage (both jobs and supply contracts), the faction had to elect a majority of the circuit court. How much simpler to elect just two county judges instead. Desire for this simplicity was surely a key motive when Truman and McElroy decided to recapture the juvenile homes for the county court.

They attacked with two county court orders. One said that no county supplies could be bought without the approval of county purchasing agent William Kirby and the county court. The other order requested the circuit court to dismiss Agnes Burke as superintendent of the Parental Home for Girls. McElroy implied that she was a thief, saying she had sold Parental Home farm animals and failed to put the proceeds in the county treasury. The circuit court called a hearing. Circuit judge Porterfield had recently pronounced McElroy a liar "from start to finish. I believe Judge McElroy is four-flushing." The hearing proved Porterfield not far from wrong. It turned out Burke had a county court order telling her to buy $232 of livestock. To generate this cash she had sold $302 of other livestock. County purchasing agent Kirby told her not to bother routing the sale money through the treasury, just buy the livestock as directed by the county court. Kirby also okayed Burke spending the extra $70 on various items for which proper receipts were filed. Burke noted that McElroy had personally approved the petty-cash fund. Burke also brought out that neither McElroy nor Truman had consulted her before demanding her job, and Judge Hayes stated that the McElroy-Truman action was based on hearsay. Cornered, McElroy suggested that the county court order for the livestock purchase was forged; but Judge Hayes testified that he remembered signing it. Character witnesses lauded Burke, and someone with a good memory noted that McElroy had been on the grand jury that praised Burke's management of the Home four years earlier. McElroy now climbed down a bit, maintaining that Burke should be fired because (on orders from McElroy's and Truman's man Kirby) she had failed to follow the proper bureaucratic procedure and deposited the $70 in petty cash without first routing it through the county treasurer. Since McElroy had recently disobeyed a direct county court order by giving a $19,000 warrant to Willie Ross instead of turning it over to the county for canceling, McElroy's argument now carried small credibility. Indeed, skeptics argued that McElroy and Truman trumped up the affair to harass Burke because she was a Shannon Democrat. The circuit judges unanimously exonerated her, and she stayed on the job.[38]

In his testimony at this fiasco McElroy touched on a point that would give him and Truman ultimate victory in the struggle for control of juvenile home patronage. He contended that the county court controlled juvenile home property. A few days earlier he and Truman had backed up this contention with an order that all county supply purchases had to be approved by William Kirby and the county court. In other words, Truman and McElroy would refuse to pay any bills the circuit court incurred for the homes. Bewildered merchants who presented the county court with bills for supplies ordered by the circuit court were browbeaten by McElroy, and accused of fraud. Newspapers enumerated anticipated sufferings of helpless children at the brutal hands of McElroy and Truman. One could almost hear the plaintive violins in the background. The circuit judges personally and civic clubs corporately guaranteed payment for juvenile home supplies, and then quickly got a writ forcing McElroy and Truman to approve county court payments. The issue then went to the Missouri Supreme Court. The circuit court's legal team included Kansas City Bar Association president A. L. Cooper. (As county counselor Cooper had helped fire road overseer Harry Truman. After Truman became eastern judge he and McElroy fired county counselor Cooper. Tit for tat. Although Truman had then backed his National Guard and oil associate Fred Boxley for county counselor, the job went to Ralph Latshaw, reputedly Boss Tom Pendergast's personal choice. Although Latshaw was perfectly competent to handle the normal routine of county litigation, Truman and McElroy decided he'd better have a helper for this case. Particularly since, as in the Koehler affair, what began as a patronage fight snowballed into a threat to the entire Pendergast county organization.) Although the ostensible dispute was over who would sign for juvenile home supplies, the real issue was whether the legislature could turn over a county institution to any agency but the county court. If the Supreme Court decided yes, Bulger and Shannon and their pals in the legislature could remove one county operation after another from the county court and make it nearly impossible for any faction to control the county government. If the Supreme Court decided no, Pendergast could seize the entire county government and its patronage simply by electing two judges. McElroy knew that he and Truman would have no political future if they lost this case. The two Pendergast judges therefore turned to General John Barker. This Kansas City attorney was one of the ablest and most famous in the state (Truman called him "expert fixer"). General Barker—his title referred to years as Missouri attorney general rather than to military accomplishments—readily took the case to the Supreme Court for Pendergast. The tribunal decided that the county court controlled all county institutions and property. With Pendergast's growing ability to generate election returns this decision guaranteed his control of Jackson County government for years. The decision came in July 1925, too late for McElroy and Truman. They had won the war for Pendergast, but lost the 1924 election.[39]

———

Although the 1924 election loss should perhaps have seemed inevitable—McElroy and Truman had, after all, alienated almost every significant voter group of the era—the upcoming defeat wasn't anticipated at the time. The county court had been handing Pendergast opponents one defeat after another. In addition, the court had been strengthening the Pendergast organization with patronage and contracts that translated into votes. A third factor was support from the business community. Pendergast chose Truman and McElroy in part for their business connections, and the two judges pursued policies designed to gain favor from the Kansas City capitalist leadership. Unlike other faction leaders Tom Pendergast was shifting his attention from voter constituencies toward the mercantile elite. This strategy was a break with the past, and would ultimately prove decisive to Pendergast's power. With Truman and McElroy, Pendergast began to demonstrate that his organization could help large corporations make more money. This profitability became so alluring that civic and business leaders, whose interests the law enforcement agencies and the judiciary served, decided to tolerate the subsequent large-scale vote frauds necessary to keep the Pendergast machine in place.

The business and banking communities would hail Truman and McElroy as financial statesmen restoring fiscal responsibility to county government. They got this reputation by paying off all current county warrants and about half the old ones. As noted earlier, a warrant authorized the county treasurer to pay an amount to the bearer from county funds. If county money ran short, warrants were numbered and registered, and paid in order. A friend of the county court might get serial number 1; Joe Citizen might get number 5,000; court enemies might get number 10 jillion. This became especially important when Miles Bulger ran the court because he also ran up county deficits. Thus the high-number warrants became IOU's. A person in a hurry could sell the warrant to someone for maybe 80 percent or 60 percent or 40 percent of face value, and the purchaser would hold the warrant until the county made good. This probably had two results. First, contractors probably padded their bids, bidding $1,000 for an $800 job. They could sell the warrant for $800 without suffering any loss. The second result was that insiders who knew that McElroy and Truman planned to pay off the old high-number warrants could buy them up at a discount and make a windfall profit. Pendergast friends were credited with profiting by this technique. This was an old maneuver, dating in the United States to Alexander Hamilton's tenure as Treasury Secretary. A particularly gratifying aspect of this ploy was that no one griped about the government paying old debts. Insiders made a killing, yet the basic transaction was legitimate. (Taxpayers took a beating if warrants for inflated contract bids were redeemed at par, but again no one could complain about the county paying its debts. The blame for this beating could be put on Bulger.) The McElroy-Truman policy of redeeming old warrants also strengthened the county's credit rating. This helped taxpayers by discouraging bid padding, reduced interest on new bank loans to the county, and improved the cash flow of merchants dealing with the county, providing a general boost to the economy. No wonder that meetings of businessmen literally cheered Truman and McElroy.[40]

The manner in which McElroy and Truman implemented the warrant redemption policy was as much a break with the past as was the policy itself, and represented a new and fundamental difference between the Pendergast Democrats and Shannon Democrats. Pendergast again demonstrated a shrewd appeal to the Kansas City capitalist leadership. To generate revenue for warrant redemption McElroy and Truman announced a retrenchment program to cut salaries of some county workers and to fire others. This meant the debt would be paid without raising taxes. Shannon forces were dominant in Kansas City municipal government, and had explicitly rejected retrenchment, instead advocating a tax increase program to pay the city debt. Mercantile leadership rallied behind McElroy and Truman, and savaged Kansas City mayor Frank Cromwell (a Shannon man). The political effectiveness of the Pendergast and Shannon policies was tested decisively in the spring 1924 Kansas City election. Despite Shannon's refusal to cut back city patronage employees and despite full campaign support from Pendergast and despite doubling the campaign lug on patronage worker salaries, Mayor Cromwell lost to Republican A. I. Beach. The county retrenchment policy, incidentally, cost Pendergast no patronage. McElroy and Truman simply betrayed the "50-50" agreement that had promised to divide county patronage between Shannon and Pendergast, and instead hogged county jobs for Pendergast followers. This meant that, in theory, McElroy and Truman could fire half the county workers in "ruthless economizing" without Pendergast losing any patronage—

the Shannon men got the ax. Thus the retrenchment policy not only gained Pendergast the backing of Kansas City and Jackson County business leadership, but was administered so as to deal the Shannon county organization a heavy blow. Truman later wrote, "This seriously hampered Joe [Shannon] financially and politically. I don't think he cared politically." The praise heaped on Pendergast fiscal responsibility had to madden the Shannon men, since they took all the sacrifices (lost jobs), and Pendergast got all the benefits. Shannon decided he would not only get mad, but get even.[41]

In the 1924 county elections Bulger and Shannon made common cause against Pendergast. Feelings ran hot. Bloodshed started in March, five months before the primary. By July Shannon himself showed the strain when he got into a fistfight with another politician on the floor of the Democrat national convention. The so-called Independent Democrats of Todd George and Harvey (or Harry) Hoffman added more zip to the county primary. Hoffman was a notorious character in Jackson County politics, so loathesome to some Democrats that in 1920 they joined the veterans in voting for Republican John Miles to replace Hoffman as county marshal. Since the close relations between Truman and Miles in that election were no secret, Hoffman had a very personal motive for defeating Truman's bid for reelection. The Pendergast organization quickly pointed out that the Independent Democrats were actually the political arm of the Ku Klux Klan, and chided Shannon for denouncing the Klan at the Democrat national convention while currying favor with the Jackson County Klan. "They threatened to kill me," Truman said, "and I went out to one of their meetings and dared them to kill me. . . . I poured it into them. Then I came down from [the] platform and walked through them to my car." Truman, of course, knew the measure of Hoffman and Todd George and many of the Klansmen, and therefore expected to get away unharmed, particularly since he brought along armed guards. Nonetheless, the confrontation was great drama and had an element of risk due to hot tempers on both sides.[42]

The Truman and McElroy victory in the August primary hampered Shannon's and Bulger's and Hoffman's revenge. The three told their followers to vote Republican in November. In this they had the aid of Walter Dickey's newspaper the *Kansas City Journal*. As noted earlier, Dickey's opinion of Truman and McElroy noticeably declined when the county court refused to take on the expense of roads in a Dickey real estate development. Dickey noted with displeasure that McElroy and Truman had been only too happy to put a county road through a real estate development promoted by McElroy's next-door neighbor, a road terminating at the James Pendergast farm. In September 1924 the *Journal* started a series of daily features probing McElroy and Truman's official conduct. The articles were strident, sometimes misleading, but mostly unshakable. Readers learned much that the *Star* and *Times* had neglected to report. For months those papers and civic groups had lauded the McElroy and Truman "business administration" of county government. Dickey now proceeded to expose that reputation as public relations puffery.[43]

Truman and McElroy had built much of their reputation on their ability to pay all current debts and some old debts, and still leave a surplus in the treasury. The existence or size of a county surplus was a crucial issue to the Shannon Democrats. They had been flayed for creating the Kansas City municipal deficit, and were anxious to show that the Pendergasts were doing no better with county finances. Particularly since the Shannon Kansas City deficit and Pendergast county surplus were big election issues. In the August primary campaign Truman said the huge Kansas City deficit would also happen in the county government if Shannon Democrats had their way, and in the county primary every Shannon candidate lost. Presiding Judge Hayes (a Shannon Democrat not up for reelection this time) had long felt that McElroy generated the county surplus with accounting tricks. McElroy bristled at these charges, and at one court session the two judges considered trading their verbal snortings for a fistfight. McElroy indeed protested too much.[44]

McElroy and Truman manufactured the county surplus through creative accounting and a godsend increase in revenue. Efficient administration had nothing to do with it. To dress up their claims, in 1924 Truman and McElroy once again hired Arthur Young & Co. to audit the county. When the results came in Judge Hayes sputtered that the accounting firm had performed its work to McElroy's specifications. (Over a half century later Jackson County officials were still using Arthur Young & Co. to back up claims, and the results were still alleged to be manufactured.) The accountants showed a 1923 surplus of $360,000—$190,000 cash and $170,000 in 1923 delinquent taxes. This surplus appeared mainly by using fourteen months of income—including 1923 taxes received in January and February 1924, which were substantial because of odd fiscal laws.* This technique wasn't used in the 1922 audit, probably because McElroy and Truman had no interest in minimizing the Bulger era deficit. Indeed, the *Kansas City Journal* showed how the 1923 audit techniques could be used to make the $1,200,000 deficit disappear. Also in 1923 property valuation increased although the tax levy stayed the same. The *Kansas City Journal* found that this alone generated over $250,000 more revenue than was available in 1922. The *Journal* also found that the $72,000 jury and election fund 1923 surplus existed simply because there were no elections that year. Truman himself admitted that the 1924 elections would cost $300,000, an expense that didn't exist in the fourteen-month year of Arthur Young & Co. Thus the 1923 surplus had nothing to do with McElroy and Truman's efficiency but was generated through their accounting techniques, an increase of revenue via higher property valuations, and a lack of $300,000 in election expenses. Observers praised Truman and McElroy for paying $610,000 of the Bulger debt. The *Journal* noted, however, that $305,000 of the payments came from delinquent tax receipts, money that could be used for nothing else. Moreover, the *Journal* reported, Truman and McElroy reduced the pauper fund and the jury and election fund, and increased the other county funds. The two Pendergast judges also switched various expenses to the pauper fund and the jury and election fund. This didn't affect the total amount of money available to the county, but it allowed Truman and McElroy to set up the circuit court (which drew from the two funds just noted) for overdraws, making the circuit court look spendthrift even if it spent no more money than the previous year. In addition to the public relations ploy, this shuffling affected the county surplus.

Because of the adjudication regarding the juvenile homes, McElroy and Truman refused to carry juvenile home expenses (normally drawn from the pauper fund) as chargeable to the county. For bookkeeping purposes this reduced county court expenses on paper, without affecting ultimate county indebtedness. Indeed, the *Journal* showed how Truman and McElroy were avoiding a 1924 deficit by asking

---

*A state law, beneficial to bankers, delayed collection of county taxes until October although fiscal-year expenditures started in January.

friendly contractors to delay work and postpone presentation of warrants for payment, and by postponing issuance of warrants. In the midst of the *Journal* exposés McElroy tried to brazen it out by declaring a $300,000 surplus for 1924. Judge Hayes quickly noted that this included no cash but was entirely uncollected delinquent taxes—money obligated exclusively for back debts. In the summer Truman had ridiculed and refused to answer questions about how the 1923 surplus had been generated. One doubts that he laughed in October after the *Journal* showed how he and McElroy had done it.[45]

The touted county surplus implied that McElroy and Truman had fought graft and political favoritism. The *Journal* took care of this impression with stories such as " 'Thrift' Court Spurns Offer to Save $9,993." In article after article the newspaper dissected what it called a "payrollers' paradise." Again and again Pendergast men and allied businesses were shown profiting from featherbed jobs and slick contracts: road inspectors who either didn't work or duplicated the work of other employees; the Hickman Mills–Lee's Summit road contract to the highest bidder; road work that increased the value of a Pendergast realtor's properties; payrolls that gave two days' pay for one day's work; a scam to change county home inmates to county employees, and thereby enfranchise them at election time; figures showing as many patronage workers under McElroy and Truman as under Bulger, and at the same expense; and on and on. The cumulative impact was devastating. Much of the information was old, reported over the past two years and lost in the shuffle of events. The *Journal*'s daily series now concentrated all this news, giving it an urgent immediacy. None of the revelations was anything more than one would expect in a political machine, but that was exactly what made them so damaging. McElroy and Truman had been promoted as scientific administrators bringing business efficiency to county government. The *Journal* showed that they were primarily Pendergast men concerned with pork barrel when not distracted by factional infighting. While incomplete, this portrayal was fair. McElroy and Truman did plenty of work that had no obvious political benefit, work that served the public well. The public interest, however, and Pendergast interest weren't necessarily incompatible. McElroy and Truman could shrewdly aid the Pendergast organization while promoting the public good. The damage of the *Journal* articles wasn't in revealing what the two judges were—Pendergast men—but in revealing what they weren't

—disinterested servants of the people. While posing as scientific administrators Truman and McElroy had been using every political gimmick to strengthen the Pendergasts. Voters who had believed the public relations puffery about Truman and McElroy likely felt cheated.[46]

Eastern judge Truman in particular had to answer for county road conditions. All county roads were in his district; none was in McElroy's western district. Part of the road story can be seen in money alone:

	New Road Construction	Total Road Work
1922 (Bulger court)	$113,000	$945,000
1923 (Truman court)	210,000	750,000
1924 (Truman court)	302,000	950,000
1925 (Republican court)	143,000	770,000

Truman and McElroy had a vigorous new road construction program. Private contractors rather than county highway engineer Koehler did most of that work, providing jobs for the Pendergast organization—many more than routine road maintenance could generate. Since total road expenditures under Truman were in keeping with the county courts preceding and following his, the emphasis on new road construction depleted money available for maintenance. Maintenance declined further because under Truman the costs accelerated:

	Miles Oiled	Total Cost	Gallons per Mile	Cost per Mile
1922 (Bulger court)	321	$113,000	4,960	$353
1923 (Truman court)	538	210,000	5,200	391
1924 (Truman court)	320	135,000	5,900	421
1925 (Republican court)	565	214,000	5,310	379

Oiling expense rose because the county court paid a premium to the Pendergast family's Eureka Petroleum Company to supply the oil, and also paid extra for patronage employees to spread the oil (a non-Pendergast contractor had offered to do the job for half the price and to post bond for faithful performance). The increase in oiling expense further cut other maintenance (scraping, pothole filling, culverts, bridges). Indeed, despite the county's bookkeeping "surplus" McElroy and Truman shut down road work after the primary election, leaving some roads blocked, because no more road money was available. In October Republican highway engineer Koehler said $1,700 would fix seven almost impassable county highways, but the county had no funds for it. The lack of funds was particularly striking because under McElroy and Truman the state took over maintenance costs of about one hundred miles of county highways, converting them to state highways. All this was a hot campaign issue in Truman's eastern district, as voters used the deteriorating roads every day. A few days before the November election Truman's supervision of road overseers blew up in his face. He had pushed through his slate of road overseers over the opposition of Judge Hayes. The *Kansas City Journal* now revealed that some of these Truman men had falsified payrolls, getting two days' pay for one day's work, and pocketing the pay of fictitious workers. The "fictitious workers" thing was explosive. It turned out that the workers were real enough, farmers who had put in hard labor helping repair roads. Sharp road overseers, however, had talked these men into donating their services to the county. The overseers then listed the farmers as workers on the payroll, and had collected their pay. The cheated farmers were livid—not over the money but over being taken as suckers. These suckers and their families and friends were voters. The revelations put some tarnish on Truman, the shining administrator. All the more so because Truman had known about such problems for years.[47]

The *Journal* twisted the knife with an article about Truman's mother. After first noting that Truman had the county build Grandview Road from the Kansas City Auto Club house in Hickman Mills south to Grandview, the *Journal* observed that Truman had the county pave Grandview's main road even though the town was incorporated and thus supposed to do its own paving. It also reported that Truman got the county to spend $2,000 on a 150-yard road through his mother's farm property to Grandview Road. In theory this thoroughfare would someday extend west to Prospect Street. Until then, however, the new road served only Martha Ellen Truman—no farm neighbor could use it without her permission since her property had to be crossed to reach or leave the road west of Grandview Road.

The *Journal* noted that Mattie's frontage on Grandview Road had been subdivided and sold. It also noted that about $1,300 of the $2,000 construction cost went for two bridges that couldn't be used because the road didn't yet go that far west. Bridges were sitting in the middle of farmland. This may have been sensible long-range planning, but it neglected current maintenance needs. Finally, the *Journal* mentioned that over $700 of the road construction money went to road overseer Vivian Truman and his crew. This was surely legitimate—Vivian had been a road overseer before Harry became eastern judge—but it made Truman look like he was funneling county money to his family. Anyone familiar with President Truman's reaction to criticism of his daughter's singing can imagine his response to *Kansas City Journal* comments about his mother. The article was entitled, "The Home Folks."[48]

Throughout the bombardment against Truman and McElroy, the *Star* and the *Times* staunchly defended the judges. These two papers were published by the same outfit and were traditional enemies of the Pendergast organization. Normally the *Star* portrayed a Pendergast man's breathing as a theft of oxygen from upright citizens, or at least from the public domain. The flip-flop on Truman and McElroy was astounding. The *Star* had much to do with creating Truman and McElroy's false image as scientific administrators of nonpartisan good government. Because of the *Star*'s traditional antipathy to the Pendergasts, its praise for Truman and McElroy has been considered important evidence of McElroy and Truman's devotion to public service. Therefore, it is well to consider a darker explanation presented by the *Kansas City Journal*. The *Journal* noted that McElroy had been on a grand jury impaneled by Judge Ralph Latshaw in 1918 to investigate tax dodging. *Kansas City Star* general manager August Seested sweated before the grand jury three times trying to explain his Jackson County tax return, changed his story twice, but in the end was let off. Previously the *Star* had condemned Latshaw's "whitewash grand juries," but the newspaper had no complaints this time. Three years later city planning commission member McElroy recommended that Seested be awarded $1,250 a foot for 101 feet of condemned frontage at Seested's 24th and McGee property. He had paid $12,000 for 164 feet in 1909, and still retained the extra 63 feet. After assorted adjustments Seested got $158,000 for the property McElroy had examined. Two years later the *Star* was booming Judge

McElroy had examined. Two years later the *Star* was booming Judge McElroy as a practitioner of modern good government. Truman himself called McElroy the *Star*'s man on the county court. The *Journal* was crude enough to ask whether the grand jury and property deals had anything to do with the warm friendship between the *Star* and McElroy the Pendergast judge.[49]

With Shannon Democrats, Bulger Democrats, Independent KKK Democrats, and all the Republicans against him, Truman surely knew how the November election would turn out. He did a little knifing of his own, secretly raising funds for the sheriff campaign of Republican John Miles to defeat the Democrat candidate. Miles had been Truman's Army major, and was currently county marshal. The jobs of marshal and sheriff were to be combined January 1, 1925, giving nearly one hundred deputies and the county's highest pay to the sheriff. This was a big patronage office, and Truman worked to throw it to the Republicans. He solicited $100 from Harry Jobes, $100 from Karl Klemm, $25 from Father Tiernan, $25 from Marvin Gates, $25 from Ted Marks, and contributions from other 129th Field Artillery veterans. Truman himself may have contributed to this substantial election fund. He got away with voting for Miles in 1920 out of friendship, but this secret fund raising was a far different matter that could have caused him tremendous political damage in later years if it had ever become known. This effort was a touching demonstration of Truman's affection for Miles, as Miles and the brother of ex-Lt. C. C. Bundschu had found the Republican candidate for eastern judge who was about to defeat Truman—fifty-nine-year-old Henry Rummel, who had made the goat harness set for Harry and Vivian three decades earlier. Truman, of course, knew from courthouse gossip that Miles and Henry Bundschu were responsible for Rummel's candidacy.[50]

On election day the Ku Klux Klan tolled Independence church bells hour after hour, and passed out sample ballots for Rummel. Truman did not have to ask for whom the bells tolled. Both he and McElroy lost. Although Truman ran far behind the Democrat governor candidate, McElroy ran far ahead of other losing Democrats, ironically because of thousands of Republicans who supported McElroy. Analysts credited the Shannon-Bulger-KKK-GOP alliance with defeating both McElroy and Truman. In addition, observers felt the harassment of county juvenile homes cost McElroy many votes from Kansas City club women who had long aided the homes. (McElroy would ignore Kansas City club women again, and they would help destroy him.) Observers felt poor road maintenance contributed substantially to Truman's defeat.[51]

The morning after the election, Boss Tom Pendergast spotted Miles Bulger at the intersection of Main and Brush Creek in Kansas City. Pendergast chased him on foot, but Bulger retreated too fast, his speed aided by Pendergast's all too clear intentions. In contrast, that same morning Truman spotted Henry Chiles near the town square in Independence and made a point to assure Chiles of continued personal friendship even though Chiles was a Shannon Democrat who had worked for Republican Rummel. The difference was that Chiles had followed the code of the professional politician, obeying the orders of his organization. Bulger and Shannon had violated that code, refusing to unite behind the party's nominee after the primary. Truman loathed such traitors, but normally showed no hard feelings toward anyone who demonstrated party or organization regularity even if the person had opposed him. Truman was a team player.[52]

A week or so later he had a cheerful supper at the City Club with sixty-five friends, about evenly divided between war associates and county politicians. Eugene Donnelly, the traditional toastmaster at Battery D reunions, surprised Truman with the gift of a gold watch. Engraved on its back was this message:

Judge Harry S. Truman
from his
Buddies and Friends
November 18, 1924

Overcome with emotion, Truman barely managed to stammer out his thanks.[53]

A close friend wrote to Truman, "I feel that if you cared to do so in two years you could run and come back with the largest majority of any candidate that ever run for the office."[54]

Young Harry
(*Harry S. Truman Library*).

The Waldo Avenue Gang. Bess Wallace is eating the watermelon
(*Harry S. Truman Library*).

Captain Harry during World War I
(*Harry S. Truman Library*).

Truman's war buddy, Sergeant Eddie Jacobson, with hand on hip. The group is in front of the regimental canteen he and Truman ran at Camp Doniphan. Later on, he would be Truman's haberdashery partner. A Zionist, Jacobson would influence President Truman's decision to recognize the state of Israel (*photo by Williard, Harry S. Truman Library*).

Truman twice invested in the city-slicker schemes of Jerry Culbertson. The mining venture was a disaster for Truman; the oil business fared slightly better (*Harry S. Truman Library*).

Jerry Culbertson (*probably Strauss-Peyton Studios, Richard Miller collection*).

ABOVE LEFT: Truman's war buddy, Spencer Salisbury, who would become Truman's hated savings-and-loan partner—a feud that would send Salisbury to federal prison (*Harry S. Truman Library*).

ABOVE RIGHT: Henry McElroy, irascible city manager of Kansas City, with a reputation for bullying the helpless (*photo by Moore, Western Historical Manuscripts Collection, University of Missouri*).

LEFT: Judge Truman asking Missouri voters to send him to the U.S. Senate in 1934 (*Harry S. Truman Library*).

The New Dealer rampant (*Harry S. Truman Library*).

Harry Truman and Boss Tom Pendergast in 1936 (*UPI, Harry S. Truman Library*).

Johnny Lazia, chief Pendergast enforcer. Truman, McElroy and Lazia were the triumvirate who ruled Kansas City for Boss Tom Pendergast (*Kansas City Star*).

Truman talks to reporters in his Senate office (with a picture of Pendergast on the wall) on the day the Big Boss was indicted for federal tax evasion. He said, "I won't desert a sinking ship." (*Associated Press, Harry S. Truman Library*).

Senator Truman on the 1939 junket to South America, a trip he took to escape the successful attacks against the Pendergast machine (*U.S. Army Signal Corps, Harry S. Truman Library*).

Policemen begin to surround an ecstatic Harry Truman as the roll call of the state delegates makes him the 1944 Democratic Vice Presidential nominee. Bess and Margaret sit by his side (*Harry S. Truman Library*).

At this meeting, according to Truman, FDR brought the Vice Presidential candidate up to date on the status of the atom bomb project (*Associated Press, Harry S. Truman Library*).

Chapter 9

BACK TO BUSINESS

When Truman and McElroy reentered private life on January 1, 1925 their financial circumstances were very different. McElroy was halfway to becoming a millionaire. Truman still had to wrestle with his haberdashery debts.[1]

These debts were more an annoyance than a burden. Percentage settlements had lawfully satisfied most of the merchandise creditors, although Cluett, Peabody & Co. got a justice of the peace judgment for $240 in January 1924. These so-called "jackrabbit" courts were universally regarded as an extortionist racket, and Truman refused to pay. No one would attempt to enforce a jackrabbit judgment on a county judge, and his county salary was immune from garnishee proceedings anyway. In September 1925, however, Cluett, Peabody seized private citizen Truman's small account at City Bank of Kansas City to settle the debt. The landlord Louis Oppenstein won a $3,200 circuit court judgment for the store lease in January 1924. This was harder to ignore, but Truman's bank accounts and other personal property were so minimal that there was nothing to seize. In theory Oppenstein could have garnisheed Truman's earnings in 1925 and 1926, but apparently he exercised forbearance, perhaps because he knew what the Pendergast city government could do to a large Republican downtown real estate operator such as himself. When Truman regained his immunity to salary garnishee proceedings in 1927 he continued to neglect the Oppenstein judgment. Truman finished repaying a $2,200 loan from Twelfth Street Bank in December 1924. This was an amicable proceeding with no court involvement. He flatly refused, however, to pay any more on the Security State Bank loan. As noted earlier, the October 1922 renewal was for $6,800, with Truman's Johnson County, Kansas, farm as security. In January 1923 Truman paid $1,000 on the principal. He paid a bit more, but the bank grew impatient and foreclosed on the farm. Truman figured that settled the debt since the farm was the security. The bank figured otherwise but got nowhere with him. When Truman returned to private life in 1925 the dispute was churning through circuit court, but a decision was years away. He voluntarily paid former merchandise creditors one hundred cents on the dollar, and achieved that goal soon after leaving county employment.[2]

Truman had no debts that concerned him. His one lawful debt to Louis Oppenstein he refused to pay. He was obligated to no one else. He had lost thousands of dollars in the haberdashery, but this was money paid and gone and not owed. He not only lacked debts, he lacked expenses. He and Bess lived in her mother's house. Truman had received pay not only as eastern judge but as ex-officio road commissioner and board of equalization member, clearing about $7,500 a year. He therefore had a life of financial ease, although like most people he groused about his income. In the Senate years he would have to scrimp, but this was due to rent, food, obligatory social entertainments, and the expense of his daughter's schooling. None of this pressed on him in 1925.[3]

While serving as eastern judge Truman planned to become a lawyer. He possibly could have received a law license as a professional courtesy, but he enrolled in the Kansas City School of Law. Tuition was $80.00 a year, and classes were at night so students could hold jobs and faculty members could pursue their legal careers. The staff included such judges and top lawyers as A. L. Cooper, Henry L. Jost, John B. Pew, John Gage, and H. G. Leedy. Truman had fired Cooper as county counselor not long before enrolling under him. Jost was the former Kansas City mayor whom Snapper Truman had harassed. Pew's associates were powerful Pendergast lawyers. Gage would become Kansas City mayor after helping to defeat the Pendergast machine. Leedy was a William Jewell College alum who would head the Federal Reserve Bank. His associate C. B. Liter would figure prominently in the denouement of Truman's last haberdashery obligation. Truman's fellow students included men like ex-Pvt. Al Ridge who stood with Captain Harry at the Battle of Who Run, Charles Whittaker who would ascend to the U.S. Supreme Court, and John E. Aylward of Commerce Trust Co.[4]

The course work was solid, including Blackstone and Kent, criminal and civil. Truman made mostly B's, a few A's, one C. He spent his days administering the county, his nights at school. How he studied is anyone's guess. In the end he gave up, complaining that people pestered him with county business all night long, even in the school library. Nonetheless, his copious notebooks indicate that he obtained a thorough understanding of law, and learned how attorneys and judges think. This background had to give him an edge later as county presiding judge and U.S. Senator. The two years were hardly wasted.[5]

Truman easily slipped back into the business world. As a county judge he mixed with businessmen, and could explore diverse business connections. His current pursuits reflected his two major interests as a county officer—roads and finance. He worked from an office in the Board of Trade building, where he daily circulated among some of the greatest powers in Kansas City finance and business.[6]

Truman hooked up with the fiercely independent Kansas City Automobile Club. This group's activities ranged from the zany (helping "Lieut. Wade, famous United States Army around-the-world flier" in "a feat never before successfully performed: namely, crossing the continent from Los Angeles to New York without once letting the wheels of his car stop turning") to the eminently practical, such as urging motorists to sweep broken glass from roads, erecting danger signs, and advocating dimmer switches for headlights. The last project brought the club into heated conflict with the Automobile Club of Missouri, which opposed the dimmer switch ordinance. Bad blood existed between the two groups over Kansas City's refusal to affiliate with the state organization. The Kansas City outfit, however, was more than an organization offering services such as free towing to members. Members had a handsome clubhouse down in Hickman Mills near the Truman farm, making it a social group. And members included some of Kansas City's biggest shots.[7]

Truman's role in all this was to sell memberships. He set up shop at the 10th and Central club office in downtown Kansas City, and hired a sales force. "I tried out 60 men, and tried them thoroughly, to get five good salesmen." Truman got about $15.00 from the club for each member brought in. He then forked over a percentage of this to the responsible salesman. "It cost me $10,000 to do the job, but I still had enough left for a living." "Enough" was around $5,000, which Truman later termed "substantial." He was irked that the Kansas City group wouldn't consolidate with the state auto club, as he felt he could have sold more memberships then. Truman did this work for about a year and a half, into mid-1926.[8]

While helping the auto club Truman also worked for Farm & Home Savings & Loan Association. His connection came about through his old artillery lieutenant colonel Arthur Elliott who was now manager of Farm & Home's Kansas City office. Another co-worker at Farm & Home was ex-Lt. N. T. Paterson, who had stood with Truman on the deck of the ship taking them to France, the two men speculating about their fate. Truman spent about eight months soliciting accounts for Farm & Home. "Almost any night you could find him calling on those he could not contact during the day," Paterson recalled. He learned about the clientele that savings and loan institutions served, and also saw that the business could be lucrative for insiders—so lucrative that he seized the chance to acquire a savings and loan company of his own. Soon after Truman left, Farm & Home came under close scrutiny due to accusations that officers were cheating borrowers and looting the company. None of this was Truman's doing.[9]

The company Truman acquired was Community Savings & Loan. Some records are missing from archives of investigating state and federal agencies, so the whole story may never be known. The tale of this adventure is twisted. For some participants the result would be financial hardship, Leavenworth Penitentiary, or suicide.

Some people associated with the company, including Truman, claimed that he organized Community Savings & Loan from scratch. This may have been true from a practical standpoint, but the company's origins can be traced to the South Central Savings & Loan Association of Kansas City, which was organized soon after Truman became eastern judge. About a year and a half later the shareholders met at Citizens Security Bank of Englewood (a district near Independence) and changed South Central's name to Community Savings & Loan. Earlier that day the directors elected John K. Hoover president. Two weeks later, in October 1924, Community was apparently reincorporated at Independence.[10]

Truman became involved in September 1925 when he signed a contract to become Community's stock sales manager. He now had his Kansas City Auto Club membership salesmen do double duty as Community stock salesmen. This contract gave Truman virtual control of Community, allowing him to choose two directors, the secretary, the loan committee, and to change Community's by-laws at will. He agreed to pick up all operating expenses of his sales force and of Community itself until the association acquired enough assets to support itself. Truman was to get a 2 percent commission on stock sales. He had big plans for these sales, and immediately raised Community's authorized capital stock from $250,000 to $1 million.[11]

Banks, savings and loan associations, and insurance companies make money in roughly the same way. Deposits and insurance policies are liabilities, debts that the institutions owe to their clients. The stocks that Truman sold were assets, incoming cash that didn't have to be paid out. The money from deposits, insurance policies, and stocks is invested in other securities, business ventures, and house loans. If these investments are sound, the financial institution will make a profit. This return is distributed to depositors as interest on their accounts. If the institution officers pay themselves liberal salaries, sales commissions, and perquisites then these "expenses" must also be paid from the investments income. Any leftover profit goes to stockholders.

Stock sales were important to Truman for generating his sales commissions and for generating assets Community Savings & Loan could use to start its investment program. As with Morgan oil, Community stock was peddled on the installment plan. Truman might sell $1,000 of stock for $20 down and $20 or $50 a month. That 2 percent down payment suggests that Truman got his commission up front. Although Community may have received only $20, this stock sale would be carried on the books as $1,000 in capital stock. This is standard practice in the finance industry, but can make an institution look stronger than it is. When Truman came on board Community had about $6,600 in assets. In February 1926 assets were nearly $28,000, and in August $45,000. In August 1927 assets were nearly $110,000 although $925,000 in stock had been sold (a good example of how the par value of stock in force can distort the true wealth of an enterprise). Stock sales were brisk. In December 1927 Community's board of directors voted to increase the capital stock 50 percent, from $1 million to $1.5 million. Director Jim Clinton— the same Jim Clinton whose drugstore bottles young Harry had dusted thirty years earlier—made the motion for the increase.[12]

Deposits, too, were solicited on the installment plan. The Class A Installment Savings Plan called for $14 a month for sixty months, yielding $1,000 at the end. The Class C Special yielded $1,000 in just thirty-seven months for a monthly deposit of $25. In the Class E Prepaid Plan $550 left for one hundred months yielded $1,000. This type of marketing shows that Community Savings & Loan was designed to serve unsophisticated depositors. Indeed, one man handed Truman $3,000, saying, "I am giving you this money to invest in your savings and loan association because I feel that if I give it to you instead of through the teller's window, you will give it back to me when I need it."[13]

In April 1926 Truman decided to take three partners into his stock selling operation: H. H. Halvorson, Arthur Metzger, and Spencer Salisbury. They called themselves Harry S. Truman & Co. Halvorson was a Kansas City businessman, a friend of Boss Tom Pendergast, and financier for Pendergast's Monroe Hotel. Metzger was a Kansas City leader of DeMolay, a young men's organization affiliated with Masonry. Metzger was also Truman's campaign manager in the 1924 primary. "Snake Eye" Salisbury was a federal Internal Revenue man in Kansas City. The Salisburys were an old-time Independence family, part of the social elite. Snake Eye and Harry served together in the war; Salisbury was captain of Battery E right next to Truman's Battery D. During inspections Salisbury would have one of his men sneak over to another battery and do a little sabotage to make sure the other unit got lower marks. That Snake Eye, what a card. If (like everyone else) he was short on horses, he'd steal them from another battery and leave that unit even shorter. "Carranza and His 40 Thieves" they called him. Snake Eye explained that the function of artillery was to support the morale of our troops rather than accomplish any tactical mission. So he wasn't too worried about hitting the target. Yet Salisbury and Truman somehow became friends in France. Back home Salisbury let Truman use Internal Revenue lists to spot prospects for Kansas City Auto Club memberships. This surely had much to do with Truman's bringing Salisbury into the partnership. Around Independence Snake Eye had a reputation for preferring to slick a dime than earn a dollar, but Truman didn't believe it, and got angry when people tried to warn him.[14]

A few months earlier, in January 1926, Truman acquired Citizens Security Bank of Englewood. His associates in this deal were Salisbury, Metzger, and E. M. Stayton. By law savings and loan institutions can't do all the things banks do, and vice versa, so Truman's idea was to have both a bank and a savings & loan to tap both markets. Citizens Security and Community Savings were already closely linked, with John K. Hoover as president of both. Pistol-packing Paul E. Cole was the Citizens cashier and the Community treasurer. Lou Holland (big in the advertising game and in the Kansas City Chamber of Commerce) was a director of both institutions. Oscar Mindrup (real estate partner of Truman's father) and John Twyman (of the medical family that treated Harry for childhood diphtheria) were other Citizens directors. For reasons not then apparent Citizens had been wheezing along for some years, barely avoiding collapse. Things would get straightened out, and a few months later the bank would be struggling to cover checks drawn on its accounts. George H. Buecking, who had watched over Truman's haberdashery loan at Twelfth Street Bank, thought Citizens cashier Russell Sheffield was untrustworthy. The Missouri Commissioner of Finance was relieved when John Hoover and Paul Cole left, and Truman and his crew came in.[15]

Truman and his people soon discovered the secret of the latest Citizens problems. Paul Cole's brother-in-law was active in Republican politics, and had been interested in acquiring the bank. Cole, however, wound up buying the bank. Missouri secretary of state Charles Becker thirsted after the governorship, and Cole turned the bank over to Truman and his group so Cole could put more time into booming Becker for governor. It turned out that Becker ("the crookedest secretary of state the world has ever seen," Truman said) had illegally deposited $25,000 of state automobile license fees in Citizens, big money for Citizens, which had only $10,000 in capital stock. This deposit had enabled Citizens to make an unsecured $7,500 loan to Becker's newspaper company, an unsecured loan of $500 to one of Becker's newspaper company employees, a $2,000 unsecured loan to Paul Cole, and a $950 loan to Cole's brother-in-law. The

Truman crew found $20,000 in questionable loans at Citizens. They were particularly irked about this because at least $10,000 of these transactions occurred between the time the books were audited on January 25 and the time Truman's group took over on February 1. In that week an additional $3,000 in cash had disappeared, and $5,000 had been paid for worthless bonds sold by the Becker newspaper company employee who had gotten the $500 loan. This meant that Truman and his associates had been cheated, and that Citizens Security Bank of Englewood would fail. The former prospect was irritating, the latter appalling since it would reflect on the stability of Community Savings & Loan, run by the same people who Cole had left holding the bag at Citizens.[16]

Truman and his men immediately set out to save the situation. First they dropped in on Cole and pointed out that these last-minute transactions exceeded his authority as cashier, leaving him personally liable. The group also informed Cole's bonding company, which concurred that he had to repay every penny. In the meantime, Truman's group confiscated $6,000 deposited by Becker's newspaper company, and applied it to the loan. They also held the newspaper company employee's new Nash auto hostage until that $500 was repaid. Cole made good the rest, but (apparently because of Becker's key and continuing role in the bank) in late April the Truman people sold out and left the institution they had spent nearly three months saving. Truman remained as a director for another thirty days to help tidy up, but instead watched the new owners undo everything. Novus Reed (a preacher and William Jewell College alum) and his brother-in-law Manly Houchens were the new owners. Despite warnings Reed and Houchens decided to bring Paul Cole back into the operation. These men let Becker and his associates replace the solid assets with chips and whetstones. The situation became public, and the state threatened to sue Truman and his associates unless Citizens paid back the $25,000 auto license money. Unlike some persons around him, Houchens was an honorable man, and he was horrified. He mortgaged and sold everything he owned, got another $12,000 from his father-in-law (a director in the First National Bank of Independence), and covered the state's $25,000. The bank failed, and with it Houchens's health. Cole's brother-in-law got a ten-year prison sentence for his handling of a St. Louis bank. Houchens committed suicide.[17]

The Citizens episode gave Truman a firsthand lesson in state-level politics. Becker obviously used Citizens to funnel money into his gubernatorial ambitions. Truman's savings and loan associate H. H. Halvorson said that the Citizens crowd was also using the bank to buy their own notes. This is an old insiders' trick. Say you borrow $1,000, and stall on repaying. Instead of suing, the bank sells your note to a friend for $200, and writes off the loss. Then you pay your friend $200 for the note, and that legally clears the debt. In effect you received an $800 gift from the bank, or more accurately, from its depositors. Banks generally fail from such deals rather than from managerial incompetence—the bankers know exactly what they're doing. Truman knew what was going on at Citizens, yet he kept the situation secret. At first this was understandable. He and his men wanted to make Citizens solvent, and this couldn't be done by publicizing insolvency. Yet after achieving that goal they didn't try to manage the bank on honest financial principles. Instead Truman sold out to a crew he knew would cause the bank to fail, and issued no warning to depositors about the past or impending situation. Such a warning in April might have caused a run on the bank, but the bank could have eventually paid all depositors, even if it closed. Instead, Truman let the depositors get reamed.[18]

On almost the same day that Truman sold his interest in Citizens he exercised the authority granted in his 1925 contract with Community Savings & Loan. He appointed Spencer Salisbury to replace Paul Cole as Community treasurer. Truman made himself general manager of Community, leaving John Hoover president in name only (a title Truman would eventually seize also). He also retained Arthur Metzger as secretary, and made H. H. Halvorson a director with a written guarantee that Halvorson would do whatever Truman ordered. Thus the four partners of the aforementioned Harry S. Truman & Co. now ran Community Savings & Loan. They agreed that all Harry S. Truman & Co. income would be deposited in Truman's personal account at the Union Avenue Bank of Commerce, not in the savings and loan association they were promoting. This decision is a telling comment about what Truman and his associates really thought about Community's safety.[19]

The Harry S. Truman & Co. stock selling operation and Community Savings & Loan also peddled insurance. A savings and loan company will typically be connected with insurance, protecting properties on which it holds mortgages. Community was an agent for Milwaukee Mechanics' Insurance Co. Community was also connected with Truman-Barr Insurance Agency, which represented Travelers Insurance Co. of Hartford, Connecticut. Major Robert Barr was a prominent member of the Pendergast Democrat faction and a director of Community Savings & Loan.[20]

The autumn 1927 audit of Harry S. Truman & Co. showed a $1,200 deficit, and revealed that Salisbury was starting to give Truman a hard time, telling the auditor that Truman had never paid $400 owed as a capital contribution to the partnership. In November the four partners changed Harry S. Truman & Co. to a limited partnership called Community Investment Co. They promised to settle all disputes by majority vote, a promise that shows the partners had been fussing. In December they agreed that Truman's contribution of his original Community Savings & Loan stock sales contract would be valued at $400. This suggests that Truman had yet to put any cash into the operation, although the other three partners had. (Truman had thus learned a little from his old oil partners Jerry Culbertson and Dave Morgan.) The bickering continued, and the partnership was dissolved in September 1930 to be replaced by a corporation.

Several interesting events then transpired. The first was an audit showing that Halvorson had lost $3,700 in Community Investment Co., Salisbury $2,200, Truman $400 ($250 in cash and $150 in unpaid commissions), and Metzger $140. The partners had agreed to share all profit and loss equally, but controversy developed on how to fulfill this agreement. Although the same four men were planning to continue Community Investment Co. as a corporation, the partnership was legally terminated. Apparently Salisbury and Metzger thought it was time to settle up. "Judge Truman," Halvorson wrote, "recognizes that the partnership is obligated, particularly to Salisbury and me." Halvorson said he and Truman agreed "that these matters can be straightened out when the [Community Savings & Loan] Association is brought to a point where it can help the Finance Company [Community Investment Co.] carry some of the expenses. The first money drawn from the Association for expenses should be applied on the debts of Salisbury and myself." In other words, Truman and Halvorson felt that Truman shouldn't have to pay off merely because the partnership had been replaced by a corporation. Instead they wanted to reimburse their losses by funneling profits from Community Savings & Loan into the four men's pockets. This was legal, and it had been the plan all along, only Community Savings & Loan wasn't generating profits. Evidently Salisbury was tired of waiting for his money from the yet-to-appear savings and loan profits, and was using the change from partnership to corporation to seek his money from Truman. Halvorson and Truman opposed this as a gyp deal, and insisted that the original plan be adhered to. Salisbury saw this as stalling, grumbling that Truman "is long on promises and short on performance." Metzger supported Salisbury, but since this made a tie vote the original plan proceeded (to reimburse themselves from Community Savings & Loan profits, if any). This division had nothing to do with financial winners and losers. Halvorson and Salisbury were the big losers, while Truman and Metzger had suffered hardly any loss. The dispute was about fairness and ethics.

Salisbury now tried a different tactic. He claimed that Truman's original contract with Community Savings & Loan had expired, permitting Truman to be thrown out of the deal. This claim was contestable since the original contract gave Truman the option to renew it on expiration. Nonetheless, the partnership was renewed without Truman, and converted to a corporation called Rural Investment Co. Rural Investment Co. was a holding company controlling Community Savings & Loan. This meant that stockholders in Community Savings & Loan had no practical say in the savings and loan association's policies. Salisbury, Metzger, and Halvorson were now the only persons whose opinions about Community Savings & Loan counted. "There is no line of demarcation between the Rural Investment Co. and the Community Savings & Loan," Halvorson wrote. (At this point the capital stock of Community Savings & Loan was at least $2.5 million, but assets were closer to $500,000. Moreover, Truman's policy of installment sales, which boosted sales volume and generated just as much commission money per sale as paid-in-full sales since the commission came from the first installment, created a chronic cash shortage in the Association since payments only dribbled in.) Halvorson insisted that Truman be issued one-fourth of the Rural Investment Co. stock. Snake Eye Salisbury, however, never seemed to get around to giving Truman the stock. Halvorson decided to drop out, writing Salisbury, "It is evident from

.

the books that there has been no friendly feeling, and to some extent a decidedly dishonest attitude." Halvorson added, "There is every indication that from the very start of your making your deal with me it has been with the intention of getting something for nothing, and I do not retract in any way that there has been dishonesty in this matter." Truman snorted, "So far as Metzger and Salisbury are concerned I am through with them in a business way, and they can take the Community [Savings & Loan Association] and run it into the ground or any place else they care to." Halvorson said Truman immediately went to work to help ruin the association: "He has done considerable to retard the growth of the Association and has caused withdrawals of stock certificates to the amount of $25,000—that is, so he states." This activity not only threatened Salisbury but also endangered the savings accounts of innocent depositors. Truman secretly wrote of his frustration. "My private business has gone to pot so that I'll be worse than pauper when I'm done. I was a Battery Commander in 1918, and I made a partner of another one in the same outfit, who used me for his own ends, robbed me, got me into a position where I couldn't shoot him without hurting a lot of innocent bystanders, and laughed at me." Over the next few years Truman would watch Salisbury's handling of Community Savings & Loan with a gimlet eye, and would one day take sudden and terrible revenge.[21]

Chapter 10

THE MASTER MACHINIST

Am I an administrator or not? Or am I just a crook to compromise in order to get the job done? You judge it, I can't.

—Harry S. Truman[1]

While Truman was making a living in private business a few changes took place on the political scene. One resulted from a chance encounter between Tom Pendergast and the leader of the rival Shannon faction. The Shannon men had joined with the Republicans to defeat Truman and McElroy in November 1924. A year later the two factional chiefs accidentally met on a downtown Kansas City sidewalk and ventilated their grievances before a fascinated and ever-growing audience. Breaking off the public argument, they met in private a day or two later and patched up their differences. So any ticket the leaders jointly endorsed would win the county elections in 1926. A second change was the new Kansas City charter establishing a city manager government. Instead of electing a mayor to run things, the people now elected a nine-member city council that hired a city manager to run things. Hailed as a good government reform, the change soon proved to be a politician's dream come true. The nadir of decadence would not be reached for another five or six decades when the council members with accountability to voters but no responsibility for city policies, and the city manager with responsibility but no accountability, would refine buck passing to a fine art. In the beginning, however, no one doubted who ran the city. The Pendergast councilmen hired Judge Henry McElroy as city manager. McElroy had supreme authority over just about every city activity, and would rule Kansas City as an irascible dictator until 1939 when Tom departed from politics. McElroy could violate any provision of the city charter, shortcut any procedure, defy any request for access to city records, as long as he had the support of the Pendergast councilmen.[2]

With the beginning of city manager government in Kansas City the Pendergast organization became the Pendergast machine, and factional chief Tom Pendergast became Boss Tom. The appellation "Boss" has been used in this book to distinguish Tom from his assorted relatives and colleagues, but not until this point has the title been earned. Other factions continued to exist, and their desires affected Pendergast machine actions; but the era of Pendergast rule had now begun in Kansas City.

In 1926 Truman aspired to be county collector, an unglamorous but lucrative job. Not everyone was diligent about paying county taxes, and the collector received fees for various receipts that he managed to bring in. Truman thought he could set a record in tax collections and earn perhaps $25,000 a year or more, enough to settle all haberdashery debts at par and pay the Grandview farm mortgage. Truman was part of the eastern Jackson County Pendergast operation, and asked the eastern leader Mike Pendergast for the collector job. Mike felt that Truman was the man, and urged his brother to slate Truman for the job. But Boss Tom felt obligated to W. T. "Banker Bill" Kemper, of the Commerce banks and former associate of Truman's father. (The choice of McElroy for city manager had been made at a conference in Kemper's office.) He insisted on one of Kemper's friends for collector, a friend who (Truman felt) split the fees with Kemper. Tom made a counteroffer, however, to slate Truman for presiding judge. Mike carried the word back to Truman and, in an extraordinary gesture of personal regard, promised to swing the eastern Jackson County Pendergast organization behind Truman if he wanted to challenge Kemper's friend in the primary. Truman refused to divide the loyalties of the Pendergast organization, and accepted the presiding judge nomination in the interests of party harmony.[3]

Truman had no primary election opposition, and the election of an all-Democrat county court in November 1926 went smoothly. The other two members of the court were Howard Vrooman and Robert Barr. Western Judge Vrooman was an insurance and real estate man, one of downtown Kansas City's live wires. "The most accomplished host I ever met," Truman said of him, "an all around good fellow." This evaluation was the more remarkable because Truman was aware of Vrooman's philandering. Normally Truman regarded such conduct as wicked, but was sympathetic about Vrooman's marital situation. Vrooman was from the Pendergast-allied Shannon Democrat faction. Some folks seemed to wonder if Barr was a Shannon man also, but he was Truman's personal choice for eastern judge, and was disowned by the Shannon faction. Major Barr was a West Pointer, a gentleman dairy farmer affiliated with Truman's Community Savings & Loan enterprise. Truman expected great cooperation from Barr, and would be bitterly disappointed.[4]

"You will no doubt have an opportunity to repay some of the old scores," Snapper told Harry. The new county court held an informal but official session on January 1, 1927 to get started on that task. On Truman's motion the court unanimously rescinded the outgoing court's appointments the previous day of two justices of the peace, one of whom was a Bulger follower. On Barr's motion the court unanimously decided to investigate, with the intention of voiding, the $9,000 purchase of a forty-acre farm from Todd George for a proposed black girls parental home. George's "Independent Democrats" were a Ku Klux Klan political arm that had helped oust Truman two years previously and had tried their damnedest to prevent his return this time. A while later Truman announced that the county livestock superintendent for the previous Republican county court was unable to account for $1,000 of transactions and that the case would be turned over to the county prosecutor unless the ex-superintendent presented a good explanation quick. The court made Truman family lawyer Fred Boxley county counselor, with Truman's Community Savings & Loan associate Rufus Burrus as assistant. Soon afterward the county court would also rent space from Truman's Community Investment Co. On January 3, 1927 the court had its first formal session. Truman announced, and the other two judges concurred, that although they intended to give Democrats jobs, the court intended for taxpayers to get full value from these workers. The *Kansas City Star* reported that Truman then "cleared his throat and said: 'Now we'll proceed to appoint some Democrats to office.' " The court appointed several dozen.[5]

Although the new county court started out little different from any of its predecessors, Truman gradually revealed some unusual—unheard of, really—plans. He seemed to have a vision of the future and of what Jackson County government should do to improve the lives of its citizens. Such vision among politicians is unusual; even more extraordinary was the ability Truman would demonstrate in implementing these plans. No misty dreamer, he had the savvy needed to accomplish these goals. In the next eight years he would prove himself to be no mere administrator, but a leader of fellow citizens, convincing them that his vision should be theirs, showing the paths that had to be used, and bringing them safely along those paths to the sought-after goals. No charisma was involved; no throngs knelt before him. To friends he was the same old Harry. And yet one can feel a sense of wonderment about what he was doing.

Even before taking office Truman announced that he wanted to create a modern road system for Jackson County. Decades later this sounds like no big deal; but at the time the announcement was audacious indeed, rather like announcing movies that talked or a campaign to make electricity available to farmers. A modern road system would change the lives of rural residents, knocking down walls of isolation between neighbors and between countryside and urban Kansas City. The latter change would have a definite, measurable effect on commerce. Keep in mind that Truman wasn't talking about mere improvement and extension of roads. He was talking about starting from zero, hiring the best engineers available, using the latest scientific knowledge in survey and construction, putting the roads where projections of traffic needs said the highways were required, linking the roads in a coherent system that enhanced the usefulness of each thoroughfare, and moreover, doing this for every section of the county simultaneously. Such a project would have an effect Truman didn't publicize at the time, but which his subsequent actions suggest he realized. The road system would encourage certain rural towns to thrive as small commercial or light industrial centers, and discourage future growth of other locales. Thus Truman was anticipating and guiding economic development of the region around Kansas City. Such intervention by a government official was specified by no statute or regulation, and was an unprecedented seizure of power. Had Truman proclaimed what he was doing, he might have been blocked. Instead his actions, step by step, made so much sense that the general populace and mercantile elite rallied around him.[6]

Barely two weeks after taking office Truman announced the appointment of Ed Stayton and N. T. Veatch to survey county road needs with highway engineer Koehler, the man who had fought Truman so vigorously before. Truman felt that Koehler had neither the professional expertise nor the personal honesty to direct such work. As a matter of politics the county's senior and Republican highway official couldn't be ignored in rebuilding the entire road system, but Koehler's role would be advisory only. Stayton—hero of the Argonne, long-time Pendergast politician, and expert public works engineer—was the same fellow that Truman and McElroy had hired to examine county roads four years earlier. Veatch was another well-regarded public works engineer, and a Republican. Veatch's participation made it hard for Koehler or any other Republican to squawk.[7]

A few days after Truman commissioned the survey he began seeking support for a bond issue to finance the survey's recommendations, sight unseen. Truman had already raised the special road and bridge fund levy from $12\sqrt[3]{4}$¢ per $100 of property valuation, to 15¢. (He also reduced the jury and elections levy, so taxes didn't rise. This was a change in allocations rather than a change in taxes or revenue.) The levy change brought road money up to about $900,000 a year, which was barely enough to maintain the current state of disrepair. The county court could raise the levy to 25¢, but this still wouldn't generate the initial capital outlay needed to build a modern road system. So Truman decided to promote a bond issue, a technique that had never been used to finance Jackson County roads. Convincing the politicians was easy since public works meant patronage jobs and profits for favored contractors. Truman made plain that he intended to give contracts only to the lowest responsible bidder, and Boss Tom voiced no objection. Had Pendergast thought Truman could actually pull off the election, the discussion about contractors might have been more heated—as indeed it became later when Truman stunned Boss Tom by winning the bond election. Bond propositions were traditional losers in Kansas City and Jackson County, largely because the opportunities for boodle were so obvious to taxpayers. Truman overcame such objections with his promise that contracts would be awarded on merit, a promise given credibility by his choice of professional engineers to plan the system. This helped get the backing of Taxpayers League president Marvin Gates, a prominent Republican and Truman's old war major. Another factor was that a coordinated road system would increase property values by several times more than the money spent on the roads—like spending $5.00 on roads to increase real estate by $30.00. It was a paying proposition, which probably influenced real estate board leader Louis Oppenstein to support the project. Passage of the $6.5 million road bonds was the more remarkable because while all the roads would be outside of Kansas City, Kansas City taxpayers would foot almost the entire tab. Nonetheless, Kansas City voters, who controlled the outcome of any countywide election, voted for Truman's road system. The election demonstrated that Truman could rally a coalition of rich and poor, Democrat and Republican, urban and rural, to support an expensive project that had demonstrable public benefits. The vote came on Truman's birthday, May 8, 1928.[8]

Truman and Boss Tom clashed over letting the contracts for the road construction. Much to his chagrin Pendergast learned that Truman intended to follow through on his commitment to award contracts on merit. Pendergast explained that bids could be rigged to give the appearance of honesty while guaranteeing the job to a particular bidder. Truman continued to insist that Pendergast keep his promise to make this project honest. Boss Tom raged at Truman when contracts actually were awarded on merit, claiming that Truman was just trying to make a national reputation for engineers Stayton and Veatch, telling Truman that the personal honor he prized was a worthless commodity. Truman continued to withstand the pressure even when Tom made him face John Pryor, William D. Boyle, and Mike Ross personally. These were road contractors who had been favored in the past. They argued that it was only fair to give some preference to local builders, businessmen whose taxes were after all helping to fund the county's greatest construction project. Truman turned them down, and Pendergast called him the contrariest cuss in Missouri. Although Truman saved the bond money from Pendergast theft, the boss used eastern judge Barr to siphon the regular revenues. "This sweet associate of mine," Truman wrote of Barr, "my friend, who was supposed to back me had already made a deal with a former crooked contractor, a friend of the Boss's who had robbed Jackson County." Truman moaned, "I had to compromise . . . I had to let a former saloon keeper and murderer, a friend of the Big Boss, steal about $10,000 from the general revenues of the county to satisfy my ideal associate [Barr] and to keep the crooks from getting a million or more out of the bond issue. Was I right, or did I compound a felony? I don't know." Truman admitted that he eventually allowed $1 million to be stolen from general revenues in order to protect $7 million of bond money. Pendergast told Truman that most men were dishonest when they had the opportunity to steal, and patiently waited for Truman to join the crowd. Truman sighed, "I hope that there are no more bond issues and no more trouble until I'm done, and then maybe I can run a filling station or something until I've run my three score and ten and go to a quiet grave."[9]

In May 1931, three years after the first road bonds were approved, voters authorized another $3.5 million in bonds to put finishing touches on the system. This was a firm expression of confidence in Truman's ability to produce high-quality public works projects. Boss Tom had ostensibly become a convert to Truman's honest county construction, and in the same election used Truman's reputation to help pass $32 million in city bonds that would be administered by the more cooperative Henry McElroy. Pendergast made Truman's honesty in the county pay off in much larger Kansas City municipal contracts. Truman immediately violated the campaign pledge to pay off one-twentieth of the new twenty-year bonds each year. The actual retirement schedule for $1 million in bonds sold by September 30 showed that nothing would be paid until 1936, with total annual payments gradually ballooning from $55,000 that year to $70,000 in 1951. Thus Truman didn't have to come up with any money to pay off the bonds. This would be left to his successors, who would have to find more and more money as the years went by.

One matter Truman did have to deal with immediately that autumn indicated the growing seriousness of the Depression. Crowds of unemployed men, two and three hundred strong, began halting road construction, protesting that contractors were importing coolie labor from Kansas at 20¢ an hour, which took work from Jackson County residents whose taxes paid for the work. The protestors demanded 40¢ an hour. County highway engineer Koehler said the current pay ranged from 22½¢ to 35¢ an hour. He suggested 45¢ an hour for two shifts of six hours, reasoning that the expense would be negligible since efficiency in cement work declined after six hours anyway. Two shifts could complete the work in fewer hours, making up for the higher wage. This would double employment and give each worker enough to scrape by with. Truman didn't seem to endorse that plan, but he did admit there was currently no minimum wage on the road project. "The next contracts will have a minimum wage provision," he promised. "We recommended that no contractor pay less than 30¢ an hour. The contracts do state specifically that 75% Jackson County men are to be employed. We allowed the contractors an optional 25% so they can use their own technical men and workers." Even if Pendergast-favored contractors failed to win bids, many patronage jobs were still available for the faithful. Apparently the interference with road construction stopped after Truman's announcement.[10]

The completed road system was a wonder. Three hundred miles had been laid, over half in concrete. Professional engineers and honest contractors did the work so economically that some extra miles were constructed. And even then money was left over. Truman transferred part to the special road and bridge fund, and blew the rest on a monster barbeque to which the entire population of Jackson County was invited. Technically this may have been a misuse of bond money, but not even the flintiest bookkeeper complained about the celebration. Appropriately the huge feed was held in a rural setting, reachable on the roads. Free maps were passed out at the event, showing off the system. The full glory had to be experienced to be appreciated; driving comfortably mile after mile over wooded hills and through lush valleys, revealing eastern Jackson County's pastoral splendor. Farmers could scarcely believe the change in their lives, with no one more than two and a half miles from an all-weather hardtop road. Generations of rural isolation ended. One orator gushed, "We no longer follow the trails of the Buffalo and the Indian. From now on we follow the Trails of Truman."[11]

When construction of the road system started Truman began to argue that Jackson County highways should be coordinated with the roads of other counties in the Kansas City vicinity. He went further yet, suggesting coordination of other activities such as sewer lines, rural parks, waterways, railroads, and land use zoning. "People have an idea, when city planning or regional planning is mentioned, that some Highbrow who spells Art with a capital A is going to tell us how everyone can live in a palace on a boulevard with no smoke-stacks, no rail yards, no tall buildings." But, Truman explained, "a regional plan is nothing less than the proper and scientific laying out of land for the proper care of large populations. . . . Cities have found that ideal factory sites have been made into poor residence sections and that good business sections have been ruined." Truman said that proper planning could save large amounts of money wasted in haphazard development, in addition to utilizing the land and resources of the region for the long-term benefit of all citizens rather than for the quick profits of real estate operators. Emphasizing that this was no crackpot theory, he ticked off a list of cities who suc-cessfully implemented such planning; he even brought in the director of Chicago's regional plan to explain how such activity had benefited that metropolitan area.

Then, to the amazement and admiration of the *Kansas City Times,* Truman proceeded with the support of civic groups to pull together such an interstate regional planning organization with representa-tives from the governments and commercial interests of six counties surrounding Kansas City in Missouri and Kansas. "Interesting and important," the *Times* called it. "It means much for the future de-velopment of a large metropolitan and semi-metropolitan area. It involves conservation of land values, the protection of residential areas and the promotion of order and attractiveness, together with the best possible relation of connecting highways and transportation facilities. His [Truman's] leadership made him the choice of the six counties for chairmanship."[12]

Under Truman's leadership the Greater Kansas City Regional Plan Association began rudimentary coordination of economic de-velopment in the six counties, just as the Jackson County road system had influenced such development in Truman's county. Highway engineers of the six counties planned road needs for each county, and the six plans were then coordinated by Truman's engineers Stayton and Veatch in cooperation with the state highway commis-sions of Missouri and Kansas. Rather than attempt major construction as Jackson County was doing, the idea was gradually to correct engineering deficiencies as regional roads wore out and were rebuilt. As president of the regional plan association, Truman asked Congressman Jim Ruffin of Missouri to get the support of Representatives John Cochran and Tuck Milligan for "a bill in which I am vitally interested. This bill is a ratification of a treaty between Kansas and Missouri regarding a toll bridge between Kansas City, Kansas, and Platte County" in Missouri. Truman explained, "The Democratic organization of Kansas City [the Pendergast machine] is very much interested in the construction of this bridge because it will make another traffic way to the [horse] race track in Platte County." Ruffin was under deep obligation to Boss Tom, and had turned down a previous invitation to show gratitude. Ruffin and Milligan pushed the bridge bill through. Probably because of Pendergast involvement the *Kansas City Star* opposed the bridge, but it was built. Truman explained the *Star*'s "selfish policy ever since they have been in town. Old Bill Nelson established a cemetery at Mount Washington to keep a beautiful residence district from being built on Blue Ridge so his Rockhill district could be properly developed." (Baron Bill Nelson was supreme ruler of the *Star* for many years.) Truman later accused the *Star* of opposing proper regional flood control due to opposition of the Union Pacific railroad, "a great advertiser in the *Star*." Truman declared, "I have tried to be fair to every section of the Greater Kansas City area, which includes three counties in Kansas and three in Missouri, and the development of which is just as important to the whole town as that section in which the *Star* is personally interested."[13]

In spring 1932 Truman got out a handsome book celebrating the benefits of county and regional planning. The book was distributed only to libraries and to government officials in Missouri and elsewhere. Even a half-century later the volume's sweeping beauty engages the reader. Lavishly illustrated with superb photos of peaceful countryside and thriving commerce, every page of *Results of County Planning* projected love for the land and towns and people. Again and again the book emphasized that such beneficial results can be achieved elsewhere, and that planning is no theoretician's dream: "The county plan was based on *practical* needs; it was carried out along *practical* lines; its effects will be for the *practical* benefit of every citizen." In a cover letter Truman invited government officials to tell him what they thought about county planning. The book was a gripping advertisement of Truman's achievements, and projected him as an extraordinary leader. Distribution to influential political leaders around the state was probably related to Truman's ambitions for higher and statewide office. "Men with vision build empires," the *Independence Examiner* said. "Presiding Judge Harry S. Truman has a vision of Jackson County as the center of such a marvelous development in roads, in manufacturing establishments, in river navigation, and in good government, that it will exceed all other parts of the United States. He is able to point out the raw materials, and suggests that all that is needed to make this vision come true is the unselfish cooperation of the people who live in this district."

Truman sighed, "OH! if I were only John D. or Mellon or Wait Phillips I'd make this section (six counties) the world's real paradise. What's the use wishing. I'm still going to do it." Yet when he went to Washington his regional planning died. Truman, and Truman alone, provided the inspiration for this activity. He had failed to make his dream that of the region's citizens, but the rise and fall of the effort demonstrated his pivotal role in making things happen.[14]

While it lasted, the planning efforts brought Truman a statewide and national reputation in the field. The Missouri State Planning Association was formed in 1930 with Truman as chairman. In December 1933 Governor Park, at the association's request, appointed a state planning board to cooperate with New Deal national planning programs. E. M. Stayton was made vice-chairman of this board. Members included Truman, his nurseryman friend Lloyd Stark, and Kansas City's mammoth real estate developer J. C. Nichols. Truman found planning regarded as an alien New Deal philosophy on the state level, and became discouraged and wondered whether to continue. "The planning organization should not be abandoned," Lloyd Stark assured him. "No worthy cause was ever won in the first fight or in the first few years." The Regional Adviser to the National Planning Board of the Federal Emergency Administration of Public Works echoed Truman's glum assessment of Missouri planning, but noted that, nonetheless, Missouri had the best operation in that region. The adviser praised Truman's Greater Kansas City association. Truman's activities won him election to the board of directors of the National Conference on City Planning in 1930, an organization founded at the turn of the century.[15]

Truman was also active as president of the National Old Trails Association, an office he gained in 1926 and held for many years thereafter. One of several national road groups, this one emphasized remembrance of the pioneer routes that modern highways followed. Truman became a mine of trivia about old-time roads. Some of Kansas City's most prominent mercantile leaders were active in Old Trails, and this work brought Truman into contact with highway officials of various states. He emphasized to local civic leaders that Jackson County roads and federal cross-country highways were vitally interrelated (indeed, the new county system was designed to integrate with and enhance national highways passing through the county). He warned that transcontinental highway traffic was being routed to avoid Kansas City. Truman accused the Kemper family's Commerce Trust Company of contributing to this situation. He urged upon civic leaders the need for a lobbyist to attend all meetings of the National Association of State Highway Officials to promote Kansas City highways to Dallas, Memphis, Omaha, Minneapolis, Chicago, and Los Angeles.[16]

In addition to the county road system Truman promoted another expensive construction project, erection of a new county courthouse in Kansas City and renovation of the one in Independence. (Jackson County had two county seats, requiring duplicate county offices although the Independence operation was on a much smaller scale.) In 1926 Truman believed the courthouse facilities were adequate, but he eventually changed his mind. Suspense-filled elevator trips in the Kansas City building may have been a factor, and the oil-soaked wooden floors definitely concerned Truman. He worried about the fire hazard. In addition to the deaths and injuries a fire could cause, Truman pondered the loss of county records, particularly real estate transactions. The cost of reconstructing such files would be appalling, and the commercial chaos unthinkable. Truman now proclaimed, "Our present courthouse has been used 45 years, and that is 40 years too long." Bond issues for a new courthouse were a perennial request submitted to voters, always failing due to expectations of graft. Truman's reputation and the demonstrated need succeeded in authorizing several million dollars this time.[17]

The great question then was where the Kansas City courthouse would be located. This would affect values and commercial development of nearby properties in a big way. A group led by big real estate operator William Scarritt wanted the location to be a few blocks south of the current location. Truman treated this proposal in a most frosty manner, favoring a location a few blocks farther south yet. Reportedly Truman was so set on the latter location that he announced selection of the site before all the property lots were acquired. Truman wasn't the sort of administrator to make such a mistake, and speculation arose about what the announcement meant if it wasn't a mistake. "Who benefits?" It was said that persons privy to Truman's intentions got options to buy land in the area, but a premature announcement should have provided no advantage to them—they would have wanted the announcement delayed, not hastened. The newspapers said Truman failed to coordinate his announcement with city manager McElroy; and since Kansas City was pretty much committed to building a new city hall adjacent to the courthouse, this boosted the price for that land since observers then knew where the city hall would have to be. So those landowners benefited. Another line of speculation, unpublicized and confidential, was that Truman may have been trying to hasten payment of the commission to the real estate man who assembled the courthouse site. Newspapers credited Thomas Y. Willock as the man who did this. Willock was a Truman relative. Another realtor, George B. Tracy, claimed that he assembled the site, and that Jackson County counselor Fred Boxley forced Tracy to cut Willock in on the deal. Tracy claimed to possess, but was never asked to produce, documentary evidence proving that he turned over two-thirds of the $24,000 commission to Willock. (Property owners paid their commissions to Kansas City Title & Trust Co., which apparently then paid Tracy and Willock.) Tracy claimed that he was told that the $16,000 would eventually go to Truman who (Tracy was allegedly told) needed to save the Grandview farm from mortgage foreclosure. Tracy said Truman's desperation about the farm caused premature announcement of the courthouse site selection.[18]

Tracy's story remains unproven, but several things give it some credibility (or at least indicate that Tracy was a shrewd guesser). Although it was a closely guarded secret, Fred Boxley actually did handle sensitive financial arrangements for Truman, constructing layers of go-betweens to hide Truman's involvement. If anyone were to arrange for the real estate commission money to go to Truman, that arranger would have been Boxley. Another secret was that

Truman actually was desperate about the farm mortgage and feared his mother would die if the land were lost. While sniffing hopefully around this story a *Kansas City Star* reporter discovered that soon after the courthouse deal was closed (and presumably the commission paid) the Grandview farm mortgage held by Bank of Belton was released on August 15, 1932, and the mortgage held by J. F. Blair was released the next day. In December 1932 Truman's mother conveyed several lots of land to Willock Realty & Loan Corp., apparently for $5,000. Willock then transferred it (presumably sold it) to Sidney Silverman of the First National Bank in Kansas City. When a *Star* reporter asked Silverman about this he suffered a lapse of memory. The reporter speculated that the transaction was to pay Tom Willock for his role in funneling the courthouse site commission money to Truman. Tracy's story is unproven, but it can't be dismissed. Yet had all of this happened, there would have been nothing illegal unless selection of the courthouse site were somehow influenced by who would get the real estate commission. The layers of go-betweens would have been to save Truman publicity and embarrassment, not to hide anything criminal.[19]

After Truman announced the courthouse site W. S. Scarritt's McCoy Land Co. filed a harassment suit to delay the project. Finally property owners in the vicinity of Truman's site paid McCoy Land Co. over $35,000 to drop the suit. Although Truman rightly noted that the money didn't come from the county, some observers feared the settlement was an invitation for further litigation that *would* raid the public treasury.[20]

A concurrent great question was the design of the building. In early 1931, before voters had even approved the bonds, Truman took a two-thousand-four-hundred-mile trip through the South and Southwest to get ideas. Upon his return he told the press he liked the Caddo Parish courthouse in Louisiana. Eventually he would hire the architect of that building to help design Jackson County's. Truman announced that the structure would be a skyscraper, the tallest building in Missouri. Labor trouble simmered throughout the construction, including one major strike before the climactic dispute in January 1934. Coincidental with the assassination of a Kansas City carpenters union leader, a Teamsters organizer who had just been indicted for bombing a local trucking company showed up at the courthouse site and did some fast and fancy brass-knuckle work on a nonunion driver. (Most truck drivers throughout town were nonunion since the Teamsters had yet to organize a single company in Kansas City.) The employer of the beaten driver was also roughed up at the site, and summoned police. This precipitated a general strike since union rules forbade members to work under police protection. Many observers, including CWA men who were working for a fraction of courthouse construction wages, were astounded that laborers would go on strike when they had no grievance about wages, job conditions, or their employer. Truman exploded, "I don't care if they don't go back at all. That's the kind of humor I'm in today. The workmen walked out for no good reason at all, and they're trying to use the county court as a catspaw in this dispute to force the unionization of a trucking company. They won't succeed." He added, "I have 3000 applications for work on my desk. The unions were given the first chance. If they intend to work the job they had better do it. It is provided in the contract that the county court can step in on a labor dispute after construction has been stopped for 10 days. And so I can say the work will start at the end of 10 days. If we have to take charge of the situation the job will be thrown open to the employment of labor on the basis of competence and skill at NRA wages, which are much lower than union wages." (Indeed, courthouse wages had been set at the 1932 level rather than the bargain Depression level that could have been obtained when construction began.) Regardless of the specifics in this dispute, Truman's declaration was the standard Pendergast machine line supporting management over labor. The machine felt less need for labor union votes than for employer money contributions. Truman's stand had the desired effect. The *Kansas City Times* reported, "A meeting of 100 employers, representing most of the larger industrial concerns in Kansas City, yesterday applauded the stand taken by Judge Truman and agreed to back him to the limit." The strike ended. The grand dedication of the nearly completed building was held in December 1934, shortly before Truman left Jackson County to take his seat in the United States Senate. Truman predicted the county wouldn't need to build a replacement courthouse for fifty years.[21]

For the much smaller job of remodeling the Independence county courthouse Truman hired his brother-in-law Fred Wallace as architect.

All these public works projects were grand for the county and the citizens and the construction workers, but there remained the not insignificant question of just how Truman was going to pay for all

JACKSON COUNTY FINANCES DURING TRUMAN'S YEARS AS EASTERN JUDGE AND PRESIDING JUDGE

Tax Levy
(¢ per $100 of Property Valuation)

Year	Current Expenses	Road and Bridge Fund	Interest and Retirement of Bonds	Total Levy
1923	28	15	0	43
1924	30	13	0	43
1927	32	13	0	45
1928	33	12	0	45
1929	35	12	4	51
1930	35	15	7	57
1931	35	15	7	57
1932	35	14	8	57
1933	33	11	15	59
1934	—	—	—	—

this. It was fine to sell bonds, but the bondholders had to be repaid—with interest. The county also had to meet all other expenses, from the sheriff's department to the old folks' home. This had to be done within the perimeters of state laws mandating certain expenses and restricting income generation, with an ever-shrinking tax base during the Depression. Truman had to find the money. This job was as important as anything else he did as presiding judge.

To grasp the scale of forces Truman had to fight, a few numbers are appropriate. These figures come from the files of a private think tank called the Civic Research Institute. Its director Walter Matscheck made the outfit a force among local reform politicians in the Pendergast era. Its studies have stood as models of objectivity and accuracy. The Institute had its own accountants; unlike various county officials and their specially hired accountants who changed from year to year (and even from department to department), the Institute used the same bases for computation—allowing a fair comparison of one year's figures with another's. To retain this fairness, no attempt has been made to fill in gaps with numbers from other sources that may have used different bookkeeping procedures.

JACKSON COUNTY FINANCES DURING
TRUMAN'S YEARS AS EASTERN JUDGE
AND PRESIDING JUDGE (CONTINUED)

% of Levy Collected in Current Fiscal Year	Taxes Received per Capita (dollars)	Total Operating Revenue from All Sources (millions of dollars)	Total Operating Expenditures (millions of dollars)
85.4	7.55	3.0	2.7
84.5	7.54	3.1	3.3
81.8	7.74	3.4	3.4
80.6	7.66	3.5	4.1
80.0	7.94	3.7	3.6
77.5	8.10	3.8	4.8
75.5	8.24	4.0	3.7
68.2	6.55	3.2	3.6
—	—	—	—
—	—	—	—

What do these numbers mean? Presiding Judge Truman steadily raised taxes as the Depression worsened; they rose by about 33 percent. Most of the increase, however, came from bond issues that voters approved. When the Depression started Truman held taxes for regular expenses steady and even reduced that levy. The same goes for the special road and bridge fund from which road maintenance was paid; part of that reduction may be attributed to the promised maintenance savings provided by the new highway system (the construction of which was funded from bonds). In every year Truman served on the court, the problem of delinquent taxes grew. It is one thing to levy taxes, and another to collect. Eventually about 10 percent of the levy would come in delinquently, and the remaining delinquency never. The figures show that more and more persons postponed this liability as the Depression worsened. Nonetheless, total county operating income showed a steady rise until 1932. The staggering drop that year was partly an artifact of the accounting system used by the Civic Research Institute, because unlike other years the 1932 figure includes no delinquent taxes eventually collected. Even taking that into consideration, however, a real drop occurred. Unlike operating revenue, operating expenditures fluctuated wildly, putting the county into the red in even-numbered years when enormous election expenses had to be absorbed (the price of democracy). The trend was ominous for county solvency, with an ever-shrinking tax base during the Depression and a growing delinquent tax problem. The Depression had begun to impoverish Jackson County.[22]

Meeting payrolls became a problem as the Depression worsened. This was aggravated by the state legislature, which in its wisdom raised the salaries of many county employees while neglecting to provide revenue to cover the raises. The crunch came in December 1930 when the county salary fund was $250,000 short and still diminishing. For the first time in years banks refused to cash salary warrants at face value. County employees had to take a 10 to 15 percent discount as Christmas approached. Since these warrants themselves drew 6 percent interest until redeemed by the county, the banks were cleaning up on the salary fund shortage. With no additional revenue in sight Truman dealt with the situation by cutting the county payroll 15 percent as 1931 began. He gave department heads a choice of firing workers or reducing pay. Although some pay reductions would later be ruled illegal (since state law set many salaries), the retrenchment went smoothly in many departments (perhaps because some employees may have been Pendergast Ghosts whose sole work was to pick up their pay). Prosecutor Jim Page balked, however. Truman took matters into his own hands, and fired five of the prosecutor's six investigators. Page was able to do a credible job demonstrating that Truman's action saved no money, since the work had to be done by sheriff employees at a slower rate, which added other expenses. Since Truman was a master of county minutiae, he surely knew this as well as Page. Questions therefore arose about Truman's motive. Some observers felt he had done this in consultation with Boss Tom to cripple Page's attacks on organized crime controlled by the Pendergast machine. (Page's work is recounted later.) The public outcry was fierce, and Truman soon allowed the investigators back on the prosecutor's staff. He continued trying to reduce the county payroll in later years. In 1932 he asked all elected officials and some others to take a 10 percent salary cut. The response was underwhelming. In 1933 he fired 139 workers.[23]

A state law requiring county budgets passed in 1933. "Gov. Park made a speech in which he told McElroy—not me, that his (Park's) budget bill for counties would cure Jackson County's going into the red. The dear governor's county budget bill is an extract from my county reorganization bill—just one of the features of it." (This reorganization is discussed shortly.) "McElroy has evidently told Park that I am a very extravagant official and need checking," Truman groused. "I'll lick the whole gang yet, and make 'em like it." The tenor of these remarks showed tensions within the Pendergast machine despite its outward monolithic appearance. Indeed, Truman feared that disgruntled county officers would talk Pendergast governor Park into vetoing the bill. At the time Truman hailed the new law's mandate for fiscal responsibility, but one wonders if he was still as enthusiastic in November 1933 when he announced the 1934 budget. The law prohibited a deficit. Faced with declining revenue and the mandatory extra expense of conducting elections that year, Truman slashed spending so drastically that even he admitted the county government could no longer function properly. He called for firing 313 of the remaining 696 employees. The county's McCune boys' home requested $75,000 for 1934. On the request Truman noted, "Can't operate for less than called for," yet spending more than $47,000 could cause a deficit. Truman had to make up the difference by shaving small amounts here and there. He cut $20 from the $200 Third District Justice of the Peace telephone and telegraph allotment, and eliminated all janitor supplies for the Sixth District Justice of the Peace, thereby saving the county $41.20. A few days after announcing the austere budget Truman led an off-the-record panel discussion about the budget law at a conference in Columbia, Missouri, attended by many government leaders from around the state. The sparse account of the proceedings indicates that participants were not altogether happy about the new era of fiscal responsibility. A year later as Truman prepared to take his U.S. Senate seat, the situation for the 1935 county budget was little different. In both years Truman blamed the state board of equalization for much of the problem by cutting real estate valuations, which in turn reduced revenue that the county levy generated. "The only remedy I can see is some other source of revenue for the county or to close out a lot of services and send some 30 percent of the paupers home or turn them out on the streets."[24]

Truman therefore felt that a new, scientific assessment of Jackson

County real estate property values was crucial. Over the years personnel of varying competence and political allegiance in the county assessor's office had created a mishmash that favored some property owners, penalized others, and cheated the county of its due. Truman traveled to St. Paul, Milwaukee, and Cincinnati searching for an assessment plan that would work. He found one: The Cincinnati plan considered types of frontages in addition to square feet, potential use of the land (farm, manufacturing, housing), and had a simple checklist for a structure's features that provided an admirable balance between just examining the exterior and tearing the building apart to determine its composition. Truman figured that a full and scientific assessment would cost $200,000, "which is a lot of money, but we must find it to do this important job." He got endorsements for the Cincinnati plan from civic groups, but the *Kansas City Star* remained cold. Truman explained, "The *Star* has gypped the county on its tax assessment ever since it has been in business, and its tremendously rich business interests have never paid what they should, nor have the new business centers and residence developments on the southwest side of town." (The last complaint was an implied criticism of mammoth real estate operator J. C. Nichols.) Truman complained with some bitterness that he was unable to push the Cincinnati plan through the opposition of such interests. He also felt that utilities such as Kansas City Power & Light Co. cheated the county on taxes. "They had one set of figures on which they paid taxes, and they had another set of figures which was four or five times as great . . . on which they based the rates. I tried my best to get the legislature of Missouri to see that rates and taxes ought to be on the same figures, but they had too big a pull in the Missouri legislature, and I couldn't get it done."[25]

Truman decided that a reorganization of county government would be the ultimate answer to most of the problems. He was not alone in this feeling. Walter Matscheck's Civic Research Institute had been promoting this notion since Truman's days as eastern judge. Despite their differing political beliefs, Truman and Matscheck coordinated efforts to give the county government, more particularly the presiding judge, fuller control over county affairs. The presiding judge would appoint a number of officials currently elected, making those now-independent departments less querulous. The presiding judge would also have more influence over departmental expenditures. "We should make the same changes in our local government for its proper functioning that Henry Ford made when he grew from a bicycle shop to the largest manufacturer of motor cars in the world," Truman told the Kansas City Real Estate Board. In the county "there are so many checks that no balance can be obtained." The real estate board's Marvin Gates played a key role in drafting the reorganization plan, so Truman addressed a friendly audience. The changes he advocated could have done much for government efficiency and, though apparently no one said it aloud at the time, could have done much to tighten Pendergast control of the county. Manvel Davis, an important Republican lawyer who helped draft the reorganization plan, expressed oblique suspicions about Truman's motive, but no one seemed to pick up on them. (Davis was later prone to be more explicit about Truman, sometimes more explicit than the facts warranted. This carelessness was a habit Davis would regret sorely one day.) Every elected official whose job would be subjugated to Truman had a vested interest in spiking the reorganization plan. Truman and Matscheck were persistent, but they never got the legislature to permit the reorganization. Truman also advocated combining some county departments (such as assessor and health) with those of the Kansas City municipal government to eliminate pointless duplication of effort. He estimated this would save the two governments $1.5 million a year, the difference between flush times and bankruptcy for the county. This idea wasn't original with Truman, and he had no more success with it than had anyone else.[26]

Truman's proposed reorganization of the state government also got nowhere. He urged that Missouri's 114 counties be consolidated into 30, townships be abolished, local school boards be consolidated into one county board, useless state agencies be abolished, the state legislature be streamlined into 60 to 75 representatives and 30 senators, and the governor be authorized to appoint cabinet members (rather than the people electing the attorney general, etc.). Truman predicted that this would cut 20 percent from government expenditures. No one predicted that any of this had a chance of happening. Truman also called for a gasoline tax to reduce the special road and bridge fund property levy, urged taxation of intangibles, and reduction of property tax exemptions. Actually, a lot of this made sense, but faced the same forces that defeated county reorganization.[27]

As the Depression worsened so did Jackson County's welfare burden, much to Truman's disgust. To the Kansas City Rotary Club he complained about the state legislature requiring the county to provide "widows pensions, boys and girls homes, and all the trimmings, but have never given us the revenue with these increases to pay for them. It must stop somewhere. Now is the time to get back to pre-war salaries and pre-war services; the cost of local government can then come down." "The tendency is toward rather socialistic and paternalistic things," he told the Kansas City Real Estate Board. "You can put out a few sobs about indigent aged or orphan children and get the tax levies raised without a whimper." Although Truman would become an ultra–New Dealer he never quite lost these sentiments. In 1942 he wrote, "We have been too much on the soft side for the past 20 years, living on a false security basis and getting a complex that the government or someone else ought to take care of us. It never was a sound doctrine, and the sooner we get away from that . . . the better off we will be." These feelings expressed in 1942 are particularly interesting because, unlike Truman, most people didn't recall the years 1922–32 as an era of welfare paradise. As a county judge Truman spent far more time on such matters than most people did, and thus the rudimentary county welfare activity loomed larger in his mind than perhaps it should have. Another factor influencing his attitude must have been the types of cases the county dealt with. Rather than upstanding citizens needing temporary aid, Truman typically saw chronic cases that could never become self-supporting. State law required Truman and the other two county judges to deal with these cases personally, and day after day the stories of the dregs of society were paraded in front of Truman with the request that he feed and house these individuals with tax money. Significantly, Truman did not speak of "welfare," a term implying a legal right, to describe this activity. He called it "charity," thereby asserting this support was a voluntary gift. Another factor shaping his view was that more than a few cases apparently were political, derelicts from the Pendergast river wards being rewarded with a few weeks' free room and board. Still another factor was his belief that many cases were fraudulent—the particular individuals had legitimate needs, but also had hidden relatives capable of financing the needs. Truman tried to smoke out these relatives, even printed some of their names and addresses in the newspaper to shame them into contributing their share of support, but he discovered some people have no shame.[28]

A quick overview of county welfare activities might be useful in understanding the background Truman took to the U.S. Senate. There was a juvenile detention home, where an average of eight youthful offenders lived in quarters that a Spartan would have found sparse. Parental homes existed for white boys, white girls, and black boys. Ordinary children put there because of neglect mixed with an ever-changing population of young criminals. The parental homes were governed by a three-headed monster—the county court, the juvenile court, and the Kansas City School Board. Tremendous political infighting crippled the homes. The county court also maintained a home for white aged and infirm, and another for black aged and infirm. In addition the county paid for the care of various persons in state and private institutions, and also provided pensions to widowed mothers. In 1929 Truman complained that the county was spending a million dollars a year on "charity." Not quite all this money was received by the county's wards. For a while as much fuel oil was bought for the old folks' homes in summer as in winter. Able-bodied inmates had to sit all day with nothing to do while the county hired workers to do laundry, tend the farm, and the like. In 1928 the Civic Research Institute found that in general the county paid one dollar for welfare services that private institutions provided for seventy cents.

Although Truman showed no concern over the cost of patronage and boodle that he controlled, he was irked by expenses he couldn't control. The juvenile court could order the county to care for delinquent and dependent children, and to pay widowed mother pensions, and Truman had to find the money. If the juvenile court ordered the children to state institutions Truman had to pay in ready money— the state wouldn't take county warrants. A judge of a court of record (not the whole court, but any one county, circuit, or probate judge, and possibly sometimes even a justice of the peace) could commit to a state hospital a poor person with mental affliction or organic brain disease. Again Truman had to find ready money for such commitments even though he had nothing to do with them. Although the various cases got cursory examination (one hapless local government official had the title "Insane Investigator"), in general, inquiries were limited to financial need. If this criterion were met, the requested relief was routinely approved even if more appropriate help might have been available from private sources. The result was appalling overcrowding, particularly at the old folks' homes. Truman was well aware of the inappropriate relief and overcrowding. A deranged man was sent to the old folks' home over Truman's protests. The facility couldn't handle such a case, and the man was beaten to death. Truman cooked up a campaign to counter the harsh publicity (publication of relatives' names and addresses was part of this campaign), trying to blame the overcrowding on inmate relatives rather than on the county court giving free room and board to Pendergast river ward derelicts. ("Inmate" was the proper term; a guard and high fence were provided to keep the infirm elderly on the grounds, a feature lacking at one home used in part for juvenile criminals.)[29]

Truman did take one positive step in improving welfare facilities when he got voters to approve construction of a county hospital. This was different from most hospitals since emphasis was on chronic illnesses. The four-story building had operating rooms, labs, psychopathic wards, occupational therapy, and 284 patient beds. Architects were Fred Gunn and Bess's brother Fred Wallace. Referring to another project Truman privately said, "Old man Gunn is in his dotage and doesn't know what it's all about, but I kidded him into believing he is necessary because Pendergast likes him." Regarding the hospital construction he complained about "my drunken brother-in-law, whom I'd had to employ on the job to keep peace in the family. I've had to run the hospital job myself and pay him for it. 'It's a great life, if you don't weaken.' " Truman squabbled with his court colleagues Barr and Bash over the electric power supply to the hospital. He privately accused Bash, former superintendent of construction for Kansas City Power & Line Co., of sharp business practices in this connection. Possibly Truman also went sour on Kansas City Power & Line vice-president A. E. Bettis over this issue. Bettis was vice-president of Truman's Greater Kansas City Regional Plan Association. Truman's ill health may also have contributed to his crankiness. In the midst of this dispute he underwent an operation at Research Hospital for rectal trouble and was, as he phrased it, "a slave to cotton" for some weeks afterward.[30]

When the Wagner Social Security Bill was introduced a few days after Truman entered the Senate his support was enthusiastic and his remarks more compassionate than before. "I am hoping that it will do away with all alms houses and place our aged poor in a respectable place in our social set-up, where they ought to be." He asserted, "A practical, properly administered Old Age Pension will not cost the taxpayer more than it costs him now to maintain these homes. . . . The whole idea is sound, human, and goes to the root of some of the failures in our present social structure. . . . Everyone with a right heart and a feeling for the welfare of the country must be for the measure."[31]

This switch in Truman's attitude about relief seems to have coincided with his tenure as National Reemployment Director for Missouri. In this work he dealt with a far different clientele from that in Jackson County, with thousands of self-reliant citizens who merely wanted a chance to earn their daily bread. The National Reemployment Service was a New Deal agency inspired by the National Industrial Recovery Act and operated under the Labor Department. Those were exhilarating times for New Dealers. "A bloodless revolution was fought at the polls last November," Harold Ickes said. "We are now in the birth throes of a new social order. . . . We are all living in an intolerable economic slavery, if, with bursting granaries on the farm and with more hogs than their owners know what to do with, people are starving; if, with our great quarries and steel plants and with rich mines of ores and forests full of lumber, people are without shelter; if, with idle textile and woolen mills and shoe factories, notwithstanding an abundance of raw materials to be turned into clothing, people are insufficiently clad. That such a type of self-imposed slavery should exist today is a reflection upon our intelligence and a challenge to our understanding." When Truman came on board as a New Deal administrator he, too, declared, "In place of permitting two or three men to get all the profit by the use of machines, we are going to distribute it over the entire community. I think that is in accord with the President's idea of the situation. We are now going about the job," he said, "of redistributing wealth that was amassed in the robust years, but, thank heaven, we are going about it more peacefully than was done in Russia, Italy, and Germany."[32]

The National Reemployment Service was a go-between for unemployed workers and federal public works contractors needing labor.

Each state had a director. The idea was for each state branch to foster a permanent state employment service to connect job seekers with employers of all kinds. Martin Lewis cranked up the Missouri program, and then moved on. Truman replaced Lewis in October 1933. This carried a salary of $300 a month, but Truman declined it so he could hold this federal position while continuing to be Jackson County presiding judge. He was a natural choice. The program emphasized public works, and Truman was probably the state's foremost administrator of such projects—famed for his handling of the road system and courthouse constructions. These Jackson County projects were pioneering efforts in the kinds of employment the New Deal made famous. Truman was also active in the statewide County Judges Association of Missouri, familiarizing him with the persons and politics throughout the state crucial to the success of any government program.[33]

This activity brought Truman into close contact with the workings of the New Deal. He and FDR's aide Harry Hopkins formed a warm, lifelong friendship as Truman helped local administrators understand and implement the strange-seeming regulations that came from Washington. Yes, veterans had preference in hiring, but only in their home county and only if they had the necessary skills. Yes, the National Reemployment Service could furnish strikebreakers but only if they were told they would be strikebreakers. Yes, highway contractors could hire only through the National Reemployment Service unless they hired through a union business office. Yes, all those numbers in the reports were important, and you couldn't just estimate or guess. Truman had (and used) an opportunity available to few men to see the New Deal in action on the local level across an entire state, in areas rich and poor, urban and rural. He learned from the inside how the New Deal really worked, and his enthusiasm grew.[34]

All these activities were useful to an ambitious politician. Truman handily won reelection as presiding judge in November 1930. The only excitement was when a gentleman appeared at Margaret Truman's school in the middle of the day and said he had come to take her home. The teacher knew the Trumans, and thought the situation fishy. While she did some double-checking the gent disappeared. Word of the possible kidnap attempt emptied Truman campaign headquarters, and squads of Truman men searched Independence for the reported would-be kidnapper. Old hands thought this was the whole point, to distract Truman workers from the polls. Rumors of planned election day kidnappings had circulated in Independence, giving the report from Margaret's teacher a sobering credibility. Indeed, one politician was snatched that day and released after hoodlums beat him up. When the new county court was sworn in, Truman's Pendergast colleague Judge Buck Purcell said the heat might be put to him. "But if a man can't stand the heat he ought to stay out of the kitchen." Purcell may have said more, but the newspaper account of Buck stops here.[35]

Truman took Purcell's advice, and fled the kitchen a month later. "I don't know whether you entirely appreciate or not the tremendous amount of strain that's been on me since November," Truman wrote to Bess from Little Rock, Arkansas, demonstrating the extent of husband-wife communication between them. "My two former associates [judges Barr and Bash] as you know were just full of anxiety to obtain any funds that they could because of their positions. The finances of the county were never in such shape since Miles Bulger handled them, and every person I've ever had any association with since birth has wanted me to take pity on him and furnish him some county money." Truman was worried that the Grandview farm might soon be lost to mortgage holders. "You and I," he told Bess, "have had our own difficulties to look after, and with it all I was becoming so keyed up that I either had to run away or go on a big drunk." So Truman ran away for a while.[36]

Truman had just taken the worst heat he had ever received. In 1930 a state law abolishing justice of the peace courts took effect. The "jackrabbit justices" had long been considered an arm of the criminal element. Typically they preyed on blacks and poor whites. One of Truman's appointees, A. P. Fonda, was a typical example. Fonda delegated his authority to clothes companies that sold on the installment plan. When a customer got in arrears the company held court, decided in favor of itself, and sent out a collection man specially deputized as a court constable. These constables weren't particular about what they seized or even whom they seized it from. A deputy constable from Marion Waltner's court decided to seize a man's property to settle a judgment against the man's son. The man understandably resisted, and the deputy constable killed him. These courts were also notorious for refusing to notify defendants in cases, which the merchants then won by default. In addition to serving the interests of these piranhas and thereby winning their support for the Pendergast machine, the justices themselves made a lucrative $600 or so a week from fees (part of which was probably kicked back to the machine). Jackson County civic leaders hailed abolition of these courts as another step in the unrelenting progress of Western Civilization.[37]

Soon after Truman's reelection he decided to reinstate a couple of these abolished courts. On November 24 Judge Bash was absent, and Judge Barr stepped out while Truman was conducting some business. As Barr returned to the courtroom he saw Marion Waltner on the way out, turning to Truman and saying, "Thank you, Judge." Barr was surprised to find the official county court record showing that he and Truman had made Waltner and Vernon Greene justices of the peace. (Truman privately bragged about how many measures he sneaked through singlehanded while his two colleagues were distracted with other matters. Democracy in action.) Soon thereafter Waltner and Greene set up shop in typical jackrabbit style and drew attention to themselves. When asked about this in early December Truman freely admitted that he had put Waltner and Greene into business, and breezily declared that his action couldn't be undone since the November county court term had now expired. While not criminal, Truman's act was patently illegal. Since the office of justice of the peace no longer existed, his appointments should have meant no more than if he appointed someone king of Siam or mayor of New York. Yet Waltner and Greene continued to operate, their "constables" (who also had no legal standing) continued merrily to "attach" property. This was literally criminal activity, but Pendergast law enforcement officers did nothing about it. There was talk in January 1931 that someone ought to ask the state Supreme Court to do something, but the excitement pretty much died.[38]

Truman came under harsh questioning about this. At first he stonewalled. "I had reasons," he said, "but I do not feel like giving them at this time." Since Boss Tom Pendergast had an intense personal interest in the well-being of jackrabbit courts, the *Kansas City Star* noted that "the general belief was that the Democratic organization to which he [Truman] is responsible cracked the whip, and he performed." Truman's subsequent explanations did nothing to lessen this belief. First he said he appointed Waltner and Greene. When the illegality of such action was pointed out, he said he merely approved the election officials' certification that Waltner and Greene had been elected in November. When the nonexistence of any such certification was pointed out, he said he appointed the two men to illustrate the evils of jackrabbits so such courts would be abolished. Since the state legislature had already abolished the courts, Truman explained that he hoped county municipal courts would be established to replace the jackrabbits. He further explained that in the meantime businessmen south of 47th Street and west of Prospect in Kansas City needed Waltner and Greene to help in account collections. Truman had the chutzpah to urge a Kansas City Bar Association committee to seek "ouster" of the illegal "judges." The *Star* was appalled by the whole episode. The paper had been presenting Truman as a remarkable public servant. Now it wiped his civic achievements from the record and for the next decade portrayed Truman as Boss Tom's stooge. Soon after all this Truman fled the heat for Little Rock, where he wrote the discouraged letter to Bess.[39]

Truman was beginning to tire of the omnipresent corruption surrounding him. He unburdened himself in a private memorandum:

There's Tom and Joe [Shannon] and Cas [Welch] and the *Star* and Newman, and among the small fry Koehler and Richardson and a host of others. What chance is there for a clean honest administration of the city and county when a bunch [of] vultures sit on the side lines and puke on the field. The *Star* does as much puking as the rest. If we only had Tom to deal with the public might have a chance, but Tom can't operate without Joe and Cas. Cas is a thug and a crook of the worst water. He should have been in the pen 20 years ago. Joe hasn't got an honest appointee on the payroll. Tom's worst influence is Mike Ross who is just a plain thief. His son Willie had his dad backed off the boards in that line, and he was also a rival of Casimir [Welch] as a thug. He's dead, and I suspect his sales of rotten paving have bankrupted the government of Hell by now. He brought Matthew Murray here from the State Highway Dept. and there hasn't been an honest letting of paving contracts since he's been here. McElroy said he'd "forced" old man Gary to let him have Murray from the State Highway

Dept., but I found out that "Willie" recommended him to McElroy; and that's how McElroy took him away from Gary. Gary no doubt heaved a big relief sigh.

Take the director of water for instance. He's a crooked building contractor who was formerly president of the old upper house of the council and was one of the "split up" men. He built a negro home for boys for Bulger (who made a half million as county judge) at a cost of $167,000. Worth probably $80,000, but Miles [Bulger] got a house out of it. He tried the same tactics on me with a negro girls home. There was an honest inspector who held his feet to the fire. He nearly died when he had to build by specifications. No wonder water bills go higher and the department has a deficit. Of course Tom Boyle helps that out, too.

Mr. Koehler is in a class by himself. His ethics were acquired in a north end precinct. He and Miles [Bulger] were partners in all Willie Ross's road contracts. He gets a rake off on road oil from the Standard Oil Company; he gets a rake off from the same outfit on asphalt. He is a partner of the Creosote Culvert Company. I'm impotent. I can't stop him. I can't catch him, and my associates have their tongues out to join him. He can't be stopped. He is a partner of Pryor and Tim Thompson. He hates Truman but is very fond of Vrooman, Barr, and Bash.

John Barker, expert fixer. He failed to fix the supreme court in the police business, and out he went. He got Mr. Terte to allow a crooked contractor Overly by name to collect some $60,000.00 on a sewer contract against the engineers' advice. I wonder how good a fixer this gentleman's successor is.

Why oh why can't we get some old Romans who are fundamentally honest and clean up this mess? It will take a revolution to do it, and it is coming.[40]

Truman never expressed such sentiments publicly, but the memo indicates that he probably knew the details of Pendergast corruption throughout the Kansas City municipal and Jackson County governments. Of his own role in the corruption he wrote: "I wonder if I did right to put a lot of no account sons of bitches on the payroll and pay other sons of bitches more money for supplies than they were worth in order to satisfy the political powers and save $3,500,000.00. I believe I did do right. Anyway I'm not a partner of any of them, and I'll go out poorer in every way than when I came into office." Perhaps Truman did take the only practical approach. Like Richard Nixon, he emphasized that he made no financial profit from the corruption he fostered, as if money were the only thing of value the public could lose. Truman's private admission that he permitted incompetent hacks to collect paychecks, and permitted purchase of goods at excessive prices is in stark contrast to every public statement he ever made on the topic. His public posture on his conduct grew more rigid as years passed, until he denied that *any* wrongdoing occurred under him. One wonders if Truman felt so guilty about what happened that he could no longer face the truth. (Such guilt feelings would suggest that his moral standards were far higher than those of his colleagues.)[41]

"I think maybe that [political] machines are not so good for the country," Truman privately wrote in his presiding judge days. "I have been doing some deep and conscientious thinking. Is a service to the public or one's country worth one's life if it becomes necessary to give it, to accomplish the end sought?" Truman saw physical danger grow in Pendergast politics. There was the apparent attempt to kidnap Margaret. Later Truman feared an attempt to poison him or his family in retaliation for his county budget decisions. A bullet thumped into city manager McElroy's house, and his daughter was abducted. Arsons and bombings of businesses and homes received the kind of newspaper coverage that other routine excitements got. Kansas City pool hall inspector Jack Dalton was murdered while he and Sam Bachman were at 103rd and State Line. A while later Bachman killed Dalton's successor and another man inside Pendergast lieutenant Cas Welch's Jeffersonian Democratic Club. Then Bachman turned up murdered. Kidnappings and beatings were common. One politician was snatched while crossing the street at 10th and Oak. During balloting for Truman's road bond election on May 8, 1928 several politicians, including a judge and a former Kansas City councilman, were kidnapped while gunmen threatened voters. The brains behind the road bond election kidnappers and pistol boys was Johnny Lazia, who assured questioners that he merely wanted the bonds to pass. Lazia soon became the top Pendergast enforcer, forming with Truman and McElroy the triumvirate directly below Boss Tom.[42]

Though Truman maintained a stoic public posture, the stress of all this forced him to flee Kansas City in February 1931 to recover his equilibrium. He began suffering from occasional nausea and apparently chronic headaches, conditions that disappeared when he went to summer camp with other U.S. Army Reserve officers.[43]

In the spring of 1931 Truman was scouting his political future even though he had only just begun his second term as presiding judge. Presiding judge was a two-term job so Truman would have to go on to something else. Occasional musings had appeared in newspapers suggesting that he might make a good governor. This had generated no public excitement, but Truman began toying with the idea. Running for governor in 1932 had particular appeal because it would be an early escape from the county politics he now found oppressive. Moreover, if he lost he would still have two years left in his term as presiding judge, plenty of time to explore other options. He would risk nothing by trying. Indeed, he could only gain because a governorship campaign would provide him with statewide publicity and political contacts.[44]

In April 1931 Truman had a series of lunches with his cousin Snapper to plan the thing. Snapper was a loose cannon but formidable when pointed in the right direction. In Kansas City while waiting to ship out to war, Snapper halted his stroll along the avenue when someone outside the IWW headquarters dropped an insult about Truman's uniform. Snapper went into action and was credited with defeating twenty-seven men singlehanded. Four reportedly escaped by leaping from the second floor, followed by the Wobblies' typewriter hurled by Snapper and last seen receding from view atop a streetcar. In France Snapper had terrible things to say about artillerymen, and even disdained pistols as the choice of wimps. He liked to get up close and personal, using a short club studded with nails. Back in the U.S. he became Chief Special Agent of the Frisco railroad's Eastern Division in Springfield, Missouri. When workers tried to strike Snapper (with Harry's active aid in one instance) sent in goons with guns and pick handles to eliminate picketing. Snapper's full nickname was "Red Snapper."[45]

This was the man Truman chose to crank up the governorship campaign. Typically the Democrat primary would have one gubernatorial candidate supported by the Pendergast machine and another supported by the St. Louis politicians. These two cities were about evenly matched in votes, so the candidate with "outstate" (rural) support would win. Truman's strategy was to demonstrate outstate support to Boss Tom. This was important since Pendergast had backed Francis Wilson in 1924 and 1928, and was expected to go with him again in 1932. So Truman couldn't declare himself a candidate because that would embarrass Pendergast, forcing him to make a very public choice between Truman and Wilson. Truman could, however, try to develop outstate demand for his candidacy. This approach would make life easy for Pendergast—he could accede to the public's demand for Truman, or he could announce for Wilson without embarrassing Truman since Truman wasn't a candidate. Such sensitivity for Tom Pendergast's feelings helped cement his friendship with Truman over the years.

To implement this strategy Truman turned to Snapper who had connections in the southwest Missouri town of Springfield (although Snapper then lived in Kansas City). Snapper was no novice to politics, having already harassed former Kansas City mayor and Pendergast opponent Henry L. Jost with a lawsuit that ran to the Missouri Supreme Court. Snapper recruited Jim Ruffin, an ambitious Springfield lawyer friendly to Pendergast but unenthusiastic about Wilson. Ruffin contacted friendly politicos around the region, and they formed the Southwest Missouri Democratic Club to promote Truman for governor. Truman relied heavily on support from members of the National Guard and American Legion. This was an excellent base, but skeptics questioned whether the support was any broader. The Truman forces recognized this problem and worked hard to give the impression that the area's old-line politicos were for Truman. Since a lot of them were for Francis Wilson this was hard to do.[46]

After his forces worked the politicos for a month Truman came to the Ozarks for a "speaking on the ground" at Houston, Missouri. Fred Boxley, Emmett O'Malley (a Tom Pendergast business associate), and Snapper accompanied Truman from Kansas City. Truman arrived in Springfield on June 5, 1931, scheduled to attend the American Legion meeting at Monett that evening and the military officers meeting in Pierce City. The next day he motored to Cabool and Mountain Grove. This was a Saturday afternoon, a chance to mix both with local businessmen and farmers who made their weekly excursion into town. At Houston Truman told a crowd of two or three hundred, "Pride should come to any man whose Army comrades and other friends feel that he has qualities which justify them in rating him as gubernatorial timber." He continued, "I have been in no sense a candidate, yet, I would hardly be human nor fair to my friends if I did not say at this time that their loyalty and interest in my behalf creates a situation which, if developed, might find me ready at their command to enter the lists." After about twenty minutes of such milquetoast rhetoric Truman finished, and someone in the crowd shouted, "Let's have some old fashioned Democratic gospel!" The reason for all his hemming and hawing had to be that just before leaving Kansas City Truman learned that Pendergast would support Francis Wilson for governor. Truman couldn't afford to whoop up a crowd for himself, yet he couldn't back out on his friends who had arranged his Ozarks political tour. The trip was bittersweet for Truman, but he had a grand time and met folks who got out votes in southwest Missouri.[47]

As a denouement to the gubernatorial boomlet Truman asked outstate friends to meet at the Sedalia state fair in August to discuss his political future. The results, if any, are unrecorded.[48]

Truman privately complained about Pendergast's decision, but he worked hard for Wilson, as he had in 1928. When he received political reports from his outstate friends he passed them along to Wilson. Because Truman had followed the proper etiquette, Wilson bore him no ill feelings. Quite the contrary, Wilson wrote to a friend, "Judge Truman is a mighty fine man and is qualified for most any office in the gift of the people of Missouri. I trust some day to see him elevated to other offices of trust." Wilson's main problem was the persistent rumor of his ill health, which he denied until he dropped dead. This expected event occurred just before the November election, and the Democrat State Committee had to hustle about appointing a new nominee. Truman's name was among those recommended in the flurry of activity, but Pendergast had decided on Guy Park while Wilson's corpse was still warm. Park was also the choice of powerful St. Louis forces, so that cinched it. Park won the election.[49]

Truman appreciated Ruffin's help, and got Boss Tom to support Ruffin for Congress in 1932. Deliberately or otherwise, the Missouri legislature had failed to draw up a satisfactory U.S. Congressional district map after the reapportionment caused by the 1930 census. Thus all U.S. congressmen in Missouri were elected at-large in 1932, which meant that all candidates had to come, cap in hand, to Boss Tom, as he controlled a crucial bloc of votes. Truman shepherded

Ruffin through the interview, and told him, "I had a talk with Mr. Pendergast since I wrote you last, and he informs me the proper thing for you to do is to see everybody in St. Louis you possibly can, particularly those whose names I mentioned in my last letter. A different brand of politics is played in St. Louis than we play up here. Most of them are bandwagon people. We don't play the game that way up here in Jackson County. We have our friends, and we stay with them bandwagon or not." In other words, a Pendergast man stuck with the organization forever. Truman's friend from the military reserves, nurseryman Lloyd Stark, drummed up outstate support for Ruffin. After Ruffin won, Boss Tom invited him to support C. W. Greenwade for Springfield postmaster. Greenwade was a political enemy of both Ruffin and Francis Wilson, and Ruffin declined the invitation. Ruffin received a plaintive request from Truman to appoint his nephew to West Point, promised to do so, then found technicalities preventing it. Truman felt Ruffin's hands were indeed tied on the matter, and held no grudge. Eventually Ruffin was able to come through with a bridge that Pendergast wanted between Kansas City and a race track across the river in Platte County.[50]

In late April 1933 Truman wrote Bess about a conversation with Boss Tom. "He told me to do as I pleased with the county payroll, make the adjustments I wanted to, and he'd put the organization in line behind me. He also told me that I could be Congressman or Collector. Think of that a while. Congressman pays $7,500 and has to live in Washington six months a year. Collector will pay $10,000 and stay at home; a political sky high career ends with eight years Collector. I have an opportunity to be a power in the nation as Congressman. I don't have to make a decision until next year. Think about it." County Collector! The gold mine Truman had sought in 1926, and now at last Pendergast was offering it. And yet—Truman felt this a comedown, an offer seven years too late. He had higher political ambitions, more likely to be achieved in Congress. Pendergast was offering a choice of money or glory. Shortly before Truman's forty-ninth birthday he mused about the choice. Though he admitted he really had done some good things in his life, he felt that he should have accomplished more.[51]

In March the Republican U.S. District Attorney in Kansas City, William Vandeventer, had begun proceedings against Johnny Lazia for tax evasion. Lazia, Truman, and McElroy were the triumvirate directly under Boss Tom. Truman's friend Jerome Walsh was attorney for Lazia, and McElroy was also formally involved in the negotiations. The Democrat Justice Department ordered Republican Vandeventer to give Democrat Lazia every chance to explain $125,000 of unreported income. Lazia maintained there was no tax liability because he had paid the money to other persons. He revealed some names but refused to identify who received the major part of the money. The Attorney General's office ordered Vandeventer to delay prosecution and give Lazia more time to explain. One of the Internal Revenue agents on this case was severely beaten at his home; others were threatened; and the Internal Revenue offices were burglarized. On May 12, 1933 Boss Tom Pendergast wrote a letter to the New Deal's political commander, Postmaster General Jim Farley:

> Jerome Walsh and John Lazia will be in Washington to see you about the same matter that I had Mr. Kemper talk to you about. Now, Jim, Lazia is one of my chief lieutenants, and I am more sincerely interested in his welfare than anything you might be able to do for me now or in the future. He has been in trouble with the income tax department for some time. I know it was simply a case of being jobbed because of his Democratic activities. I think Frank Walsh spoke to the proper authorities about this. In any event, I wish you would use your utmost endeavor to bring about a settlement of this matter. I cannot make it any stronger, except to say that my interest in him is greater than anything that might come up in the future.
>
> Thanking you for any and everything you can do, I remain,
>
> Sincerely, your friend,
>
> T. J. Pendergast.

Pendergast later told a questioner, "I asked Mr. Farley to help Lazia in an honorable way. Other citizens have been accorded the privilege of having their incomes adjusted in a perfectly legitimate way without going to court. Lazia offered to pay without argument. Why should he have been made an exception of? It was a plain case of political persecution." Pendergast added, "Whenever I get to the stage when I accept the help of an organization—no matter if it is composed of Jews or Italians, anybody—and then won't go to bat for it in an honorable way, I ought to have my head cut off."[52]

Shortly after Pendergast wrote the letter to Farley he was consoling Henry McElroy over the kidnapping of Henry's daughter Mary. Johnny Lazia raised the ransom, and the young woman was released. (She was unharmed physically, but the psychic wounds persisted and eventually she killed herself.)[53]

A month later Johnny Lazia attracted the attention of J. Edgar Hoover with an incident remembered as the Union Station Massacre. According to the feds, on June 16, 1933 Johnny arranged a get-together at which Verne Miller, Adam Richetti, and Pretty Boy Floyd planned how to rescue another hoodlum from law officers in the parking lot of Kansas City's Union Station the next morning. The rescue went awry, with four lawmen and their prisoner shot to death and several other persons wounded, including Pretty Boy. Michael James "Jimmy Needles" LaCapra told federal investigators that Lazia arranged safe escort out of the city for Richetti and Pretty Boy. Verne Miller reportedly left town on his own initiative. Squealer LaCapra later turned up murdered.[54]

The next month, July 1933, Machine Gun Kelly and Harvey Bailey staged a big kidnapping, and some of the ransom money turned up in the hands of Kansas City mobster Ferris Anthon.[55]

Enter Jackson County sheriff Thomas B. Bash. "I wonder what the B stands for," Truman huffed, " 'Bull' or 'Baloney.' " Truman claimed that Bash of the Shannon faction had been a grafter while serving with Truman on the county court. If so, Bash underwent a sudden conversion to law abiding and law enforcement when he moved from being county judge to county sheriff. While Henry McElroy's Kansas City police rounded up the usual suspects, Bash earned a fearsome national reputation for tracking down the real perpetrators. (Bash was only a few miles behind Pretty Boy Floyd when the FBI caught up with Floyd.) At 1:15 on the morning of August 12, 1933 Bash and his wife and a teenage girl and a deputy sheriff were motoring from an ice cream social to the Bash home. At the corner of Forest Avenue and Armour Boulevard Bash was distracted by machine gunners murdering Ferris Anthon a block away. Perhaps demonstrating more guts than brains, Bash leaped from his car and went after the assassins. He killed two of them before their car rammed his. The third coolly ran toward the sheriff while emptying a pistol at Bash. The assassin became less cool when he ran out of bullets and Bash didn't. The arrest was made, and the gunman turned out to be Pendergast enforcer Charles Gargotta.[56]

This was a blatant case, and the Pendergast machine had to do something. In testimony later revealed as perjury, Henry McElroy's police maintained that Gargotta's revolver was recovered so far away from the scene that he had to have been unarmed when Bash encountered him. The Pendergast county prosecutor W. W. Graves refused to prosecute further. (Much later Gargotta confessed that he did try to shoot Bash.) Truman lopped the sheriff's budget and thereby put a crimp in his crime fighting. Bash went to court and got the money restored. Truman then fumed that Bash was going to bankrupt the county.[57]

Truman had a similar encounter with Jim Page (the county prosecutor who preceded Graves) when Truman fired a bunch of Page's investigators. In addition to throwing small-time hoodlums into the slammer Page reached to the upper command of the Pendergast machine, taking on Lazia, McElroy, and Truman. Page had a grand jury investigate Truman's handling of county affairs, and accused McElroy of having the police protect rather than suppress underworld gamblers. Page declared outright that McElroy was helping gangsters. McElroy was unruffled by all this, and felt free to have his police raid and destroy evidence that Page had accumulated against Pendergast underworld activities. Now the interesting thing was that Page himself was part of the Pendergast machine and continued to receive full electoral support of the organization up to and including the election that promoted him to a circuit judgeship. Truman called prosecutor Page "about as unscrupulous and heartless a man as ever held that job." Yet the main reason for Truman's ire was probably that Page gave the lie to Truman's defense of his own loyalty to the Pendergast machine. After Gargotta tried to kill Truman's opponent Tom Bash, Truman privately defended his silence about the crime with this assertion: "You can get farther cleaning up a political organization from the inside than you can from the out. At least, I can in the position I am in. If I came out against the organization and tried to wreck it, people would say I was a yellow dog, and they'd be right." Page did not come out against the Pendergast machine, but he did take out after the criminals who hid within it. Despite sabotage from Truman (who once tried to gut the prosecutor's force of investigators) and McElroy, Page still managed to achieve convictions and rally the public behind him while retaining the electoral support of Boss Tom. Truman claimed he had no choice but to stay silent. Page exposed this as a rationalization, and Truman never forgave him.[58]

In both the Bash and Page incidents Truman may have been correct that budget economies were necessary for all county departments. Nonetheless, Truman was perfectly willing to waste a million dollars, by his own admission, on corrupt contracts and incompetent patronage employees rather than reduce that Pendergast boodle and assure efficient suppression of the gangsters on whom the Pendergast machine depended more and more.

Truman decided he wanted out of Jackson County, and began making arrangements to get the Congressional seat that Boss Tom had promised. Truman participated in the redrawing of district lines in 1933, and gerrymandered the Fourth District to guarantee him an easy election. In January 1934 he met with Pendergast to formally accept the offer of a seat in the U.S. House of Representatives. Boss Tom, the man who never went back on his word, told Truman that he had decided to give the seat to circuit judge Jasper Bell. Truman explained that despite the financial appeal of county collector, he regarded it as a demotion after all the things he'd accomplished as presiding judge. Pendergast asked Truman if he might want to enter Congress as a senator instead of a representative. Pendergast explained that Joe Shannon and Jim Aylward were going to turn down the invitation, and Truman could then have the machine's support. Truman told Pendergast to save his breath, both men knew Missouri would never elect a county judge to the Senate. Boss Tom became a bit peeved and said the offer was serious and that Truman just needed to be patient and allow things to work out. Truman left feeling steamed, and tried to resign himself to being county collector.[59]

At the time of that discussion, Pendergast, McElroy, and Lazia were cranking up the ultimate example of democracy under machine rule—the Kansas City municipal election of March 27, 1934. Lazia had finally been convicted of tax evasion and had been sentenced on February 28, but he was out on appeal. The municipal election had generated more excitement than usual. The anti-Pendergast elements (or "uplifters" as Truman derisively labeled them) were well-organized, and need was felt to demonstrate the futility of such opposition. The demonstration began on election day when Pendergast enforcers chased a car containing two uplifter politicians and a *Kansas City Star* reporter, shooting into it and then forcing the car to a stop. The gangsters apprehended the three men and beat them. One politico had to be hospitalized, but the bloodied *Star* reporter in a terrific stroke of luck managed to leap into the passing auto of an uplifter. Two armed enforcers gave chase in their own vehicle all the way to the steps of the *Star* building. About the same time two more Pendergast enforcers pulled a similar scenario on the chauffeur of *Star* editor H. J. Haskell while the driver was attempting to give voters a ride to the polls. Henry McElroy's police refused to intervene. Pendergast enforcers shot and killed a precinct captain trying to prevent the beating of an election judge. (Fair election judges make fair elections *if* the people want them, Truman declared much later. He said citizens got the kind of elections they wanted.) Uplifters asked Pendergast governor Guy Park to call out the National Guard, but he refused. Gangsters then shot one of sheriff Bash's deputies near a polling place in a quiet residential area. Mortally wounded, the deputy managed to take one Pendergast enforcer with him as the gangsters killed an innocent bystander with return fire. Literally hundreds of armed enforcers cruised the streets in cars without license plates. The police took no notice. They did arrest uplifter politicos, however.[60]

When asked to comment on the election day events Truman said he was an Independence voter; he had nothing to do with Kansas City politics.[61]

The day after the killings Truman was scheduled to be in Jefferson City. Around this time Governor Park asked him to join a road show promoting a constitutional amendment to provide a bond issue for statewide public works projects. Truman agreed. The amendment could pass by a simple majority and was a ploy to get around the two-thirds majority required for bond authorizations. Lloyd Stark was vice-chairman of the campaign, and Kansas City banker James M. Kemper was on the finance committee. The proposal passed in May, some Pendergast precincts voting unanimously for the bonds.[62]

Truman was stumping the state for the bonds when Democrat state chairman Jim Aylward and Boss Tom's nephew Jim caught up with him at Sedalia. Jim Pendergast told Truman that Truman was Boss Tom's choice for senator if he wanted to run. The newspapers had been full of how Joe Shannon and Jim Aylward had turned down the chance, and how Boss Tom was desperately looking for someone willing to be a senator. Truman now remembered his January conversation with Pendergast, and realized he had been serious. The intricate dance Pendergast had described was now reaching its climax, and only awaited Truman's assent to reach completion. Truman agreed. The date was May 8, 1934, his fiftieth birthday.[63]

Awake with excitement in the predawn hours before he announced his candidacy, Truman wrote, "I have come to the place where all men strive to be at my age, and I thought two weeks ago that retirement on a virtual pension in some minor county office was all that was in store for me." He continued writing on page after page of Pickwick Hotel stationery. Here he maintained a secret hideaway from Jackson County politicians (the hotel register even lacked his name), a refuge where he could read and write and think without distraction. On that early morning he wrote out nothing less than the story of his life, his hopes, his dreams. He knew he was close, very close, to achieving the goal of his life plan. And that seems to have prompted the predawn reflections. This life plan, which he perhaps had confided to no one but his mother, was a deliberate attempt to achieve political power. He had decided to go as far in politics as a man could. This decision was probably made in his haberdashery days. Truman wanted to be elected eastern judge of Jackson County, then presiding judge, then U.S. congressman, then governor of Missouri, then U.S. senator. "And now I am a candidate for the United States Senate," Truman wrote. "If the Almighty God decided that I go there I am going to pray as King Solomon did, for wisdom to do the job."[64]

The Pendergast endorsement didn't guarantee success. Pendergast had endorsed Charles Howell in the previous Senate election, and little had been heard of Howell since. Truman, however, had some definite advantages beyond the assured Jackson County vote. For one thing, he had an amazing record as presiding judge, with unheard of achievements. His Greater Kansas City Regional Plan Association developed solid political contacts in Clay and Platte counties. His work on the Missouri State Planning Board put him into state government circles. His veterans and Masonic and abortive gubernatorial and recent state bond issue activities built grassroots contacts throughout the state. His service as Missouri's National

Reemployment director combined grassroots contact with county politicos across the state, and left more than a few persons feeling they owed their jobs and homes to Truman. He had an important advantage with his activity in Missouri's county judges association. Through this he had developed friends in the courthouse crowds across the entire state. Truman explained, "They appointed the judges and clerks of election. So when I ran for the Senate there was not a precinct in Missouri in which I did not have at least one friend at the polls." Thus Truman claimed the Pendergast machine had someone in each precinct throughout Missouri. This was crucial outstate, where the electorate didn't have to register. No registration meant no upper limit on ballot stuffing. Anyone could show up at the polls and vote if the election judges raised no objection. In later years a quaint notion grew among some folks that outstate vote totals were more honest than Jackson County or St. Louis totals. They never voted in outstate Missouri.[65]

Truman put on a slam-bang campaign, having the time of his life hitting a dozen or more towns a day. On July 6 his Plymouth hit a Chevy amidship, throwing Truman's head into the windshield and catching his side on the gearshift. He suffered a couple of broken ribs, a sprained wrist, and a nasty bruise on his forehead, but carried on nonetheless, albeit with difficulty.[66]

Three days later Truman was coincidentally back in Kansas City when Johnny Lazia suffered a mishap while stepping from his car into the path of numerous machine-gun bullets from a weapon used in the Union Station Massacre. "Doc," he said to an attending physician, "what I can't understand is why anybody would do this to me. Why to me, to Johnny Lazia, who has been the friend of everybody?" Lazia spoke of his love for Boss Tom, and died. Tom Pendergast and Henry McElroy were conspicuous at the funeral. Truman wasn't remembered as present. If Lazia ever had any dealings with Truman as he did with Pendergast and McElroy, they remained secret. Such contacts surely would have been professional, as were Truman's contacts with Marion Nigro, Lazia's successor as North Side political chieftain. Nigro would bring in batches of tax abatement requests, and (according to Truman's county judge colleague Buck Purcell) Truman would have them routinely approved without examination. Purcell grumbled that Truman was just giving away county money. When Purcell took over the county court for

Pendergast he confidentially stated, "We have been doing too many illegal things in the past." Fred Boxley disagreed, explaining, "The old court had a Truman at the head of it, and that makes the difference."[67]

As the Senate campaign peaked a couple weeks after Lazia's demise, Truman's old haberdashery debts entered the news. Apparently the point was to show up Truman as a deadbeat, but the effect was to demonstrate that he had no hidden income and had made no money from the multi-million-dollar public works projects he supervised. The newspapers explained his settlements with merchant creditors and revealed the small bank account that had been seized to satisfy a jackrabbit judgment. Louis Oppenstein confirmed that Truman finally had paid off the 1924 circuit court judgment on his lease, but didn't remember the exact settlement. Truman said he paid Oppenstein fifty cents on the dollar around 1933. Truman's sole remaining haberdashery debt was an $8,900 circuit court judgment won by Security State Bank in 1929. This was for the $6,800 loan on which Truman had pledged his Johnson County, Kansas, farm. That mortgage had been foreclosed, the farm lost, and the matter settled as far as Truman was concerned. The bank didn't view it that way since other mortgages on that farm (mortgages that the bank knew of when it accepted the farm as collateral) exceeded Truman's equity. Thus the bank gained nothing by foreclosing. Over the years several bank consolidations left W. T. Kemper's Commerce Trust Company controlling this debt in the name of Continental National Bank & Trust Co. Kemper was a Pendergast machine bankroller, and Truman knew him well. Commerce Trust raised no small amount of ire from Truman when it began pressing him to settle the Security State loan at par even though Commerce Trust had acquired the debt without any expenditure. In 1929 attorney Omar Robinson got a judgment of $8,900 for the loan plus interest. Truman refused to pay. Since his county judge salary was immune to garnishee proceedings there was little Robinson could do. He did seize a $250 account that Truman had in a Leeds, Missouri, bank; but as of the Senate campaign Robinson and Commerce Trust had received nothing more. Senator's salaries couldn't be garnisheed either, and Truman frankly declared he would pay nothing because he viewed this lawful debt as unjust. Robinson was one of the men to whom Truman had to explain his illegal jackrabbit judge appointments, and Truman would cross paths with him again. The day after the *St. Louis Post-Dispatch* ventilated Truman's haberdashery debts, attachment orders were served on Independence banks where Truman was suspected of having accounts.[68]

The Pendergast machine was in grand form when election day arrived. After some prodding by Truman, Pendergast governor Guy Park apparently motivated state employees to do their bit. From St. Joseph an attorney reported, "The [state] Grain Department and [city] Police Department are thoroughly organized, and there are few who have not fallen in line." The president of Spalding's Commercial College sent Truman literature to one thousand five hundred graduates in Missouri. Lloyd Stark sat out the primary, but in the general election threw a roast pig buffet supper for Truman and the Pike County political powers. Truman claimed to understand Stark's delay, and at this time apparently agreed to back Stark for the 1936 gubernatorial nomination. "I'm mum on how much of the state Truman will carry outside of Kansas City and Jackson County," Boss Tom said, "but I will guarantee him a larger majority in the primaries than [his opponent John] Cochran will get in St. Louis. Neither Cochran nor [Truman's other opponent Tuck] Milligan can expect many votes here." (In 1932 Bennett Clark's Jackson County total reputedly was smaller than the number of Jackson County members in his Clark-for-Senator club.)[69]

Truman gave his last speech of the primary campaign in Independence, a speech filled with themes he had expounded across the state. He noted that the machine age had made farmers a minority, now only 25 percent of the population; they had to be put on a parity with industry. He supported a national old-age pension. "It means protection of home and security in old age. Many of these old people face disaster through no fault of their own." Truman wanted immediate payment of the cash bonus promised to world war veterans, and advocated extending it to Spanish-American War veterans as well. He said the bonus would boost the national economy. Truman called himself a New Dealer. "We have a great humanitarian in the White House," Truman said. "President Roosevelt is working out the New Deal with the one and only objective of restoring this country and its government to the common people."[70]

On election day Truman checked the voting. At one polling place he watched men going round and round in a circle, casting one ballot after another. Situation normal. Gunfire and a bomb explosion wracked Marion Nigro's North Side Democratic Club as Truman soared to victory.[71]

"Am I proud of him?" Mattie Truman asked. "Say, I knew that boy would amount to something from the time he was nine years old. He never did anything by halves." After winning the general election Truman went to Washington, D.C., in early December to scout the territory. He also sought a million-dollar loan to keep the county running until he took his Senate seat. Accompanied by Missouri Democrat chairman Jim Aylward, Truman spent several days being introduced to the people who ran the federal government. The two men, along with Missouri's U.S. Senator Bennett Clark, then went to the White House. There Harry Truman visited President Roosevelt.[72]

When sworn into the Senate on January 3, 1935, Harry Truman achieved the pinnacle of his ambition. The highest office voters of Missouri could bestow. He had come as far as he could, journey's end, nowhere else to go.

Chapter 11

NEW DEALER
RAMPANT

I began to have the conviction that I was now where
I really belonged.

—Harry S. Truman[1]

When the *Kansas City Journal Post*'s
Washington man caught up with Truman on his first day in the
Senate, Truman was in an unusually solemn mood. He spoke of the
great obligations he felt to the nation in holding such a position. He
spoke also of the suffering in the Depression and how he wanted to
help the average citizen.[2]

To accomplish the most he could, Truman sought acceptance as
one of the Senate's regular fellows. Personal relationships determined
whether a senator's proposals got a decent hearing or disappeared
many fathoms deep. In addition, Truman enjoyed people and naturally wanted to be friends with those around him. So he felt hurt
when only a handful of senators welcomed him—Ham Lewis, Carl
Hayden, and Burton Wheeler. The rest of that august assemblage
snubbed him as a stooge for Boss Tom Pendergast. Truman was
irked when a colleague went to Boss Pendergast seeking Truman's
vote. The error was easy enough to commit, considering the large
framed picture of Boss Tom that Truman displayed in his office. In

case anyone had failed to make the connection, Senator Huey Long reminded them in a February 20, 1935 floor speech. Truman listened and seethed as the Kingfish laid bare Tom's relationship with Johnny Lazia. As things turned out, the Kingfish probably did Truman a favor, creating sympathy for him as another of Long's victims. Truman recalled, "He did the same thing to Senator Carter Glass. 'You're the orneriest man in this Senate,' Glass told him, 'and I'd just as soon get my knife and cut your heart out.' He actually started after Long, but Senator Joe Robinson stopped him."[3]

Truman took pains to minimize his Pendergast connection, declaring that Boss Tom "only talked to me once about my work in the Senate" when FDR was hustling votes for election of a majority leader. "On no other occasion did T. J. Pendergast ever talk to me about my actions in the Senate." These statements appear straightforward, but are actually carefully hedged. Just before the Huey Long speech Truman wrote to Pendergast, "I have your telegram regarding the Borah resolution, and I feel and always have felt very favorable to that resolution." This was Senate business, but Truman could truthfully say he didn't talk with Pendergast. "Charley Howell," Pendergast wrote in 1939, "will talk with you about some matters in which Braniff Airways, Inc., are interested. I hope you are in a position to help him out as it means considerable to him. . . . P.S. It means a great deal to more than Howell." Truman replied he would "do anything I can to help," but could later truthfully declare this wasn't Senate business. After a secret meeting with Pendergast in New York City Truman wrote, "We talked for three hours about everything under the sun. Discarded a couple of prominent candidates for governor." After another New York City discussion he reported, "I talked about county affairs, too, and he's going to straighten them out along lines I suggested." Despite lengthy political strategy sessions between the two men, Truman could truthfully claim they didn't cover Senate matters. Truman and Pendergast also communicated via go-betweens, therefore Truman could truthfully state that he hadn't discussed this or that matter with Pendergast.[4]

All of Truman's narrowly truthful assertions about his lack of contact with Pendergast add up to one big deceit. Why should Truman lie about this? After all, he wasn't taking orders from Pendergast. But that's exactly the point. The personal meetings, in particular, demonstrate that Truman and Pendergast were coequals plotting out the course of Missouri and Jackson County politics during Truman's Senate years. They were equally responsible for the corruption used to implement these plans. Truman may never have ordered an election stolen, but neither did Pendergast (Boss Tom was convicted of income tax fraud, not vote fraud). They didn't have to give such orders. The precinct workers knew what to do.

Truman hunkered down to his job, determined to make himself a valued member of the Senate. He carefully observed the complex etiquette, remaining silent on the floor for his first year as tradition required. He offered little legislation then or at any other time— perhaps a couple bills a month, often private relief measures for constituents (pensions, permissions to seek compensation, and the like). The respect of colleagues grew from Truman's mastery of committee assignments, particularly Appropriations and Interstate Commerce—"two big committees," Truman told his good friend Lloyd Stark, "it looks like I have just let myself in for a lot of work." Such work was crucial to the functioning of the Senate, as busy members often had to rely on committee reports in deciding how to vote. Truman's background in finance, law, and county administration allowed him to grasp the intricacies of proposed legislation. These efforts went unnoticed by the press but gradually gained the respect of his colleagues.[5]

In that era the president of the United States was an awesome personage, and in February 1935 Truman found himself tongue-tied when he called on Roosevelt socially for the second time. The senator quickly proved he was more of a New Dealer than FDR himself. Truman was in an unusual position to do so due to his seat on the Appropriations Committee, which ruled on every government measure that cost money. He had as much power over the New Deal as some senior senators had.[6]

The first big money fight was over FDR's $4.8 billion relief bill. "There seems to be some deep political maneuver in connection with it, for what reason I don't know," Truman wrote to Governor Park. Chances are Truman's letter itself was a political maneuver because the issue was whether state governors or U.S. senators would control the patronage. The Washington lawmakers resolved that issue in favor of themselves. Truman felt the scope of the bill too limited. FDR wanted the jobs for destitute people. Truman wanted the unemployed made eligible even if they weren't already on Welfare, saying it was unfair to penalize people who were using up their savings, or borrowing money to live on. Broadening the scope in this way would also allow patronage administrators more flexibility in passing out the jobs. Truman talked about amending the bill along this line and even took up the matter with Roosevelt personally, but eventually let FDR's limitation stand. Truman did, however, doggedly stick by the American Federation of Labor in support of an amendment to pay public works employees the wage prevailing in the city where the job was. FDR demanded the amendment be dropped. Most New Dealers backed off under that pressure, but Truman defied the president and went to defeat with the labor unions. Thus began the Works Progress Administration.[7]

Harry Hopkins became the WPA chief. He and Truman had known and liked each other since Truman's days as National Reemployment director for Missouri. They had kept in touch during the WPA funding fight, even to the extent of discussing specific people to run the federal relief set-up in Missouri. This personal relationship seemed to portend a big edge for the Pendergast machine in WPA patronage. To create WPA patronage, however, specific public works projects had to be submitted to Frank Walker, and then be recommended to President Roosevelt by Harold Ickes. "Donald Duck" Ickes had already proved himself a curmudgeon, nixing Truman's request to bend federal hiring regulations requiring preference to residents of the county where work was performed. Truman had argued that Kansas City and St. Louis had the most population and paid most of the taxes in Missouri, and therefore those city dwellers should be hired no matter where federal public works projects were constructed in the state. Truman's plan also would have guaranteed jobs for hundreds of Pendergast loyalists from Jackson County. Ickes insisted that rules were rules, and insisted in a frosty manner. "There is nothing more I can do about it," Truman moaned to a Pendergast lieutenant. Frank Walker had a finer understanding of Democrat patronage needs than did Ickes (who was not only a Republican but a Bull Moose traitor). Walker and Truman and Senator Bennett Clark had a satisfactory meeting on May 7, and things moved fast. By the time the Pendergast organization could respond to Truman's report on that meeting Matt Murray was appointed Missouri WPA director.[8]

Murray's appointment was a Pendergast machine triumph. He

had been the Kansas City Public Works director ever since McElroy took over the municipal government for Pendergast in 1926. The *Kansas City Star* commented dryly, "Mr. Murray is thoroughly familiar with Kansas City's needs and the possibilities for government spending in the community." Truman was ecstatic, "Murray is the best man in the entire state to help Missouri get its share of relief money and aid the unemployed in getting work." Great were the cries from Pendergast opponents such as Assistant Commerce Secretary Ewing Mitchell of Missouri, who soon found himself fired from the Roosevelt subcabinet. Truman accused Mitchell of trying to make a corrupt deal with him over county warrants in 1927, with Mitchell offering to split the proposed $100,000 profit. While at the White House on other business, Truman found Roosevelt a receptive audience for criticisms of Mitchell. Murray came to Washington and dined with Harry Hopkins. Of all the state WPA directors, Truman wrote, "Murray was the only one of the 48 who had that honor. It looks as if we are really in good now." Truman exulted as a recipient of White House largess. Of a Murray opponent Truman declared, "I don't have any interest in her affairs, and I didn't see why she should have any in mine." He added, "It was a matter for Missouri's two Senators, and we agreed on Murray. It seems that a family that has two $10,000 jobs would do well to just look after their own affairs. Mrs. Blair, Mr. Blair, and their son Newell, all have government jobs." When a constituent protested the criminal background of a Murray deputy, Truman retorted, "There are always people in every community who like to tear people down whenever it is possible, and it seems you belong to that class." To Truman, Murray's stewardship of millions of tax dollars was a private matter in which the public was entitled to no input. Regarding WPA, Truman's confidential operative Fred Canfil frankly stated to another Pendergast operative, "We have tried in this work to place only good [i.e., Pendergast] Democrats in the key positions." Canfil claimed that "the pick and shovel jobs" were handed out regardless of the recipient's politics, but Truman and his staff repeatedly told persons seeking WPA employment to apply through local Democrat Party leaders. Raymond Clapper in the *Washington Daily News* estimated that Pendergast "probably gets 100% of the WPA vote, if not more." This patronage added to Pendergast strength statewide, and would be important to Truman's 1940 reelection campaign.[9]

In forming the WPA Truman found himself aligned with labor unions and against FDR in the method of determining wage rates. Truman later mused privately about persons who were "against labor and for unlimited hours. My father was the same way. They honestly believe that every man ought to have to work from daylight to dark and that the boss ought [to] have all the profit." Truman proclaimed his sentiments in 1936: "Instead of passing the profits of the machine around, they have become concentrated in the hands of a small number, and a great class of working people have been made idle. . . . With a minimum wage and maximum hour law in force, the manufacturer who could obtain the whole-hearted support of his workers, and who used his brain to cut the legitimate corners without exploiting his labor would be the man who would prosper and survive, and the profits of the machine would be more widely distributed. Something is radically wrong with a distribution system which causes people to be fed and clothed by the government when there is an over-abundance of everything necessary to make life worth living." Thus Senator Truman viewed wages and hours as something going far beyond productivity and profits, and as something crucial to the definition of democracy. He went even further, condemning business management that refused to spend less than $1,000 to correct conditions that killed several workers. Truman called on management to "realize and acknowledge their great responsibility," arguing that business functions extended beyond the strictly economic realm to the well-being of society. This responsibility wasn't charity but an integral part of business operations, as necessary as raw materials and labor. These sentiments were backed up by Truman's voting record, and attracted notice from organized labor.[10]

"Industry and labor, while viciously fighting each other, have done all they can to strangle agriculture, which is more important to the country than both of them." Truman could sound like an Old Testament prophet on this point: "We who live in cities sometimes feel proud of our huge skylines and mistakenly believe that they are conclusive proof of independent wealth producing power. . . . City expansion is but a reflection of the growth of wealth on the farms. Left to itself, the city would soon collapse. The city's prosperity is the result of the sweat, muscle, and brain of the country." And, he warned, "Man has not reached the point where he can live abundantly and virtuously in stone and macadam, clustered around elevator shafts, in the midst of a synthetic flora and fauna created by the captains of industry."[11]

Truman was deeply troubled by the plight of farmers, and baffled as to a solution. As willing to experiment as any New Dealer, he was more impatient than some. "There is no desire on my part to be critical or to question the motives of Secretary Wallace and his various farm remedies. The farm bill as passed by the last Congress apparently is not working." Truman glumly indicated that he was ready to give new proposals a try, "Conditions would be no worse for the farmer no matter what legislation we may pass." The basic problems were beyond the control of the farmer, who "sells on a world market. He buys on a closed market. His machinery, his clothing, and everything he buys is on a price fixed by monopoly." Because the U.S. was a creditor nation after World War I, and because of "our mutton-headed tariff policy under past [Republican] administrations," many countries could no longer afford U.S. agricultural products. Truman said this created a big surplus of agricultural products and brought on the 1921 depression, which continued for the farmer even though other businessmen appeared to recover. "No effort was ever made to bring him out until the creation of the Agricultural Adjustment Administration. That was an effort to limit production to the point of consumption, just as the manufacturers limit production to what they can sell." Truman said that the AAA was starting to provide a decent living for farmers when the Supreme Court struck down the AAA, declaring "agriculture is not a national and interstate business but is one that the states must regulate." Truman's explanation of the farm situation was easy to understand, yet showed a mind able to correlate diverse and seemingly unrelated matters (from clothing prices to French war debts), a mind able to explain these complex interrelations to the average person.[12]

After the Supreme Court decision on AAA Truman began some heavy thinking about the tribunal's role in American life. Six months earlier he had been satisfied with the court's destruction of the National Recovery Administration even though he had supported that New Deal program. "The NRA decision was all right," he then told an applauding audience. "It upheld the Constitution. Emergency measures should be made to fit the Constitution and not the Constitution to fit the emergency measures." He went on, "I thank God we have a Supreme Court that can tell us what the Constitution is and how to keep within its bounds." The AAA decision, however, took Truman aback. To him the issue was so clearly national that he could scarcely believe the case had been considered on its merits when the court put agriculture under state regulation. At first Truman thought the answer was to amend the Constitution, but eventually he decided that nothing could stop the court from twisting even the most forthright language. Not yet declaring himself openly, and over a year before the issue leaped into national consciousness, Truman nonetheless placed a January 7, 1936 *St. Louis Star-Times* editorial into the *Congressional Record*. The editorial said the opinion of Justice Roberts showed there was nothing sacred about the law, that the "Constitution [merely] means what the court majority says." The newspaper characterized the AAA decision as "undoubtedly the narrowest and most restrictive interpretation of the Constitution since the Dred Scott decision of 1857 and remarkably like it in logic." Roberts's reasoning "holds that farm prosperity benefits nobody but farmers" while upholding government aid to manufacturers through tax breaks. "Six justices say they can see no connection between agricultural prostration and the flow of interstate commerce." It would follow from Roberts's reasoning that "Noah's flood was of local concern, since at each spot on Earth only one spot was under water." The newspaper warned that "the Guffey Coal Act seems doomed, with chaos lying ahead. The narrowing of the [Constitution's] general welfare clause suggests that the Wagner Social Security Act will be destroyed" because "the plight of each victim of insecurity is a local matter, not affecting the general welfare." In conclusion, the newspaper proclaimed, "The real need is what it was when a similar situation existed in the days of Abraham Lincoln—new blood in the Supreme Court."[13]

Some years later, and again in the context of agricultural matters, Truman revealed that he knew of another way in which the Constitution was being used to thwart democratically expressed desires. "The dry lands Senators are a majority on the Agriculture Committee . . . , and it is almost impossible to hold up a project that has to do with the irrigation of land in these Western States. Montana, Idaho, Wyoming, Colorado, Utah, Arizona, and New Mexico have 14 Senators in the Senate, and they spend most of their time getting special privileges from the rest of the country. The population of all seven of them [combined] is less than the population of Missouri, Iowa, or Indiana. . . . As far as the Senate is concerned the tail wags the dog." The Supreme Court problem could be solved by attrition or simple legislation, but Truman's complaint about the Senate involved the most basic part of the Constitution and dealt with one of the greatest debates in the Constitutional Convention of 1787: How shall the states be represented in Congress? Indeed, the "flaw" he observed—that a tightly organized minority can control the overwhelming majority of the people via the Senate—has been traditionally viewed as one of the Constitution's great strengths. Even Truman had no desire to reopen an issue supposedly settled by the Founding Fathers.[14]

The AAA decision opened the fourth year of the New Deal, 1936, an election year. In politics nothing is certain. Although the results that year seemed to strengthen Truman and Pendergast, in the deep woods beyond their stronghold the sound of snapping twigs grew ominously loud and ever closer.

Appropriations Committee member Truman started off the year with a call for increased taxes to balance the federal budget. "The money has been spent, and the bill must be paid," he said. "Now is as good a time as any to start the unpleasant ordeal." Instead the New Deal responded by reducing spending. This did not go down well with Missouri Democrats. When FDR turned down twenty WPA projects in Missouri, using the excuse that not enough skilled workers were available, Truman quickly telegraphed public works administrator Ickes that plenty of skilled workers were available. Truman called Missouri's $100,000 Public Works Administration allotment "almost nothing," and tried to get twelve school projects added. These particular projects were a sore point. Senator Clark warned the New Deal's political commander Jim Farley that the projects were authorized in a bond election campaign "encouraged and steamed up by the PWA itself." He continued, "If, after voting these bonds the money should be refused on purely technical grounds it certainly will have a most disastrous effect. . . . Harry Truman has just left a few minutes ago and has authorized me to say that he agrees thoroughly with every word that I have expressed." (After FDR's renomination in Philadelphia Senator Clark got the Democratic Convention to abandon the two-thirds majority rule. This change would become crucial to the political futures of both Roosevelt and Truman.)[15]

Truman found breezes from the White House no longer quite so warm. Routine patronage appointments started becoming damnably complicated, often impossible. Truman's phone calls to White House aides went unanswered. His repeated requests for an FDR campaign stop in the Kansas City area went unheeded until shortly before the voting when Truman bluntly wired Farley, "Have other reasons besides those outlined you before." Jim Aylward, then a Pendergast ally, also telegraphed Farley, "Have many more reasons which cannot be explained by wire." Roosevelt came. Despite the snubs Truman gave fire-breathing speeches for the New Deal: "When, thanks to this burst of intelligent action for which we had waited in vain while his predecessor fiddled and grouched, we finally got our feet on solid ground again, what happened? Why, grave doubts arose as to whether we had done the right thing or not! White-lipped, terrorized men, who had begged him [FDR] to save them, and whom he had saved, began to question the means of their salvation. It hadn't been done according to the Constitution, they said. . . . One by one, these critics began to cut the ropes [NRA and AAA] that hauled us up from the sides of the bottomless pit." Truman also praised the New Deal's Reconstruction Finance Corporation for saving banks and insurance companies and railroads, somehow neglecting to say that the RFC was created by that old fiddler Herbert Hoover. Alluding to the John Paul Jones fighting ship *Bonhomme Richard,* Truman proclaimed, "President Roosevelt believes the government belongs to the whole American nation, not just to Morgan, DuPont, and the Liberty League. . . . We can choose between the Jolly Roger and the Bonhomme Roosevelt."[16]

Missouri had yet another choice, between the Pendergast gubernatorial candidate Major Lloyd Stark and his opponents. Stark had lusted after the governorship for years, and in February 1935 he asked Truman how to get Boss Pendergast's endorsement. Truman and Stark had both been active in veterans organizations and the Field Artillery Reserve, and Stark had thrown his Pike County political support to Truman late in the 1934 election. Truman felt both political and personal friendship toward Stark, and advised him to use the same tactics Truman had used four years earlier when *he* sought Pendergast's gubernatorial endorsement. Namely, demonstrate outstate support. Truman felt obligated enough toward Stark also to give him a list of Truman supporters in sixty or seventy counties, with the recommendation that Stark ask them to send their endorsements of him to Pendergast. Things puttered along until Stark and other hopefuls put in the mandatory appearance at Father Wogan's annual July picnic up in Cameron, Missouri. From Washington Truman looked the field over and declared, "We don't have any real politicians yet for candidates. I hope we get a good one." Truman and Pendergast met in New York soon thereafter to narrow down the list of contenders. Truman figured the final choice might be made in a couple of weeks. Sometime after this meeting Stark made one of his frequent visits to Truman's Washington office and revealed that Senator Clark was ready to urge Stark upon Pendergast. Since Clark represented the St. Louis machine, this was powerful news and apparently clinched Truman's decision to back Stark. Clark and Pendergast had been feuding, and Clark was reluctant to go calling on the big boss unless Truman came along. Truman immediately phoned Pendergast in New York and set up an appointment for the next day. Truman chuckled, "He couldn't do anything else but see us. Two United States Senators can see anyone." (Pendergast, of course, would have been glad to see Truman any time.) The two senators and Stark chatted with Pendergast a while. Stark then excused himself, and the three men discussed him in private. Clark's praise turned out to be faint, Truman recalled, and "Pendergast kept saying to me, 'He won't do, Harry.' 'I don't like the so-and-so.' 'He's a no-good.' " Truman put forward an enthusiastic pitch for Stark, and brought Pendergast around: Boss Tom would endorse Stark that autumn if the outstate support held. When Truman broke the news to Stark on the train back to Washington, "I almost had to leave the drawing room to prevent his hugging and kissing me." Truman's feelings were scarcely different. He told Stark, "I want to see you nominated and elected by such an overwhelming majority that it will make Missouri Democratic for the next 20 years."[17]

Despite the Pendergast endorsement a few glitches arose in the Stark campaign. The most important was "a bull-headed Irishman by the name of O'Malley who is [Missouri's] insurance commissioner. He has taken a notion that fraternal insurance societies are cheating the public, and he has taken after them. They may be wrong for all I know, but it hasn't made the Democrats in Missouri any votes." So said Truman to Jim Farley, adding that O'Malley had cost Stark fifty to a hundred thousand votes in the primary. Fraternal insurance companies promote social fellowship among members in addition to insurance coverage, and their social activities were a big deal in rural Missouri. O'Malley's attack could easily be portrayed as an attack on members and their fellowship. The societies mounted a vigorous campaign against Stark since both he and O'Malley were Pendergast adherents. Emmett O'Malley's Pendergast loyalties went back at least twenty years. U.S. Senator Jim Reed, also a Pendergast man, wanted O'Malley to be postmaster of Kansas City, but President Wilson blocked this patronage request. Reed's vilification of Wilson, which culminated in blocking U.S. membership in the League of Nations, dated from that incident. O'Malley and other factors pulled a good two hundred thousand votes against Stark in the primary. Even Truman admitted this meant that "there is a large anti [Pendergast] feeling in the state, and that it is growing." Senator Clark agreed, noting that the vote total was even more significant considering the difficulty of getting such ballots counted in St. Louis and Kansas City. Stark won the general election handily, amid Republican charges of Pendergast vote fraud and Pendergast pressure on WPA and Civilian Conservation Corps workers. "We have an excellent county ticket here in Jackson County, my friends," Truman said over the *Kansas City Star* radio station in October, "one that will carry on the tradition of good government under Democratic rule. Kansas City and Jackson County have had efficient government ever since the Democrats took charge some 12 years ago, and that is the reason they stay in power."[18]

Truman's old prewar militia captain George Collins was a Pendergast operative, and he watched Truman's social philosophy and 1936 political maneuvers with admiration, "If I had the necessary money to build up the kind of propaganda essential, I could make you President just as easily as I made you corporal, and if you live you will make it anyway." Truman scoffed at the prophecy, "I know that is something that cannot possibly happen."[19]

On his return to Washington after the election, Truman introduced his pet piece of legislation: a bill to require driver's license examinations. Truman spent a lot of time on the road, and saw a lot of crazy driving. (Some passengers even felt "a little uneasy" with Truman at the wheel.) "About 4:00 in the afternoon, on High-way 66, about 40 miles out of St. Louis, I observed your familiar license number—369—upon your Chrysler coupe. . . . However, you were going so fast, before I could turn around and even attempt to overtake you, you would have been several miles away." One of Truman's stenographers observed, "He made mighty good time." This is borne out by Truman's records of gas station stops, showing times and cities. Truman felt that drivers should have to pass tests of vision, highway sign recognition, and actual driving skills. The driver is the main cause of road collisions. "We kill and injure more people . . . every year in automobile accidents than were killed and injured for us in a year of the World War." He added, "There are more innocent children killed in America every year than have been injured by the bombing of Madrid." Also, "Every kind of accident except automobile accidents shows a steady decrease from 1914 to 1936. The motor accidents have increased." Some of Truman's Senate colleagues supported this legislation. Yet Truman found that driver's licenses were considered a radical innovation, too revolutionary for solid citizens to stomach. He introduced this legislation in session after session of Congress, and each time the bill failed.[20]

Soon after Truman introduced his driver's license bill Roosevelt introduced the Supreme Court packing plan. This was his solution to the court's rulings that the New Deal was unconstitutional. Ostensibly FDR merely wanted to reduce the case load by appointing a new justice for each member of the court whose efficiency had been presumably slowed by reaching the age of seventy. The allegedly coincidental effect would be to put justices friendly to the New Deal on the court. Truman felt this trickiness a tactical error, that Roosevelt should have proposed a straightforward increase of court membership. Nonetheless, Truman was excited by the audacity of the plan. "This issue will split both the old parties, and I'm of the opinion that is what F.D.R. wants. He, you know, reads a lot of history, and I think would like to be a Monroe, Jackson, and Lincoln all in one—and is probably succeeding."[21]

Truman's first statement on the Supreme Court packing plan was forthright, "I am for it 100%." Although he claimed his position never changed, his next declaration said: "There should be a retirement age for justices and judges. I am not in favor of packing any court to explain any set of decisions any more than I am in favor of jury fixing." He added, "If, therefore, the condition of the docket warrants it, I see nothing against increasing the membership of the court. It should be very cautiously approached, however." Truman was receiving thousands of letters on the subject, with sentiment running at least ten to one against the plan. He claimed slyly, "I read all the letters I receive"—which didn't mean he received all letters that his staff opened, despite the implication. Apparently shaken by the size of protest, Truman became mum on how he'd vote, and exploded when Traders Gate City National Bank vice-president R. L. Dominick released correspondence he received from Truman indicating the senator intended to support FDR. Dominick "had no authority to print any correspondence of mine without my specific permission," Truman fumed, "he really had no right to publish my letter because it is my property." Truman announced that he needed more information before deciding how to vote.[22]

A few days later Truman stopped pussyfooting. "I think the President has offered one of the simplest solutions to one of the greatest problems facing the country," he told a gathering of Missouri Democrats. "They talk about packing the court," Truman said. "The court has been packed for 30 years against the everyday people of the United States. . . . The court has changed numerous times, and the country has not gone to the bow wows. . . . I think the country would be better off by following the President." The crowd gave him a standing ovation. When asked about the thousands of letters against the plan, Truman dismissed them as unrepresentative of Missouri feelings.[23]

A few days later Roosevelt nominated Missouri Supreme Court justice John Caskie Collet to a federal bench. Though both Missouri senators had endorsed Collet, FDR's action was viewed as both a Truman victory and a reward for his loyalty on the packing plan. Senator Clark was already steamed about what he regarded as Truman treachery on federal judge appointments, but Clark's opposition to the Supreme Court plan put him in a bad position to argue with the White House.[24]

"A little study of history is all anybody needs to come to the conclusion that the Supreme Court should not under any circumstances be allowed to become the final arbiter of legislative acts," Truman wrote privately. Publicly he roared: "By a 'twistification of words,' neither the Congress nor the states can legislate on hours and wages. Yet, according to the opinions of certain great dissenters on the Supreme Court, the Constitution does not hinder what is sought to be done." He declared, "Only twice before the Civil War did the Supreme Court try to declare laws passed by the Congress unconstitutional. In neither instance were the decisions of the court effective." Truman explained how the 14th Amendment was "intended strictly to give the negro equal political rights with the whites in the South. It has been used by the Supreme Court to nullify progressive legislation that is as foreign to the intention of the amendment as it could possibly be." He told a Kansas City rally how Jefferson increased the number of justices from five to seven to alleviate Federalist predominance and how Jackson increased them from seven to nine; how Lincoln increased the justices to ten, and how Congress reduced the number back to seven so Andrew Johnson couldn't fill vacancies; and then increased the number to nine again so Grant could appoint friends of legal tender laws. FDR was proposing nothing new.

Truman called forth the memory of Old Hickory for the position that the Supreme Court had no authority over actions of Congress or the Executive. He cited Lincoln for the argument that to obey the Supreme Court was to abandon self-rule. Starting "about 50 years ago," Truman proclaimed, "we began to get government by special privilege and by the great corporations and by injunction." He concluded, "The cry is that the President wants to pack the court. Well, if that were possible, the court is packed now, and has been for 50 years, against progressive legislation. If you don't believe it, read some of the dissenting opinions of Justices Clark, Harlan, Holmes, and Stone, and even Chief Justice Hughes, in whose beard certain people in this city believe reposes more wisdom than Daniel Webster had in his head."[25]

Just before Truman expressed these sentiments he and Governor Lloyd Stark went to see FDR about a $2.5 million PWA project to rehabilitate the Missouri penitentiary and prison farm. FDR had recently asked Truman to line up Stark as a Midwestern governor favoring the court packing—a delicate job since Missouri had two senators, and Stark's endorsement could be viewed as a slap to Senator Clark (with possibly dire political consequences in Missouri). Truman managed to finesse the situation, and now he and

Stark asked FDR personally to approve this PWA project. The three men compromised on $1,276,000 to rehabilitate the pen but dropped the farm. FDR said he'd tell public works administrator Ickes to expedite, and Truman followed through to make sure Ickes did. This was an especially sweet task for Truman, as Ickes had earlier snubbed Truman on preference on public works hirings. Soon thereafter Truman got PWA help for schools at Fulton, Missouri, and a municipal building at Neosho despite declining PWA funds. A few days later Appropriations Committee member Truman called for an end to wild New Deal spending, saying the budget could be balanced without hurting the deserving needy. Truman complained that some Welfare recipients were too lazy to work.[26]

While Truman was out of the office working on all this, a death threat letter came to his office. His staff and Capitol police took the matter seriously, and over his protests special guards were assigned to him. The letter promised that Truman would die between noon and 11:59 P.M., April 22, 1937. During those hours extra guards were posted at Capitol entrances and the Senate chamber, and were also sent to a Missouri DAR dinner Truman attended in Washington that night. Truman felt it a lot of bother over nothing, that all senators got nut mail. "If I had been here on Monday when the letter was received I would have thrown it away." Senator Clark joked that he ought to be entitled to a bodyguard, too—which suggests that Truman took quite a ribbing from his colleagues.[27]

In the midst of FDR's losing battle for the court packing plan Senate majority leader Joe Robinson died. Roosevelt took an intense and personal interest in promoting Senator Alben Barkley as the successor. A substantial number of senators, including Truman, favored Senator Pat Harrison. Sentiment was about evenly divided, and FDR's interest made the close race a hot affair. As the vote was about to come up Boss Tom Pendergast was in Colorado Springs on vacation. Lloyd Stark showed up there, and on July 19 they had a showdown. Pendergast was livid over Stark's decision to fire Missouri insurance commissioner Emmett O'Malley. Although O'Malley was a Pendergast man, Truman and others had regarded him as a political liability and a prime candidate for dumping ever since his attack on fraternal insurance societies that had cost Stark so many votes the year before. Yet Boss Tom was vehement about retaining O'Malley as insurance commissioner, a vehemence that made no sense at the time. Pendergast and Stark became enemies over the issue.

On that same day the boss got a call from New Deal political commander Jim Farley asking him to line up Truman for Barkley in the majority leader election. Pendergast phoned Truman and asked him to vote for Barkley, giving Truman the impression that he had talked with Roosevelt about it. Truman explained that he was pledged to Senator Harrison. Pendergast tried to ease the awkwardness, saying he really didn't care about the majority leader race anyway, but that he had promised the White House he would ask. Reporter Bill Helm saw Truman about an hour later and found him visibly disturbed. "You could never guess what happened to me," Truman said. "Tom Pendergast phoned me and asked me to vote for Barkley for majority leader. And I had to turn him down. Jim Aylward phoned me, too. I didn't mind turning Jim down, not so much anyhow, but to say no to Tom was one of the hardest things I ever had to do." Truman was miffed by the White House action, feeling it implied that he took orders from Pendergast. Truman was sensitive on this point. Farley, of course, had simply contacted the two big Kansas City Democrat leaders, but Truman chose to interpret the call to Pendergast as a personal affront. The press soon publicized the incident. Roosevelt said he knew nothing about the rumor that the White House had called Pendergast—which wasn't a denial of a call by Farley. Pendergast outright denied having asked Truman to vote for Barkley. Truman said nothing about a phone call from Pendergast, but spoke instead of a telegram: "Pendergast's wire said Barkley was a fine fellow, but at the end of his telegram he said for me to use my own judgment. Pendergast has never asked me to vote for or against any legislation." Barkley won by one vote. Truman took pains to display his marked ballot before depositing it, so colleagues would know he voted for Harrison.[28]

Truman's impatience with such treatment was easy to understand since he had already demonstrated his independence from Pendergast in the Public Utility Holding Company Act of 1935. Holding companies are set up to control assets (and thereby policies) of other companies. The money that customers and investors put into an electricity company could go straight to the holding company above it. Stockholders in the electricity company could vote any change they wanted, but such a vote would be meaningless because the holding company was really in charge. Truman had firsthand experience with this technique on a small scale with his old oil companies. Without getting into the subterranean details, suffice to say that for a small capital outlay financiers could control millions of dollars with no accountability. Since their own money was not at risk, financiers attempted reckless gambles. If the gamble went sour, investors and customers took the loss; if the gamble worked, the financiers took the profit. Holding companies allowed great abuses that threatened the availability of gas and electricity service to business and residential customers throughout America. Truman attended and occasionally presided over the hearings on legislation to deal with this situation. "The hearings on the bill were the most remarkable that I ever had anything to do with." Truman watched in amazement as Wendell Willkie (1940 GOP presidential nominee), John W. Davis (1924 DEM presidential nominee), John Foster Dulles (future secretary of state), Hopson, the Whitneys, and other Wall Street financiers tried to explain away their manipulations of utility companies, manipulations that customers had to pay for. Truman declared, "Public utility operating companies are gold mines—oil wells—bonanzas, really, when it comes to making money, and like everything of that kind they attracted the pirates of finance." Hopson "couldn't tell which end of him was up" when testifying, Truman said. "So many of these utility executives know so little about the bill they cannot talk about it intelligently, and others are worrying about what will happen to holding companies that should have been dissolved long ago."[29]

Truman's forthright stand against holding company abuses was in direct contradiction to the wishes of the Pendergast organization in Kansas City, which was hooked up with utility interests. National utility representatives tried to influence Truman directly in Washington without success, though Truman gleefully enjoyed dinners furnished by lobbyists giving him their pitches. The utilities then tried to influence him through the Pendergast machine. The most visible approach from this angle was through the *Kansas City Journal Post,* now allied with Pendergast despite its Republican ownership. This was the newspaper that had helped defeat Truman in his reelection bid for eastern judge. The Dickey family still had a large say in the paper, but had taken on Harry Doherty as a half-owner.

Doherty had been well-publicized in the Teapot Dome scandal investigations. Thus Truman could care less about what the Dickeys or Doherty printed against him. He shrugged off the stories as an effort to sell newspapers. The utilities then resorted to direct mail, which also left Truman unmoved. "I knew that the 'wrecking crew' of Wall Street was at work behind the scenes and that it was responsible for the 30,000 requests which eventually piled up on my desk. I burned them all." The bill passed handily, so easily that Truman felt comfortable going out of town and missing the vote. This wasn't a cave-in to pressure. He had repeatedly declared his support for limiting holding company activities and was ready to rush to Washington if necessary for the voting.[30]

Truman began to make himself felt in airline development. He was excited by the potential of commercial aviation: "Air transport will make Europe, Asia, South America, and Polynesia our nextdoor neighbors. Shanghai is not as far from San Francisco by air as New York is by rail. Rio de Janeiro is closer to Miami by air than Chicago is by rail. We must realize what this means to our foreign trade." He spoke also of a need to integrate airline development into national security: "A policy which will make commercial aviation a second line of defense, just as the merchant marine is the second line of the Navy, and the Reserve Corps is the second line of the Regular Army and the National Guard. . . . Large numbers of trained pilots will be most essential, should an emergency ever come." In the 1930s Truman was one of the most influential senators in drafting and shepherding airline development legislation. He worked hard to shift air safety regulation from the Commerce Department to the Interstate Commerce Commission. One of his strong allies in this, Senator Wheeler, said the public couldn't depend on good safety policy and enforcement from the Commerce Department because the responsible personnel changed every four years and then sought jobs in air transportation companies. Wheeler said air safety should be under the ICC, which changed railroad journeys from risky to routine. Truman went further yet, trying to put all airline matters—not just safety—under the ICC. He urged his case on FDR in writing, but the president refused to support him. Truman sighed, "I tried for two years to have the regulation of air transportation under the Interstate Commerce Commission, but we finally had to compromise and place it in the Civil Aeronautics Authority, which is supposed to have the same rules and regulations governing air transportation that the Interstate Commerce Commission has for other methods of transportation. I think the time will come, however, when every method of transportation will be under the same regulatory body." Time and again Truman found himself pitted against Roosevelt, opposing the president's attempts to abolish the Air Safety Board and his transformation of the Civil Aeronautics Authority from an independent agency into a branch of the Commerce Department. Truman noted the increase of air fatalities following the latter move. He thought his leadership in air transport matters entitled him to patronage favors from the Civil Aeronautics Authority, but he found out otherwise when he approached the agency. In addition to his work for the aviation industry in general, Truman worked specifically to boost Transcontinental and Western Air, Inc. (TWA).[31]

Although Truman's work with aviation was noticed by the industry, the public's imagination was caught by his work with railroads. He was acknowledged as one of the nation's foremost experts in railroad finance, known and feared throughout New York financial circles. The excitable public thrilled to his revelations of how railroads worked. The thoughtful public discussed his proposals for correction of abuses. His Senate colleagues discovered his formidable investigative abilities. Truman the railroad expert and tenacious investigator for the first time became a national figure.

Scarcely a month after he entered the Senate in 1935 Truman horned in on Senator Wheeler's railroad investigation. "Wheeler knew all railroads were guilty of something wrong," newsman Bill Helm recalled, and Wheeler "suspected each was guiltier than the others. In Truman he found a disciple; and while Truman didn't go the full road of Wheeler's philosophy, he did go along for at least two looks and a jump." Truman wasn't chosen as a member of the investigating committee, but he asked Wheeler for permission to attend hearings. Wheeler consented, probably more out of senatorial courtesy than in anticipation of the expertise Truman would bring. Truman crammed for the first committee meeting. "I ransacked the Library of Congress for every book on the subject of railroad management and history, and at one time had 50 volumes sent by the Library to my office." His knowledge took the other senators aback at the first session, and he quickly moved from hanger-on to vice-chairman. The committee had to be frugal since the Senate had allowed only $10,000 for the inquiry. Truman's expertise was almost like getting a free extra counsel. Truman also watched and learned how to stretch money while hiring a clerical staff and obtaining supplies. Of the spadework he said, "Documents had to be impounded, witnesses subpoenaed, and all legal technicalities carefully checked in advance. All this was required before the real work of gathering testimony and holding hearings could begin." He learned how to organize a major Senate investigation.[32]

As the months of testimony proceeded Truman thought a lot about what the investigation uncovered, and the more he thought the madder he got. Toward the end of May 1937 he chewed out seven top railroad executives in the hearing room. A week later he made his first speech on the Senate floor. This was a major effort. Truman began by explaining the relationships of holding companies to operating companies. Railroad operating companies were the organizations that ran locomotives, hauled the freight and passengers, paid wages to employees and (sometimes) dividends to investors. The operating companies were what people thought of when they thought of railways—Missouri Pacific, Great Western, Frisco. Truman went on to explain how operating companies were controlled by holding companies set up by financiers. These two kinds of companies had conflicting interests. The operating companies wanted to make profits by moving traffic. The holding companies wanted to make profits by manipulating stock prices, and to do this they could force the operating companies to do things that harmed the railroads.[33]

Truman ticked off example after example of financiers abusing railroads. He related how Speyer & Co. bankers looted the St. Louis & San Francisco Railway Co. via purchase of $951,000 of Gulf, Mobile & Northern stock. Speyer & Co. were the Frisco's bankers, and when the stock declined to $344,000, Speyer & Co. claimed that the purchase had been on behalf of the Frisco, and forced the rail line to take the loss even though no Frisco records ordering such a stock purchase could be presented. "If the market had gone up as much as it went down, would the Frisco Railway have participated in profits? I leave Senators to draw their own conclusions." Truman noted that Jesse James risked death by robbing the the Rock Island of $3,000, but that thirty years later respected financiers used holding companies to rob the Rock Island of at least $70 million. "Senators can see what 'pikers' Mr. James and his crowd were alongside of some real artists." Truman praised the competency of Missouri Pacific's president L. W. Baldwin, but condemned the men who ran Alleghany Corp., the holding company that ruled MoPac. "Control of 23,000 miles of railroad, with two and a half billions of assets, was bandied about like a plug horse; contrary to the intent of the Interstate Commerce Act, but done nevertheless; and control is held by about one-hundredth of one per cent of investment." Truman inserted a *New York Post* editorial into the *Congressional Record* about the money necessary to gain control of Alleghany and thereby MoPac— that it was the same as spending $2.55 to acquire a $30,000 business. The editorial suggested that such a small stake could encourage carelessness about the business's best interests. The newspaper noted that taxpayers (via government loans to railroads) had a stake in the railroads hundreds of times larger than the manipulators had, and that ordinary investors had more of a stake yet. Truman protested that when Alleghany was first listed on the New York Stock Exchange, insiders could buy at a price lower than that offered to the general public. "A public official who would be a party to such a transaction involving public funds would be called a plain grafter." Truman said, "The Missouri Pacific and the Frisco both serve the richest farming section of the United States. If their operating management had been allowed to operate the railroads for the benefit of their owners, the stockholders, and for the benefit of the territory they serve, it is my opinion that neither road would ever have been in any very serious difficulty. The railroad holding company has proven almost as disastrous to operators of railroads and railroad investors as public utility holding companies have proven to plant operators and investors."[34]

The Senate had been investigating such abuses for at least forty-five years. "Here is a situation which needs attention and which needs a remedy. The able and experienced members of this body ought to be thinking of some sort of cure for railroad holding companies and railroad wholly owned subsidiaries. Both of these devices are used to get around regulations by the Interstate Commerce Commission and to defy the laws of Congress." Truman concluded, "When one of these great transportation companies fails, lawyers and investment bankers sit around like vultures at the death of an elephant. When the receivership comes they get all the flesh, and the stockholders and the public get the bones."[35]

This speech reverberated across the country. "More power to you!" Missouri governor Stark told Truman. "You were certainly right about the small stockholders getting nothing but the 'bones and carcass.' " Truman replied, "I hope eventually some good will come out of it. The federal court in St. Louis has ordered suit brought against Speyer & Company and [bankers] J. & W. Seligman for the various Frisco deals, and I understand that the same procedure will be followed with the Missouri Pacific. If we can get judgment in a few cases like this, maybe we can stop these vultures from carrying on their trade."[36]

The investigations and revelations continued. Truman said that the Chesapeake & Ohio cheated the federal Reconstruction Finance Corp. out of $700,000. He said the money was lent to the Chicago & Eastern Illinois Railway to pay a fraudulent debt to the Chesapeake & Ohio generated from a dummy transaction through Cleveland's Midland Bank. Both roads were part of the Alleghany Corp. that had devastated the Missouri Pacific. The Senate committee found that when Chesapeake & Ohio acquired Chicago & Eastern Illinois "fake documents, including a promissory note which was not a promissory note, a purchase contract which was not a purchase contract, a dummy depository contract, and fake extending contracts, were drafted by leading financial and railroad lawyers and solemnly signed." Testimony showed that Alleghany Corp. sold to Chesapeake & Ohio an option to buy control of the Erie and the Nickel Plate. The sale was because Alleghany urgently needed $5 million to pay off debts to Boston brokers Paine, Weber, & Co. Truman noted that the ICC hadn't approved Chesapeake & Ohio control of Erie and Nickel Plate, and that indeed Chesapeake & Ohio feared such control would violate antitrust laws. The purchase of an option to buy, however, got around this. Chesapeake had no formal control over the two roads, but could continually intimidate the two managements with threats to exercise the option if the roads did anything to displease Chesapeake & Ohio. Of the manipulators behind these schemes Truman's committee asked, "Is their attitude toward government regulation and control so hostile as to justify in their minds such means, or any means, for defeating laws of Congress and administrative regulation? Is the ingenuity of promoters, financiers, and lawyers sufficiently fertile to provide such hostility with devices enabling them to get around the law and to make themselves to this extent more powerful than government itself?"[37]

Testimony also ventilated the Bremo holding company which, Truman's committee said, "was designed to seize control of the Chicago Great Western on a shoestring. The stocks . . . were bought on margin, and even some of the margin was obtained on margin."* Paine, Weber & Co. were the brokers in the Bremo scheme, and had trouble calling the margin after the 1929 stock market crash. Fortunately for Paine, Weber they also happened to be brokers for the manipulators behind Alleghany. The president and treasurer of Bremo were one man, who happened to be the Paine, Weber partner running the Alleghany stock transactions. The Alleghany manipulators were convinced to strip assets from Chesapeake & Ohio to cover Bremo. The men behind Bremo holding company included traffic managers of Shell Oil and Standard Oil of Indiana, of Dodge, Hupp, and Oakland automobile companies, of Libby foods, of Kroger groceries, of Swift meats and Wilson meats, and other corporations with large railroad usage. Truman's committee found that the traffic managers' role was to cheat their companies by diverting freight to Great Western, even though other railways could serve the companies better, and thereby increase profits Bremo could take from Great Western. This cheated investors and customers, and hurt the other railroads.[38]

In summer 1937 "sweltering hours of testimony—during which witnesses and Senate experts alike shed coats and neckties" revealed more wheels within wheels. Great Western got a federal Reconstruction Finance Corp. loan to make a multi-million-dollar purchase of Kansas City Southern railway stock at twice the market price, a huge gift to Kansas City Southern. At the same time Great Western started paying dividends on its own stock for the first time in twenty years when, Truman said, "almost immediately afterwards it had to borrow money from the government to meet its interest pay-

---

*"Margin" is a friendly arrangement with a stockbroker. A buyer wanting $100 of stock might pay $40, the broker paying the other $60. If the broker needed the $60 later he would call for it. This would be "calling the margin." In this hypothetical example, a buyer got $100 of stock for a cash outlay of only $40, although the buyer promised to pay $60 to the broker whenever the broker called for it. Such promises cost nothing—and were sometimes worth exactly what they cost.

ments." He noted that many of these dividends went to Bremo and from there to Virginia Transportation, a holding company controlled by the people behind Alleghany. Thus the traffic managers cheated their companies to acquire Great Western through Bremo, and the Alleghany interests cheated the traffic managers by looting Great Western and Bremo. Truman peeled back layer after layer of corruption.[39]

Just as the committee prepared for autumn 1937 hearings on the Missouri Pacific situation, Senator Wheeler decided to go speechmaking, and left Truman in charge. Truman was irked at Wheeler for leaving the committee a man short, and for putting him on the spot. These MoPac hearings could be expected to excite powerful persons in Truman's home state, particularly since the railroad interests of Pendergast organization associates would be explored. Indeed, Truman began receiving pointed suggestions that a "once over lightly" treatment would be the best approach. The committee staff knew political realities; they offered to bury important evidence. Truman adamantly insisted that the hearings be thorough. Committee counsel Max Lowenthal, aware of the kinds of pressure brought against Truman, was amazed at the senator's strength of character. Lowenthal doubted that many of Truman's colleagues could have resisted such opposition. Truman had no choice: "If I quit this thing now they'll say that Kemper and the Boss pulled me off." Truman confided, "It is a mess and has created a terrible furor in New York. Guaranty Trust and J. P. Morgan have used every means available to make me quit. I'm going to finish the job or die in the attempt. I sure hate it." Truman's health had indeed declined under the past months' strain. "I'm getting jittery, and maybe a chance to sit down a minute would help," he said. "I never needed rest as badly in my life." A journalist who saw Truman noted "black rings under his eyes, and his face is seamed and drawn." Truman's letters to Bess contained chronic complaints of fatigue and headaches, and in the weeks before the MoPac hearings he was afflicted with a heart abnormality. "One valve is smaller than it should be, but it isn't the one that gives trouble, so they say," he wrote from the hospital. Physicians disagreed about whether his heart condition was a problem, and Truman opted for the optimistic view.[40]

As the MoPac hearings progressed Truman became more and

more upset by the revealed corruptions. The October 28 testimony of MoPac treasurer William Wyler made Truman so angry that he recessed the hearing. The next day he wrote, "It has been a most trying and patience straining week. I wanted to punch the witnesses rather than question them because they'd robbed and abused a great property and a lot of the 'widows and orphans' you hear so much about. I really had to pulverize the ring leader yesterday. New York papers had my picture on the financial page and really gave me a nice write up. Even Mr. Hearst gave me the best of it. So I'm calming down somewhat."[41]

Behind MoPac's troubles the committee once again found the Alleghany Corp. In March 1930 Alleghany learned that Missouri law required the Missouri Public Service Commission to consent to Alleghany's acquisition of Missouri Pacific. The commission was pressured to act on twenty-four hours' notice without listening to opponents of the acquisition. Instead, the commission delayed the action seven days but failed to notify likely opponents that the acquisition hearing was scheduled. The committee found that pressure on St. Louis and Kansas City newspapers elicited editorials supporting the acquisition. The committee found that one of the most influential members of the Missouri legislature, Senator Michael Kinney, received $1,000 for unexplained services. Truman's group concluded, "The activities of Alleghany Corporation in winning consent from the Missouri commission indicate the difficulty, if not the impossibility, of state regulation of holding companies." Truman said that in 1931 MoPac began "desperate cutting of expenses and deferred maintenance" to "pay the Van Swearingens money which ought to have gone into additions and betterments" for the railroad. (The Van Swearingen brothers masterminded Alleghany Corp.) Despite denials, the committee concluded that in 1934 Price, Waterhouse & Co. accountants discovered and attempted to keep secret a discrepancy of over $3 million in Missouri Pacific's listed assets. "Price, Waterhouse & Co. violated the specific instructions of the trustee, and the confidence of the public in certifying a report that departed from even minimum standards of correctness, accuracy, and truth." Truman revealed that the St. Louis, Brownsville & Mexico and the New Orleans, Texas & Mexico railroads generated money that MoPac sent to Alleghany. On the day of that revelation

Truman wrote, "I have a notion it didn't please Mr. Kemper very much. But I can't help it. I'm not working for him. I'm working for Missouri."[42]

"I'm not so sure that even after I've aired all the Missouri Pacific dirty linen that anything but another chance to dirty some more will come of it," Truman sighed. "The money boys control the country, and there's no use trying to keep 'em from it. All we can do is to make the yoke as easy as possible." Indeed, he discovered that the current MoPac reorganization plan included bankers and insurance men whom J. P. Morgan & Co. had favored with Alleghany Corp. shares at $15.00 under the market price. Committee investigators claimed the reorganization would leave the Alleghany crowd still in control of Missouri Pacific. Regarding the so-called "reform" of Alleghany Corp., they found the changes merely cosmetic, and concluded that even under intense scrutiny and wide publicity the financial community was incapable of self-reform.[43]

On December 17, 1937 Truman announced to the Senate that he intended to make a railroad speech December 20. He was nervous about it, and had been vacillating about whether to go ahead. "It probably will catalogue me as a radical, but it will be what I think," he confided to Bess. Some Senate speeches are delivered to a nearly empty chamber, but the advance publicity for this one attracted a crowd that probably expected quite a show. They got one. In reading the official transcript you can almost hear the gasps from the audience. The content of questions from fellow senators shows their attention riveted on Truman.[44]

Truman started off denouncing favored persons who bought Alleghany or other rail securities below market prices, a feat made possible courtesy of J. P. Morgan & Co. and Kuhn, Loeb bankers. "Why, it is almost a racket, or I might say, the biggest racket on Earth." Since large banks don't just give away assets, the implication was that such bargains were payments for services rendered. Truman had in his hand a list of the favored persons, and while he refrained from reading it aloud he did print it as part of his remarks:

Charles Francis Adams (Hoover's Navy secretary)
Newton Baker (Baltimore & Ohio director, Wilson's war secretary)
Russell C. Leffingwell (Wilson's assistant treasury secretary)

William Gibbs McAdoo (senator from California in 1937 and Wilson's treasury secretary)
Hornblower & Weeks (brokerage firm of Harding's war secretary)
John W. Davis (1924 DEM presidential nominee)
Calvin Coolidge
Edgar Rickard (personal financial agent for President Hoover)
William Woodin (FDR's treasury secretary)
Edward R. Stettinius, Jr. (FDR's future secretary of state)

Truman had hundreds of names, a veritable *Who's Who* of government and finance. "Some of the so-called investment bankers had a gratuity list. This consisted of high rail officials. One in particular was E. N. Brown, chairman of the board of the Frisco. . . . Speyer & Co. paid him a gratuity of $100,000 per year, and the poor old Frisco paid him as chairman of the board to help Speyer & Co. loot it."[45]

Truman waxed indignant about the Cravath law firm's involvement in various railroad receiverships. For generations the Cravath organization had been a shadow government. The firm's alumni included:

John P. Crosby (son-in-law of Jackson's and Van Buren's attorney general)
Richard Blatchford (tutor in the Robert R. Livingston family; adviser to Zachary Taylor; estate executor of Daniel Webster, who was secretary of state under William Henry Harrison, Tyler, and Fillmore)
Abraham Lincoln (local counsel for Springfield, Illinois, litigation; father of President Garfield's and President Arthur's war secretary)
William H. Seward (Lincoln's and Andrew Johnson's secretary of state)
Samuel Blatchford (Supreme Court justice and private secretary to William H. Seward)
Clarence A. Seward (nephew of William H. Seward)
Maxwell Evarts (son of Andrew Johnson's attorney general and Rutherford Hayes's secretary of state)
James McReynolds (U.S. Supreme Court justice and Wilson's attorney general)
Russell C. Leffingwell
Paul D. Cravath (law partner of Charles Evans Hughes, who was

U.S. chief justice, the 1916 GOP presidential nominee, and sec-
retary of state for Harding and Coolidge)
Joseph P. Cotton (Hoover's undersecretary of state and law partner
of one of Wilson's treasury secretaries)
Roswell Magill (FDR's treasury undersecretary)
John J. McCloy (FDR's assistant war secretary)
William O. Douglas (FDR's Securities & Exchange Commission
chairman and Supreme Court justice)

The Cravath organization was one of the nation's largest law firms,
and many more of its associates could be found throughout the three
branches and many agencies of the federal government. Truman had
already demanded that the New York City Bar Association investigate the conduct of Cravath partner Robert T. Swaine in the 1925
Chicago, Milwaukee & St. Paul railroad receivership. (This was
rather like demanding that the House of Representatives impeach
FDR, and Truman was amazed when the Bar Association president
actually started an inquiry. "Maybe I've done some good after all.")[46]
Truman explained that the St. Paul receivership was arranged by
"Mr. Shaw, of Winston, Strawn & Shaw—this is the Mr. Silas
Strawn, past president of the National Chamber of Commerce, and
a great uplifter—to have Judge Wilkerson, the most notorious receivership judge on the federal bench, take charge of the St. Paul
bankruptcy and appoint receivers and the attorneys for the receivers.
All these arrangements were secretly fixed up, and Mr. Shaw claims
this was done to keep out the sharpshooters." Truman had earlier
called on the Chicago Bar Association to investigate Ralph Shaw,
who Truman said was getting instructions from Kuhn, Loeb attorney
Swaine. Truman's investigators found evidence that Judge James
Wilkerson secretly considered one reorganization plan months before
the official proceedings. Kuhn, Loeb lawyer Paul Cravath asked
Shaw to explain the plan to Wilkerson so the judge wouldn't "get
any wrong notions about the plan." Shaw told Cravath the situation
had been dealt with. Truman sputtered, "If it goes as it appears on
the surface, it is a matter for impeachment." Indeed, the House
Judiciary Committee chairman began looking into the advisability
of impeaching Wilkerson. To his Senate colleagues Truman proclaimed, "Judge Wilkerson had a Milwaukee & St. Paul private
[railway] car at his beck and call in which to take his pleasure. The

receivers also had a grand time in this respect. One or more of them even took their families and their friends on long jaunts in the poor old busted St. Paul's private cars to San Diego, to New York, to Florida, and on trips extended on free passes to Alaska."[47]

Appalled by huge fees obtained by persons in the St. Paul receivership, Truman now presented a list of receipts accruing to the Cadwalader, Wickersham & Taft law firm, the Davis, Polk, Wardwell, Gardiner & Reed firm, the Sullivan & Cromwell firm, the Root, Clark, Buckner & Ballantine firm, the Shearman & Sterling firm, and the Cravath firm. Again the firmament trembled. The Cadwalader firm was organized in 1796, and had served some corporate clients for over a century. Chief Justice Hughes had declined an offer to take Cadwalader's place when that partner died. Wickersham was attorney general under Taft (who preceded Hughes as chief justice). Taft's brother was a member of the firm. The Davis of Davis, Polk was the 1924 DEM presidential nominee John W. Davis whom Truman had already encountered in probes of public utility scandals. Davis had formerly been with Grover Cleveland's law firm along with the brother-in-law of J. P. Morgan. Polk was a relative of President James K. Polk. Sullivan & Cromwell was the firm of Harlan Stone, Coolidge's attorney general whom FDR would appoint chief justice to succeed Hughes. The firm's best-known partner was John Foster Dulles, whom Truman had also encountered in the public utilities scandals inquiry. Thomas Dewey briefly accepted a partnership offer from Dulles, but immediately had to decline due to the press of political activity with which Truman became all too familiar. About the time Truman made his railroad speech Richard Nixon tried to enter Sullivan & Cromwell, but was rejected. Root, Clark was the firm of Elihu Root, secretary of war for McKinley and Theodore Roosevelt. Root's law partner Henry Stimson held the same job under Taft, FDR, and Truman, in addition to being secretary of state under Hoover. Root and Paul D. Cravath were Thomas Fortune Ryan's attorneys. The Ballantine of Root, Clark was a Harvard classmate of FDR and of Hoover's treasury secretary Mills. The Clark of Root, Clark was in the class ahead of them. Clark was once with the law firm of Chief Justice Hughes's father-in-law. The Shearman & Sterling firm had the same connections. Truman was exposing some mighty powerful people: "Now, the St. Paul is only one receivership of some dozen or two. Do you see how it pays to know all about these things from the inside? How these gentlemen, the highest of the high-hat in the legal profession, resort to tricks that would make an ambulance chaser in a coroner's court blush with shame?"[48]

Decades later we can still sense Truman's emotion:

We worship money instead of honor. A billionaire, in our estimation, is much greater in these days in the eyes of the people than the public servant who works for the public interest. It makes no difference if the billionaire rode to wealth on the sweat of little children and the blood of underpaid labor. No one ever considered Carnegie libraries steeped in the blood of the Homestead steel workers, but they are. We do not remember that the Rockefeller Foundation is founded on the dead miners of the Colorado Fuel & Iron Company and a dozen other similar performances. We worship mammon; and until we go back to ancient fundamentals and return to the Giver of the Tables of the Law and His teachings, these conditions are going to remain with us.

It is a pity that Wall Street, with its ability to control all the wealth of the nation and to hire the best law brains in the country, has not produced some financial statesmen, some men who could see the dangers of bigness and of the concentration of the control of wealth. Instead of working to meet the situation, they are still employing the best law brains to serve greed and selfish interest. People can stand only so much, and one of these days there will be a settlement. . . .

I believe the country would be better off if we did not have 60% of the assets of all the insurance companies concentrated in four companies. I believe that a thousand insurance companies, with $4 million each in assets, would be just a thousand times better for the country than the Metropolitan Life, with its $4 billion in assets. The average human brain is not built to deal with such astronomical figures. I also say that a thousand county seat towns of 7000 people each are a thousand times more important to this Republic than one city of 7 million people. Our unemployment and our unrest are the result of the concentration of wealth, the concentration of population in industrial centers, mass production, and a lot of other so-called improvements. We are building a Tower of Babel . . . .

Wild greed along the lines I have been describing brought on the depression. When investment bankers, so-called, continually load great transportation companies with debt in order to sell securities to savings banks and insurance companies so they can make a commission, the well finally runs dry. . . .

I do not think we can solve the problem by pouring more government money into broken down financial structures or by merely tinkering with rates. The whole structure must be overhauled. Rates, finances, management, coordination, consolidation must be studied. The problem can be solved, but not through the kind of panacea Wall Street has put forward in the past—panaceas that are basically and fundamentally unsound, which have been proved in experience to be unsound, and which simply serve the interest of Wall Street at the expense of the public interest. There is no magic solution to the condition of the railroads, but one thing is certain—no formula, however scientific, will work without men of proper character responsible for physical and financial operations of the roads and for the administration of the laws provided by Congress.[49]

Truman's emotional denunciation of financiers who destroyed railroads was all the more telling because listeners knew he had facts to support every statement. He found himself being accepted into the "Progressive Establishment," an exciting experience. He bubbled, "Last night I went out to call on Mr. Justice Brandeis, a wonderful old man. It was his 81st birthday. One of my investigators had been his secretary, and I went out with him. Nobody there but just the three of us, and we discussed anti-trust laws and holding companies." Brandeis started inviting Truman to Sunday teas, and he became a fixture at them for years. "The justice spent more time with me than any of his other guests and seemed very much interested in what we are doing to the railroad and insurance companies. . . . It was a rather exclusive and brainy party. I didn't exactly belong, but they made me think I did." Truman also got to know Justice Stone, "another great progressive on the Supreme Court. He'd written a dissenting opinion on railroad reorganization, and I got a lot of information from him." Truman felt he had really arrived when old Senator Norris began paying attention to him.[50]

The White House now acknowledged Truman's expertise in railroad matters, and over the coming years Truman presented various proposals intended to eliminate the abuses he had revealed. "This is the day of appeasement," he said in 1939. "Appeasement seems to be in the air. . . . I shall not attempt or even consider a policy of appeasement for the railroads." He explained how the mere refunding of old debts had to stop and be replaced by an amortization program. He showed how competitive bidding could yield better prices for bonds. He proposed a method by which the federal Reconstruction Finance Corp. could buy bonds of railroads facing bankruptcy or reorganization. The formula of purchase would both bail out the railroads and seemingly guarantee repayment of the RFC loan. He called for simplification in freight rates. "Railroads exist for one purpose only, to transport passengers and freight around the country. It is a sales proposition, and if they cannot sell transportation to the country and their competitors can, the railroads will go out of business just as the old river packets did." Truman expressed confidence, however, that young imaginative managers could revamp the rail system. He scoffed at railroad complaints about government interference. "I will say that for every regulation there was an abuse to cure, which the railroads themselves could have cured but did not." He noted that railroad purchases of supplies had declined $1 billion a year since 1923. "Any time a billion dollars a year . . . is taken from the stream of commerce, you have the difference between prosperity and a so-called depression or recession. A billion dollar purchase is a pretty good pump primer in itself." Truman saw railroads not only in their transportation function but in their relation to a healthy economy. His work to correct abuses was not so much to right wrongs, as to enable railroads to make money in a way that would benefit the entire economy and all businesses. In the broadest sense he was the ally of businessmen large and small. This was eventually realized by some financiers themselves. Of a 1939 visit to New York bankers, Truman wrote, "Last night I had dinner at the University Club with . . . a lot of millionaires. There were 13 at the table. . . . They were trying to impress the country boy, I guess, but the country banker told me as we went to the train that the sale had been the other way." Indeed, financiers such as Cyrus Eaton began turning to Truman for confidential advice.[51]

An opportunity arose for Truman directly to correct one example of an abuse. The occasion was satisfying because he had no direct authority over the corporation lawyers he criticized for excessive fees in receivership cases. In Kansas City, however, the federal district attorney Maurice Milligan (brother of Tuck Milligan who ran against Truman in 1934) had been cleaning up with receivership fees that exceeded his salary. These cases were assigned by judges Otis and Reeves, and the amount of income raised questions about whether Milligan was under some sort of obligation to the judges. This wouldn't be such a big deal with a corporation lawyer, but with Milligan an obligation to the judges could affect the prosecutions he pursued. So in Truman's view the situation was doubly offensive. Milligan's term was running out, and under normal patronage courtesies Truman could expect to choose the replacement. Truman could also expect acclaim for personally eliminating an outrage on public sensibilities. Nothing is certain in politics, however, and several factors coming together would change Truman's no-lose situation into a no-win proposition that would cost him dearly.[52]

Chapter 12

NEW DEALER
AT BAY

Enter *dramatis personae:* Franklin Delano Roosevelt, Bennett Champ Clark, Lloyd Crow Stark, Albert L. Reeves, *Kansas City Star*.

Roosevelt was having nightmares over California politics. "I had lunch with [William Gibbs] McAdoo," Truman told Bess one day. "He's been treated shamefully by the President. He said people had been appointed in California who were his (McAdoo's) bitterest enemies." McAdoo was Woodrow Wilson's son-in-law, and had been his treasury secretary. FDR had been in Wilson's subcabinet (assistant Navy secretary) and had known McAdoo for years. California had a lot of electoral votes, which would affect the 1940 presidential election, so FDR had a strong incentive to stay on top of the murky California politics—waters further muddied by Truman's revelation that McAdoo had accepted rail securities at bargain prices (the revelation came some months after his lunch with McAdoo). A 1932 McAdoo Senate campaign manager, Peirson Hall, became U.S. district attorney for southern California. He and McAdoo quarreled, and in late 1937 McAdoo refused to support Hall for reappointment. In the outcome Hall filed for the 1938 Democrat Senate nomination against McAdoo, later withdrawing to become campaign manager for the man who would defeat McAdoo. This dismal drama was underway when Roosevelt's acute antennae sensed tremors in Missouri, and he turned to Attorney General Cummings for confirmation.[1]

Cummings reported that the Pendergast organization supposedly opposed Milligan's reappointment as district attorney, but that Cummings had yet to hear anything from Truman or Senator Clark on the matter. FDR was not reassured. He told Cummings, "I have very good reason to believe that he [Milligan] ought to be reappointed, and I think if you and I from now on take the position that we have heard no valid reason against his reappointment, it will help him to be confirmed next February [1938]. McAdoo is in all kinds of hot water over his insistence that Hall be not reappointed, and if either of the Missouri Senators were to oppose Milligan it is my judgment that it would hurt them and the Democratic Party in the same way." Senator Clark had originally wanted Carl Ristine for the Missouri U.S. district attorney job. Congressman Tuck Milligan was pushing for his brother Maurice. The Justice Department sent word that Ristine was unacceptable, but that Maurice Milligan was okay. Clark then forced the Justice Department to give Ristine an $8,500-a-year job before Clark would support Milligan. Thus FDR knew that Milligan was the first choice of neither Truman nor Clark. Indeed, Truman wrote, Clark and Maurice Milligan "almost came to blows the last time they met, and now the Pres and Stark are thinking of running him for Senator against Clark."[2]

Bennett Champ Clark was up for reelection in 1938. Whenever FDR came over to Congress with a New Deal proposal Clark stuck a knife in his back. Roosevelt always pulled it out, and handed it back to Clark with a jaunty grin, saying, "Bennett, I believe you misplaced this knife." Clark smiled, too, "Thank you, Mr. President, I believe I did," and immediately stuck the blade into Roosevelt again, a little deeper and with a twist. Truman, on the other hand, was one of the most loyal New Dealers in the Senate. FDR the canny politician responded by giving Clark all the Missouri patronage, and leaving Truman in the cold. Truman resented this bitterly, yet he remained unwavering in support of the New Deal—demonstrating incidentally that Roosevelt was correct in seeing no need to thank Truman. Truman thought the president's policy would backfire, strengthening opposition to him in Missouri instead of support. To an extent Truman was right—Clark's people disbelieved in the New Deal and administered its Missouri programs in a ham-handed way inciting many voters against the New Deal. On the other hand, Roosevelt proved himself politician enough to get elected president four times, so he may have known what he was doing with Missouri patronage.[3]

Interestingly enough Clark was mad at Truman over patronage. Back in the early days when the White House was cutting Truman in on patronage, he and Clark made agreements on patronage matters, which Truman then ignored. For instance, they agreed to keep mum on an upcoming federal judge appointment until they agreed on candidates, and Truman then recommended Guy Park, Al Ridge, and Daniel Bird as the men to choose from. (Park was occupying the governor's mansion for Pendergast; "Uncle Tom's Cabin" it was called. Circuit Judge Ridge was one of the cannoneers who stood by Truman at the Battle of Who Run. Circuit Judge Bird had been quashing suits that Pendergast opponents were still attempting against Truman over his conduct as presiding judge.) Then there was the months-long matter of attempting to engineer the appointment of Columbia National Bank vice-president Charles L. Aylward to the Federal Reserve Board. Congressman Jasper Bell of Kansas City received word in February 1936 that "Clark and Truman have both been advised by James Aylward [Charles's brother] and Pendergast to do the necessary. They are now trying to get in touch with Farley." Clark was still out on this Pendergast limb when Truman publicly announced for Jake Vardaman, son of the old Mississippi U.S. Senator. This was particularly embarrassing for Clark since Vardaman was a St. Louis banker—Clark appeared to be neglecting his hometown. So when the Milligan matter arose Clark was in no mood to help out Truman the New Dealer with any patronage desires.[4]

His Excellency the Governor of Missouri and Protector of Its Liberties Lloyd Crow Stark professed to be shocked, utterly shocked, by evidence that the Pendergast machine may have stuffed ballot boxes to elect Stark in 1936. His Excellency pledged himself to eradicate this threat to democracy. He started off by revamping the election boards supervising Kansas City and Jackson County, a move that crippled ballot stuffing. He also began checking the political endorsements of state workers, and those who had gotten jobs through Pendergast and Truman (there were actual printed forms kept by the state showing these data) found themselves unemployed. Before the Pendergast machine caught on to the game, Boss Tom's nephew

Jim would go down to Jeff City at Stark's request. His Excellency would ask Jim to look over a list of names and recommend which ones should get choice patronage plums. Jim would ride back to Kansas City thinking warm thoughts about that swell Mr. Stark, and the men Jim recommended would wait and wait and wait but never get hired. When the Pendergast organization finally figured the score, the reaction was fierce. After all, how did His Majesty the Royal Ingrate think he got elected anyway? It turned out Stark had plans to run for the U.S. Senate in 1940, plans that required the Pendergast organization to produce few votes in that election for Truman. It also turned out that His Excellency had been cultivating FDR, and that Roosevelt's "very good reason" to support Milligan may have had something to do with Stark's White House visits. "The Gov. and the Pres would like to be heroes and boss busters," Truman groaned. And Milligan was out to bust Pendergast.[5]

He was assigned this job by federal judge Albert L. Reeves. He had once been part of the Kansas City law firm Humphrey, Boxley & Reeves. This was the firm that had looked after Truman's personal and commercial business for so many years. The firm dissolved when Warren Harding appointed his Republican friend Reeves to the federal bench. Boxley was a machine Democrat who thrived as county counselor under presiding judge Truman. The two had been watching Reeves for some time. Boxley reported "considerable talk that Judge Reeves is much worried about his status and particularly since E. Mont Reilly [Hardings's governor of Puerto Rico] has been after him pretty strong showing up some of his past and some things which have occurred since he has been judge." Boxley alerted Truman that "Governor Reilly may have Reeves impeached," adding "I will not detail here the things which have been told to me, but if you ever need to know a lot of details which sound unsavory, I will furnish them to you." Boxley did note one case in which Reeves reportedly "is very much worried because some of the parties have taken an appeal. In another case of a receivership, I was told by one of the attorneys the other day that he expects to start a Congressional investigation. . . . The U.S. Court of Appeals has already criticized Judge Reeves in a number of cases." Reeves's friends grew increasingly worried about him in the latter 1930s. Boxley reported reason to believe Humphrey had gotten Kansas City Life Insurance vice-president Ed. Villmoare to go to Washington in Reeves's behalf.

Truman mentioned, "Mr. Kemper was in town the other day, but did not come to see me. . . . I could not find out what he wanted, but imagine I will find out when it is too late to do anything about it." Boxley responded immediately, "I would not doubt but that Mr. Kemper was there on some mission for Judge Reeves as he has been quite close to him, and Reeves permitted him to do a great many things about which he has been censured. This is very confidential, of course."[6]

So Judge Reeves was in the market for favorable publicity when the 1936 ballots were counted for Stark and the other Pendergast candidates. The totals seemed questionable, but Jackson County totals always seemed questionable. Reeves himself felt the Pendergasts had robbed him of a seat in Congress when he ran in 1918. Starting a foray against Pendergast Democrat vote frauds would not only settle an old grudge but put Republican Reeves in the headlines as a defender of democracy. District Attorney Maurice Milligan, to whom Reeves had been throwing those lucrative bankruptcy receivership fees, was cooperative. "When a man casts a dishonest ballot, he cocks and fires a gun at the heart of America," Reeves told the grand jury. "Gentlemen, reach for all, even if you find them in high authority. Move on them!"[7]

The *Kansas City Star* followed all this with great interest, and reported those parts which would harm Pendergast and Truman. By September 1937 the *Star* was saying that Truman would oppose reappointment of Maurice Milligan, the fearless D.A. who was exposing Pendergast depredations. In October the *Star* reported that FDR would back Milligan. The stage was set for an epic confrontation of evil against good, hometown boy against the Supreme Leader, a confrontation that would sell newspapers. Truman was scrambling, with calls to Jim Farley and efforts to see FDR. Truman tried to curry favor by rushing to Kansas City solely to introduce Eleanor Roosevelt at a speech she gave, but didn't even get a thank you. On January 22, 1938 Truman announced that Farley had squelched Milligan's reappointment, but the *Star* noted that FDR hadn't yet agreed. This was exciting. The formal submission of Milligan's name would be in less than two weeks . . . if it occurred. One could hardly wait to buy the next edition. On January 27 the *Star* heightened suspense by reminding readers that the White House "is under heavy obligations to Senator Truman," which was certainly news to him.

The next day readers learned that Governor Stark had twice spoken to FDR about Milligan, and had urged the D.A.'s retention. The same day Truman revealed that the Justice Department was probing Milligan's receivership fees, and the department confirmed this. Two days later the *Star* announced that Truman was speeding home to consult with Boss Tom. On January 31 Truman, Boss Tom, and Jim Pendergast met for an hour at 1908 Main Street. Truman declined comment on the meeting but said he would speak on the matter in Washington. Boss Tom told the *Star* only, "Whatever is said will be by Senator Truman on the floor of the Senate." The next night Truman attended the St. Louis Advertising Club gridiron dinner. A skit lampooned Truman, Stark, and other Missouri politicians. In one skit an FDR character asked a Charlie McCarthy character, "What is Senator Truman's relationship to Tom Pendergast?" Charlie replied, "You know my relationship to Edgar Bergen—weell—." The audience roared with laughter.[8]

From St. Louis Truman went to Chicago where he received a telephone call from the president of the United States. Roosevelt told him that he had formally submitted Milligan's reappointment to the Senate and asked Truman, as a personal courtesy, to permit confirmation. (Under Senate tradition Truman theoretically could have blocked Milligan by declaring the nomination "personally obnoxious.") Truman unhappily agreed. This call showed FDR's sensitivity, allowing Truman to extricate himself gracefully from an awkward situation. No one, neither critics nor even Boss Tom Pendergast, could accuse ultra-New Dealer Truman of surrendering the fight by acceding to a personal request from Roosevelt. Almost immediately afterward the White House announced that Truman, federal Reconstruction Finance Corp. chairman Jesse Jones, Securities & Exchange Commission chairman William O. Douglas, and nine others would soon meet with the president to discuss the railroad industry. This was a strong message that the president discounted the current media portrayal of Truman as a corrupt political hack, but instead still valued the senator as one of the nation's leading authorities on railway finance and management.[9]

Truman had worked himself into a fury when the Senate voted on the nomination. He privately exploded that Milligan was "a drunkard, libertine, and a grafter, but he's helping them [*Kansas City Star* and *St. Louis Post-Dispatch*] now so he is a great man." Truman's remarks to the Senate were scarcely less intemperate. He began calmly, emphasizing that he supported honest elections, and calling for the conviction of persons involved with corrupt balloting. He further called for the retention of Milligan as a special prosecutor to finish the job. (Indeed, Milligan's predecessor had been in the middle of the Johnny Lazia investigation, and was retained as a special prosecutor to finish that job. There were no cries then that changing district attorneys was a plot to protect Pendergast.) Truman then outlined his complaints about Milligan's receivership fees and about judges Reeves and Otis. Truman noted an old *Kansas City Star* editorial condemning Reeves as unfit for the federal bench. Of Merrill Otis, he said, "Mr. Otis has spent his time since he has been a federal judge in going up and down the country making partisan speeches, which I do not think is the right thing for a federal judge to do." Truman went on:

These two judges have made it perfectly plain to Mr. Milligan—and he has been able to see eye to eye with them, due to the bankruptcy emoluments—that convictions of Democrats is what they want. Lawyers in Kansas City have been afraid to act as defendant attorneys in these cases because it was plainly intimated to them that the Federal judges did not consider it the proper thing to do. Lawyers all expect to practice in the federal court. In fact, a good friend of mine told me that he did not dare to act as a defendant lawyer in these cases because he had important matters pending in Judge Otis's court.

No one in Jackson County is allowed on the jury panels. Everyone in a community of 600,000 people is barred from jury service in the federal court of western Missouri on these cases. Grand juries were hand-picked and the attitude of the grand jury men was ascertained by the court in advance.

Petit jury panels are investigated by the Secret Service, and if a man is found to have acquaintances in Jackson County he is barred from service.

I say to the Senate, Mr. President, that a Jackson County, Missouri, Democrat has as much chance of a fair trial in the Federal District Court of Western Missouri as a Jew would have in a Hitler court or a Trotsky follower before Stalin. Indictments have been wholesale. Convictions have been a foregone conclusion. Verdicts have been directed. This is federal court justice in western

Missouri, on the face of it a conspiracy between the partisan federal judges and their bought and paid for district attorney.[10]

At this point Senator H. Styles Bridges, a brash New Hampshire Republican, began taunting Truman, enumerating some of the widespread Kansas City vote frauds, noting that one of Truman's 1934 campaign managers, Alfred R. (Dick) Hendricks, had been imprisoned for later WPA payroll padding. (Earlier when someone tried to warn Truman about Hendricks, the senator snapped, "There are always people in every community who like to tear people down whenever it is possible, and it seems you belong to that class.") Truman's Senate remarks invited a partisan response, since his excitement had caused him to veer from questions of Milligan's receivership fees. In addition, several of Truman's assertions were incorrect (or highly questionable): about the Secret Service, about the selection of grand jury members, about the political allegiance of defendants. Truman sounded like his main concern was that Pendergast machine frauds were being exposed. Senator Clark made the classic defense of scoundrels, pointing out that even if the Milligan-Reeves-Otis receivership fee arrangement was immoral, it was legal. Truman's shrill speech, which he read from a carefully prepared and revised typescript, only accentuated the news media scenario that the Milligan nomination was a vote for or against honest elections. After proclaiming that innocent men were being imprisoned, Truman cast the only vote against Milligan. All his colleagues, Republican and Democrat, voted to confirm.[11]

The *Kansas City Star* ranted, "The people of Kansas City know that in all the history of rotten elections in this city, Senator Truman never once has done anything to help clean them up." This was quite true, and was the theme of the newspaper's coverage of the Truman-Milligan controversy. Day after day the *Star* presented Truman as the Pendergast machinist seeking to thwart the vote fraud prosecutions. This was quite untrue, and Truman resented it. Unquestionably some of the precinct and ward boys wanted Milligan out of the way for that reason. Truman, however, was simply trying to correct an example of the receivership fee abuses that he had condemned in the railroad hearings. Indeed, had he failed to act in this hometown instance theoretically under his control, critics could have claimed he pursued a double standard. Truman had no intention of hampering the vote fraud prosecutions, as demonstrated by his insistence that Milligan be retained as a special prosecutor until the investigation and adjudication were completed. Even if a Pendergast stooge had replaced Milligan as district attorney, that would have had no effect on the vote fraud cases. Yet the *Star* continually charged that Truman wanted a new district attorney in order to stop those cases. This was a bum rap. Truman didn't encourage those prosecutions, but when the process began he made no attempt to obstruct justice. "I do not care to be put in the position of supporting fraudulent elections," he told the *Star*.[12]

A related patronage dispute arose during the Milligan affair, this one over the job of U.S. marshal. The *Kansas City Star* declared that the jobs of district attorney and marshal were vitally linked, and that Marshal Henry Dillingham should be retained. Governor Stark also urged FDR to retain Dillingham, purring, "My only interest in this matter is in the cause of honest elections." Observers felt Truman had been after that patronage since 1936, and indeed Truman was pushing Fred Canfil for that job in the middle of the Milligan business even though Dillingham was a Truman relative and had been vice-president of Truman's Greater Kansas City Regional Plan Association. Canfil had a murky background, and took pains to keep it that way. He was another of Truman's Army Reserve buddies, and had been big in the 1934 Senate campaign. In temperament he was like Truman's cousin Snapper, a trait all the more fearsome because of Canfil's size—"Bull of the Woods" was one nickname. Some people had doubts about the Bull. Fred Boxley told Truman, "I went into the Kansas City Club for luncheon today, and Judge McElroy motioned me to sit down at his table and have lunch with him. He was alone, and one of the first things he asked me was who this fellow Canfil was. I told him." McElroy then said, "Well, Harry knows what he is doing, I guess, but I would not want anybody making the statements he (F.C.) is making." Boxley warned Truman, "I hope you remember what I had told you before, and, at least, caution him [Canfil] to be more careful." Time passed, and Truman's faith in Canfil remained unshaken, "While he is somewhat peculiar in his actions, he is 100% loyal and would cut a throat for me." The Bull's fists were known to flatten opponents without orders from the senator. Canfil handled many patronage matters for Truman and also did sensitive political liaison and intelligence work. A

Truman associate recalled, "I know of instances where, when Mr. Truman didn't want to send anyone else out, he would send Fred Canfil; because Fred would do exactly what he asked him to, and he'd take the word back exactly the way that he found it." Canfil served as go-between for Boss Pendergast and Senator Truman, and stayed with Truman into the White House. Truman was adamant that Canfil would become U.S. marshal, "This one will not end like the Milligan affair." The Justice Department told Truman that it opposed Canfil, and favored the incumbent Dillingham. Apparently this attitude was influenced by an FBI investigation of Canfil's mysterious background. Truman became livid, and implied that the FBI talked only to Canfil's political enemies. He raised such a stink that Assistant Attorney General Carl Ristine (whom Senator Clark had once preferred for Milligan's district attorney job) went to Kansas City to investigate Canfil further. In the end Dillingham stayed. Truman was mad at the White House over this, feeling that his New Deal loyalty had been rewarded with slaps over Milligan and Canfil. This feeling was unjustified; the White House merely wanted to avoid the kind of damage that Truman brought on himself by opposing Milligan and Dillingham. FDR's telephone call to Truman in Chicago, and the White House railroad conference showed that Roosevelt understood Truman's political needs and that the president was doing the best he could to help the senator. Truman showed no such sensitivity for Roosevelt's position. (Truman's support for Canfil remained tenacious, and years later Canfil finally became U.S. marshal.)[13]

Truman snorted, "All this hullabaloo is simply about the Kansas City election, and as soon as we win that in the usual manner all controversy will cease." Those sentiments are hard to beat in cynicism, conceit, and ignorance of one's environment. Yet true enough, in the midst of the Milligan and Canfil controversies Kansas City was holding a municipal election. This was touted as the big test of Pendergast against his opponents, winner take all. The assorted anti-Pendergast factions and reform groups were in full battle array. Governor Stark's election board had eliminated tens of thousands of fraudulent Pendergast votes, and zealots were enforcing an honest ballot count. In addition, Pendergast's authentic support had eroded. Labor was mad about City Manager McElroy's handling of the Ford Motor Company's threat to close its Kansas City operation unless the police ran off CIO picketers. McElroy went to Detroit and discussed the matter with Henry Ford himself. On McElroy's return the police attacked the CIO pickets with tear gas and gunfire, and the union men resisted as best they could. The outcome was inevitable but it had not yet been reached on election day. The Ford matter was only one of several labor disputes, and in Washington Truman privately recognized the political problem: "Had dinner with Paul Nachtman and Mr. Pratt of the labor relations board last night and found out all the low down on the Ford, Montgomery Ward, and Nell Donnelly situations. There is a lot more behind the scenes in all those troubles than publicly appears. . . . Our city manager has had a finger in most of those things and sometimes a sledge hammer." Even more important was the growing alienation of J. C. Nichols, James M. Kemper, and other members of Kansas City's mercantile elite who had earlier supported the Pendergast machine. Part of the disenchantment was the machine's inability to resist the rising labor union strength; bribes and thugs no longer did the trick. Part of the disenchantment was the growing expense of supporting the machine in return for declining benefits. Walter Matscheck's indomitable Civic Research Institute had been thoroughly demonstrating how McElroy and his crew were juggling the city's account books and misspending bond money. Businessmen became all too aware that the machine was no longer cost effective. Since the judicial system exists to protect businessmen, this accounts for much of the Pendergast organization's growing legal problems. Still another factor against Pendergast was the Great Fear that had been used so effectively for so many years, the continual threats against the livelihood and lives of people who failed to cooperate with the machine. People were getting fed up with goons and gangsters.[14]

Thus consternation was great in March 1938 when Pendergast won the Kansas City election as Truman had predicted, despite the well-organized opposition and a fair ballot count. Truman gleefully inserted Boss Tom's victory statement into the *Congressional Record*:

If it is true, as the *Kansas City Star* and the Coalition speakers reported, that the Democratic President of the United States was against us, that the Attorney General of the United States was against us, that the Governor of the state of Missouri was against us, that the independent *Kansas City Star* newspaper was against us—I think under those circumstances we made a wonderful showing.

The only further thing I have to say is that the Democratic officeholders elected yesterday will go on doing their duty to Kansas City business interests and to Kansas City generally.

There never has been and there never will be any reprisals, as was stated by the Coalition speakers, and the Democratic organization which I represent will do its utmost for the best interests of Kansas City now, and for all times in the future.

Jim Farley sent congratulations—probably the last good news Pendergast would hear from the federal government.[15]

"Now in reference to the governor of this state," Boss Tom said a few days later, "Stark will have to live with his conscience the same as the rest of us. If his conscience is clear—I know mine is. I now say, let the river take its course." The river was flowing toward the August 1938 primary. Unlike the March local election, the August contest would be statewide and include votes from St. Louis and outstate. Pendergast and Stark both treated this as their supreme test, and focused their efforts on just one office—the election of a Missouri Supreme Court justice. The previous year Stark had appointed James M. Douglas to the court to fill a vacancy, and Douglas was now up for election in his own right. During his brief tenure the court had voted four to three against a rate settlement that insurance commissioner Emmett O'Malley had made with insurance companies doing business in Missouri. This was the politically inept O'Malley who had cost Stark so many votes in 1936, whom Stark had then fired in defiance of Boss Tom's wishes. Just as Pendergast was strangely interested in O'Malley's welfare, Pendergast was reported to have an inexplicable anger about the Supreme Court decision invalidating O'Malley's rate settlement. Douglas was part of the one-vote majority in that ruling. Amid much head scratching by observers, Pendergast chose the normally placid Supreme Court contest as the ultimate test between him and Stark. Boss Tom backed James V. Billings, and Stark backed Douglas.[16]

Governor Stark came on strong, exhibiting oratory and political savvy that took opponents aback. Journalist William Reddig captured the atmosphere:

Three thousand men, women and children gathered in Shaffer's Grove for the speakin' and a fish fry. Neighbors visited happily together under the trees. Crowds stood before the refreshment booths and hurried through the eating to rush for the best seats arranged in tiers before a lighted speakers' platform. The speaking began and gradually the throng settled down. A full moon shed glory on Shaffer's Grove and a voice, amplified to unnatural volume and quality by loud speakers, charged the night air with a feeling of alarm and calamity. . . .

"A sinister and ominous shadow is raising its ugly head in an attempt to destroy the sanctity of our highest court," the Governor said.

Reddig noted that listeners "were quiet for a long period. They did not seem to be in a hurry to leave when the meeting ended. Watching them, the politicians knew that a ground swell was coming." Although St. Louis bosses such as Robert Hannegan backed Douglas, and although the Pendergast organization made full use of its control over WPA jobs (such as a rumor that Truman would end WPA if the machine lost), Truman and Pendergast no longer had the decisive statewide power they once enjoyed. In addition, as Truman grudgingly admitted years later, "Stark had made an able governor and was well liked by many Missourians." Stark also imposed a lug on some state employee salaries, forced some workers to display Douglas stickers on their cars, had them labor for Douglas on state time, and ordered them to transport Douglas voters to the polls. On top of that, just when "it looked like Billings was a sure winner," a Pendergast WPA official recalled, "O'Malley made his announcement that a victory in the supreme court race would be a 'referendum' on his compromise of that insurance suit." (Why in heaven's name were O'Malley and his insurance rate settlement so important?)[17]

Stark's man Douglas won big. "We have crushed the Pendergast machine by a landslide," the governor exulted to President Roosevelt. FDR decided Stark was now the coming political power in Missouri, and so informed Farley.[18]

Some weeks later circuit judge Allen Southern, a Truman relative and brother of the *Independence Examiner* editor, cranked up a grand jury against Pendergast gambling operations. Judge Southern "is always sticking his nose into something that doesn't concern him," Truman had tartly observed earlier. County prosecutor W. W. Graves tried to halt the probe, and wound up being indicted himself for failures to prosecute. "His continued failure to prosecute ghastly felonies," Stark proclaimed, "justifies his immediate removal from office." The indictment charged, in part, that Graves was criminally negligent in refusing to prosecute the Pendergast enforcer who tried to kill Truman's political opponent Tom Bash. Graves was also notorious for his inability to find anything illegal about Pendergast vote frauds. County presiding judge David Long was also indicted for corruption, as was former county judge J. W. Hostetter. Sheriff James L. Williams would be ousted. Stark shoved tremendous state resources behind the Southern grand jury while federal judge Albert Reeves convened a new federal grand jury. Targets of the federal investigation included Charley Carollo, who had rescued Johnny Lazia's wife when the machine gunners opened fire. Carollo eventually admitted that he collected the protection money from the illegal multi-million-dollar Kansas City gambling industry, personally delivering hundreds of thousands of criminal dollars to Boss Tom Pendergast and his secretary. Gradually, as observers analyzed the meaning of the federal grand jury subpoenas, people realized that there was yet another target of federal investigators. The Treasury Department intelligence unit chief later said, "Stark . . . asked us to put Pendergast in jail."[19]

The Internal Revenue boys had discovered why Pendergast was so touchy about Emmett O'Malley and the insurance rates. In 1929 fire insurance companies announced a huge rate increase for Missouri policyholders. The protest was so strong that the courts impounded the money generated by the rate increase. Policyholders paid the higher rates, but the extra money went into special accounts rather than into the companies. By 1935 about $11 million had accrued, and the insurance companies were getting impatient. Wise in the ways of Missouri government, the insurance industry offered Boss Tom $750,000 cash if he would turn the impounded millions over to the companies. Pendergast and O'Malley worked out an 80-20 split, with 80 percent of the impounded premiums going to the companies and 20 percent refunded to policyholders. In the end the insurance men welshed on the full bribe, but Pendergast managed

to collect $315,000, and O'Malley got $62,500. For reasons easy to
understand, the two gentlemen failed to include these sums in their
federal income tax returns.[20]

Great alarms went forth from the Pendergast organization when
it realized the feds had unraveled the conspiracy. When the smoke
cleared, Truman wrote, "That income tax outfit are worse than the
OGPW or the GESTAPO either. Someday I hope I can help to put
some of them where they belong." He also muttered, "Looks like
everybody got rich in Jackson County but me."[21]

Events soon to unfold suggested that Truman was informed about
desperate maneuvers to get the Roosevelt administration to abandon
the investigation. According to Emmett O'Malley's wife Truman
himself was supposed to participate in those efforts. As the situation
climaxed Truman returned to Kansas City ostensibly for the St.
Patrick's Day reunion of Battery D. He also held secret meetings
about Boss Tom's predicament. On March 21 Truman addressed a
joint session of the Missouri legislature revealing none of the rage
that would soon erupt:

> I had no legislative experience and only about two and a half years
> of law school when I went to Washington. My whole experience
> in public service had been executive and administrative. . . . The
> fact that I have been a lifelong student of world and United States
> history has been a very great help.
>
> The business of a good legislator is not to get things done quickly
> and efficiently, as a good administrator has to do, but to prevent,
> if possible, the enactment into law of the land many crazy and
> crackpot measures. . . . The man whose interests are of most im-
> portance to the country is not usually represented in the lobbies
> of Congress and . . . the bill on which the lobbyist and propa-
> gandist expend the greatest efforts is the one that needs the most
> deliberate consideration and, perhaps, obstruction.
>
> I've had to answer personally thousands and thousands of let-
> ters, see hundreds of people, and act as a sort of national em-
> ployment agency for all the thousands of Missourians who feel
> that it is their patriotic duty to become attached to the payroll of
> the federal government. It has been necessary for me to get up
> early in the morning and burn considerable electric energy at night,
> both at the government's and my own expense, but it has been a

grand experience, and no one can say I haven't honestly tried to make you a proper representative in the Senate.

Governor Stark failed to attend Truman's speech, and Truman failed to call on him in the capitol. Truman and Stark did attend a Jefferson City luncheon. Neither spoke to the other.[22]

In Jefferson City Truman received an emergency telephone call from Jim Farley, member of the president's cabinet and key man in the Pendergast organization's attempts to stop the investigation. Farley informed Truman that the Senate would decide on the administration's executive branch reorganization bill the next day, and that the vote looked close. Farley asked Truman to return for the vote. Steve Early, personal secretary to the president, phoned Truman with the same message. But what was the *real* message? Was Truman supposed to prove his New Deal loyalty one more time if he wanted anything done about Pendergast? Truman caught a risky night airplane flight back to Washington through a terrible snowstorm, and arrived in time to cast the deciding vote.[23]

The more Truman thought about the situation the madder he got. He regarded the federal investigation against Pendergast as political persecution, plain and simple, inspired by Stark in a power grab and conducted by the Roosevelt administration as revenge for Pendergast support of Senator Clark's 1938 reelection. (After all, other Kansas City and St. Louis factions, equally blatant with vote frauds over the years, weren't targeted by federal prosecutors.) Truman also noted that Assistant District Attorney Thomas Costolow had been the lawyer for Truman's old nemesis Louis Oppenstein in the haberdashery rent settlement. This prosecution was FDR's reward to Kansas City Democrats for Truman's steadfast New Deal votes. Moreover, Roosevelt had continually slighted Truman on patronage. And now Truman had jumped through the hoop when FDR's men cracked the whip. For what? Truman went haywire, and telephoned Steve Early.

TRUMAN: Well, I'm here, at your request, and I damn near got killed getting here by plane in time to vote, as I did on another occasion. I don't think the bill amounts to a tinker's damn, and I expect to get kicked in the — just as I always have in the past in return for my services.

EARLY: Well, Senator, what is it you want?

TRUMAN: I don't want a God-damned thing. My vote is not for sale. I vote my convictions, just as I always have, but I think the President ought to have the decency and respect to treat me like the Senator from Missouri and not like a God-damned office boy, and you can tell him what I said. If he wants me to, I'll come down and tell him myself.

EARLY: All right, Senator, I'll tell the President.[24]

FDR responded by inviting Truman to come visit the next day. Roosevelt showed goodwill toward Truman, and during the visit demonstrated awareness and sympathy about the strain Truman was under. Afterward the senator had little to say about the meeting. In an apparent gesture of friendliness, however, the White House seems to have leaked details to the press—knowing that the senator's best interests would be served. Roosevelt warmly thanked Truman for the hurried trip to Washington that saved the New Deal bill. A discussion of Missouri politics began. Truman said the state would go Democratic in 1940 and reelect him to the Senate. The president inquired about Pendergast's health, and Truman said it was excellent (which was incorrect). Roosevelt emphasized that he wanted Kansas City politics cleaned up, but at the same time expressed personal friendship for Truman and appreciation for his steadfast support—thus indicating that Roosevelt distinguished between Truman's political backing and his public service. The conversation must have shaken Truman. Although he appreciated FDR's assurances of friendship and gratitude, the president demonstrated intimate knowledge of the Kansas City situation—from the indictment of county prosecutor Graves to the cover-up manipulations Kansas City police director Otto Higgins was unsuccessfully attempting with various Washington officials. This meant that federal investigators were working under the full authority of the president of the United States and that no deals would be possible without Roosevelt's personal approval. And FDR had bluntly stated he intended to clean up Kansas City politics.[25]

Truman, nonetheless, did what he could in Washington to save Boss Tom. Some observers felt that Truman's emergency airplane journey for the New Deal entitled him to a big favor. The day Truman met with Roosevelt, Emmett O'Malley's wife wrote, "Jimmy [Pendergast] is flying to see our big friend [Farley] in Washington tonight. Truman's publicity has been a Godsend to them." Truman told the Internal Revenue commissioner that the grand jury probe against Pendergast was politically motivated, and the commissioner assured the senator, "If Pendergast is as innocent as you say he is, he has nothing to worry about." Five days after the White House meeting Truman called on Attorney General Murphy. The same day Jim Pendergast and Truman consulted with Farley. Truman told the press that Jim Pendergast was in town about a tax case, nothing dramatic, and that the meeting with Murphy was unconnected and coincidental. Murphy, however, announced that Pendergast men were trying to squelch a grand jury investigation of the Missouri insurance rate settlement. The attorney general pledged that the investigation would continue. A few days later Murphy and FBI director J. Edgar Hoover flew to Kansas City where they consulted with district attorney Milligan. Three days later, on the Friday before Easter 1939, the federal grand jury indicted Boss Tom and Emmett O'Malley. Pendergast snapped, "There's nothing the matter with me. They persecuted Christ on Good Friday, and nailed him to the Cross."[26]

"My relationships with Mr. Pendergast have always been purely political," Truman announced, and reportedly added, "I am not going to desert a ship that is going down." He soon denied making the latter statement, claiming that he said instead, "I won't desert a ship in distress." The new version asserted Truman's belief that the Pendergast organization could survive. City manager McElroy, the immovable dictator of municipal government for Pendergast ever since the machine seized control in 1926, resigned on April 13. On or about May 2 a top official of seven Pendergast family companies disappeared. His body was found in the Missouri River five days later. Some observers called it suicide; some didn't. On May 22 Boss Tom pleaded guilty to all federal charges, and was sentenced to prison, with a proviso that he could have no involvement in politics when he got out. The next day Truman's old Community Savings & Loan associate Rufus Burrus sent word of a growing consensus that only Truman could save the Pendergast organization. Truman refused a trip home to rebuild the machine for Pendergast, telling someone else, "If I do any reorganizing it will be on my own hook." Four days later O'Malley pleaded guilty, and was sentenced to prison.

Four days after that, Pendergast man Shannon Douglass informed Truman that Kansas City mayor Bryce Smith was doing well enough with damage control at city hall that most local operatives could concentrate on saving the county organization. Douglass also informed Truman of retaliations planned against members of circuit judge Southern's grand jury. Matt Murray, who had headed the WPA program in Missouri for Pendergast, got a two-year prison sentence, as did John Pryor, one of the road contractors who tried to pressure presiding judge Truman to deviate from competitive bidding. Kansas City police director Otto Higgins was replaced and imprisoned. Governor Stark called this "the final blow in the destruction of the Pendergast organization's death grip on that city and of its insidious influence in state and national affairs." Privately Stark credited FDR's "timely aid" with ending Kansas City police partnership with the gangster underworld.[27]

Of Stark, Truman later said, "He should have been a member of the Spanish Inquisition or of the Court of Louis XI of France. Someday when I have time I'll write a character sketch of him that will be very interesting." He added, "Stark had neither honor nor loyalty." In contrast, Truman typically referred to Pendergast as an honest man because he kept his word. In politics Truman viewed honesty and honor in terms of keeping promises. Pendergast may have violated law after law, been in partnership with notorious gangsters who intimidated and murdered, cheated the public by bribing public officials, yet Truman viewed Pendergast as honest and upstanding because he had told various persons he would do these things and then kept his word. Stark may have stood for truth, justice, and the American way, but Truman viewed him as garbage because when Stark realized he had hooked up with criminals and thieves he broke off from them. In politics a man had to stand by his friends no matter what, even if the circumstances that formed the friendship radically changed, even if the friends were exposed as crooks. The bond between political friends was eternal, for richer for poorer, for better for worse, in sickness and in health. Friendship was more important than the good of the community. Now, Truman had a far different view of morality among businessmen—he had awful things to say about men who conspired to cheat private and governmental customers, even though the conspirators honestly stood by their word to steal. Truman's curious double standard may have had an arcane philosophical rationale, but Truman was never known for intro-spection. More likely he was soothing his conscience for his crucial assistance in maintaining one of the nation's most notorious corrupt political machines.[28]

"The terrible things done by the high ups in K.C. will be a lead weight to me from now on," Truman told Bess. "I took your advice and went to see *Goodbye Mr. Chips*. It was well worth seeing. I almost cried over it. I've been fool enough to believe that things are really like that, and for some reason I still believe it in spite of O'Malley, Stark, and McElroy."[29]

Plenty of Truman's friends thought his reelection impossible. Ru-mors circulated that they were asking President Roosevelt to give the senator a good job to spare him an election defeat. Initially Truman had been so mortified by the springtime revelations that he had considered resigning from the Senate. He eventually decided, however, that he needed to run for reelection as a matter of personal vindication and revenge. "I'm going to lick that double crossing lying governor if I can keep my health." In addition, Truman felt he deserved another term: "I had worked hard. I had worked very hard. I felt that I had made a good record." Nonetheless, the portents were grim. Truman's daughter Margaret wrote, "Never before or since can I recall my father being so gloomy as he was in those latter months of 1939." Truman himself confided at the time, "It is a miserable state of affairs when a man dreads showing up in his hometown because all his friends are either in jail or about to go there." Attempting to forget his troubles for a while, he went to see *Mr. Smith Goes to Washington,* in which a bespectacled white-haired senator wins the respect and admiration of his colleagues and the public, only to be exposed as the office boy of a corrupt big city boss. Truman did not enjoy the show. He began toying with the idea of going on what he called "the greatest trip ever by the military affairs subcommittee on appropriations," a junket through Central America and Mexico. "I might be better off making this inspection of national defense than being there [in Kansas City] taking it on the chin with the Long trial, Mr. Higgins, and Mr. Murray. At least they can get no interviews from me." The more Truman thought of the trip the better it sounded, particularly since he had declined a 1937 congres-sional jaunt to Europe, and the Central American travel would prob-ably be his last opportunity to junket. "It won't cost a penny," he wrote to Bess, "and will not add to the government cost. What do you really think. Love to you. Fix your teeth. Harry."[30]

So Truman headed off on what he frankly described as "a pleasure trip" courtesy of U.S. taxpayers. The congressional party stopped at Ft. Sill, Oklahoma, to observe artillery fire. The general was a friend of Truman and knew his military background, while Truman's congressional colleagues apparently didn't. The general asked if the senator would like to try his hand at a target problem. Without a blink Truman took over professionally, gave the proper aiming and firing commands, and made a perfect score. Truman recalled gleefully, "These Senators and Representatives stood around open-mouthed."[31]

Truman's letters home were a potpourri of tourist observations. San Salvador "is not beautiful to see—too much poverty, although there are no beggars. Vera Cruz was full of 'em." He thrilled at going 225 M.P.H. during one airplane flight, and reported losing a dental bridge but not the contents of his stomach. He found President Somoza of Nicaragua "a regular fellow," and was impressed with the tommy guns, machine guns, and other firepower that Central American presidents kept around them. The president of Costa Rica and the entire diplomatic corps came to the reception thrown by the American minister. "The Italians celebrated their Fascist Birthday with a reception not long ago, and no one went." Truman failed to report the party afterward, which climaxed in an orgy with whores furnished by the government of Costa Rica, an event Senator Shay Minton bragged about. When sexual activity got underway Truman left immediately, but didn't condemn his colleagues who stayed. He avoided similar hijinks in Mexico City, reporting dryly, "It is some town. Paris or New York can't touch it." Toward the end of the junket, in San Francisco, Truman sounded impatient with such shenanigans. "I came back to the hotel to write you," he told Bess. "The rest went on a slumming expedition. I guess I'm not built right. I don't enjoy 'em—never did even in Paris, and I was 20 years younger then." In Los Angeles the congressional group inspected national defense at the MGM studios, where Truman was excited to see famous movie stars and to get their autographs for Margaret.[32]

Fellow junketeers noticed and often commented about Truman's voluminous letter writing to Bess. Truman was a devoted husband, yet there was an undertone of needling in his correspondence. "The plane had to go back to the post at Montgomery because some slouchy soldier left the cap off the oil pressure feed tank." Truman told Bess that the Army had provided all the junketeers with parachutes in case the plane went down in the jungle. He assured her that the plane was perfectly safe, however, that even the fire the other day only required a hand extinguisher. Such "reassurances" were a rhetorical trick, such as telling an audience, "I shall not mention my opponent's criminal record." Bess apparently did the same thing to Harry. Family correspondence over the years shows many references to things being fine at home, that Harry shouldn't worry about Margie hurting her arm last night, that Bess is sure Margie must understand deep down that her father loves her even if he isn't around much. Truman's absences caused friction, but they weren't all initiated by him. During the Senate years Bess spent great amounts of time, months at a stretch, living apart from her husband. Harry sent her numerous letters telling of his loneliness and practically pleading with her to come back. One gets the impression that the marriage was under a strain. When Bess was living with Harry in Washington he often had little time for her. He found her presence a comfort, but one can see how she might have felt ignored. Though she had looked forward to life in Washington when Harry was first elected to the Senate, Bess eventually decided to spend enormous blocks of time living in Independence. There she had a circle of friends to ease any loneliness. Another factor may have been her mother, an exasperating person with a seemingly untoward hold on her daughter. Madge Wallace may have devised excuses to keep Bess in Independence. Madge may well have thrived on attempts to throw discord into her daughter's marriage, and Bess may have been more concerned about mollifying her mother than about any grief such mollification caused Harry.[33]

Before leaving for Central America Truman settled accounts with Spencer Salisbury, who had run Truman out of Community Savings & Loan Association. Truman had followed the association's activities with interest over the years, and by summer 1939 believed he had Salisbury nailed. "There was not anything I could do when I found out what Salisbury was doing but report it to the federal authorities," he said (an attitude far different from what he thought of persons who reported Pendergast machine illegalities). Truman began seeking a federal investigation of Salisbury before leaving on a Colorado vacation in August. The senator's secretary dispatched a telegram to him there: "Federal department here has agreed to make immediate investigation of Loan Association Independence if urgent or if not urgent October First. Unless specific information regarding irregularities is available it is sometimes difficult for examiners to make discoveries. If you can wire me confidential information of any particular case or specific irregularity it will be a big help and source will not be disclosed." Truman replied instantly: "Businessmen in Independence inform me that manager [Salisbury] is using association funds for personal use, proper income returns have not been made. A complete and thorough investigation of association and the manager should be made as soon as possible. All well, walking up mountains now." The next day Truman's secretary wrote that federal savings and loan officials were at work on the matter. By mid-October the feds had verified Truman's allegations, and a more intense examination of Salisbury's affairs began. Truman's old associate in this savings and loan enterprise, Rufus Burrus, wrote to the senator, " 'Snake Eye' is on a hot spot."[34]

Salisbury pleaded guilty to federal charges. Burrus chortled, "He has already taken some considerable punishment by reason of his humbling himself and personally asking the mayor and the postmaster to be character witnesses. Some say that would be equal to a year's time." Truman grumbled that Salisbury had better not ask *him* to be a character witness, "We all know that he would steal the pennies off his grandmother's eyes." The newspapers listed Mayor Roger Sermon (but not postmaster Edgar Hinde), Harry Jobes, Jay M. Lee, and C. C. Bundschu among the character witnesses—all were 129th Field Artillery officers. E. M. Stayton also testified for Salisbury, "He served under me at the Mexican border. I, too, invested money in his company, and I do not regret it." The court disregarded all of this. "Judge Reeves said there was no doubt Salisbury had practiced deception to hide the condition of the association, and that he had used funds of the association for speculation and that he had used 'short cuts' to try to offset losses." Salisbury got fifteen months in Leavenworth. Years later another 129th Field Artillery officer, Father Curtis Tiernan, interceded with the president of the United States and asked him to restore Salisbury's citizenship. "Let him poop it out," Truman said.[35]

Community Federal Savings & Loan went into receivership, and its accounts were distributed among six Kansas City area savings and loan associations. Truman successfully urged federal authorities to include Blue Valley Federal Savings & Loan and Independence Savings & Loan in the transfers. He was particularly adamant about Independence Savings & Loan, whose directors included Henry Rummel (who defeated Truman for eastern judge in 1924). Accounts also went into Standard Federal Savings & Loan of Kansas City, whose president Conrad Mann was a well-known Pendergast operative. Salisbury later made much of the fact depositors lost nothing. This says nothing about how investors fared, nor does it reflect the efforts of federal authorities and the six other savings and loan institutions in saving depositor accounts. Without FSLIC insurance the outcome might have been far different.[36]

By July 1938 Truman had Stark spotted as the man to beat in 1940. Truman was busy undercutting Stark's position in the state Democratic committee and was even at work devising anti-Stark slogans and cartoons. Truman *was* surprised by the Pendergast collapse, but was already protected against any untoward disclosures. "I looked carefully through the [county counselor] files," Fred Boxley wrote to Truman in 1935. "Some of them might have embarrassed us, because there were communications between yourself and myself about some of the bond issues, contracts, etc., in which we designated some people by their right names." Boxley continued, "I referred to various people who were trying to 'horn' in on contracts and quoted your opinions on same." Boxley assured Truman that all such materials had been removed. Truman replied gratefully, "I certainly appreciate the way you handled the files. I think you were entirely correct in it." Boxley's correspondence about this went to Truman's apartment, not his office (this was Truman's standard procedure for confidential written communications. Truman also continued to use Vivian for secret communications). Eric O. A. Miller, who had done the accounting for part of Truman's Community Savings & Loan operation, later wrote to him, "Please tell me what to do about the audit working papers and reports I have in my files concerning the audit of the Jackson County Court and the county assessor's office. I had them hidden away in case they would have called for them during the rumpus here. Shall I burn them all up, or shall I turn them over to you? I talked to Jim Pendergast, but he did not seem to understand." Truman replied instantly, "Burn them up." Another

Pendergast man informed Truman, "In regard to the matter of embezzlement and forgery of which we talked, will say it seems to be working out satisfactorily, although the danger is not over. I have done all I could to keep the case from doing the organization further damage." Truman could be confident that nothing embarrassing would turn up about his administration of Jackson County.[37]

Truman wasn't nearly as optimistic about the 1940 election as he sounded in public. Just after Boss Tom's indictment the *Kansas City Star* quoted Truman as saying, "If Governor Stark runs against me in 1940 I'll beat the hell out of him." Truman denied saying that, but he did say, "Anyone who opposes me will know he has been through a fight when the primary campaign is over." In May 1939 he vowed, "I am a candidate for re-election, and nothing can stop me." Truman was actually glum about his situation, losing sleep, and eventually so beat down that he couldn't bear any more questions about the Pendergast organization prosecutions.[38]

The Latin America trip, however, seems to have been a tonic. In January 1940 he met with friends in Kansas City and St. Louis to organize his reelection campaign. A couple dozen supporters met with Truman at the St. Louis Statler Hotel. Steve Early phoned during the meeting and asked for Truman. Truman told his secretary to talk to the president's secretary. Early said that Roosevelt would appoint Truman to the ICC if the senator would let Stark have the nomination. This bribe did not go down well with Truman, and the group had a frank discussion of election realities. Truman's Senate record, particularly his railroad work, was viewed as a plus. Railroad unions were friendly toward him. The usefulness of WPA workers was discussed. Also despite the Pendergast prosecutions and bad press, the Pendergast organization had done a lot of favors and still had a lot of friends around Missouri. Truman also stood out as a man of presumed honesty since none of the grand juries or prosecutions had touched him. Moreover, Stark was no Mr. Congeniality; he had angered important elements of the Democrat Party. On the minus side Stark had fanatically organized state employees on his behalf, the support of the Kansas City and St. Louis press, and apparently the support of the New Deal administration. Truman also lacked campaign funds and had few eager contributors. The consensus of the meeting was that Truman would try to put on the damnedest losing campaign possible. And one or two persons there even suspected he might win.[39]

Truman returned to Washington with Secretary of War Woodring in his private plane. There Truman met with a few more supporters at the New Willard Hotel. They considered many of the same factors discussed in St. Louis, and also discussed the effects of anti–third term sentiment against FDR. Roosevelt's ICC offer to Truman was mentioned, too. Although the newspapers were promoting Stark as "Missouri's crime-busting chief executive," the New Willard group thought this claim would prove mighty thin in the campaign since others, such as Maurice Milligan, had done the real work against Pendergast. The meeting closed with Truman confidently citing ancient history as a portent: "You fellows know that Nero was a great Roman politician and for a long time was very successful. I have studied his career very closely, and for a long time wondered why, having started out as he did, he should have come down in ruin in the end. I think I located the place in history where he began to take his friends for granted and tried to buy his enemies, and at that point I think his road to ruin began. I believe Lloyd Stark has already been guilty of that same error."[40]

Truman ran two campaigns simultaneously—a public, up-front effort that emphasized his and the New Deal's services to Missouri, and a sub-rosa campaign with much clinking of metal blades in the night. Regarding the latter a Truman man up in Nodaway County wrote to another politician, "I would far rather for Truman's benefit to see Milligan to get into the race. . . . There are those who are for the machine and those who are against it. . . . Those who hate Stark for trying to bust the machine and those who are glad that he did. I don't know, but I think those who hate Stark are in the majority. If Stark and Milligan would divide the minority, there would not be any threat to beating Truman in the primary." Although this letter wasn't directed to Truman it wound up in his files with a blue-pencil notation indicating that the matter was discussed with him. In mid-1939 Truman was telling newspapers that Milligan might be a more formidable opponent than Stark. Truman had Senator Clark's cooperation in trying to bring Milligan into the race—Roosevelt and Stark had reportedly planned to run Milligan against Clark in 1938. Indeed, Milligan had planned to run against Stark this time, but hesitated when Truman announced for reelection. When Milligan finally decided he was man enough to beat both Stark and Truman this was a piece of luck Truman found hard to believe. He later declared innocently, "As to Milligan being the reason for my winning the election, I have never thought that."[41]

Roosevelt's role in this primary was murky although pleasing to Stark and infuriating to Truman. In 1937 Truman got Farley's promise that the New Deal would do nothing to help Stark against him. This, of course, was before the downfall of Pendergast and Farley. Still, soon after Boss Tom's indictment Roosevelt reportedly said he supported Truman for reelection. This report was questioned, but in August rumors appeared again and were given credibility this time. On this occasion several senators apparently reported that FDR "believes that the Missouri Senator was in a sense a victim of Pendergastism, a courageous, public-spirited official who had been accidentally involved in Pendergast's downfall." Truman knew that FDR had indeed expressed such sentiments (but not to Truman), and had even promised (but not to Truman) to get Stark out of the race—the assumption was that Roosevelt might appoint Stark Secretary of the Navy. In a private conversation (but not with Truman) Roosevelt called Stark "an egotistical fool." All these messages tossed over the fence were fine, but Truman started getting a little impatient waiting for Roosevelt to say something publicly. He privately likened FDR's conduct to Stark's. Finally, in August 1939, Truman had a most satisfactory interview with Roosevelt. "Yesterday was some day. Went to see the President about a bill, and he insisted on talking Missouri politics and telling me what a funny governor we have. He didn't say phony, but that's what he meant. Actual quotation: 'I do not think your governor is a real liberal. . . . He has no sense of humor. . . . He has a large ego.' " The president "invited me to ride on his train across Missouri. Said, 'Be sure and get on that train for you can rest assured your governor will without any invitation.' " As late as December things between Roosevelt and Truman were good enough for Truman personally to ask the president to give Fred Canfil a job, and for FDR to agree.[42]

By the end of January, however, Roosevelt was trying to keep Truman from filing for reelection. (Also, the job for Canfil never materialized.) This probably had something to do with FDR's third-term ambitions. Until Truman announced his candidacy in February, Stark was the sole candidate. Roosevelt probably wanted to avoid a bitter Senate primary battle in Missouri, which might leave the losers inclined to sulk in November. Stark tried to convince FDR that Truman was working against a third term, but the evidence was surely too thin to be convincing. (Truman's statements supporting the two-term tradition were tempered with the proviso that he would support Roosevelt if he desired a third term.) FDR simply withdrew from the Missouri Senate contest, surely realizing that Truman and Stark were about evenly matched and that the winner was far from certain. Roosevelt felt no need to back a potential loser and thereby alienate the winner's supporters in November. Truman's people tried to get Roosevelt to declare for Truman, but the man in the White House refused to say anything. Both Truman and Stark seemed confident that Roosevelt was backing Stark, so perhaps they were privy to information that they shared with no one. More likely Stark's inflated self-esteem was at work. Truman seems to have based his own belief on Roosevelt's refusal to express his private sentiments about Stark and on Roosevelt's ICC offer that was coupled with the requirement that Truman not oppose Stark in the election. Truman felt Roosevelt had turned traitor and couldn't be trusted, a feeling reinforced after a personal conference when the president agreed to support a bill Truman wanted, let Truman tell the Senate that Roosevelt wanted the legislation, and then vetoed the measure.[43]

In contrast, Truman's Senate colleagues went on the line for him, most unusual behavior in a primary. Truman's opponents carped about these senators from other states telling Missouri Democrats how to vote, but the general effect was to promote Truman as a national statesman. These testimonials did much to lessen the Pendergast stigma. Senators Barkley, Hatch, Minton, and Schwellenbach made personal appearances in Missouri. Some senators helped by inserting material in the *Congressional Record* that could then be mailed under their frank. Senator Gillette orchestrated investigations of the Stark campaign finances and later the GOP nominee's campaign finances. On the Senate floor Connally of Texas gave Bridges a verbal thrashing for criticizing Truman. A St. Louis Jewish Zionist named David Berenstein worked himself into a top position in Truman's campaign by having Truman's Senate colleagues write letters of endorsement, which were then publicized. These letters went far beyond the minimum courtesy fellow Democrats show a colleague, and demonstrated that Truman had become a man of influence in the Senate. In all, a couple dozen colleagues dispatched messages to Missouri. If opinions of fellow workers mean anything, Truman was highly regarded indeed.[44]

Reservists, Guardsmen, and veterans were an important source of Truman strength. "I belong to every veteran organization in the United States." Truman became president of the 35th Division Association in October 1939, a group with many Missouri members. John Snyder, who succeeded Truman as commander of the 379th Field Artillery, was big in the 1940 campaign. Stark had been active with veterans, too, but Truman had a voting record to prove his usefulness to ex-servicemen. He had been particularly insistent about immediate payment of the bonus—IOU's the U.S. government had given to veterans—and had voted for this despite Roosevelt's opposition and his own secret opinion that the bonus was unwise.[45]

Freemasons were another large group intertwined with the campaign. Truman was in the standard line of succession to become Grand Master of the Grand Lodge of Missouri. Year after year Truman and the others ahead and behind in the line received routine votes of approval to move up a notch. In 1939, after Boss Tom's indictment and subsequent revelations, opposition developed against allowing Truman to continue upward. The September 1939 Grand Lodge meeting was an ordeal, with the opposition organized by two of Truman's oldest Masonic associates—Tom Reynolds who helped Truman start the Grandview Lodge and a Mr. Foster whom Truman had personally raised to the third degree in 1919. Prominent among Truman's friends at this meeting were his brother Vivian, Henry Chiles, John Snyder, and Harry Vaughan. Feelings ran hot, and Vivian "came very nearly whipping Foster." Truman needed 427 votes, and got 436. The divided opinion over Truman was illustrated by the votes received by the new Grand Master—845. Truman noted that the St. Louis contingent voted against him in force, but that strong outstate support carried the election for him. He felt this battle was symbolic of the upcoming Senate race.[46]

The next autumn Truman routinely became Grand Master. The general election was then underway. The GOP gubernatorial candidate Forrest Donnell was in line of succession behind Truman, and one day Donnell himself would become Grand Master. Even in the midst of the fall campaign Truman and Donnell were cooperating in Masonic affairs, such as a project to reduce anti-Catholic feeling in one area of the state. (Truman took care not to cancel any campaign appearances before Roman Catholic groups.) One of the senator's friends attended a GOP rally featuring appearances by Donnell and Republican Senate nominee Manvel Davis, the same Davis who had helped Truman draft the reorganization plan for Jackson County government. Davis made a slashing speech, and afterward Truman's friend buttonholed Donnell to ask how such a low-down scum as Davis described could be Grand Master. Donnell answered that what Davis said about Truman was untrue. Donnell's remark received wide publicity and reportedly cost Davis many votes.[47]

One old-time Missouri politico recalled Truman's 1940 campaign as the first time large numbers of blacks were active in a statewide election. Truman's campaign kept a card file of about eight hundred blacks in Missouri, including some card notations of the kinds of work people were willing to do for Truman. In a close election anything can make the difference, but Truman credited black voters with his victory. Governor Stark had thoroughly alienated this part of the electorate by firing black state workers and by signing a bill that blacks felt was intended to evade a Supreme Court decision in favor of equal education opportunity. This influenced Truman's support from the black community, but this support was as much a pro-Truman phenomenon as anti-Stark. Therefore, Truman's racial attitudes are worth examining at this point both for an understanding of him and of his times.[48]

Truman's attitudes were bigoted. It was more than a matter of using racial epithets, as the connotations of such words change over the years. (Indeed, the word "black" had a vulgar connotation in the 1950s but is perfectly acceptable in the 1980s.) Truman frankly disliked blacks, and his private writings (and some of his public statements) imply that he viewed the abilities of blacks in general as inferior to those of whites. His sister put it bluntly: "Harry isn't any more in favor of nigger equality than I am." He felt that blacks should be of subservient demeanor—the Truman family servants were black, and anecdotes such as this are also revealing: "My desk is a mess, just killed a cockroach. He walked right out on the armrest where I'm writing this, as impudently as a sassy nigger."[49]

Truman was also insensitive to the realities of life in black Missouri. "I got to thinking about the Negro problem [while] in the

Senate. We had no real problem at home." While he was presiding judge Missouri hosted one of the nation's most notorious lynchings at Maryville, one of the mean-spirited towns in the northwest corner of the state. The event was well-advertised in advance. Rabbi Samuel Mayerberg of Kansas City telephoned Governor Park (a Pendergast man) and convinced him to call out the National Guard. The weekend warriors preserved order while the townspeople took a black inmate from jail, chained him to the roof of a schoolhouse, and set fire to the building. Decades later the good citizens told details of the murder with relish, citing it as one of the proudest moments in a town that the chamber of commerce touted as the "All-American City." Yet Truman believed there was "no real problem" in Missouri.[50]

The circumstances of the Maryville lynching are particularly interesting when seen in the light of Truman's approval of a speech Senator Borah made against the antilynching bill in January 1938. A quorum call followed Borah's speech. Truman described what happened next:

> Borah just made a wonderful speech on the anti-lynching bill. I'll tell my mother to read the *Record* today. She'll agree entirely with him on it. So do I, but I may have to vote for the bill.
>
> Met Colonel Halsey at my desk just as Borah was about to finish. He invited me to have lunch in his office. Joe Guffey, Pat Harrison, Alben Barkley were also invited. We had quail. Key Pittman came in to have a drink. The story telling started after the coffee . . . there was no hurry about getting back into the chamber.
>
> Barkley told one about a big old country boy at a Kentucky barbecue who was very anxious to have intercourse with a big corn fed girl. They wandered away from the crowd, and she informed him that she had a weak heart and was afraid to proceed. "Oh! come on," he told her, "I'll go easy as I pass your heart."
>
> We asked Pat if he would speak today on the anti-lynching bill. Pat said, "Did you ever get billed as a speaker—the principal speaker at a meeting and arrive after several others had spoken and then be introduced by a long winded chairman, do your best and then have the papers say the next day, 'Pat Harrison also spoke'? No, I'll not speak after Borah. The newspaper boys have already done a day's work."

Key Pittman took his bourbon and soda and after listening awhile was reminded by Barkley's story of a negro who started to walk from Baltimore to Washington one snowy night. He stopped at a negro woman's house about halfway on the road and asked her for a cup of coffee. She was pleased with his appearance and asked him to stay all night. He told her he couldn't, that he must go on to Washington. At the door she put her arm around him, unbuttoned his pants, and discovering that he was not interested in her dropped his organ of joy rather contemptuously. He remarked to her, "Now you needn't throw it in the snow just because I'm tired and not interested."

Truman's essay is enlightening not only about Senate conviviality and his sense of humor (he enjoyed such humorless smutty stories so much that he occasionally wrote them down). What is revealing is that neither Truman nor his Senate buddies felt it inappropriate to tell demeaning jokes about blacks, just off the Senate floor, while the antilynching bill was under consideration. (Truman eventually voted with a majority to table the bill.)[51]

Truman's prejudice makes his civil rights record all the more remarkable. It is one thing to favor civil rights because one believes in racial equality and integration. Truman promoted civil rights despite his dislike of blacks and his possible feeling that they were inferior humans. This shows not only a genuine tolerance for others but a firm belief in the ideal of America as a land of opportunity. Truman believed that inferiors had a right to seek the good life even if they lacked the inherent ability to achieve it. In a word, Truman's attitude toward blacks was paternalistic.

Excerpts from three speeches of this era clearly show Truman's public stance on the rights of blacks. In 1938 he told a Kansas City audience, "I am not one who believes that you require white uplifters to solve your problems. . . . If you are given the opportunity, you are perfectly capable of solving them yourselves." He called race prejudice a "misunderstanding. And misunderstanding is the right word." The senator continued, "When anyone tells me that the colored people of this country are turning Communist, I tell him that I saw you tried in 1917–18. You did your part honorably and well at that time, and besides, Communists do not believe in God. Where can you find a truer religious spirit than among the colored race of this nation?" Truman declared, "I want to see you solve your own problems, and I am here to tell you that I'll help to attain that end with all my might. Just the other day I learned that your race were being discriminated against in Fort Leavenworth. The proper authorities were informed, and I am assured that the discrimination has ceased." In conclusion he asserted, "There is no other country under the sun where a minority such as you are could live in peace and protection, and where the people in high places are anxious to see you succeed and are doing things for your good and welfare. Now it is up to you and your leaders to live up to that confidence and to show us by your acts that you can make good on that confidence. I'm one who believes you can and will do it."[52]

The opening speech of his 1940 reelection campaign was given at Sedalia, a moderate-size town with light industry surrounded by a rural area.

When we speak of man and his labor, at least in this country and, more particularly, in this locality, we must consider the problem of our Negro population and bend our every effort that, at least under law, they may claim their heritage of our Bill of Rights to "life, liberty, and the pursuit of happiness." Their social life, will, naturally, remain their own, but as freemen they must have their equality before law. . . .

I believe in the brotherhood of man; not merely the brotherhood of white men, but the brotherhood of all men before law. . . . If any class or race can be permanently set apart from, or pushed down below, the rest in political and civil rights, so may any other class or race when it shall incur the displeasure of its more powerful associates, and we may say farewell to the principles on which we count our safety. . . .

Negroes have been preyed upon by all types of exploiters, from the installment salesman of clothing, pianos, and furniture to the vendors of vice. The majority of our Negro people find but cold comfort in shanties and tenements. Surely, as freemen, they are entitled to something better than this.[53]

A month later Truman traveled to Chicago for the Democratic National Convention. There he gave a black audience his boldest statement on civil rights, going beyond anything he had said before. Truman declared that blacks were behind whites in accomplishments only because of educational differences and denial of opportunities. "If white men wish to do better for themselves, it would be well for them to give more definite attention to the education of the Negro" so society could benefit from that unused source of creative talent. Reflecting Masonic beliefs, Truman observed, "When we are honest enough to recognize each other's rights and are good enough to respect them, we will come to a more Christian settlement of our difficulties." The senator warned, "All dark people, except the Negroes, are against the white race." (The implication was that civil rights had a national defense function. Years later from the White House Truman said, "The top dog in a world which is 90% colored ought to clean his own house.") Truman emphasized, "I am not appealing for social equality of the Negro. The Negro himself knows better than that, and the highest types of Negro leaders say quite frankly that they prefer the society of their own people. Negroes want justice, not social relations." He went beyond platitudes and advocated a practical, bricks-and-mortar expression of civil rights: "Every community owes the Negro a fair deal in regard to public utilities, lights, sewers, street improvement, and water mains. We owe the Negro legal equality . . . because he is a human being and a natural born American." Truman summed up his remarks by saying the white man couldn't drag the black man down without standing below him to do so.[54]

Although Truman openly courted the black vote in 1940 he recognized the political danger of attracting the label "nigger lover." He was gratified when C. A. Franklin, editor of the large-circulation weekly *The Call,* indicated that his paper was sensitive about this in presenting Truman to its black readership. When a sociology professor asked Truman for his views on the black situation in Missouri in late 1942, he replied, "It is a most difficult problem to discuss because of its repercussions politically, and I would prefer not to discuss it with you until I have had a chance to give it a great deal of thought, which I have been doing for the last 10 years."[55]

Truman's campaign had a women's division, but he never showed any sensitivity to women's issues. The president of the Women's Trade Union League in Kansas City asked for help in getting women jobs as railway postal clerks: "One official has made the statement that he will not hire a woman until he is unable to find a man." Truman replied merely that Railway Mail Service officials told him that there was no discrimination against women and that qualified women could get jobs. Truman seemed chilly toward the proposed Equal Rights Amendment to the Constitution. His Senate secretary sent noncommittal responses to women's organizations requesting Truman's support for the amendment. Senator Truman sent personal noncommittal replies to women asking him to vote no. (Truman opposed birth control, believing procreation was "one of our principal reasons for being here, I think." He also felt "divorces are a disgrace. I think, when you make a contract, you should keep it." Period.)[56]

Labor unions, particularly the railroad brotherhoods, did crucial work for the campaign. Truman's pro-labor work and his efforts to restore railroads to good health (thereby generating jobs) were obvious factors. Truman, however, had put in special effort to thwart a rail management plan to cut wages in 1938. Management claimed that high pay was preventing railroad recovery. Truman easily demonstrated that labor costs had nothing to do with railway financial troubles, and showed that workers were actually underpaid. He called for the roads to raise wages and cut prices. "The lawyers and economists who are in charge of the railroads today couldn't sell gold dollars for 95 cents." The railroad unions provided crucial manpower to the campaign, recruited help from other trade unions, and printed up a special Truman-appreciation issue of the railway union newspaper, *Labor*. This issue was aimed at all voters, not just union workers, and at least half a million copies were distributed throughout Missouri just before the primary voting, including a copy to every RFD mailbox. This was all donated, didn't cost the Truman campaign anything. The unions did still more, raising money for the campaign. David Berenstein, who thought up the endorsement letters from Truman's Senate colleagues, came up with another idea— printing up booklets of Truman-for-Senator tickets, and trying to peddle them by mail at $1.00 per ticket. Hundreds were mailed out, and apparently about $100 came back. This didn't even cover the postage, and Truman turned livid about Berenstein's blunder. The booklet fiasco was discussed at a July 8 strategy session of railroad union political operatives, and the unions immediately bought up the booklets, which put $17,000 into the campaign at an urgent moment. The unions in turn tried to recover the donation by peddling the tickets to locals across the United States and in Canada, saying it was crucial to send in the money by July 16.[57]

The campaign was strapped for funds. A northwest Missouri politico said, "I am strong for Truman . . . but it would incur a lot of cost which I could not afford. You know yourself what the fourth ward is in Maryville. Nobody ever got many votes down there without spending a lot of money." Truman was touchy about the financial shortage, and felt "shortage" was indeed the proper word. According to him the 1934 campaign raised enough money to cover 1940 as well, but somehow the overflow all disappeared. Thus he was suspicious in 1940, and apparently suspected top campaign officials Vic Messall and David Berenstein of embezzling. Truman went over the accounts after the primary but was unable to find anything amiss. Yet the figures literally don't add up. Truman's official campaign expenditure report showed (in rounded figures) $21,500 of expenses, with $17,900 cash income, $2,800 in donated services, and a deficit of about $3,700 (most of which Truman absorbed personally). The campaign's bank statements showed an $18,125 income from June 20 to October 2. Money continued to come in after that date—for instance, $500 from the Democratic Senatorial Campaign Committee on October 25. Berenstein said $17,000 came in from railroad unions alone. Nothing anywhere close to that amount appears in the campaign bank statements, let alone between July 8 (when the unions discussed the ticket booklets) and primary day. Truman's official campaign report listed fifty-seven contributors of $100 or more (the largest being $800). His private campaign files show about two hundred contributors of $1 to $25 apiece. Possibly the railroad union money went directly to recipients without passing through the campaign treasury (obviously the printing and distribution of half a million or more copies of *Labor* exceeded the $2,800 of donated services Truman listed, so the cash may have bypassed the campaign committee as well). Loans were a source of funds that would not be listed as donations, even though the loans may later have been forgiven. Truman also apparently had personal bank accounts opened in his name in various towns, and local supporters deposited money in those accounts for the campaign.[58]

The financial chaos was exceeded by the staff confusion. A three-headed monster ran the campaign. Vic Messall, Truman's old Senate secretary, was campaign chairman. David Berenstein was director general. Fred Canfil was Fred Canfil. A Truman supporter explained how the triumvirate worked: "[Fundraiser] John Snyder hated Vic Messall, see, and [treasurer] Harry Vaughan hated him, because he was John Snyder's boy. So, they decided that they were going to have to get rid of Vic [remove him from St. Louis campaign head-quarters]. So Truman told me, he said, 'Now, we're going to have Vic to set up an outstate office and we'll have all our campaign literature and everything in Sedalia. Vic don't know anybody in St. Louis, and he'll run that office there in Sedalia.' Well, that plowed old Vic under, you see. He was really teed off. Canfil never did like Vic either, and Canfil said he would be a handicap up there, and I think he pretty well sold Truman on the idea, too. . . . I remember Berenstein, and nobody ever knew what happened to him. The next thing that anyone knew, why, Vaughan was in charge, and no one knew who in the hell he was. It was a messed up thing. I don't know sometimes how Truman ever got elected." Truman was tying knots in flagpoles: "Vic has no brains, the Jew has too many, and Canfil has too much every and no balance wheel." Truman fumed, "We ought to have lost with such a set up," and he vowed, "The next time I have a campaign I'll run it myself."[59]

While the chiefs quarreled, the lower echelon knew what to do without waiting for orders. Defying the Hatch Act some postmasters went to work for Truman, the more faint-hearted using their spouses as fronts. Other workers solicited help from people the senator had helped over the years. A card file was available to expedite this work:

Bates Co. Butler, Missouri. Paul B. Levy. Assisted in obtaining sister's furniture from K.C. Customs. April 1939.

Buchanan County. St. Joseph, Missouri. Frank S. Gillette. Assisted in obtaining approval of his railroad retirement annuity. April 1939.

Green Co. Springfield, Missouri-530 W. College St. Arnes, Anthony Francis (Veteran). Award of $17.00 from 6-25-35 to 9-18-35 $42.00 from 9-19-35 Interest[ed] Party: M. Emmett Hogan, Landers Building, Springfield.

Pettis County. Houstania, Missouri. Ralph Hanley. Helped him to obtain corn-hog check. April to July 1935.

Another file showed PWA grants awarded to communities. Still another meticulous file was kept of people who refused to help the senator.[60]

The bleak reports of February and March turned bright in June and July. June 3: "I have been in Springfield, Joplin, Carthage, and Nevada since seeing you and unless there are an awful lot of liars in these places you are going to receive a lot of votes." June 8: "Couldn't look any better . . . going over strong." June 20: "The fact that the [Kansas City] Star would come out with a dirty editorial such as the one published last Monday shows very conclusively that they are uneasy." On July 30, a week before the balloting, one of Truman's Kansas City stenographers exclaimed, "We have won the election!"[61]

Yet despite the shift toward Truman the outcome was far from certain as balloting began. Truman was glad that his ally Charles Hay was on the St. Louis election board, "I know we will have fair elections in one big city, anyway." The Jackson County situation was complicated by the pending forced departure of county prosecutor W. W. Graves who had winked at Pendergast vote frauds. Truman was uneasy about an honest ballot count. Perhaps fifty thousand of votes for him in 1934 had been fraudulent. Fortunately for Truman the Pendergast organization could still intimidate voters by inserting identifying marks on the ballots to check how individuals voted. (When this practice was outlawed the next year Truman exclaimed, "I read House Bill 37 with sort of a gasp. I don't know what [Representative] Gene Munger is thinking about to do a trick like this.") In addition, St. Louis boss Robert Hannegan switched from Stark to Truman at the last minute. On election night Truman and Edgar Hinde were together in Independence. Hinde recalled, "He said, 'Well, Hinie, I guess this is one time I'm beaten.' And I said, 'Aw, it's a long time 'til morning; you're not beat yet.' I figured he was, too, to be right honest with you, I figured he was gone. And 'long about two or three o'clock in the morning St. Louis turned loose some returns it had been holding back, and he won the election." Truman's winning margin was less than 8,000 out of 665,000 votes.[62]

Truman immediately returned to Washington. When he stepped on the Senate floor, business stopped and colleagues rushed to greet him. They threw an impromptu luncheon where "they sang his praise in lusty song." Truman was especially touched by the interest capitol employees took in his election. An old hand on The Hill said the universal interest in Truman's election had never been seen before with anyone else. Truman was confident of success in November. Of President Roosevelt's role in the primary Truman huffed, "Frank will need me a lot more in Missouri than I'll need him this fall, so I should worry." He added, "I am not going to see the President any more until February 1, and then he's going to want to see me. I rather think from here out I'll make him like it." Of the whole experience Truman said, "I hope some good fact finder will make a record of that campaign. It will be history someday."[63]

Chapter 13

THE SENATOR'S PRIVATE INCOME

Ironically, at the moment of Truman's greatest political triumph he suffered perhaps his worst personal defeat—the loss of the family farm at Grandview. Although he would face accusations of political corruption in his efforts to protect the farm, ultimately the loss proves Truman's personal integrity. Dozens of banks across the nation would have carried the mortgage as a favor to a U.S. senator, but Truman didn't ask. Moreover, his inability to raise the necessary cash demonstrates that he had no secret sources of income. There are several angles to the farm loss.

When Truman took office as senator he still owed one haberdashery debt, the 1929 circuit court judgment of $8,900 for the old Security State Bank loan. Security State Bank had consolidated with Continental National Bank, which became Continental National Bank & Trust Co., which affiliated with the Kemper family's Commerce Trust Co., and then went bankrupt (although Commerce Trust stayed open). As part of the liquidation process, Continental's assets were to be converted into cash to satisfy debts owed to Holland Banking Co. Those Continental assets included the $8,900 Truman owed. Since Truman refused to pay this judgment and couldn't be garnished, this Continental "asset" was worth little on the open market.[1]

As the sale of Continental assets approached in January 1935

Truman secretly arranged to buy the judgment from Continental. Fred Boxley coordinated the delicate maneuvers. Continental attorney Omar Robinson had diddled Vivian day by day, promising that Vivian could buy the judgment for $1,000. On the day of the court-ordered sale of Continental assets Robinson told Vivian the deal was off. (On behalf of Continental, Robinson had sued Truman for the original judgment. Truman viewed this as a personal attack by Robinson. A lawyer associated with Robinson in important litigation leading to the sale of Continental assets was listed as "Harry L. Jost." This was probably a misprint for longtime Pendergast opponent Henry L. Jost.) Robinson was also attorney for about half the people whose judgments (owned by Continental) were being sold that day. After consulting with Boxley, Vivian rushed over to William T. Kemper. Kemper telephoned Federal Reserve Bank general counsel H. G. Leedy and offered to lend him enough money to buy all of the Continental assets. Leedy had taught Truman at the Kansas City School of Law and was the brother of Missouri Supreme Court justice C. A. Leedy. H. G. Leedy and former U.S. Senator Roscoe Patterson, whom Truman had defeated in 1934, were attorneys opposing Robinson and Jost in the litigation that led to the sale of Continental assets. Another lawyer in Leedy's office, Clifton B. Liter, bought the assets later that day for a grand total of $4,300. Thus, although everything was done under Truman's orders, several layers of go-betweens prevented outsiders from discovering his involvement.

Boxley had promised Leedy $1,000 for the Truman judgment, not a bad deal since *all* the judgments in the Continental assets went to Liter for $1,075. Robinson predicted that his brother-in-law J. F. Meade, Continental president, would have John T. Barker (the Pendergast fixer who saved McElroy's and Truman's political scalps in the parental home litigation back in Truman's eastern judge days) protest the sale, but that the Truman judgment would be excluded from any protest. Roscoe Patterson's brother and Judge John Farrington apparently were two more attorneys opposing Robinson in the litigation leading to the sale; the two Springfield men monitored the sale and felt it was okay. (Farrington was a top Truman operative in Springfield.) Continental attorney Robinson stalled final settlement of the deal for a few weeks, demanding court costs in addition to the bid; and H. G. Leedy watched closely to be sure that Meade didn't somehow wind up with the judgment. At the end of February

1935 Truman finally bought the judgment against him for a straight $1,000. All his haberdashery debts were now paid. "This cleans me up entirely, and it is certainly a burden off my shoulders."[2]

In the midst of these maneuvers Truman and Boxley were also dealing with a filling station the senator's sister Mary Jane had. She didn't run it personally but leased it out. The income was important for her support. "I can't get a bit of satisfaction out of Standard," she told her brother. "Mr. Boxley says Wilson is still going to do something, but I think he is just stalling." Truman, who fretted over her health, wrote back, "Don't get too badly discouraged over it." The nature of the dispute with Jay Wilson is unclear from surviving records, but it was fierce and continued for years. During World World II Truman met Wilson and, "I told him in one-word syllables that I didn't like the way he had acted with regard to that contract. He said that he was going to work it out some way so it would be of benefit to Mary."[3]

Truman supported other family members in addition to his wife and daughter. "Thanks for the check," his mother wrote, "but— have always hoped you could lay up something for a rainy day instead of helping everybody." Truman also supported Bess's mother, whose reputation for personal wealth was apparently as inflated as her ego. Truman tried to throw architectural business to Bess's brother Fred, as had been done with the design of the county courthouse in Independence. In 1936 Truman complained to Governor Park that Fred had so far gotten only $2,500 of business from the $13 million bond issue Truman had promoted. "I didn't expect him of course, to get the biggest jobs in the whole layout, but I was hoping that he would get one that would make him a little money. . . . If there is anything you can do in this matter, I will certainly appreciate it." Park replied, "I have been doing everything possible to get another architectural job for Fred. It was with difficulty that I got him the Algoa job. His filing the claim which he did file seems to have offended some of the officials. The Board will meet tomorrow, and I will again take the matter up." Fred tried to get Governor Stark's backing for the State Office Building and Cancer Clinic contracts, but Stark gave him the brush-off: "Senator Truman is one of my warmest friends. Of course, in cases of this kind, even our friends and closest relatives must stand on their own two feet." Fred eventually landed a federal bureaucrat job in Kansas City. Independence mayor Roger Sermon, a Truman war buddy and uneasy political ally, helped keep Vivian and Bess's brother George on the county payroll during the Senate years.[4]

Truman usually felt strapped for funds. He gave Bess a verbal lashing for running up a $9.53 grocery bill one month. While he had no avarice of "the get," he suffered from avarice of "the keep." Much has been written of Truman's supposed terrible financial privations as senator, how at one point Bess not only had to hold down a $4,500-a-year clerical job in Truman's office but had to do household chores as well (because Truman could no longer afford enough domestic servants). Many other wives have held jobs and done household chores without anyone thinking it remarkable. Truman had enough money to support his mother, his mother-in-law, a large Independence residence with full-time servants, a modest Washington apartment with occasional domestic help, private school tuition for Margaret, and obligatory social entertainments for political colleagues and big shots. He may have had no trouble keeping expenses current to income, but that's not the same as being poor. If Truman felt poor, and his private writings show that he did, it was only a relative measurement against the far wealthier people he dealt with every day.[5]

While Truman was the 1944 nominee for vice-president his monthly net from his Senate salary was $687. He fretted about possibly bouncing checks, but the Hamilton National Bank of Washington assured him that an overdraft would be permitted. By September 1941 Truman was buying $300 to $500 of U.S. defense bonds every month. This suggests that he was not only a patriot but that Bess's clerical salary was providing the family with more than enough income—otherwise the bonds would have been an impossible financial drain. Thus in his second Senate term the family income exceeded expenses by a comfortable margin.[6]

Truman believed that his financial situation proved his personal goodness. "The reason for my lack of worldly goods [is] I just can't cheat in a trade or browbeat a worker. Maybe I'm crazy, but so is the Sermon on the Mount if I am." "I have always believed in doing as I'd be done by, and to make money and keep it you must be a pirate or strike an oil well or gold mine." Such statements are found throughout Truman's private writings. He felt superior to any wealthy person, even to a trusted personal friend like John Snyder, of whom he wrote: "I'm too much enamoured of the Sermon on the Mount to be a good banker." Such an attitude was far different from the common American belief that wealth was a sign of God's approval, poverty a sign of sin and sloth. Since Truman thought rich people were robbers he was comfortable with proposals that would tax those ill-gotten gains for projects to help ordinary folk.[7]

Despite his desire for additional income Truman declined opportunities that he viewed as profit from his public office. This included speeches about public affairs. "Just the other day I refused an offer to make 10 speeches for a fee of $4000 and expenses. Of course Martin Dies has followed a program of that sort, but I think when he does he sells the country down the river. No one cares about hearing me speak, and the Chairman [Truman] of this Committee is not for sale." He also declined to do celebrity product endorsements, such as for Lucky Strike cigarettes. "Wouldn't my friends, who know my love for cigarettes, have a grand time wondering how much it takes to buy me."[8]

Considering Truman's criticism of railroad securities manipulations, his own efforts to make a stock market killing (sometimes with aid of insider tips) were all the more remarkable. "Maybe I can make a gamble next fall and hit a pot of gold," he told Bess in 1935. "If I'd played my hunch last fall we'd have had enough to build two houses." In that instance Truman thought faintheartedness had cost him $30,000. His caution proved more fortunate when Roosevelt announced the Supreme Court packing plan: "I've been hesitating on the investment, and it was well I did, because everything went down after the Court message." Of course, Truman wasn't intending an "investment" reflecting a belief in a company's product or service and an expectation that the stock would therefore pay dividends. He was simply gambling. In this activity he worked through his secretary Vic Messall. "When I was in Kansas City," Messall wrote Truman in 1938, "I said something about selling the Superior Oil Stock. I talked to my brother-in-law, Pat, while I was in Chicago, and he told me that the directors of the company were holding 275,000 shares that set them back $3.75. Pat suggested that we ought to sell the stock any place between $3.75 and $4.00. It is about $3.50 now, and think I will sell mine at the market and take a chance on buying some more when it gets down to $2.00, if it ever does. I am giving you this information for what it is worth, so you can use your own judgment in what you may care to do." Truman replied, "When you sell your Superior Oil stock, sell mine, too. Since we've got a profit in it, we had better take it. We made a mistake not selling that Cities Service when it was up to 10. If we get a chance to get 3/4 or a dollar for the Croft, I think we had better let that go, too." The next year Truman confided to Bess, "Vic was taking a lot for granted on that Crown [Drug] thing, but there is already a profit of $250 on it, so I guess he did me a favor at that." A few days later Truman bubbled, "It looks as if the Crown will buy us each a car. It looks awful good." (Crown Drug's chief Tom Evans was a trusted Pendergast ally.) In July 1943 Truman wanted McDonald & Co. to sell three hundred of his shares in Crown Drug Co. if the price reached $2.00 a share.[9]

Thus in his first Senate term Truman lacked the personal funds necessary to pay off the Grandview farm mortgage. In that era monthly payments covered only interest, and the entire principal was due at the end of a loan. In 1937 Truman was being pressed hard to pay the $25,000 five-year mortgage given to his mother in 1932 by Anna Lee Rosier, wealthy director of the Bank of Belton. Apparently demands were also being made about the additional $3,000 mortgage Bank of Belton gave to Truman's mother in 1933. Still a third mortgage was evidently due, a loan of $5,500 made in 1935 by Kansas City Life Insurance Co. Technically the Kansas City Life mortgage was on land owned by Vivian, but this was a legal subterfuge, and the land was in fact Mattie's. The son of Kansas City Life vice-president Ed. Villmoare moved in the same Kansas City political circles as did Harry's cousin Snapper, Robert Ryland (closely associated with Truman's later lawyer Arthur Mag), and Jerome Walsh (son of Jim Reed's nemesis Frank Walsh). While the controversy over District Attorney Milligan's reappointment was heating in November 1937, Truman was gratified by Vivian's efforts to get a new water plant near Grandview: "It may mean that we could get a buyer for that 200 acres and save the farm which as you know is my greatest worry because of Mamma. She knows nothing of the extremity to which the mortgage holders have been pressing us for payment. In fact when Vivian and I went to see them last when I was at home they told us point blank if something wasn't done by December 1 they'd take over. Well I'm afraid it would kill her, and I want to keep her alive as long as I can."[10]

Truman discovered an escape hatch in the Jackson County School Fund. State law permitted county judges to lend out school money not currently needed. Truman explained, "While I was in Washington Buck Purcell and other judges suggested the loan to Vivian as a good one for the county. I didn't know anything about it." How Buck suggested this is unclear since he died in May 1936 before any need arose to renew the mortgages. Truman's assertion that Vivian was simply trying to do the county a favor by accepting the loan also seems far-fetched. Since Harry and Vivian kept in close touch about the mortgage situation, the senator's profession of ignorance about the loan is hard to believe, especially since Fred Canfil participated in the arrangements. The arrangements indicate the county was doing the Trumans a favor, not the other way around. The loan was approved in April 1938 by the two Pendergast county judges David Long and J. W. Hostetter while the Pendergast opponent judge, Battle McCardle, was out of the courtroom. This was the last school fund loan the county ever made, which also suggests a certain favoritism. Another interesting factor was that although state law prohibited the mortgage from exceeding 50 percent of the property's value, the loan was for $35,000 on property valued at $22,680. (The $35,000 figure is particularly interesting since Kansas City Life was reportedly willing to lend only $15,000 to $16,000. Of course, with the $5,500 Kansas City Life mortgage already outstanding, that could mean Kansas City Life was willing to go for approximately the total valuation.) The law also required the loan to be endorsed by people owning property with assessed valuation equal to the mortgaged land. The endorsers were Vivian Truman and Fred Canfil, neither of whom had such property. Vivian later explained that he and Canfil gave bonds for the necessary amount. These bonds were surely a worthless Pendergast organization subterfuge to get around the law, since when the crunch came neither Vivian nor Canfil presented any money.[11]

This school fund loan was a mighty fine deal for the Trumans, allowing them to pay off or extend the $3,000 Bank of Belton mortgage and the $5,500 Kansas City Life mortgage. The school fund loan was to be repaid with 6 percent interest on December 31, 1938. Those nine months passed, and no money arrived from the Trumans. When the county became cranky about this, Truman made a sudden trip to Kansas City in late June 1939. He explained, "We are having some difficulty, but I hope to work out arrangements to pay off the note this month. You know how it is when you seem to owe more than you can pay. The farm has been mortgaged many years, and in the recent drought years its income hasn't been up to normal." The "arrangements" apparently were attempts to sell the farm. These efforts were complicated by the fall of Boss Pendergast, the forced resignation of indicted presiding judge David Long in November, and a new Pendergast opponent, Presiding Judge George S. Montgomery. Since Judge Fred Klaber was also a Pendergast opponent, the three-member county court was now distinctly unfriendly toward Truman, and only too happy for a chance to cause him damnable problems. Now, anyone who has participated in the adventure of real estate sales knows that negotiations can be delicate. Truman blew up at Klaber: "You have completely ruined any opportunity I might have had to save the equity in it. We had several offers on it . . . that would have paid off the indebtedness. Every time one of them would come near to being closed old Montgomery would run to the [*Kansas City*] *Star* and J. C. Nichols and get it knocked out." Nichols was already a Kansas City legend and had a national reputation as a city planning expert. His mammoth real estate company would continue to dominate some residential and ritzy commercial districts decades later. His company had been approached by J. W. Perry for an estimate on the Truman property. Perry was in charge of liquidating the school fund loans for the county; he was also chairman of the Forward Kansas City Committee representing the wealthy mercantile interests that had turned on the Pendergast machine and driven it from power. Thus Perry, like Judge Montgomery, had no interest in helping the Trumans. Perry got Ray Jones of the Nichols company to give an informal opinion of what the Grandview property would bring in a depressed real estate market after heavy publicity forced the Trumans to accept just about any offer to prevent a sheriff's sale. Jones gave the same informal opinion that any knowledgeable person would, that the land if sold now wouldn't realize the mortgage. On the basis of this casual guess Perry left Vivian and Vivian's attorney Omar Robinson with the impression that Mr. J. C. Nichols formally appraised the land as worth less than the mortgage—which (without the qualifiers to Jones's guess) implied that the county school fund had been cheated by the loan. This soured Truman on Nichols for life. Nichols was livid when he learned that

Jones had violated company policy by giving an informal opinion, and that Perry had used the J. C. Nichols name to put the squeeze to the Trumans. By the time J. C. Nichols learned what had happened, however, the farm had been lost, and Truman had small interest in protestations of innocence from "the great Mr. Nichols."[12]

After sabotaging all Truman's efforts to sell the farm and pay off the school fund loan, the county court foreclosed the mortgage in June 1940. Admittedly the county had allowed the loan to go delinquent for eighteen months before foreclosing, a generous grace period, especially considering that the Trumans had paid absolutely nothing on the obligation—no interest, no taxes, no anything. Nonetheless, the foreclosure and sheriff's sale came in the midst of Truman's 1940 reelection campaign, and Truman felt the action had political rather than fiscal motivations. Indeed, much was made about the Pendergast favoritism that granted the loan, particularly since this was as close as anyone had ever come to finding Truman receiving monetary gain from his Pendergast connections. Further credence to the political motive theory can be found in the identity of the purchaser at the sheriff's sale. Jackson County itself bought the farm for $36,500, sat on it until the real estate market strengthened, and then sold it at a profit five years later. Thus the county was in no hurry whatsoever to get its money. The only beneficiary from the foreclosure was Truman's opposition.[13]

Truman was displeased. "I only hope I can catch old Montgomery, J. C. Nichols, and Roy Roberts where I can take the heart out of 'em." (Roberts was managing editor of the *Kansas City Star.*) "Under a forced sale with everything against it the farm brought $1,600 more than the original lien. The damned *Star* never mentioned that." Truman mused about his mother, "No matter how much front she puts on she hates to leave the farm even if it has been nothing but a source of worry and trouble to us for about 50 years. The place has brought bad luck and financial disaster to everyone connected with it since my grandfather died in 1892. If we'd been smart and sold it right after the World War when I had the [live]stock sale we could have been no worse off if we'd spent all the money in riotous living. Well it's gone anyway, and may the jinx go with it."[14]

Unfamiliar with the house she moved into, Truman's eighty-eight-year-old mother fell down the stairs and broke her hip the month after she was forced off the farm. His own health weakened, Truman had arrived in Hot Springs, Arkansas, two days earlier to recuperate from the strain of the campaign and foreclosure. Truman rushed back to Kansas City in such a panic that he forgot to pay his hotel tab. A broken hip is often fatal to an elderly person, but Mattie gradually recovered in the ensuing months. Truman blamed the suffering and doctor bills on Judge Montgomery and J. C. Nichols.[15]

Truman was excited about the prospects for his next Senate term. "I've made some good friends up here, and we'll go to town in accomplishment." This was a matter of great satisfaction for him, and he vowed, "I'm going to do as I please. . . . I've spent my life pleasing people, doing things for 'em and putting myself into embarrassing positions to save the Party and the other fellow. Now I've quit. To hell with 'em all."[16]

Chapter 14

CALL TO ARMS

Truman had scarcely settled into his Senate seat in 1935 when he began to learn how Hitler was affecting the lives of Kansas Citians. Plea after plea arrived in his office imploring him to help the homefolk's European relatives escape territory coveted or seized by the Nazis. The requests came from strangers and friends: from Frank Spina, the Italian barber of Battery D; from Eddie Jacobson; from Jackson County highway engineer Alex Sachs; from insurance man Thomas McGee; from clothiers Otto Hess and Sig Harzfeld; from Phillip Wang of Alaskan Fur; from Arthur Eisenhower of Commerce Trust (Truman's old boarding-house companion from bank clerk days, whose Army brother would later do a little work of his own liberating people from Hitler's rule); from politico Jim Aylward; from Pendergast city councilman Ruby Garrett; from Boss Tom's nephew Jim; and from Boss Tom himself. Sometimes Truman succeeded, sometimes he failed. Any pattern seems elusive. Truman could get Secretary of State Hull to intervene personally without results, and other times a routine expression of interest by Truman's office would do the trick. In apparent recognition of the seriousness of these situations Truman was willing to forego personal grudges. He felt Lee Erb of Grandview was sabotaging Mary Jane's filling station business but he nonetheless attempted to get Erb's relatives out of Berlin (and learned that Erb had been doing nothing against Mary Jane).

Truman's work raised questions about whether the State Department and particularly U.S. Consul General Douglas Jenkins in Berlin gave a damn about Hitler's victims. For instance, Truman was told that Jenkins would reject visa applications from Jews because he didn't like the way they filled in their names. On one occasion Jenkins refused a family's visa request, saying they might have to go on Welfare in the United States. When shown proof that $100,000 of resources stood behind this family Jenkins said that wasn't enough to guarantee they would stay off Welfare. Truman complained, but Secretary Hull backed Jenkins.

For some reason Truman seemed generally unconcerned about this State Department conduct. He assured two troubled correspondents, "Everything that can be done is being done to relieve this shocking situation by providing the means for these people to go to places of refuge." This seems to have been Truman's honest opinion. He seemed unwilling to believe that State Department officials would allow personal anti-Semitism to affect their work. (Truman's personal writings were sprinkled with anti-Jewish epithets, but Jews seemed satisfied with his public work, just as blacks were.) As a member of the Appropriations Committee, Truman could have put considerable pressure on the State Department if he believed a problem existed. He used this clout to make the Navy name a new battleship for his home state.[1]

Truman did some hard thinking about what led up to all this. In a 1938 Armistice Day address he declared that any of four men could have prevented the present European situation had their plans succeeded. Julius Caesar was murdered before he could colonize northern Europe with Romans. Henry IV of France was murdered just as he was ready "to completely pacify Germany and northern Europe and make it part of a united plan for peace." Napoleon and Woodrow Wilson failed also. "Europe's troubles . . . are racial and economic. France and the old Austro-Hungarian empire were the only two really self-contained nations on the continent." Germany, Truman said, always sought to drive east toward the Black Sea or to follow the Danube, but Britain and Russia always stood in the way. "I still hope that some sort of a world arrangement along the lines laid out by Henry IV and Woodrow Wilson may be worked out. Eventually it will have to be, or our civilization will end as all other great civilizations have, and we'll just start over from another dark age." Truman made no such analysis of the Asian situation, but he was well aware of Japan's depredations in China. In June 1938 he inserted a *Washington Post* editorial into the *Congressional Record:* "It is an unparalleled indictment which the Tokyo Government is steadily assembling against itself. And it will be in Japan's long-run interests if her rulers begin to realize that the points in this indictment are being noted carefully by peoples other than their Chinese victims." Later he warned, "We cannot escape our responsibility this time." "We looked back in 1920, and that's what's the matter today. Lot's wife looked back, and see what happened to her."[2]

Truman had no doubts about what needed to be done. "We are facing a bunch of thugs, and the only theory a thug understands is a gun and a bayonet." He elaborated:

It has never been my policy to try to satisfy either isolationists or interventionists. I have had an idea and a program of my own, which I have been trying to carry out ever since 1921, and that was to awaken the country to the necessity of an adequate and efficient defense program.

Senator Copeland and I made an endeavor in 1935 to get anti-aircraft guns, modern planes, and heavy artillery. We didn't succeed. We tried it again in '36, and in '37 we succeeded in getting an authorization of 169 anti-aircraft guns, the first ones of which were delivered in December 1939.

Pacifists, isolationists, and followers of the old Henry Cabot Lodge school of thought have very nearly ruined the country, but I still think we can defeat our enemies, and I am going to devote the rest of my life in trying to do it.[3]

Congress and the public thoroughly dissected various government policies to determine whether they might lead the nation to war, but Truman found all these arguments superfluous. "It is not a case of being for or against the war that is going to cause our difficulty. There was no enthusiasm for war in Belgium, Holland, and France, and that is the situation we are up against, and it is not our making." He added, "Denmark and Norway tried to be neutral, determined to take no action until actually attacked. Their condition today is not enviable."[4]

Truman felt it crucial to hamper the Japanese and Nazi war effort while doing everything feasible to defend the British Empire. "I have always been in favor of cutting off the shipments of war materials to Japan, and I hope the United States and England will effectually prevent her receiving any more materials with which to murder the Chinese. I am sure if that is done an honorable peace can be worked out between Japan and China and the needless slaughter stopped." Truman's concern went beyond China; he inserted a newspaper clipping into the *Congressional Record* warning that the scrap iron America sold to Japan "may be returned to us in a very unacceptable form." Truman recognized, however, that such a boycott required finesse. When fourteen hundred Kirksville, Missouri, Teachers College students called for an end to *all* economic dealings with Japan, he warned that such a move could provoke Japan to war against the United States. (Of the students Truman said, "I have an idea that nearly all of them are pacifists and would not want to see a war in the Orient carried on by this country, although my sympathies, just as theirs, are with the Chinese." In Truman's vocabulary "pacifist" was a term of contempt, as bad as "uplifter.")[5]

Influenced by Senator Nye's investigation of how financiers and munitions makers (the "merchants of death") affected U.S. entry into World War I, Truman voted for the Neutrality Act of 1937 banning arms sales to countries at war—and then kicked himself a hundred times. Truman explained that he thought this would discourage American involvement in the Spanish Civil War, and he was right. He later decided Nye had misled him, and he turned on Nye bitterly. Truman decided the 1937 Neutrality Act had become neutral against England. "We should not help the thugs among nations by refusing to sell arms to our friends." In September 1939 he called for FDR to summon a special session of Congress to revise the Neutrality Act. "The present act gives Hitler an advantage," Truman said. "We should change it as soon as possible to put us on a cash and carry basis with all European nations." "Cash and carry" was a well-known phrase meaning that people with ready money and their own transportation could buy certain war goods from the U.S. The idea was to help Britain without getting U.S. merchant ships sunk, as such sinkings would tend to bring the United

States into the war. Truman declared, "We should insist upon Americans and American shipping remaining out of the war zone. That is one of the best ways to keep us out of war." The "cash and carry" policy had been used before, but Truman went farther yet with that call to end freedom of the seas. This idea wasn't a Truman innovation; he was merely announcing support for one side of the neutrality controversy. A majority of Congress now shared Truman's views, and enacted such legislation. Truman's advocacy of restrictions on American freedom of the seas was surely a sop to nervous public opinion, to relieve anxieties that arms sales might bring the United States into the war. At the moment Truman was more worried about defending England than about defending freedom of the seas. "As old [President] Cleveland said, we have got a condition to face, and not a theory." In November 1941 Truman and a majority of Congress removed most restrictions on freedom of the seas, allowing American merchantmen to arm themselves and sail anywhere with any cargo. He felt aid to the British Empire was the crucial thing, by whatever means American public opinion would allow.[6]

Truman was gravely troubled by the isolationist element of American public opinion, fearing its effect not only on American policy but on Nazi policy. "The Germans in 1916," he said, "thought we wouldn't fight and that if we made the attempt we couldn't." He felt the Huns "were misled by the talkers and publicity hounds here at home," and warned:

> Pressure groups and the distributors of propaganda are a bad thing for the stability of our form of government. With the radio we are almost back to the old demagogy government of Athens. The situation as it is developing now, if my history is correct, caused the downfall of the Roman Republic. Every time a Senator had a pet measure to put through the Senate and if the Senators didn't like it, he would run out to the Forum and bring pressure to bear by haranguing the people. That is what Fish and his crowd are attempting to do with the America First Program Movement.

Of the America First crowd Truman wrote, "I think there are some people who are out [of] step with the Government, as they have been all the time . . . as demonstrated in New York the other night at Mr. Lindbergh's meeting." He now believed it un-American to oppose the president's desires. "There is another phase of national defense which is of vital interest to our country and its welfare. That is the disloyal inhabitants who are enjoying peace and freedom here and yet who would like to overthrow our form of government. I believe those people should be sent to the countries they admire and that every effort should be made to eliminate any 'fifth column' activities." Truman proclaimed, "There must be no other 'ism' than Americanism," and explicitly demanded "immediate deportation of all undesirables who are not American citizens." He complained of receiving "nutty letters . . . nearly all from St. Louis and nearly all have German names. The Bund is working."[7]

Truman misunderstood the isolationist sentiment. Unquestionably there was a "head in the sand" element that wanted to ignore danger, just as the interventionists had a "purify the nation through war" element. Neither extreme represented the best thinking of either group. The mainstream of isolationism questioned whether helping Britain and France retain their empires served the interests of freedom. If America didn't help liberate the colonies, some nastier outfit might gain the friendship of these oppressed peoples. Another problem was that up to and including Munich, German demands were often viewed as reasonable adjustments for unfairness in the Versailles Treaty. Hitler's diplomatic triumphs in that period had little to do with his bellicosity, but were achieved because the European diplomatic corps felt Germany had legitimate beefs. The great debate was whether Hitler was seeking fair play or using legal means for territorial expansion merely until legal means no longer worked. The question baffled the upper-class striped-pants diplomats, but Truman and many of his fellow politicians had dealt with creeps like Hitler in politics, and had him spotted for what he was.

Truman called for a massive U.S. arms buildup. "Don't let us be caught napping as Great Britain was. Let us prepare. Another billion dollars for the security of our liberty and independence would be cheap insurance as compared to the cost of the last war." He said American weapons were good, but pitifully few, not even plentiful enough for U.S. forces to train with. Truman stated, "An army of 400,000 men is adequate for the first line of defense on land and to act as instructors to the citizen army. I think we should have a navy second to none, and the necessary air force to support it. If it takes 50,000 planes and 100,000 pilots, let's build the planes and train the pilots. I think we should have a citizen army, trained on the Swiss plan, subject to call in case of an emergency, and the necessary tanks, armament, and other material to equip these forces." He warned, "Every bulwark of democracy in the world has been eliminated except Britain . . . , and it will be a most difficult world in which to live by our democratic way if Britain is conquered. . . . A nation such as ours, with all the resources that are necessary for a happy and contented population, will not be allowed to smugly enjoy these resources if the totalitarians win the war." Truman noted, "I am certain that American geniuses can create a bombing plane that can travel 10,000 miles and accomplish its mission. What then happens to impregnable Atlantic and Pacific barriers?"[8]

Truman became concerned that the accelerated defense expenditures weren't properly supervised. In summer 1940 he started a quiet tour of defense projects, and as the months went by he drove his car thirty thousand miles across the South and Midwest and back East. From his Jackson County years Truman knew every contract scam in the book, and in November he sounded the alarm to Assistant War Secretary Robert Patterson: "While I believe it is conceded that 94 or 95% of the people are honest, it has been my experience with contracts that the percentage is exactly reversed when public funds are at stake. As you know I have had considerable experience with public construction and it requires a most extreme vigilance on the part of public officials to prevent the robbery of the treasury and immense scandals." Truman observed no increase in War Department vigilance.[9]

He also became uneasy about the contract award process. To mobilize American industry, executives from major corporations had become government officials authorizing defense contracts. The billions of tax dollars then tended to flow into these major corporations. Truman disliked the obvious favoritism. He also feared this slowed defense preparations, since his railroad investigations had convinced him that top industrial executives didn't necessarily know much about what their corporations did—they were policy rather than production men. Most serious of all, however, Truman suspected that the major corporations and their alumni who now poured into the government were using the defense emergency as a smokescreen hiding a conspiracy to undo the New Deal. He sensed that big corporations were planning to use tax dollars (defense contracts) to ruin smaller competitors, to establish the greatest monopolies the world had ever seen, to gain a stranglehold over the very citizens who were working to avoid domination by foreigners. Armies and navies clearly threatened America from without, and Truman now discovered an enemy within.

Truman took his suspicions to the president of the United States on February 3, 1941. He also took with him a plan he had devised with his old associate from the Citizens Security Bank of Englewood, Lou Holland. This plan would coordinate the capabilities of small manufacturers in various geographical regions, so that defense contracts could be awarded to these consortia, which could produce items just as well as the big boys could. Moreover, this plan would produce the goods cheaper and faster since the consortia used existing facilities, while contracts for the big boys too often included funds to build manufacturing plants to produce the item (thus using tax money to expand the ability of major corporations to challenge small competitors that had created innovative products). Truman and Roosevelt discussed the situation for a good half hour, and the senator departed in frustration. "I don't know whether I made any impression or not, because the President is always courteous and cordial when anyone calls on him, and when you come out you think you are getting what you wanted, when nine times out of ten you are just getting cordial treatment. Anyway, I am going to lay it before the Senate."[10]

Truman had been expressing his concerns to colleagues for several weeks, laying a foundation for a committee to investigate the situation. A week after seeing FDR, Truman announced he would soon introduce a resolution calling for such an investigation. He noted how contract awards were squeezing small business, how big corporations with defense contracts were allowed to buy machine tools from small competitors and ship the tools to big city plants. This ruined the little business, wrecked the small-town economies, delayed manufacturing, and caused housing shortages in big cities as small-town workers sold their homes at a sacrifice to follow the jobs. Truman complained that defense contracts were awarded through friendships of government officials with big manufacturers rather than through analysis of contract applicant competence. He bluntly charged a conspiracy: "It undoubtedly is the plan to make the big manufacturers bigger, and let the little men shift for themselves."[11]

A few days later Truman introduced his formal resolution calling for an investigating committee. Despite his outstanding New Deal credentials there were concerns that such a committee could turn into a harassing operation against the White House. Great straining among Truman, Vice-President Wallace, Senator Jimmy Byrnes (who controlled initial funding), Majority Leader Barkley, Minority Leader McNary, and President Roosevelt yielded a committee of five New Deal Democrats, two cordial Republicans (one of whom would support FDR for reelection in 1944), and $15,000 to make a complete investigation of the nationwide multi-billion-dollar defense industry. "I have had some difficulty in getting a committee," Truman sighed, "and even after it is appointed some of the people on it don't want to serve." Truman's old friend Lewis Schwellenbach exploded over the funding: "The appropriating of only $15,000 for this task is ridiculous. The idea of expecting anybody to do a job as important as this . . . and as far-reaching for that sum is just silly. Between ourselves, I would spend it all as quickly as possible and go back and ask for some more. With the $15,000 you can work out plans for committee work of such an important nature that they won't dare turn you down on it." This view turned out to be correct, and Truman got more money by unanimous consent whenever he asked (although that consent occasionally required delicate behind-the-scenes maneuvers). The committee eventually spent $400,000. Expenses were held down by getting federal agencies to lend staff members who remained on the agency payroll while doing committee work. Truman also quietly received advice from Supreme Court justices Brandeis and Black on how to proceed. For committee counsel Truman hired Hugh Fulton, formerly of Cravath.[12]

Much to Truman's surprise the committee's first big task was to deal with a coal miners' strike. In April 1941 the coal operators contract with miners ended, and with it, the production of coal. This hampered national defense work, and Truman announced he would call the responsible parties before his committee if production failed to resume by April 25. The deadline passed. Representatives of management and labor were summoned, the latter in the person of John L. Lewis (whom *Time* magazine dubbed "last of the great ham tragedians of politics"). "We had a show almost as big as the one when the hearings were up on the Lend-Lease Bill," Truman proudly told a friend the next day. "It was due to our grilling of the fellows on the coal strike that they arrived at a settlement." Truman found all sides at fault, but that Southern operator intransigence was the immediate cause of the strike. "While I don't pose as an admirer of John L. Lewis you will have to give him credit for trying to help his people. . . . I think the extreme selfishness of the people who control the contracts can hardly be equaled by a few laboring men who feel they are not being paid enough." Yet Truman grumbled, "It is about time people on both sides of this controversy are giving up what they are clamoring for and think a little about the United States of America."[13]

Immediately after the coal strike settlement Truman began investigating Army camp construction. "I do think that we all have to expect a certain amount of waste because of the emphasis on speed," Truman told a CBS radio audience. "But I for one have been amazed at the extent." He explained to listeners how "you can't expect an electrician, for example, who has been drafted at $21 a month to find pleasure in watching an Army camp building being completely wired three times. And you can't blame soldiers who were professional carpenters before the Army got them, for being indignant when they see a gang of highly paid novices standing around leaning on their ladders." Truman told the Senate that generals assumed no mobilization would ever occur, that they had declined available WPA funds to finance camp planning and lost the plans that had been developed to avoid problems encountered during the war construction. Truman revealed that the Army had lied to Congress when estimating construction costs, that building plans weren't good enough for contractors to use, that Army failure to coordinate lumber supply purchases had wasted $13 million as contractors bid against one another for lumber and thereby raised the price, that the same folly had occurred with contractors bidding up the price of construction equipment rentals, and that cost-plus contracts had provided astounding windfall profits.* The Truman committee estimated a $200 million waste in camp construction by the War Department.[14]

---

*In cost-plus contracts the government agrees to pay all costs plus a profit. Thus any incentive to hold down costs disappears, and the contractor's suppliers can freely boost their prices for windfall profits, which can be shared with the contractor through kickbacks.

The committee's work started slowly, but Truman was now satisfied. "We really, I think, did a job in connection with the coal strike, and we also have shown that millions of dollars have been shoveled out by both the Army and Navy on these contracts. In other words we have justified the existence of the Committee, and I don't believe there will be any serious difficulty for us to get the necessary funds from now on to carry out our work. I had to justify the existence of the Committee in the preliminary stage, and that is the reason I stayed shy of the real controversial issues."[15]

One of Truman's next targets was "labor racketeering," his term for charging defense workers fees to join unions. On the surface Truman's concern was odd since the practice of charging money to join a union was nothing new, and assorted federal regulations made life easier for defense contractors if they hired union labor exclusively. Yet Truman ranted against the tyranny of labor "racketeers" who prevented patriotic Americans from working in defense projects without first paying to join the union. He voiced no complaints about federal regulations that encouraged hiring of union members, nor any criticism of contractors who voluntarily decided to use union labor exclusively. Instead he condemned unions that benefited from policies they didn't make.

Truman's concern about all this may have been related to problems Kansas City unions were causing in his efforts to rebuild the Pendergast organization. Despite explicit denials Truman and his Pendergast allies were rewarding loyalists with jobs at the Remington Arms Lake City defense plant near Independence. If loyalists didn't have the up-front money to join the union they didn't get the jobs. Truman didn't like this. He told Bill Kirby, Kansas City manager of the Missouri State Employment Service, "I am informed that a man cannot get a job unless he is willing to pay McElroy and Jim Mack anywhere from $50 to $120." Jim Mack was an old union antagonist of Truman's. Perrin D. McElroy was secretary and business manager of the Kansas City metro area Building & Construction Trades Council, and he would later attempt to get elected Jackson County presiding judge over a Pendergast candidate. Truman's complaint to Kirby was a matter of wheels within wheels, as Truman felt Kirby himself was thwarting his plans to reward Pendergast loyalists with jobs. Truman told Independence mayor and shaky political ally Roger Sermon, "The difficulty with the employment situation [at Remington Arms] is Mr. Kirby. . . . If he wanted to be cooperative in this matter I think we could get everyone in at the plant in whom we are interested." Truman told Vivian, "The situation at the Remington plant has been brought about by the pinheaded actions of Bill Kirby and no one else. You are perfectly right about a lot of people being put to work there who are not our friends, and I think it was done with malice and forethought." Regarding Kirby, Truman urged a friend to "make it as unpleasant for him as possible, and you have my cooperation in it." In response to Truman's complaint about Jim Mack and Perrin McElroy, Kirby assured him that nothing untoward was going on, that even the newspapers had been unable to find anything wrong. But the Pendergast organization believed Perrin McElroy was close to the *Kansas City Star*, so Truman would have little surprise about the *Star* finding nothing wrong. More wheels within wheels.

Kirby took the matter up with Mack and McElroy. Truman had phrased his accusation so as to imply the payments were going into the pockets of McElroy and Mack, which the two men easily disproved. The unions also showed that the fees were the same as had been charged for years and in many cases much less than what Truman claimed. The unions also demonstrated that the fees didn't yield a profit and that joining the union didn't guarantee a job at Remington Arms or anyplace else. Mack didn't appreciate the accusations, and reminded Truman, "Organized labor went down the line 100% in both your elections; if it had not been for organized labor's taking an active part in your last campaign, you would be just another citizen of Kansas City today instead of a member of the United States Senate." Truman didn't deny that his accusations were unfounded, and claimed amusement at Mack's reaction: "I imagine it hit him where he lives."[16]

Truman's enthusiasm for placing Pendergast loyalists in defense jobs was matched by his lagging interest in the plight of operatives from other factions. Albert Norton had been a Pendergast precinct captain for many years. Eventually he could stomach the corruption no longer, joined the United Democrats, and helped end Pendergast control of Kansas City government. He got a city job, but the reform government fired him to make way for a Republican. Now he asked Truman to help find him a war job so he could support his family, noting, "I have a hernia which I received while loading six-inch shells into an ammunition truck while under fire in the rain and while my loading detail was hiding from the shells." Truman replied: "I cannot appreciate a supposed Goat [slang for Pendergast faction] precinct captain who joined the United Democrats. It looks to me as if you really got what they usually give people who go in and help them. No one could approve of some of the things that were done by people in control of the city government in Kansas City, and no one can condone crookedness and stealing, but the Democratic Party is still the Democratic Party, and the time is coming when we are going to need all the loyal Democrats to rally around and save it. I hope we will find you in that category when the real time comes." Though Truman talked glowingly, almost lyrically, of Andrew Jackson's loyalty to veterans regardless of their political affiliations, Truman's heart was cold to this veteran's plea. In his reply he admitted that the Pendergast machine was a criminal organization, but insisted that was no reason to oppose it. Interesting, too, was Truman's exclusion of all factions but Pendergast's from the Democratic Party.[17]

Men with more power than Albert Norton took Truman to task. Independence mayor Roger Sermon lectured: "You and I have paid our debt to the Organization, and it is now only a burden rather than a help to us. I think if the Organization boys in Jackson County had started out on a carefully planned program of mistakes they could not have been any more successful. I have worked too hard and too long to continue to associate myself with people who do not have any thought of public service, who destroy people to serve their own ends, and consider a promise or pledge something to be kept only in event that it is advantageous to them." Truman wrote back only, "If you and I could sit down for a few minutes, it wouldn't take long to straighten things out." He had no patience for anyone, great or small, who felt honesty and public service more important than aid to the Pendergast organization. In 1942 Truman told Pendergast operative Bill Kitchen (of the Kansas City Public Service streetcar company for which Truman had occasionally introduced special legislation), "You could expect the leeches to fall away rather swiftly after the defeat in the city election, but the real boys will stay with us." The fanatic, unthinking, and eternal devotion Truman demanded from anyone ever associated with the Pendergast machine has no justification in normal American political practice or in the history of Kansas City politics. Clearly he protested too much, perhaps to ease his own guilty conscience about his role as an honest front protecting the power of thieves and murderers. The ultimate explanation, however, hides in a portion of Truman's soul elusive to biographers.[18]

Truman's activity in preserving and rebuilding the Pendergast organization was remarkable for both its intensity and its duplicity. While running the Senate national defense investigation Truman was involved in every facet of Kansas City and Jackson County politics, from selecting county road overseers and garage employees to assembling slates of candidates. He did whatever he felt expedient to promote the Pendergast organization. As noted, he worked against Bill Kirby while using Kirby to work against Perrin McElroy and Jim Mack with unfounded allegations that they were embezzling union funds. While keeping in close touch with Pendergast operatives Shannon Douglass and Russell Gabriel, Truman told Pendergast man Bill Kitchen, "I have not heard from anyone with regard to the political situation in Jackson County but you, and I have made no effort to get in touch with anyone because I have been too busy." Regarding a political agreement that had become inopportune, Truman devised a way out of it—"Don't quote me," he advised Russell Gabriel, "I don't want to be in the position of double-crossing."[19]

Truman was probably glad to consider complaints about hiring practices at Kansas City, Kansas's North American Aviation plant, since he'd heard that the rival Shannon faction was rewarding its followers with jobs there. The controversy was about racial rather than political discrimination, however. Just before the bond election to build a bomber test field for North American Aviation, the mayor promised black taxpayers that North American's top man J. H. "Dutch" Kindleberger had pledged to hire blacks in the plant. When hiring day arrived Kindleberger would accept blacks all right, but only for janitorial positions. Truman agreed to hear complaints, but seemed to brush them off. "I have absolutely no control over the North American Airplane Corporation, and I don't think there is any chance of doing anything about it." He had "absolutely no control" over any of the corporations his committee investigated, but he seemed to get results at those companies when he cared to. Truman admitted that he was well aware of discrimination against blacks in defense jobs, but was disinclined to hold hearings even when Senate colleagues asked about the national situation. He called critics of his position "half-cocked," and said they didn't consider that if he had allowed a hearing it would have been a fair one. On October 14, 1941 Independence mayor Roger Sermon wrote to Truman, apparently about the Remington Arms plant, "I had a letter from [Truman's secretary] Harry Vaughan about Mrs. Odell Berry. She is a negro, and I think it very unlikely that she could get a job." Truman replied, "I don't suppose Harry Vaughan knew that he was recommending a Negro." On October 23 *St. Louis Call* editor Chester Stovall accused the Truman committee of whitewashing the situation of blacks in national defense jobs. On October 31 Harry Vaughan huffed, "Mr. Stovall is one of the particular class of humans to which I am allergic—an Ethiopian graduate of Harvard. We have had a score of claims that negroes were being discriminated against, and in every case that we have investigated, we have found the facts fail to justify or substantiate the claims." (But how many cases, and which ones, were investigated?) When persons informed Truman that Jews were being refused jobs at North American and Remington he replied, "I have never heard of any race prejudice existing either at Lake City or the bomber plant."[20]

Truman's attitude toward organized labor was becoming less friendly. Brown Harris, who had chauffeured the reinforcements that prevented theft of the ballot box that elected Truman eastern judge in 1922, complained that North American and Remington were hiring nonunion men from rural localities hundreds of miles away rather than taking skilled union workers from local Ford and Chevrolet operations that had closed. Ford complicated the situation by refusing to process paperwork that laid-off workers needed to get new jobs. Harris complained that these unemployed union men were losing their homes, and that J. C. Nichols was apparently making money by reselling them. Truman replied, "These labor people will drive you to drink permanently. Two-thirds of them are interested only in skinning their fellow workers, and the rest of them have not much interest in the country's welfare. I have always been friendly to them because it has been the policy of the smart people on top to mistreat them and browbeat them, and I say very frankly to you when they get in control they are just as bad as the big boys you and I have been fighting." On another occasion Truman told an old friend, "There isn't any difference in the manner in which John L. Lewis is trying to overturn the Government and the manner in which the New York bankers tried to do it in the 1920's. We got the banking situation cleaned up, and now we have a worse one on our hands. The only language Mr. Lewis can understand is a pick-handle, and that is what ought to be used on him." He continued, "Our administration—and I say 'our' advisedly—has built a Frankenstein at the other end of the economic scale, just as bad as the one that Harding and Mellon built up at the top of the scale. It is going to take 10 or 15 years to get a readjustment on a right basis."[21]

Truman's new attitude toward unions could be seen in his committee's work. Sidney Hillman had done important work for Franklin Roosevelt and for organized labor. In 1941 Hillman was codirector of Office of Production Management, the federal agency supposedly coordinating defense production. He was a man of talent, respected by unions and despised by Republican congressmen. Labor strife was no stranger to Detroit, and Hillman saw an opportunity to keep the peace by spending an extra $216,000 to have three hundred Detroit houses constructed by AFL workers. Genial John L. Lewis, innocent as a sleeping volcano, said CIO men could have done the job at the lower price. Truman then put Hillman on the griddle for squandering defense money. Hillman explained that the AFL and CIO were unfriendly, and that Detroit was a town filled with uninhibited union men who would violently disrupt a housing project using CIO labor. Therefore, in the interests of getting the job done, avoiding bloodshed, and saving the expense of putting down a riot and replacing destroyed property, Hillman decided to spend an extra $216,000 for AFL labor on the contract. Truman thundered on the Senate floor, "The United States does not fear trouble from any source," and proclaimed that if Hillman "cannot or will not protect the interests of the United States, I am in favor of replacing him with someone who can and will." Since Truman felt the interests of the United States required the Michigan National Guard to knock some AFL heads, Senator Robert Taft rose to ask Truman if the Michigan National Guard or any other state agency was in fact available for such a purpose. Truman admitted that he didn't know, and thereby admitted that Hillman's approach may have been entirely proper. Truman had been tearing into Hillman and organized labor without knowing the facts. Even after holding a hearing he didn't have the facts.[22]

Truman's attitude toward strikes also took a dramatic shift. He said that labor threatened strikes and demanded higher wages because the defense contractors in question were making exorbitant profits. Nonetheless, he felt that wage increase requests were unjustified because privates drafted into the Army made far less. Truman never insisted on reducing his Senate pay to buck private level, yet workers were unpatriotic for wanting a share of the windfall profits that their sweat and, yes, blood produced. Soon after Pearl Harbor Truman delivered a savage comment about "selfish" defense workers: "Twelve or fifteen hundred laborers were sent to Guam to build the defenses on Guam. They were paid $15 a day and transportation, and time and a half for overtime. They used to brag to the soldiers over there that they got in one day what the soldiers got in a month. Guam now has changed hands. Those men still are going to work, and will have to be happy and satisfied to get a little rice to eat." Be content with what you've got, he told defense workers, even if the plant owner brags about making as much in one hour as a laborer makes in one month. Indeed, Truman heard testimony from a Navy admiral advocating legislation to freeze labor relationships for the war's duration. The admiral said if workers realized their conditions would never change "you can improve the morale . . . and the productivity will be materially increased." What hurts production, he said, is workers' belief that they can change their lot.[23]

Months before Pearl Harbor Truman warned, "Drastic action must be taken if the mediation method doesn't become more effective in settling labor disputes." On December 9, 1941 he announced, "Strikes and any stoppage of the national defense program cannot be tolerated now that the country is at war." At the same time mail like this was arriving at Truman's office: "Eliminate the fetters of the wage and hour bill so that industry can operate at maximum capacity" (from the president of American Box Corp., San Francisco). "If we need a seven day week, let's have it, but why pay labor overtime for doing their part. . . . Now is the definite time to stop these labor union demands" (from the executive vice-president of Missouri Insurance Co.). Truman indeed questioned whether defense workers should be paid overtime, and declared, "Labor will have to work longer and harder hours. There must be no strikes." General George Marshall called a railroad strike and a steel strike together "the damndest crime ever committed against America," saying these two strikes may have added half a year to the war. The

War Department shouted that soldiers were dying for lack of ammunition, and the Truman committee castigated labor unions for costing twenty-six million man-days in strikes. Rumblings grew that people would have to be drafted into defense jobs if the civilian population didn't begin to act like there was a war on.[24]

All this was a bum rap. All of it. The civilian population didn't care that there was a war on? Didn't notice those fellows missing from the neighborhood, or see those gold stars in the windows? The men on strike didn't care about their sons? The women (who, Truman warned, might seek to retain their jobs in peacetime) didn't care about their brothers and husbands? Secret testimony before the Truman committee in early 1942 showed that a forty-hour week didn't hurt war efforts because whenever a forty-eight-hour week was needed it could be gotten at no expense to employers—either covered by cost-plus provisions or contract renegotiations. (Although the Navy complained about "excessive" shipyard worker wages, the cost-plus contracts allowed companies to make a fortune from labor "costs." One executive even admitted, "If it hadn't been for taxes we couldn't have handled our profits with a steam shovel.") And so what if a defense employer had to absorb overtime—weren't workers told to take the same loss to prove their patriotism? The railroad strike General Marshall condemned had no effect on transportation—the trains ran normally—and was caused by Roosevelt administration interference with the National Mediation Board. The steel strike that gave Marshall such a spasm lasted four days and was due in part to shutdowns caused by declining War Department orders. The lack of ammo at the front was caused by the Army's inability, to transport it in field conditions, not by a lack of manufacturing. The Truman committee's figure of twenty-six million man-days lost through strikes was for the *entire economy;* the Office of Production Management's figures showed the time lost to *defense work* as less than one-tenth the amount Truman implied. The talk of having to draft people into defense work grew as canceled contracts left unemployed war workers seeking defense jobs (and, indeed, although Truman once toyed with such conscription he now argued against it since no need could be shown).[25]

Obviously something was up. Bruce Catton tells the ugly story in his beautiful book *The War Lords of Washington,* so only highlights need be mentioned here. Corporations great and small were using the cry "war emergency" as a smokescreen to permit business as usual in labor relations. In real life a strike is usually such an ordeal for workers that the tactic is used only as a last resort. How much more so when the workers believe their labor vital to the safety of their sons and brothers and husbands. Thus conditions had to be intolerable indeed to cause a strike, yet the *workers* were portrayed as selfish villains. Interestingly, strikes had no appreciable effect on war production. Any deficiencies were from lack of manufacturing capacity, not lack of labor. Yet the people of America were continually browbeaten by the government as slothful ingrates who cared nothing about their fellow citizens in the armed forces.

This propaganda, in which Truman played an unthinking part, grew from two fundamental decisions by the federal government. First, the government decided citizens were neither brave nor intelligent enough to face the truth about the war, yet were also (as reaction to the Truman committee would demonstrate) ready to hold corporations and government agencies accountable for their actions. Thus Roosevelt administration spokesmen began to lie about why various actions were taken. When those lies were shaken, further lies had to be constructed. Etc. Since the rationale behind the deceit was that citizens were too selfish and stupid to accept and deal with the truth, they had to be made to believe this themselves. A great propaganda campaign pummeled and scolded the American people, and lies about defense workers were part of the campaign. The second fundamental decision behind this propaganda was the giving of de facto authority to the military to halt civilian production interfering with military needs. The military felt that *any* civilian production interfered. Thus, as the war situation became brighter and defense contracts were canceled, the military kept the factories and workers idle even though the raw materials and labor weren't needed for battlefield supplies. Since the government mistakenly feared that the remaining defense workers would slack off because the war was going well, a phony labor shortage had to be invented. For this strictly political reason Selective Service chief General Hershey announced huge new draft quotas. These quotas would cause a labor shortage, which would then create the necessary atmosphere for civilians to accept conscription into defense jobs. People like Truman prevented that scenario from playing out, but the military retained control over the U.S. economy. As we shall see, this meshed with the plans of great corporations when conversion from war goods to civilian goods became appropriate.

Truman's acceptance of the propaganda against workers had much to do with his enthusiasm for Moral Re-Armament. This organization evolved from Frank N. D. Buchman's soul saving at Cambridge, England, where students ridiculed him as "Old Moral Uplift" and jokingly confessed outrageous sins to him. In time he developed a packaged formula for creating pseudomystical experiences among confused university students, foreshadowing the techniques used so successfully by American religious cults in the 1970s. Buchman moved beyond the collegiate crowd, and in the late 1930s was accumulating endorsements for a program he called Moral Re-Armament.[26]

Moral Re-Armament resonated with some of Truman's most cherished beliefs, claiming that everyone shared the same basic interests, and that strife could be reduced or even eliminated if these interests were uncovered. This fit in with sentiments he had been expressing in speeches, with his Masonic knowledge, with the remarks of Theodore Roosevelt that Truman had heard and admired long ago in Kansas City, with the unsigned editorial in his high-school yearbook. Moral Re-Armament was also permeated with nonsectarian religiosity that Truman found appealing. The very name grabbed Truman's interest, as he felt a sick world would soon be cleansed by fire unless people awakened to their moral responsibilities.[27]

Truman played a featured role in the June 1939 meeting at Constitution Hall in Washington, which started Moral Re-Armament in the United States. Truman read President Roosevelt's greeting to the throng: "The underlying strength of the world must consist in the moral fiber of her citizens. A program of moral rearmament for the world cannot fail, therefore, to lessen the danger of armed conflict. Such moral rearmament, to be most highly effective, must receive support on a worldwide basis." A few days later Truman told the Senate about this meeting. "It is rare in these days, Mr. President, to find something which will unite men and nations on a plane above conflict of party, class, or political philosophy. I am sure that I voice the sentiment of all of us here today in expressing gratification at a response so remarkable to a need so urgent, and confidence that America will play her full part in this cause on whose fortunes the future of civilization must largely depend."[28]

Truman was a busy man and no philosopher, and Moral Re-Armament was endorsed by respected government and civic leaders. Buchman's words, however, should have disquieted anyone who cherished freedom. Inner liberty is true democracy? This is what the chaps in Berlin were saying, suppressing lust for material well-being, freeing Aryan souls to soar unfettered by concern over personal self-interest. Submit, submit, submit, Buchman cried. Don't grasp after the illusion of individual happiness; trade it for the reality of your group's welfare. The individual must sacrifice to help his group, and the group must never be asked to sacrifice for a meaningless individual.

On October 29, 1939 a prerecorded speech by Truman was included in a worldwide broadcast promoting Moral Re-Armament. "I speak from the nation's capital at Washington, where four months ago I first met Dr. Buchman at the great national meeting for Moral Re-Armament at Constitution Hall." He continued, "The World Assembly for moral rearmament, which took place on the West Coast, began with the gathering of some 25,000 people in the Hollywood Bowl at Los Angeles in July. It brought leading representatives from over 20 nations to its deliberations and closed with the day for moral rearmament at the Golden Gate International Exposition in San Francisco. That assembly marked a great contribution to the life of America and all the world." He concluded, "I believe that the future of civilization must largely depend upon the success of moral rearmament." Frank Buchman responded, "I am grateful for the statesmanlike words in which Senator Truman has referred to the widespread work and influence of moral rearmament in this and other countries. He has struck a brave blow for that realistic reordering of world affairs of which he spoke." Buchman proclaimed, "The morally rearmed have learned to live under a crisis-proof, fear-free discipline. They are a panic-proof, single-minded, and intelligent trained force at the disposal of all who put their country before selfish interest." A more explicit declaration of Moral Re-Armament's purpose could hardly be desired. The goal was to produce a population whose members had given up independent thinking, who were unaware of personal harm, who could be manipulated to do any ruler's bidding. Yet Truman remained unalarmed. He wrote excitedly about the important people around the world who listened to his October 29 speech, and worked to have three million copies of his broadcast distributed via *Congressional Record* reprints.[29]

Truman felt his Moral Re-Armament work promoted world peace, and in early November 1939 asked Roosevelt to participate in a world broadcast scheduled for the first three days of December. Truman told Bess, "I'm trying to get the President to join with the Queen of Holland, the King of Belgium, and the three Scandinavian kings." FDR's refusal surprised Truman. The president said, "Timing is of the very essence of any action I should take in behalf of world peace," and he felt this was an inopportune time. Truman had also asked Roosevelt to meet with Frank Buchman, but the president didn't consent to this either.[30]

In 1940 Moral Re-Armament distributed a booklet called "You Can Defend America!" The booklet was slick, very slick. It claimed that enemies merely bribed gatekeepers to get through the Great Wall of China, and that the Maginot Line did France no good because "Employers refused to sacrifice. Men refused to work." The booklet stated, "Today America builds her wall. A ring of steel. Ships and planes and guns. But is this enough? Does America have what China lacked? What France lacked?"[31]

Professional public relations talent was at work promoting Moral Re-Armament, skillfully perverting elements from the American dream to hide a most undemocratic philosophy. "Fathers who know how to unite their families will take that spirit into their jobs. If they can settle private strikes and lockouts at home, they know the way to industrial cooperation." Father is the boss at home. His happy family obeys the boss. Father should obey the boss at work. The boss cares about him as father cares about his own family. Boss and father share the same interests, the same goals. This paternalistic dogma about industrial relations had no basis in real-world experiences. "Every man works not just for himself, but for his country, whatever his job." This was news to a lot of folks who thought they worked for their employers. Thus, to go on strike against a vicious boss was to be disloyal to one's country, whatever one's job. Patriots did whatever the boss wanted. "America does not need to be divided and quarreling at home, just to prove she is a democracy." The Pendergasts could have gotten along with Stark if only they had tried. The black fellow in Maryville could have been friends with the lynch mob. Only vanity prevented the New Dealers from accepting Liberty League principles. If only people would do what they were told to do they could enjoy inner liberty. "Either we sacrifice our personal selfishness for our nation, or we sacrifice the nation for our personal selfishness." Everyone's interests are the same, and everyone's interests conflict with America's.[32]

The goal of Moral Re-Armament doubletalk had less to do with morality than with increasing industrial output while pacifying labor. Truman thought this was Moral Re-Armament's most important work: "They have rendered great assistance to the all-out war program by creating the spirit of cooperation between management and labor, reducing absenteeism, heightening all-around efficiency and increasing production. There is not a single industrial bottleneck I can think of which could not be broken in a matter of weeks if this crowd were given the green light to go full steam ahead." Said Truman, "Moral Re-Armament on the West Coast, and also in Detroit and Philadelphia, did some excellent work in creating a friendly feeling between employers and employees. In fact I think a general strike was avoided in Detroit and in an airplane factory on the West Coast." He praised Moral Re-Armament for "yeoman service in keeping good understanding between labor and management since this war started, and I am willing to see any procedure followed that will accomplish that purpose."[33]

Truman's involvement in Moral Re-Armament was intense. He did favors for this group that he attempted for no one else. He made speeches even when physically worn down. He tried to arrange a meeting between FDR and Buchman. He sent out press releases. He interceded with the British government to lengthen a British Moral Re-Armament staffer's permission to remain in the United States. He sought draft exemptions for Moral Re-Armament staff members—an unheard of favor from Truman—and asked the Army to assign men specified by Moral Re-Armament to the traveling patriotic revue "You Can Defend America," taking up these matters with General George Marshall, Assistant War Secretary Patterson, and FDR himself. His files show warm friendship with Moral Re-Armament leaders. "I wish I were 30 years younger to see this thing work out. I know it is going to," Truman said. "It would make the world a very different place."[34]

By the time Truman was the Democrat vice-presidential nominee in 1944 Moral Re-Armament had received some close scrutiny. George Seldes, one of Truman's leftist political supporters, warned him that Moral Re-Armament had notorious fascist and anti-Semitic involvements. Seldes was knowledgeable about such topics. Truman now apparently ordered his staff to investigate Moral Re-Armament, and the report raised serious questions about the politics and (ironically) the morality of Moral Re-Armament. To questioners Truman explained, "I know nothing about the past attitudes or connections of the MRA group." He waffled, "I do not happen to be a member of that organization." Moral Re-Armament, however, had no formal membership, so the denial meant nothing. Truman explicitly lied, "I am not personally acquainted with Dr. Buchman, and I don't think I ever saw him in my life." Yet even if that statement had been true, it wouldn't have explained away Truman's former fervent support of Moral Re-Armament. There were far bigger questions in the campaign, and if Truman had been duped so had many other civic and governmental leaders. So he was never called to an accounting. His 1944 statements, however, are interesting to compare with his insistence on loyalty to political friends. He accepted no explanation for anyone parting from the Pendergast organization, but he himself had no scruples about dumping Moral Re-Armament and its leaders when they became political liabilities. The campaign of 1944, however, comes later in our story.[35]

Chapter 15

THE BUSINESS
OF WAR

Before Pearl Harbor, when Truman's committee was just starting its criticisms of organized labor, the committee also began investigating the defense contract award process. As noted, this was ostensibly why the Senate approved Truman's defense industry inquiry. The probe started modestly enough, but as often happens when great abuses are discovered, the inquiry gained an importance no one had foreseen. What started as routine questions about contract award favoritism evolved into debate about the meaning of democracy.

The favoritism was easy enough to document. Corporate executives became government contract award officials. They typically served without compensation or for a dollar a year. Truman had no objection to dollar-a-year men per se: "I served once in that capacity, and never did get my dollar. It has been owing to me since 1933." Truman recognized that an economy mobilized for military requirements needed industrialists to do the mobilizing—airhead bureaucrats would accomplish nothing. Truman's objection was dollar-a-year men with authority to award contracts to their old corporations or industry, who often continued to receive their huge executive salaries from the companies while ostensibly working for the government. The latter instances were blatant evidence of favoritism, since rather few corporations pay someone $100,000 a year without getting something in return. The executives thought it okay for hillbillies to get themselves shot for $21.00 a month, but they simply couldn't afford the financial sacrifice of $10,000 federal salaries. These were the same fellows who called on defense workers to be patriotic and accept whatever wages were offered. The industrialist demand was simple, "Meet our terms, or lose the war." Truman didn't like this attitude, and declared, "The committee does not like to have procurement matters entrusted to men who have given such hostages to fortune. Those who cannot forego large incomes temporarily cannot reasonably be expected to take a chance of foregoing them permanently by taking positions on behalf of the government with which the controlling officials of their corporations are not in sympathy." Truman's fussing and fuming had no effect.[1]

Truman also lost the battle over giving these executives Army commissions. Contract award agencies became infested with colonels whose military experience was limited to watching parades. This irked Truman who had worked hard for his colonelcy. The regular Army was friendlier toward corporation executives than toward National Guard officers. Truman saw dark motives at play. If the ordnance department colonel in charge of munitions contract awards received word from an ordnance department general that more shells were needed from XYZ corporation, could the colonel instead award the contract to ABC corporation? Of course not. Through these officer commissions the military was gaining the power to decide which corporations lived or died. Few people admired the military more than Truman did, but he felt the military had no right to control a democracy's economy—indeed, such control meant abandonment of democracy. Such control also imperiled the defense effort. Perhaps XYZ corporation was at maximum production. To deliver more shells, XYZ's factories would have to be expanded, taking time and labor and materials from other defense needs, while ABC corporation could deliver immediately.

Efficiency was the point in Truman's demands that small business participate fully in the war effort. Were small businesses merely ornaments to whom Rotary Club speakers pointed with pride? An ornament that couldn't be afforded when the economy had to produce the material needed to defeat and destroy Hitler and Hirohito? Or were small businesses a national resource, the very foundation of democracy rather than a decoration? If their role was crucial to our society, then they should have the capability to produce needed material faster and cheaper than the great corporations could; maybe not assemble one hundred thousand airplanes in a year, but provide the spark plugs and cockpit instrument gauges. Truman proved that small business had this capability, that it could be coordinated to rise in democracy's finest hour, leading America to military and spiritual victory over the fascist governments who argued that monopolies and cartels would rule the world.[2]

Instead, the dollar-a-year men, civilians and colonels, put down democracy at home while they sent hillbillies to fight foreign armies. Oh, the Roosevelt administration paid lip service to Truman's argument, even putting a man in charge of implementing the program Truman advocated. One man in a city of ten thousand colonels. He described his experience:

"You know what they're doing to me, don't you?" he rasped. "They started on the roof, and they took rubber hoses and beat me, on top of the roof, and then they threw me down that chute— you know—and then they threw me down the steps to the third floor, and then they kicked me, on that escalator, and I got a leg cut off and both of my ears. Then they laid me down on the floor, and if it hadn't been for sulfa drugs and penicillin and injections of blood transfusion I'd have expired. Of course, they gave me sulfa drugs and penicillin, and I got in the center of the Cross and said twelve Hail Mary's, and God preserved my life. But that's all. I just came out with my life."

Truman watched dumbfounded as FDR allowed the dollar-a-year crowd to strengthen their corporations and crush their competitors through defense contract awards, which involved not only money but allocations of raw materials. Eventually the Roosevelt administration even made a colonel director of Truman's small business program. Truman wrote in anguish to an old New Dealer friend, "I fear very much that the economic situation has gone right back to 1920. Everything that you and I have fought for for the last 10 years has been knocked into a cocked hat." He sorrowfully admitted, "Little business is simply being slaughtered, and we seem practically helpless to prevent it."[3]

Even if he couldn't stop the slaughter, Truman would make sure all the free world knew what was happening. There were those who tried to stop him. After Pearl Harbor the unfriendly Assistant War Secretary Robert Patterson told FDR that the Truman committee had to disband, that the Civil War's Committee on the Conduct of the War had been a devastating handicap to Lincoln's generals. But Truman couldn't be stopped. He reminded the president that the committee always had and always would avoid any inquiry into military tactics, unlike the Civil War committee. Truman did not remind the president, because he did not have to, that the committee was getting very good reviews from the public, the press, and the Congress. As had been foretold when the committee was established, once started its work couldn't be halted.[4]

Now Truman investigated the great defense industries, one after another, demonstrating that major corporations were using the war to make fortunes from taxpayers and defense bond purchasers, were using the war to destroy smaller competitors, and, moreover, were literally unable to produce the goods.

"It is just a bit easier to walk off with one of the statues out of the Capitol than to get an allotment of aluminum at this time," said Truman's secretary Harry Vaughan. Aluminum Company of America (Alcoa) was the nation's source of aluminum. This corporation was built by Andrew Mellon, the Republican treasury secretary whom Truman blamed for the failure of his haberdashery. Alcoa gained a monopoly in its product and worked hard to retain this status. The company all too easily assured the federal dollar-a-year men that no expansion in the nation's aluminum industry would be needed if America entered the war. "How they expected to take care of the situation when the shortage would become apparent is not clear," the Truman committee reported. Indeed, when the war came Alcoa couldn't provide enough aluminum. "Rather than surrender their monopoly rights they were perfectly willing to let the country go to pot," Truman snorted. Alcoa was none too pleased about the committee's revelations of how the company put profits ahead of national security, and Truman knew the committee was on target when Alcoa's president tried to avoid testifying by invoking the influence of a Democratic National Committee vice-chairman. (The committee hired staff members recommended by the Democratic National Committee.) The committee found that two factors prevented military disaster from Alcoa's actions. One was the Reynolds

Metal Company's belief that America would enter the war and that Alcoa would then lack sufficient capacity. On this assumption Reynolds Metal mortgaged every manufacturing plant it had to build aluminum production facilities. When the crisis came Reynolds was ready. The other factor was government electricity. Private utilities could provide less than one-third of the power needed to manufacture aluminum. The New Deal's electricity projects proved crucial to national defense. Even after such revelations Truman found Alcoa and the dollar-a-year men still thwarting aluminum industry expansion despite Army and Navy pleas for more metal.[5]

The committee noted that the automobile industry said it couldn't convert its factories to make anything but cars. So the industry used huge defense contracts to construct new manufacturing plants to compete with small factories that could make the same goods. This construction not only delayed production, it used up vital raw materials and labor. Then when civilian auto manufacture had to stop due to military needs for the raw materials, the auto industry smoothly converted its car assembly facilities into weapons assembly. This conversion delay hurt defense but ensured that no smaller companies captured any of the civilian car market. These competitors were put down even during the war. For instance, American Bantam Car Company devised a vehicle called the jeep. The prototypes passed Army tests, but American Bantam was cut out of the ensuing massive contracts. The company president said that Maj. Gen. R. C. Moore decided American Bantam shouldn't get so much business. Orders shifted to Ford, which delayed production since it had to go to the American Bantam plant and copy the jeep design (according to American Bantam's president). Willys-Overland then got subsequent huge orders.[6]

"Ford's vaunted production ability didn't show up in his construction of Army bombers," Truman complained. "He was supposed to turn out one plane an hour from September First, and he hasn't turned out over 30 all together." Fred Canfil found that the North American Aviation "bomber assembly plant we have in Kansas City is not doing much; to date they have assembled one plane, and it has been turned down three times by the Army." Truman later received accusations that North American foremen were telling workers to loaf if they wanted to keep their jobs—the cost-plus contract paid for featherbedding. A similar situation developed in

North American's Dallas operation. Curtiss-Wright supplied engine parts that failed to meet the company's own specifications. Newly manufactured planes sat idle because Bendix couldn't manufacture enough radios and wouldn't let small companies supply them. The armed forces "have merely purchased what the manufacturers had to offer," Truman thundered, "instead of planning to use available facilities to produce what they needed at maximum capacity. There is no planned and coordinated program for the production of aircraft."[7]

"The steel situation," Truman wrote, "is much worse than the aluminum or copper or lead. We have been sending tremendous quantities, of course, to Russia for their plane program, and we have had immense amounts of that cargo steel buried at the bottom of the Atlantic. That actually is the main reason for our domestic shortage right at this time. The fundamental reason is, however, that the steel people used the same tactics to maintain control as the aluminum and copper people did. United States Steel and Bethlehem and the group known as Little Steel were very reluctant to do any expanding, and they are extremely anxious not to open any new ore beds for the reason that they fear competition when the war is over. The aluminum people were very frank on that score, as were the big three who control copper. We must take some action on this situation, but you can see that from the standpoint of unity and whole-hearted support of the Commander-in-Chief, a blow-up in steel at this time might be extremely bad for the war effort. Yet I can't sit idly by and let the country lose the war because of a lack of facilities for making steel when we have all the necessary raw materials with which to produce it."[8]

Truman showed no such hesitations in public. He demonstrated that "certain interests undoubtedly are much more interested in what their position is going to be after the war than they are right now in furnishing the materials with which to win the war." And he found that the steel industry had difficulty even furnishing the needed materials. United States Steel subsidiary Carnegie-Illinois Steel Corporation faked steel plate tests in order to sell substandard plate to the U.S. military. (Congress found the company had done the same thing with steel sold to the Navy in 1894.) *Time* magazine assured readers that no one was upset about this. In resulting criminal prosecution the judge found that U.S. Steel records had been destroyed;

Truman committee witnesses took the Fifth Amendment in court; the Navy and the Maritime Commission were uncooperative with the Justice Department; yet the corporation admitted faking the tests and supplying substandard steel. With much vital evidence and testimony missing, however, the corporation won acquittal, claiming this was an exoneration from "unfair and unsubstantiated accusations made by the Truman Committee." Six months later FDR made U.S. Steel chairman Edward Stettinius, Jr., secretary of state. President Truman fired him as soon as feasible.[9]

Gasoline rationing raised a fateful question. The U.S. had plenty of oil and gasoline. Spot shortages occurred here and there because the normal distribution system was disrupted—Nazi U-boats ate East Coast tankers for breakfast. Nonetheless, gasoline supplies were ample. The problem was rubber. The national transportation system was designed to collapse if private automobiles were unavailable. Such a collapse would do war production no good. Because the dollar-a-year men had seen no need to stockpile natural rubber before the war, tires were now in short supply. So short that no civilian tires would be available again until after the war. To keep autos and the transportation system running tires had to be conserved. Thus nonessential driving had to end, and the easiest way to do this was to ration gas. People groused, but as Truman said, "It is a part of the war, and we have just got to take it and like it."[10]

The question was: Why couldn't the United States produce all the synthetic rubber it needed from oil, just as Nazi Germany could? The question was put to some top rubber corporation executives at a closed hearing of a Truman committee subcommittee.

SENATOR TRUMAN: Did you have negotiations with Standard as to the use of their patents?

JOHN COLLYER (president B. F. Goodrich Rubber): Yes, going back first I think with the I. G. [Farben] Company in Germany as far back as 1932.

SENATOR BREWSTER: What was the fruit of those discussions?

COLLYER: I think that Mr. Litchfield summed that up very well. I have nothing to add to what he said.

BREWSTER: He didn't speak of I. G. Farben. He only spoke of Standard.

The rubber executive was unable to distinguish the Standard Oil Company of New Jersey from the I. G. Farben chemicals company of Germany. The Justice Department and the Truman committee had already discovered a sinister reason for this.[11]

U.S. defense efforts were hamstrung by a collaboration between Standard Oil of New Jersey (later renamed Exxon) and I. G. Farben. Standard NJ's work for the Nazis left the United States hanging for rubber supplies when war broke out with Japan, cutting off natural rubber. This work for Hitler was illegal, and after the war Standard NJ was fined for it.

Truman also found that I. G. Farben and Alcoa set up Magnesium Development Co. in 1931 to hold magnesium patents. As part of the agreement I.G. got authority to limit Alcoa's magnesium production. I.G. wanted to bring Dow into this (Dow was America's other chief magnesium producer). Alcoa had other agreements with Dow, and now put the screws to Dow to force compliance with I.G.'s wishes. Dow complied in 1933.

Truman wondered if Dow had supplied magnesium to the Nazis in 1939 via Dutch and Polish brokers, but Dow had destroyed any records of those sales. Truman did confirm that Dow had sold magnesium to Japan in 1938 at a price cheaper than England had to pay. Dow destroyed key records of these transactions after Pearl Harbor, but Truman assumed that Japan used most of the magnesium for aircraft and incendiary bombs.[12]

Reluctant to publicize information that might hurt American morale, Truman was discreet about his knowledge that these and other U.S. firms had been collaborating with Hitler and Hirohito. Although his committee did reveal some specifics of the Nazi connections of U.S. business, Truman's private correspondence had only cautious comments that omitted company names. His public statements sometimes were so careful as to be nearly meaningless to anyone unaware of the story; for example, that investigation of patent agreements revealed "many interesting facts" about a situation, which "gives cause for reflection." Nonetheless, he realized what was going on, and America's corporations knew that he did. Since a few words from him might have destroyed the sales of these companies in postwar America, President Truman may have had a secret leverage over some of the nation's most powerful businessmen.[13]

For the most part, cartel agreements among U.S. and Nazi corporations remained in force during World War II. The corporations planned to resume business as usual after the war, whoever won. These cartel agreements had much to do with American and British unpreparedness for the war. Many of the agreements were illegal. Lax enforcement of U.S. antitrust laws permitted the Nazis to gain strategic advantages. This was an important but little recognized lesson of World War II: Vigorous enforcement of antitrust laws can be vital to U.S. military security.[14]

The larger lesson in all this, however, was that the leading American businessmen cared more about profits than democracy. Indeed, Hitler counted on this, providing U.S. corporations with arrangements so lucrative that it was in their interests to support his conquest of Europe. He believed America would stay out of the war not because of fear, but because of friendship. In later years U.S. support of dictatorships around the world proved Hitler's thinking not far from wrong.[15]

In 1942 Truman commended to the American people a book written by Guenter Reimann, one of the foremost experts on Nazi ties with American business. Reimann warned that if U.S. corporation policies failed to change, then the postwar world "would require permanent occupation by [U.S. or allied] military forces of all key positions in the world and the support of foreign dictatorships." Reimann foresaw that a "return to the status quo for industry would not mean return to an era of peace. On the contrary, huge armies and military expenditure on an unprecedented scale would become permanent peacetime affairs." Regarding the "so-called backward nations" Reimann declared that "not all the force in the world will hold back their will to live," and predicted a postwar "vacuum into which the forces of the future or of the past must rush."[16]

Significantly, one of the nation's foremost experts on the fate of small business in World War II reached the same conclusions independently, studying the dollar-a-year men without any reference to ties between U.S. corporations and the Nazis. Bruce Catton glumly concluded:

Because we retreated during the war—because we did not, in the very process of winning the war, take the opportunity to give modern democracy a new meaning, a new vigor, a triumphant and eternally hopeful awareness of its own everlasting vitality—

we are today in the exceedingly curious position of being at once the strongest and the most nervous nation on earth. We won an overwhelming victory and we have not the least notion what to do with it. And so, in a world where more profound, far-reaching, and lasting changes are taking place than at any time since the breakup of the Roman empire, we can think of nothing better to do than to strike hands with those men, in whatever quarter of the earth, who are struggling for a season against all change. We are afraid of communism, and with right good reason, but we are also afraid to use the irresistible weapon of democracy which lies ready to our hands. Instead we are relying on words, dollars, and guns, and none of them will turn the trick for us.[17]

These words were said in 1948. But in 1944 the battle for democracy had yet to be lost, and Senator Truman would carry the colors to defeat, fighting to restore America to her own people.

The final struggle was over converting the economy from war to civilian production. In 1942 Truman warned that a "ghost . . . haunts every businessman, every employee, every farmer, every American citizen. What will happen to our jobs, to our businesses, to our farmers, after the war? . . . Tremendous damage . . . is being done to our nation when men say to themselves,—I can't do this, or I don't want to do that, because it will leave me in the ditch after the war is over. If we run our war in that spirit, we have two strikes against us at the outset." Go full out, Truman told workers and employers, and have faith that the federal government will protect your job and your business after the war.[18]

"What is to be done with the great bulk of our war plants?" Truman asked, only four days before the Normandy landings in 1944. "The great bulk of the plants, tools, and facilities can be converted to the production of civilian goods." Truman noted, "The population of the United States has been reshuffled from one end of the country to the other. New communities have sprung up around war plants. . . . It is no answer to say that war workers will return to their former peacetime jobs." He added, "Our returning fighting men and our vast numbers of war workers are entitled to earn a good living at the jobs they have been trained for." Truman declared that government must decide how to terminate war contracts, how much notice of this can be given, how to clear government property out of plants so plants can reconvert, what loans government may provide to business, and how government will lease or sell war plants it built. The government, he believed, must coordinate war contract cancellations with increase of civilian production to prevent unemployment. The government must reduce inventories to provide these materials to the civilian economy without disruptions by heedless dumping of inventories. The government needed to supplement private banking resources for business loans. If necessary, contracts given to corporations early in the war for postwar lease or sale of government-built facilities must be renegotiated in light of current conditions. Truman called for state and local government to plan public works projects to take up civilian economy slack as veterans returned. He said that labor must accept fair wage cuts reflecting peacetime economic realities—this should be compensated by lower prices for food and clothing and other goods now that the war demand was ending. Truman foresaw programs to rebuild war-torn countries, and urged "every precaution that unemployment and business depression do not gain headway before the major task of readjustment has even begun."[19]

Truman's plan for orderly transition from a wartime to a peacetime economy made sense. Too damn much sense. Corporations discovered that their dominance of war contracts left them vulnerable to the remaining small competitors as war contracts declined. Say the War Department reduced orders for airplanes by 25 percent. The huge factories had to reduce output by that amount, and still had to remain tooled to produce airplanes. The small radio manufacturer, however, might find his contract canceled completely if he was supplementing the great factory's output of airplane radios. This left him free to make home radios and establish himself in the civilian market while the big factory was trapped with War Department manufacturing. The kind of economic reconversion that Truman and others were promoting would coordinate that very thing, putting small businessmen in the forefront of a soon-to-boom civilian market. The dollar-a-year men and the military joined to stop this. The method was simple. There was a war on, and the military established priorities in allocations of raw materials and component parts. The small manufacturer was unable to get tubes for making home radios because the Army said radios were a military necessity. Truman discovered the military accumulating huge stockpiles of such items, in quantities that could never be exhausted during the war, while steadfastly refusing to allow any such items into the civilian market. And thus when war contracts of a small business ended, so did the small business. The dollar-a-year men and the military in partnership ensured domination of the peacetime economy by the monopolies that seized the war economy. Truman's struggle to make small business the bulwark of American democracy was over. He had lost.[20]

There were those, however, who noticed Truman's work. Men who glanced guardedly at one another after meetings with the palsied and weakening Franklin Roosevelt. Men who saw in Truman's determination and energy a chance to keep the New Deal strong.

Chapter 16

PROMOTED TO
GLORY

At some time, the precise moment
probably unknown even to himself, Senator Truman began considering that he might become president of the United States. His
memoirs indicate that he began to realize this in 1941, perhaps
earlier. His private writings as chairman of the Truman committee
indicate awareness of his growing national stature. "It scares me to
death, the things they say to me and about me." Truman showed
no thirst for the presidency, but nonetheless he demonstrated an
unerring knack for propelling himself in that direction when opportunities began to arise. This was in keeping with his life plan of being
open to possibilities. He would claim truthfully that he never wanted
to be vice-president—truthfully, because that was not his goal.[1]

Many politicians of national repute get mentioned as vice-
presidential possibilities. Such speculations are entertaining at the
time, and mostly meaningless. Truman scoffed as his name began
to appear in early 1943, an appearance encouraged by a *Time* magazine cover story featuring him. He explained repeatedly that he
could do more for the country as a senator than as vice-president,
an assessment with unshakable historical precedents. Some people
also suggested him as a presidential candidate if FDR didn't run,
and Truman just as adamantly disclaimed desire for that job. None
of his disclaimers for either post contained an explicit refusal to

accept the nomination, thus he permitted speculation to build. Truman often said he was not a candidate, but as with his 1931 gubernatorial ambitions, that didn't mean that friends couldn't promote his candidacy. This activity increased Truman's power and influence, but he was reluctant to believe anything would come of it, a reluctance caused in part by his fear that he might otherwise start playing to the gallery in his Senate work and thereby lose the very attributes that made his work valuable.[2]

It is one thing for the ordinary citizen to fantasize about what he or she would do if president; but for someone who actually might get the job, the prospects can be sobering, especially if the United States is in the middle of a war. Truman was all too aware of what the burdens would be, and already felt overwhelmed by the work on his investigating committee. To Bess he confided that the labor reminded him of the Argonne, "trying to fire a barrage with which I could never catch up." Truman was entering his seventh decade of life, and the pace of his Senate work threatened his health. The Senate physician thought Truman would live only a few years at best. The senator's private correspondence showed references to chronic fatigue and occasional unpublicized hospitalizations. "I was sincerely sorry I had to see you in [my] bed, but it couldn't be helped." "I spent the last two weeks in the hospital." "I went to bed at five and didn't wake up until seven the next morning." "Been a little tired myself during the last six months, but I just don't seem to be able to find the time to sit down." "I am limp physically and mentally." "I've been worrying about all the responsibility." On April 18, 1941 War Secretary Stimson authorized an abdominal X-ray exam of Truman at Walter Reed Hospital. Three days later Truman had an electrocardiogram taken at the Hot Springs, Arkansas, military hospital, which was sent to Washington apparently for review there as well. (A heart abnormality had been diagnosed in 1937.) "There seem to be some rocks in my liver," Truman now told Vivian. A month later, "Have not been feeling as well as I should." Around July 1941 he was hospitalized for three weeks. His stomach was found to lack essential acids, apparently causing chronic nausea after meals. The staff was confident of remedy, but in July 1942 Truman again had trouble holding down food for long. His family occasionally became fearful. "I am not much on dreams," Vivian wrote, "but I awoke with a start the other morning thinking you were over at the old place and feeling exceptionally bad, so please let us hear from you." Truman concealed his afflictions as best he could, lying even to close political associates. Problems continued right up to his nomination as vice-president—around May 1944 he apparently had some sort of grueling oral surgery.[3]

Vice-President Henry Wallace was a swell guy with a brilliant and practical mind who nonetheless exuded an air of befuddlement. By early 1944 concerns about Wallace had spread far beyond the *Chicago Tribune* crowd, and brave men shuddered when they saw Roosevelt's failing health and considered the alternative. More than a few politicians now made an avocation of dumping Wallace. Each had his personal choice for a replacement, and infighting left no replacement candidate in a commanding position. Yet all were united against the common enemy, and Wallace reeled under the blows. He was a canny politician of no small ambition, and he had formidable allies. He would play out his string to the end, but in the end would lose because Roosevelt didn't care to fight for him. Roosevelt knew the Southern state delegations would be a monolith against Wallace at the Democratic Convention, and FDR didn't relish the prospect of the Confederates stalemating the Yankee and throwing the vice-presidential nomination to whoever could cut the slickest deal on the spot. Roosevelt also knew that border states such as Missouri had formidable electoral college strength that could be nudged either way, and therefore he desired a running mate with wide appeal. So with a warm embrace and expressions of fond regard Roosevelt sent Wallace on a fact-finding mission to China in the crucial weeks of preconvention maneuvering, and relieved of his interference the politicians looked for a replacement.[4]

Roosevelt acted as if he had no strong preference in the matter, but he decided firmly on Truman a week or so before the convention. There are several stories about how Roosevelt made up his mind. But, basically, he felt that Truman was more of a political asset than any other contender. Truman appealed to the same groups that liked Wallace, and appealed to some groups that hated Wallace. The Missourian could be expected to have strength in the Midwest and South, and had spent months making nationwide political contacts as a sought-after Democratic speechmaker. He was known to the professional politicos. The general public gave Truman credit as troubleshooter for the nation's war production, making sure the military got what it needed when it needed it. All this added up to votes, many votes. Roosevelt also recognized Truman's popularity in the Senate, where he would need all the help he could get in continuing the New Deal and in ratifying postwar diplomatic agreements.[5]

In the maneuverings to nominate Truman the "Hannegan switch" entered American political folklore. Truman credited Bob Hannegan with crucial help in the 1940 election, and managed to reward Hannegan with appointment as Democratic National Committee chairman. Hannegan had worked hard to promote Truman for vice-president; and when FDR announced his choice to a gathering of advisers a week before the convention, Hannegan thought it useful to get a note in the president's handwriting to convince delegates that Truman was the man. What the note said, where and when Hannegan got it, and even how many notes Roosevelt provided, became unclear as ensuing decades passed. Some stories say that all Hannegan got was a statement that FDR would be willing to run with either U.S. Supreme Court Justice William O. Douglas or Senator Harry Truman, and that Hannegan then tricked the president's secretary into typing the statement with the order of names switched to make Truman look like first choice. The "Hannegan switch" is a delightful story of skulduggery, but several things should be kept in mind. A carbon copy of the typed note was preserved, and shows clearly that Roosevelt was endorsing neither Truman nor Douglas, so the order of names didn't indicate first or second choice. Also, Douglas was neither a candidate nor a contender, so anything Roosevelt said about him was irrelevant to the convention. Given the note's ambiguity and the irrelevancy of Douglas, why would Hannegan risk switching the names when a quick double-check with Roosevelt (a certainty in a situation of such high stakes) would reveal the fabrication? And if the note were signed (which surely it was, else it would be valueless), Roosevelt approved the order of names anyway. Allegations of the "Hannegan switch" were widely distributed at the convention, which suggests that the story was merely a ploy in a "stop Truman" effort. Indeed, fear of a "stop Truman" movement probably explains the note's ambiguity despite Roosevelt's explicit choice of Truman—the longer the contenders fought Wallace and one another, the more time Truman forces had to arrange the nomination. A public endorsement by Roosevelt would have galvanized all competing factions against the senator.[6]

What Truman thought about all this is unclear. In January 1944 he was organizing his 1946 senatorial reelection campaign. He was well aware of the Truman for vice-president boom, and did all the right things to remain a contender. A week before the convention he told intimates that Bob Hannegan expected him to become vice-president. Since Hannegan had been in touch with Truman, the senator had probably heard that he was FDR's choice. Yet Truman had not heard this from FDR, and knew that several contenders in their enthusiasm thought they were the anointed. Thus Truman may have discounted any such assurance from Hannegan. Nonetheless, he now began telling his oldest and most trusted friends to come to the Chicago convention, that he would need their assistance there. Every one of these men, without known exception, planned to do anything necessary to win the vice-presidential nomination for Truman.[7]

As Truman loaded his suitcases into the family car at Independence, for the trip to Chicago and glory, he received a phone call from Mr. Justice Senator Assistant President of the United States Jimmy Byrnes. Byrnes said that Roosevelt had selected him (Byrnes) for vice-president, and Byrnes offered Truman the honor of placing the chosen name in formal nomination. Truman said he'd be delighted to do that, and was later delighted to visit every delegation, faction, pressure group, power broker, and wheelhorse at the convention on Byrnes's behalf. Truman the master machinist just seemed to lack the old touch—every time he went on a mission for Byrnes he came away with another endorsement for Truman instead.[8]

To everyone Truman protested much, much too much, that he didn't want to be vice-president. Deep toward midnight at one "nonstrategy" session Truman's old Battery D friend Eddie McKim nailed him: "I think, Senator, that you're going to do it." "What makes you think that I'm going to do it?" "Because there's a little old 90-year-old mother down in Grandview, Missouri, that would like to see her son President of the United States." Truman began to weep, and left his friends.[9]

And there was the rub, uttered by Eddie McKim and known to every conventioneer and newspaper reader—this time the Democrats were to nominate not one president, but two. Truman's old friend Cactus Jack Garner would grumble that the biggest mistake of his life was his service as Roosevelt's spare tire. But after twelve years the treads had worn bald, and the road ahead appeared worse yet.[10]

Truman saw it coming, had done everything a practical man could do to receive it, yet still could scarcely believe the gift would actually arrive. Despite all the work of his friends, despite all their assurances, he refused to believe. He refused to believe because he had heard no assurance from the one voice with power to bestow the gift. Now, with everything being orchestrated for a second-ballot victory, Bob Hannegan beckoned Truman to the telephone to hear the voice of the president of the United States. Truman heard himself anointed, and uttered, "Jesus Christ."[11]

The next night Truman walked quietly through the stadium, unnoticed for the last time in his life. He sat with the Missouri delegation, and photographers soon discovered him. Politicos surged around him, and told him all was in readiness for the second ballot before the first even began. Truman then joined Bess and Margaret in a box, Bess to his right and John Snyder to his left. The senator appeared in good spirits, conversing with persons around him as he failed to win a first-ballot nomination. Politicos continued to assure him that the second ballot was his. The call of the states began again, and flashbulbs exploded from every direction. Truman rose, and uniformed men appeared in front of him, in back of him, on every side, forced the crowd to give way, as arms reached out and frenzied voices screamed, "That's Truman! That's Truman!" The call of the states continued as Truman reached the platform. Senate colleagues and old friends embraced him again and again as he moved toward the podium. Unrecognized on the convention floor, Vivian watched his brother walk forward to a destiny far removed from the Grandview farm. The call of the states ended, and Harry Truman stood at the podium with a page from someone else's speech, on which he had scribbled hasty notes of his own. The nation gazed at him, and he gazed back, and he opened his mouth and said nothing memorable, and didn't have to. More flashbulbs, more reporters, more ado, and Truman declared an end to the proceedings. "I am quite tired," he said.[12]

"In presenting Franklin Delano Roosevelt as the Democratic candidate for President," Truman would declare, "I am presenting him for the BIGGEST job in the world. From 1944 to 1948 the President of this country is going to have responsibilities such as few men in history have faced. He's going to have the job of leading us through the final stages of victory in this war. And this war—as our fighting men in Germany and in Italy and in the Pacific can tell you—is far from being over. He's going to have the job of helping to make and to secure a worldwide and lasting peace. He's going to have the job of getting us back on the march of progress we began in 1932. We agree, then—it's a mighty big job." And Truman had some definite ideas about how to do it.[13]

The final victory. "I don't think enough can be said in praise of the Red Army," Truman wrote. "As long as the Russians keep the . . . Germans busy in Europe that certainly is a war effort that cannot be sneered at." He added, "I am perfectly willing to help Russia as long as they are willing to fight Germany to a standstill." Truman was intrigued by the idea of continued postwar U.S.-U.S.S.R. cooperation, with America trading machine tools for stockpiles of minerals. He was intrigued, but not committed: "I still think they are as untrustworthy as Hitler and Al Capone."[14]

Truman believed that Germany would be defeated before Japan, sometime in 1946. "That will be a time of great danger to the future cause of peace," because people might feel that Hitler's defeat meant the war was over, allowing Japan to offer terms attractive to war-weary Americans. Truman insisted on unconditional surrender, accompanied by measures to impress knowledge of defeat on the Japanese. Only that course, he believed, would guarantee that Japan could never attack again. "The action of the Japs at Nanking is known, and a full accounting will be made." Full indeed. Apparently in mid-1943 Senator Wallgren became upset that the U.S. military had seized two hundred thousand American agriculture acres. Truman began looking into this, but stopped when Secretary Stimson and General Marshall asked him to leave the project alone, saying this was a personal request from President Roosevelt. In July 1943 Truman told a judge in Washington State not to worry about the propriety of vast land condemnations benefiting a DuPont corporation enterprise. "I know something about that tremendous real estate deal," Truman told the judge, "and I have been informed that it is for the construction of a plant to make a terrific explosion for a secret weapon that will be a wonder. I hope it works." In

November 1943, however, Truman resumed investigation following complaints from Senator John Thomas and others about waste and inefficiency in the project. A Truman committee staff member reported, "The guise of secrecy is being resorted to by the War Department to cover what well may be another shocking example when the lid is finally taken off." From the scene Fred Canfil reported to Truman, "Colonel Matthias, commanding officer DuPont plant, told me that you and the Secretary of War had an understanding that none of your committee would come into the plant. Through another agency I found that within the last 10 days a confidential letter was received from the War Department . . . to Army officers and to high ranking civilian engineers . . . to the effect that these people were to see that no Senator or anyone connected with the Senate was to be given any information about the project." Nonetheless, Canfil did ferret details of "the internal workings of this plant, food, living conditions, and labor." This apparently was the last Truman committee inquiry about the atom bomb project. Truman claimed to have received a general outline of the research from Roosevelt himself. Much would be written about the "agonizing" decision to use the weapon, but Adm. William D. Leahy (liaison between the president and the joint chiefs) scoffed at this: "I know FDR would have used it in a minute to prove that he hadn't wasted two billion dollars." Truman maintained that the purpose was to destroy military targets. "Of course," Leahy remarked, "then they went ahead and killed as many women and children as they could, which was just what they wanted all the time." Japan would know the feel of defeat, and pay a full accounting. Full indeed.[15]

Looking ahead to the postwar world Truman had strong feelings about France's role. Even before the war he wrote, "I spent a year in France, the hardest work that any man ever did, trying to save their country from the Germans, and after it was all done, I sincerely wished I had been on the side of the Germans, and I still feel that way." Truman explained, "Just to show you what a petty larceny outfit they are, one of the companies of the 140th Infantry, while we were stationed in Commercy, cut down a tree on the farm of President Poincare to keep from freezing in the cold weather; and they were there, you understand, to keep the Germans from coming over and taking the whole place. The President of France raised such a howl about that tree that we had to take up a collection and pay him for it." Regarding World War I debts Truman fumed, "I still feel like the 'frogs' should pay us what they owe us."[16]

When Truman looked to China he felt it "hard for a straight-thinking Westerner to appreciate the situation," which he felt derived from China's isolationist foreign policy. He explained it this way:

> The Chinese government which we recognize is supposed to be on friendly terms with Russia. Russia is at peace with Japan, yet Russia and Japan both have policies which are inimicable to a united China. If you remember, the Russia-Japan war of 1904 was fought for the maritime provinces in northwest China. . . .
>
> I am sure that neither Great Britain or Russia would want to see a strong China, and neither am I thoroughly convinced Great Britain or Russia want to see Japan completely crushed. I am very sure they would like to maintain the balance of power in East Asia which would not be too friendly to the United States of America and still maintain the balance of power.
>
> All these deep, dark ramifications are entirely too much for me to work out. . . . Diplomacy has always been too much for me— especially diplomacy as it is practiced by the great powers. They always have some deep, dark ulterior motive for everything they do.

Later President Truman called the Nationalist regime "corrupt" and the "most terrible government in the history of the world." He declared, "Chiang apparently did not want to make any concessions and did not do anything for the agrarian population, which is the vast majority of the citizens of China. And so they turned him out. And the relatives of Chiang sifted the aid we sent to them, and I have been reliably informed that they have got 700 million dollars in real estate in the United States, and it all came out of the Treasury of the United States. Well, I thought it was about time to quit that kind of business." President Truman knew who "lost China."[17]

Truman felt that the postwar world had a special obligation to Jewish victims of Hitler. In 1939 he alluded to Munich when he said, "The British government has used its diplomatic umbrella again, this time on Palestine. It has made a scrap of paper out of Lord Balfour's promise to the Jews. It has just added another to the long list of surrenders to Axis powers." Truman quoted with approval an article by Barnet Nover from the May 18 *Washington Post*.

Nover: "Having by the Balfour declaration and her assumption of the mandate encouraged the Zionist experiment to go forward, Great Britain now washes her hands of declaration and mandate and forces the experiment to fend for itself in what is certain to be an extremely hostile environment." Nover wondered if Zionists would be massacred as were the Assyrians in Iraq when Britain granted Iraq independence. Nover was particularly disturbed that Britain was limiting Jewish immigration in Palestine to an average of fifteen thousand a year now. He asked where Jewish victims of Hitler could go. "The other areas Mr. Chamberlain would open to harassed Jews are no substitute. Where bread is called for, Mr. Chamberlain offers a stone."[18]

When in February 1941 Senator Robert Wagner asked Truman "to lend moral support to the Zionist cause and encourage the settlement of large numbers of Jewish refugees in the Jewish National Home," Senator Truman gladly joined the American Palestine Committee. Truman also supported the United Palestine Appeal. In the first half of 1942 Truman was unenthusiastic about calls for a Palestine-based Jewish army to fight alongside the Allies, but he signed a two-page December 7, 1942 *New York Times* ad calling for just such a thing. The ad was by the Committee for a Jewish Army of Stateless and Palestinian Jews.[19]

On the evening of April 14, 1943 Truman addressed an audience of twenty-one thousand at a Chicago United Rally to Demand Rescue of Doomed Jews, a meeting sponsored by high-powered establishment-type Jewish organizations. "Jews," Truman cried,

are being herded like animals into the ghettos, the concentration camps, and the wastelands of Europe. The men, the women and the children of this honored people are being starved, yes! actually murdered by the fiendish Huns and Fascists.

No one can any longer doubt the horrible intentions of the Nazi beasts. We know that they plan the systematic slaughter throughout all of Europe, not only of the Jews but of vast numbers of other innocent peoples. The streets of Europe, running with the blood of the massacred, are stark proof of the insatiable thirst of the Nazi hordes.

Today—not tomorrow—we must do all that is humanly possible to provide a haven and place of safety for all those who can be grasped from the hands of the Nazi butchers. Free lands must be opened to them. Their present oppressors must know that they will be held directly accountable for their bloody deeds. . . . This is not a Jewish problem. It is an American problem.

"When I got through," Truman wrote, "I was practically mobbed by a host of Jewish rabbis who had whiskers ranging in style all the way from Moses to Jeff Davis."[20]

Three weeks after this emotional rally, the Committee for a Jewish Army of Stateless and Palestinian Jews placed another ad in *The New York Times*. This ad called not only for a Jewish army but for acceptance of offers by Nazi allies Rumania, Hungary, and Bulgaria to ship Jews to havens elsewhere in the world. The ad said Britain opposed this because it feared the refugees would go to Palestine. The ad criticized the Bermuda Conference at which Senator Scott Lucas was a delegate, but didn't mention him or anyone else who attended. The ad had two separate lists of endorsers. One list was of people endorsing action to save Jews, and included Truman's name, but the layout implied that Truman endorsed the whole ad. Truman exploded, inaccurately claiming that the ad criticized members of Congress, but accurately stating that the ad wasn't cleared with him or any other Senator listed. "I am withdrawing my name from your committee, and you are not authorized under any circumstances to make use of it for any purpose in the future. This does not mean my sympathies are not with the down-trodden Jews of Europe, but when you take it on yourself without consultation to attack members of the Senate and House of Representatives who are working in your interest I cannot approve of that procedure." Truman sent copies of this letter to various Jewish organizations, and Senator Lucas seemed thankful. A month later Truman complained that the May 4 ad "was used by all the Arabs in North Africa in an endeavor to create dissention among them and caused them to stab our fellows in the back." Truman—who was always fuzzy about distinguishing among Zionists, Jews, Israelites, and (later) Israelis—received a warning from a former president of a large Reform Jewish congregation, who was also a good friend of Senator Lucas. The warning was that the Committee for a Jewish Army of Stateless and Palestinian Jews was a Zionist organization, and that "hundreds of thousands, and perhaps millions, of Americans of Jewish faith are deeply and strongly opposed to the creation of a national entity under the flag of David."[21]

In December 1943 the United Hebrew Congregation of Joplin asked Truman to help convince Britain to allow Palestinian immigration after March 1944. Truman replied, "I do not think it is the business of Senators who are not on the Foreign Relations Committee to dabble in matters that affect our relations with our Allies at this time. There is nobody on Earth who dislikes more than I do the actions of Hitler and Mussolini; but it is of vital importance that the Jewish congregations be patient and support wholeheartedly the foreign policy of our government. I think you will find that every effort is being made by the government to accomplish just what you have in mind."[22]

In early 1944 various people requested Truman to support U.S. Senate resolution #247 introduced by senators Wagner and Taft regarding "Establishment in Palestine of a National Home for the Jewish People." Truman declared that the resolution

> affects the foreign relations program between Great Britain, the United States, and the Middle East. My sympathy of course is with the Jewish people, but I am of the opinion a resolution such as this should be very circumspectly handled until we know just where we are going and why.
>
> With the difficulty looming up between Russia and Poland, and the Balkan States and Russia, and with Great Britain and Russia absolutely necessary to us in financing this war I don't want to throw any bricks to upset the apple cart, although when the right time comes I am willing to help make the fight for a Jewish homeland in Palestine.[23]

Truman felt some sort of world government would be needed in the postwar years. Some of his colleagues introduced a resolution calling for the United Nations to organize a permanent postwar peacekeeping military force, for the UN to prevent territorial aggression, and for the group to take in new members. Under this scheme military force would be used against anyone threatening peace, not only against members. Truman didn't quite endorse the measure, but did say in July 1943, "We intend to assume our full responsibility toward the building of a postwar world in which each nation shall have its rights." By the end of the year Truman called for "an organization with power to act in order to prevent aggression of . . . outlaw nations." He warned, "A worse war will follow this one, unless the United Nations and their allies, and all the other sovereign nations, decide to work together for peace as they are working together for victory." In early 1944 he outlined a specific proposal:

> The only logical basis for erecting a lasting peace and reconstructing a war-torn world must be in a new "improved" League of Nations made up of the United Nations, and controlled by Britain, China, Russia, and the United States, in the name of all and for the welfare of all. We must see to it that there is no postwar scramble for the spoils of war, for more power at the expense of other nations. . . . We must outlaw war by creating a new machine of peace, more powerful than any machine of war. The means of enforcement is a powerful international police force. The question is this: Do we really want international law and order and peace . . . ? No government at any level, local, state or federal, however limited its functions, ever functioned successfully without having somewhere the force necessary to enforce its rules and punish violations.[24]

With the welcome support of a War Production Board official named J. A. Krug, vice-presidential candidate Truman continued his losing battle to reconvert the war economy to civilian production in an orderly way. He said the federal government "must see to it that a full production program is maintained when peace comes. It must see to it that war plants are not junked. If private industry fails to operate them, then the government must." He added, "There are now many public works projects needed by communities throughout the country. These should be planned now, and arrangements made to put to work on them war workers who are displaced from jobs during the changeover. These should be financed by local communities with federal assistance."[25]

Early in 1944 Truman and two of his Senate colleagues made this statement on the broader role of the United States in the world economy:

The future peace depends on an economically healthy United States, and we cannot have economic health without a volume of foreign trade above and beyond anything we have ever had before. A large volume of foreign trade will contribute to the peace by insuring full production and full employment at home. It will contribute to the general peace because it will insure a basis for friendly collaboration between nations all over the earth. . . .

. . . It becomes all the more incumbent upon this country, in our own interest and for the future of nations, to lead the world into a great era of productive peace. No other nation can match our preeminent responsibility, not Great Britain whose industrial output is only one-fifth that of ours, nor Russia with its reconstruction and growth before it.

We cannot help but be sobered when we realize, on the basis of present facts, that this country has within its grasp a leadership which will determine the happiness and prosperity not only of our own 130-odd million but hundreds of millions of people in the years to come. . . .

The author of Ecclesiastes said in his wisdom many years ago that "the profit of the earth is for all." We have an opportunity now to implement this bit of ancient wisdom, making the earth and the fullness thereof a boon instead of a war-causing burden upon the back of mankind.[26]

As the ballots were tabulated on that November evening, Truman sat at a piano and played Mozart's Ninth Sonata. He knew what was coming. After lunching with Roosevelt in August Truman confided, "I had no idea he was in such a feeble condition. In pouring cream in his tea, he got more cream in the saucer than he did in the cup. His hands are shaking, and he talks with considerable difficulty." On trips back to Kansas City and Independence Truman began to seek out trusted friends and to indicate he would soon become president. Truman would keep the friends awake sometimes deep into the night, asking for advice and reassurance. Over and over he asked variations of the same question, "What am I going to do?" His war buddy Roger Sermon offered an answer that seemed to give relief, telling Truman to keep on doing what he had always done—to hire the best men available for each job, and to let them do it. Truman "looked thoughtful, then smiled. 'Yes,' he said, 'that's always been my policy.' "[27]

The vice-presidency changed Truman's routine little. He had a secretary, four stenographers, and perhaps four clerks. He retained his old Senate office. Perhaps the main noticeable change was in the favors requested of him—"I trust that you are not telling your constituents that Mr. Houdini is connected with the office at 240 Senate Office Building," an exasperated aide wrote to one supplicant. Truman scoffed at suggestions that he was becoming a darling of high society, noting that a string of obligatory functions had merely happened to come up all at once. Truman was amazed when Secret Service bodyguards were assigned to him. No vice-president had ever before received such protection.[28]

January 1945. Truman asked the news media to use common sense while the war continued. He declared that journalists had the right to be stupid, but questioned the point of exercising that right with stories helpful to Germany or Japan. To an NBC radio audience Truman predicted that civilian wants would fuel postwar business expansion. This was the radio program "America United."[29]

February 1945. A black soldier writes to the vice-president. "Despite the fact that I have given up my civilian freedom, last week I had to exchange seats on a bus in Waynesville because the seat I was riding in was for white only. . . . Thousands of others . . . are risking and giving their lives in every theater of operation, and the only way for all that we are doing not to be in vain is for you . . . to go to work and sponsor laws that will end this discrimination in a peaceful way because even those boys that have lived in the South all their lives aren't going to find it easy to ignore the things the Army has taught them to fight against, and stand being shoved around." Truman's aide Harry Vaughan replied that racial discrimination "has existed in this country for some time, and has existed in the world for a million years. That it is wrong—all right-thinking people agree. You may count upon Harry Truman to do his utmost toward righting this wrong. You must realize that your people have progressed further in the last 100 years in America than the black race have progressed in the previous thousand years. They will continue to progress, but conditions which have existed for centuries cannot be changed overnight. But with patience, tolerance and understanding, this matter, like many others, will be worked out." America United?[30]

Truman proclaimed, "A few days ago, from Yalta on the Black

Sea coast, we received good news. Another long stride had just been made not only toward victory, but toward a lasting peace. The agreement, like those reached before, is a product of good common sense." He added, "As the American philosopher, Emerson, well stated, 'Nothing can bring you peace but yourself. Nothing can bring you peace but the triumph of principles.' In the long run, the same basic philosophy applies to nations. America must live up to its highest principles, otherwise peace and security become impossible."[31]

February also brought a bittersweet real estate transaction—the Grandview farm was returned to the Truman family. The county, which now owned the land, had made half-hearted efforts to sell a portion of the property for $52,500 in 1942. This indicated that despite 1940 election campaign howls, Truman had hardly cheated the school fund by getting a $35,000 mortgage on the place. The matter laid dormant until Truman became vice-president. His old enemy George Montgomery was still presiding judge, and word began circulating that the county court would try to embarrass Truman by quietly selling the property far below market value to imply that the school fund mortgage had been a bad deal for the county. Charles F. Curry decided to do something about this. (Curry fought in the Argonne with Stayton's 110th Engineers, and returned home to make a fortune in real estate. His son would one day be the county presiding judge, and go on to prominence in national Democrat Party affairs.) Curry organized a small syndicate to offer a bid too high for the county to refuse. This was done not as a real estate investment but as a personal favor to Truman, with the understanding that at least part of the property would be sold back to the Truman family. Curry bid $43,500, and the county court accepted it. After computing various income and outgo on the property while the county held it, and obligations to the school fund, the county ended up with a $6,100 profit. Truman shoved this figure up the nose of *Kansas City Star* boss Roy Roberts, but neglected to tell Roberts that the profit accrued in part because Curry had deliberately submitted a high (though reasonable) bid. Harry and Vivian paid Curry $20,000 for eighty-seven acres including the old farmhouse. Curry held the remainder. He could have sold it for a handsome profit, but he held it intact as a courtesy to Truman until he could afford to buy it—at Curry's cost price. Eventually a shopping center development made the property one of Truman's major financial assets.[32]

March 1945. On the night of March 9/10, U.S. aviators attacked Tokyo with incendiary bombs. The toll was 267,171 buildings destroyed, 83,793 people killed and 40,918 wounded, over 1 million homeless. Through the 1970s at least, this would rank as the most devastating air raid ever known. Even the atom bombs would not cause so much destruction, making the decision to use them almost routine in retrospect.[33]

In March Truman proved FDR right in believing the Missourian could be crucial to the New Deal in Congress. Roosevelt had appointed Henry Wallace secretary of commerce. Wallace had had four years to make enemies while presiding over the Senate, and he used the time well. It took every glimmer of Truman's personal charm along with his savvy experience in parliamentary duels to push the nomination through.[34]

Controversy arose that month when Truman referred a bill on the proposed Missouri Valley Authority to an unfriendly committee. Truman crankily noted that he assigned the bill to where the rules required it to go. "As long as I am Vice President those rules will be strictly adhered to, and I don't care whether anyone likes it or not." To a critic of this action, Truman mentioned the parliamentary necessities, and then in one of his longest letters delivered a thoughtful exposition on the needs of the Missouri River Valley. He explained geographical constraints to dam construction and how those would alter the pattern of flood control dams. He talked also of associated reclamation projects, and how markets must be assured for the crops. "Get on a train and go to Fort Peck, Montana, alongside the river in daylight, and then get into an automobile and drive over Montana and look at the various proposed power dam sites and reclamation projects in Montana and the Dakotas, and you can then begin to have some idea of what a tremendous project the proposed Missouri Valley Authority is. . . . I have been working on it for 12 years, and we have some prospects now of getting the plans worked out." The critic replied that if Truman had been working on this for a dozen years he sure didn't have much to show for it. One can almost feel the pain as Truman replied, "My Dear Mr. — ——: I wasted my time. I am sorry. Sincerely yours."[35]

April 1945. Seven days into the month Truman spoke about the postwar economy. Again he called for planned conversion from war goods to consumer goods. He called for public works projects to provide employment. Veterans should be given cash, tuition payments, special loans, preference in government jobs, and other benefits. "This time our fighting men will *not* have to fight again for justice on the home front!" Truman then had fun with statistics, arguing that returning veterans would cause no massive unemployment:

11,000,000	armed forces personnel
− 2,000,000	students
− 2,000,000	farmers, lawyers, and other self-employed
− 1,000,000	local government jobs such as police and teachers
− 2,000,000	staying in military
4,000,000	needing jobs

Compare with:

3,500,000	women war workers anxious to return to their homes
+ 500,000	elderly workers anxious to retire
+ 2,000,000	teenagers who should be sent back to school
6,000,000	people leaving job market

Thus he predicted a shortage of two million workers after all the soldiers came home. Plentiful jobs, soaring wages as employers bid for scarce labor, a consumer's paradise with good cars priced under $400, houses young couples could afford, luxury railroad passenger service, new types of food packaging and storage, television. Boom times ahead.[36]

April 12, 1945. Truman presided with one ear over a tedious afternoon Senate session, taking advantage of the torpor to catch up on family correspondence. His old buddy Eddie McKim was in town, and Truman was looking forward to a poker game with him and other cronies that evening. The Senate recessed at 4:56 P.M., and Truman walked over to Speaker Rayburn's private hideaway in the Capitol to relax for a few minutes before finishing up work for the day. The Capitol was almost deserted, the corridors silent, and the telephone bells loud in Mr. Sam's hideaway. Rayburn took the call from Steve Early, the White House secretary Truman had chewed out years ago when he felt FDR was treating him like an office boy. Early had called Truman's office, and was told that Truman was walking over to Rayburn's place. Rayburn promised to have Truman return the call, and had barely replaced the receiver when Truman walked in wearing a bow tie and a grin. About this time Truman's aide Harry Vaughan telephoned Eddie McKim to see how preparations were going for the poker game. McKim had talked the hotel manager into moving him from a sardine tin–sized cubbyhole to a full suite. The green poker table was set up. McKim had laid in a supply of liquor from Truman's office; mixers and ice were on hand. Vaughan was delighted. "The V-P says to tell you that the Senate has adjourned. He is going over to Sam Rayburn's office; then he's coming here to the Senate Office Building and sign the mail. He's got a call from the White House; he'll have to answer that, and after that we'll be down."[37]

Eddie waited. The ice melted. Captain Harry never came.

Bibliographic Note

Detailed references appear in the Notes Section. Here I guide interested readers to archives containing manuscript sources for Truman's prepresidential years.

At the Harry S. Truman Library in Independence, Missouri, the Senate papers have crucial information but are filed to meet the needs of a senator's office staff. Researchers soon learn that their needs are different from a U.S. senator's. Truman's "Family, Business, Personal" papers at the library are also filled with useful data. The library staff and the citations in Notes can guide researchers into other collections with smaller amounts of prepresidential material.

Equally important is the Western Historical Manuscripts Collection of the University of Missouri, housing papers of Truman's Missouri colleagues and opponents. The collections are well indexed and are accessible from any branch of the university throughout the state.

The Jackson County government has retained more records about Judge Truman than is commonly realized. However, they are not indexed, and to find them one must know exactly what items are sought. One must then go from department to department and floor to floor in the courthouse. But patience often yields the desired information.

The Missouri Valley Room of the Kansas City, Missouri, Public Library contains much about Truman's Missouri heritage, but the material is nearly inaccessible. One uncooperative staff member proclaimed, "We don't need another rehash on Truman." Such attitudes, voiced loudly and repeatedly, make research difficult.

The Snyder Collection of the University of Missouri at Kansas City (housed in the Volker Campus General Library) has material useful to understanding Truman's Kansas City environment. The Liberty Memorial Archives in Kansas City, Missouri, are a valuable source for all military aspects of World War I, and include material on Captain Harry. The Jackson County Historical Society Research Library in Independence, Missouri, contains much about Truman's Independence background.

The *Kansas City Star* library may be used only by newspaper staffers, but its collection of Truman clippings is invaluable—particularly since some clippings are from editions that weren't microfilmed. These disintegrating clippings are a valuable resource that should be preserved and somehow made available to outside researchers.

Kansas City and Jackson County newspapers are crucial to understanding the context of Truman's Missouri activities. Microfilm copies are available at various libraries, but no index has been prepared (an awkward index does exist for the *St. Louis Post Dispatch*). St. Louis newspapers give another perspective to Truman's Senate years.

The Congressional Record and various committee hearings and reports trace Truman's Senate activities.

Three books deserve special mention. Bruce Catton's *The War Lords of Washington* (New York: Harcourt Brace Jovanovich, 1948) puts Senator Truman's national defense committee in proper context. Pseudonymous author Frank Mason raised controversy in Kansas City with *Truman and The Pendergasts* (Evanston, Ill.: Regency Books, 1963), but the book holds to the general truth despite specific errors. No one interested in Truman's Missouri heritage should fail to consult William M. Reddig's *Tom's Town* (New York: J. B. Lippincott Company, 1947). This is a superior volume, with almost no factual mistakes (and those few are inconsequential). *Tom's Town* can be relied on as authoritative.

William L. Riordon's classic *Plunkitt of Tammany Hall* may provide helpful insight into the thinking of machine politicians. ▾

Notes

Quotations are generally edited to conform with modern grammar and spelling.

The following abbreviations are used:

FDRL: Franklin D. Roosevelt Library

HSTL: Harry S. Truman Library

WHMC,MU: Western Historical Manuscripts Collection, University of Missouri

Chapter 1 MOVING TOWARD INDEPENDENCE

1. Edward W. Potts, "The President's Mother," *The Christian Advocate,* undated article in "Truman, Martha Ellen Young," vertical file, HSTL; *Kansas City Star* clipping, undated but near time of Martha Ellen Truman's death, in "Truman, Martha Ellen Young," vertical file, HSTL.

2. Jonathan Daniels, *The Man of Independence* (Philadelphia: J. B. Lippincott, 1950), pp. 34–35, 40; Mary Ethel Noland oral history, pp. 3–4, 15–16, 19–20, HSTL. Truman collaborated with Daniels in the writing of *The Man of Independence,* giving Daniels extensive interviews and access to associates who normally would refuse to tell a writer about their dealings with Truman. Daniels made manuscript changes at Truman's request. Therefore the published version of *The Man of Independence* has Truman's *nihil obstat.*

3. Differing versions of the fatherly advice to John Anderson Truman are found in Daniels, *Man of Independence,* pp. 41–42, in Jonathan Daniels's interview with Vivian Truman, September 23, 1949, *The Man of Independence* research notes (hereafter cited as MOI notes), Jonathan Daniels papers, HSTL; and in Alfred Steinberg, *The Man from Missouri* (New York: G. P.

Putnam's Sons, 1962), p. 16. Truman reportedly disagreed with numerous statements in Steinberg's book.

4. Mary Martha Truman to Nan Bentley, October 1, 1882, April 15, 1883, explanatory note appended to Mary Martha Truman to Nan Bentley, July 14, 1887, Jordan Bentley papers, HSTL; Harry S. Truman, *Year of Decisions* (Garden City, N.Y.: Doubleday, 1955), p. 113 (hereafter cited as *Memoirs*); Mary Ethel Noland oral history, pp. 21, 164–65, HSTL.

5. Truman, *Memoirs*, p. 112; Jonathan Daniels interview with Harry S. Truman, August 30, 1949, p. 4, MOI notes, Jonathan Daniels papers, HSTL; "Truman's Home in Lamar," *The Midwest Motorist*, February 1972, in "Truman, Harry S.—Homes," vertical file, HSTL; Miscellaneous Historical Document 271, HSTL. The house was purchased from Simon Blethrode.

6. Meyer Berger, *Kansas City Star*, June 30, 1946 (reprint of *New York Times Magazine* article).

7. "Truman's Home in Lamar"; Richard Eaton and LaValle Hart, "Meet Harry S. Truman," in "Truman, Harry S.—Personal Information," vertical file, HSTL; "Harry Truman's Missouri," *Life*, June 25, 1945; Frank McNaughton and Walter Hehmeyer, *This Man Truman* (New York: McGraw-Hill, 1945), pp. 9–10. Harry Truman personally checked the galleys of *This Man Truman* for factual errors, and his corrections were incorporated in the printed version of the book. Yet the book has many inaccuracies. A set of galleys reflecting his corrections is in the Harry S. Truman Library; Vere C. Leigh oral history, p. 74, HSTL.

8. "Truman's Home in Lamar"; McNaughton and Hehmeyer, *This Man Truman*, p. 9; Mary Martha Truman to Nan Bentley, April 7, 1885, Jordan Bentley papers, HSTL.

9. Mary Martha Truman to Nan Bentley, April 7 and May 12, 1885, Jordan Bentley papers, HSTL.

10. *Kansas City Times*, June 14, 1971, p. 4A; Miscellaneous Historical Document 91, HSTL; *The First Hundred Years: History of Belton, Missouri*, in "Truman, Harry S.—Homes," vertical file, HSTL.

11. Harry S. Truman, *The Autobiography of Harry S. Truman*, ed. Robert H. Ferrell (Boulder, Colo.: Colorado Associated University Press, 1980), p. 3 (hereafter cited as Truman, *Autobiography*). Jhan Robbins, *Bess and Harry: An American Love Story* (New York: G. P. Putnam's Sons, 1980), p. 15 (this book should be used with caution); Steinberg, *Man from Missouri*, p. 21; Berger, *Kansas City Star; Kansas City Times*, June 14, 1971, p. 4A.

12. Mrs. Francis H. Montgomery oral history, p. 30, HSTL; Truman, *Memoirs*, pp. 114–115; Truman, *Autobiography*, pp. 3–5.

13. John W. Meador oral history, pp. 14, 33–34, Gaylon Babcock oral history, pp. 17–18, HSTL.

14. Mary Ethel Noland oral history, p. 52, HSTL; Henry A. Bundschu,

"Harry S. Truman, 'The Missourian,' " manuscript pp. 4–5, Biographical file, PSF, Harry S. Truman papers (hereafter cited as HST papers), HSTL (the manuscript dates the California property during the Civil War; the printed version dates it as antebellum); Jonathan Daniels interview with Harry S. Truman, November 12, 1949, p. 57, MOI notes, Jonathan Daniels papers, HSTL; John W. Meador oral history, pp. 15, 20, HSTL; Mrs. Francis Montgomery oral history, p. 37, HSTL; memorandum of conversation among Mary Jane Truman, Milton Perry, and Benedict Zobrist, May 25, 1973, Miscellaneous Historical Document 189, HSTL; Truman, *Memoirs*, p. 114; Elsie Spry Davis, *Descendants of Jacob Young of Shelby County, Kentucky* (Coronado, Calif.; Elsie Spry Davis, 1980), pp. 127, 133–134. This book can be found in the vertical file, HSTL. The Youngs had several houses on this property over the years, and the antebellum dining scene wasn't necessarily at the mansion Harry Truman knew.

15. Truman, *Memoirs*, p. 115.

16. Margaret Truman, *Harry S. Truman* (New York: William Morrow, 1973), p. 46; Truman, *Autobiography*, p. 6.

17. Margaret Truman, *Harry S. Truman*, p. 46; Davis, *Descendants of Jacob Young*, p. 127; Harry S. Truman to Margaret Truman, June 25, 1943, Margaret Truman, *Letters from Father* (New York: Arbor House, 1981), p. 47; Harry S. Truman, September 5, 1949, *Public Papers of the President 1949* (Washington, D.C.: U.S. Government Printing Office), p. 460; Truman, *Memoirs*, p. 114; Truman, *Autobiography*, p. 6.

18. Truman, *Autobiography*, p. 6; Davis, *Descendants of Jacob Young*, p. 127.

19. Truman, *Memoirs*, pp. 113, 115; Truman, *Autobiography*, pp. 5–6; Daniels, *Man of Independence*, p. 45; Steinberg, *Man from Missouri*, p. 21; Mary Martha Truman to Nan Bentley, July 14, 1887 (with appended explanatory note), Jordan Bentley papers, HSTL; Mary Ethel Noland oral history, pp. 22, 23, 165, HSTL; Margaret Truman, *Harry S. Truman*, p. 46.

20. Margaret Truman, *Harry S. Truman*, p. 46.

21. Davis, *Descendants of Jacob Young*, pp. 128, 132–34; Truman, *Memoirs*, p. 113; Steinberg, *Man from Missouri*, p. 22; Truman, *Autobiography*, p. 28. Frictions existed in the household. To the horror of her sister Sallie, Mattie would box the ears of Sallie's daughter Suda, claiming the child was too noisy while descending stairs. After Mattie burned Sallie's portrait of her late husband "Jim Crow" Chiles, Sallie and her children moved out. Suda later outraged her Confederate family by marrying a Union army officer. None of her Missouri kin attended the wedding.

22. Truman, *Memoirs*, p. 113.

23. Truman, *Autobiography*, p. 6; John W. Meador oral history, p. 12, HSTL; Truman, *Memoirs*, p. 113.

24. McNaughton and Hehmeyer, *This Man Truman*, p. 12; Truman, *Autobiography*, pp. 6–8, 33; Truman, *Memoirs*, p. 115.

25. Truman, *Memoirs*, p. 114.

26. Ibid.

27. Ibid.

28. Harry S. Truman in William Hillman, *Mr. President* (New York: Straus and Young, 1952), p. 236.

29. Mary Ethel Noland oral history, p. 47, HSTL.

30. "History—interest in," Memoirs File, Post-Presidential File, HST papers, HSTL; Truman, *Autobiography*, p. 8; Margaret Truman, *Harry S. Truman*, p. 47; Daniels, *Man of Independence*, p. 49; Steinberg, *Man from Missouri*, pp. 23–24; Mary Ethel Noland oral history, pp. 63–64, HSTL; Jonathan Daniels interview with the Trumans of Grandview, September 24, 1949, p. 16, MOI notes, Jonathan Daniels papers, HSTL; Merry Optical Co. prescription, "Miscellaneous 1922–1953" folder, box 15, FBP, HST papers, HSTL; Harry S. Truman to Bess Truman, July 20, 1930, box 5, FBP, HST papers, HSTL. In *Memoirs* (p. 116) Truman said his mother had him fitted with glasses because he had trouble reading newspaper print. In 1952 Truman told the publishers of *National Cyclopedia of American Biography* that he began wearing glasses at age eight, for nearsightedness (Harry S. Truman handwritten notation in 4/24/52 draft of *National Cyclopedia of American Biography* article, "Correspondence relating to Harry S. Truman—biographical," Biographical File, PSF, HST papers, HSTL). Truman called his affliction "short sight" in "Memories—early" folder, Memoirs File, Post-Presidential File, HST papers, HSTL. Years later he speculated that proper eye exercises at this time might have improved his vision (Harry S. Truman interview with Jonathan Daniels, July 28, 1949, p. 2, MOI notes, Jonathan Daniels papers, HSTL).

31. Mary Ethel Noland oral history, p. 74, HSTL; Truman, *Autobiography*, p. 8; Bela Kornitzer, "The Story of Truman and His Father," *Parents' Magazine*, March 1951.

Chapter 2 SCHOOL DAYS

1. Truman, *Memoirs*, p. 114; John W. Meador oral history, p. 14, HSTL.

2. *Circuit* judges held trials. *County* judges such as Richard Chiles had nothing to do with trials but were the top county executives, administrators running county government. Each county had three such judges—eastern, western, and presiding. Richard Chiles is omitted from some lists of presiding judges, but the Henry Chiles oral history (HSTL) makes this identification.

3. The family claimed Jim Crow's nickname came from his agility performing a dance step called Jim Crow, but the racist connotation had to be apparent to townsfolk who knew nothing of his antebellum dancing. Accounts of his death conflict; Pearl Wilcox, *Jackson County Pioneers* (n.p., 1975), pp. 461–63; Harry S. Truman to Mrs. Phil A. Long, May 10, 1960,

"Correspondence—Biographical," PPF, HST papers, HSTL; Jonathan Daniels interview with William H. Southern, September 26, 1949, p. 24, MOI notes, Jonathan Daniels papers, HSTL; Davis, *Descendants of Jacob Young*, pp. 130, 133; O. C. Sheley, "James Peacock and 'Jim Crow' Chiles," *Frontier Times*, April-May 1963, pp. 29, 46–47; George Creel, *Rebel at Large: Recollections of Fifty Crowded Years* (N.Y.: G. P. Putnam's Sons), p. 16. One of the good citizens terrorized by Jim Crow was George Porterfield Gates, whose granddaughter would marry Harry Truman (Mary Paxton Keeley oral history, pp. 39–40, HSTL).

4. Kornitzer, "The Story of Truman."

5. Margaret Truman, *Harry S. Truman*, p. 49; Mary Ethel Noland oral history, p. 55, HSTL; J. R. Fuchs memorandum of June 27, 1972, "Harry S. Truman—Homes" folder, vertical file, HSTL; Thomas H. Madden to Jonathan Daniels, February 8, 1950, Jonathan Daniels papers, University of North Carolina. Deeding property to close relatives in order to evade creditors was an old Young family technique (John Meador oral history, p. 20, HSTL).

6. Truman, *Memoirs*, p. 115; Daniels, *Man of Independence*, p. 47; Mary Ethel Noland oral history, pp. 55–56, HSTL; Kornitzer, "The Story of Truman."

7. Daniels, *Man of Independence*, p. 47; Jonathan Daniels interview with Ethel Noland and Nellie Noland, September 25, 1949, p. 18, MOI notes, Jonathan Daniels papers, HSTL; Jonathan Daniels interview with Harry S. Truman, November 12, 1949, p. 56, MOI notes, Jonathan Daniels papers, HSTL; Truman, *Autobiography*, p. 9; Mary Ethel Noland oral history, p. 81, HSTL.

8. Truman, *Memoirs*, p. 115; Harry S. Truman, "Early 1900's and Late 1890's," personal notes folder, desk file, Post-Presidential File, HST papers, HSTL; Darrell Garwood, *Crossroads of America* (New York: W. W. Norton, 1948), p. 305.

9. Truman, *Memoirs*, p. 115; Daniels, *Man of Independence*, pp. 48–49; Jonathan Daniels interviews with Vivian Truman, September 23, 1949, p. 15, and with Henry Bundschu, October 3, 1949, p. 39, and with Harry S. Truman, November 12, 1949, p. 56, MOI notes, Jonathan Daniels papers, HSTL; Kornitzer, "The Story of Truman."

10. Daniels, *Man of Independence*, p. 55; Truman, *Memoirs*, p. 116; Mary Paxton Keeley oral history, pp. 23, 27, HSTL; Harry's mother had withdrawn her membership from Blue Ridge Baptist Church "because she felt that there were too many liars and hypocrites in it," her older son later wrote (Harry S. Truman, "Pickwick Papers," p. 1 of "The Ideals," typed copies in "Senatorial Campaign—1934" folder, County Judge 2, HST papers, HSTL).

11. Harry S. Truman quotation, February 5, 1953, "Independence, Missouri—life in" folder, Memoirs File, HST papers, HSTL; Mize Peters oral

history, p. 21, HSTL; Henry P. Chiles oral history, p. 21, HSTL; Harry S. Truman, "My First 80 Years," *Saturday Evening Post*, June 13, 1964; Truman, *Autobiography*, p. 11; Truman, *Memoirs*, p. 116; Elizabeth Paxton Forsling, "Remembering Delaware Street," Jackson County Historical Society, May 1962, appendix to Sue Gentry oral history, p. 24, HSTL.

12. Truman, *Memoirs*, p. 116; Mize Peters oral history, pp. 1, 3, 22–24, HSTL; Mrs. W. L. C. Palmer oral history, p. 3, HSTL; Robert Martin Redding and Jimmie O'Bryan Shepard, "The Formal Education of Harry S. Truman," "Biographical Information—Harry S. Truman" folder, vertical file, HSTL; Potts, "The President's Mother." Truman habitually misremembered Ewin's name as "Ewing," just as he misremembered the names Mamie Dunne and Ardelia Hardin. He didn't seem to make such mistakes with names of his male teachers.

13. Truman, *Autobiography*, pp. 8–9, 11; Mary Ethel Noland oral history, pp. 56–57, HSTL; Jonathan Daniels interview with the Trumans of Grandview, September 24, 1949, p. 16, with Harry S. Truman, November 12, 1949, p. 56, and with Ethel Noland and Nellie Noland, September 25, 1949, p. 18, MOI notes, Jonathan Daniels papers, HSTL; Truman, *Memoirs*, pp. 116–17; Daniels, *Man of Independence*, pp. 52–53. Mary Jane Truman also missed sharing her brothers' later episodes of measles and mumps. Later Harry and Vivian took care of Grandma Vaile and Caroline Simpson as long as the women lived.

14. Jonathan Daniels interview with Vivian Truman, September 23 and 24, 1949, pp. 15, 17, MOI notes, Jonathan Daniels papers, HSTL; Mary Ethel Noland oral history, p. 51, HSTL; Davis, *Descendants of Jacob Young*, p. 143; memorandum of conversation among Mary Jane Truman, Milton Perry, and Benedict Zobrist, May 25, 1973, Miscellaneous Historical Document 189, HSTL.

15. Redding and Shepard, "Formal Education"; Mrs. W. L. C. Palmer oral history, p. 12, HSTL; Truman, *Memoirs*, p. 117; McNaughton and Hehmeyer, *This Man Truman*, p. 15; Mize Peters oral history, p. 2, HSTL; Truman, *Autobiography*, pp. 9, 11; Daniels, *Man of Independence*, p. 53; Miscellaneous Historical Document 292, HSTL. The Harry S. Truman Library identifies this report card as second grade. The school, teacher, and absences are inconsistent with second grade while consistent with fourth grade.

16. Harry S. Truman, October 16, 1951, *Public Papers 1951*, p. 579.

17. Truman, *Autobiography*, p. 11; Mize Peters oral history, pp. 2, 6–7, HSTL; Bundschu, "Harry S. Truman." Truman reviewed Bundschu's manuscript for accuracy before it was printed.

18. Case # 24214 *F. M. Burkett* v. *J. A. Truman*, Jackson County Circuit Court, Jackson County, Missouri; index of cases notation for Book L, p. 280, Jackson County Circuit Court, Jackson County, Missouri; Pearl Wilcox, *Independence and 20th Century Pioneers* (n.p., 1979), pp. 41–42; Charles Robbins, *Last of His Kind: An Informal Portrait of Harry S. Truman* (New York:

William Morrow, 1979), p. 17; Independence city directories for 1888–89, 1898, and 1900–01, in Missouri Valley Room of Kansas City, Missouri, Public Library; *Jackson Examiner*, May 31, 1901; *The Illustrated World*, April 1899 (in collection of Jackson County Historical Society); *Independence as It Is* (n.p., c. 1902); Jonathan Daniels interview with William H. Southern, Jr., September 26, 1949, p. 23, MOI notes, Jonathan Daniels papers, HSTL; Davis, *Descendants of Jacob Young*, p. 147; McNaughton and Hehmeyer, *This Man Truman*, p. 62; Thomas Joseph Heed, "Prelude to Whistlestop: Harry S. Truman the Apprentice Campaigner," Ed.D. dissertation, Columbia University, 1975, p. 5.

19. Steinberg, *Man from Missouri*, p. 17; Daniels, *Man of Independence*, p. 48; Mary Ethel Noland oral history, p. 167, HSTL; Jonathan Daniels interview with Harry S. Truman, November 12, 1949, p. 56, MOI notes, Jonathan Daniels papers, HSTL.

20. Steinberg, *Man from Missouri*, pp. 17, 25; Daniels, *Man of Independence*, p. 48; Jonathan Daniels interviews with Henry Bundschu, October 3, 1949, p. 39, and with Harry S. Truman, November 12, 1949, p. 56, MOI notes, Jonathan Daniels papers, HSTL; Mize Peters oral history, pp. 18–19, HSTL; Esther M. Grube oral history, pp. 48–49, HSTL; Kornitzer, "The Story of Truman."

21. Steinberg, *Man from Missouri*, p. 15; Jonathan Daniels correspondence in Harry S. Truman papers and Truman family correspondence (Noland) referring to Daniels's treatment of John Anderson Truman in *The Man of Independence*, HSTL; Harry S. Truman to Ethel Noland, August 13, 1949, Mary Ethel Noland papers, HSTL; Truman, *Memoirs*, pp. 124–25.

22. Anthony Leviero, "Harry Truman, Musician and Music Lover," *New York Times Magazine*, June 18, 1950; Kornitzer, "The Story of Truman"; Jonathan Daniels interviews with the Trumans of Grandview, September 24, 1949, p. 17 and with Harry S. Truman, November 12, 1949, p. 57, MOI notes, Jonathan Daniels papers, HSTL; enclosure with John Conly to Joseph Short, December 28, 1951, and enclosure with Joseph Short to Bela Kornitzer, May 1, 1951, "5928" folder, PPF, HST papers, HSTL; Mary Ethel Noland oral history, p. 159, HSTL; Hillman, *Mr. President*, p. 200; Harry S. Truman to Mrs. Don Scarbrough, late 1964, "Truman, Harry S.—Music Interest," vertical file, HSTL; Harry S. Truman to Bess Wallace, November 1, 1911, in Robert H. Ferrell, ed., *Dear Bess* (New York: W. W. Norton, 1983).

23. J. R. Fuchs memorandum of June 27, 1972, "Truman, Harry S.—Homes," vertical file, HSTL; "Abstract of title to North 100 feet of Lot 3, Woodland Place, an addition to the City of Independence, in Jackson County, Missouri," "Truman, Harry S.—Homes," vertical file, HSTL; Thomas H. Madden to Jonathan Daniels, February 8, 1950, Jonathan Daniels papers, University of North Carolina.

24. Forsling appendix to Sue Gentry oral history, pp. 23–24, 26–27,

HSTL (appendix reprinted from Jackson County Historical Society newsletters of May 1962 and November 1963).

25. Ibid., p. 32; Sue Gentry oral history, *passim; Independence as It Is;* Truman, *Memoirs,* p. 117; Truman, *Autobiography,* pp. 11–12; Steinberg, *Man from Missouri,* p. 26; Mary Ethel Noland oral history, pp. 78–79, 169, HSTL; Henry P. Chiles oral history, pp. 19, 90–91, HSTL; Truman, *Memoirs* draft, p. 2885, HST papers, HSTL; Jonathan Daniels interview with Ethel Noland and Nellie Noland, September 24, 1949, p. 18, MOI notes, Jonathan Daniels papers, HSTL.

26. Truman, *Memoirs,* pp. 117–18; Harry S. Truman interview with William Hillman, December 14, 1951, interviews folder, "Mr. President" file, box 269, PSF, Harry S. Truman Papers, HSTL.

27. Henry P. Chiles oral history, pp. 1, 5–6, HSTL; Henry Bundschu, in CBS broadcast "Closed Ranks," 6:30–7:30 P.M., quoted in *Kansas City Star* or *Times,* c. April 1945, Biographical File, PSF, HST papers, HSTL; Bundschu, "Harry S. Truman."

28. Henry P. Chiles oral history, p. 9, HSTL; Truman, "Early 1900's and Late 1890's"; Jonathan Daniels interview with Vivian Truman, September 23, 1949, MOI notes, Jonathan Daniels papers, HSTL; Mary Paxton Keeley oral history, pp. 32, 35, HSTL; Harry S. Truman to Bess Truman, May 6, 1933, box 5, FBP, HST papers, HSTL.

29. Truman, *Memoirs,* pp. 117–18.

30. Henry P. Chiles oral history, pp. 9–11; Steinberg, *Man from Missouri,* p. 25; Jonathan Daniels interview with Vivian Truman, September 23, 1949, MOI notes, Daniels papers, HSTL; Kornitzer, "The Story of Truman."

31. Truman, *Memoirs,* p. 118.

32. Truman, *Autobiography,* p. 9; Redding and Shepard, "Formal Education"; Forsling appendix to Sue Gentry oral history, p. 29, HSTL.

33. Stoll, "Closed Ranks"; Mize Peters oral history, p. 10, HSTL; Mary Ethel Noland oral history, pp. 58–59, HSTL. Harry's grade school graduation certificate lists Rose Shepherd as his teacher, but he never credited her as an instructor (Miscellaneous Historical Documents 46 and 62, HSTL). *Life* magazine listed Principal Caroline Stoll as Harry's seventh-grade teacher ("Harry Truman's Missouri," *Life,* June 25, 1945, p.79).

34. Truman, *Memoirs,* p. 125.

35. Steinberg, *Man from Missouri,* p. 24; McNaughton and Hehmeyer, *This Man Truman,* p. 15; Daniels, *Man of Independence,* p. 50; Berger, *Kansas City Star,* June 30, 1946; Mary Ethel Noland oral history, p. 71, HSTL; Grace Summer comment in Kornitzer, "The Story of Truman."

36. Jonathan Daniels interviews with Harry S. Truman, July 28, 1949, p. 2, and with William Southern, September 26, 1949, p. 22, MOI notes, Jonathan Daniels papers, HSTL; Truman, *Memoirs,* p. 116; Harry S. Truman, "My Impressions of The Senate, The House, Washington, etc.,"

holograph, HSTL; William Hillman interview with Harry S. Truman, October 1, 1951, "Mr. President" File interviews folder, PSF box 269, HST papers, HSTL; "History—interest in" folder and "Masonic Lodge" folder, Memoirs File, Post-Presidential File, HST papers, HSTL; Robert Underhill, *The Truman Persuasions* (Ames, Iowa: Iowa State University Press, 1981), pp. 21–22; Mrs. W. L. C. Palmer oral history, pp. 17–18, HSTL; Henry P. Chiles oral history, p. 13, HSTL; Harry S. Truman to Cyril Clemens, August 28, 1944, "Harry S. Truman—Personal May 1944—August 1944" folder, box 170, SV, HST papers, HSTL; Cyril Clemens, "The School Days of Harry S. Truman: Typical American," *School and Society*, September 1, 1945, "Truman, Harry S.—Musical Interests" folder, vertical file, HSTL; Mary Ethel Noland oral history, pp. 170–72, HSTL.

37. Truman, *Memoirs*, p. 119; Margaret Truman, *Harry S. Truman*, p. 52; William Hillman interview with Harry S. Truman, October 1, 1951, "Mr. President" File, interviews folder, PSF box 269, HST papers, HSTL.

38. "History—interest in" folder, Memoirs File, Post-Presidential File, HST papers, HSTL; Robbins, *Last of His Kind*, p. 42.

39. Truman, *Autobiography*, pp. 27, 118–19; Harry S. Truman to Ethel Noland, January 2, 1953, Mary Ethel Noland papers, HSTL; Truman, "Pickwick Papers" (p. 1 of May 14, 1934, p. 1 of "The Ideals I've tried to make work and perhaps haven't"), HST papers, HSTL.

40. Truman, *Memoirs*, p. 124.

41. Truman, *Autobiography*, p. 120.

42. Harold F. Gosnell, *Truman's Crises: A Political Biography of Harry S. Truman* (Westport, Conn.: Greenwood Press, 1980), p. 51; Berger, *Kansas City Star*, June 30, 1946; McNaughton and Hehmeyer, *This Man Truman*, pp. 18–19; Truman, *Autobiography*, p. 11; Mrs. W. L. C. Palmer oral history, pp. 58–60, HSTL; Louis W. Truman to Richard L. Miller, June 22, 1982, author's files; Daniels, *Man of Independence*, p. 54; Steinberg, *Man from Missouri*, p. 26; Harry S. Truman, "Two Years in the Army" essay, "Military Service, Longhand notes by Harry S. Truman regarding" folder, box 21, FBP, HST papers, HSTL.

43. Mrs. W. L. C. Palmer oral history, pp. 7–8, 14, HSTL; Sue Gentry oral history, pp. 14–15, HSTL; Henry P. Chiles oral history, pp. 2–3, HSTL; *Independence Examiner*, July 1, 1950.

44. Redding and Shepard, "Formal Education"; Mrs. W. L. C. Palmer oral history, pp. 3, 11–12, HSTL; "Harry Truman's Missouri," p. 79; Truman, *Memoirs*, pp. 118, 153; Steinberg, *Man from Missouri*, p. 28; Henry P. Chiles oral history, p. 75, HSTL; *Kansas City Times*, April 21, 1945; Charles Ross, editor, *The Gleam* (Independence, Mo.: Independence High School class of 1901, 1901), pp. 1–2, 17–20.

45. Mrs. W. L. C. Palmer oral history, pp. 15–16, 32–33, HSTL.

46. *Kansas City Star*, June 12, 1955; Truman, *Memoirs*, pp. 121–22; Harry S. Truman, *Memoirs* draft, p. 2890; Miscellaneous Historical Document 86,

HSTL; McNaughton and Hehmeyer, *This Man Truman,* p. 19; Mary Ethel Noland oral history, pp. 108–09, HSTL; Henry P. Chiles oral history, p. 71, HSTL; Roy Roberts to Jonathan Daniels, October 20, 1949, Jonathan Daniels papers, University of North Carolina; Truman, "Two Years in the Army"; Harry S. Truman to Margaret Truman, June 23, 1941, box 10, FBP, HST papers, HSTL. Harry bought a present for his mother before offering the remainder of the first week's wages to his father. Harry's drugstore job has also been dated as 1895 or 1896 when he was eleven years old. Truman approved that dating as correct, and also confirmed the high-school date. Ethel Noland said it was a high-school job. Would Jim Clinton hire a fourth or fifth-grade boy, with high-school help available for surely the same price? Henry Chiles had an uncertain memory that Harry worked there in seventh grade and in high school.

47. Truman, *Memoirs,* p. 122; Harry S. Truman to Bess Wallace, February 10, 1913 and January 12, 1914, in Ferrell, *Dear Bess.*

48. Bundschu, "Harry S. Truman"; Mrs. W. L. C. Palmer oral history, p. 11, HSTL; Daniels, *Man of Independence,* p. 55; Steinberg, *Man from Missouri,* p. 27; Henry Bundschu to Harry S. Truman, April 21, 1945, box 1, Henry Bundschu papers, HSTL.

49. Harry S. Truman interview with William Hillman, December 10, 1951, "Mr. President" File, interviews folder, PSF box 269, HST papers, HSTL; Truman, *Memoirs,* pp. 115, 122; Harry S. Truman to Ethel Noland, January 2, 1952, Noland papers, HSTL; Mary Ethel Noland oral history, pp. 70–71, HSTL; Ross, *The Gleam,* pp. 1–2, 17–20.

50. Harry S. Truman, "Pickwick Papers," May 14, 1934 and "The Ideals"; Truman, *Memoirs,* pp. 115, 124–25.

51. Truman, "Early 1900's and Late 1890's"; Elizabeth Berry, "Harry Truman's Christmas," "Truman Family—General" folder, vertical file, HSTL; Edgar Hinde oral history, pp. 13, 111, HSTL; Jonathan Daniels oral history, pp. 43–44, HSTL; Harry S. Truman to Ethel Noland, January 2, 1952, Noland papers, HSTL. Harry Truman's many references to Bess and to their daughter Margaret are replete with "pedestal/protectiveness" comments.

52. Henry P. Chiles oral history, pp. 23–24, HSTL; Mary Ethel Noland oral history, pp. 72–73, HSTL; Mrs. W. L. C. Palmer oral history, pp. 24–25, HSTL; Truman, "The Ideals"; Mary Paxton Keeley oral history, pp. 34–35, HSTL. Steinberg (*Man from Missouri,* p. 28) reports an anecdote supposedly showing that Harry's Aunt Ella Noland knew that Harry was sweet on Bess. Reportedly Truman felt the Steinberg book was filled with inaccuracies, so the story must be viewed cautiously. Few persons, if any, shared Aunt Ella's supposed knowledge of Harry's feelings.

53. Truman, *Autobiography,* p. 22; Steinberg, *Man from Missouri,* p. 26; Leviero, "Harry Truman, Musician"; unattributed newspaper article, September 4, 1949, Harry S. Truman to Mrs. Don Scarbrough, late 1964,

"Truman, Harry S.—Music Interest," vertical file, HSTL; Daniels, *Man of Independence*, p. 56; Harry S. Truman to Mrs. Joseph Lhévinne, November 4, 1950, quoted in Hillman, *Mr. President*, p. 43; Harry S. Truman to Randolph Adams, November 17, 1944, "Harry S. Truman—Personal September–November 1944" folder, box 170, SV, HST papers, HSTL; Harry S. Truman to Thomas Sherman, December 11, 1944, "Harry S. Truman—Personal December 1944–January 1945" folder, box 170, SV, HST papers, HSTL.

54. Daniels, *Man of Independence*, pp. 58, 107; Steinberg, *Man from Missouri*, pp. 27, 29; *New Yorker*, May 9, 1959, p. 37; William M. Reddig, *Tom's Town* (Philadelphia: J. B. Lippincott, 1947), pp. 50–51, 272; Anon., *Political History of Jackson County Biographical Sketches of Men Who Have Made It* (Marshall & Morrison, 1902), pp. 55, 189–90; Harry S. Truman, *Years of Trial and Hope* (Garden City, N.Y.: Doubleday, 1956), p. 200; Harry S. Truman interview with Jonathan Daniels, November 12, 1949, p. 58, August 30, 1949, p. 4, MOI notes, Jonathan Daniels papers, HSTL; Harry S. Truman, July 12, 1960, personal notes folder, desk file, HST papers, HSTL; Gosnell, *Truman's Crises*, p. 21, citing Bela Kornitzer, *American Fathers and Sons*, chap. 1.

55. Clemens, "School Days of Harry S. Truman"; *Kansas City Times*, April 21, 1945; *Jackson Examiner*, May 31, 1901, pp. 6, 9; Mrs. W. L. C. Palmer oral history, pp. 8–10, 19–20, 56, HSTL; Independence High School graduation program, May 30, 1901, correspondence relating to Harry S. Truman—biographical, Biographical File, PSF, HST papers, HSTL; Harry S. Truman interview with William Hillman, October 4, 1951, "Mr. President" File, interviews folder, PSF box 269, HSTL; Truman, *Memoirs*, pp. 122–23; Truman, *Autobiography*, p. 12; Ross, *The Gleam;* Steinberg, *Man from Missouri*, p. 28; Margaret Truman, *Harry S. Truman*, p. 53; *New York Post*, December 29, 1972; Harry S. Truman, *Public Papers 1952*, pp. 203 and 330.

Chapter 3   CITY LIGHTS

1. Truman, *Memoirs*, p. 122; "Memories—early" folder, Memoirs File, Post-Presidential File, HST papers, HSTL; Daniels, *Man of Independence*, p. 56; Jonathan Daniels interview with Harry S. Truman, November 12, 1949, p. 57, MOI notes, Jonathan Daniels papers, HSTL; Bryant E. Moore to Gordon Gray, September 6, 1949, Jonathan Daniels papers, University of North Carolina; Steinberg, *Man from Missouri*, p. 29; McNaughton and Hehmeyer, *This Man Truman*, pp. 20–21. The McNaughton and Hehmeyer account says that Truman actually received a West Point appointment from Rep. William S. Cowherd, a powerful Kansas City politician who had succeeded Truman's relative Benjamin Holmes as Kansas City mayor. Daniels said no appointment was tendered. Truman approved the accuracy

of both accounts, but West Point records agree with Daniels. An appointment, however, would still mean that Truman had to pass the eye exam.

2. Truman, *Autobiography*, p. 21; Mary Jane Truman papers, box 1, folder 10, HSTL; advertisement in Hoye's *Kansas City Directory 1900*, "Truman, Harry S.—1900," vertical file, HSTL; Leviero, "Harry Truman, Musician"; Personal expense book of Harry S. Truman, Mary Jane Truman papers, HSTL. If Truman correctly stated that he attended Spalding into 1902, this must have been despite his father's 1901 financial disaster if (like many schools) autumn tuition included a few weeks of the next calendar year.

3. Truman, *Memoirs*, p. 123; Daniels, *Man of Independence*, pp. 58–59; Jonathan Daniels interview with Harry S. Truman, November 12, 1949, p. 58, MOI notes, Jonathan Daniels papers, HSTL; Davis, *Descendants of Jacob Young*, pp. 135–36.

4. Biographical sketch of Ralph E. Truman, Ralph E. Truman papers, HSTL; Ralph E. Truman to Ralph Truman, May 27, 1943, Family Correspondence File, Ralph Truman and family folder, Post-Presidential File, HST papers, HSTL; Harry S. Truman to Ralph Truman, February 3, 1923, Ralph E. Truman folder, Family Correspondence File, Post-Presidential File, HST papers, HSTL.

5. Daniels, *Man of Independence*, pp. 59, 70; Truman, "My Impressions," p. 17; Margaret Truman, *Harry S. Truman*, pp. 52, 54; Leviero, "Harry Truman, Musician"; Harry S. Truman interview with William Hillman, October 1, 1951, "Mr. President" File, interviews folder, box 269, PSF, HST papers, HSTL; Harry S. Truman interview with Jonathan Daniels, August 30, 1949, p. 4, MOI notes, Jonathan Daniels papers, HSTL; Harry S. Truman to Bess Wallace, May 23, 1911, in Ferrell, *Dear Bess*; Truman, "Two Years in the Army." Truman's stint as office boy for a grain company at the Board of Trade must have been during his father's heyday there (Harry S. Truman, September 30, 1947, *Public Papers 1947*, p. 449). In several accounts Truman said the piano lessons ended before he left high school. This is incorrect. One wonders if this adjustment in memory was another effort to forget the pain of his father's financial calamity. Truman's comment about his lack of education could easily be misinterpreted. Truman had more knowledge than many college graduates, and he realized it. The comment was the wistful exclamation of a man who ruled a nation, yet could feel how much more he might have been able to do.

6. Truman, *Memoirs*, pp. 123–24; Harry S. Truman, "Memories—early" folder, Memoirs File, Post-Presidential File, HST papers, HSTL; Steinberg, *Man from Missouri*, p. 30.

7. Truman, *Autobiography*, p. 18; Truman, *Memoirs*, p. 124; McNaughton and Hehmeyer, *This Man Truman*, p. 20; Harry S. Truman, "Memories—early" folder, Memoirs File, Post-Presidential File, HST papers, HSTL; Daniels, *Man of Independence*, p. 58; Truman, "Two Years in the Army";

Edward R. Schauffler, *Harry Truman Son of the Soil* (Kansas City: Schauffler Publishing Company, n.d.), p. 20.

8. Truman, *Autobiography*, pp. 17–18; Truman, *Memoirs*, p. 123; Truman, "Memories—early" folder, Memoirs File, Post-Presidential File, HST papers, HSTL; "Personal Data" memorandum, "Biography" folder, Box 17, Eben Ayers papers, HSTL; Steinberg, *Man from Missouri*, p. 30; Daniels, *Man of Independence*, pp. 57–58; Harry S. Truman interview with Jonathan Daniels, July 28, 1949, Jonathan Daniels interview with the Noland sisters, September 25, 1949, MOI notes, Jonathan Daniels papers, HSTL; Truman, "Two Years in the Army"; Truman, "My Impressions"; McNaughton and Hehmeyer, *This Man Truman*, pp. 21–22; Personal expense book of Harry S. Truman 1902–1904, Mary Jane Truman papers, HSTL; Harry S. Truman to Roy Roberts, June 17, 1950, "Roberts, Roy A." folder, PSF—personal, HST papers, HSTL; Truman, "Pickwick Papers"; Miscellaneous Historical Document 308, HSTL; Mary Ethel Noland oral history, pp. 91–92, HSTL; Roy Roberts to Jonathan Daniels, October 20, 1949, Jonathan Daniels papers, University of North Carolina. Although Truman's pride as an amateur historian approached arrogance, his autobiographical accounts can be treacherous. For example, Truman approved assorted contradictory descriptions of his railroad employment. The main problem is determining the dates of employment. In a 1905 job application Truman wrote that he did the railroad work from August 23, 1902 to February 1903. That dating was given so soon after the event that it is surely correct. In a 1903 job application Truman listed his railroad pay as $50 a month, but this surely includes the $15 value of his board plus the $35 salary. Since Truman said later that he netted about $100 from the entire railroad job after deductions for his errors in figuring the hobos' pay, that is the basis of figuring Truman's average weekly net. Truman also approved contradictory versions of whether his *Kansas City Star* employment preceded or followed the railroad experience. Truman's earlier accounts indicate that he worked at the *Star* first, and *Star* records verify that his employment there ended between August 15 and 22, 1902; so that is the chronology accepted here. All this effects the dating of the trip to John's forty acres in Oregon County. Truman remembers the trip as a springtime excursion. His high school and business college studies tend to make 1901 unlikely. That leaves 1902, which is the date Truman claimed, and also fits with his father's need to generate cash by selling the land—a need that sacrificed the Waldo Street house in early autumn 1902. One doubts that the family could have afforded John and Harry both to take time off in spring 1903, and one is disinclined to think Harry's notorious Bank of Commerce boss Charles H. Moore would have tolerated such a trip. Since no version indicates that the trip occurred after the bank job, the dating of spring 1902 is used here. Incidentally, in Truman's many sermonettes on world history he omitted dates.

9. Miscellaneous Historical Documents 151 and 308, HSTL; Abstract of title to North 100 feet of Lot 3, Woodland Place, in "Harry S. Truman—Homes," vertical file, HSTL; Truman, *Memoirs,* p. 124; "Documents relating to Harry S. Truman," folder 15, Mary Jane Truman papers, HSTL; Daniels, *Man of Independence,* p. 60; Mary Ethel Noland oral history, p. 93, HSTL; Hillman, *Mr. President,* p. 220; Thomas H. Madden to Jonathan Daniels, February 8, 1950, Jonathan Daniels papers, University of North Carolina.

10. Truman, *Memoirs,* pp. 124–125; Truman, *Autobiography,* pp. 18–20; Harry S. Truman, "Memories—early" folder, Memoirs File, Post-Presidential File, HST papers, HSTL; Daniels, *Man of Independence,* p. 67; Steinberg, *Man from Missouri,* pp. 30–31; McNaughton and Hehmeyer, *This Man Truman,* p. 22; Miscellaneous Historical Documents 308 and 309, HSTL; Bundschu, "Harry S. Truman," p. 8. None of Truman's contradictory claims about his Commerce salary agreed with the bank's records. His first supervisor at Commerce, Fred Grossbeck, was the only official who left any critical comments about Truman's performance.

11. Daniels, *Man of Independence,* pp. 59–60, 66–67; Miscellaneous Historical Document 408, HSTL; Mary Ethel Noland oral history, p. 99, HSTL; Truman, *Autobiography,* p. 18. Plutarch wrote, "They are wrong who think that politics is like an ocean voyage or a military campaign, something to be done with some end in view, something which levels off as soon as that end is reached. It is not a public chore, to be got over with; it is a way of life." Like Truman, Plutarch criticized physical excess (sex and drink), thirst for money, a showy lifestyle, and questing for titles and honors. Plutarch also admired men who became great military men first and politicians later. Did the avid reading of Plutarch influence Harry's ideals of personal conduct?

12. Ross, *The Gleam,* p. 28; Truman, *Years of Trial and Hope,* p. 201; Truman, November 6, 1951, *Public Papers 1951,* p. 621; *The New York Times,* May 2, 1903, p. 2. Some details of Truman's memory are contradicted by contemporary accounts in Kansas City newspapers.

13. Truman, *Memoirs,* p. 124; Truman, *Autobiography,* p. 18; *St. Clair County Democrat,* July 12, 1934; *Clinton Eye,* June 7, 1934; Charles G. Ross to Fred E. Ashcraft, September 29, 1950, PPF, HST papers, HSTL; Miscellaneous Historical Document 308, HSTL; Thomas M. Madden to Jonathan Daniels, February 8, 1950, Jonathan Daniels papers, University of North Carolina.

14. Miscellaneous Historical Document 308, HSTL.

15. Truman, *Autobiography,* pp. 22–23; Daniels, *Man of Independence,* p. 69; Hillman, *Mr. President,* p. 231; Harry S. Truman to Mr. Ross, September 14, 1949, "Correspondence relating to Harry S. Truman—biographical," Biographical File, PSF, HST papers, HSTL; Harry S. Truman to Roy A. Roberts, June 12, 1950, "Roberts, Roy A." folder, PSF—personal, HST

papers, HSTL; Mary Ethel Noland oral history, pp. 99–100, HSTL; Margaret Truman, *Harry S. Truman*, p. 151. Cousin Ethel Noland said Harry ushered at the Shubert.

16. Mary Ethel Noland oral history, pp. 94–96, HSTL; Schauffler, *Harry Truman*, pp. 21–22, 25–30. Did Harry get a certain satisfaction from seeing other young men in a hopeless romantic situation? He tried a similar prank on his sister (Harry S. Truman to Bess Wallace, December 14, 1911, in Ferrell, *Dear Bess*). The Noland and Schauffler accounts are authoritative and contradictory, with Schauffler portraying the prank's victims as receiving a well-earned comeuppance.

17. Mary Ethel Noland oral history, p. 97, HSTL; Truman, *Memoirs*, p. 124; Truman, *Autobiography*, p. 18; Daniels, *Man of Independence*, pp. 69–70; Harry S. Truman to Margaret Truman, May 13, 1944, quoted in Margaret Truman, *Letters from Father*, pp. 51–52; John McCallum, *Six Roads from Abilene* (Seattle: Wood & Reber, 1960), p. 36; J. T. C. to Harry S. Truman Library director, June 14, 1971, in "Harry S. Truman—Homes" folder, vertical file, HSTL.

18. Daniels, *Man of Independence*, p. 70; Mary Ethel Noland oral history, pp. 98, 102, HSTL; Truman, "Two Years in the Army." In the "Pickwick Papers" of May 14, 1934 Harry seems to confirm Ethel Noland's belief that he and Bess had no contact for years after high school: "Soon after we moved back to the farm I began going to call on my school girl sweetheart." That move was in 1906, but Truman probably began calling in 1910.

19. Miscellaneous Historical Document 308, HSTL; Truman, *Autobiography*, pp. 18–20; Truman, *Memoirs*, p. 124; Harry S. Truman, "Memories—early" folder, Memoirs File, Post-Presidential File, HST papers, HSTL; Daniels, *Man of Independence*, p. 69; Truman, "My Impressions." Truman claimed that his departing salary at Union National was $125 a month (Harry S. Truman interview with Jonathan Daniels, November 12, 1949, p. 59, MOI notes, Jonathan Daniels papers, HSTL).

20. Truman, *Autobiography*, p. 27; Truman, *Memoirs*, p. 125; Harry S. Truman, *Memoirs* draft, p. 2898; George R. Collins to Harry S. Truman, July 25, 1935, May 27, 1936, February 1, 1940, Miscellaneous Historical Document 403, HSTL; Truman, "Two Years in the Army."

21. *Kansas City Star*, June 15, 1905, p. 6; *Kansas City Journal*, June 15, 1905; Truman, "My Impressions"; Truman, "Pickwick Papers," December 3, 1930, May 14, 1934; Harry S. Truman, "Memories—early" folder, Memoirs File, Post-Presidential File, HST papers, HSTL; George Collins to *Kansas City Star*, September 28, 1939, Miscellaneous Historical Document 403, HSTL; records from the office of the adjutant general, state of Missouri, pertaining to Harry S. Truman, HSTL; Truman, "Two Years in the Army."

22. Truman, *Autobiography*, p. 28.

23. Ibid., pp. 28–30; Truman, "Pickwick Papers," May 14, 1934; Harry

S. Truman to Mrs. M. M. Hood, May 24, 1961, Correspondence—biographical, Biographical File, Post-Presidential File, HST papers, HSTL; Miscellaneous Historical Documents 114 and 115, HSTL; Davis, *Descendants of Jacob Young,* pp. 127, 134–35; Harry S. Truman, notes on manuscript, reproduced in Kornitzer, "The Story of Truman"; December 21, 1945 clipping and Berger, *Kansas City Star* in "Truman, Martha Ellen Young" folder, vertical file, HSTL; U.S. House of Representatives document 901, 59 Cong., 1 Sess., "Findings in Harriet L. Young, administratrix of Solomon Young, deceased, against the United States"; Margaret Truman, *Harry S. Truman,* pp. 49–50. Harry Truman claimed that Jim Lane burned the Young house, but this didn't happen (Harry S. Truman to John Barker, November 13, 1947, folder 2, John Barker papers, Western Historical Manuscripts Collection, University of Missouri). Thus family accounts of Yankee depredations may be exaggerated.

24. Truman, *Autobiography,* p. 27; Truman, "My Impressions"; Truman, *Memoirs,* p. 124; Daniels, *Man of Independence,* p. 72; McNaughton and Hehmeyer, *This Man Truman,* p. 23; Charles G. Ross to Fred Ashcraft, September 29, 1950, PPF, HST papers, HSTL; Harry S. Truman, "Masonic Lodge" folder, Memoirs File, Post-Presidential File, HST papers, HSTL.

25. Truman, *Autobiography,* p. 27; Daniels, *Man of Independence,* pp. 72–73; Truman, "My Impressions"; Truman, *Memoirs,* p. 125; Harry S. Truman, *Memoirs* draft, p. 2898; Harry S. Truman to John Gage, April 2, 1943, "John B. Gage" folder, box 60, SV, HST papers, HSTL; Harry S. Truman to Bess Truman, February 1, 1937, box 6, FBP, HST papers, HSTL.

26. Harry S. Truman interview with William Hillman, October 16, 1951, "Mr. President" File, interviews folder, box 269, PSF, HSTL; Truman, *Autobiography,* p. 27; McNaughton and Hehmeyer, *This Man Truman,* p. 23; Truman, "My Impressions"; Daniels, *Man of Independence,* p. 71.

Chapter 4 ANGLES OF ASCENT

1. Gaylon Babcock oral history, pp. 21, 45, 51–52, HSTL; Regna Vanatta oral history, p. 10, HSTL.

2. Richard S. Kirkendall, "Harry S. Truman A Missouri Farmer in the Golden Age," *Agricultural History,* October 1974, pp. 470, 473, 476; Folders 7, 9, and 10, box 1, Mary Jane Truman papers, HSTL; Gaylon Babcock oral history, p. 52, HSTL; Mrs. Francis Montgomery oral history, pp. 9–10, HSTL. Truman scholars are indebted to Kirkendall's work. "Home Phone" was a company competing with Bell, and telephones on one system couldn't be reached from the other. Thus persons had to give their phone number and the company in order to receive calls.

3. Folders 8 and 9, box 1, Mary Jane Truman papers, HSTL; Bill Renshaw article in *The Prairie Farmer,* May 12, 1945; Samuel R. Guard, "From

Plowboy to President," *Breeder's Gazette,* June 1945; John W. Meador oral history, p. 36, HSTL; Mrs. Francis Montgomery oral history, pp. 9–10, HSTL; Robert B. Wyatt oral history, p. 5, HSTL; McNaughton and Hehmeyer, *This Man Truman,* p. 32.

4. Harry S. Truman interview with William Hillman, October 16, 1951, interviews folder, "Mr. President" File, box 269, PSF, HST papers, HSTL; Renshaw, *The Prairie Farmer;* McNaughton and Hehmeyer, *This Man Truman,* pp. 29–30, 33; Harry S. Truman to Nellie Noland, September 26, 1952, Mary Ethel Noland papers, HSTL; Harry S. Truman to Captain, May 12, 1911, Miscellaneous Historical Document 403, HSTL; Truman, "My Impressions"; Miscellaneous lists folder, Memoirs File, Post-Presidential File, HST papers, HSTL; Harry S. Truman to Bess Wallace, April 24, May 9, May 23, June 22, and September 5, 1911, in Ferrell, *Dear Bess;* Gaylon Babcock oral history, p. 43, HSTL. Truman farm neighbor Gaylon Babcock felt Harry's veterinary prowess was overrated and perhaps nonexistent (Gaylon Babcock oral history, pp. 43–48, HSTL). Truman's care to vaccinate animals as insurance against disaster was also reflected in his membership in Missouri Farmers Mutual Crop Insurance Co., protecting against $6,000 in losses by "destructive hail, wind or rain storms."

5. Folder 7, box 1, Mary Jane Truman papers, HSTL; Renshaw, *The Prairie Farmer;* Roderick Turnbull, June 1945 magazine article, Biographical File—correspondence folder, PPF, HST papers, HSTL; Truman, *Autobiography,* pp. 31–32; Robert B. Wyatt oral history, p. 16, HSTL; Joseph R. Stewart to Harry S. Truman, March 20, 1961, Correspondence—biographical, Biographical File, Post-Presidential File, HST papers, HSTL; Harry S. Truman to Carol Taylor, printed in *New York World-Telegram & Sun,* July 24, 1959(?), newspaper clipping folder, Desk File, Post-Presidential File, HST papers, HSTL.

6. Renshaw, *The Prairie Farmer;* Truman, *Autobiography,* pp. 30–31; Margaret Truman, *Harry S. Truman,* p. 23; Gaylon Babcock oral history, pp. 49–50, HSTL.

7. Renshaw, *The Prairie Farmer;* Truman, "My First 80 Years."

8. John J. Strode oral history, pp. 24–30, HSTL; Renshaw, *The Prairie Farmer;* Robert B. Wyatt oral history, pp. 13–15, HSTL; B. F. Ervin, Sr., "He was a Good Man with a Pitchfork, Too," *Kansas City Times,* July 10, 1963; Esther Grube oral history, p. 25, HSTL; Gaylon Babcock oral history, pp. 7, 56–57. Another Grandview area resident said it was the other way around—other men had to help Truman keep up with the threshing machine (John Meador oral history, p. 35, HSTL).

9. Guard, "From Plowboy to President"; still photographs 72–3569, 72–3585, 77–3970-A, HSTL; Pansy Perkins oral history, p. 34, HSTL; Gaylon Babcock oral history, pp. 20–21, 48–49, HSTL; Ervin, *Kansas City Times,* July 10, 1963; Harry S. Truman interview with Jonathan Daniels, November 12, 1949, p. 59, MOI notes, Jonathan Daniels papers, HSTL.

10. Guard, "From Plowboy to President"; Esther Grube oral history, p. 34, HSTL; Pansy Perkins oral history, p. 5, HSTL.

11. Kirkendall, "A Missouri Farmer," p. 477; Daniels, *Man of Independence*, p. 78; Mize Peters oral history, p. 4, HSTL; Guard, "From Plowboy to President"; Turnbull June 1945 article in Biographical File—Correspondence folder, Post-Presidential File, HST papers, HSTL; Harry S. Truman interview with Jonathan Daniels, July 28, 1949, p. 2, MOI notes, Jonathan Daniels papers, HSTL; J. M. Slaughter to Jonathan Daniels, October 27, 1949, Jonathan Daniels papers, University of North Carolina; Harry S. Truman to Bess Wallace, March 12, March 18, and March 23, 1912, November 4, November 19, 1913, January 12, January 20, January 26, and April 1914 (second letter that date), in Ferrell, *Dear Bess*; Benefit Certificate, Modern Woodmen of America, and Benefit Certificate, Royal Neighbors of America, "Membership applications & Cards" folder, box 14, FBP, HST papers, HSTL.

12. Gosnell, *Truman's Crises*, p. 24, citing Kornitzer, *American Fathers and Sons*, p. 20; Harry S. Truman interview with William Hillman, January 2, 1952, interviews folder, "Mr. President" File, box 269, PSF, HST papers, HSTL; Truman, *Autobiography*, p. 36; Truman, "My Impressions"; Truman, *Saturday Evening Post*, June 13, 1964; Miscellaneous Historical Documents 49, 78, and 160, HSTL; *U.S. Civil Service Commission Letter*, July 1949; 4/24/52 draft of *National Cyclopedia of American Biography* article, Biographical File, PSF, HST papers, HSTL; Daniels, *Man of Independence*, p. 78; Steinberg, *Man from Missouri*, p. 34; Gaylon Babcock oral history, p. 35, HSTL; Jesse Donaldson to Jonathan Daniels, October 11, 1949, Jonathan Daniels papers, University of North Carolina; Harry S. Truman to Bess Wallace, February 13 and August 6, 1912, January 6 and February 4, 1913, August 18, August 31, and September 8, 1914, 1915 (p. 181), July 25 and August 4, 1916, in Ferrell, *Dear Bess;* Kornitzer, "The Story of Truman."

13. Harry S. Truman interview with William Hillman, January 2, 1952, interview folder, "Mr. President" File, box 269, PSF, HST papers, HSTL; Truman, "My Impressions"; Truman, *Autobiography*, pp. 34–36; Robert B. Wyatt oral history, pp. 6–9, HSTL; *Independence Examiner*, November 3, 1914, p. 1; Wilcox, *Jackson County Pioneers*, p. 473; Harry S. Truman interview with Jonathan Daniels, November 12, 1949, p. 59, MOI notes, Jonathan Daniels papers, HSTL; Gaylon Babcock oral history, pp. 39–40, 58, HSTL; Jackson County Court orders, February 21, 1913 and February 26, 1914, Jackson County Clerk's office; Harry S. Truman to Bess Wallace, March 23 and August 6, 1912, February 4, May 26, and July 14, 1913, postmark illegible (p. 132), January 20, January 26, and August 18, 1914, in Ferrell, *Dear Bess.*

14. Mize Peters oral history, pp. 4, 17, HSTL; Gosnell, *Truman's Crises*, p. 25; Truman, *Autobiography*, pp. 34–36; Harry S. Truman to Allen C. Southern, August 3, 1915, folder 10, and folders 12, 13, and 14, box 1,

Mary Jane Truman papers, HSTL; *Independence Examiner*, April 19, 1929; Truman, "My Impressions"; Reddig, *Tom's Town*, pp. 104–05; Lyle W. Dorsett, *The Pendergast Machine* (New York: Oxford University Press, 1968), pp. 55–57, 63–64; Jackson County Court orders, February 13, 1915 and February 8, 1916, Jackson County Clerk's office; "Jackson County—Longhand notes by Harry S. Truman regarding road work 1915" folder, box 13, FBP, HST papers, HSTL.

15. Steinberg, *Man from Missouri*, pp. 34–35; Heed, "Prelude to Whistlestop," p. 7; Anon., *The History of Jackson County, Missouri . . .* (Kansas City: Union Historical Company, 1881 [reprint: Cape Girardeau, Mo.: Ramfre Press, 1966]), p. 986; school board minutes, "Truman—Harry S., School Board," vertical file, HSTL; Mike Davis, "Truman Was a School Board Member First," *Raytown News*, February 1, 1973. The Davis article says that Truman served on the school board until May 1918, but the context of the statement suggests the date should be May 1917. The Tom Evans oral history (HSTL) contains valuable memories of life in the Mike Pendergast club.

16. Gaylon Babcock oral history, p. 15, HSTL; Truman, *Autobiography*, p. 32; Truman, *Memoirs*, pp. 125–26; "Masonic Lodge" folder, Memoirs File, Post-Presidential File, HST papers, HSTL; "Masonic Biography" folder, Biographical File, PSF, HST papers, HSTL; Harry S. Truman's petition for initiation into Belton Lodge No. 450, Miscellaneous Historical Document 234, HSTL; Harry S. Truman petition for initiation into AAONMS, Miscellaneous Historical Document 241, HSTL; Esther Grube oral history, pp. 6–8, HSTL; Regna Vanatta oral history, pp. 5–6, 25, HSTL; *The Royal Arch Mason*, spring 1973 and spring 1975; "Harry S. Truman—Masonic Information," vertical file, HSTL; *Modern Woodmen*, July 1945, p. 7; Harry S. Truman to Bess Wallace, March 10, 1918, in Ferrell, *Dear Bess*.

17. Joseph Fort Newton, *The Builders* (New York: Macoy Publishing and Masonic Supply Co., 1930), p. 238 quoting C. R. Kennedy, *The Servant in The House*.

18. Ibid., pp. 69–70, 243–44; Truman, February 21, 1952, *Public Papers 1952*, p. 169.

19. Newton, *The Builders*, pp. 229, 229n, 241.

20. Daniels, *Man of Independence*, p. 69; Truman, *Autobiography*, pp. 33–34; *Liberty Advance*, April 16, 1945; Pauline Sims oral history, p. 9, HSTL; Harry S. Truman to Bess Wallace, February 7, 1911, in Ferrell, *Dear Bess*, p. 22.

21. Truman, "Pickwick Papers"; Harry S. Truman, September 26, 1952, *Public Papers 1952–1953*, p. 591; Harry S. Truman, October 30, 1953, quoted in *Royal Arch Mason*, spring 1975, p. 268.

22. August 13, 1959 interview in publications folder, Desk File, Post-

Presidential File, HST papers, HSTL; Truman, September 28, 1951, *Public Papers 1951*, pp. 548–50; Harry S. Truman to Noyes in Truman interview with William Hillman, January 9, 1952, interviews folder, "Mr. President" File, box 269, PSF, HST papers, HSTL; Harry S. Truman to Bess Wallace, February 18, 1913, in Ferrell, *Dear Bess*; Harry S. Truman to Margaret Truman, October 9, 1939, box 10, FBP, HST papers, HSTL.

23. Harry S. Truman, March 6, 1946, *Public Papers 1946*, pp. 143–44; Truman, September 28, 1951, *Public Papers 1951*, pp. 548–50.

24. Folder 10, box 1, Mary Jane Truman papers, HSTL; Harry S. Truman interview with Jonathan Daniels, November 12, 1949, p. 59, MOI notes, Jonathan Daniels papers, HSTL; Daniels, *Man of Independence*, pp. 74–75; Gaylon Babcock oral history, pp. 30–31, 49–50, HSTL; Truman, "My Impressions," HSTL; Renshaw, *The Prairie Farmer;* Truman, "Pickwick Papers"; Tom L. Broad to Richard L. Miller, February 7, 1983, author's files; Harry S. Truman to Bess Wallace, August 31, September 8, September 17, September 28, and November 1914 (second letter), in Ferrell, *Dear Bess; Independence Examiner*, November 3, 1914, November 3, 1924, p. 2. Truman said he had been awake a long time the night his father died. He dozed off, and awoke to find a corpse where his father had been. This is consistent with Huber's account, as the kitchen scene was probably predawn, and Truman could have fallen asleep in the next room while Huber ate. Huber's version is as reliable as Truman's. After all, in the "Pickwick Papers" account Truman said his father died in 1915, and in "My Impressions" he said his father died November 9, 1916. The actual date was November 2, 1914. Earlier that year Truman witnessed his mother's emergency hernia operation at the farm home, holding a lamp to provide light for the surgeons. He found the experience unnerving (Harry S. Truman to Bess Wallace, March 20, 1914, in Ferrell, *Dear Bess*).

25. *Independence Examiner*, November 3, 1914, p. 1; Harry S. Truman interview with William Hillman, December 14, 1951, interviews folder, "Mr. President" File, box 269, PSF, HST papers, HSTL. The *Examiner* obituary said that John Anderson Truman formerly had a grocery business in Independence. This confusion was probably caused by his business partnerships with Oscar Mindrup and J. W. Mercer, who each dealt in groceries. Ethel Noland remembered Bess accompanying her to John Truman's funeral at the Grandview farm home (Mary Ethel Noland oral history, pp. 84–85, HSTL). Harry's letter afterward to Bess suggests otherwise, but doesn't rule out attendance by Bess (Harry S. Truman to Bess Wallace, November 1914, in Ferrell, *Dear Bess*). Bess did send flowers to John in the hospital, and Harry spoke movingly of how his father pointed them out to visitors and refused to let the nurse remove wilted ones.

26. Mary Ethel Noland oral history, pp. 84–85, 98, 102–03, HSTL; Truman, "Pickwick Papers"; Henry Chiles oral history, p. 23. The cake

plate incident occurred no earlier than 1906 and no later than 1910. The start of Harry's early correspondence with Bess would imply that it happened around Thanksgiving in 1910.

27. "Wallace Family General" folder, vertical file, HSTL (including *York Rite Masonic News,* spring 1973); Miscellaneous Historical Document 42, HSTL; Mrs. W. L. C. Palmer oral history, pp. 53–54, HSTL; Mary Paxton Keeley oral history, pp. 40–41, HSTL; Sue Gentry oral history, p. 24 (Forsling article), HSTL; Robbins, *Bess and Harry,* pp. 17, 21–22, 24; William M. Southern, Jr., interview with Jonathan Daniels, September 26, 1949, p. 21, MOI notes, Jonathan Daniels papers, HSTL; Underhill, *Truman Persuasions,* pp. 38–39; Dave Wallace obituary clipping, vertical file, HSTL; telephone conversation between May Wallace and Richard Lawrence Miller, August 29, 1983, author's files.

28. *Kansas City Star,* May 17, 1959, p. 1G; *Kansas City Times,* November 22, 1975; Margaret Cousins, "Valentine for Bess Truman," *McCall's,* February 1975, p. 91.

29. "Ten Years Ago Today" column, *Independence Examiner,* April 23, 1913; *Jackson Examiner,* August 10, 1906; Jonathan Daniels interview with Harry S. Truman, November 12, 1949, p. 55, MOI notes, Jonathan Daniels papers, HSTL.

30. Reddig, *Tom's Town,* pp. 64–66, 102–103; Garwood, *Crossroads of America,* pp. 207ff; George Collins to Harry S. Truman, February 1, 1940, Miscellaneous Historical Document 403, HSTL; Jonathan Daniels interview with Harry S. Truman, November 12, 1949, p. 55, MOI notes, Jonathan Daniels papers, HSTL; Underhill, *Truman Persuasions,* pp. 39–41.

31. Robbins, *Bess and Harry,* pp. 24, 28–29, 32–34; Mary Ethel Noland oral history, pp. 103–04, HSTL; Vivian Truman interview with Jonathan Daniels, September 23, 1949, p. 15, MOI notes, Jonathan Daniels papers, HSTL; Mrs. W. L. C. Palmer oral history, p. 29, HSTL; Harry S. Truman, "I have had two wonderful associates" essay, "Pickwick Papers," (Memoirs File copy); Lillian Rogers Parks, *My Thirty Years Backstairs at the White House* (New York: Fleet Publishing Corporation, 1961), p. 293; Margaret Truman, *Letters from Father,* p. 220; Harry Vaughan interview with Harold F. Gosnell, July 7, 1966, background interviews folder, box 11, Harold F. Gosnell papers, HSTL; Mary Paxton Keeley oral history, p. 44, HSTL.

32. Mary Ethel Noland oral history, pp. 86, 104, HSTL; Ardis R. Haukenberry to Richard L. Miller, May 26, 1982, author's files; Miscellaneous Historical Document 189, HSTL; Renshaw, *The Prairie Farmer;* John J. Strode oral history, pp. 44–45, HSTL; Esther Grube oral history, pp. 6–8, HSTL; Daniels, *Man of Independence,* p. 77; Jonathan Daniels interview with the Trumans of Grandview, September 24, 1949, p. 16, Harry S. Truman interview with Jonathan Daniels, November 12, 1949, p. 59, MOI notes, Jonathan Daniels papers, HSTL; Margaret Truman, *Harry S. Truman,* p. 151; Harry S. Truman to Bess Wallace, February 16, May 9, November

1, and November 22, 1911, May 20, July 30, and September 17, 1912, February 4, May 12, and July 7, 1913, January 26, March 24, April (both letters), April 7, July (both letters), September 28, and November 1914 (first letter), January 26, 1915 and 1915 (p. 181), undated (p. 183), November 10, 1918, in Ferrell, *Dear Bess.*

33. Harry S. Truman to Bess Wallace, January 26 and October 27, 1911, January 30 and September 9, 1912, in Ferrell, *Dear Bess;* Harry S. Truman to Bess Truman, April 15, 1933, box 5, FBP, HST papers, HSTL.

34. Daniels, *Man of Independence,* p. 104.

35. Margaret Truman, *Harry S. Truman,* p. 61; Harry S. Truman to Bess Wallace, January 25, 1912, April 28, 1915, February 16, 1916, in Ferrell, *Dear Bess.*

36. Harry S. Truman to Bess Wallace, June 22, July 10, and July 12, 1911, in Ferrell, *Dear Bess;* Harry S. Truman to Bess Wallace, July 1, 1911, box 1, FBP, HST papers, HSTL.

37. Harry S. Truman to Bess Wallace, August 14, August 27, September 5, and December 14, 1911, January 12, 1912, November 4, 1913, in Ferrell, *Dear Bess.*

38. Gaylon Babcock oral history, pp. 36, 38, HSTL; Davis, *Descendants of Jacob Young,* pp. 127–29, 132–34, 147; John Meador oral history, pp. 14, 30–31, 33–34, HSTL; Daniels, *Man of Independence,* pp. 77, 79–80; National Register of Historic Places Inventory—Nomination Form, "Grandview" folder, vertical file, HSTL; Mary Jane Truman to Doris Faber, Mary Jane Truman folder 2, Family Correspondence File, Post-Presidential File, HST papers, HSTL; Harry S. Truman interview with Jonathan Daniels, November 12, 1949, p. 58, MOI notes, Jonathan Daniels papers, HSTL. Harriet Louisa Young had so lost touch with her family that her will misspelled Ada's name as Van Cluster.

39. Harry S. Truman, October 30, 1953, quoted in *Royal Arch Mason,* spring 1975, p. 268; Daniels, *Man of Independence,* pp. 77, 79–80, 86; Harry S. Truman interviews with Jonathan Daniels, July 28, 1949, p. 2 and November 12, 1949, p. 58, Vivian Truman interview with Jonathan Daniels, September 23, 1949, p. 15, MOI notes, Jonathan Daniels papers, HSTL; Gaylon Babcock oral history, p. 68, HSTL; "Memories—early" folder, Memoirs File, Post-Presidential File, HST papers, HSTL; Truman, *Autobiography,* p. 55; Harry S. Truman to Bess Wallace, November 28 and December 21, 1911, January 3, February 27, and May 12, 1912, February 4, March 10, March 12, March 26, April 7, November 4, and November 10, 1913, February 3, February 24, March 24, May 12, undated (p. 169), and September 17, 1914, April 28, 1915, and undated (p. 186), in Ferrell, *Dear Bess.* The assertion about Frank Blair is based on Truman's statement that Blair "believed that my father and I were good risks for loans." Since John Truman was dead when Blair helped refinance the mortgage in 1917, this suggests that Blair was involved with the initial mortgage. Harry Tru-

man maintained a checking account at Bank of Belton, and the Trumans also had a checking account at O. V. Slaughter's Farmers Bank of Grandview (enclosures with Mary Jane Truman to Harry S. Truman, March 23, 1962, Mary Jane Truman folder 2, Family Correspondence Files, Post-Presidential File, HST papers, HSTL; Pansy Perkins oral history, p. 16, HSTL; Allen Glenn, *History of Cass County Missouri* [Topeka: Historical Publishing Co., 1917], p. 314). The Trumans also borrowed and diligently repaid sums from neighbor farmer C. W. Babcock (Gaylon Babcock oral history, pp. 3, 59, HSTL).

40. Harry S. Truman to Nellie Noland, October 19, 1911 and September 1913, Mary Ethel Noland papers, HSTL; Gaylon Babcock oral history, pp. 22–24, HSTL; Harry S. Truman to Bess Wallace, June 22, October 7, October 16, October 22, and October 27, 1911, undated (p. 133), September 17, September 30, and November 18, 1913, May 4, May 12, and September 8, 1914, in Ferrell, *Dear Bess*. Harry Truman actually drew a Montana claim in 1913 but didn't follow through with a homestead. He, too, was skeptical of the climate. If he had a notion about selling the Montana land, apparently nothing came of it.

41. *Gallager* v. *Chilton et al.* (192 SW 409); *Chilton* v. *Cady* (298 Mo. 101); *Truman* v. *Chilton et al.* (197 SW 346); John K. Hulston, *An Ozarks Lawyer's Story 1946–1976* (published by the author, 1976), pp. 464–67; John K. Hulston to Richard L. Miller, March 17, 1982 and January 4, 1983, Lucille Orchard to Richard L. Miller, January 1982, D. A. Divilbiss to Richard L. Miller, December 30, 1981, all in author's files. Harry S. Truman to Bess Wallace, January 3, 1912, February 17, 1914, in Ferrell, *Dear Bess*, may refer to this litigation.

42. Harry S. Truman, *Memoirs* draft p. 2902, HSTL; Harry S. Truman to Bess Wallace, March 4, 1912, may describe this trip. Yet Harry S. Truman to Bess Wallace, January 6, 1913, might conflict with such a hypothesis. (Both letters in Ferrell, *Dear Bess*.)

43. *Harriet L. Young, administratrix de bonis non of Solomon Young* v. *The United States*, U.S. Court of Claims, Congressional 7843 (U.S. House of Representatives Document 901, 59 Cong., 1 Sess.); Frank T. Peartree to Richard Lawrence Miller, September 27, 1982, Harold D. Williams to Richard Lawrence Miller, November 18, 1982, author's files; U.S. Senate Report 770, p. 24, 106, 62 Cong., 2 Sess.; *Congressional Record*, 63 Cong., 3 Sess., pp. 5287–89, 5294, 5515, 5521, 5523; Davis, *Descendants of Jacob Young*, pp. 127, 145–46. Efforts to locate U.S. Court of Claims and U.S. District Court for Western Missouri files for this case have been unsuccessful. The account in Davis, *Descendants of Jacob Young* (written by Solomon Young's great great granddaughter Betty Strong House), says that Martha Ellen Truman sued the United States in 1915 for $20,000 of gold stolen from Solomon Young by Union troops, and got a decision for $3,800. These amounts are so similar to the Court of Claims case as to suggest a connection—possibly

Martha Ellen Truman had to sue for the $3,800 to be delivered at last, or possibly the family's account confuses her with Louisa Young in this litigation.

44. Harry S. Truman to Ethel Noland, September 13, 1950, Mary Ethel Noland papers, HSTL; Mary Ethel Noland oral history, p. 90, HSTL; Davis, *Descendants of Jacob Young*, p. 134; Harry S. Truman interview with William Hillman, December 10, 1951, interviews folder, "Mr. President" File, box 269, PSF, HST papers, HSTL; various postcards of Harry S. Truman to Ethel Noland and Nellie Noland, February 1916, Mary Ethel Noland papers, HSTL; Harry S. Truman to Bess Wallace, February 17, February 20, and February 24, 1914, in Ferrell, *Dear Bess*.

45. Harry S. Truman, *Saturday Evening Post*, June 13, 1964; Truman, "My Impressions"; Renshaw, *The Prairie Farmer;* Mary Jane Truman to Doris Faber, Mary Jane Truman folder 2, Family Correspondence File, Post-Presidential File, HST papers, HSTL; Harry S. Truman, September 23, 1948, *Public Papers 1948*, p. 550 and May 24, 1950, *Public Papers 1950*, p. 438; Harry S. Truman to Bess Wallace, September 17, 1914 and undated (p. 186), in Ferrell, *Dear Bess;* Harry S. Truman to Edward McKim, June 10, 1942, "Edward McKim" folder, box 81, SV, HST papers, HSTL.

46. Truman, "My Impressions."

47. Margaret Truman, *Harry S. Truman*, p. 61.

Chapter 5   A PURITAN IN BABYLON

1. Harry S. Truman to Bess Wallace, February 19, 1916, in Ferrell, *Dear Bess*.

2. Harry S. Truman to Bess Wallace, April 7, 1913, May 12, 1914, April 28, 1915, undated (p. 186), in Ferrell, *Dear Bess*.

3. Harry S. Truman to Bess Wallace, November 4, 1915, undated (p. 183), February 4, February 16, 1916, undated (p. 185), and February 19, 1916, in Ferrell, *Dear Bess*.

4. Harry S. Truman to Bess Wallace, February 16, 1916, in Ferrell, *Dear Bess;* Harry S. Truman interview with William Hillman, December 14, 1951, interviews folder, "Mr. President" File, box 269, PSF, HST papers, HSTL; folder 12, Mary Jane Truman papers, HSTL; Truman, *Memoirs* draft, p. 2901; Truman, "My Impressions"; Truman, *Autobiography*, pp. 36–37; Heed, "Prelude to Whistlestop," p. 26; Steinberg, *Man from Missouri*, pp. 38–39; Daniels, *Man of Independence*, p. 81; Harry S. Truman notes inscribed on a letter of Theodore C. Box to Harry S. Truman, October 13, 1960, Correspondence—Biographical, Biographical File, Post-Presidential File, HST papers, HSTL; Harry S. Truman interview with Jonathan Daniels, July 28, 1949, p. 2, MOI notes, Jonathan Daniels papers, HSTL; Truman, *Memoirs*, p. 126; David H. Morgan to Jonathan Daniels, November

25, 1949, Jonathan Daniels papers, University of North Carolina; Katherine Baxter, *Notable Kansas Citians of 1915–1916–1917–1918* (Kansas City: Kellogg-Baxter Printing Co., 1925), pp. 213–15; Arthur Alkire, *Men of Affairs in Greater Kansas City* (Kansas City: Kansas City Press Club, 1912), p. 104.

5. Harry S. Truman to Bess Wallace, February 19 and March 5, 1916, May 27, 1917, in Ferrell, *Dear Bess;* Articles of Agreement, April 14, 1916, "Mining Company" folder, box 15, FBP, HST papers, HSTL; Truman, *Memoirs* draft, p. 2901.

6. Harry S. Truman to Bess Wallace, March 15, 1916, in Ferrell, *Dear Bess;* Articles of Agreement, April 14, 1916, stock certificates, and Articles of Incorporation of T-C-H Mining Company, J. A. Clark to Harry S. Truman, September 14, 1916, C. A. Gish to Harry S. Truman, September 22, 1916, "Mining Company" folder, box 15, FBP, HST papers, HSTL; List of names on T-C-H Mining Co. stationery, "Mining Company—Truman, Culbertson, Hughes—Time and Payroll Book—1916" folder, box 15, FBP, HST papers, HSTL.

7. Harry S. Truman to Bess Wallace, March 18, undated (p. 192), undated (p. 193), and March 1916, in Ferrell, *Dear Bess.*

8. "Mining Company—Truman, Culbertson, Hughes—Time and Payroll Book—1916" folder, box 15, FBP, HST papers, HSTL; Harry S. Truman to Bess Wallace, undated (p. 192), March, April 2, April 9, April 16, April 24, April 27, May 23, June 10, and July 25, 1916, in Ferrell, *Dear Bess;* Articles of Incorporation of T-C-H Mining Company, "Mining Company" folder, box 15, FBP, HST papers, HSTL.

9. Harry S. Truman to Bess Wallace, March 23, April 2, April 24, April 27, June 3, June 10, June 29, July 13, July 25, August 5, August 26, August 29, and September 7, 1916, in Ferrell, *Dear Bess.*

10. Harry S. Truman to Bess Wallace, May 19, 1916, in Ferrell, *Dear Bess;* "Mining Company—Truman, Culbertson, Hughes—Time and Payroll Book—1916" folder, box 15, FBP, HST papers, HSTL.

11. Harry S. Truman to Bess Wallace, April 16, May 23, May 26, June 3, June 10, June 24, August 19, and August 26, 1916, in Ferrell, *Dear Bess.*

12. Harry S. Truman to Bess Wallace, July 16, July 28, July 30, August 4, August 5, August 19, August 29, and September 7, 1916, in Ferrell, *Dear Bess;* "Mining Company—Truman, Culbertson, Hughes—Time and Payroll Book—1916" folder, box 15, FBP, HST papers, HSTL; Murdock Hardware Co. to T-C-H Mining Co., September 30, 1916, Consumers Gas Co. to T-C-H Mining Co., October 1, 1916, Manager of Atlas Powder Co. to T. R. Hughes, October 4, 1916, in "Mining Company" folder, box 15, FBP, HST papers, HSTL.

13. Harry S. Truman to Bess Wallace, July 25, August 5, and August 29, 1916, in Ferrell, *Dear Bess;* list of expenses on T-C-H Mining Co., stationery, "Mining Company—Time and Payroll Book—1916" folder, box 15, FBP, HST papers, HSTL; Davis, *Descendants of Jacob Young,* p. 132;

Harry S. Truman interview with Jonathan Daniels, July 28, 1949, p. 2, MOI notes, Jonathan Daniels papers, HSTL; Truman, *Memoirs* draft, p. 2901.

14. Harry S. Truman to Bess Wallace, April 24, 1916, in Ferrell, *Dear Bess.*

15. Harry S. Truman to Bess Wallace, undated (p. 169) and August 29, 1916, in Ferrell, *Dear Bess;* Truman, *Memoirs* draft, p. 2902; Davis, *Descendants of Jacob Young,* p. 132; Truman, "Pickwick Papers"; Steinberg, *Man from Missouri,* pp. 41–42; Daniels, *Man of Independence,* p. 105; National Register of Historic Places Inventory—Nomination Form, "Grandview" folder, vertical file, HSTL.

16. David H. Morgan to Eben A. Ayers, August 5, 1951 (autobiographical sketch and pp. 1 and 2 of "A Factual Narrative Relating to the Business Activities Etc. of David H. Morgan & Harry S. Truman 1916–1919"), PSF—Personal, David H. Morgan, HST papers, HSTL (hereafter cited as Morgan, "Narrative"). Truman reviewed the Narrative, and wrote to Morgan, "Your recollection parallels mine, and I think you have stated the facts as clearly as they can be stated in the case" (Harry S. Truman to David H. Morgan, August 8, 1951, PSF—Personal, David H. Morgan, HST papers, HSTL). In Truman's *Memoirs* his account of his oil business follows Morgan's Narrative almost verbatim in spots.

17. Harry S. Truman to Bess Wallace, undated (p. 193), March 23, May 23, May 26, June 3, July 25, and August 5, 1916, January 23 and May 27, 1917, in Ferrell, *Dear Bess;* Morgan, "Narrative," p. 2; Truman, *Memoirs,* p. 126; Steinberg, *Man from Missouri,* p. 39; Harry S. Truman interview with Jonathan Daniels, July 28, 1949, p. 2, MOI notes, Jonathan Daniels papers, HSTL; Gaylon Babcock oral history, pp. 13, 44–45, 51, 64, HSTL; Pansy Perkins oral history, p. 4, HSTL; "Miscellaneous," p. 191, MOI notes, Jonathan Daniels papers, HSTL; David H. Morgan to Jonathan Daniels, November 25, 1949, Jonathan Daniels papers, University of North Carolina. Daniels (p. 81) says that Truman put up $5,000 cash in addition to the notes, but this is probably incorrect as Culbertson requested only $5,000. Steinberg (pp. 41–42) says that the mortgage was on Harrison Young's farm, and that Harry had given his mother the quitclaim deed for his interest in exchange for the five $1,000 notes. This loan added $5,000 of debt to the family homestead. On February 10, 1917 Mattie had to borrow $25,000 on her land (without the oil loan, that mortgage conceivably could have been $20,000 instead). The mortgage was held by T. P. Green and James Frank Blair. Harry said that most of this money went to lawyers and to Truman kinfolk contesting the Louisa Young will (Harry S. Truman interview with Jonathan Daniels, November 12, 1949, p. 58, MOI notes, Jonathan Daniels papers, HSTL).

18. Morgan, "Narrative," pp. 1–2; David H. Morgan to Harry S. Truman, June 11, 1945, PPF llll, HST papers, HSTL; Daniels, *Man of Inde-*

pendence, p. 81; Truman, *Memoirs,* pp. 126–27; Truman, *Memoirs* draft, pp. 2830–32; Steinberg, *Man from Missouri,* p. 39; "Amended Agreement and Declaration of Trust of the Morgan Oil & Refining Company. (formerly Atlas-Okla Oil Lands Syndicate)," instrument 116257, book 1759, p. 280, Office of the Recorder of Deeds, Jackson County, Missouri (hereafter cited as "Amended Agreement"). The contract Truman signed said he would devote full time to the oil business, but in reality the other partners allowed him to spend time supervising the Grandview farm. For this reason he didn't take the $250 monthly salary the contract provided for him.

19. Morgan, "Narrative," pp. 2, 5; Baxter, *Notable Kansas Citians,* pp. 213–15 (see also Alkire, *Men of Affairs,* p. 104); Articles of Incorporation Morgan & Company Oil Investments Corporation, corporation 33127, Corporation Division, Office of the Secretary of State of Missouri. The articles of incorporation gave the company power to "engage in the business of manufacturing, mining, prospecting for, developing, buying, selling and dealing in oil, gas, timber, coal, and all products and by-products thereof; to engage in manufacturing, purchasing, and supplying for and to themselves and others, oils, gas, electricity, and any other agent for light, heat, power, or other purposes." The articles also gave the corporation power to acquire mills, factories, and refineries. Company records ("Amended Agreement," pp. 278–79) say that Truman proposed the change from Atlas-Okla to Morgan Oil & Refining, but Truman's role had to be mere window dressing for the official record. The declaration of trust was a lengthy legal document that only a lawyer would have devised. Both Morgan and Truman credit Culbertson with devising the trust. The trust was given basically the same powers that Morgan & Company Oil Investments Corp. possessed. Unlike Morgan & Company, neither Atlas-Okla nor Morgan Oil & Refining was registered with the Missouri Secretary of State Corporation Division since they were common law trusts rather than corporations. Journalist Fulton Lewis, Jr. ("Washington Report," *Washington Times Herald,* July 11, 1951) claimed that the trust's date of filing was backdated in courthouse records, but the alteration he claims to have seen was invisible thirty years later. Such alteration could have been a crime, but such records were kept lackadaisically in that era; why would the Recorder object to correcting a lawyer's oversight? On March 21, 1917 the stockholders of Morgan & Company (Truman, Morgan, and Culbertson) voted to increase the number of directors from three to four. The identity of the fourth director is unrecorded (Affidavit of Increase of Directors, Morgan & Company Oil Investments Corporation), but he may have been old mining partner Tom Hughes, as Truman wrote that "Hughes and I were suckers enough to go into" Culbertson's oil company (Truman, *Autobiography,* p. 37). The installment stock purchase plan is mentioned in an Atlas-Okla installment contract receipt, and the exchange of Atlas-Okla shares for Morgan shares in Harry S. Truman to Mrs. J. H. Best, March 31, 1917 (both documents

in "Truman, Harry S.," Westbrook Pegler papers, Herbert Hoover Presidential Library).

20. Morgan, "Narrative," p. 2; Truman, *Memoirs,* p. 127; "Amended Agreement," pp. 284, 286–87; Lewis, "Washington Report," July 11 and 12, 1951, include an analysis of the trust agreement by Bernard T. Hurwitz who is identified as a former securities commissioner for the state of Missouri.

21. Morgan Oil & Refining Co. advertisement in *Kansas City Star,* April 1, 1917; Morgan, "Narrative," p. 2; W. S. Lynn to Mr. Moore, May 17, 1917, Miscellaneous Historical Document 45, HSTL; Lewis, "Washington Report," July 2, 3, 9, and 11, 1951; Henry Bundschu interview with Jonathan Daniels, October 3, 1949, p. 39, MOI notes, Jonathan Daniels papers, HSTL; Harry S. Truman to Clara Erickson, February 5, 1917, "Truman, Harry S.," Westbrook Pegler papers, Herbert Hoover Presidential Library.

22. Morgan, "Narrative," pp. 2–3, 5–7; David H. Morgan to Fulton Lewis, Jr., July 5, 1951, PSF—Personal, Morgan, David H., HST papers, HSTL; Truman, *Memoirs,* p. 127; Truman, *Memoirs* draft, pp. 2828–32; "The Foundation of Fortunes—Oil Investment Opportunities" prospectus for Morgan & Company Oil Investments Corp., Miscellaneous Historical Document 45, HSTL; Truman, *Autobiography,* p. 37; Lewis, "Washington Report," July 12, 1951; Harry S. Truman to Bess Wallace, January 23, 1917, in Ferrell, *Dear Bess.* A 5 percent commission on all stock sales went to Morgan & Co. Over thirty-four thousand shares were issued by mid-1917, but that doesn't mean they were sold. Fulton Lewis, Jr., in "Washington Report," July 11, 1951, refers to a sales pitch letter signed by Truman, although both Truman and Morgan claimed that the future president took no part in stock selling. Photocopies of two such letters exist. In one, Truman's signature appears to be in his handwriting, but the angle is so strange that one wonders if the letter were added to a blank piece of stationery that Truman had signed (or perhaps a rubber stamp was used). The "Truman signature" on the other letter was clearly from some other hand (Harry S. Truman to Clara Erickson, February 5, 1917, and Harry S. Truman to Mrs. J. H. Best, March 31, 1917, "Truman, Harry S.," Westbrook Pegler papers, Herbert Hoover Presidential Library).

23. Morgan, "Narrative," p. 8; Truman, *Memoirs* draft, pp. 2830–32; Truman, *Autobiography,* pp. 36–37; Harry S. Truman to Bess Wallace, May 27, 1917, in Ferrell, *Dear Bess.*

24. Morgan, "Narrative," pp. 2, 5; David H. Morgan to Harry S. Truman, March 8, 1946, PSF—Personal, Morgan, David H., HST papers, HSTL. Morgan & Co. Oil Investments Corp. stationery carried the warning: "ALL COMMUNICATIONS TO BE ADDRESSED TO THE COMPANY AND NOT TO INDIVIDUALS" (W. S. Lynn to Mr. Moore, May 17, 1917, Miscellaneous Historical Document 45, HSTL). This suggests that a certain mistrust had grown among the partners. Although this

particular letter was written after Truman had ceased active involvement with the company, the stationery had been printed while Culbertson was still involved. An indication that other partners viewed Culbertson's salesmen with distrust is found in the printed warning on a receipt for Atlas-Okla stock: "NOTE—No agent is authorized to collect any part of the purchase price of the shares herein sold except when the check, draft or money order, is made payable direct to Morgan & Company, Oil Investments Corporation" ("Truman, Harry S.," Westbrook Pegler papers, Herbert Hoover Presidential Library). Truman wanted to unload the old Commerce, Oklahoma, mine on Mullen (Harry S. Truman to Bess Wallace, May 27, 1917, in Ferrell, *Dear Bess.*) A brief account of Mullen's career up to 1916 can be found in Joseph B. Thoburn, *A Standard History of Oklahoma* (New York, 1916), p. 1201.

25. David H. Morgan to Harry S. Truman, March 8, 1946, PSF—Personal, Morgan, David H., HST papers, HSTL; J. K. Brelsford to Jonathan Daniels, memorandum, February 12, 1950, PSF—Biographical File, HST papers, HSTL; Harry S. Truman to Bess Wallace, November 16, 1916, in Ferrell, *Dear Bess.* The 1917 Kansas City Directory lists Brelsford as treasurer of Morgan & Company Oil Investments Corporation, and Truman as treasurer of Morgan Oil & Refining Co.

26. Morgan, "Narrative," pp. 4–5, 7, and *passim;* Lewis, "Washington Report," July 2, 3, 9, 11, and 12, 1951; Harry S. Truman to Nellie Noland, December 19, 1916, Mary Ethel Noland papers, HSTL; David H. Morgan to Fulton Lewis, Jr., July 5, 1951, PSF—Personal, Morgan, David H., HST papers, HSTL; Harry S. Truman to Bess Wallace, January 23, 1917, in Ferrell, *Dear Bess.* In addition to his business conduct, further evidence of Truman's seriousness can be found in his March 31, 1917 petition for initiation and membership in Ancient Order Nobles of the Mystic Shrine Ararat Temple (Miscellaneous Historical Document 241, HSTL) in which he described his profession as "Farmer & Oil Business" and gave his business address as 703 Ridge Arcade—the same address of Morgan Oil & Refining. Truman the Freemason wouldn't have called himself an oilman unless he felt the description were accurate. One wonders if the oil business influenced his Masonic activity, if Truman coveted the secular business advantages that could accrue from admission into higher Masonic circles. Photos of the "refinery" graced the Morgan Oil stock prospectus even though the company never had enough oil to put the plant into operation. The prospectus stated baldly that the "refinery has an established reputation over the State of Kansas with over 1,200 customers; it has the reputation of putting out the highest grade of gasoline of any refinery in the State of Kansas, and our markets for its products are already established, and is not an unknown quantity" ("The Foundation of Fortunes—Oil Investment Opportunities" prospectus for Morgan & Company Oil Investments Corp., Miscellaneous Historical Document 45, HSTL). M. M.

Fulkerson of Ten Strike turned up owning 998 shares of Morgan Refining in December 1919, just three shares short of what Dave Morgan then owned (Statement Increasing Capital Stock of Morgan & Company Oil Investments Corporation). In 1919 Ten Strike had an office at 704 Ridge Arcade. Morgan Investments was at 703 Ridge Arcade.

27. Morgan, "Narrative," pp. 3–4, 6; David H. Morgan, "Facts Relating to the Business Association between Harry S. Truman and David H. Morgan," Jonathan Daniels papers, University of North Carolina; Harry S. Truman interview with William Hillman, January 9, 1952, interviews folder, "Mr. President" File, box 269, PSF, HST papers, HSTL. On some occasions Truman expressed mellow sentiments about the lost fortune (Morgan, "Narrative," p. 3; Daniels, *Man of Independence,* p. 83; Truman, *Memoirs,* p. 127; Truman, *Memoirs* draft, pp. 2830–32). On less mellow occasions Truman crankily blamed his partners for the loss of the Teter fortune (Truman, *Autobiography,* p. 37; Steinberg, *Man from Missouri,* p. 40; Truman, "My Impressions"; Harry S. Truman, "The Military Career of a Missourian," holograph manuscript, HSTL; David H. Morgan to Jonathan Daniels, December 23, 1949, Jonathan Daniels papers, University of North Carolina; Harry S. Truman interview with Jonathan Daniels, November 12, 1949, p. 59, MOI notes, Jonathan Daniels papers, HSTL). Vivian also felt that Harry's oil partners had acted badly (Vivian Truman interview with Jonathan Daniels, September 23, 1949, p. 15, MOI notes, Jonathan Daniels papers, HSTL).

28. Morgan, "Narrative," pp. 2, 7; Lewis, "Washington Report," July 2, 9, 11, and 12, 1951; David H. Morgan, "Facts Relating the Business Association between Harry S. Truman and David H. Morgan," Jonathan Daniels papers, University of North Carolina.

29. Harry S. Truman, *Memoirs* draft, pp. 2828–29.

30. David H. Morgan to Jonathan Daniels, November 25, 1949, Jonathan Daniels papers, University of North Carolina.

31. Truman, "My Impressions."

32. Margaret Truman, *Harry S. Truman,* p. 59.

Chapter 6 BLOOD BROTHERS

1. Daniels, *Man of Independence,* p. 90; Jonathan Daniels interview with Harry S. Truman, November 12, 1949, MOI notes, p. 60, Jonathan Daniels papers, HSTL.

2. Truman, "My Impressions"; Truman, "Military Career." Although Truman's heroes were military, he didn't study military campaigns until after joining the militia (Harry S. Truman handwritten correction, 4/24/52 draft of *National Cyclopedia of American Biography* article, Biographical File, PSF, HST papers, HSTL).

3. Truman, *Autobiography*, p. 21. *Report of the Adjutant General of Missouri* for 1910 notes that in 1909 Battery B had thirteen minors who had enlisted without written parental consent (pp. 187–88). Only fragmentary records exist to show who joined the Guard with Truman, but a check of the Kansas City city directory for those few names shows that the enlisted recruits were young fellows with junior positions in downtown businesses. Possibly, too, Truman was interested specifically in artillery, and rejected the Independence unit because it was infantry.

4. Truman, "My Impressions"; Truman, *Memoirs* draft, p. 2898; *Kansas City Star*, June 15, 1905; *Kansas City Journal*, June 15, 1905; Anon., *History of the Missouri National Guard* (Missouri National Guard, 1934), pp. 204–05; *Report of the Adjutant General of Missouri* for 1905–1906 (pp. 115–16) and for 1910; Edward D. McKim oral history, p. 6, HSTL; "Record of Battery A, 129th Field Artillery," Liberty Memorial Archives, Kansas City, Missouri. In this era National Guard units elected their officers. The elections were often a formality—Dr. Pittam had become first lieutenant in another unit the previous year, and no one could have been surprised that George Collins was elected captain on June 14 after having organized the battery April 25. The men elected had to pass examinations and evaluations before getting commissions, so the elections weren't final.

5. *Kansas City Star*, June 15, 1905; *Kansas City Journal*, June 15, 1905; Anon., *History of the Missouri National Guard*, pp. 204–05; *Report of the Adjutant General of Missouri* for 1905–1906, pp. 17, 21, 47–48, 55, 61; Gaylon Babcock oral history, pp. 44–45, HSTL; Harry S. Truman, autobiographical sketch, pp. 17–18, Biographical File, PSF, HST papers, HSTL; Truman, September 6, 1951, *Public Papers 1951*, p. 509; Harry S. Truman to George Collins, May 23, 1934, Miscellaneous Historical Document 403, HSTL; folder 2, box 1, Mary Jane Truman papers, HSTL; Harry S. Truman to Edward Morris, December 5, 1952, PPF Personal, D Battery—1949 Presidential Inaugural, HST papers, HSTL; Harry S. Truman War Dept. Identification Card, Miscellaneous Historical Document 289, HSTL. In his September 1951 speech Truman seems to have said he made sergeant in Battery B, but he surely misspoke himself.

6. Truman, "Military Career"; Truman, *Autobiography*, p. 27; *Report of the Adjutant General of Missouri* for 1905–1906, pp. 17, 35, 62–63; Harry S. Truman to John L. Blue, December 26, 1952, correspondence folder, "Mr. President" File, box 268, PSF, HST papers, HSTL; Harry S. Truman to Mr. Cavasin, April 12, 1951, quoted in Hillman, *Mr. President*, p. 44; "Memories—early" folder, Memoirs File, Post-Presidential File, HST papers, HSTL. Truman generally said he attended his first Guard camp at Cape Girardeau in August 1905. There was no camp at Cape Girardeau in 1905; it opened in July 1906. Truman said that the name of the first camp he attended was DeArmond, he evidently didn't attend the St. Joseph camp

in 1905. As noted earlier, such inconsistencies abound in Truman's auto-biographical writings. To list all of them would be impractical.

7. Truman, "Military Career"; Harry S. Truman National Guard discharge papers, June 14, 1908, folder 3, box 1, Mary Jane Truman papers, HSTL; George Collins draft of letter to *Kansas City Star*, September 28, 1939, Miscellaneous Historical Document 403, HSTL; Harry S. Truman to Nellie Noland, August 14, 1907, Mary Ethel Noland papers, HSTL; *Report of the Adjutant General of Missouri* for 1907–1908, pp. 6–7, 30–31; Truman, "Pickwick Papers," December 3, 1930.

8. Harry S. Truman to Mary Ethel Noland, July 21, 1906, Mary Ethel Noland papers, HSTL; *Report of the Adjutant General of Missouri* for 1905–1906, pp. 22–23, for 1907–1908, pp. 12, 25, 27, for 1910, pp. 187–88, and for 1912, pp. 41–42; *Independence Examiner*, November 29, 1954; Jay M. Lee, *The Artilleryman* (Kansas City: Spencer Printing Company, 1920), p. 16; Ted Marks oral history interview, pp. 6–12, HSTL; Truman, "Two Years in the Army." In an era that preceded both commercial radio and sound movies Truman may actually have been baffled by the British accent. Yet his theater going would argue otherwise. Indeed, the *Kansas City Times* c. April 19, 1945 quoted Marks as saying that Truman realized he was from England.

9. *Report of the Adjutant General of Missouri* for 1910, pp. 187–89, 403–04.

10. *Report of the Adjutant General of Missouri* for 1907–1908, pp. 7–8, 28, and for 1910, pp. 175–77; Truman, "Military Career"; Harry S. Truman to Mary Ethel Noland, August 25, 1908, Mary Ethel Noland papers, HSTL; Truman, "Pickwick Papers," December 3, 1930. Truman's "Military Career" account suggests that his battery missed the July 1909 brigade camp, but this conflicts with the official *History of the Missouri National Guard*. Most likely only Truman missed.

11. Truman, "Military Career"; George Collins draft of letter to *Kansas City Star*, September 28, 1939, Miscellaneous Historical Document 403, HSTL; Harry S. Truman, autobiographical sketch, pp. 17–18, Biographical File, PSF, HST papers, HSTL; Harry S. Truman June 22, 1917 enlistment papers, records of the Missouri Adjutant General, HSTL; Harry S. Truman War Dept. Identification Card, Miscellaneous Historical Document 289, HSTL; Harry S. Truman to Bess Wallace, May 17, 1911, in Ferrell, *Dear Bess*.

12. Truman, *Autobiography*, p. 41; Truman, "The Ideals."

13. Unidentified newspaper article, "Record of Battery A, 129th Field Artillery," Liberty Memorial Archives, Kansas City, Missouri; Vere Leigh oral history, pp. 2, 4, HSTL; Floyd Ricketts oral history, pp. 2–4, HSTL; Walter Menefee oral history, pp. 1–2, HSTL; James S. Huston, " 'Captain Harry' Truman, Battery D, 129th Field Artillery, 35th Division," historical sketch in records from the office of the Missouri Adjutant General pertaining

to Harry S. Truman, HSTL; Edward McKim oral history, p. 5, HSTL; Harry S. Truman interview with William Hillman, October 16, 1951, interviews folder, "Mr. President" File, box 269, PSF, HST papers, HSTL; Harry S. Truman to Edward Morris, December 5, 1952, "D Battery—1949 Presidential Inaugural," PPF Personal, HST papers, HSTL.

14. Ted Marks oral history, pp. 15–16, HSTL; Harry S. Truman, June 22, 1917 enlistment papers, records from the Missouri Adjutant General pertaining to Harry S. Truman, HSTL; Lee, *Artilleryman*, p. 14; advertisement for *The Artilleryman*, "Truman, Harry S.—Military Career" folder, vertical file, HSTL; Bundschu, "Harry S. Truman," p. 9; Frederick Bowman oral history, pp. 5–6, HSTL; Harry S. Truman acceptance of commission, July 23, 1917 (effective since June 22), Missouri Adjutant General records pertaining to Harry S. Truman, HSTL; Truman, *Autobiography*, p. 41; Robbins, *Last of His Kind*, p. 35; Edgar Hinde in "Harry Truman The Soldier" pamphlet (New York: Veterans Advisory Committee, 1948), "Truman, Harry S.—Military Career" folder, vertical file, HSTL; Harry S. Truman to Mary Ethel Noland, August 5, 1918, Mary Ethel Noland papers, HSTL; Harry S. Truman to Bess Wallace, February 23 and March 21, 1981, in Ferrell, *Dear Bess*; Gaylon Babcock oral history, p. 44, HSTL; Harry S. Truman interview with William Hillman, January 9, 1952, interviews folder, "Mr. President" File, box 269, PSF, HST papers, HSTL. A later exam in less friendly surroundings revealed Truman's vision trouble, but he convinced officialdom to retain him as an Army officer. In the advertisement cited for Lee's sanitized but authoritative account Truman said, "Your facts and details as regards the positions of the regiment are absolutely accurate. It is the best history of the war I have seen."

15. Lee, *Artilleryman*, p. 16; Harry S. Truman interview with William Hillman, October 4, 1951, interviews folder, "Mr. President" File, box 269, PSF, HST papers, HSTL; Edward Jacobson to Harry S. Truman, April 19, 1951, Correspondence—General 1937–1955, Correspondence File, Edward Jacobson papers, HSTL.

16. Harry S. Truman to Vic Housholder, November 1, 1962, Correspondence between Harry S. Truman and Vic Housholder, 1960–1964, Vic Housholder papers, HSTL; October 27, 1967 memo of conversation between Philip Brooks and Mary Ethel Noland, Miscellaneous Historical Document 23, HSTL; *Report of the Adjutant General of Missouri* for 1917–1920; James B. Agnew, "Go To Hell! . . . but I'll try," *Field Artillery Journal*, March-April 1974, p. 34.

17. Battery A was then captained by Roy Olney who had enlisted in the old Kansas City militia battery with Truman on June 14, 1905. Olney was made acting sergeant that day. *Kansas City Journal*, June 15, 1905; August 25 and 27, September 29, 1917, and undated clippings in "Record of Battery A, 129th Field Artillery," Liberty Memorial Archives, Kansas City, Missouri; Maj. John Miles journal, August 25, 1917, Miscellaneous Historical

Document 29, HSTL; Anon., *The Service of the Missouri National Guard on the Mexican Border* (Jefferson City, Mo.: [state of Missouri], n.d.), p. 425; Fred Schmidt to Harry S. Truman, July 19, 1948, and Harry S. Truman to Fred Schmidt, July 28, 1948, folder 2, D Battery—35th Division, PPF Personal, HST papers, HSTL; Harry S. Truman, autobiographical sketch, pp. 23–24, Biographical File, PSF, HST papers, HSTL; L. L. Bucklew oral history, p. 28, HSTL; Paul Marsh to Truman Library Director, October 1, 1970, HSTL; Harry S. Truman interview with William Hillman, January 9, 1952, interviews folder, "Mr. President" File, box 269, PSF, HST papers, HSTL.

18. Tommy Murphy in *Daily Oklahoman*, c. March 1949, enclosed with John Thacher to Harry S. Truman, March 19, 1949, folder 2, D Battery—35th Division, PPF Personal, HST papers, HSTL; Lee, *Artilleryman*, pp. 19–23, 28, 36; *Report of the Adjutant General of Missouri* for 1917–1920; Floyd Ricketts oral history, pp. 4–5, HSTL.

19. Harry S. Truman to Mary Ethel Noland and Nellie Noland, postmark December 24, 1917, Mary Ethel Noland papers, HSTL; Truman, *Autobiography*, pp. 41–43; McNaughton and Hehmeyer, *This Man Truman*, p. 40; Arthur Wilson oral history, pp. 4–5, 11–13, HSTL; Truman, *Memoirs*, p. 128; Joe Whitley manuscript accompanying c. 1946 letter of Ernest C. Havemann to Edward Jacobson, Correspondence—General 1937–1955, Correspondence File, Edward Jacobson papers, HSTL; Floyd Ricketts oral history, p. 6, HSTL; Frederick Bowman oral history, pp. 7–9, HSTL; Harry S. Truman to Bess Wallace, September 29, October 15, and November 11, 1917, January 27 and March 10, 1918, in Ferrell, *Dear Bess*; Ted Marks oral history, pp. 17–17A, HSTL; Lee, *Artilleryman*, pp. 32–33; Truman, "Pickwick Papers," May 14, 1934 essay; Harry S. Truman interview with William Hillman, October 16, 1951, interviews folder, "Mr. President" File, box 269, PSF, HST papers, HSTL; Ferrell, *Dear Bess*, p. 162; Harry S. Truman to Margaret Truman, November 13, 1939, box 10, FBP, HST papers, HSTL.

20. Truman, *Autobiography*, pp. 41, 45; Miscellaneous Historical Document 189, HSTL; "Morgan, David H.," PPF 1111, HST papers, HSTL; Miscellaneous Historical Document 437; Truman, "Pickwick Papers," May 14, 1934; Harry S. Truman to Mary Ethel Noland and Nellie Noland, postmark December 24, 1917, Mary Ethel Noland papers, HSTL; Harry S. Truman to Bess Wallace, November 24, 1917, in Ferrell, *Dear Bess*.

21. *Kansas City Times*, January 3, 1958; Maj. John Miles journal, Miscellaneous Historical Document 29, HSTL; Battery F pay records and Harry S. Truman military pay records, HSTL; Harry S. Truman War Dept. Identification Card, Miscellaneous Historical Document 289, HSTL. Truman paid $7.20 a month for $10,000 of War Risk Insurance.

22. Ted Marks oral history, pp. 17A–19, HSTL; Truman, "Military Career"; Haven, *Battery "C"*, pp. 10–11; February 1, 1918 newspaper article, "Record of Battery A, 129th Field Artillery," Liberty Memorial Ar-

chives, Kansas City, Missouri; Lee, *Artilleryman*, pp. 26–27, 34–35; *Report of the Adjutant General of Missouri* for 1917–1920; Army War College report cited in Agnew, "Go To Hell," p. 35; Edward McKim oral history, pp. 8–12, HSTL; "Report of investigation concerning the tactical employment and conduct of the 35th Division in the recent operations," October 15, 1918, pp. 7–10, Records of the 35th Division, Records of the American Expeditionary Forces, HSTL; McKim entry, personnel notebook, "Battery D—129th Field Artillery" folder 2, Desk File, Post-Presidential File, HST papers, HSTL.

23. Truman, *Autobiography*, pp. 43–44; Joe Whitley manuscript accompanying c. 1946 letter of Ernest C. Havemann to Edward Jacobson, Correspondence—General 1937–1955, Correspondence File, Edward Jacobson papers, HSTL; *Report of the Adjutant General of Missouri* for 1917–1920; Truman, "Pickwick Papers," May 14, 1934; Truman, "My Impressions"; Harry S. Truman to Margaret Truman, November 13, 1939, box 10, FBP, HST papers, HSTL; Richard Eaton and LaValle Hart, "Meet Harry S. Truman," p. 36, in "Truman, Harry S.—Personal Information," vertical file, HSTL.

24. Lee, *Artilleryman*, p. 34; Truman, "Military Career"; Harry S. Truman holograph notes, probably October 16, 1933, Harry S. Truman correspondence for 1937, 1938, HSTL; Harry S. Truman to Mary Ethel Noland, postmarked March 26, 1918, Mary Ethel Noland papers, HSTL.

25. Truman, "Military Career."

26. Harry S. Truman to Mary Ethel Noland, May 7, 1918, Mary Ethel Noland papers, HSTL.

27. Truman, "Military Career"; Harry S. Truman to Mary Ethel Noland, May 7, 1918, Mary Ethel Noland papers, HSTL.

28. Truman, "Military Career"; Truman, *Autobiography*, pp. 44–45; Truman, *Memoirs*, p. 128; James Huston, *National Guardsman*, February 1950, p. 3; Harry S. Truman interviews with William Hillman, October 1 and October 16, 1951, interviews folder, "Mr. President" File, box 269, PSF, HST papers, HSTL; Vere Leigh oral history, p. 12, HSTL; Anon., *Provisional Drill and Service Regulations for Field Artillery (Horse and Light) 1916* (Washington, D.C.: U.S. War Dept., 1917), vol. 3, pp. 128–29; Mrs. W. L. C. Palmer oral history, p. 26, HSTL; Robert Sullivan article, *Denver Post*, May 20, 1945, Biographical File, PSF, HST papers, HSTL.

29. Edgar Hinde oral history, pp. 16–18, HSTL.

30. Truman, "Military Career"; Truman, *Memoirs*, pp. 130–31; Truman, *Autobiography*, pp. 45–48; folder 5, box 1, Mary Jane Truman papers, HSTL; John Thacher letter, June 26, 1918, Miscellaneous Historical Document 442, HSTL; various items about captain's pay, "Military Service, Miscellaneous material regarding Harry S. Truman's" folder, box 21, FBP, HST papers, HSTL.

31. Truman, *Autobiography*, p. 46; Harry S. Truman to Bess Wallace,

July 14 and July 22, 1918, in Ferrell, *Dear Bess*; Harry S. Truman to Bess Truman, July 12, 1928, box 5, FBP, HST papers, HSTL.

32. Edward McKim oral history, pp. 7–12, HSTL; Vere Leigh oral history, p. 7, HSTL; Edgar Hinde oral history, p. 9, HSTL; Frederick Bowman oral history, pp. 3–4, 10, 28–29, HSTL; Miscellaneous Historical Document 331, HSTL; Walter Menefee oral history, pp. 4–5, HSTL; "President Harry S. Truman Private, Captain, Commander-in-Chief" manuscript, July 6, 1957, "Battery D" folder, vertical file, HSTL; Harry S. Truman to Vic Housholder, c. 1957, Correspondence between Harry S. Truman and Vic Housholder 1953–1959, Vic Housholder papers, HSTL; Harry Murphy oral history, p. 20, HSTL; Lee, *Artilleryman*, p. 332.

33. Vere Leigh oral history, pp. 7, 36, HSTL; Harry Murphy oral history, pp. 17, 30, HSTL; Edward McKim oral history, pp. 13, 15, 20–21, HSTL; Harry S. Truman interview with Jonathan Daniels, November 12, 1949, p. 60, MOI notes, Jonathan Daniels papers, HSTL; Truman, "My Impressions"; Frederick Bowman oral history, pp. 2–4, 9, 32, HSTL; *Life*, January 31, 1949; Floyd Ricketts oral history, pp. 3, 6–7, HSTL; *Los Angeles Times*, December 28, 1972; Harry S. Truman autobiographical sketch, pp. 24–25, Biographical File, PSF, HST papers, HSTL; McNaughton and Hehmeyer, *This Man Truman*, p. 41; *Report of the Adjutant General of Missouri* for 1917–1920, pp. 23–25; Arthur Wilson oral history, p. 9, HSTL; Miscellaneous Historical Document 189, HSTL; Truman, "Pickwick Papers," December 3, 1930 essay; *Kansas City Star*, November 28, 1930; *Kansas City Journal Post*, November 28, 1930; 1916 and 1920 Kansas City city directories; Directors of Southwest National Bank of Commerce to Comptroller of the Currency, October 5, 1920, "Citizens Security Bank of Englewood" folder, box 20950, Lou Holland papers, WHMC, MU; Dorsett, *Pendergast Machine*, p. 29; Harry S. Truman to Bess Wallace, July 14, 1917, in Ferrell, *Dear Bess*; *Jackson Examiner*, July 13, 1917.

34. Frederick Bowman oral history, pp. 12–13, 40–41, HSTL; *Los Angeles Times*, December 28, 1972; Vere Leigh oral history, pp. 10–12, HSTL; Floyd Ricketts oral history, pp. 7–8, HSTL; Tommy Murphy in *Daily Oklahoman*, enclosed with John Thacher to Harry S. Truman, March 19, 1949, folder 2, D Battery—35th Division, PPF Personal, HST papers, HSTL; Edward McKim oral history, pp. 12, 15–16, HSTL. Bowman added, "We never figured Pete [Allen] was too smart as far as firing data and so on was concerned. We always kind of accused Truman of more or less kind of looking out for him, and helping him with his firing problems and a few more things. But Truman would never admit it. Although, you know, in a way you could tell by his saying that he knew what we were talking about. We always figured that Truman not only had to take care of the firing of Battery D, but also he helped out in Battery F, although their gun position would be entirely different, naturally" (Frederick Bowman oral history, pp. 40–41, HSTL).

35. Truman, "Military Career"; Truman, *Autobiography*, p. 46; Mc-Naughton and Hehmeyer, *This Man Truman*, pp. 41–42; Steinberg, *Man from Missouri*, p. 45; Miscellaneous Historical Document 189; Schauffler, *Harry Truman*, pp. 44–45.

36. Truman, "Military Career"; Harry S. Truman, autobiographical sketch, pp. 24–25, Biographical File, PSF, HST papers, HSTL; Daniels, *Man of Independence*, p. 95; Steinberg, *Man from Missouri*, p. 45; Harry Murphy oral history, p. 20, HSTL; Schauffler, *Harry Truman*, pp. 44–45.

37. McNaughton and Hehmeyer, *This Man Truman*, p. 43; Truman, "Military Career"; Harry S. Truman to Mary Ethel Noland, August 5, 1918, Mary Ethel Noland papers, HSTL; Vere Leigh oral history, pp. 24–25, HSTL; biographical sketch of Ralph E. Truman, p. 24, Ralph E. Truman papers, HSTL; Lee, *Artilleryman*, pp. 52–53; Harry S. Truman to Bess Wallace, July 31, 1918, in Ferrell, *Dear Bess*.

38. Truman, "Military Career"; Housholder memoir, Vic Housholder papers, HSTL; Lee, *Artilleryman*, pp. 54, 56–57; 129th Field Artillery Daily Operations Reports, August 24, 1918, 35th Division Records, History of Operations September 11, 1918–March 26, 1919, American Expeditionary Forces Records, HSTL.

39. Lee, *Artilleryman*, p. 64; Frederick Bowman oral history, pp. 14–15, HSTL.

40. Frederick Bowman oral history, p. 11, HSTL; Truman, "Military Career."

41. Truman, "Military Career"; Ted Marks oral history, p. 24, HSTL; Walter Menefee oral history, p. 8, HSTL; Vere Leigh oral history, pp. 21–23, HSTL; McNaughton and Hehmeyer, *This Man Truman*, p. 46; Harry S. Truman to Vic Housholder, undated c. 1957, Correspondence between Harry S. Truman and Vic Housholder 1953–1959, Vic Housholder papers, HSTL; *Columbus Daily Advocate*, Columbus, Kansas, August 16, 1950, Kenneth Arline, "The Day Truman Almost Got His!," *The Phoenix Gazette*, February 20, 1971, "Articles about Harry S. Truman and Vic Housholder" folder, Vic Housholder papers, HSTL; Lee, *Artilleryman*, pp. 62–63.

42. Vere Leigh oral history, pp. 20–23, HSTL; Truman, "Military Career"; Walter Menefee oral history, pp. 8–9, HSTL; McNaughton and Hehmeyer, *This Man Truman*, p. 46; Edward McKim oral history, pp. 18–19, HSTL; Steinberg, *Man from Missouri*, p. 46; *Life*, January 31, 1949; Harry S. Truman interview with Jonathan Daniels, July 28, 1949, MOI notes, Jonathan Daniels papers, HSTL; Harry Murphy oral history, pp. 11–12, HSTL; Floyd Ricketts oral history, pp. 10–11, HSTL; Daniels, *Man of Independence*, p. 96; 129th Field Artillery Daily Operations Reports, August 29, 1918, 35th Division Records, History of Operations September 11, 1918–March 26, 1919, American Expeditionary Forces Records, HSTL; Lee, *Artilleryman*, pp. 62–63; Harry S. Truman, "The night of the 29th of August 1918" essay, "Military Service, Longhand notes by Harry S. Truman re-

garding" folder, box 21, FBP, HST papers, HSTL; Harry S. Truman to Bess Wallace, September 1, 1918, in Ferrell, *Dear Bess*. Although his men may not have heard Truman use foul language before, he used it in exasperating moments at Camp Doniphan and during his farm years (Harry S. Truman to Bess Wallace, May 12, 1914 and February 3, 1918, in Ferrell, *Dear Bess*).

43. Floyd Ricketts oral history, pp. 10–11, HSTL; Haven, *Battery "C"*, p. 19. Higinbotham later earned fame at a formal review of the 35th Division by the Prince of Wales, shouting, "Captain, ask that little son of a bitch when he's going to free Ireland" (Frederick Bowman oral history, pp. 38–39, HSTL; Daniels, *Man of Independence*, p. 99; Lee, *Artilleryman*, p. 242).

44. Haven, *Battery "C"*, pp. 18–20; Ted Marks oral history, p. 24, HSTL.

45. Floyd Ricketts oral history, p. 12, HSTL; Truman, "Military Career."

46. Truman, "Military Career"; Ted Marks oral history, p. 41, HSTL; 129th Field Artillery Daily Operations Reports, August 30, 1918, HSTL; Vere Leigh oral history, pp. 11–12, HSTL; Walter Menefee oral history, p. 8, HSTL; "Woolridge" entry, personnel notebook, "Battery 'D'—129th Field Artillery" folder 2, Desk File, Post-Presidential File, HST papers, HSTL. Of Woolridge, Truman said, "Later in the war he stood firm under the fiercest fire" (Harry S. Truman interview with Jonathan Daniels, November 12, 1949, MOI notes, Jonathan Daniels papers, HSTL).

47. *The New Yorker*, May 9, 1959, p. 37; Harry S. Truman, July 12, 1960, personal notes folder, desk file, HST papers, HSTL; Harry S. Truman interview with Jonathan Daniels, August 30, 1949, MOI notes, Jonathan Daniels papers, HSTL; Truman, "Military Career"; Arthur Wilson oral history, pp. 10–11, HSTL; Harry S. Truman, March 15, 1952, *Public Papers, 1952*, p. 63, and January 21, 1951, *Public Papers, 1951*, p. 17.

48. Truman, "Military Career."

49. Ibid.; 129th Field Artillery Daily Operations Reports, September 6 and 7, 1918, HSTL; John Thacher letters, September 10 and 14, 1918, Miscellaneous Historical Document 442, HSTL; Lee, *Artilleryman*, p. 68.

50. Arthur Wilson oral history, p. 17, HSTL. Lieutenant Lee noted that reveille at Camp Doniphan was "Over There," and the band actually could play still other songs (Lee, *Artilleryman*, pp. 37–38; John Thacher letter, July 20, 1918, Miscellaneous Historical Document 442, HSTL).

51. Truman, "Military Career"; John Thacher letter, September 14, 1918, Miscellaneous Historical Document 442, HSTL; Haven, *Battery "C"*, p. 21; Lee, *Artilleryman*, pp. 70–74.

52. Edward Jacobson's personal copy of *Readings from the Holy Scriptures for Jewish Soldiers and Sailors*, Edward Jacobson papers, HSTL; Lee, *Artilleryman*, pp. 75, 79; Truman, "Military Career."

53. Floyd Ricketts oral history, pp. 14–15, HSTL; Edward McKim oral history, p. 3, HSTL; Harry Murphy oral history, p. 15, HSTL; Harry

Vaughan oral history, p. 10, HSTL; Keith Dancy diary, September 11 and 18, October 3 and 4, 1918, Liberty Memorial Archives, Kansas City, Missouri; biographical sketch of Ralph E. Truman, p. 32, Ralph E. Truman papers, HSTL; Lee, *Artilleryman*, p. 82; Truman, "Military Career." The pace of the march was criticized in a wartime Army investigation (Recommendation section of "Argonne-Meuse Operation Report of 35th Division, file 13503.07," History of Operations September 11, 1918–March 26, 1919, HSTL).

54. Edward McKim oral history, pp. 20–21, 24–25; Lee, *Artilleryman*, pp. 66, 77; Frances Burns article, *Chicago Sun*, April 19, 1945, p. 10, Democratic National Committee Clipping File, HSTL; Floyd Ricketts oral history, pp. 14–15, HSTL; Truman, "Military Career"; Mary Jane Truman quotation regarding injured man on horse, *St. Louis Globe-Democrat*, November 4–5, 1978; Harry S. Truman quotation on Doherty, unidentified news clipping, and Jim Doherty quotation, *Courier-Journal*, c. January 1949, "Battery D" folder, vertical file, HSTL; Ted Marks oral history, p. 41, HSTL; Harry Murphy oral history, pp. 17–18, HSTL. The colonel in the incident of the injured man on Truman's horse was probably Klemm, since he was regarded as having authority to demote Truman, but accounts don't use Klemm's name.

55. Truman, "Military Career"; Lee, *Artilleryman*, p. 83.

56. Truman, "Military Career"; Lee, *Artilleryman*, pp. 88–89.

57. "Report of investigation concerning the tactical employment and conduct of the 35th Division in the recent Operations," October 15, 1918, pp. 1–10, Records of the American Expeditionary Forces, HSTL.

58. Vic Housholder to Harry S. Truman, September 1951, Correspondence between Harry S. Truman and Vic Housholder 1950–1953, Vic Housholder papers, HSTL; Truman, "Military Career"; 129th Field Artillery Daily Operations Reports, September 26, 1918, Harry S. Truman memorandum c. October 9, 1918, HSTL; Lee, *Artilleryman*, p. 91; Truman, *Autobiography*, p. 48.

59. McNaughton and Hehmeyer, *This Man Truman*, p. 44; Edward McKim oral history, pp. 17–18, HSTL.

60. Floyd Ricketts oral history, pp. 20–22, HSTL; Truman, "Military Career"; Lee, *Artilleryman*, pp. 94, 211; Vere Leigh oral history, p. 54, HSTL; Harry Murphy oral history, p. 14, HSTL; John Thacher letter, December 22, 1918, Miscellaneous Historical Document 442, HSTL; Truman, "The Ideals," in "Pickwick Papers"; *Kansas City Journal Post*, September 25, 1938, p. 1A; Harry S. Truman to Dave, September 29, 1951, "Mr. President" File, *Reader's Digest* folder, box 269, PSF, HST papers, HSTL.

61. Lee, *Artilleryman*, p. 104.

62. This and all subsequent battle messages are from "Argonne-Meuse Operation Item 'C' Sub-Item 4, Enclosure No. 10, Messages Sent and Received During the Argonne-Meuse Operation," Report of 35th Division,

File 13503.04, 35th Division Records, American Expeditionary Forces Records, HSTL.

63. Truman, *Autobiography*, p. 48; Truman, "Military Career"; Lee, *Artilleryman*, p. 107; Karl Klemm to Peter Traub, October 9, 1918, and Marvin Gates memorandum, October 9, 1918, 129th Field Artillery Daily Operations Reports, HSTL; Harry S. Truman to Bess Truman, September 27, 1942, box 8, FBP, HST papers, HSTL; Harry S. Truman, "The 129th F.A. moved into position" essay, rough and polished drafts, "Military Service, Longhand notes by Harry S. Truman regarding" folder, box 21, FBP, HST papers, HSTL.

64. Truman, "Military Career"; 129th Field Artillery Daily Operations Reports, September 26 and 26–27, 1918, and 2nd Battalion Operations Reports, 129th Field Artillery, September 26, 1918, and Karl Klemm to Peter Traub, October 9, 1918, and Marvin Gates memorandum, October 9, 1918, all in 129th Daily Operations Reports, HSTL; chapter 2, file 13503.1, Report of 35th Division, Argonne-Meuse Operation, Detailed Operation Reports September 26, Detailed Operation Reports September 26 (two documents with same title), Colonels Hawkins and Nuttman to Gen. Traub, and sworn statement of Brig. Gen. L. G. Berry, October 7, 1918 in "Report of investigation concerning the tactical employment and conduct of the 35th Division in the recent operations," October 15, 1918, all in Records of the 35th Division, History of Operations September 11, 1918–March 26, 1919, American Expeditionary Forces Records, HSTL; Truman, "The 129th F.A. moved into position," polished draft, HSTL.

65. Lee, *Artilleryman*, pp. 116–19; chapter 2, file 13503.01, Report of the 35th Division, Argonne-Meuse Operation, and "Report of investigation concerning the tactical employment and conduct of the 35th Division in the recent operations," October 15, 1918, p. 4, both in Records of the 35th Division, HSTL.

66. Truman, "Military Career"; Truman, *Autobiography*, p. 48; Lee, *Artilleryman*, pp. 118–19.

67. Truman, "Military Career"; *Kansas City Journal Post*, September 25, 1938, p. 5A; Truman, "The 129th F.A. moved into position" polished draft, HSTL. Meisburger said the dead men were victims of artillery, not of machine gunners.

68. Vere Leigh oral history, pp. 30–32, HSTL; Lee, *Artilleryman*, pp. 125–32; Truman, *Autobiography*, p. 49; Richard J. Keogh, "The Truman Colts," *Arms Gazette*, September 1980, "Truman, Harry S.—Military Career" folder, vertical file, HSTL; Harry S. Truman, memorandum c. October 9, 1918, 129th Field Artillery Daily Operations Reports, HSTL; Edward McKim oral history, p. 24, HSTL; Floyd Ricketts oral history, pp. 8–9, HSTL; 129th Field Artillery Daily Operations Reports, September 27–28, 1918 and 2nd Battalion September 27, 1918, 129th Field Artillery Daily Operations Reports, HSTL.

69. Lee, *Artilleryman*, pp. 125, 129, 136; Edward McKim oral history, pp. 17–18, HSTL; Vere Leigh oral history, pp. 24–25, HSTL; McNaughton and Hehmeyer, *This Man Truman*, p. 50; Truman, *Autobiography*, pp. 48–49; Truman, memorandum c. October 9, 1918, 129th Field Artillery Daily Operations Reports, HSTL; Statement of Peter E. Traub, September 30, 1918, file 13503.06, 35th Division Records, American Expeditionary Forces Records, HSTL. Lee (p. 136) notes that everyone thought there was an order prohibiting firing at targets out of division sector, but Lee questioned whether such an order existed. Commanding general of the 35th Division Peter Traub said the order existed.

70. Edward McKim oral history, p. 24, HSTL; Harry Murphy oral history, pp. 12–13, HSTL; Floyd Ricketts oral history, pp. 8–9, HSTL; Lee, *Artilleryman*, p. 130.

71. Lee, *Artilleryman*, p. 135; Truman, memorandum c. October 9, 1918, 129th Field Artillery Daily Operations Reports, HSTL; Harry S. Truman to Mary Ethel Noland, postmark January 25, 1919 and Harry S. Truman to Mary Ethel Noland, March 25, 1919, Mary Ethel Noland papers, HSTL.

72. 2nd Battalion Operations Reports, September 28, 1918, 129th Field Artillery Daily Operations Reports, HSTL.

73. Lee, *Artilleryman*, pp. 163–64; Truman, memorandum, c. October 9, 1918, 129th Field Artillery Daily Operations Reports, HSTL; Statement of Peter E. Traub, September 30, 1918, American Expeditionary Forces Records, HSTL; "Report of investigation concerning tactical employment and conduct of the 35th Division in the recent operations," October 15, 1918, pp. 7–10, HSTL.

74. Keith Dancy diary, "General" entry after October 2, 1918, Liberty Memorial Archives, Kansas City, Missouri; Haven, *Battery "C"*, pp. 26–27; Lee, *Artilleryman*, pp. 165–66; John Thacher, memoir of 1923 visit to France, pp. 12–13, Miscellaneous Historical Document 442, HSTL. Thacher may not have referred to the same moment described in the text, but the sentiments were appropriate.

75. *Kansas City Journal Post*, September 25, 1938, p. 5A; Lee, *Artilleryman*, pp. 150–52, 167–68. In a postwar parade, "when the 110th Engineers, which had held the line on that fateful 29th day of September, the year before, came down Grand Avenue with the modest man who bore himself so gallantly leading it, Kansas City rose as one man and cheered Col. Stayton and his fighting Engineers" (*Report of the Adjutant General of Missouri for 1917–1920*, *Independence Examiner*, May 3, 1919).

76. Laurence Stallings, *The Doughboys* (New York: Harper & Row, 1963), pp. 239–40; Truman, memorandum c. October 9, 1918 and 2nd Battalion Reports, October 1–2, 1918, 129th Field Artillery Daily Operations Reports, HSTL; Harry S. Truman to Mary Ethel Noland, postmark January 25, 1919, Mary Ethel Noland papers, HSTL; Vere Leigh oral history,

p. 21, HSTL; U.S. Army—copies of notes—U.S. Army field messages—1918, Biographical File, PSF, HST papers, HSTL.

77. Harry S. Truman to Nellie Noland and Mary Ethel Noland, November 1, 1918, Mary Ethel Noland papers, HSTL.

78. *Washington Times Herald*, April 20, 1945, Democratic National Committee Clipping File, HSTL; *Kansas City Star*, November 9, 1958; Truman, *Autobiography*, pp. 49–50.

79. Harry S. Truman to Mary Ethel Noland and Nellie Noland, December 18, 1918, Mary Ethel Noland papers, HSTL; Haven, *Battery "C"*, p. 32; Vere Leigh oral history, p. 68, HSTL; "The Rhyme of the Prize Goofs," part three, M. R. Evans papers, HSTL; *Kansas City Star*, November 12, 1980, p. 5A; Truman, *Autobiography*, p. 50; Lee, *Artilleryman*, p. 229n.

80. Harry S. Truman to Mary Ethel Noland and Nellie Noland, December 18, 1918, Mary Ethel Noland papers, HSTL; Truman, *Autobiography*, pp. 50–51. The "Casino de Paris" may have been Monaco's Hotel de Paris.

81. *The Catholic Reporter*, December 22, 1961; John Thacher letter, January 19, 1919, Miscellaneous Historical Document 442, HSTL; *Kansas City Post*, February 26, 1919.

82. Harry S. Truman to Mary Ethel Noland, January 20, 1919, Harry S. Truman to Mary Ethel Noland, postmark January 25, 1919, Harry S. Truman to Mary Ethel Noland, postmark March 25, 1919, Mary Ethel Noland papers, HSTL; Truman, *Autobiography*, p. ix; Tommy Murphy in *Daily Oklahoman*, clipping enclosed with John Thacher to Harry S. Truman, March 19, 1949, D Battery—35th Division, folder 2, PPF Personal, HST papers, HSTL; Harry Murphy oral history, p. 9, HSTL; *Washington Times Herald*, April 20, 1945, Democratic National Committee Clipping File, HSTL; Edgar Hinde oral history, pp. 10–11, HSTL; Miscellaneous Historical Document 420, HSTL; Hillman, *Mr. President*, p. 230.

83. Floyd Ricketts oral history, p. 24, HSTL; Frederick Bowman oral history, p. 38, HSTL; Edward McKim oral history, pp. 25–26, HSTL; Arthur Wilson oral history, p. 9, HSTL; Tommy Murphy in *Daily Oklahoman*, clipping enclosed with John Thacher to Harry S. Truman, March 19, 1949, HSTL; Truman, May 14, 1932, "Pickwick Papers," HSTL.

84. Edgar Hinde oral history, pp. 20–21, HSTL.

85. "Record of Battery A, 129th Field Artillery," newspaper clipping, Liberty Memorial Archives, Kansas City, Missouri; *Independence Examiner*, May 3, 1919; Miscellaneous Historical Document 331, HSTL; Lee, *Artilleryman*, pp. 252–53.

Chapter 7   VETERAN BUSINESSMAN

1. Harry S. Truman to Bess Wallace, July 14, 1917, in Ferrell, *Dear Bess*.

2. Mary Ethel Noland oral history, p. 114, HSTL; Truman, "Military

Career," HSTL; Edgar Hinde oral history, pp. 14–15, HSTL; Arthur Wilson oral history, p. 12, HSTL; Truman, "The Ideals."

3. Jane Schermerhorn, "Bess and Harry's 50 Golden Years," *The Detroit News,* June 26, 1969, pp. 1D–2D; Mary Ethel Noland oral history, pp. 115–17, HSTL; Ted Marks oral history, pp. 27–28, HSTL; Floyd Ricketts oral history, pp. 25–26, HSTL; Vere Leigh oral history, p. 50, HSTL; Harry Murphy oral history, p. 22, HSTL.

4. Morgan, "Narrative"; David H. Morgan to Harry S. Truman, July 10, 1951, "David H. Morgan," PSF—Personal, HST papers, HSTL; Steinberg, *Man from Missouri,* p. 40; Daniels, *Man of Independence,* p. 85; book B-2184, p. 55, Office of the Recorder of Deeds, Jackson County, Missouri; Bess Truman to Benedict Zobrist, July 5, 1980, telephone call, "Harry S. Truman—Homes" folder, vertical file, HSTL; Statement Increasing Capital Stock of Morgan & Company Oil Investments Corporation, corporation 33127, Corporation Division, Office of the Secretary of State of Missouri; David H. Morgan, "Facts Relating to the Business Association between Harry S. Truman and David H. Morgan," Jonathan Daniels papers, University of North Carolina, cover of *Kansas City Street and Avenue Guide and Directory of Householders* (Kansas City: Gate City Directory Co., 1918[?]), hereafter cited as *KC City Directory; Oil and Gas Journal,* September 1916–May 1919; J. H. Conrad to Harry S. Truman, June 19, 1919, Harry S. Truman to J. H. Conrad, June 26, 1919, Harry S. Truman to David H. Morgan, July 28, 1919, "D. H. Morgan" folder, General File, box 15, FBP, HST papers, HSTL; Harry S. Truman to Bess Wallace, March 17, 1918 and November 2, and November 11, 1918 and January 7, 1919, in Ferrell, *Dear Bess.*

5. Morgan, "Narrative," pp. 2, 6; David H. Morgan to Harry S. Truman, July 10, 1951, "David H. Morgan," PSF—Personal, HST papers, HSTL; Daniels, *Man of Independence,* p. 85; Morgan, "Facts Relating to the Business Association between Harry S. Truman and David H. Morgan."

6. Truman, *Memoirs* draft, pp. 2833–34; Lease—Louis Oppenstein to Harry S. Truman and Edward Jacobson, Truman-Jacobson Haberdashers file, Edward Jacobson papers, HSTL; Schauffler, *Harry Truman,* p. 52. Jacobson was once quoted as saying, "We agreed during the war to go into business together." This would make the decision less hasty, but most accounts explicitly or by implication say the decision was made after the return to civilian life. (Unidentified newspaper clipping, April 18, 1945, Newspaper Clippings folder, Biographical File, PSF, HST papers, HSTL.)

7. Truman, *Memoirs* draft, pp. 2833–34; Truman, *Memoirs,* p. 133.

8. Truman, *Memoirs* draft, pp. 2833–34; Truman, *Memoirs,* p. 133; "Merchandising venture 1919–1921" folder, Memoirs File, Post-Presidential File, HST papers, HSTL; Joe Whitley manuscript with undated letter of Ernest C. Havemann to Edward Jacobson, c. 1946, Correspondence—general,

1937–1955, Correspondence File, Edward Jacobson papers, HSTL; Truman, "My Impressions"; news item and advertisement, *Independence Examiner*, September 22, 1919; Schermerhorn, *The Detroit News*, June 26, 1969; Miscellaneous Historical Document 189, HSTL; Mary Jane Truman correspondence with Doris Faber, Mary Jane Truman folder 2, Family Correspondence File, Post-Presidential File, HST papers, HSTL; Gaylon Babcock oral history, pp. 13, 44–45, 51, 64, HSTL; Elizabeth Berry, "Harry Truman's Christmas," "Truman Family—General" folder, vertical file, HSTL; miscellaneous p. 191, MOI notes, Jonathan Daniels papers, HSTL; Daniels, *Man of Independence*, p. 105; Truman, "Pickwick Papers," May 14, 1934, HSTL; Harry S. Truman to D,762 Star, November 4, 1919, "Correspondence—general 1919" folder, box 12, FBP, HST papers, HSTL.

9. Lease—Louis Oppenstein to Harry S. Truman and Edward Jacobson, Truman-Jacobson Haberdashers file, Edward Jacobson papers, HSTL; *KC City Directory*, 1923 and 1924.

10. Daniels, *Man of Independence*, p. 106; unidentified newspaper clipping, April 18, 1945, Newspaper Clippings folder, Biographical File, PSF, HST papers, HSTL; Truman, *Memoirs*, p. 132; Joe Whitley manuscript with letter of Ernest C. Havemann to Edward Jacobson, c. 1946, Correspondence—General 1937–1955, Correspondence File, Edward Jacobson papers, HSTL; Harry S. Truman to Victor Housholder, November 28, 1919, "Correspondence—general 1919" folder, box 12, FBP, HST papers, HSTL; Ted Marks oral history, p. 33, HSTL; P. H. Neyhart to Harry S. Truman, c. July 1919, Desk File, Post-Presidential File, HST papers, HSTL; Schauffler, *Harry Truman*, p. 52; Eaton and Hart, "Meet Harry S. Truman," pp. 44–45; Kansas City Club 1919 membership card, "Membership applications and cards" folder, box 14, FBP, HST papers, HSTL; P. H. Neyhart to Harry S. Truman, October 1, (bill) and October 3, 1919, "Correspondence—general 1919" folder, box 12, FBP, HST papers, HSTL; W. G. Randall to Harry S. Truman, September 22, 1920, "Correspondence—general 1920" folder, box 12, FBP, HST papers, HSTL. Truman was also a member of the Kansas City Athletic Club and the Lakewood Golf & Country Club at this time. He dropped all or most of these memberships in late 1920, possibly for financial reasons. The list of items carried by the store is from various receipts and reports in the Truman-Jacobson Haberdashers file (Edward Jacobson papers, HSTL) and from photos of the store. The store hired a professional window trimmer to change displays every week, and he kept Truman and Jacobson informed about their competitors. Truman didn't like to wait on tough 12th Street characters, and assigned those sales to a clerk. The Neyhart letter shows Truman's business address c. July 1919 as 703 Ridge Arcade, the address of Morgan & Co. Oil Investments. He may still have had an interest in Morgan oil then, or may just have used the office as a mail drop.

11. Harry Murphy oral history, p. 6, HSTL; Vere Leigh oral history, pp. 52–53, HSTL; Frederick Bowman oral history, pp. 25–26, HSTL; Edward McKim oral history, pp. 25–27, HSTL; Arthur Wilson oral history, pp. 13–14, HSTL; Ted Marks oral history, p. 33, HSTL; "Harry Truman The Soldier" pamphlet (New York: Veterans Advisory Committee, 1948), "Harry S. Truman—Military Career" folder, vertical file, HSTL (a similar quotation from Meisburger is in *Washington Times Herald,* April 20, 1945); F. C. Hirsch to Harry S. Truman, January 19, 1920, "Correspondence—general 1920" folder, box 12, FBP, HST papers, HSTL; Harry S. Truman to James A. Burkhardt, August 14, 1922, C. L. Quinn to Harry S. Truman, August 7, 1922, and Harry S. Truman to C. L. Quinn, August 14, 1922, "Correspondence—general August-September 1922" folder, box 12, FBP, HST papers, HSTL; Edgar Hinde oral history, pp. 27–28, HSTL; Steinberg, *Man from Missouri,* pp. 54–55; Joe Whitley manuscript with letter of Ernest Havemann to Edward Jacobson, c. 1946, Correspondence—General 1937–1955, Correspondence File, Edward Jacobson papers, HSTL; Charles F. Curry oral history, pp. 3–5, HSTL. A small list of Truman's personal loans to Battery D veterans and other persons while he was a haberdasher can be found in County Judge Notebook, box 2, Desk File, Post-Presidential File, HST papers, HSTL. Truman's loans were affectionately noted in the printed program from the notorious 1921 Battery D reunion (Miscellaneous Historical Document 284, HSTL).

12. Harry Murphy oral history, pp. 24–26, HSTL; Walter Menefee oral history, p. 11, HSTL; Vere Leigh oral history, pp. 51–52, HSTL; Edward McKim oral history, pp. 32–34, 39, HSTL; Drew Pearson, "Washington Merry-Go-Round," c. January 1949, "Battery D" folder, vertical file, HSTL; Harry S. Truman to Ethel Noland, January 31, 1959, Mary Ethel Noland papers, HSTL; E. J. Becker to Harry S. Truman, March 22, 1921, "Programs 1914–1925" folder, box 16, FBP, HST papers, HSTL; *Kansas City Star,* June 28, 1945; Robbins, *Last of His Kind,* caption to photo of Truman and Frank Spina; Frederick Bowman oral history, p. 33, HSTL; Harry S. Truman to Bess Wallace, February 18, 1919, in Ferrell, *Dear Bess;* Ted Marks oral history, HSTL; Edgar Hinde oral history, pp. 24–25, HSTL; *Kansas City Times,* March 16, 1959; Mrs. Sam Ray, "Postcards from Old Kansas City," *Kansas City Times,* November 7, 1980; Truman speech at Battery D dinner, November 3, 1953, "Personal—Battery D, 35th Division" folder 2, Post-Presidential File, HST papers, HSTL. The "Third Annual St. Patrick's Day Banquet" program of Battery D listed Spina as "the next presidential barber" in 1920 (Miscellaneous Historical Document 284, HSTL).

13. Edward F. Witsell memo, September 6, 1949, Jonathan Daniels papers, University of North Carolina; Edward Thelen oral history, pp. 3, 15, 33, 62–63, HSTL; Miscellaneous Historical Document 173, HSTL; Harry Vaughan oral history, p. 22, HSTL; Truman, September 6, 1951, *Public*

Papers 1951, pp. 509–10; *Kansas City Post*, September 28, 1923, p. 3; *Kansas City Star*, November 29, 1938.

14. Sara Mullin Baldwin, *Who's Who in Kansas City* (Hebron, Neb.: Robert M. Baldwin Corp., 1930); *Independence Examiner*, July 18, 1922; Richard Lawrence Miller to Rufus Burrus, January 31, 1983, Rufus Burrus to Richard Lawrence Miller, February 1, 1983, author's files; Roy Ellis, *A Civic History of Kansas City, Missouri* (Springfield, Mo.: Elkins-Swyers Co., 1930), pp. 231–33; Brown Harris to Harry S. Truman, January 7, 1947, correspondence relating to Harry S. Truman—biographical, Biographical File, PSF, HST papers, HSTL. Reputedly, Miles was the only candidate who ever prompted Truman to deviate from the straight Democrat ticket. In 1912, however, Truman apparently voted for a Republican and a Bull Moose (Harry S. Truman to Bess Wallace, November 6, 1912, in Ferrell, *Dear Bess*).

15. "Correspondence—Oliver M. Solinger, 1920–1921" folder, Truman-Jacobson Haberdashers file, Edward Jacobson papers, HSTL; Joe Whitley manuscript with undated letter of Ernest C. Havemann to Edward Jacobson, c. 1946, "Correspondence—general 1937–1955" folder, Correspondence File, Edward Jacobson papers, HSTL; "Truman-Jacobson Haberdashery" folder, box 17, FBP, HST papers, HSTL. In a different situation years later Truman wrote, "If we could bring it home to the kid that he is reflecting on his mother it would be a good thing" (Harry S. Truman to Fred Canfil, June 6, 1944, "Fred Canfil" folder, box 51, SV, HST papers, HSTL).

16. Truman, *Autobiography*, p. 55.

17. Penciled note stapled to correspondence to Edward Jacobson, confidential memo by Eben A. Ayers, sheet with heading "The Security State Bank Loan—$5,000.00, and the judgment against Harry S. Truman," all in "Personal—Ayers, E.—trip to Kansas City (June 19–30, 1951)," Eben Ayers papers (23), HSTL; Harry S. Truman to Edward Jacobson, May 24, 1950, "Correspondence—general 1937–1955" folder, Correspondence File, Edward Jacobson papers, HSTL; Harry S. Truman to Edward Jacobson, June 17, 1950, "Eddie Jacobson" folder, General File, PSF, HST papers, HSTL; Harry S. Truman to Bess Truman, June 28, 1942, box 8, FBP, HST papers, HSTL; Baldwin, *Who's Who in Kansas City*, pp. 26, 219; Lee, *Artilleryman*, pp. 37, 194, 202; Miscellaneous Historical Document 462, HSTL; transcript of instrument # A3782, pp. 263–66, book 2154, Recorder of Deeds, Jackson County, Missouri; Fred Boxley to Charles Becker, February 23, 1921, Truman & Jacobson, Inc. File, Corporation Division, Missouri Secretary of State; Dick Fowler, *Leaders in Our Town* (Kansas City, 1952), Reeves biographical sketch; Morgan & Co. Oil Investments stationery, "Military Service, Miscellaneous material regarding Harry S. Truman's" folder, box 21, FBP, HST papers, HSTL. Truman recalled the

original Security State Bank loan as $12,500, which he and Jacobson eventually reduced to $5,000. Jacobson thought the original loan was $5,000. Truman's version would make the 1920 note a renewal of the original, but Jacobson said the 1920 note was the first loan and was renewed with two years' interest for $5,600 in October 1922. (Eben Ayers memo, July 16, 1951 [there are two memos with that date] and pencil note stapled to Edward Jacobson correspondence, "Personal—Ayers, E.—trip to Kansas City [June 19–30, 1951]," Eben Ayers papers [23], HSTL.) Material from the Ayers folder states that the original Security State Bank loan was secured by Truman's Johnson County, Kansas, farm, but Jonathan Daniels found that the farm wasn't put up as collateral until January 1922 (abstract from Register of Deeds, Johnson County, Kansas, MOI notes, Jonathan Daniels papers, University of North Carolina). The records found by Daniels were surely correct. The chairman of Security State Bank in 1920 was W. S. Woods, who had been president of National Bank of Commerce when Truman was a clerk there.

18. Journal Entry of Judgment in *Qupaw Supply Co.* v. *Harry S. Truman, J. T. Hughes and J. Culbertson,* case no. 1471, District Court of Ottawa County, Oklahoma, A. Scott Thompson to Harry S. Truman, November 16, 1920, and receipt from George M. Henderson to Harry S. Truman, May 6, 1921, "Mining Company" folder, box 15, FBP, HST papers, HSTL.

19. Book B-2184, p. 55, book 2177, p. 253, Recorder of Deeds, Jackson County, Missouri; memorandum of telephone call Bess Truman to Benedict Zobrist, July 5, 1980, "Harry S. Truman—Homes" folder, vertical file, HSTL; abstract from Johnson County, Kansas, Register of Deeds, MOI notes, Jonathan Daniels papers, University of North Carolina; Daniels, *Man of Independence,* p. 108; Exchange contract between Harry S. Truman and Samuel C. See, March 26, 1921, "Miscellaneous 1921" folder, box 15, FBP, HST papers, HSTL; Warranty Deed, Swofford Realty Co. to William I. Rush, Jr., "D. H. Morgan" folder, box 15, FBP, HST papers, HSTL; Deed and Burns & Watts attorneys to Taylor Realty Co., June 21, 1921, and Partnership agreement between Harry S. Truman and Ed Beach, August 5, 1921, "Correspondence—general 1921" folder, box 12, FBP, HST papers, HSTL; Ed Beach page, county judge notebook, box 2, Desk File, Post-Presidential File, HST papers, HSTL.

20. Geo. H. Snyder Realty Co. memorandum, Jessie P. Crump to Harry S. Truman, March 21, 1922, and J. F. Blair to Harry S. Truman, June 29, 1922, "Correspondence—general January–July 1922" folder, box 12, FBP, HST papers, HSTL; Geo. H. Snyder Realty Co. memorandum, and Phil C. Lee to Harry S. Truman, August 31, 1922, "Correspondence—general August–September 1922" folder, box 12, FBP, HST papers, HSTL; Geo. H. Snyder Realty Co. memorandum, "Correspondence—general October–December 1922" folder, box 12, FBP, HST papers, HSTL.

21. Account book—vouchers payable, Truman-Jacobson Haberdashers

file, Edward Jacobson papers, HSTL; transcript of instrument #A 3782, pp. 263–66, book 2154, Recorder of Deeds, Jackson County, Missouri; Truman, *Memoirs,* p. 134; Truman, *Autobiography,* p. 55.

22. Truman, *Memoirs,* p. 134; Truman, *Autobiography,* p. 55; transcript of instrument #A 3782, pp. 263–66, book 2154, Recorder of Deeds, Jackson County, Missouri; Harry S. Truman note on letter of Dickson Jay Hartwell to Charles Ross, May 16, 1949, "Business Ventures—Harry S. Truman" folder, vertical file, HSTL; "Merchandising Venture 1919–1921" folder, Memoirs File, Post-Presidential File, HST papers, HSTL; Sam O'Neal article, *St. Louis Post-Dispatch,* July 24, 1934. The haberdashery bookkeeping is accepted as accurate here, although Truman secretly admitted cooking the figures when he audited the books of the Grandview Commercial Club (Harry S. Truman to Bess Wallace, January 20, 1914, in Ferrell, *Dear Bess*). Daniels (*Man of Independence,* p. 108) lists the debt to Oppenstein as $3,900, but this is likely due to interest charges that accrued between the January 1924 circuit court judgment of $3,200 and the February 1925 bankruptcy petition of Eddie Jacobson that Daniels cites.

23. Charles G. Ross to Dickson J. Hartwell, June 15, 1949, "Business Ventures—Harry S. Truman" folder, vertical file, HSTL; Rufus Burrus to Richard Lawrence Miller, December 29, 1981, author's files; I. H. Kalis to Eben Ayers, June 25, 1951, Charles Hipsh to Eben Ayers, June 25, 1951, Isadore Steinberg to Eben Ayers, July 9, 1951, statement of Phineas Rosenberg, June 25, 1951, "Personal—Ayers, E.—trip to Kansas City (June 19–30, 1951)," Eben Ayers papers (23), HSTL; "Merchandising Venture 1919–1921" folder, Memoirs File, Post-Presidential File, HST papers, HSTL; Joe Whitley manuscript with letter of Ernest C. Havemann to Edward Jacobson, c. 1946, "Correspondence—general 1937–1955" folder, Correspondence File, Edward Jacobson papers, HSTL. The Rosenberg statement can also be found in "Jacobson, Eddie," General File, PSF, HST papers, HSTL. Truman followed this document closely in his memoirs (p.134). The corporation charter was forfeited January 1, 1923 (Truman & Jacobson, Inc. file, Corporation Division, Missouri Secretary of State). Jacobson went through lean years, eventually prospered, and then paid Truman $20,000 as his half of the haberdashery indebtedness (Edgar Hinde oral history, pp. 30–31, HSTL; Harry S. Truman interview with Jonathan Daniels, July 28, 1949, MOI notes, Jonathan Daniels papers, HSTL). This would mean the haberdashery debts totaled $40,000. This is higher than Truman's 1922 $35,000 figure because he didn't include interest charges that accrued over the years. Truman figured his own total losses, both debts and money previously invested, at $28,000 (Daniels, *Man of Independence,* p. 108).

24. Truman, "The Ideals"; Truman, *Memoirs,* pp. 134, 136; "Merchandising Venture 1919–1921" folder, Memoirs File, Post-Presidential File, HST papers, HSTL.

Chapter 8 JOURNEYMAN JUDGE

1. Truman, "I have had two wonderful associates" essay, "Pickwick Papers," HSTL.

2. Dorsett, *Pendergast Machine*, p. 87; John Barker to Jonathan Daniels, August 10, 1949, Jonathan Daniels papers, University of North Carolina (Barker was a top Pendergast faction lawyer); Harry S. Truman interview with Jonathan Daniels, August 30, 1949, p. 6, MOI notes, Jonathan Daniels papers, HSTL.

3. John Barker to Jonathan Daniels, August 10, 1949, Jonathan Daniels papers, University of North Carolina.

4. John Oliver, "An Examination of Elections Under the Kansas City Charter of 1925," "Kansas City—Elections" folder, box 8, Civic Research Institute records, WHMC, MU.

5. Harold W. Luhnow, speech to 47th Annual Conference on Government of the National Municipal League, November 17, 1941, speech (probably by Luhnow) to Business Day Dinner, University of Kansas, April 24, 1940, John B. Gage, speech to American Municipal League, October 24, 1941, "Miscellaneous—Local and Non-Local 6. Speeches" folder, box 5, Civic Research Institute records, WHMC, MU; Walter Matscheck oral history, p. 38, HSTL; Gosnell, p. 67; John Fennelly, "Kansas City: 1925 to 1951," senior thesis, Princeton University, 1952; E. Y. Mitchell memorandum, c. July 17, 1934, folder 2986, and G. H. Foree to E. Y. Mitchell, September 14, 1934, folder 3004, E. Y. Mitchell papers, WHMC, MU; *Kansas City Times,* March 27, 1984, p. A-6.

6. A. Theodore Brown and Lyle W. Dorsett, *K.C.: A History of Kansas City, Missouri* (Boulder, Colo.: Pruett Publishing Co., 1978), p. 179; Henry C. Haskell, Jr. and Richard B. Fowler, *City of the Future* (Kansas City: Frank Glenn Publishing Co., 1950), p. 120; *Kansas City Post*, April 17, 1923, p. 1.

7. George Collins, draft of letter to *Kansas City Star*, September 28, 1939, Miscellaneous Historical Document 403, HSTL. Of this account Truman wrote, "Your statements are correct" (Harry S. Truman to George Collins, October 2, 1939, Miscellaneous Historical Document 403, HSTL). Truman, *Autobiography,* pp. 56, 81; Schauffler, *Harry Truman,* pp. 59–60; Harry S. Truman interview with Jonathan Daniels, November 12, 1949, pp. 61–62, MOI notes, Jonathan Daniels papers, HSTL; Truman, *Memoirs,* p. 136; Program, March 17, 1921 Battery D reunion, Miscellaneous Historical Document 284, HSTL; Heed, "Prelude to Whistlestop," pp. 45, 63–64; Harry S. Truman to Bess Wallace, November 1, 1918 and November 2, 1918, in Ferrell, *Dear Bess;* Harry S. Truman, "My Impressions"; Harry S. Truman interview with William Hillman, January 9, 1952, interviews folder, "Mr. President" file, box 269, PSF, HST papers, HSTL; Harry S. Truman to Ethel Noland and Nellie Noland, December 18, 1918, Mary Ethel Noland papers, HSTL; "Missouri politics" folder, Memoirs File,

Post-Presidential File, HST papers, HSTL; Reddig, *Tom's Town*, pp. 266–67; Truman, "Pickwick Papers," May 14, 1934; Henry Chiles oral history, pp. 33–36, HSTL; Mary Ethel Noland oral history, pp. 129–31; Edgar Hinde oral history, pp. 64–68, HSTL; Brown Harris to Harry S. Truman, March 6, 1943, and Harry S. Truman to Brown Harris, March 13, 1943, " 'Time' Magazine Article" folder, box 166, SV, HST papers, HSTL.

8. William Southern interview with Jonathan Daniels, September 26, 1949, p. 20, MOI notes, Jonathan Daniels papers, HSTL; Heed, "Prelude to Whistlestop," pp. 43–45, 129.

9. Sue Gentry interview with Harold Gosnell, August 29, 1964, "Background interviews" folder, box 11, Harold Gosnell papers, HSTL; Edward Rogge, "The Speechmaking of Harry S. Truman," Ph.D. dissertation, University of Missouri, 1958, pp. 53–54; Heed, "Prelude to Whistlestop," pp. 60–62; Truman, *Autobiography*, p. 57.

10. Edgar Hinde oral history, pp. 56–61, HSTL; Heed, "Prelude to Whistlestop," pp. 63–64.

11. Harry S. Truman interview with Jonathan Daniels, November 12, 1949, p. 62, MOI notes, Jonathan Daniels papers, HSTL; Truman, *Memoirs*, p. 136; Harry S. Truman interview with William Hillman, January 9, 1952, interviews folder, "Mr. President" File, box 269, PSF, HST papers, HSTL.

12. Truman, *Autobiography*, p. 57; "Missouri politics" folder, Memoirs File, Post-Presidential File, HST papers, HSTL; Charles F. Curry oral history, pp. 4–5, HSTL; Henry Chiles oral history, p. 72, HSTL; Truman, "My Impressions"; Edgar Hinde oral history, pp. 44–47, HSTL; Vere Leigh oral history, pp. 69–70, 73–74, HSTL; Mize Peters oral history, pp. 3–4, HSTL; Mrs. W. L. C. Palmer oral history, pp. 31–32, HSTL.

13. Gosnell, *Truman's Crises*, pp. 21–22 (citing Joseph Short to Mrs. Lichty, January 14, 1952, HSTL); "New Road and Precinct Map Showing Where to Vote for Harry S. Truman," in "Printed Material" folder, box 2, County Judge papers, Harry S. Truman papers and in "Correspondence 1960–1963" folder, Biographical File, Post-Presidential File, HST papers, HSTL; Edward McKim oral history, pp. 42–43, HSTL; Harry S. Truman to Margaret Ann Kurt, cited in Hillman, *Mr. President*, pp. 30, 32; Edgar Hinde oral history, pp. 44–47, HSTL; Margaret Truman, *Harry S. Truman*, p. 24; Harry S. Truman, May 14, 1952, *Public Papers 1952*, p. 125.

14. A few of the many Klan articles are in *Kansas City Star*, January 9, 1923, p. 1, January 10, 1923, p. 10, January 12, 1923, p. 5, January 20, 1923, p. 2, January 22, 1923, p. 2, *Kansas City Times*, January 27, 1923, p. 1, *Kansas City Journal*, January 2, 1923, p. 1, *Kansas City Post*, January 8, 1923, p. 1, January 13, 1923, p. 1, January 22, 1923, p. 2, January 23, 1923, p. 3; Margaret Truman, *Harry S. Truman*, p. 66; Harry S. Truman to Lou Holland, October 25, 1944, "Personal Correspondence—Harry S. Truman—Senator," Lou Holland papers, HSTL; Edgar Hinde oral history, pp. 50–55, HSTL; Heed, "Prelude to Whistlestop," pp. 73, 120; Reddig,

Tom's Town, pp. 267–69; Edgar Hinde interview *Kansas City Star* or *Kansas City Times,* April 20, 1945, Biographical File, PSF, HST papers, HSTL.

15. Heed, "Prelude to Whistlestop," p. 97; *Independence Examiner,* July 29, 1922; *Kansas City Star,* June 23, 1960. Truman also received labor support (see Resolution by Building Laborers Local Union No. 303, "Correspondence—general January-July 1922" folder, box 12, FBP, HST papers, HSTL; [printed as a handbill in "newspaper clippings folder 1," box 16, FBP, HST papers, HSTL]); L. A. Lohman to Harry S. Truman, October 14, 1922, "Correspondence—general October–December 1922" folder, box 12, FBP, HST papers, HSTL.

16. Heed, "Prelude to Whistlestop," pp. 95, 100–01; Bundschu, "Harry S. Truman," pp. 17–19; Brown Harris to Harry S. Truman, January 7, 1947, "Correspondence relating to Harry S. Truman—biographical," Biographical File, PSF, HST papers, HSTL; Truman, "My Impressions."

17. Harry S. Truman interview with William Hillman, January 9, 1952, interviews folder, "Mr. President" File, box 269, PSF, HST papers, HSTL; Daniels, *Man of Independence,* pp. 112–13; *Kansas City Times,* May 8, 1924, p. 3; Harry S. Truman to Ralph E. Truman, August 6, 1922, "Ralph E. Truman" folder, Family Correspondence File, Post-Presidential File, HST papers, HSTL; Affidavit, August 19, 1922, "Correspondence—general August–September 1922" folder, box 12, FBP, HST papers, HSTL; Affidavit, November 24, 1922, and Harry S. Truman to Democratic Finance Committee, October 18, 1922, "Correspondence—general October–December 1922" folder, box 12, FBP, HST papers, HSTL. Truman said that the Pendergast organization "didn't think I could do it" and that he had no campaign funds in 1922 ("Missouri politics" folder, Memoirs File, HST papers, HSTL; Harry S. Truman interview with Harold Gosnell, June 25, 1963, background notes folder, box 11, Harold Gosnell papers, HSTL).

18. *Lee's Summit Journal,* August 3, 1922, cited in Heed, "Prelude to Whistlestop," p. 102; Heed, "Prelude to Whistlestop," pp. 77–78, 115–116; *Independence Examiner,* July 17 and July 18, 1922.

19. Sam O'Neal article, *St. Louis Post-Dispatch,* July 24, 1934; Harry S. Truman interview with Jonathan Daniels, July 28, 1949, p. 2, MOI notes, Jonathan Daniels papers, HSTL; Eben Ayers memo, August 3, 1951, "Personal—Ayers, E.—trip to Kansas City (June 19–30, 1951)," Eben Ayers papers (23), HSTL. Note that Truman's living arrangements freed him from any rent or mortgage payments. A prewar example of Truman refusing to pay a lawful debt can be found in Harry S. Truman to Bess Wallace, July 7, 1913, in Ferrell, *Dear Bess.*

20. George Buecking to Harry S. Truman, June 25, 1951, pencil note stapled to correspondence to Edward Jacobson, George Powell to Harry S. Truman, May 31, 1951, Eben Ayers memo and sheet with heading "The Security State Bank Loan—$5,000.00, and the judgment against Harry S. Truman," all in "Personal—Ayers, E.—trip to Kansas City (June 19–30,

1951)," Eben Ayers papers (23), HSTL; Truman, *Memoirs* draft, p. 2836; Harry Miller to Harry S. Truman, July 17, 1922, "Correspondence—general January–July 1922" folder, box 12, FBP, HST papers, HSTL; Central Trust Co. to H. L. Truman, August 1, 1922, DeSoto Bank to Harry S. Truman, August 8, 1922, F. E. Goodway to C. S. Hambleton, August 9, 1922, Harry S. Truman to William Boydston, September 27, 1922, William Boydston to Harry S. Truman, September 25, 1922, "Correspondence—general August–September 1922" folder, box 12, FBP, HST papers, HSTL; C. S. Hambleton to Harry S. Truman, January 26, 1923, Harry S. Truman to C. S. Hamilton, February 3, 1923, William Boydston to Harry S. Truman, January 15, 1923, Harry S. Truman to William Boydston, February 3, 1923, "Correspondence—general 1923" folder, box 12, FBP, HST papers, HSTL; C. W. Sheldon to Ed Beach, February 14, 1924, "Correspondence—general 1924–1925" folder, box 13, FBP, HST papers, HSTL; Delinquent tax notice, July 19, 1922, "Miscellaneous 1922–1953" folder, box 15, FBP, HST papers, HSTL. Truman first put up the farm as security in January 1922 (abstract from Recorder of Deeds, Johnson County, Kansas, MOI notes, Jonathan Daniels papers, University of North Carolina).

21. Carl B. Jenkins to Harry S. Truman, September 15, 1922, Harry S. Truman to Carl B. Jenkins, September 16, 1922, "Correspondence—general August–September 1922" folder, box 12, FBP, HST papers, HSTL.

22. *Independence Examiner*, December 1 and December 7, 1922, January 1 and January 2, 1923. The judges took the oath of office on December 6 although they didn't assume office until January 1.

23. Harry S. Truman to J. H. Twyman, July 9, 1922, "General correspondence—January–July 1922" folder, box 12, General File, FBP, HST papers, HSTL; Edgar Hinde oral history, pp. 50–55, HSTL; Truman, *Autobiography*, p. 57; Truman, *Memoirs*, p. 137; *Independence Examiner*, January 2, January 3, and January 5, 1923; *Kansas City Star*, January 2, 1923, p. 1, January 3, 1923, pp. 1, 22, January 5, 1923, p. 1, January 11, 1923, p. 5, January 13, 1923, p. 1, January 16, 1923, p. 2, January 17, 1923, p. 2; *Kansas City Times*, January 3, 1923, p. 1, January 4, 1923, p. 3, January 6, 1923, p. 3; *Kansas City Post*, January 3, 1923, p. 2, January 4, 1923, p. 2, January 6, 1923, p. 1, March 2, 1923, p. 1. A list of persons Truman apparently appointed to low-level patronage jobs (including the names of their faction sponsors) can be found in county judge notebook, box 2, Desk File, Post-Presidential File, HST papers, HSTL.

24. *State ex rel. Leo E. Koehler* v. *Elihu W. Hayes et al.*, no. 185, 263, Jackson County Circuit Court, Order to show cause why writ of prohibition should not issue, January 22, 1923, decision, May 21, 1923, and Motion for a New Trial and Defendants' Suggestions in Support of Motion to Quash, "Jackson County Court 1923" folder, box 13, General File, FBP, HST papers, HSTL; *Kansas City Star*, January 22, 1923, p. 2, January 27, 1923, p. 1, January 29, 1923, p. 5, February 7, 1923, p. 3, March 3, 1923, p. 1, March 5, 1923,

p. 2, March 15, 1923, p. 3, March 16, 1923, p. 1, March 18, 1923, p. 2, March 21, 1923, p. 2, May 21, 1923, p. 1, May 20, 1923, p. 1, October 19, 1923, p. 1; *Kansas City Times,* January 25, 1923, p. 1, February 8, 1923, p. 3, February 9, 1923, p. 3, March 3, 1923, p. 3, March 9, 1923, p. 3, March 13, 1923, p. 5, March 19, 1923, p. 3, March 20, 1923, p. 2, May 26, 1923, p. 1; *Kansas City Journal,* January 4, 1923, p. 1, January 28, 1923, p. 2, February 6, 1923, pp. 1–2, February 8, 1923, pp. 1–2, February 9, 1923, p. 1, March 3, 1923, p. 1, March 17, 1923, p. 1, March 18, 1923, pp. 1–2, March 20, 1923, p. 2, June 1, 1923, p. 2; *Kansas City Post,* January 26, 1923, p. 2, January 28, 1923, p. 2, February 5, 1923, p. 1, February 7, 1923, p. 2, March 3, 1923, p. 1, March 5, 1923, p. 1, March 15, 1923, p. 2, March 19, 1923, p. 2, March 21, 1923, p. 2, April 13, 1923, p. 2, May 21, 1923, p. 1, May 25, 1923, p. 4, May 29, 1923, p. 3; Harry S. Truman interview with William Hillman, January 9, 1952, interviews folder, "Mr. President" File, box 269, PSF, HST papers, HSTL; Alfred N. Gossett to Elihu Hayes, Henry McElroy, and Harry S. Truman, January 22, 1923, "Jackson County Court 1923" folder, box 13, General File, FBP, HST papers, HSTL. Gossett would become one of the best-known Kansas City councilmen keeping McElroy in power. Pendergast opponent Walter Matscheck termed Gossett "very, very capable and a shrewd man" (Walter Matscheck oral history, p. 21, HSTL). "It's my belief," Gossett said, "that all a man needs is one knife, one fork, one teaspoon, one book, one wife or sweetheart, and one million dollars" (Reddig, *Tom's Town,* p. 154).

25. *Independence Examiner,* January 24, 1923; *Kansas City Star,* February 14, 1923, p. 3, February 15, 1923, p. 3, March 8, 1923, p. 2, March 11, 1923, p. 1, March 21, 1923, p. 2, March 23, 1923, p. 1, March 23, 1923, pp. 1–2, March 30, 1923, p. 1, April 3, 1923, pp. 1–2, July 6, 1924, p. 4A; *Kansas City Times,* January 23, 1923, p. 3, February 21, 1923, p. 2, March 3, 1923, p. 3, March 9, 1923, p. 3, March 22, 1923, p.1, March 23, 1923, p. 1, March 24, 1923, p. 1, March 27, 1923, p. 1, March 29, 1923, p. 2, April 5, 1923, p. 1; *Kansas City Journal,* January 4, 1923, p. 1, January 25 1923, p. 2, February 6, 1923, pp. 1–2, March 3, 1923, p. 1, March 9, 1923, p. 1, March 15, 1923, p. 2, March 24, 1923, p. 1, March 27, 1923, p. 1, March 29, 1923, pp. 1, 3; *Kansas City Post,* March 8, 1923, p. 1, March 23, 1923, p. 1, March 24, 1923, p. 2 (two articles), March 27, 1923, p. 2, April 3, 1923, p. 1; letter to Harry S. Truman, January 27, 1923, "General Correspondence 1923" folder, box 12, General File, FBP, HST papers, HSTL; Jackson County Court order, February 19, 1923, Jackson County Clerk's office; Henry Chiles oral history, p. 28, HSTL.

26. *Kansas City Journal,* February 20, 1923, p. 1, March 3, 1923, p. 1; *Kansas City Star,* March 1, 1923, p. 1, March 2, 1923, p. 1, March 5, 1923, p. 2; *Kansas City Post,* March 1, 1923, p. 1, February 1, 1923, p. 2, February 16, 1923, p. 1, March 2, 1923, p. 1; Jackson County Court order, February 19, 1923, Jackson County Clerk's office.

27. Arthur Young & Co. to Honorable County Court, February 5, 1923, "Jackson County Audit 1922" folder, box 13, General File, FBP, HST papers, HSTL; *Kansas City Star,* February 6, 1923, p. 1, February 14, 1923, p. 3, February 19, 1923, p. 1, February 20, 1923, p. 3, March 10, 1923, pp. 1–2, March 11, 1923, p. 1; *Kansas City Post,* February 1, 1923, p. 2, February 6, 1923 p. 1, March 9, 1923, p. 1, March 10, 1923, pp. 1–2, May 4, 1923, pp. 1–2; *Kansas City Times,* March 12, 1923, p. 4; *Kansas City Journal,* March 24, 1923, p. 1.

28. Estimated Cost of Operation for the Jackson County Industrial Home for Negro Boys for One Year, "Jackson County Court 1924" folder, General File, FBP, HST papers, HSTL; Jackson County Court order, March 29, 1923, Jackson County Clerk's office; *A Survey of the Welfare Activities of Jackson County Government 1928* (Kansas City: Civic Research Institute, 1928), p. 89; *Kansas City Star,* March 1, 1923, p. 1, March 10, 1923, pp. 1–2, March 22, 1923, p. 1, April 5, 1923, p. 1, March 29, 1923, p. 1, May 11, 1923, p. 1; *Independence Examiner,* January 29, 1923; *Kansas City Journal,* January 27, 1923, p. 3, January 18, 1924, p. 1; *Kansas City Times,* April 6, 1923, p. 3, November 2, 1923, p. 3; *Kansas City Post,* March 22, 1923, p. 1, April 7, 1923, p. 3, March 26, 1923, p. 2, April 5, 1923, p. 1, April 6, 1923, p. 1.

29. Jackson County Court orders April 6, April 20, April 23, April 25, June 12, 1923, Jackson County Clerk's office; *Kansas City Times,* April 6, 1923, p. 1, April 10, 1923, p. 3, April 19, 1923, p. 1, April 20, 1923, p. 1, April 23, 1923, p. 1, April 25, 1923, p. 1, April 27, 1923, p. 1; *Kansas City Journal,* April 25, 1923, p. 2, May 20, 1923, p. 1, August 22, 1923, p. 3; *Kansas City Post,* February 1, 1923, p. 2, April 20, 1923, p. 1, April 23, 1923, p. 1, April 25, 1923, p. 1, April 27, 1923, p. 1, May 21, 1923, p. 1, May 31, 1923, p. 1, August 21, 1923, p. 1, August 22, 1923, p. 1, October 5, 1923, p. 1; *Kansas City Star,* May 20, 1923, p. 1, May 21, 1923, p. 1, March 7, 1923, p. 1, August 22, 1923, p. 1.

30. Jackson County Court orders May 28, May 29, and June 1, 1923; *Kansas City Post,* April 24, 1923, p. 1, May 11, 1923, p. 3, June 1, 1923, pp. 1, 18, June 5, 1923, p. 3, June 13, 1923, p. 1; *Kansas City Journal,* June 1, 1923, p. 2; *Kansas City Star,* April 24, 1923, p. 1, May 28, 1923, p. 1, June 2, 1923, p. 1, June 6, 1923, p. 6, June 13, 1923, p. 1; *Kansas City Times,* June 1, 1923, p. 1, June 2, 1923, p. 1, June 6, 1923, pp. 2, 6, June 13, 1923, p. 3.

31. Ralph E. Truman to Harry S. Truman, January 3 and January 23, 1923, and Harry S. Truman to Ralph E. Truman, February 3, 1923, "Ralph E. Truman" folder, Family Correspondence File, Post-Presidential File, HST papers, HSTL; Biographical sketch, pp. 43–44, 56–57, Ralph E. Truman papers, HSTL; *State of Missouri ex rel. Ralph E. Truman* v. *Henry L. Jost et al.,* case 74,634, Jackson County Circuit Court. The Charlie Ross who served under Snapper and the Charlie Ross who attended high school with Harry Truman were two different persons. Judge Latshaw presided

over the trial of B. C. Hyde for the Swope murders. He was also Exalted
Ruler of the Elks Lodge where the notorious Battery D reunion was held
(E. J. Becker to HST, March 22, 1921, "Programs 1914–1925" folder, box
16, FBP, HST papers, HSTL).

32. Jackson County Court order, September 21, 1923, Jackson County
clerk's office; *Kansas City Times,* April 25, 1923, p. 1, June 7, 1923, p. 1,
September 21, 1923, p. 2, September 22, 1923, p. 2, September 24, 1923,
p. 1, September 27, 1923, p. 3; *Kansas City Star,* September 20, 1923, p. 1,
September 21, 1923, p. 1, September 25, 1923, p. 1, September 26, 1923,
p. 2, October 25, 1923, p. 4; *Kansas City Post,* March 29, 1923, p. 1, September 20, p. 1 (two articles), September 21, 1923, p. 1, September 24,
1923, p. 1, September 25, 1923, p. 1, September 26, 1923, p. 1.

33. Jackson County Court order, August 31, 1923, Jackson County Clerk's
office; *Kansas City Star,* August 19, 1923, p. 1, August 30, 1923, p. 1, August
31, 1923, p. 2; *Kansas City Journal,* September 26, 1923, p. 3; *Kansas City
Post,* February 13, 1924, p. 5.

34. Harry S. Truman to Bess Truman, July 22, July 24, July 25, July
28, 1923, "Correspondence from Harry S. Truman to Bess Wallace Truman—July 1923" folder, Family Correspondence File, box 5, FBP, HST
papers, HSTL; *Kansas City Star,* February 16, 1923, p. 3, February 25, 1923,
p. 3, September 28, 1923, p. 1, September 29, 1923, p. 1, September 30,
1923, p. 4A, July 30, 1923, p. 1; *Kansas City Journal,* February 22, 1923, p.
3, September 28, 1923, p. 2; *Kansas City Post,* September 27, 1923, p. 3,
September 29, 1923, p. 2; *Kansas City Times,* September 29, 1923, p. 2, July
14, 1923, p. 6.

35. Jackson County Court orders, May 10 and August 31, 1923, Jackson
County Clerk's office; Truman, "More Character Sketches" and "More
about government," "Pickwick Papers"; *Kansas City Journal,* October 2,
1923, p. 1, March 18, 1924, p. 1, March 19, 1924, p. 1, March 6, 1923, p.
1, May 20, 1923, pp. 1–2; *Kansas City Star,* November 9, 1923, p. 1, April
21, 1924, p. 4, January 16, 1923, p. 2, September 1, 1923, p. 2, September
16, 1923, p. 4A; *Kansas City Times,* February 11, 1924, p. 1, March 18, 1924,
p. 3, April 21, 1924, p. 1, May 30, 1924, p. 3, February 27, 1923, p. 1,
March 6, 1923, p. 1, July 4, 1923, p. 1, July 9, 1923, p. 1, July 31, 1923,
p. 2; *Kansas City Post,* January 15, 1923, p. 2, July 30, 1923, p. 1, August
7, 1923, p. 3, August 9, 1923, p. 1, January 16, 1923, p. 3.

36. Margaret Weddle oral history, pp. 35–39, HSTL; *Kansas City Journal,*
May 20, 1923, pp. 1–2.

37. *Kansas City Post,* October 23, 1923, p. 1, October 27, 1923, p. 1,
October 29, 1923, p. 1, October 31, 1923, p. 1; *Kansas City Times,* October
29, 1923, p. 3, November 7, 1923, p. 1; *Kansas City Journal,* October 28,
1923, pp. 1, 5, November 18, 1923, pp. 1, 7; *Kansas City Star,* October 27,
1923, p. 1, October 28, 1923, p. 1, October 31, 1923, p. 1, November 1,
1923, p. 1, November 18, 1923, p. 1, November 21, 1923, p. 2.

38. Jackson County Court order, November 6, 1923, Jackson County Clerk's office; *Kansas City Post,* November 6, 1923, p. 2; *Kansas City Times,* November 3, 1923, p. 2, November 5, 1923, p. 4, November 7, 1923, p. 1, November 17, 1923, p. 3; *Kansas City Star,* November 1, 1923, p. 1, November 12, 1923, p. 2; *Kansas City Journal,* October 28, 1923, p. 1. Burke was also cleared of charges of payroll irregularities.

39. *Independence Examiner,* March 7, 1924; *Kansas City Star,* January 4, 1923, p. 3, March 9, 1924, p. 2A, May 17, 1924, p. 2, March 25, 1923, p. 2A, April 17, 1923, p. 1, November 28, 1923, p. 2, December 5, 1923, p. 2, December 14, 1923, p. 3, February 1, 1924, p. 2, February 29, 1924, p. 2; *Kansas City Post,* November 6, 1923, p. 2, April 17, 1923, p. 1, January 5, 1924, p. 3, March 18, 1924, p. 1; *Kansas City Times,* November 17, 1923, p. 3, November 29, 1923, p. 1, December 20, 1923, p. 3, January 5, 1924, p. 6, March 1, 1924, p. 1; *Kansas City Journal,* November 29, 1923, p. 1, December 14, 1923, p. 1, January 5, 1924, p. 2, January 18, 1924, p. 1, March 7, 1924, p. 1, March 14, 1924, p. 1, May 15, 1924, p. 1, October 19, 1924, p. 8, October 29, 1924, p. 1, October 31, 1924, pp. 1–2; John T. Barker, *Missouri Lawyer* (Philadelphia: Dorrance & Co., 1949), pp. 219–20; Fred Boxley to Harry S. Truman, March 8, 1923, "Jackson County Court 1923" folder, box 13, General File, FBP, HST papers, HSTL; Ralph Latshaw to E. W. Hayes, January 29, 1924, "Jackson County Court 1924" folder, General File, FBP, HST papers, HSTL; Harry S. Truman, "More about Government," "Pickwick Papers"; *State ex rel. D. A. Holmes et al.* v. *Elihu W. Hayes et al.,* case 203,565, Jackson County Circuit Court; *State ex rel. Thomas B. Buckner et al.* v. *Henry F. McElroy et al.* (309 Mo. 595); *A Survey of the Welfare Activities of Jackson County Government, 1928* (Kansas City: Civic Research Institute, 1928), pp. 51–52, Civic Research Institute records, WHMC, MU.

40. Heed, "Prelude to Whistlestop," pp. 34–35, 156, 163–64, 224, 173–74; Henry Chiles oral history, pp. 37–38, HSTL; *Kansas City Post,* March 29, 1923, p. 1; *Kansas City Star,* March 22, 1923, p. 1, March 26, 1923, p. 4; *Kansas City Times,* December 14, 1923, p. 1, May 21, 1924, p. 1; *Independence Examiner,* July 18 and July 28, 1922, March 3, March 15, March 20, April 15, and July 14, 1924; William Schilling to Westbrook Pegler, October 24, 1946, and Herbert Simpson to Westbrook Pegler, March 14, 1950, Westbrook Pegler papers, Herbert Hoover Presidential Library. (The Simpson letter has a handwritten notation, "Ask Milligan.")

41. Heed, "Prelude to Whistlestop," pp. 160–62, 217, 230; Truman, "My Impressions"; Harry S. Truman interview with William Hillman, January 9, 1952, interviews folder, "Mr. President" File, box 269, PSF, HST papers, HSTL; unidentified clipping, "HST—1924 Election" folder, vertical file, HSTL; *Kansas City Post,* January 8, 1923, p. 1, January 18, 1923, p. 4, January 27, 1923, p. 2, May 9, 1923, p. 1, January 1, 1924, p. 2, June 17, 1924, p. 1, November 5, 1924, October 31, 1924; *Independence Examiner,*

January 29, 1923; *Kansas City Star,* January 9, 1923, p. 3, January 14, 1923, p. 4A, January 17, 1923, p. 2, January 23, 1923, p. 1, January 31, 1923, p. 1, March 21, 1924, p. 1; *Kansas City Times,* January 8, 1923, p. 1, January 9, 1923, p. 2, January 19, 1923, p. 6, January 23, 1923, p. 3, January 26, 1923, p. 2, January 27, 1923, p. 1, May 8, 1924, p. 3; *Kansas City Journal,* January 9, 1923, p. 2, October 22, 1924, p. 7.

42. Harry S. Truman interview with Jonathan Daniels, October 12, 1949, p. 61, MOI notes, Jonathan Daniels papers, HSTL; *Kansas City Star,* March 7, 1924, p. 1, March 8, 1924, p. 1, March 11, 1924, p. 1, March 12, 1924, pp. 1–2, June 30, 1924, p. 1; *Kansas City Times,* March 8, 1924, pp. 1–2, March 13, 1924, pp. 1, 2, February 20, 1924, p. 3, February 28, 1924, p. 2 (two articles), May 8, 1924, p. 3, July 4, 1924, p. 4; Reddig, *Tom's Town,* pp. 107–09, 113–14; Margaret Truman, *Harry S. Truman,* p. 68; Daniels, *Man of Independence,* p. 126.

43. Harry S. Truman to Bess Truman, July 22, 1923, "Correspondence from Harry S. Truman to Bess Wallace Truman—July 1923" folder, Family Correspondence File, box 5, FBP, HST papers, HSTL; *Public Affairs* (bulletin of the Civic Research Institute), July 17, 1924; Heed, "Prelude to Whistlestop," pp. 156, 169, 186–87, 214; *Independence Examiner,* July 18, 1924, May 9, 1924; *Kansas City Journal,* February 23, 1924, p. 1, June 12, 1924, p. 2, September 29, 1924, pp. 1–2; *Kansas City Star,* January 3, 1923, p. 22, March 22, 1923, p. 1; *Kansas City Post,* March 28, 1923, p. 3; *Kansas City Times,* June 26, 1924, p. 1.

44. *Kansas City Star,* January 24, 1924, p. 5; *Kansas City Journal,* December 28, 1923, p. 1, February 23, 1924, p. 1, March 14, 1924, p. 1; *Kansas City Times,* May 29, 1924, p. 3, July 1, 1924, p. 4, January 17, 1924, p. 4, January 19, 1924, p. 1, June 30, 1924, p. 1; Reddig, *Tom's Town,* p. 113; Heed, "Prelude to Whistlestop," pp. 170–71, 221.

45. Unidentified clipping, newspaper clipping envelope, "Jackson County Court Election 1924" folder, box 13, FBP, HST papers, HSTL; Heed, "Prelude to Whistlestop," p. 209; Statement of Financial Condition of Jackson County, May 31, 1924, Statement of Condition of Funds, June 30, 1924, and Ralph Latshaw to E. W. Hayes, January 29, 1924, "Jackson County Court 1924" folder, General File, FBP, HST papers, HSTL; Walter Matscheck oral history, p. 32, HSTL; *Kansas City Journal,* January 22, 1924, p. 2, February 23, 1924, p. 1, March 14, 1924, p. 1, April 2, 1924, p. 1, September 28, 1924, pp. 1A, 8A, September 29, 1924, pp. 1–2, October 1, 1924, pp. 1–2, October 8, 1924, p. 1, October 11, 1924, p. 14, October 14, 1924, p. 6, October 15, 1924, p. 14, October 21, 1924, p. 12, October 31, 1924, pp. 1–2; *Kansas City Post,* January 23, 1924, p. 2, March 13, 1924, p. 1, March 18, 1924, p. 1; *Kansas City Star,* January 18, 1923, p. 1, January 23, 1924, p. 1, January 24, 1924, p. 5, February 1, 1924, p. 2, March 13, 1924, p. 1, March 31, 1924, p. 1; *Kansas City Times,* March 20, 1924, p. 3,

June 24, 1924, p. 5; *Independence Examiner*, August 13, 1924, and July 1, 1926.

46. Jackson County Court orders August 3 and October 11, 1923, Jackson County Clerk's office; Heed, "Prelude to Whistlestop," pp. 167–68, 180–81; *Kansas City Star*, September 25, 1923, p. 1, March 2, 1924, p. 5A, March 10, 1924, p. 5; *Kansas City Post*, September 25, 1923, p. 1, November 1, 1923, p. 1, February 12, 1924, p. 1, March 10, 1924, p. 1; *Kansas City Journal*, March 2, 1924, pp. 1–2, March 3, 1924, pp. 1–2, March 4, 1924, pp. 1–2, March 7, 1924, p. 1, September 28, 1924, p. 8A, October 3, 1924, p. 14, October 4, 1924, p. 1, October 6, 1924, p. 14, October 7, 1924, p. 14, October 9, 1924, p. 14, October 12, 1924, p. 12A, October 14, 1924, p. 14, October 17, 1924, p. 14, October 18, 1924, p. 3, October 19, 1924, pp. 1, 8, October 26, 1924, pp. 1A, 6A. The *Independence Examiner* defended Truman on October 25, October 27, October 29 and November 3, 1924.

47. Anon., *Report on the County Highway Department and County Road System of Jackson County, Missouri* (Kansas City: Civic Research Institute, 1926), pp. 12, 22, 33–36; Ralph Truman to Harry S. Truman, May 7, 1924, "Ralph E. Truman" folder, Family Correspondence, Post-Presidential File, HST papers, HSTL; Heed, "Prelude to Whistlestop," pp. 164–65, 171, 182, 204–05, 218, 223; *Kansas City Star*, April 8, 1923, p. 2A, August 6, 1923, p. 5, October 22, 1923, p. 3; *Kansas City Post*, May 9, 1923, p. 1, July 3, 1923, p. 2, October 22, 1923, p. 3, November 9, 1923, p. 1, February 20, 1924, p. 3, June 13, 1924, p. 1; *Kansas City Journal*, July 31, 1923, p. 1, August 6, 1923, p. 3, September 8, 1923, p. 2, September 30, 1924, October 2, 1924, pp. 1–2, October 6, 1924, p. 14, October 7, 1924, p. 14, October 8, 1924, p. 1, October 13, 1924, p. 16, October 20, 1924, p. 14, October 22, 1924, p. 14, October 23, 1924, p. 14, October 24, 1924, p. 5, October 25, 1924, p. 1, October 27, 1924, p. 5, October 28, 1924, p. 16, October 29, 1924, p. 3, October 30, 1924, p. 16, October 30, 1924, p. 1, October 31, 1924, p. 14, November 1, 1924, p. 14, November 3, 1924, pp. 1, 3, November 4, 1924, pp. 1, 2, 3; *Kansas City Times*, October 22, 1923, p. 1, February 26, 1924, p. 3; J. R. Knorpp to Harry S. Truman, July 20, 1924, "Jackson County Court 1924" folder, General File, FBP, HST papers, HSTL; Jackson County Court order, August 8, 1924, Jackson County Clerk's office; Truman, *Autobiography*, pp. 34–36; Harry S. Truman interview with Jonathan Daniels, November 12, 1949, p. 62, MOI notes, Jonathan Daniels papers, HSTL.

48. Jackson County Court orders, February 25, 1921, February 16, 1922, Jackson County Clerk's office; *Kansas City Journal*, October 5, 1924, p. 8A.

49. *Kansas City Journal*, November 2, 1924, p. 1A; *Kansas City Times* editorials June 26, July 21, and October 31, 1924; *Kansas City Star* editorial, July 17, 1924; Heed, "Prelude to Whistlestop," p. 224; Truman, *Autobiography*, p. 57.

50. "John Miles for Sheriff" contributions list, county judge notebook, box 2, Desk File, Post-Presidential File, HST papers, HSTL; Edgar Hinde oral history, pp. 27, 50, HSTL; *Independence Examiner*, November 6 and November 7, 1924; Bundschu, "Harry S. Truman," pp. 19–20; General Historical Document 70, HSTL.

51. Heed, "Prelude to Whistlestop," pp. 225–30; unidentified clipping, "HST—1924 Election" folder, vertical file, HSTL; *Kansas City Post*, November 4, 1924; Margaret Truman, *Harry S. Truman*, p. 68; Edgar Hinde oral history, pp. 50–55, HSTL.

52. *Kansas City Times*, November 7, 1924, p. 8, cited in Heed, "Prelude to Whistlestop," p. 235; Reddig, *Tom's Town*, pp. 114–15; Henry Chiles oral history, p. 29, HSTL; John Strode oral history, pp. 9–13, HSTL; Harry S. Truman to J. W. Corn, August 14, 1922, and J. W. Corn to Harry S. Truman, August 6, 1922, "Correspondence—general August–September 1922" folder, box 12, FBP, HST papers, HSTL.

53. Heed, "Prelude to Whistlestop," pp. 235–36; *Independence Examiner*, November 19, 1924.

54. Ralph Truman to Harry S. Truman, November 7, 1924, "Ralph E. Truman" folder, Family Correspondence File, Post-Presidential File, Harry S. Truman papers, HSTL.

Chapter 9   BACK TO BUSINESS

1. Unidentified clipping, scrapbook 4, John T. Barker papers, WHMC, MU.

2. *St. Louis Post-Dispatch*, July 24, 1934; I. H. Kalis to Eben Ayers, June 25, 1951, Charles Hipsh to Eben Ayers, June 25, 1951, Isadore Steinberg to Eben Ayers, July 9, 1951, George H. Buecking to Harry S. Truman, June 25, 1951, "The Security State Bank Loan—$5,000.00 and the judgment against Harry S. Truman" memo, all in "Personal—Ayers, E.—trip to Kansas City (June 19–30, 1951)," Eben Ayers papers (23), HSTL; Harry S. Truman interviews with Jonathan Daniels, July 28 and November 12, 1949, MOI notes, Jonathan Daniels papers, HSTL.

3. Harry S. Truman to Bess Truman, July 15, 1925, July 5, 1926, Family Correspondence File, box 5, FBP, HST papers, HSTL.

4. Barker, *Missouri Lawyer*, pp. 226–27; *Catalog of the Kansas City School of Law*, June 1923, p. 38, June 1924, pp. 12–13; *The Pandex* (Kansas City: Kansas City School of Law, 1924), pp. 8, 28, 70, 88; Sales exam, March 7, 1924, Torts final exam, May 5, 1924, "Kansas City School of Law, Harry S. Truman Examinations 1923–1924" folder, Kansas City School of Law, General File, box 14, FBP, HST papers, HSTL.

5. Harry S. Truman law school notebooks in Miscellaneous Historical documents, HSTL, in box 2, Desk File, Post-Presidential file, HST papers,

HSTL, and in Kansas City School of Law, General File, box 14, FBP, Harry S. Truman papers, HSTL; "Miscellaneous," Desk File, Post-Presidential File, HST papers, HSTL; Harry S. Truman interview with Jonathan Daniels, August 30, 1949, MOI notes, Jonathan Daniels papers, HSTL; Miscellaneous Historical Document 17, HSTL; Edgar Hinde oral history, p. 87, HSTL; Mize Peters oral history, pp. 48, 51, HSTL.

6. Daniels, *Man of Independence*, p. 132; H. H. Halvorson oral history, pp. 20–21, HSTL; Vera Henthorn to Harry S. Truman, July 8, 1926, "General Correspondence 1926–1953" folder, General File, box 13, FBP, HST papers, HSTL.

7. *Kansas City Star*, May 29, 1923, p. 3, May 31, 1923, p. 1, July 4, 1923, p. 1, July 8, 1923, p. 2A, September 13, 1923, p. 1; *Kansas City Journal*, August 18, 1923, pp. 1–2; *Kansas City Times*, June 5, 1923, p. 5; Meverell Good to Albert Beach, July 25, 1925, "Clubs" folder, box 2, Albert Beach papers, WHMC, MU.

8. Truman, *Autobiography*, p. 59; Truman, *Memoirs*, p. 138; Truman, "Pickwick Papers," May 14, 1934; Harry S. Truman interview with Jonathan Daniels, November 12, 1949, p. 61, MOI notes, Jonathan Daniels papers, HSTL; Daniels, p. 133; McNaughton and Hehmeyer, *This Man Truman*, pp. 64–65; Harry S. Truman, speech to sales conference of Shirtcraft Co., December 19, 1936, "Speeches by Sen. Harry S. Truman 1935–1939 (Folder 1)" folder, box 163, SV, HST papers, HSTL.

9. "Farm & Home Savings & Loan" folder, H. H. Halvorson papers, HSTL; Frederick Bowman oral history, p. 32, HSTL; N. T. Paterson to Harry S. Truman, December 19, 1955, "N. T. Paterson" folder, HST papers, HSTL; *Farm & Home News*, October 1977, "Battery D" folder, vertical file, HSTL; N. T. Paterson, "The President's Savings and Loan Background," *Savings and Loans*, June 1945, Biographical File, PSF, HST papers, HSTL; Rufus Burrus to Richard Lawrence Miller, April 15, 1982, telephone call, author's files; Charles F. Curry oral history, pp. 25–27; *Kansas City Post*, July 14, 1917; *Kansas City Star*, November 28, 1930.

10. Rufus Burrus to Richard Lawrence Miller, April 15, 1982, telephone call, author's files; Harry S. Truman interview with Jonathan Daniels, November 12, 1949, p. 61, MOI notes, Jonathan Daniels papers, HSTL; South Central Savings & Loan incorporation papers and Change of Name document (book 423, p. 638), "Community Savings & Loan Association and personal business" folder, H. H. Halvorson papers, HSTL; John O'-Brien to O. K. LaRoque, October 5, 1949, Jonathan Daniels papers, University of North Carolina.

11. Rufus Burrus to Richard Lawrence Miller, April 15, 1982, telephone call, author's files; Limited partnership agreement and contract, November 18, 1927, "Rural Investment Company" folder, H. H. Halvorson papers, HSTL; Tom Evans oral history, p. 191, HSTL.

12. Rufus Burrus to Richard Lawrence Miller, April 15, 1982, telephone

call, author's files; Community Savings & Loan brochure, "Community Savings & Loan Association and personal business" folder, HSTL; excerpt from Community Savings & Loan Association board of directors minutes, December 31, 1927, Corporation Division, Missouri Secretary of State; Rufus Burrus to Richard Lawrence Miller, February 1, 1983, author's files; H. H. Halvorson oral history, pp. 6–7, HSTL. Another director was Truman's cousin Murray Colgan.

13. Community Savings & Loan Association brochure, "Community Savings & Loan Association and personal business" folder, HSTL; Paterson, *Savings and Loans.*

14. *Kansas City Journal,* September 28, 1924, pp. 1A, 8A; Heed, "Prelude to Whistlestop," pp. 220–21; Partnership Agreement, April 21, 1926, "Rural Investment Company" folder, H. H. Halvorson papers, HSTL; Frederick Bowman oral history, pp. 36–38, HSTL; Walter Menefee oral history, p. 12, HSTL; Edward McKim oral history, p. 48, HSTL; Harry Vaughan oral history, p. 21, HSTL; Edgar Hinde oral history, pp. 79–83, HSTL; Harry Vaughan and Edward McKim interview with Jonathan Daniels, September 29, 1949, p. 33, Henry Bundschu interview with Jonathan Daniels, October 3, 1949, p. 38, Harry S. Truman interview with Jonathan Daniels, November 12, 1949, p. 55, MOI notes, Jonathan Daniels papers, HSTL; Charles F. Curry oral history, p. 24, HSTL; Arthur Wilson oral history, p. 32, HSTL; Daniels, *Man of Independence,* pp. 131–33; H. H. Halvorson oral history, pp. 14–16, 26, HSTL. Tom Pendergast was in favor of Truman prospering with Community, but he didn't want it to solicit deposits from the city hall and county courthouse crowd that his nephew Jim's North American Savings & Loan was hitting. Salisbury claimed Truman tried to consolidate Community with North American in 1932 (Daniels, *Man of Independence,* p. 136). Salisbury's credibility is questionable, although after both men left Community Truman did work to help North American (Harry S. Truman to Mildred Dryden, December 13, 1940, Mildred Dryden to Harry S. Truman, December 17, 1940, "Harry S. Truman—Personal [October 1940–December 1941]" folder, box 168, SV, HST papers, HSTL). Peter J. Kelley, a top Shannon Democrat faction leader who was observed running from the house where Shannon men were trying to steal the crucial ballot box in Truman's 1922 election, eventually became president of North American Savings & Loan.

15. George Buecking to Lou Holland, September 20, 1921, letter to Lou Holland, February 16, 1926, Lou Holland to C. E. French, February 1, 1926, A. C. Watkins to Lou Holland, June 26, 1919, February 27, 1920, Russell Sheffield to Lou Holland, November 30 and December 3, 1920, and October 5, 1921, Lou Holland to C. F. Enright, September 17, 1920, C. E. French to Lou Holland, February 3, 1926, Lou Holland to John Seward, January 11, 1921, "Citizens Security Bank of Englewood" folder, box 20950, Lou Holland papers, WHMC, MU; "Forty Years Ago" column, *Kansas*

City Times, July 15, 1964; *Kansas City Star,* March 13, 1923, p. 1, August 15, 1926.

16. Letter to Lou Holland, February 16, 1926, "Citizens Security Bank of Englewood" folder, box 20950, Lou Holland papers, WHMC, MU; Rufus Burrus to Richard Lawrence Miller, April 15, 1982, telephone call, author's files; Harry S. Truman, "More about government" essay, "Pickwick Papers"; *Kansas City Star,* August 13, August 15, and August 26, 1926; unidentified memo, "Lou E. Holland" folder, H. H. Halvorson papers, HSTL.

17. *Kansas City Star,* August 15, 1926; Rufus Burrus to Richard Lawrence Miller, April 15, 1982, telephone call, author's files; Harry S. Truman interview with Jonathan Daniels, November 12, 1949, p. 61, MOI notes, Jonathan Daniels papers, HSTL; Lou Holland to C. E. French, April 27, 1926, North T. Gentry to Charles Becker, Lou Holland, Harry Truman, Spencer Salisbury, Arthur Metzger, and Rufus Burrus, undated, "Citizens Security Bank of Englewood" folder, box 20950, Lou Holland papers, WHMC, MU; Daniels, *Man of Independence,* pp. 134–35. Offhand the state's threat to sue Truman and his associates seems ironic. Yet the situation is clouded by Lou Holland's apparent need to keep Becker informed about the bank (Lou Holland to Charles Becker, April 23, 1926, "Citizens Security Bank of Englewood" folder, box 20950, Lou Holland papers, WHMC, MU), and the bank attorney's letter to Holland, "Send me a copy of the correspondence that you had with Mr. Becker so I may put them away in our files and be prepared to meet whatever action is taken in this matter" (Rufus Burrus to Lou Holland, August 26, 1926, "Citizens Security Bank of Englewood" folder, WHMC, MU).

18. H. H. Halvorson oral history, pp. 28–29, HSTL.

19. Partnership Agreement, April 21, 1926, "Rural Investment Co." folder, H. H. Halvorson papers, HSTL. While Truman was eastern judge Union Avenue Bank of Commerce was a depository for Jackson County funds (*Kansas City Post,* May 9, 1923, p. 1; Jackson County Court order, May 9, 1923, Jackson County Clerk's office).

20. Partnership Agreement, April 21, 1926, reverse side of Community Investment Co. Balance Sheet, September 1–December 31, 1927, and Articles of Association of the Community Investment Co., "Rural Investment Co." folder, H. H. Halvorson papers, HSTL; *Independence Examiner,* March 2, 1927, George F. Kern to Harry S. Truman, November 29, 1948, Harry S. Truman to George F. Kern, December 15, 1948, correspondence relating to Harry S. Truman—biographical, Biographical File, PSF, HST papers, HSTL; Edgar Hinde oral history, p. 78, HSTL; Mize Peters oral history, p. 40, HSTL.

21. Increase of stock, book 525, p. 349, and unidentified newspaper clipping, March 14, 1931, "Community Savings & Loan Association and personal business" folder, H. H. Halvorson papers, HSTL; Rufus Burrus to Richard Lawrence Miller, April 15, 1982, telephone call, author's files;

Audit of Harry S. Truman & Co. by Eric O. A. Miller & Co., August 31, 1927, limited partnership agreement and contract, November 18, 1927, articles of association of the Community Investment Co., October 1930, Community Investment Co. Financial Statements, September 30, 1930, H. H. Halvorson to Harvey Burrus, November 18, 1930, December 19 and December 31, 1931, Spencer Salisbury to H. H. Halvorson, December 30, 1931, H. H. Halvorson to Harry S. Truman, October 22 and November 3, 1931, H. H. Halvorson to Spencer Salisbury, October 15, May 7, February 27, and May 13, 1932, Harry S. Truman to H. H. Halvorson, October 28, 1931, all in "Rural Investment Co." folder, H. H. Halvorson papers, HSTL; Harry S. Truman, "I have had two wonderful associates," "Pickwick Papers" (Memoirs File copy).

Chapter 10   THE MASTER MACHINIST

1. Truman, "I have had two wonderful associates."
2. Reddig, *Tom's Town*, pp. 120–22.
3. Truman, *Autobiography*, p. 59; Truman, "My Impressions"; Edgar Hinde oral history, pp. 88–89, HSTL; Harry S. Truman interview with Patrick Ellen Maher, June 27, 1962, "Harry S. Truman interview notes," box 4, Sister Patrick Ellen Maher papers, HSTL; Truman, "I have had two wonderful associates"; Reddig, *Tom's Town*, p. 122; Tom Evans oral history, p. 175, HSTL.
4. Anon., *Who's Who in Kansas City* (1921), Vrooman sketch (book can be found in Kansas City, Missouri, Public Library); Edgar Hinde oral history, pp. 99–101, HSTL; Truman, "I have had two wonderful associates," and "More character sketches" essay, "Pickwick Papers"; *Independence Examiner*, May 8, 1926.
5. Ralph Truman to Harry S. Truman, November 24, 1926, "Ralph Truman and Family" folder, Family Correspondence File, Post-Presidential File, HST papers, HSTL; *Kansas City Times*, September 14, 1926, January 24, 1927, p. 1; *Kansas City Star*, January 1, and January 3, 1927, p. 2; Community Investment Co., Statement of Assets and Liabilities, February 28, 1930, "Community Savings & Loan correspondence" folder, H. H. Halvorson papers, HSTL.
6. *Kansas City Times*, December 3, 1926 editorial, p. F.
7. Ibid., January 28, 1927, pp. 1, 2; Truman, "I have had two wonderful associates," "Thomas B. Bash (I wonder what the B stands for . . .)," and "More about government," "Pickwick Papers"; Edgar Hinde oral history, p. 40, HSTL; Harry S. Truman, speech to Club Presidents Round Table, June 16, 1930, "Kansas City (Missouri) Road System and Old Trails" folder, box 3, County Judge papers, HST papers, HSTL.

8. *Kansas City Times,* January 6, 1927, p. 1, and January 22, 1927, p. 1; Anon., *Report on the County Highway Department and County Road System of Jackson County, Missouri* (Kansas City: Civic Research Institute, 1926), pp. vi, viii, 29, 50; Harry S. Truman (probably), speech to Rotary Boys Camp, October 1, 1930, Personal Correspondence—Harry S. Truman—County Judge, Lou Holland papers, HSTL; Harry S. Truman, speech to Club Presidents Round Table, June 16, 1930, Lou Holland speech, "Road Program," October 12, 1932, "Kansas City (Missouri) Road System and Old Trails" folder, box 3, County Judge papers, HST papers, HSTL; "Report on County Highway System of Jackson County, Missouri, by Edward M. Stayton [&] N. T. Veatch, Jr., [May 14] 1927," Personal Correspondence—Harry S. Truman—County Judge, Lou Holland papers, HSTL; Lou Holland diary, January 21, 1927, Lou Holland papers, HSTL; Margaret Truman, *Harry S. Truman,* p. 71; Harry S. Truman, "The Greater Kansas City Regional Plan," speech to Women's Government Study Club, March 10, 1930, "County Judge" folder, Lou Holland papers, HSTL. Truman received praise for refusing to allow the county to pay for a road right-of-way taken from the Truman farm at Grandview. Truman, however, apparently refused to pay anyone for rights-of-way, because the roads markedly increased the value of adjoining property rather than causing owners any loss. This increase in value could increase revenue generated by property taxes, and to an extent the road system could therefore literally pay for itself. This principle of public administration was rediscovered decades later and hailed as a bold new innovation. (Robert Wyatt oral history, pp. 21–22, HSTL; E. M. Stayton, "The Jackson County Road System," speech to Highway Engineers Association of Missouri, February 12, 1932, HSTL; Esther Grube oral history, pp. 26–28, HSTL; Margaret Truman, *Harry S. Truman,* p. 73; *Kansas City Star,* August 12, 1934, p. 1C.

9. Truman, "Politics, Life, etc.," "More character sketches," "I have had two wonderful associates"; Truman, "My Impressions"; Truman, *Autobiography,* p. 82; Harry S. Truman interviews with William Hillman, January 9 and January 10, 1952, interviews folder, "Mr. President" File, box 269, PSF, HST papers, HSTL; Daniels, *Man of Independence,* pp. 144–47; Edgar Hinde oral history, pp. 105–06, HSTL; Tom Evans oral history, pp. 177–79, HSTL; William Reddig to Jonathan Daniels, May 12, 1950, and Henry Bundschu to Jonathan Daniels, May 9, 1950, Jonathan Daniels papers, University of North Carolina; Margaret Truman, *Harry S. Truman,* p. 72. Daniels (p. 144) says W. A. Ross, not Mike, was one of the three contractors who confronted Truman in Pendergast's office. This is surely incorrect. The Evans oral history account of the confrontation is noteworthy because he was an eyewitness.

10. "The Ten-Year Bond Funds—To Sept. 30, 1931" report in folder of Civic Research Institute trustee meeting minutes, box 1, Civic Research Institute records, WHMC, MU; Civic Research Institute board minutes,

September 23, 1931, "1-3-Minutes" folder, box 6, Civic Research Institute records, WHMC, MU; *Kansas City Star,* September 3, 1931, p. 5; *Kansas City Times,* September 3, 1931, p. 3; newspaper clippings in Annie scrapbook A, Jackson County Historical Society, identified as *Kansas City Post,* August 2, 1931, *Kansas City Journal Post,* August 1, 1931, *Kansas City Star,* September 6, 1931, *Kansas City Times,* September 2, 1931, unidentified clipping August or September 4, 1931 (the Annie scrapbooks are a valuable record of Shannon Democrat activities and interests). Truman proudly announced a reduction in the special road and bridge levy because of maintenance savings with modern roads ("Address made to the Real Estate Board of Kansas City, September 25, 1931, by Harry S. Truman, Presiding Judge of the County Court, Jackson County, Missouri," Personal Correspondence—Harry S. Truman, Lou Holland papers, HSTL).

11. Lou Holland, "Road Program," speech, October 12, 1933, "Kansas City (Missouri) Road System and Old Trails" folder, box 3, County Judge papers, HST papers, HSTL; Margaret Truman, *Harry S. Truman,* p. 73; Haskell and Fowler, *City of the Future,* pp. 146–47; Mize Peters oral history, p. 41, HSTL; *Kansas City Star,* October 28, 1930; *Kansas City Times* editorial, October 29, 1930; Harry S. Truman, draft of "Jackson County's Road System," speech to be delivered July 24, 1928, "County Judge" folder, Lou Holland papers, HSTL; F. E. Gallup to Harry S. Truman, September 15, 1932, Harry S. Truman to F. E. Gallup, September 23, 1932, Lou Holland to Harry S. Truman, November 2, 1932, Lou Holland papers, HSTL; Miscellaneous Historical Document 430, HSTL; Truman, *Autobiography,* p. 71.

12. Harry S. Truman, speech to Club Presidents Round Table, June 16, 1930, and Harry S. Truman, speech to Engineers Club, February 15, 1929 (including handwritten notes), "Kansas City (Missouri) Road System and Old Trails" folder, box 3, County Judge papers, HST papers, HSTL; Anon., *Results of County Planning* (1932), p. 122; *Kansas City Times,* January 22, 1927, p. 1, May 26 and October 17, 1930; Harry S. Truman, "The Greater Kansas City Regional Plan" speech to Women's Government Study Club, March 10, 1930, "County Judge" folder, Lou Holland papers, HSTL; *Kansas City Star,* January 24, 1927, p. E, December 19, 1928, p. 3; Harry S. Truman to H. H. Halvorson, October 29, 1929, Miscellaneous Historical Document 425, HSTL.

13. *Kansas City Star,* January 24 and January 27, 1930 editorial; Harry S. Truman to James Ruffin, May 6, 1933, James Ruffin to Harry S. Truman, May 19, 1933, folder 12, James Ruffin papers, WHMC, MU; Harry S. Truman to Howard Huselton, July 26, 1941, "Missouri River" folder, box 112, SV, HST papers, HSTL; handwritten notes for Harry S. Truman speech to Engineers Club, February 15, 1929, "Kansas City (Missouri) Road System and Old Trails" folder, box 3, County Judge papers, HST

papers, HSTL; Harry S. Truman to Roy Roberts, June 12 and June 17, 1950, "Roy A. Roberts" folder, PSF—Personal, HST papers, HSTL.

14. Anon., *Results of County Planning*, p. 9 (Truman's cover letter is with the copy of the book at the Snyder Collection of University of Missouri at Kansas City); *Kansas City Journal Post*(?), clipping c. May 1932, Annie scrapbook G, Jackson County Historical Society; *Independence Examiner*, December 15, 1928; Truman, "The Ideals"; Harry S. Truman to Jonathan Daniels, June 5, 1950, "Jonathan Daniels" folder, Presidential Papers, HST papers, HSTL (also in Jonathan Daniels papers, University of North Carolina); Harry S. Truman, "Plans. Personal Plans, City Plans, County Plans, Regional Plans, National Plans" essay, folder 3, Desk File, Personal File, PSF, HST papers, HSTL; Harry S. Truman, speech to Kansas City Rotary Club, *Buzz Saw*, November 24, 1932, "Speeches" folder, box 2, County Judge papers, HST papers, HSTL.

15. Harry S. Truman to Lloyd Stark, March 19, 1933, Lloyd Stark to Harry S. Truman, March 23, 1933, folder 7616, Lloyd Stark papers, WHMC, MU; R. W. Selvidge to Lloyd Stark, October 11, 1934, folder 7623, Lloyd Stark papers, WHMC, MU; Miscellaneous Historical Document 130, HSTL; National Planning Board, Federal Emergency Administration of Public Works, Third Circular Letter, October 25, 1933, "PWA" folder, box 3, County Judge papers, HST papers, HSTL; "State Planning Board" folder, box 2, County Judge papers, HST papers, HSTL; *Independence Examiner*, June 27, 1930.

16. *Independence Examiner*, March 2, 1927, February 26 & February 11, 1930, July 6, 1934, April 27, 1926; Harry S. Truman, "for reference use on Tuesday, March 24, 1931," Harry S. Truman, speech April 13 or 19, 1929, "Kansas City (Missouri) Road System and Old Trails" folder, box 3, County Judge papers, HST papers, HSTL; Margaret Truman, *Harry S. Truman*, pp. 68, 77; Frank Davis to Harry S. Truman, September 18, 1936, "Speaking Engagements" folder, box 162, SV, HST papers, HSTL; *Kansas City Times*, May 9, 1924, p. 6, July 24, 1926, pp. 6, 7; *Kansas City Star*, April 16, 1929, p. 5; Frank Davis to Harry S. Truman, March 11, 1946, "National Old Trails Association" folder, Biographical File, PSF, HST papers, HSTL; Harry S. Truman, notes and text for speech on WDAF radio, July 24, 1928, about Jackson County's road system, "County Judge" folder, Lou Holland papers, HSTL; Harry S. Truman to Lloyd Stark, February 17, 1934, folder 7616, Lloyd Stark to Scott Wilson, March 19, 1934, folder 8378, Lloyd Stark papers, WHMC, MU; Harry S. Truman to Bess Truman, November 1926 and February 1927, box 5, FBP, HST papers; Harry S. Truman notes on history of national trails, Miscellaneous Historical Document 129, HSTL.

17. Schauffler, *Harry Truman*, pp. 69–70; *Kansas City Star*, May 17, 1931, p. 2A.

18. *Kansas City Star*, November 26, 1931, p. 1, December 8, 1931, p. 3;

Kansas City Journal Post, undated editorial, Annie scrapbook A, Jackson County Historical Society; "McCoy—Office Report, June 20, 1939" in "Harry S. Truman 1939 envelope #1," *Kansas City Star* Library, Kansas City, Missouri; telephone conversation between May Wallace and Richard Lawrence Miller, August 29, 1983, author's files.

19. Harry S. Truman to Bess Truman, February 12, 1931, box 5, FBP, HST papers, HSTL; "McCoy—Office Report, June 20, 1939" in "Harry S. Truman 1939 envelope #1," *Kansas City Star* Library.

20. *Kansas City Journal Post,* May 25, 1932, *Kansas City Star,* May 25, 1932, *Kansas City Times,* May 25, 1932, unidentified clipping, Annie scrapbook G, Jackson County Historical Society; Brown Harris to Harry S. Truman, January 7, 1947 (with enclosure), Harry S. Truman to Brown Harris, January 10, 1947, "Correspondence Relating to Harry S. Truman—biographical," Biographical File, PSF, HST papers, HSTL.

21. *Kansas City Star,* February 20, 1931, p. 3, November 26, 1931, p. 1, January 17, 1934, p. 1, January 18, 1934, p. 2; Harry S. Truman, speech on WOW radio, Omaha, Nebraska, August 6, 1938, box 5, Speech File, SV, HST papers, HSTL; Daniels, *Man of Independence,* p. 153; *Kansas City Times,* September 24, 1930, p. 9, January 16, 1934, p. 1, January 17, 1934, p. 1, January 18, 1934, p. 3, January 19, 1934, p. 1, January 20, 1934, p. 1; Fred Wolferman to Harry S. Truman, January 20, 1934, "W" folder, Fred Canfil papers, HSTL; Margaret Truman, *Harry S. Truman,* p. 82; Schauffler, *Harry Truman,* pp. 69–70. See also *Independence Examiner,* March 11, 1930, for another labor dispute.

22. "Jackson County Finances" folder, box 1, Civic Research Institute records, WHMC, MU; "Trends in County Finance, Jackson County, Missouri, September 1933," pp. 1–2, 6, 10, 20–22, box 13, Civic Research Institute records, WHMC, MU; Ray Wilson to Francis Wright, November 10, 1932, "5-3-C Chamber of Commerce" folder, Civic Research Institute records, WHMC, MU; *Kansas City Star,* June 13, 1927, pp. 1–2; *Kansas City Times,* April 30, 1929, p. 1. County officials listed 1933 total income as $3.2 million and total expenses as $2.9 million. Their 1934 figures were $3.0 million total income and $3.3 million total expenditures. (*Inter-City News,* April 5 and April 13, 1934.)

23. *News Notes,* Kansas City Public Service Institute, June 1929, Civic Research Institute records, box 12, WHMC, MU; *Kansas City Star,* December 14, 1930, p. 2, December 29, 1930, p. 3, December 31, 1930, p. 2, April 1, 1931, p. 3, April 3, 1931, p. 12; *Kansas City Post,* December 14, 1930, March 30, April 2, and April 3, 1931, *Kansas City Post*(?), April 4, 1931, *Kansas City Star,* March 31, 1931, *Kansas City Times,* April 15, 1932, and unidentified clipping, Annie scrapbook A, Jackson County Historical Society; Rufus Burrus to Harry S. Truman, December 7, 1940 (with enclosure), "Jackson County" folder, box 71, SV, HST papers, HSTL; Schauffler, *Harry Truman,* p. 69.

24. Harry S. Truman to Bess Truman, April 15, 1933, box 5, FBP, HST papers, HSTL; Senate Bill 154, "House Bill 257" folder, box 1, County Judge papers, HST papers, HSTL; "Budget Fiscal Year, 1934, Jackson County, Missouri" in unidentified folder, box 1, County Judge papers, HST papers, HSTL; printed copies of Jackson County, Missouri, budgets for fiscal years, 1934 and 1935, box 1, County Judge papers, HST papers, HSTL; Report of the Secretary—Second Government Conference (Conference on Financial Administration in Missouri), "Legislative 57th General Assembly" folder, box 2, County Judge papers, HST papers, HSTL; Preliminary list of members of Conference on Financial Administration in Missouri, List of members of the Conference on Financial Administration in Missouri, Conference information sheet, Conference on Financial Administration in Missouri agenda (November 20, 1933), "Conferences—Miscellaneous" folder, box 1, County Judge papers, HST papers, HSTL; Harry S. Truman, budget comments, unidentified folder, box 1, County Judge papers, HST papers, HSTL; Budget Fiscal Year, 1935, Jackson County, Missouri, unidentified folder, box 1, County Judge papers, HST papers, HSTL; *Independence Examiner*, July 30 and September 7, 1934; "Trends in County Finance, Jackson County, Missouri, September 1933," pp. 1–2, box 13, Civic Research Institute records, WHMC, MU; *Kansas City Times*, November 16, 1932, p. 8; *Kansas City Star*, November 28, 1931, p. 2; Harry S. Truman, testimony before Committee on Taxation and Governmental Reforms, November 28, 1931, "Speeches" folder, box 2, County Judge papers, HST papers, HSTL; Harry S. Truman to Bess Truman, April 22, April 23, April 24, April 28 (both letters that date), April 29, May 5, and May 9, 1933, box 5, FBP, HST papers, HSTL. Correspondence between Truman and Park on the budget bill showed no friendliness, particularly compared to the warm comradeship in the early Truman–Governor Lloyd Stark correspondence (Harry S. Truman to Guy Park, May 2, 1933, Guy Park to Harry S. Truman, May 3, 1933, folder 2199, Guy Park papers, WHMC, MU; in the same folder see also Harry S. Truman to Guy Park, April 28, 1933 and Guy Park to Harry S. Truman, April 29, 1933 for another example of cool politeness).

25. *Independence Examiner*, October 31, 1924; *Kansas City Post*(?), April 17, 1932, Annie scrapbook A, Jackson County Historical Society; Harry S. Truman to Howard Huselton, July 26, 1941, "Missouri River" folder, box 112, SV, HST papers, HSTL; *Citizen's League Bulletin*, May 7, 1932, folder 219, V. E. Phillips papers, WHMC, MU; "Proposed Plan of Revaluation and Appraisement of Real Property in Jackson County, Missouri," "Legislation 57 General Assembly" folder, box 2, County Judge papers, HST papers, HSTL; Harry S. Truman, May 26, 1952, *Public Papers 1952–1953*, p. 373; *Kansas City Times*, November 16, 1932, p. 8; Truman, *Buzz Saw*, November 24, 1932; Harry S. Truman to Roy Roberts, June 12, 1950 and June 17, 1950, "Roy A. Roberts" folder, PSF—Personal, HST papers, HSTL.

26. *Public Affairs*, December 28, 1922, and July 17 and December 21, 1924, Civic Research Institute, Missouri Valley Room, Kansas City, Missouri, Public Library; *Kansas City Times*, January 24, 1924, p. 6, October 16, 1929, p. 11, October 3, 1930, editorial; *Kansas City Star*, September 16, 1923, p. 4A, March 29, 1927, p. 7; A Bill to Reorganize the Administrative government of Jackson County, Missouri, "County Organization" folder, box 7, Civic Research Institute records, WHMC, MU; *News Notes*, May 1929, box 12, Civic Research Institute records, WHMC, MU; Minutes of Subcommittee on County Reorganization, Kansas City Chamber of Commerce, May 3, May 23, September 16, October 3, November 28, and December 1, 1932, "5-3-C Chamber of Commerce" folder, Civic Research Institute records, WHMC, MU; A Proposed Bill Providing for the Reorganization of the government of Jackson County, Missouri, "Kansas City Courthouse Construction Fund" folder, box 1, County Judge papers, HST papers, HSTL; Ray Wilson to Walter Matscheck, January 26, 1933, "County Organization" folder, box 7, Civic Research Institute records, WHMC, MU; Civic Research Institute trustees meeting, July 14, 1924, box 1, Civic Research Institute records, WHMC, MU; Walter Matscheck, "Methods of Reducing the Cost of Government," pp. 5–7, 10, box 12, Civic Research Institute records, WHMC, MU; Harry S. Truman, speech to Club Presidents Round Table, October 7, 1929, "County Judge" folder, Lou Holland papers, HSTL (also in "Speeches" folder, box 2, County Judge papers, HST papers, HSTL); Harry S. Truman, speech to Rotary Boys Camp, October 1, 1930, Personal Correspondence—Harry S. Truman—County Judge, Lou Holland papers, HSTL; Harry S. Truman, speech to Kansas City Real Estate Board, September 25, 1931, Personal Correspondence—Harry S. Truman—County Judge, Lou Holland papers, HSTL; "Tax Assessments and collections in Kansas City and Jackson County, August 1932," p. 1, Civic Research Institute Report, box 12, Civic Research Institute records, WHMC, MU; *Independence Examiner*, September 7, 1934; Truman, *Buzz Saw*, November 24, 1932; *Kansas City Times*, November 16, 1932, p. 8.

27. Harry S. Truman, testimony before Committee on Taxation and Governmental Reforms, November 28, 1931, "Speeches" folder, box 2, County Judge papers, HST papers, HSTL; *Kansas City Star*, November 28, 1931, p. 2; Harry S. Truman, speech to Kansas Real Estate Board, September 25, 1931, Personal Correspondence—Harry S. Truman—County Judge, Lou Holland papers, HSTL; Truman, *Buzz Saw*, November 24, 1932.

28. *Kansas City Journal Post*(?), April 4, 1931, Annie scrapbook A, Jackson County Historical Society; Harry S. Truman to J. A. Seck, March 27, 1942, "National Defense—Rubber Situation" folder, box 117, SV, HST papers, HSTL; *Kansas City Times*, August 8, 1929, p. 1; "A Survey of the Welfare Activities of Jackson County Government 1928," pp. 111–13, Civic Re-

search Institute records, box 12, WHMC, MU; Truman, *Buzz Saw*, November 24, 1932; Truman, speech to Rotary Boys Camp, October 1, 1930.

29. *Kansas City Times*, August 8, 1929, p. 1; Harry S. Truman to Bess Truman, July 12, 1929, box 5, FBP, HST papers, HSTL; Fred Boxley to Harry S. Truman, July 12, 1929, "Correspondence, general 1926–1953" folder, box 13, FBP, HST papers, HSTL; Truman, speech to Kansas City Real Estate Board, September 25, 1931; Truman, *Buzz Saw*, November 24, 1932; "General Statement of Findings and Recommendations from the Survey of the Welfare Activities of Jackson County Government (1928)," box 12, Civic Research Institute records, WHMC, MU; "A Survey of the Welfare Activities of Jackson County Government 1928," *passim*, box 12, Civic Research Institute records, WHMC, MU; Civic Research Institute trustees meetings, April 16 and May 17, 1928, box 1, Civic Research Institute records, WHMC, MU; *Independence Examiner*, February 28, 1924, March 2, 1927; *Kansas City Star*, May 28, 1923, p. 1; *Kansas City Post*, November 13, 1923, p. 3, November 14, 1923, p. 3, February 22, 1924, p. 4, February 28, 1924, p. 1; M. E. Ballou, *Jackson County Missouri Its Opportunities and Its Resources* (Rural Jackson County Chamber of Commerce, 1926), p. 302, "Jackson County Missouri Its Opportunities and Its Resources" folder, box 1, County Judge papers, HST papers, HSTL; Anon., *Results of County Planning*, pp. 18, 38–39, 57; Earl W. Beck in CBS broadcast "Closed Ranks" described in *Kansas City Star*(?) or *Kansas City Times*(?), April 1945, Biographical File, PSF, HST papers, HSTL.

30. Truman, "I have had two wonderful associates," and "Thomas B. Bash"; "Jackson County Hospital for the Poor," "County Judge" folder, Lou Holland papers, HSTL; *Independence Examiner*, February 28, 1924, April 8, 1930, October 3, 1930; *Kansas City Post*, February 28, 1924, p. 1; Harry S. Truman to Bess Truman, July 13, July 14, and July 16, 1929, c. July 8, 1932, August 21, 1933, box 5, FBP, HST papers, HSTL.

31. Harry S. Truman, speech to Kansas City Chamber of Commerce, September 11, 1935, and undated speech on Wagner Bill, "Speeches" folder, box 163, SV, HST papers, HSTL.

32. Harold Ickes, speech to Conference of Mayors at A Century of Progress Exposition, Chicago, September 23, 1933, p. 2, "PWA" folder, box 3, County Judge papers, HST papers, HSTL; Daniels, *Man of Independence*, p. 167.

33. "Proceedings the Indianapolis Conference State Reemployment Directors," September 30 and October 1, 1933, p. 11, "Conferences—Miscellaneous" folder, box 1, County Judge papers, HST papers, HSTL; Daniels, *Man of Independence*, p. 166; Dorsett, *Pendergast Machine*, p. 109; Harry S. Truman to Lloyd Stark, October 31, 1933, folder 7616, Lloyd Stark papers, WHMC, MU; Truman, "My Impressions."

34. Daniels, *Man of Independence*, p. 166; "Proceedings of Conference of Central State Reemployment Directors," Kansas City, Missouri, July 25–

26, 1933, pp. 3–4, 12–13, "Conferences—Miscellaneous" folder, box 1, County Judge papers, HST papers, HSTL; "Proceedings the Indianapolis Conference State Reemployment Directors," pp. 6–7, 110–12; Harry S. Truman to all Relief and Reemployment Committee Chairmen, November 15, 1933, R. B. Browning to all statisticians and reemployment clerks, February 26, 1934, "N.R.S. 'Rules and Regulations' " folder, box 2, County Judge papers, HST papers, HSTL; "Veterans" folder, box 2, County Judge papers, HST papers, HSTL; Harry S. Truman interview with Jonathan Daniels, November 12, 1949, p. 63, MOI notes, Jonathan Daniels papers, HSTL.

35. Edgar Hinde oral history, pp. 62–63, HSTL; Reddig, *Tom's Town*, p. 174; *Kansas City Star*, January 1, 1931, Annie scrapbook A, Jackson County Historical Society.

36. Harry S. Truman to Bess Truman, February 12, 1931, box 5, FBP, HST papers, HSTL. The letter indicates the "big drunk" was a rhetorical option and not seriously considered.

37. Harry S. Truman, speech to Club Presidents Round Table, October 7, 1929, Lou Holland papers, HSTL; *Kansas City Times*, December 13, 1930, Annie scrapbook A, Jackson County Historical Society; *Kansas City Times*, December 10, 1930, p. 1, December 11, 1930, pp 1–2; *Independence Examiner*, September 24, 1924.

38. *Kansas City Star*, December 10, 1930, January 11, 1931, and *Kansas City Post*(?), December 30, 1930, Annie scrapbook A, Jackson County Historical Society; *Kansas City Times*, December 10, 1930, December 11, 1930, pp. 1–2; *Kansas City Star*, December 13, 1930, p. 1, January 3, 1931, p. 2; Truman, "More character sketches"; Edgar Hinde oral history, pp. 69–70, HSTL.

39. *Kansas City Star*, December 10, 1930, December 11, 1930 editorial, December 14, 1930 cartoon, *Kansas City Times*, December 16, 1930, December 17, 1930 editorial, and unidentified clipping, December 14, 1930, Annie scrapbook A, Jackson County Historical Society; *Kansas City Times*, December 10, 1930, p. 1, December 17, 1930, p. E; *Kansas City Star*, December 15, 1930, p. 2; T. J. Pendergast to Guy Park, October 16, 1933, cited in Eugene F. Schmidtlein, "Truman the Senator," Ph.D. dissertation, University of Missouri, 1962, p. 48.

40. Truman, "More about government." This is constructed from the versions in the Eben Ayers papers, Memoirs File, and "Longhand Notes" County Judge (PSF), which differ in small particulars. Truman's original handwritten version has several corrections and changes, and thus differs from the various typed copies. The Eben Ayers version of the "Pickwick Papers" is normally served to researchers at the Truman Library and is censored in spots, as is the PSF version. The Memoirs File copy is uncensored.

41. Truman, "More character sketches"; Harry S. Truman interview

with William Hillman, October 3, 1951, interviews folder, "Mr. President" File, box 269, PSF, HST papers, HSTL.

42. Truman, "I have had two wonderful associates"; Harry S. Truman to Bess Truman, April 27, 1933, box 5, FBP, HST papers, HSTL; *Kansas City Times,* January 12, 1932, *Kansas City Journal Post,* January 12 and January 15, 1932, January 5, 1933, *Kansas City Star,* February 5, 1931 (1932?), February 2, 1932, *Kansas City Star* or *Kansas City Times,* November 18, 1931, Annie scrapbook A, Jackson County Historical Society; *Kansas City Star,* June 10, 1932, Annie scrapbook G, Jackson County Historical Society; William Reddig to Jonathan Daniels, May 12, 1950, Jonathan Daniels papers, University of North Carolina; Report to Chamber of Commerce, February 15, 1932, "Personal Correspondence—56—Crime Prevention Bureau" folder, box 20950, Lou Holland papers, WHMC, MU; *Kansas City Times,* November 16, 1939; *Kansas City Star* or *Kansas City Times,* May 8, 1928; Reddig, *Tom's Town,* p. 247; E. Y. Mitchell memorandum, c. July 17, 1934, folder 2986, E. Y. Mitchell papers, WHMC, MU.

43. Harry S. Truman to Bess Truman, July 19, 1928, August 9, 1930, February 12, April 26, April 28 (first letter that date), May 5, August 18, and August 22, 1933, box 5, FBP, HST papers, HSTL.

44. *Clinton Eye,* September 19, 1929; *Independence Examiner,* September 27, 1929, November 7, 1930; *Inter-City News,* November 14, and November 21, 1930; *Odessa Democrat,* November 21, 1930.

45. Appointment book, April 1931, box 3, County Judge papers, HST papers, HSTL; biographical sketch of Ralph Truman, pp. 12–15, 29–30, 56–58, Ralph E. Truman papers, HSTL; *Kansas City Times,* May 2, 1962 editorial; James Burkhardt ("Abie") to Harry S. Truman, August 9, 1922 and Harry S. Truman to James Burkhardt, August 14, 1922 and James Burkhardt to Edward Jacobson, August 12, 1922, "Correspondence, general August–September 1922" folder, box 12, FBP, HST papers, HSTL; Harry S. Truman to Ethel Noland, postmark March 25, 1919, Mary Ethel Noland papers, HSTL.

46. *State of Missouri Ex Rel. Ralph E. Truman* v. *Henry L. Jost et al.,* case 74634, Jackson County, Missouri, Circuit Court; Francis M. Wilson to J. W. McCammon, May 18, 1931, folder 488, Francis Wilson papers, WHMC, MU; *Kansas City Times,* December 18, 1930, May 12, 1931, Annie scrapbook A, Jackson County Historical Society; James Ruffin to Robert Fyan, April 28, 1931, minutes of Southwest Missouri Democratic Club, May 4, 1931, folder 3, James Ruffin papers, WHMC, MU; James Ruffin to David Impey, May 2, 1931, James Ruffin to M. N. White, May 5, 1931, James Ruffin to Ernest Mayberry and to Pete O'Brien, May 7, 1931, James Ruffin to Frederic Lamar, May 8, 1931, Ralph E. Truman to James Ruffin, May 8, 1931 (two letters), folder 4, James Ruffin papers, WHMC, MU; James Ruffin to William Raupp, May 16, 1931, James Ruffin to Carl L. Ristine, May 26, 1931, folder 5, James Ruffin papers, WHMC, MU; Peter O'Brien to

James Ruffin, June 2, 1931, James Ruffin to Pete O'Brien, June 3, 1931, folder 6, James Ruffin papers, WHMC, MU; W. Y. Foster to Francis M. Wilson, May 21, 1931, J. W. McCammon to Francis M. Wilson, June 9, 1931, folder 488, Francis Wilson papers, WHMC, MU; Will H. Zorn to Francis M. Wilson, August 8, 1931, W. F. Schlict to Francis M. Wilson, July 7, 1931, folder 910, Francis Wilson papers, WHMC, MU; Mary Gray to Francis M. Wilson, June 14, 1931, folder 528, Francis Wilson papers, WHMC, MU; *Kansas City Star*, February 15, 1924, p. 1, March 26, 1924, p. 2; *Kansas City Times,* February 15, 1924, p. 1; *Kansas City Journal Post*(?), April 22, 1931, April 23, 1931 editorial, Annie scrapbook A, Jackson County Historical Society.

47. *Independence Examiner*, June 8, 1931; Hulston, *Ozarks Lawyer's Story*, pp. 455–58; Margaret Truman, *Harry S. Truman*, pp. 80–81; James Ruffin to Ralph Truman, May 29, 1931, folder 5, James Ruffin papers, WHMC, MU; Pete O'Brien to James Ruffin, June 2, 1931, James Ruffin to Pete O'Brien, June 3, 1931, Harry S. Truman to James Ruffin, June 12, 1931, folder 6, James Ruffin papers, WHMC, MU; Will H. Zorn to F. W. Wilson, August 8, 1931, folder 545, Francis Wilson papers, WHMC, MU; Frank Mitchell, "Who is Judge Truman? The Truman-for-Governor Movement of 1931," Miscellaneous Historical Document 30, HSTL; *Kansas City Star*, May 31, 1932(?), Annie scrapbook A, Jackson County Historical Society. Years later Ruffin said that Truman didn't arrive in Springfield until shortly before noon Saturday, and that only Boxley came with him. The *Independence Examiner* version is accepted because it appeared the day after Truman arrived back in Independence. Truman apparently still had some glimmers of hope for the gubernatorial nomination in late July (Harry S. Truman to Bess Truman, July 28, 1931, box 5, FBP, HST papers, HSTL).

48. H. G. Cherry to James Ruffin, August 21, 1931, James Ruffin to H. G. Cherry, August 25, 1931, folder 7, James Ruffin papers, WHMC, MU.

49. Francis M. Wilson to Charles Dickey, December 10, 1931, folder 492, Francis Wilson papers, WHMC, MU; Harry S. Truman to Francis M. Wilson, March 16 and April 2, 1932, folder 551, Francis Wilson papers, WHMC, MU; Harry S. Truman to James Ruffin, June 19, 1931, folder 6, James Ruffin papers, WHMC, MU; Hulston, *Ozarks Lawyer's Story*, p. 458; Harry S. Truman to Francis M. Wilson, July 23, 1928, folder 86, Francis Wilson papers, WHMC, MU; Margaret Truman, *Harry S. Truman*, pp. 80–81.

50. Francis M. Wilson to J. W. McCammon, May 18, 1931, folder 488, Francis Wilson papers, WHMC, MU; Harry S. Truman to James Ruffin, October 12, 1931, folder 7, James Ruffin papers, WHMC, MU; James Ruffin to Pete O'Brien, 1932, Harry S. Truman to James Ruffin, January 11, January 12, February 5, February 9, April 6, and April 26, 1932, James

Ruffin to Harry S. Truman, January 12, January 20, January 29, February 3, and April 8, 1932, folder 8, James Ruffin papers, WHMC, MU; Lloyd Stark to James Ruffin, August 1, 1932, Harry S. Truman to James Ruffin, August 6 and August 13, 1932, folder 10, James Ruffin papers, WHMC, MU; T. J. Pendergast to James Ruffin, February 20, 1933, James Ruffin to T. J. Pendergast, March 11, 1933, Harry S. Truman to James Ruffin, February 6 and March 27, 1933, James Ruffin to Harry S. Truman, February 8, 1933, folder 11, James Ruffin papers, WHMC, MU; James Ruffin to Harry S. Truman, July 26, 1933, Harry S. Truman to James Ruffin, July 28, 1933, folder 12, James Ruffin papers, WHMC, MU.

51. Harry S. Truman to Bess Truman, April 23, April 30, May 3 (one of two letters that date), and May 7, 1933, box 5, FBP, HST papers, HSTL; Truman, "My Impressions."

52. *Congressional Record* 74:1, p. 2278; *St. Louis Post-Dispatch*, November 30, 1934, reprinted in *Congressional Record* 74:1, pp. 2281–82.

53. Reddig, *Tom's Town*, pp. 255–56.

54. Ibid., pp. 257–59, 263.

55. Ibid., p. 259.

56. Truman, "Thomas B. Bash," and "I have had two wonderful associates"; Harry S. Truman to Bess Truman, February 12, 1931, box 5, FBP, HST papers, HSTL; Reddig, *Tom's Town*, pp. 260–61; *Kansas City Times*, June 14, 1983, p. 4A.

57. Reddig, *Tom's Town*, p. 260; *Independence Examiner*, September 7, 1934. See also Harry S. Truman to Bess Truman, May 3 (both letters that date), May 4, and May 5, 1933, box 5, FBP, HST papers, HSTL.

58. Reddig, *Tom's Town*, pp. 158–60, 215–16; Harry S. Truman to John Barker, September 26, 1949, folder 8, John Barker papers, WHMC, MU; Schauffler, *Harry Truman*, pp. 71–73; *Kansas City Star*, May 23, 1930, p. 2.

59. Daniels, *Man of Independence*, p. 167; Truman, "My Impressions"; Truman, *Autobiography*, pp. 63–64; *Kansas City Star*, August 12, 1934, p. 2C; Harry S. Truman interview with William Hillman, January 2, 1952, interviews folder, "Mr. President" File, box 269, PSF, HST papers, HSTL.

60. *St. Louis Post-Dispatch*, November 30, 1934, reprinted in *Congressional Record* 74:1, p. 2282; Harry S. Truman to Charles Blackmar, January 31, 1941, "Miscellaneous" folder, box 82, SV, HST papers, HSTL; Reddig, *Tom's Town*, pp. 237–42; *Kansas City Times*, March 27, 1984, pp. A-1, A-6.

61. Daniels, *Man of Independence*, p. 170.

62. Rogge, "Speechmaking of Harry S. Truman," pp. 127–28; Harry S. Truman, 1934 appointment book and 1934 election diary, box 3, County Judge papers, HST papers, HSTL; *Independence Examiner*, May 16 and May 19, 1934; Daniels, *Man of Independence*, p. 168; Citizens State Bond Committee for Missouri Eleemosynary and Penal Institutions stationery, folder 7656, Lloyd Stark papers, WHMC, MU.

63. Truman, "My Impressions"; Truman, *Autobiography*, pp. 64, 67; Lloyd Stark to Harry S. Truman, c. May 8, 1934, folder 7616, Lloyd Stark papers, WHMC, MU.

64. Harry S. Truman to Bess Truman, April 28, 1933 (second letter that date), box 5, FBP, HST papers, HSTL; Truman, "May 14, 1934" essay, "Pickwick Papers"; John T. Wenne letter to the editor, *Kansas City Star*, December 6, 1957, p. 12D, Biographical File, booklets & clippings, Correspondence—biographical, Post-Presidential File, HST papers, HSTL; *Kansas City Star*, August 12, 1934, p. 2C; Truman, "My Impressions."

65. Daniels, *Man of Independence*, p. 169.

66. Harry S. Truman, 1934 election diary, box 3, County Judge papers, HST papers, HSTL; *Independence Examiner*, August 7, 1934; *Kansas City Star*, August 12, 1934, p. 2C.

67. Reddig, *Tom's Town*, pp. 261–63; Fred Boxley to Harry S. Truman, February 15 and April 18, 1935, "Fred A. Boxley" folder, box 239, PSF, HST papers, HSTL.

68. Truman, "My Impressions"; "The Bank Liquidations" memorandum and Jonathan Daniels to Eben Ayers, May 31, 1951, "Personal—Ayers, E.—trip to Kansas City (June 19–30, 1951)," Eben Ayers papers (23), HSTL; *St. Louis Post-Dispatch*, July 24 and July 26, 1934; Harry S. Truman interview with Jonathan Daniels, November 12, 1949, p. 60, MOI notes, Jonathan Daniels papers, HSTL; Truman, *Memoirs* draft, pp. 2836–37; *Security State Bank of Kansas City, Missouri* v. *Harry S. Truman and Edward Jacobson,* Jackson County, Missouri, Circuit Court case 203262, Record Book 68, p. 407, Record Book 92, p. 88, Record Book 419, pp. 8, 238, 248, 296, Record Book 420, p. 629, Record Book 422, pp. 546, 548, 553; Appearance Docket notes, Record of Circuit Court, Jackson County, Missouri, at Kansas City with Respect to Cause 203262, Security State Bank vs. Harry S. Truman et al., "Personal—Ayers, E.—trip to Kansas City (June 19–30, 1951)," Eben Ayers papers (23), HSTL (also in Edward Jacobson papers, HSTL).

69. Gaty Pallen to Guy Park, August 8, 1934, Harry to Guy Park, July 12, 1934, D. R. Spalding to Homer Duvall, July 11, 1934, C. M. Buford to Guy Park, July 21, 1934, Guy Park to Orestes Mitchell, July 23, 1934, Orestes Mitchell to Guy Park, July 25, 1934, folder 2200, Guy Park papers, WHMC, MU; Harry S. Truman to Guy Park, June 6, 1934, Guy Park to William Job, July 7, 1934, folder 2199, Guy Park papers, WHMC, MU; Samuel Fordyce to Ewing Mitchell, July 13, 1934, folder 2981, E. Y. Mitchell papers, WHMC, MU; *St. Louis Globe-Democrat*, July 30, 1934 (cited in R. C. Schroeder to Woodson K. Woods, October 23, 1934), folder 3027, E. Y. Mitchell papers, WHMC, MU; Carl Smith to Lloyd Stark, July 30, 1938, folder 4187, Lloyd Stark papers, WHMC, MU; Lloyd Stark to Clarence Cannon, July 6, 1934, folder 7620, Lloyd Stark papers, WHMC, MU; T. W. Griffith note, October 11, 1935, folder 7888, Lloyd Stark papers, WHMC, MU; Lloyd Stark to Harry S. Truman, Oc-

tober 10, 1934, Lloyd Stark to W. M. Ledbetter, October 13, 1934, folder
7623, Lloyd Stark papers, WHMC, MU; Lloyd Stark to Harry S. Truman,
c. May 8, 1934, folder 7616, Lloyd Stark papers, WHMC, MU; Lloyd Stark
to Harry S. Truman, July 11, 1934, folder 7620, Lloyd Stark papers, WHMC,
MU; *Independence Examiner*, June 1, July 28, July 30, and August 3, 1934;
St. Louis Post-Dispatch, July 12, 1934, typed quotation in folder 2980, E. Y.
Mitchell papers, WHMC, MU.

70. *Independence Examiner*, August 7, 1934.

71. *Kansas City Times*, August 8, 1934; Miscellaneous Historical Document 312, HSTL.

72. *Kansas City Star*, August 12, 1934, p. 1C; *Independence Examiner*, December 11, 1934; Harry S. Truman interview with Jonathan Daniels, November 12, 1949, p. 63, MOI notes, Jonathan Daniels papers, HSTL.

Chapter 11 NEW DEALER RAMPANT

1. Truman, *Memoirs*, p. 143.

2. Ibid., pp. 143–144; William P. Helm, *Harry Truman: A Political Biography* (New York: Duell, Sloan & Pearce, 1947), pp. 64–65.

3. Harry S. Truman to Bess Truman, June 26, 1935, box 6, FBP, HST
papers, HSTL; *Kansas City Times*, January 15, 1935; Truman, *Memoirs*, pp.
144, 146; *Congressional Record* 74:1, pp. 2276, 2278. Truman answered a
quorum call just before Long's speech. This and Truman's comments about
the speech indicate he was on the floor, although a senator could answer
a quorum call without being present (see *Congressional Record* 75:2, pp. 209–
11).

4. Truman, *Autobiography*, p. 83; Miscellaneous Historical Document 457,
HSTL; Tom Pendergast to Harry S. Truman, January 13, 1939, Harry S.
Truman to Tom Pendergast, January 17, 1939, "Charles M. Howell" folder,
box 63, SV, HST papers, HSTL; Harry S. Truman to Bess Truman, July
24, July 29, and August 11, 1935, box 6, FBP, HST papers, HSTL; *Kansas
City Star*, June 18, 1935; Harry S. Truman interview with William Hillman,
January 9, 1952, interviews folder, "Mr. President" File, box 269, PSF,
HST papers, HSTL. The Howell letter was an example of a go-between.
Truman had extensive contacts with other Jackson County political figures
who met with Tom Pendergast and his associates. Regarding the Braniff
matter there is some reason to believe it could have involved airmail contracts. Also, a few months after Howell's visit Truman amazed Kansas
City by asking the Civil Aeronautics Authority to favor Braniff over the
Missouri-based Mid-Continent Airlines for the Kansas City–Minneapolis
route (*Kansas City Star*, July 16, 1939).

5. Truman, *Memoirs*, pp. 144–49; *Kansas City Times*, January 17, 1935;

Harry S. Truman to Lloyd Stark, February 9, 1935, folder 7656, Lloyd Stark papers, WHMC, MU.

6. Margaret Truman, *Harry S. Truman,* pp. 90–91; *Kansas City Times,* February 15, 1935.

7. Harry S. Truman to Guy Park, March 4, 1935, folder 2202, Guy Park papers, WHMC, MU; *Kansas City Times,* February 15 and March 6, 1935; *Kansas City Star,* February 25 and April 14, 1935; Harry S. Truman to Fred Boxley, April 30, 1935, "Fred A. Boxley" folder, box 239, PSF, HST papers, HSTL.

8. Harry S. Truman to Guy Park, February 16, 1935, Harry S. Truman to Harold Ickes, February 15, 1935, Harold Ickes to Harry S. Truman, February 23, 1935, folder 2201, Guy Park papers, WHMC, MU; Harry S. Truman to Guy Park, May 8, 1935, Guy Park to Harry S. Truman, May 10, 1935, folder 2203, Guy Park papers, WHMC, MU; *Kansas City Times,* May 10, 1935; Harry Vaughan to J. K. Vardaman, May 26, 1941, "J. K. Vardaman, Jr." folder, box 175, SV, HST papers, HSTL.

9. *Kansas City Star,* May 10, May 15, and June 18, 1935; Harry S. Truman to Bess Truman, June 18 and June 19, 1935, box 6, FBP, HST papers, HSTL; Harry S. Truman to William Diehl, June 6, 1935 (quoted in William Diehl to Harry S. Truman, July 1, 1935), Franklin D. Roosevelt Library (hereafter cited as FDRL); Associated Press dispatch, May 15, 1935, folder 7931, Lloyd Stark papers, WHMC, MU; Fred Canfil to Harry Easley, August 29, 1935, "E" folder, Fred Canfil papers, HSTL; "WPA Applicants" folder, box 224, SV, HST papers, HSTL; *Washington Daily News,* May 9, 1938, reprinted in *Congressional Record* 75:3, appendix, pp. 1883–84.

10. Harry S. Truman to Bess Truman, February 25, 1937, box, 6, FBP, HST papers, HSTL; Harry S. Truman, speech to Sales Conference of Shirtcraft Company, December 19, 1936, "Speeches by Sen. Harry S. Truman 1935–1939 (folder 1)" folder, box 163, SV, HST papers, HSTL; Harry S. Truman, undated speech on "The Value of Industrial Safety," undated speech at Portland Cement Company, "Speeches" folder, box 163, SV, HST papers, HSTL. Truman's labor sentiments also attracted attention from William Allen White, famed journalist from Kansas, who wrote that Truman "is a perfect product of the Pendergast machine . . . innocent with a good front and a kind heart and nothing under his head but hair." White later explained, "I happen to disagree with him about many fundamental matters in national labor politics." (Enclosure with Rufus Burrus to Harry S. Truman, June 18, 1940, "Rufus Burrus" folder, box 51, SV, HST papers, HSTL.)

11. Harry S. Truman, speech to Clay County Historical Society, October 11, 1937, "Speeches by Sen. Harry S. Truman 1935–1939 (Folder 1)" folder, box 163, SV, HST papers, HSTL; Harry S. Truman, undated speech on agriculture, "Campaign Speeches" folder, box 163, SV, HST papers, HSTL.

12. *Congressional Record* 76:1, appendix, p. 799; Harry S. Truman, radio speech at Schenectady, New York, March 20, 1936, printed in *Congressional Record* 74:2, pp. 4373–74.

13. *Kansas City Star,* June 8, 1937, June 13, 1935; *Kansas City Times,* January 7, 1936; *Congressional Record* 74:2, pp. 1344–45.

14. Harry S. Truman to John Gage, July 15, 1941, "Waterways" folder, box 216, SV, HST papers, HSTL.

15. *Kansas City Star,* March 14, July 29, and August 27, 1936; *Kansas City Times,* February 1, 1936, September 28, 1939, October 7 and October 9, 1936; Bennett Clark to James Farley, August 7, 1936, FDRL; Helm, *Harry Truman,* pp. 37–38; Harry S. Truman to Bess Truman, September 24, 1939, box 7, FBP, HST papers, HSTL.

16. Harry S. Truman to Jim Farley, July 9, 1936, Miscellaneous Historical Document 401, HSTL; Harry S. Truman to Marvin McIntyre, April 16, 1936, Harry S. Truman to James Farley, October 3, 1936, James Aylward to James Farley, October 3, 1936, Harry S. Truman to Franklin D. Roosevelt, October 16, 1936, Franklin D. Roosevelt to Harry S. Truman, October 30, 1936, FDR papers microfilm, HSTL; Harry S. Truman, speech to St. Louis Chamber of Commerce, February 7, 1936, "Speeches" folder, box 163, SV, HST papers, HSTL; Harry S. Truman, speech to Missouri Democratic Convention, Joplin, Missouri, May 5, 1936, printed in *Congressional Record* 74:2, pp. 7458–59.

17. Harry S. Truman to Bess Truman, July 24, July 28, July 29, August 24, 1935, Box 6, FBP, HST papers, HSTL; Truman, *Autobiography,* pp. 70–73; Daniels, *Man of Independence,* p. 181; Lloyd Stark to Harry S. Truman, September 15, 1935, September 17, 1936, folder 8536, Fred Canfil to Lloyd Stark, June 9, 1936, folder 8388, Harry S. Truman, list of key men, folder 8956, Harry S. Truman to Lloyd Stark, January 11 and January 20, 1936, folder 8019, Lloyd Stark to Harry S. Truman, August 28, 1937, folder 7228, Lloyd Stark to Harry S. Truman, March 19, April 10, and c. May 8, 1934, Harry S. Truman to Lloyd Stark, March 31, and April 21, 1934, folder 7616, Lloyd Stark to Harry S. Truman, July 11, 1934, Harry S. Truman to Lloyd Stark, May 14, 1934, folder 7620, Lloyd Stark to Harry S. Truman, February 19, 1935, folder 7656, Harry S. Truman to Lloyd Stark, c. March 1935, folder 7690, Lloyd Stark to Harry S. Truman, June 24, 1935, folder 7756, Lloyd Stark to Harry S. Truman, September 17, 1935, folder 7869, confidential memo, folder 7974, Lloyd Stark to Scott Wilson, March 19, 1934, folder 8378, Lloyd Stark papers, WHMC, MU; *Kansas City Times,* March 26, 1935.

18. Harry S. Truman to James Farley, July 9, 1936, Miscellaneous Historical Document 401, HSTL; Harry S. Truman to James Farley, October 23, 1936, FDRL; Mary Jane Truman to Harry S. Truman, February 8, 1935, "Mrs. Martha Ellen Truman and Mary Jane Truman" folder, box 173, SV, HST papers, HSTL; *Stop Tax Grab* campaign newspaper of Fra-

ternal Protective Association of Missouri, folder 9096, Lloyd Stark papers, WHMC, MU; Omar E. Robinson to Lloyd Stark, August 5, 1936, folder 8469, Fred Canfil to Lloyd Stark, April 29, 1936, folder 8568, Lloyd Stark papers, WHMC, MU; Bennett Clark to James Farley, August 7, 1936, FDRL; *Kansas City Star*, October 15, 1936; Harry S. Truman, speech over WDAF radio, Kansas City, Missouri, October 30, 1936, "Speeches in Campaign of 1936" folder, box 4, Speech File, SV, HST papers, HSTL. Omar Robinson was at one point attorney for Vivian Truman, and Vivian did confidential political work for the senator. Therefore, when Robinson advised Stark to fire O'Malley this may have been a message on Truman's behalf.

19. George Collins to Harry S. Truman, May 12, 1936, Harry S. Truman to George Collins, May 15, 1936, Miscellaneous Historical Document 403, HSTL.

20. Helm, *Harry Truman*, pp. 37, 116–19; Mildred Dryden oral history, pp. 14–15, HSTL; Mize Peters oral history, p. 76, HSTL; Rufus Burrus to Harry S. Truman, November 6, 1941, "Rufus Burrus" folder, box 51, SV, HST papers, HSTL; Margaret Truman, *Harry S. Truman*, pp. 97–98; Miscellaneous Historical Document 61, HSTL; 1926 appointment book, end pages and "Miscellaneous Records" folder, 1934 election diary, box 3, County Judge papers, HST papers, HSTL; *U.S. Senate Report 938* (75:1); *New York Herald Tribune*, February 7, 1937, reprinted in *Congressional Record* 75:1, appendix pp. 174–75; Harry S. Truman, radio speech, January 31, 1937, printed in *Congressional Record* 75:1, appendix pp. 165–66; Harry S. Truman, radio speech, February 7, 1939, printed in *Congressional Record* 76:1, appendix pp. 473–74; *Kansas City Times*, January 9, January 22, April 19, and December 5, 1937, December 4, 1936; Tom Evans oral history, p. 764, HSTL; Harry S. Truman to Bess Wallace, November 10, 1918, in Ferrell, *Dear Bess;* Robbins, *Last of His Kind*, p. 21.

21. Harry S. Truman to Bess Truman, February 13, and February 21, 1937, box 6, FBP, HST papers, HSTL.

22. Harry S. Truman to Bess Truman, February 12, February 24, and February 25, 1937, box 6, FBP, HST papers, HSTL; Mildred Dryden oral history, pp. 54–55, HSTL; *Kansas City Times*, February 6, February 9, February 24, and March 2, 1937; *Kansas City Star*, February 21, February 22, and February 28, 1937.

23. T. H. Van Sant to Lloyd Stark, March 5, 1937, folder 10909, Lloyd Stark papers, WHMC, MU; *Kansas City Times*, March 5, March 10, and March 13, 1937 (editorial); *Kansas City Star*, March 14 and April 4, 1937. An example of Truman's hostility toward judges is in Barker, *Missouri Lawyer*, p. 224.

24. *Kansas City Times*, January 1 and March 10, 1937; Rex Moore to Lloyd Stark, February 9, 1937, folder 528, Lloyd Stark papers, WHMC, MU; *Kansas City Star*, December 24, 1936.

25. Harry S. Truman to Price Wickersham, February 15, 1937, "Speech on Supreme Court" folder, box 4, Speech File, SV, HST papers, HSTL; Harry S. Truman, speech at Kansas City, Missouri, April 19, 1937, folder 7226, Lloyd Stark papers, WHMC, MU; *Kansas City Times*, April 16, 1937.

26. Lloyd Stark to Harry S. Truman, April 6, 1937, Harry S. Truman to Lloyd Stark, April 7, 1937, folder 7226, Lloyd Stark to Harry S. Truman, April 19, 1937, folder 2894, Harry S. Truman to Lloyd Stark, April 22, 1937, Lloyd Stark to Harry S. Truman, April 27, 1937, folder 2895, Lloyd Stark papers, WHMC, MU; *St. Louis Post-Dispatch,* April 19, 1937; *Kansas City Times,* April 14, April 16, and May 1, 1937; *Kansas City Star,* April 28, 1937.

27. *Kansas City Star,* April 20 and April 22, 1937; *Kansas City Times,* April 21 and April 22, 1937.

28. Omar E. Robinson to Lloyd Stark, August 5, 1936, folder 8469, Lloyd Stark papers, WHMC, MU; Harry S. Truman to James Farley, July 9, 1936, Miscellaneous Historical Document 401, HSTL; Harry S. Truman to James Farley, October 23, 1936, FDRL; Reddig, *Tom's Town,* p. 295; Helm, *Harry Truman,* pp. 47–52; Harry S. Truman to Bess Truman, June 26, 1935, box 6, FBP, HST papers, HSTL; Truman, *Autobiography,* p. 83; *Kansas City Times,* July 21, 1937; *Kansas City Star,* July 22, 1937; Daniels, *Man of Independence,* p. 180; Harry S. Truman interviews with William Hillman, January 9 and January 10, 1952, interviews folder, "Mr. President" File, box 269, PSF, HST papers, HSTL.

29. Harry S. Truman, May 26, 1952, *Public Papers, 1952–1953,* pp. 371, 373; Truman, *Memoirs,* pp. 150–52; *Kansas City Times,* May 24, 1935; *Kansas City Star,* April 14, April 15, September 11, and September 12, 1935; Harry S. Truman, speech to Kansas City Chamber of Commerce, September 11, 1935, "Speeches" folder, box 163, SV, HST papers, HSTL.

30. Harry S. Truman to Bess Truman, December 6, 1937, box 6, FBP, HST papers, HSTL; Truman, *Memoirs,* pp. 151–52; Helm, *Harry Truman,* pp. 76–79; Margaret Truman, *Harry S. Truman,* p. 92; *Kansas City Star,* April 15, 1935. One of Truman's stenographers doubted that anyone destroyed this mail (Mildred Dryden oral history, pp. 54–55, HSTL).

31. Harry S. Truman, speech, July 2, 1937, *Congressional Record* 75:1, pp. 6743–45; *U.S. Senate Reports 1329 (74:1), 686 (75:1), 687 (75:1);* Harry S. Truman to Franklin D. Roosevelt, June 1, 1937, Franklin D. Roosevelt to Harry S. Truman, May 29, 1937, FDR papers microfilm, HSTL; *Washington Herald* article and editorial, August 20, 1937, printed in *Congressional Record* 75:1, appendix pp. 2206–07; *Congressional Record* 76:1, p. 5961; *Congressional Record* 76:3, pp. 5162 ff.; *Congressional Record* 77:1, appendix p. A1195; Harry S. Truman to Clinton Hester, August 22, 1938, "Victor R. Messall" folder, box 81, SV, HST papers; Harry S. Truman to Henry McElroy, June 6, 1938, "Harry S. Truman folder #1" folder, box 2, Bryce Smith papers, HSTL; "Transcontinental & Western Air, Inc." folder, box 167, SV, HST

papers, HSTL; *Kansas City Star,* August 13 and August 19, 1937; Victor Messall to Harry S. Truman, July 21 and August 19, 1938, Harry S. Truman to Victor Messall, August 10 and August 22, 1938, "Harry S. Truman Correspondence 1937–1938," HST papers, HSTL.

32. Truman, *Memoirs,* pp. 157–58; Helm, *Harry Truman,* pp. 73–74; Harry S. Truman interview with Jonathan Daniels, November 12, 1949, p. 63, MOI notes, Jonathan Daniels papers, HSTL.

33. *Kansas City Times,* May 25, 1937; *Kansas City Star,* June 3, 1937; *Congressional Record* 75:1, pp. 5271–74.

34. *Congressional Record* 75:1, pp. 5271–75.

35. Ibid., p. 5274.

36. Lloyd Stark to Harry S. Truman, June 8, 1937, Harry S. Truman to Lloyd Stark, June 16, 1937, folder 7227, Lloyd Stark papers, WHMC, MU.

37. *Kansas City Star,* May 13 and May 25, 1937; *Kansas City Times,* May 25, 1937; *U.S. Senate Report 25,* part 4, (76:3), p. 16.

38. *U.S. Senate Report 25,* part 12 (76:3), pp. 54–56; *Kansas City Times,* June 3, 1937.

39. *Kansas City Times,* June 9, 1937.

40. Harry S. Truman to Bess Truman, December 1935, various letters, January 4 and June 29, 1936, March 10 (two letters), September 14, September 15, September 16, November 9, November 25 and December 15, 1937, box 6, FBP, HST papers, HSTL; Daniels, *Man of Independence,* p. 185; Helm, *Harry Truman,* p. 13; Harry S. Truman interview with William Hillman, January 9, 1952, interviews folder, "Mr. President" File, box 269, PSF, HST papers, HSTL; Max Lowenthal interview with Jonathan Daniels, August 31, 1949, p. 11, MOI notes, Jonathan Daniels papers, HSTL. Helm quotes Truman's secretary Vic Messal as saying Truman had a drinking problem at this time, but Messal denied those quotations (Victor R. Messall interview with Jonathan Daniels, October 27, 1949, MOI notes, Jonathan Daniels papers, HSTL). Truman's letters to Bess in the 1930s contain veiled references that can be interpreted as concern about his drinking, although the contexts allow other interpretations (two of several examples are February 6 and November 18, 1937, box 6, FBP, HST papers, HSTL).

41. *Kansas City Times,* October 29, 1937; Harry S. Truman to Bess Truman, October 29, 1937, box 6, FBP, HST papers, HSTL.

42. *Kansas City Star,* October 28 and November 3, 1937; *Kansas City Times,* October 21, 1937; *U.S. Senate Report # 25,* part 3 (76:1), p. 13; *U.S. Senate Report #25,* part 8 (76:3), p. 19; Harry S. Truman to Bess Truman, November 3, 1937, box 6, FBP, HST papers, HSTL.

43. Harry S. Truman to Bess Truman, November 7, 1937, box 6, FBP, HST papers, HSTL; *Kansas City Times,* November 11, 1937; *U.S. Senate Report # 26,* part 1 (77:1), pp. 50–53.

44. *Congressional Record* 75:2, pp. 1769, 1912–24; Harry S. Truman to Bess Truman, December 12 and December 14, 1937, box 6, FBP, HST papers, HSTL.

45. *Congressional Record* 75:2, pp. 1912–19.

46. Ibid., p. 1920; *Kansas City Times,* December 7, 1937; Harry S. Truman to Bess Truman, December 16, 1937, box 6, FBP, HST papers, HSTL.

47. *Kansas City Times,* December 7, 1937; *Kansas City Star,* December 8, 1937; Harry S. Truman to Bess Truman, December 16, 1937, box 6, FBP, HST papers, HSTL; *Congressional Record* 75:2, p. 1920.

48. *Congressional Record* 75:2, pp. 1920–22.

49. Ibid., pp. 1923–24.

50. Daniels, *Man of Independence,* pp. 185–187; Harry S. Truman to Bess Truman, December 10, December 11, December 12, and December 13, 1937, box 6, FBP, HST papers, HSTL; Harry S. Truman to Margaret Truman, November 10, 1937, box 10, FBP, HST papers, HSTL; Harry S. Truman to Max Lowenthal, April 1, 1940, "Max Lowenthal" folder, box 79, SV, HST papers, HSTL; Max Lowenthal interview with Jonathan Daniels, August 31, 1949, p. 11, MOI notes, Harry S. Truman interview with Jonathan Daniels, November 12, 1949, p. 63, MOI notes, Jonathan Daniels papers, HSTL.

51. Harry S. Truman, speech to Brotherhood of Railroad Trainmen, Kansas City, Missouri, August 23, 1939, Miscellaneous Historical Document 110, HSTL; Harry S. Truman, speech to Maryland Motor Truck Association, "Speeches by Sen. Harry S. Truman 1935–1939 (Folder 1)" folder, box 163, SV, HST papers, HSTL; *Congressional Record* 75:3, pp. 9534–35, appendix pp. 864–65, 76:1, pp. 5956, 11127–28, appendix pp. 1160–61, 76:3, p. 328, 77:1, appendix pp. A443–44; Harry S. Truman to Bess Truman, November 4, 1939, box 7, FBP, HST papers, HSTL; Cyrus Eaton to Harry S. Truman, February 15, 1943 and various Harry S. Truman–Cyrus Eaton correspondence, June–August 1943, "Interstate Commerce Commission" folder, box 67, SV, HST papers, HSTL.

52. *Congressional Record* 75:3, pp. 1962–64.

Chapter 12   NEW DEALER AT BAY

1. Harry S. Truman to Bess Truman, June 15, 1936 (one of two that date), box 6, FBP, HST papers, HSTL; *New York Times,* December 15, 1937, p. 52, col. 5, August 24, 1938, p. 9, col. 3.

2. Typed copies of Homer Cummings to Franklin D. Roosevelt, November 1, 1937, Franklin D. Roosevelt to Homer Cummings, November 3, 1937, "Milligan" folder, Eben Ayers, papers, HSTL; Daniels, *Man of Independence,* pp. 189–90; *Kansas City Times,* October 3, 1937; Harry S. Truman to Bess Truman, November 28, 1937, box 6, FBP, HST papers, HSTL.

3. Harry S. Truman to Roy Harper, February 8, 1943, "Roy Harper" Folder, box 62, SV, HST papers, HSTL.

4. *Kansas City Star*, March 5, 1935, December 24, December 27, December 29, and December 30, 1936; Fred Boxley to Harry S. Truman, February 12, 1935, Harry S. Truman to Fred Boxley, February 15, 1935, "Fred A. Boxley" folder, box 239, PSF, HST papers, HSTL; Jasper Bell to Charles Aylward, June 19, 1936, Charles Aylward to Jasper Bell, June 20, 1936, Jasper Bell to Paul Buzard, January 28, 1936, Paul Buzard to Jasper Bell, February 5, 1936, folder 32, C. Jasper Bell papers, WHMC, MU.

5. Harry S. Truman to Bess Truman, November 1 and November 28, 1937, box 6, FBP, HST papers, HSTL; Daniels, *Man of Independence*, p. 190; Harry S. Truman to Charles Hay, October 20, 1939, "Charles Hay" folder, box 62, SV, HST papers, HSTL; Dorsett, *The Pendergast Machine*, p. 125; *Kansas City Times*, February 27, 1940; *Kansas City Star*, January 28, 1938 (one of several articles that date).

6. Fred Boxley to Harry S. Truman, February 12, February 15, and March 1, 1935, Harry S. Truman to Fred Boxley, February 26, 1935, "Fred A. Boxley" folder, box 239, PSF, HST papers, HSTL.

7. Reddig, *Tom's Town*, p. 287; *Hearings before Committee on Elections Number One on the Memorial of Albert L. Reeves*, "Miscellaneous" folder, H. H. Halvorson papers, HSTL; Richard B. Fowler, *Leaders in Our Town* (Kansas City: Burd and Fletcher, 1952), Albert L. Reeves section.

8. Harry S. Truman to Bess Truman, November 16, November 18, November 22, and November 23, 1937, box 6, FBP, HST papers, HSTL; Harry S. Truman to Bess Truman, October 28, 1939, box 7, FBP, HST papers, HSTL; *Kansas City Star*, September 2, October 15, and November 13, 1937, January 22, January 27, January 28 (several articles), January 30, and January 31, 1938; *Kansas City Times*, February 2, 1938.

9. *Kansas City Star*, February 3, 1938; *Kansas City Times*, February 5, 1938.

10. Harry S. Truman to Bess Truman, December 4, 1937, box 6, FBP, HST papers, HSTL; *Congressional Record* 75:3, pp. 1962–64.

11. W. L. Diehl to Harry S. Truman, July 1, 1935, FDRL; *Kansas City Star*, February 25, 1938; *Kansas City Times*, February 26, 1938; *Kansas City Journal Post*, March 8, 1938, cited in Gene Powell, *Tom's Boy Harry* (Jefferson City, Mo.: Hawthorn Publishing Co., 1948), pp. 98–99; "Statement on Reappointment of Maurice Milligan as U.S. Attorney" folder, box 165, SV, HST papers, HSTL; *Kansas City Star*, February 25 and 26 (no year), Annie Scrapbook E, Jackson County Historical Society.

12. *Kansas City Times*, February 16, 1938, editorial; *Kansas City Star*, February 3, 1938.

13. Lloyd Stark to Franklin D. Roosevelt, February 10, 1938, FDRL; Granville Richart to Kimbrough Stone, December 4, 1936, folder 255, Kimbrough Stone papers, WHMC, MU; *Kansas City Star*, February 8, February 20, March 6, and March 21, 1938, January 5 and July 26, 1939;

Kansas City Times, February 25 and March 16, 1938, July 22 and July 27, 1939; Fred Boxley to Harry S. Truman, March 19, 1935, "Fred A. Boxley" folder, box 239, PSF, HST papers, HSTL; Harry S. Truman to Bess Truman, July 25 and December 1, 1939, box 7, FBP, HST papers, HSTL; Harry Easley oral history, pp. 19, 73, HSTL; Edward McKim oral history, p. 64, HSTL; Mr. and Mrs. Randall Jessee oral history, p. 2, HSTL; William Boyle to Fred Canfil, March 3, 1944 (two telegrams), "Fred Canfil" folder, box 51, SV, HST papers, HSTL; various correspondence, box 1, Harry Easley papers, HSTL; "Truman" folder, box 1, Tom Van Sant papers, HSTL; Fred Canfil to W. Lyle Ellis, January 29, 1935, Fred Canfil to Harry Easley, October 21, 1935, "E" folder, Fred Canfil papers, HSTL; Fred Canfil to Guy Park, February 23, 1935, folder 2202, Guy Park papers, WHMC, MU; Anon., *Results of County Planning,* pp. 122 ff.

14. Harry S. Truman to Guy McAvoy, February 15, 1935, Miscellaneous Historical Document 335, HSTL; Harry S. Truman to Bess Truman, November 19, 1937, box 6, FBP, HST papers, HSTL; Reddig, *Tom's Town,* pp. 300–03; A. Theodore Brown and Lyle W. Dorsett, *K.C.: A History of Kansas City, Missouri* (Boulder, Colo.: Pruett Publishing Co., 1978), pp. 211–12; Garwood, *Crossroads of America,* pp. 303–04.

15. *Congressional Record* 75:3, appendix pp. 1243–44. The version quoted in the text is from Reddig, *Tom's Town,* pp. 303–04.

16. Reddig, *Tom's Town,* pp. 305–06.

17. Ibid., p. 308; Truman, *Memoirs,* p. 160; Dorsett, *Pendergast Machine,* pp. 130–31; Lyle W. Dorsett, "Kansas City Politics: A Study of Boss Pendergast's Machine," *Arizona and the West* (n.d.), box 100, files of Jackson County, Missouri, Historical Society; J. W. Hunolt to Clare Magee, August 16, 1938, folder 407, Dwight Brown papers, WHMC, MU.

18. Lloyd Stark to Franklin D. Roosevelt, August 3, 1938, FDR papers microfilm, HSTL; Gosnell, *Truman's Crises,* p. 120.

19. Harry S. Truman to Fred Boxley, March 4, 1935, "Fred A. Boxley" folder, box 239, PSF, HST papers, HSTL; Dorsett, *Pendergast Machine,* p. 129; Reddig, *Tom's Town,* pp. 311–22; Franklin D. Roosevelt conversations with Henry Morgenthau, Jr., June 8, 1938, Morgenthau Diaries, container 128, p. 122, FDRL; *Kansas City Star* or *Times,* July 6, 1948.

20. Reddig, *Tom's Town,* pp. 275–77.

21. Harry S. Truman to Bess Truman, October 25 and October 27, 1939, box 7, FBP, HST papers, HSTL; Harry S. Truman interview with William Hillman, January 9, 1952, interviews folder, "Mr. President" File, box 269, PSF, HST papers, HSTL.

22. Powell, *Tom's Boy,* p. 113; *Congressional Record* 76:1, appendix pp. 1105–06; *Kansas City Star,* March 21, 1939.

23. *Kansas City Times,* March 23, 1939; *Kansas City Star,* March 23, 1939.

24. Enclosure with Rufus Burrus to Harry S. Truman, June 18, 1940, "Rufus Burrus" folder, box 51, SV, HST papers, HSTL; Harry S. Truman

to Eddie Jacobson, May 22, 1951, "Personal—Ayers, E.—trip to Kansas City (June 19–30, 1951)," Eben Ayers papers (23), HSTL; *Kansas City Times*, May 13, 1939; Statement of Senator Truman to Secretary Early, March 22, 1939, "Personal Notes" folder, Family Correspondence File, Post-Presidential File, HST papers, HSTL.

25. *St. Louis Star-Times*, March 24, 1939; *Kansas City Star*, March 23, 1939; *Kansas City Times*, March 24 and March 30, 1939.

26. *St. Louis Star-Times*, March 24, 1939; Powell, *Tom's Boy*, pp. 113–15; *Kansas City Times*, March 24 and May 4, 1939; Reddig, *Tom's Town*, pp. 324–27; John Hanes telephone conversation with Lloyd Stark, March 29, 1939, Group Meeting, April 6, 1939, Morgenthau Diaries, container 171, pp. 182–86, FDRL.

27. *Kansas City Star*, April 9, April 23, and June 14, 1939; Rufus Burrus to Harry S. Truman, May 23, 1939, Harry S. Truman to Rufus Burrus, May 25, 1939, "Rufus Burrus" folder, box 51, SV, HST papers, HSTL; Harry S. Truman to Bess Truman, July 26, 1939, box 7, FBP, HST papers, HSTL; Shannon Douglass to Harry S. Truman, May 31, 1939, Miscellaneous Historical Document 272, HSTL; Lloyd Stark to Edwin Watson, c. June 14, 1939, FDR papers microfilm, HSTL; Reddig, *Tom's Town*, pp. 328–31.

28. Truman, *Autobiography*, pp. 72–73, 83; Harry S. Truman interviews with William Hillman, January 9 and January 10, 1952, interviews folder, "Mr. President" File, box 269, PSF, HST papers, HSTL.

29. Harry S. Truman to Bess Truman, July 11 and October 1, 1939, box 7, FBP, HST papers, HSTL.

30. *Kansas City Star*, July 13, 1937, May 28, 1939; Gosnell, *Truman's Crises*, p. 122; Harry S. Truman to Bess Truman, July 5, October 1, October 18, November 5, November 6, November 7 and December 15, 1939, box 7, FBP, HST papers, HSTL; Margaret Truman, *Harry S. Truman*, pp. 117–18; *St. Louis Post-Dispatch*, February 4, 1940; Harry S. Truman to George Collins, July 17, 1939, "George R. Collins" folder, box 53, SV, HST papers, HSTL.

31. Harry S. Truman to Bess Truman, November 6 and November 13, 1939, box 7, FBP, HST papers, HSTL; James A. Huston, " 'Captain Harry' Truman, Battery D, 129th Field Artillery, 35th Division" historical sketch in records from the office of the adjutant general, state of Missouri, pertaining to Harry S. Truman, HSTL; Harry S. Truman to John Snyder, November 7, 1939, "John W. Snyder" folder, box 162, SV, HST papers, HSTL.

32. Harry S. Truman to Bess Truman, November 13, November 16, November 19, November 22, November 24, November 28, November 30, December 1, December 3, and December 5, 1939, box 7, FBP, HST papers, HSTL; Harry S. Truman to Margaret Truman, November 17 and Novem-

ber 21, 1939, box 10, FBP, HST papers, HSTL; Walter Trohan, *Political Animals* (Garden City, N.Y.: Doubleday, 1975), pp. 216–17.

33. Harry S. Truman to Bess Truman, November 11, November 12, November 14, and November 16, 1939, box 7, FBP, HST papers, HSTL; Mary Paxton Keeley oral history, p. 44, HSTL; *Kansas City Star*, August 12, 1934, pp. 1C–2C.

34. Victor R. Messall to Harry S. Truman, August 15 and August 17, 1939, Harry S. Truman to Victor R. Messall, August 16, 1939, "Harry S. Truman—Correspondence for 1939" folder, box 168, SV, HST papers, HSTL; Daniels, *Man of Independence,* p. 136; Rufus Burrus to Harry S. Truman, undated (but filed between November 7, 1939 and April 18, 1940), November 6, 1941, Harry S. Truman to Rufus Burrus, November 22, 1941, "Rufus Burrus" folder, box 51, SV, HST papers, HSTL; John A. O'Brien to O. K. LaRoque, October 5, 1949, Jonathan Daniels papers, University of North Carolina; Harry S. Truman to Bess Truman, December 4, 1939, box 7, FBP, HST papers, HSTL; Harry S. Truman to John Childress, December 13, 1941, John Childress to Harry S. Truman, December 11, 1941, Harry S. Truman to Louisa P. Johnston, December 13, 1941, Louisa P. Johnston to Harry S. Truman, November 26, 1941, "Federal Home Loan Banks" folder, box 56, SV, HST papers, HSTL; Harry S. Truman to Louisa P. Johnston, November 25, 1941, Harry S. Truman to O. R. Kurtz, November 26, 1941, "Federal Savings & Loan Insurance Corporation" folder, box 57, SV, HST papers, HSTL; Roger Sermon to Harry S. Truman, March 25, 1944, "Roger Sermon" folder, box 161, SV, HST papers, HSTL.

35. Rufus Burrus to Harry S. Truman, February 6, 1941, Harry S. Truman to Rufus Burrus, February 10, 1941, Harry S. Truman to Eddie Jacobson, February 17, 1941, "Harry S. Truman—Personal (October 1940–December 1941)" folder, box 168, SV, HST papers, HSTL; *U.S.* v. *Spencer Salisbury* cases 14976, 14977, 14978, U.S. District Court for Western Missouri; *Kansas City Times,* October 25, 1940; *Kansas City Star* or *Times,* February 8, 1941; L. Curtis Tiernan interview with Jonathan Daniels, October 2, 1949, p. 34, MOI notes, Jonathan Daniels papers, HSTL; Edgar Hinde oral history, pp. 83–84, HSTL. Salisbury at first claimed that the prosecutions were politically motivated, punishment for his role as Tuck Milligan's eastern Jackson County campaign manager against Truman in 1934. Simultaneously with the savings and loan trouble, Salisbury also faced accusations of stealing from his mother's estate. Fidelity & Deposit Company of Maryland, in which FDR had once been an executive, escaped liability as Salisbury's surety because he failed to pay the 1940 premium. (*Kansas City Journal Post,* May 8, 1932, November 30, 1940; *Kansas City Times,* October 25, 1940; *Kansas City Star,* December 20, 1940.)

36. John O'Brien to O. K. LaRoque, October 5, 1949, Jonathan Daniels

papers, University of North Carolina; Daniels, *Man of Independence*, p. 138; *Kansas City Star,* June 11, 1940; *Kansas City Star* or *Times*, February 8, 1941; Harry S. Truman to John Fahey, May 24, 1944, "Federal Home Loan Banks" folder, box 56, SV, HST papers, HSTL; Harry S. Truman to John W. Childress, July 6, 1940, William West to Joseph J. McGee, July 1, 1940, "Jackson County" folder, box 71, SV, HST papers, HSTL; Independence Savings & Loan Association annual report, December 31, 1939, John Childress to Harry S. Truman, July 25, 1940, various other correspondence, "N. D. Jackson" folder, box 71, SV, HST papers, HSTL. Henry Rummel and E. M. Stayton had both been directors of Home Deposit Trust Co. of Independence (*Independence Examiner*, November 5, 1924; E. M. Stayton to President and Directors of Home Deposit Trust Company, March 6, 1926, "Citizens Security Bank of Englewood" folder, box 20950, Lou Holland papers, WHMC, MU).

37. Victor R. Messall to Harry S. Truman, August 12 and August 19, 1938, Harry S. Truman to Victor R. Messall, August 10, August 15, and August 22, 1938, "Harry S. Truman Correspondence 1937–1938" folder, HSTL; Fred Boxley to Harry S. Truman, February 15 and April 18, 1935, Harry S. Truman to Fred Boxley, April 25, 1935, "Fred A. Boxley" folder, box 239, PSF, HST papers, HSTL; Frank H. Lee to Harry S. Truman, July 24, 1941, Harry S. Truman to Frank H. Lee, July 30, 1941, "Frank H. Lee" folder, box 74, SV, HST papers, HSTL; Clara McCulley to Harry S. Truman, July 27, 1941, Harry S. Truman to Clara McCulley, July 30, 1941, "Liberty Bend Cutoff" folder, box 76, SV, HST papers, HSTL; Henry Chiles oral history, pp. 26–27, HSTL; John Strode oral history, pp. 9–13, HSTL; Ralph E. Truman to Harry S. Truman via Vivian Truman, August 5, 1943, "Ralph E. Truman" folder, box 173, SV, HST papers, HSTL; Harry S. Truman to Bess Truman, October 18, 1942, box 8, FBP, HST papers, HSTL; Eric O. A. Miller to Harry S. Truman, February 10, 1941, Harry S. Truman to Eric O. A. Miller, February 12, 1941, "Harry S. Truman—Personal Correspondence for February–September 1941" folder, box 168, SV, HST papers, HSTL; Ralph Depugh to Harry S. Truman, February 5, 1940, "Ralph Depugh" folder, box 55, SV, HST papers, HSTL; typed copy of Mrs. Fred Boxley to Eben Ayers, "Personal—Ayers, E.—trip to Kansas City (June 19–30, 1951)," Eben Ayers papers (23), HSTL.

38. *Kansas City Star*, April 23, 1939; *Kansas City Times*, May 13, 1939; Harry S. Truman to Bess Truman, September 29 and December 2, 1939, box 7, FBP, HST papers, HSTL.

39. *Kansas City Times*, January 26, 1940; *Kansas City Star*, January 26, 1940; Harry Easley oral history, pp. 42–46; Truman, *Memoirs*, p. 159; Daniels, *Man of Independence*, pp. 204, 211; Victor Messall interview with Jonathan Daniels, October 27, 1949, pp. 52–53, Roger Sermon interview with Jonathan Daniels, September 26, 1949, p. 22, Harry S. Truman interview with Jonathan Daniels, August 30, 1949, p. 5, MOI notes, Jonathan

Daniels papers, HSTL; Ralph Depugh to Harry S. Truman, February 5, 1940, "Ralph Depugh" folder, box 55, SV, HST papers, HSTL; Harry S. Truman, press release, February 3, 1940, "1940 Senatorial Campaign" folder, box 51, SV, HST papers, HSTL; Miscellaneous Historical Document 272, HSTL; attachment with Frank Monroe to Harry S. Truman, September 30, 1949, "Jonathan Daniels" folder, Biographical File, PSF, HST papers, HSTL. Truman immediately filed his candidacy with the Democratic Party state treasurer in St. Louis. The fee was $100. Truman didn't have to file with the Missouri secretary of state until June. (*Kansas City Star,* February 3, 1940.)

40. Helm, *Harry Truman,* pp. 127–28; Daniels, *Man of Independence,* p. 204; *Kansas City Star,* September 15, 1939; attachment with Tom Van Sant to Harry S. Truman, September 21, 1949, "Jonathan Daniels" folder, PSF, HST papers, HSTL. In Truman's view the same "error" could be attributed to FDR, yet his political career would continue to thrive.

41. William Heekins (or Heetins) to Joe Guilfoyle, undated, "1940 Senatorial Campaign" folder, box 51, SV, HST papers, HSTL; *Kansas City Times,* May 13, 1939; Harry S. Truman to Bess Truman, November 28, 1937, box 6, FBP, HST papers, HSTL; Harry S. Truman to Bess Truman, July 24 and July 27, 1939, box 7, FBP, HST papers, HSTL; Daniels, *Man of Independence,* p. 199; Leslie Fulkerson to Harry S. Truman, May 31, 1940, "Campaign Contributions" folder, box 51, SV, HST papers, HSTL; Roger Sermon interview with Jonathan Daniels, September 26, 1949, p. 22, MOI notes, Jonathan Daniels papers, HSTL; Harry S. Truman to B. D. Smiley, July 26, 1941, "National Defense Committee—General" folder, box 119, SV, HST papers, HSTL; Schmidtlein, "Truman the Senator," p. 217; Tom Evans oral history, pp. 262–65, HSTL.

42. Harry S. Truman to Bess Truman, November 22, 1937, box 6, FBP, HST papers, HSTL; Harry S. Truman to Bess Truman, September 24, July 5, July 7, July 10, August 8, December 13, and December 14, 1939, box 7, FBP, HST papers, HSTL; *Kansas City Times,* May 26 and May 27, 1939; *Kansas City Star,* August 27, 1939; *St. Louis Post-Dispatch,* August 27, 1939; *Kansas City Times,* February 1, 1940.

43. *Kansas City Times,* February 1, 1940; Lloyd Stark to Franklin D. Roosevelt, February 7, 1940, FDR papers microfilm, HSTL; *Kansas City Star,* February 5, 1940; Harry S. Truman to Frank McMurray, February 14, 1940, Harry S. Truman to Wilbert McCune, February 14, 1940, "Third Term Correspondence" folder, box 166, SV, HST papers, HSTL; Truman, *Memoirs,* p. 159; Harry S. Truman to Bess Truman, June 19, 1940, box 7, FBP, HST papers, HSTL; Stephen Early to R. H. Wadlow, July 30, 1940, FDR papers microfilm, HSTL; Lloyd Stark press release, July 3, 1940, folder 4019, Lloyd Stark papers, WHMC, MU; *Congressional Record* 76:3, pp. 8652, 8787, 8789.

44. Harry S. Truman to Bess Truman, June 17, June 19, July 5, August

12, and September 12, 1940, box 7, FBP, HST papers, HSTL; Lloyd Stark, press release, June 22, 1940, folder 4059, Lloyd Stark papers, WHMC, MU; Guy Gillette, press release, June 20, 1940, Harry S. Truman to Charles Wilson, May 2, 1940, Harry S. Truman to Guy Gillette, May 14, 1940, Guy Gillette to Harry S. Truman, May 16, 1940, "Gillette Investigating Committee" folder, box 61, SV, HST papers, HSTL; Harry S. Truman to C. D. Hicks, January 24, 1940, "C. D. Hicks" folder, box 62, SV, HST papers, HSTL; *Congressional Record* 76:3, pp. 540–41; Harry S. Truman to John Snyder, March 11, 1940, "John W. Snyder" folder, box 162, SV, HST papers, HSTL; various U.S. senators to David Berenstein, "1940 Senatorial Campaign" folder, box 51, SV, HST papers, HSTL; Helm, *Harry Truman*, pp. 135–36.

45. Harry S. Truman to Harold Bowen, February 1, 1941, "Harry S. Truman—Personal Correspondence for February–September 1941" folder, box 168, SV, HST papers, HSTL; *Kansas City Star*, October 21, 1939; Truman, *Memoirs*, p. 152.

46. Harry S. Truman to Bess Truman, September 28, 1939, box 7, FBP, HST papers, HSTL; Harry S. Truman to Bess Truman, September 24, 1941, box 8, FBP, HST papers, HSTL.

47. R. V. Denslow to Forrest Donnell, October 23, 1940, folder 2769, Forrest Donnell papers, WHMC, MU; "Invitations accepted by Senator Truman" memorandum, "1940 Senatorial Campaign" folder, box 51, SV, HST papers, HSTL; "Masonic Lodge" folder, Memoirs File, Post-Presidential File, HST papers, HSTL; Truman, *Memoirs*, pp. 162–63.

48. Harry Easley, oral history, pp. 105–106, HSTL; Harry S. Truman to C. A. Franklin, November 18, 1940, "Negroes" folder, box 131, SV, HST papers, HSTL; *The Call*, October 13, 1939, May 12, 1939, pp. 1, 7, 18; Harry S. Truman to C. A. Franklin, May 18 and October 25, 1939, C. A. Franklin to Harry S. Truman, May 15 and October 19, 1939, "C. A. Franklin" folder, box 60, SV, HST papers, HSTL; Box 26, 1940 Election Card File, SV, HST papers, HSTL.

49. Mary Jane Truman interview with Jonathan Daniels, October 2, 1949, p. 35, MOI notes, Jonathan Daniels papers, HSTL; Harry S. Truman to Bess Truman, September 15, 1940, box 7, FBP, HST papers, HSTL; Mary Paxton Keeley oral history, p. 49, HSTL.

50. Harry S. Truman interview with Jonathan Daniels, August 30, 1949, MOI notes, Jonathan Daniels papers, HSTL; Reddig, *Tom's Town*, pp. 191–92. Rabbi Mayerberg was incensed by the Pendergast state administration's connivance in this murder, and by Governor Park's refusal—based on politics—to commute a death sentence for a Jewish man convicted for the same crime that resulted in a prison sentence for a gentile associate. The rabbi vented his outrage in a political manner that the Pendergast machine found most unpleasant, but that is a story told elsewhere. Tru-

man's insensitivity to racial discrimination was further demonstrated when the Jefferson City NAACP protested the rumored appointment of James Byrnes to the Supreme Court, saying he was against legislation that helped blacks. Truman replied, "I am very sure you are misinformed about his attitude toward colored people." (M. G. Hardiman to Harry S. Truman, March 26, 1941, Harry S. Truman to M. G. Hardiman, April 2, 1941, "Miscellaneous October 1940–April 1941" folder, box 82, SV, HST papers, HSTL.)

51. *Congressional Record* 75:3, pp. 138, 140–43, 2210; Harry S. Truman, holograph, January 7, 1938, "Harry S. Truman Correspondence 1937–1938" folder, HSTL. Truman called Joe Guffey and Nate Bachman "two of the Senate's most expert storytellers." Here is one of the "wonderful" Bachman stories that Truman jotted down: "He related a story about a woman who was prosecuting a man for rape. He said the woman was a decided blond, in fact too decided. That she had on a black silk dress and long white kid gloves reaching to her elbows and, according to Nathan looked very much like a bawd. She claimed the gentleman had assaulted her while she was asleep. The judge became interested and asked her, 'Madam, just how far did this man penetrate your person before you woke up.' The lady raised up one of her white gloved arms and measured off a distance with the other hand about half way to her elbow. The old judge leaned back in his chair and said to the clerk, 'Mr. Clerk, just dismiss this case; and Madam, don't you go to sleep in this courtroom for there's no one here who can wake you up.' " Truman claimed that Bachman became the Senate's peacemaker, able to smooth over any dispute by buttonholing the arguing Senators and telling such stories until good spirits were restored. Truman credited Benjamin Franklin with the same technique. (Truman, *Memoirs*, p. 145; Harry S. Truman interview with William Hillman, October 4, 1951, interviews folder, "Mr. President" File, box 269, PSF, HST papers, HSTL; Truman, "My Impressions"; A. J. Granoff oral history, pp. 25–26, HSTL.) The Bachman story and similar items by other Senators may be found in Harry S. Truman, holographs, April 25 and July 28, 1937, "Harry S. Truman Correspondence for 1937–1938" folder, HSTL, and in Harry S. Truman to Mr. Dye, September 18, 1964, Desk File, Post-Presidential File, HST papers, HSTL.

52. Harry S. Truman, speech to National Alliance of Postal Employees, Kansas City, Missouri, October 2, 1938, box 1, Speech File, SV, HST papers, HSTL.

53. Harry S. Truman, speech at Sedalia, Missouri, June 15, 1940, reprinted in *Congressional Record* 76:3, appendix p. 4546. The phrase "life, liberty, and the pursuit of happiness" that Truman credited to the Bill of Rights is from the Declaration of Independence. Note also Truman's use of "freemen" rather than "free men," terms with different meanings.

54. Harry S. Truman, speech to National Colored Democratic Association, Chicago, July 14, 1940, reprinted in *Congressional Record* 76:3, appendix pp. 5367–69.

55. C. A. Franklin to Harry S. Truman, October 19, 1939, Harry S. Truman to C. A. Franklin, October 25, 1939, "C. A. Franklin" folder, box 60, SV, HST papers, HSTL; Rudoph Schwenger to Harry S. Truman, December 8, 1942, Harry S. Truman to Rudolph Schwenger, December 16, 1942, "Negroes" folder, box 131, SV, HST papers, HSTL.

56. Marion Burns to Harry S. Truman, February 9, 1944, Harry S. Truman to Marion Burns, February 11, 1944, "Railway Mail Service" folder, box 157, SV, HST papers, HSTL; "Equal Rights Amendment" folder, box 55, SV, HST papers, HSTL; Harry S. Truman to L. B. Thompkins, October 11, 1941, "Miscellaneous" folder, box 83, SV, HST papers, HSTL; Harry S. Truman to Bess Truman, August 19, 1935, c. April 5, 1937, box 6, FBP, HST papers, HSTL; Harry S. Truman interview with William Hillman, October 4, 1951, interviews folder, "Mr. President" File, box 269, PSF, HST papers, HSTL; Harry S. Truman to Bess Wallace, June 16, 1911, May 20, 1912, April 23, 1913, in Ferrell, *Dear Bess*.

57. *Kansas City Times*, June 17 and October 15, 1938; attachment with Frank Monroe to Harry S. Truman, September 30, 1949, "Jonathan Daniels" folder, Biographical File, PSF, HST papers, HSTL; unused draft of Harry S. Truman statement to Railroad Labor Conference, October 12, 1938, box 5, Speech File, SV, HST papers, HSTL; *Congressional Record* 75:3, pp. 6881–82, 9534–35, appendix p. 864; Daniels, *Man of Independence*, p. 204; Floyd Ricketts oral history, pp. 29–30, HSTL; *Kansas City Labor Herald*, August 2 and August 9, 1940; *Labor*, special issue, "Missouri Political Situation" folder, box 112, SV, HST papers, HSTL (also in 1940 campaign files, HST papers); C. A. Schutty to C. O. Crebbs, July 10, 1940 anonymous pencil notes of July 8, 1940 campaign meeting, "Missouri Political Situation" folder, box 112, SV, HST papers, HSTL; Harry S. Truman to Daniel Tobin, January 30, 1941, "Miscellaneous" folder, box 82, SV, HST papers, HSTL; Harry S. Truman to Bess Truman, August 23 and October 24, 1939, box 7, FBP, HST papers, HSTL; Helm, *Harry Truman*, pp. 132–34; Mildred Dryden oral history, pp. 88–89, HSTL; Boxes 11, 19, 27, 1940 Election Card File, SV, HST papers, HSTL; David Berenstein to Edwin Watson, August 9, 1940, FDR papers microfilm, HSTL; various Truman Club ticket correspondence, "Campaign Contributions" folder, box 51, SV, HST papers, HSTL; various railroad union endorsements, October 1940, "Labor Situation" folder, box 73, SV, HST papers, HSTL.

58. William Heekins (or Heetins) to Joe Guilfoyle, undated, "1940 Senatorial Campaign" folder, box 51, SV, HST papers, HSTL; Mildred Dryden oral history, pp. 68, 82, HSTL; Harry S. Truman to Bess Truman, August 14, August 29, September 1, and September 4, 1940, box 7, FBP, HST papers, HSTL; Victor R. Messall to Harry S. Truman, August 12, 1938,

Harry S. Truman to Victor R. Messall, August 22, 1938, "Harry S. Truman Correspondence 1937–1938" folder, HSTL; Helm, *Harry Truman*, pp. 146–47; Edwin Halsey to Harry S. Truman, October 25, 1940, "Harry S. Truman—Personal Correspondence for February–September 1941" folder, box 168, SV, HST papers, HSTL; Boxes 27, 28, 1940 Election Card File, SV, HST papers, HSTL; David Berenstein to Edwin Watson, August 9, 1940, FDR papers microfilm, HSTL; Harry Easley oral history, p. 55, HSTL; Edgar Hinde oral history, pp. 138–39, HSTL; Tom Evans oral history, pp. 268–71, 274, HSTL. The $18,125 figure excludes bad checks and items that appear disputed.

59. Daniels, *Man of Independence*, p. 198; Mildred Dryden oral history, p. 64, HSTL; Harry Easley oral history, pp. 49–50, HSTL; Harry S. Truman to Bess Truman, June 11, August 13, August 29, August 31, September 1, September 3, September 5, and September 6, 1940, box 7, FBP, HST papers, HSTL.

60. Mrs. Goebel Ray to Truman Headquarters, July 29, 1940, W. H. Ward to Victor R. Messall, July 10, 1940, F. L. Decker to Victor R. Messall, June 29, 1940, "Campaign Contributions" folder, box 51, SV, HST papers, HSTL; Box 27, 1940 Election Card File, SV, HST papers, HSTL; Harry Easley oral history, pp. 51–52, HSTL.

61. Ralph Depugh to Harry S. Truman, June 3, 1940, "Ralph Depugh" folder, box 55, SV, HST papers, HSTL; I. H. Severn, June 8, 1940, "Campaign Contributions" folder, box 51, SV, HST papers, HSTL; Harry S. Truman to Rufus Burrus, June 20, 1940, "Rufus Burrus" folder, box 51, SV, HST papers, HSTL; Elizabeth (Tillman?) to Rethal Odum, July 30, 1940, "WPA—Missouri Office, B. M. Casteel" folder, box 224, SV, HST papers, HSTL.

62. Harry S. Truman to Charles Hay, October 16, 1939, "Charles M. Hay" folder, box 62, SV, HST papers, HSTL; Harry S. Truman to Bess Truman, November 7, 1939, box 7, FBP, HST papers, HSTL; Harry S. Truman to Frank Briggs, March 24, 1941, "Miscellaneous" folder, box 82, SV, HST papers, HSTL; *Kansas City Journal*, July 31, 1941, p. 2; *Kansas City Star*, June 17, 1940 (editorial); Edgar Hinde oral history, pp. 112–13, HSTL.

63. Helm, *Harry Truman*, p. vi; Harry S. Truman to Bess Truman, August 9, August 10, August 11, August 12, and September 15, 1940, box 7, FBP, HST papers, HSTL.

Chapter 13   THE SENATOR'S PRIVATE INCOME

1. "The Bank Liquidations" memorandum, Eben Ayers to Phineas Rosenberg, July 3, 1951, Phineas Rosenberg to Eben Ayers, July 11, 1951, "Personal—Ayers, E.—trip to Kansas City (June 19–30, 1951)," Eben

Ayers papers (23), HSTL; Victor R. Messall to R. B. Wood, January 24, 1941, "Miscellaneous" folder, box 82, SV, HST papers, HSTL.

2. Harry S. Truman to Eddie Jacobson, May 22, 1951, "Personal—Ayers, E.—trip to Kansas City (June 19–30, 1951)," Eben Ayers papers (23), HSTL; Fred Boxley to Harry S. Truman, January 8, January 17, February 1, February 8, February 15, February 26, and March 1, 1935, Harry S. Truman to Fred Boxley, January 11, February 6, February 26, and March 2, 1935, "Fred A. Boxley" folder, box 239, PSF, HST papers, HSTL; enclosure with Phineas Rosenberg to Eben Ayers, July 11, 1951, typed version of data from Phineas Rosenberg, typed sheet containing Vivian Truman statement of June 26, 1951, June 25, 1951 memorandum, "The Security State Bank Loan" memorandum, "Personal—Ayers, E.—trip to Kansas City (June 19–30, 1951)," Eben Ayers papers (23), HSTL; Harry S. Truman, *Memoirs* draft, p. 2839; Mildred Dryden oral history, p. 84, HSTL; Harry S. Truman to Ethel Noland, June 22, 1949, Mary Ethel Noland papers, HSTL.

3. Harry S. Truman to Mary Jane Truman, May 17, 1935, Mary Jane Truman to Harry S. Truman, February 21, 1935, "Mrs. Martha Ellen Truman and Mary Jane Truman" folder, box 173, SV, HST papers, HSTL; Harry S. Truman to Vivian Truman, January 29, 1942, "J. Vivian Truman" folder, box 173, SV, HST papers, HSTL; Fred Boxley to Harry S. Truman, February 15, February 26, and April 26, 1935, "Fred A. Boxley" folder, box 239, PSF, HST papers, HSTL; Harry S. Truman to Bess Truman, December 28, 1941, box 8, FBP, HST papers, HSTL; Harry S. Truman to Margaret Truman, April 9, 1944, box 10, FBP, HST papers, HSTL.

4. Martha Ellen Truman to Harry S. Truman, February 14, 1935, "Mrs. Martha Ellen Truman and Mary Jane Truman" folder, box 173, SV, HST papers, HSTL; Harry S. Truman to Bess Truman, July 25, 1939, box 7, FBP, HST papers, HSTL; Harry S. Truman to Guy Park, October 12, 1933, Guy Park to Harry S. Truman, October 14, 1933, folder 2199, Guy Park papers, WHMC, MU; Harry S. Truman to Guy Park, March 23, 1936, Guy Park to Harry S. Truman, March 26, 1936, folder 2204, Guy Park papers, WHMC, MU; D. F. Wallace to Lloyd Stark, June 17, 1937, Lloyd Stark to D. F. Wallace, June 19, 1937, folder 3078, Lloyd Stark papers, WHMC, MU; "David F. Wallace" folder, box 186, SV, HST papers, HSTL; Roger Sermon to Harry S. Truman, March 5, 1943, "Roger Sermon" folder, box 161, SV, HST papers, HSTL; William Southern, Jr., to Harry S. Truman, February 10, 1941, Harry S. Truman to William Southern, Jr., February 13, 1941, "William Southern, Jr." folder, box 162, SV, HST papers, HSTL. There seems little doubt that Truman also provided important financial help from his own pocket to Bess's brothers George and Frank.

5. Harry S. Truman to Bess Truman, June 18, June 21, June 26, and

July 3, 1935, box 6, FBP, HST papers, HSTL; Helm, *Harry Truman*, pp. 66, 110; Harry S. Truman to Thomas Fitzgerald, December 18, 1941, "Harry S. Truman—Personal October–December 1941" folder, box 169, SV, HST papers, HSTL; *St. Louis Post-Dispatch*, July 26, 1944 newspaper reference, p. 101, MOI notes, Jonathan Daniels papers, HSTL.

6. Oco Thompson to Harry S. Truman, July 31, 1944, "Harry S. Truman—Personal May 1944–August 1944" folder, box 170, SV, HST papers, HSTL; Edgar Hinde to Harry S. Truman, September 22 and October 31, 1941, Harry S. Truman to Edgar Hinde, October 11 and November 4, 1941, William Boyle to Edgar Hinde, July 6, 1942, "Edgar Hinde" folder, box 63, SV, HST papers, HSTL; Harry S. Truman to Edgar Hinde, January 8 and June 23, 1942, "Harry S. Truman—Personal January–October 1942" folder, box 169, SV, HST papers, HSTL.

7. Harry S. Truman to Bess Truman, June 28, 1935, February 7 and February 25, 1937, box 6, FBP, HST papers, HSTL.

8. Harry S. Truman to Lewis Schwellenbach, April 21, 1942, "(Hon.) Lewis B. Schwellenbach" folder, box 159, SV, HST papers, HSTL; Harry S. Truman to Bess Truman, February 10, 1937, box 6, FBP, HST papers, HSTL; Helm, *Harry Truman*, pp. 210–11; Victor Messall interview with Jonathan Daniels, October 27, 1949, p. 52, MOI notes, Jonathan Daniels papers, HSTL.

9. Harry S. Truman to Bess Truman, July 12, 1935, February 6, 1937, box 6, FBP, HST papers, HSTL; Victor R. Messall to Harry S. Truman, August 19, 1938, Harry S. Truman to Victor R. Messall, August 22, 1938, "Harry S. Truman Correspondence 1937–1938," HSTL; Harry S. Truman to Bess Truman, September 25, September 28, and October 4, 1939, box 7, FBP, HST papers, HSTL; report of January 8, 1940 Pendergast faction meeting, Miscellaneous Historical Document 272, HSTL; Victor R. Messall to Claude McDonald, July 3, 1943, "Harry S. Truman—Personal for January–July 1943" folder, box 169, SV, HST papers, HSTL; Victor R. Messall interview with Jonathan Daniels, October 27, 1949, p. 52, MOI notes, Jonathan Daniels papers, HSTL.

10. McCoy—Office Report, June 20, 1939, Harry S. Truman 1939 envelope #1, *Kansas City Star* library, Kansas City, Missouri; Thomas Madden to Jonathan Daniels with enclosure, January 25, 1950, box 1, Arthur Mag papers, HSTL; *Kansas City Journal Post*, April 17, 1932, Annie scrapbook A, Jackson County Historical Society; Fred Boxley to Harry S. Truman, April 26, 1935, and Harry S. Truman to Fred Boxley, April 30, 1935, "Fred A. Boxley" folder, box 239, PSF, HST papers, HSTL; Harry S. Truman to Bess Truman, November 6, 1937, box 6, FBP, HST papers, HSTL; *Kansas City Star*, April 5, 1938.

11. Harry S. Truman interview with Jonathan Daniels, November 12, 1949, pp. 64–65, MOI notes, Jonathan Daniels papers, HSTL; Powell,

Tom's Boy, pp. 125–27; *Kansas City Star*, June 14, 1940; Memorandum of Omar Robinson statements, June 25, 1951, "Personal—Ayers, E.—trip to Kansas City (June 19–30, 1951)," Eben Ayers papers (23), HSTL.

12. *Kansas City Star*, June 22, July 7, and December 8, 1939, June 14, 1940; Powell, *Tom's Boy*, pp. 125–27; Harry S. Truman to Bess Truman, November 7, 1939, August 22, 1940, box 7, FBP, HST papers, HSTL; Harry S. Truman to Fred Klaber, July 25, 1941, "Harry S. Truman—Personal (October 1940–December 1941)" folder, box 168, SV, HST papers, HSTL; J. C. Nichols to Harry S. Truman, December 11, 1940, J. C. Nichols to J. W. Perry, December 1940, Harry S. Truman pencil note on V. R. Messall to Lou Holland, October 7, 1940, "National Defense—Lou E. Holland" folder, box 116, SV, HST papers, HSTL; W. T. Grant to Harry S. Truman, January 3, 1942, Harry S. Truman to W. T. Grant, January 6, 1942, "Harry S. Truman—Personal Telegrams" folder, box 173, SV, HST papers, HSTL.

13. *Kansas City Star*, June 14 and June 15, 1940 (editorial), February 5, 1945; *Kansas City Times*, July 17, and July 17, 1940 (editorial); Powell, *Tom's Boy*, pp. 125–27; Harry S. Truman to William Coe, November 17, 1944, "Campaign 1944–November 1944" folder, box 1, 1944 Campaign File, SV, HST papers, HSTL; Harry S. Truman interview with Jonathan Daniels, November 12, 1949, pp. 64–65, and miscellaneous notes, p. 191, MOI notes, Jonathan Daniels papers, HSTL; Harry S. Truman to Roy Roberts, December 12, 1945, PSF—Personal, HST papers, HSTL. Truman's old Community Savings & Loan associate H. H. Halvorson gave him a further explanation for the foreclosure. Halvorson dealt in industrial and commercial real estate transactions, and in January 1925 was a broker who sold a Kansas City site at 15th and Cleveland to Sears, Roebuck for a huge Midwest warehouse. Halvorson said the St. Louis–Kansas City Short Line Railroad was organized to prevent Sears from moving its operations to that site. He didn't specify the details, but some right of way may have been created for which Sears had to pay the Short Line. Halvorson told Truman, "Who put up the money for the hearings before the Public Service Commission and the Interstate Commerce Commission, who incorporated the railroad, who represented the former owners of the site, the building material combination, and other seemingly extraneous matters are most interesting." The Short Line's greatest promoter was George Collins, a Pendergast operative who was Truman's prewar militia captain. At the request of Collins, Truman pushed legislation through Congress to help the Short Line. Another figure in Short Line was Charles H. Apple, business associate of William Volker and Joseph J. Heim. Volker and Heim were both immensely wealthy businessmen, and Heim was the father-in-law of Col. Karl Klemm. Halvorson believed Sears had a long memory and was behind the foreclosure. Halvorson told Truman that Sears "does a lot of reprisal punishment to its enemies." (H. H. Halvorson to Harry S. Truman,

October 25, 1941, "Harry S. Truman—Personal October–December 1941" folder, box 168, SV, HST papers, HSTL; Harry S. Truman to George Collins, April 2, 1937, "Major George Collins" folder, H. H. Halvorson papers, HSTL; Fred Boxley to Harry S. Truman, May 22, 1935, Harry S. Truman to Fred Boxley, May 27, 1935, "Fred A. Boxley" folder, box 239, PSF, HST papers, HSTL; *U.S. House of Representatives Report 765 & 766*, 75 Cong, 1 Sess; *U.S. Senate Report 1893*, 75 Cong, 3 Sess; "St. Louis–Kansas City Short Line Railroad Co." folder, *Kansas City Journal*, February 17, 1922 clipping, "Miscellaneous" folder, H. H. Halvorson papers, HSTL; *Kansas City Star* or *Times*, January 8, January 11, July 5, and August 27, 1925; undated clipping about Sears specifications for property, "Sears, Roebuck & Co., Cleveland at Truman Road" envelope # 1, *Kansas City Star* library.)

14. Harry S. Truman to Bess Truman, August 13, and October 1, 1940, box 7, FBP, HST papers, HSTL. A few months after the foreclosure, school fund agent L. C. Miller developed a scheme to cut the farm into small lots, which could gross $85,000 for the county. Truman advised Vivian, "You ought to have a conversation with [county judge] Les George and with [county judge] Klaber and see that that fellow Miller is properly taken care of. I have already talked to George about him." To Jim Pendergast, Truman wrote, "It would be a good thing for us to fire Miller out of that job and turn all the land business over to Russell Gabriel and let him handle it in a common sense manner. It is my honest opinion that Miller is no good, and that the longer we keep him the more trouble we are going to get into." (Vivian Truman to Harry S. Truman [with *Kansas City Star* clipping], January 4, 1941, Harry S. Truman to Vivian Truman, January 6, 1941, "J. Vivian Truman" folder, box 173, SV, HST papers, HSTL; Harry S. Truman to Jim Pendergast, August 8, 1941, "Harry S. Truman Personal Correspondence for February–September 1941" folder, box 168, SV, HST papers, HSTL.)

15. Harry S. Truman to Edgar Hinde, January 10, 1941, "Edgar Hinde" folder, box 63, SV, HST papers, HSTL; C. B. Francisco to Harry S. Truman, April 11, 1941, "Miscellaneous" folder, box 82, SV, HST papers, HSTL; Harry S. Truman to Frank N. D. Buchman, November 20, 1940, "Moral Rearmament" folder, box 113, SV, HST papers, HSTL; Harry S. Truman to Lou Holland, March 11, 1941, box 116, SV, HST papers, HSTL; Harry S. Truman to Fred Klaber, July 25, 1941, Harry S. Truman to Earl Cheeseman, December 27, 1940, J. C. Nichols to Harry S. Truman, November 27, 1940, Harry S. Truman to J. C. Nichols, November 30, 1940, Harry S. Truman to William G. McAdoo, November 29, 1940, Harry S. Truman to Lester Cox, November 19, 1940, Harry S. Truman to Fred Colgan, Sr., November 16, 1940, Harry S. Truman to Mary Romine, November 18, 1940, "Harry S. Truman—Personal (October 1940–December 1941)" folder, box 168, SV, HST papers, HSTL; Harry S. Truman to

E. J. Short, November 18, 1940, "E. J. Short" folder, box 161, SV, HST papers, HSTL; Robert Schauffler to Harry S. Truman, February 13, 1941, "Harry S. Truman—Personal Correspondence for February–September 1941" folder, box 168, SV, HST papers, HSTL; Harry S. Truman interview with Jonathan Daniels, November 12, 1949, pp. 64–65, MOI notes, Jonathan Daniels papers, HSTL; Mildred Dryden oral history, pp. 78–79, HSTL.

16. Harry S. Truman to Bess Truman, August 1, 1939, September 15, 1940, box 7, FBP, HST papers, HSTL.

Chapter 14   CALL TO ARMS

1. Harry S. Truman to Mr. & Mrs. Arthur Karbank, March 4, 1943, "Jews" folder, box 71, SV, HST papers, HSTL; Harry S. Truman to Lloyd Stark, August 21, 1937, John Cochran to Lloyd Stark, August 14, 1937, folder 10912, Lloyd Stark papers, WHMC, MU; "Jacob Abt," "Francisco Biondo," "Erich Blumenfeld," "Charlotte Cahn," "Erwin Cahn," "Sally Cheim," "Hersz Eckstein," "Ettlinger Family," "Siegfried & Paula Finkelstein," and "Berke Glickstein" folders, box 64, SV, HST papers, HSTL; "Jurajka Antonia Grunstein" and "Phillip Kaliski" folders, box 65, SV, HST papers, HSTL. Some anti-Jewish epithets can be found in Harry S. Truman to Bess Truman, June 29, 1935, box 6, FBP, HST papers, HSTL; Harry S. Truman to Bess Truman, September 18, 1941, box 8, FBP, HST papers, HSTL. A derogatory reference (in context though without epithets) is in Harry S. Truman to Roger Sermon, August 30, 1940, "Independence" folder, box 67, SV, HST papers, HSTL, responding to S. Charles Enfeld to Harry S. Truman, August 28, 1940 in the same folder.

2. *Kansas City Star*, November 11, 1938; *Congressional Record* 75:3, appendix p. 2794; Harry S. Truman to Luther Ely Smith, February 6, 1941, "National Defense—Projects in Missouri" folder, box 125, SV, HST papers, HSTL; Harry S. Truman to Bess Truman, October 2, 1943, FBP, HST papers, HSTL.

3. Harry S. Truman to Luther Ely Smith, February 6, 1941, "National Defense—Projects in Missouri" folder, box 125, SV, HST papers, HSTL; Harry S. Truman to A. M. Hitch, December 13, 1941, "Miscellaneous" folder, box 83, SV, HST papers, HSTL.

4. *Congressional Record* 76:3, appendix p. 2518; Harry S. Truman to Ben Couch, May 12, 1941, "Miscellaneous" folder, box 82, SV, HST papers, HSTL; Harry S. Truman to J. P. Wilhelm, June 4, 1941, "National Defense Commission—General" folder, box 119, SV, HST papers, HSTL.

5. Harry S. Truman to A. L. Meredith, January 6, 1941, Harry S. Truman to Theo. Farry, August 4, 1941, "War Situation" folder, box 215, SV,

HST papers, HSTL; *Congressional Record* 76:1, appendix p. 87; *Congressional Record* 76:3, appendix pp. 4192–93; *Kansas City Star,* June 24 or 25, 1939. Examples of Truman's contempt for "pacifists" can be found in *Congressional Record* 75:3, appendix pp. 945–46, 76:2, appendix p. 202, and in Harry S. Truman to A. M. Hitch, December 13, 1941, "Miscellaneous" folder, box 83, SV, HST papers, HSTL.

    6. Truman, *Memoirs,* p. 153; *Congressional Record* 76:2, appendix p. 202; *Kansas City Times,* September 4, 1939, November 8, 1941; *Kansas City Star,* October 21 and October 28, 1939; Harry S. Truman to Ralph W. Smith, October 18, 1941, "National Defense Committee Contract Investigation—November 1941" folder, box 123, SV, HST papers, HSTL; Harry S. Truman to Luther Ely Smith, February 6, 1941, "National Defense—Projects in Missouri" folder, box 125, SV, HST papers, HSTL.

    7. Harry S. Truman, speech to National Aviation Forum, February 20, 1939, printed in *Congressional Record* 76:1, appendix pp. 642–43; Harry S. Truman to Clarence Chilcott, June 21, 1941, Harry S. Truman to John Lyon, May 26, 1941, "Miscellaneous" folder, box 82, SV, HST papers, HSTL; Harry S. Truman, speech on KMOX radio, St. Louis, Missouri, June 30, 1940, printed in *Congressional Record* 76:3, appendix pp. 4192–93; *Kansas City Star,* July 7, 1940; Harry S. Truman to Bess Truman, September 23, 1939, box 7, FBP, HST papers, HSTL; *Congressional Record* 76:1, appendix p. 1106. After Pearl Harbor Truman cautioned against hysteria against American citizens of Italian and German heritage. He seemed relieved, however, that Japanese-Americans were interned in concentration camps. ("Japanese" folder, box 71, SV, HST papers, HSTL; Harry S. Truman to Edward McKim, December 16, 1941, "Edward McKim" folder, box 81, SV, HST papers, HSTL; Harry S. Truman to Alice Thompson, January 16, 1942, "Miscellaneous" folder, box 83, SV, HST papers, HSTL; Harry S. Truman to Karl Vetsburg, December 18, 1941, "Harry S. Truman—Personal October–December 1941" folder, box 169, SV, HST papers, HSTL; L. C. Kirkman to Harry S. Truman, December 11, 1941, Harry S. Truman to L. C. Kirkman, December 16, 1941, "War Situation" folder, box 215, SV, HST papers, HSTL; Harry S. Truman to Bess Truman, March 10, 1942, box 8, FBP, HST papers, HSTL.)

    8. *Kansas City Star,* July 7, 1940; Truman, speech on KMOX radio, June 30, 1940; Truman, speech to National Aviation Forum, February 20, 1939; *St. Louis Post-Dispatch,* January 13, 1939, reprinted in *Congressional Record* 76:3, p. 6874.

    9. Harry S. Truman to Robert Patterson, November 19, 1940, quoted in Roger Edward Willson, "The Truman Committee," (Ph.D. dissertation, Harvard University, 1966), p. 28; Truman, *Memoirs,* p. 165; Daniels, *Man of Independence,* p. 218; Harry S. Truman interview with Jonathan Daniels, November 12, 1949, pp. 63–64, MOI notes, Jonathan Daniels papers, HSTL.

10. Harry S. Truman to Lou Holland, February 4, 1941, "National Defense—Lou E. Holland" folder, box 116, SV, HST papers, HSTL.

11. Truman, *Memoirs*, p. 166; Helm, *Harry Truman*, pp. 153–54; *Congressional Record* 77:1, pp. 830–38; Lou Holland to Mason Brittain, March 5, 1941, "National Defense—Lou E. Holland" folder, box 116, SV, HST papers, HSTL; Harry S. Truman interview with Jonathan Daniels, November 12, 1949, p. 64, MOI notes, Jonathan Daniels papers, HSTL. Let history note that Truman credited journalist Bill Helm for coming up with the idea of a resolution calling for an investigating committee.

12. Harry S. Truman to Lou Holland, March 7 and March 11, 1941, "National Defense—Lou E. Holland" folder, box 116, SV, HST papers, HSTL; Lewis Schwellenbach to Harry S. Truman, March 3, 1941, Harry S. Truman to Lewis Schwellenbach, March 10, 1941, "Harry S. Truman—Personal Correspondence for February–September 1941" folder, box 168, SV, HST papers, HSTL; Harry S. Truman to Mon Walgren, July 28, 1941, "National Defense Investigating Committee—Items for Report" folder, box 123, SV, HST papers, HSTL; *Kansas City Star*, February 13 and March 2, 1941, May 10, 1943; Helm, *Harry Truman*, pp. 162–63, 171; Harry S. Truman to David Proctor, July 29, 1942, "National Defense Committee" folder, box 120, SV, HST papers, HSTL; *Business Week*, June 26, 1943, pp. 19–22.

13. *Time*, April 5, 1943, pp. 14–15; Harry S. Truman to Lewis Schwellenbach, April 29, 1941, "Harry S. Truman—Personal Correspondence for February–September 1941" folder, box 168, SV, HST papers, HSTL; Truman, *Memoirs*, pp. 169–70; Harry S. Truman to S. M. Woodson, May 27, 1941, Harry S. Truman to Charles A. Bruun, June 9, 1941, "Labor Situation" folder, box 73, SV, HST papers, HSTL; Harry S. Truman to Roger Sermon, April 28, 1941, "Roger Sermon" folder, box 161, SV, HST papers, HSTL; Harry S. Truman to E. B. Berkowitz, May 27, 1941, "National Defense Projects—In Missouri April 1941" folder, box 125, SV, HST papers, HSTL; *Congressional Record* 77:1, appendix p. A3628; Helm, *Harry Truman*, pp. 171–72.

14. *Congressional Record* 77:1, pp. 7116, 9998, appendix pp. A3630, A4482; Fred Canfil to Harry S. Truman, December 19, 1941, "Fred Canfil" folder, box 51, SV, HST papers, HSTL; Harry S. Truman to William Southern, Jr., September 9, 1941, "Labor Situation" folder, box 73, SV, HST papers, HSTL; *Kansas City Times*, July 23, and August 6, 1941; *Kansas City Star*, August 14, 1941; *The Nation*, August 23, 1941, pp. 153–54.

15. Harry S. Truman to Lou Holland, April 24 and May 1, 1941, "National Defense—Lou E. Holland" folder, box 116, SV, HST papers, HSTL; Harry S. Truman to Lewis Schwellenbach, April 22, 1941, "Harry S. Truman—Personal Correspondence for February–September 1941" folder, box 168, SV, HST papers, HSTL.

16. Harry S. Truman, speech to Interstate Conference of Employment

Security Agencies, Kansas City, Missouri, October 21, 1942, printed in *Congressional Record* 77:2, appendix pp. A3804–05; Harry S. Truman to Nellie Noland, June 22, 1942, Mary Ethel Noland papers, HSTL; Helm, *Harry Truman,* pp. 150, 178–81; Harry S. Truman to William Southern, Jr., May 28, 1941, "Labor Situation" folder, box 73, SV, HST papers, HSTL; William Southern, Jr., to Harry S. Truman, February 11, 1941, "William Southern, Jr." folder, box 162, SV, HST papers, HSTL; Harry S. Truman to Roger Sermon, April 28, 1941, "Roger Sermon" folder, box 161, SV, HST papers, HSTL. The latter two items include references to the union fees at Remington Arms. More on that dispute can be found in Roger Sermon to Harry S. Truman, April 23, 1941, "Roger Sermon" folder, box 161, SV, HST papers, HSTL; L. S. Brayton to Perrin McElroy, February 14, 1941, "National Defense Commission—General" folder, box 119, SV, HST papers, HSTL; J. O. Mack to Harry S. Truman, April 7, 1941, Harry S. Truman to J. O. Mack, April 16, 1941, "Labor Situation" folder, box 73, SV, HST papers, HSTL; Harry S. Truman to Edgar Hinde, April 17, 1941, "Edgar Hinde" folder, box 63, SV, HST papers, HSTL; Bryce Smith to Harry S. Truman, June 18, 1943, "Bryce B. Smith" folder, box 162, SV, HST papers, HSTL; Powell, *Tom's Boy,* pp. 153, 155; Harry S. Truman to William H. Kirby, March 31, and April 18, 1941, William H. Kirby to Harry S. Truman, April 4, 1941, "Missouri State Employment Service" folder, box 112, SV, HST papers, HSTL. Evidence of Truman and Pendergast organization efforts to place loyalists at Remington Arms can be found in Harry S. Truman to William Stone, February 27, 1941, Harry S. Truman to J. J. Rode, March 19, 1941, "Missouri State Employment Service" folder, box 112, SV, HST papers, HSTL; Harry S. Truman to Vivian Truman, August 11, 1941, "Vivian Truman" folder, box 173, SV, HST papers, HSTL; Russell Gabriel to Harry S. Truman, October 29, 1941, Harry S. Truman to Russell Gabriel, November 3, 1941, "Russell Gabriel" folder, box 60, SV, HST papers, HSTL; Harry S. Truman to Roger Sermon, February 18, 1941, "Jackson County" folder, box 71, SV, HST papers, HSTL; Roger Sermon to Harry S. Truman, April 24, 1941, and several other letters in "Roger Sermon" folder, box 161, SV, HST papers, HSTL. Truman's denials of this activity are in Mildred Dryden to Michelo Calderono, December 23, 1940, "Veterans of Placement Service" folder, box 185, SV, HST papers, HSTL; Harry S. Truman to Tilford Goslin, April 17, 1941, "William Hourigan" folder, box 63, SV, HST papers, HSTL.

17. Albert Norton to Harry S. Truman, May 12, 1942, Harry S. Truman to Albert Norton, May 23, 1942, "Kansas City" folder, box 72, SV, HST papers, HSTL; Harry S. Truman, speech to Jackson Day Dinner, Charleston, West Virginia, January 7, 1939, box 1, Speech File, SV, HST papers, HSTL.

18. Roger Sermon to Harry S. Truman, February 25, 1941, Harry S. Truman to Roger Sermon, March 1, 1941, "Roger Sermon" folder, box

161, SV, HST papers, HSTL; Harry S. Truman to William Kitchen, April 10, 1942, "William Kitchen" folder, box 73, SV, HST papers, HSTL; Powell Groner to Harry S. Truman, February 7, 1941, Harry S. Truman to Powell Groner, February 14, 1941, "Special Bills—Introduced by Senator Truman 1941" folder, box 162, SV, HST papers, HSTL.

19. Harry S. Truman to William Kitchen, August 21, 1942, "William Kitchen" folder, box 73, SV, HST papers, HSTL; Harry S. Truman to Russell Gabriel, February 10, 1942, "Russell Gabriel" folder, box 60, SV, HST papers, HSTL. Information on Truman's Pendergast activities in the 1940s is scattered throughout his Senate papers. Among the more fruitful places are Harry S. Truman to Rufus Burrus, January 18 and February 22, 1941, "Rufus Burrus" folder, box 51; "Russell Gabriel" folder, box 60; "Shannon Douglass" folder, box 55; "William Kitchen" folder, box 73; "Jackson County" folder, box 71; Harry S. Truman to John H. Thompson, July 25, 1941, "Liberty Bend Cutoff" folder, box 76; "Missouri Employment Service" folder, box 112; "Roger Sermon" folder, box 161; "Edgar Hinde" folder, box 63. Other prime sources include "Fred A. Boxley" folder, box 239, PSF, HST papers, HSTL, and Miscellaneous Historical Document 72, HSTL.

20. Harry S. Truman to A. F. Schopper, December 18, 1941, "Harry S. Truman—Personal Telegrams" folder, box 173, SV, HST papers, HSTL; Harry S. Truman to Walter Maloney, March 24, 1941, "National Defense Commission—General" folder, box 119, SV, HST papers, HSTL; *The Call* editorial, week of May 19, 1941; C. A. Franklin to Don McCombs, March 5, 1941, C. A. Franklin to Harry S. Truman, May 19, March 5, and January 2, 1941, Harry S. Truman to C. A. Franklin, January 31 and January 8, 1941, "C. A. Franklin" folder, box 60, SV, HST papers, HSTL; Planning Committee of Negro National Defense Committee to Harry S. Truman, January 20, 1941, Harry S. Truman to Robert Owens, February 14, 1941, Jean Monroe to Harry S. Truman, March 22, 1941, Harry S. Truman to Jean Monroe, March 31, 1941, Harry S. Truman to C. A. Franklin, January 16, 1942, James Mead to Harry S. Truman, July 10, 1941 (with enclosure), Harry S. Truman to James Mead, July 18, 1941, Warren Barbour to Harry S. Truman, July 16, 1941, Harry Vaughan to Walter Hilliker, October 31, 1941, "Negroes" folder, box 131, SV, HST papers, HSTL; Roger Sermon to Harry S. Truman, October 14, 1941, Harry S. Truman to Roger Sermon c. late October 1941, "Roger Sermon" folder, box 161, SV, HST papers, HSTL; *St. Louis Star-Times,* October 23, 1941; Brown Harris to Harry S. Truman, May 22, 1942, "Brown Harris" folder, SV, HST papers, HSTL; Dorothy Masell to Harry S. Truman, February 24, 1942, Harry S. Truman to Dorothy Masell, February 27, 1942, "Miscellaneous" folder, box 83, SV, HST papers, HSTL; Harry S. Truman to James Pouncey, July 28, 1941, "Jackson County" folder, box 71, SV, HST papers, HSTL. Harry Vaughan's pious claim that the Committee failed to verify discrimination against

blacks in the defense industry has even less credibility when read with Truman's complaints about the difficulty of verifying questionable activities of labor unions (which were as involved in racial discrimination as were employers): "When we try to get the facts and the sworm testimony to prove it, it evaporates into thin air, because the people affected are afraid of assault and battery, and you can't blame them much. The gang that does that sort of thing in organized labor are the thug class and are very difficult to run to earth." (Harry S. Truman to E. J. Wallace, December 22, 1941, "National Defense Contract Investigation" folder, box 122, SV, HST papers, HSTL.)

21. Brown Harris to Morris Ernst, May 9, 1942, Brown Harris to C. Harold Mann, May 14, 1942, Brown Harris to Harry S. Truman, May 22, 1942, Harry S. Truman to Brown Harris, May 28, 1942, "Brown Harris" folder, SV, HST papers, HSTL; Brown Harris to Harry S. Truman, March 6, 1943, Harry S. Truman to Brown Harris, March 13, 1943, " 'Time' Magazine Article" folder, box 166, SV, HST papers, HSTL; Gene Minshall to Harry S. Truman, November 30, 1942, "Ford Plant" folder, box 59, SV, HST papers, HSTL; Harry S. Truman to Edward McKim, November 22, 1941, "Edward McKim" folder, box 81, SV, HST papers, HSTL.

22. Helm, *Harry Truman*, pp. 174–75; *Kansas City Times*, October 27 (editorial) and October 29, 1941; *Kansas City Star*, October 19 and October 29, 1941; *Congressional Record* 77:1, pp. 8302–05.

23. Harry S. Truman to C. R. Mooney, September 8, 1941, "C. R. Mooney" folder, box 113, SV, HST papers, HSTL; Harry S. Truman to Hugart F. Norman, June 12, 1941, "Labor Situation" folder, box 73, SV, HST papers, HSTL; *Congressional Record* 77:2, p. 384; "Investigation of the National Defense Program, Executive Session, March 23, 1942" transcript, pp. 4–5, "National Defense—Rubber Situation" folder, box 117, SV, HST papers, HSTL; Edgar Hinde to Harry S. Truman, May 29, 1941, Harry S. Truman to Edgar Hinde, June 3, 1941, "Edgar Hinde" folder, box 63, SV, HST papers, HSTL; *U.S. Senate Report 480,* part 5, p. 52, 77 Cong., 2 Sess.

24. Bruce Catton, *The War Lords of Washington* (New York: Harcourt, Brace, Jovanovich, 1948), pp. 211–12, 238, 267; *New York Times* editorial, November 14, 1942, printed in *Congressional Record* 77:2, p. A3955; *The Nation,* January 24, 1942, pp. 80–81; Harry S. Truman, speech dedicating American Legion Monument, St. Louis, Missouri, September 6, 1942, box 1, Speech File, SV, HST papers, HSTL; W. H. Schlueter to Harry S. Truman, June 20, 1941, Harry S. Truman to W. H. Schlueter, June 30, 1941, "National Defense Commission—General" folder, box 119, SV, HST papers, HSTL; Walter S. Johnson to Harry S. Truman, December 8, 1941, H. G. Zelle to Harry S. Truman, December 13, 1941, Harry S. Truman to H. E. Knight, December 9, 1941, "Labor Situation" folder, box 73, SV, HST papers, HSTL.

25. *Congressional Record* 77:2, p. 385; "Investigation of National Defense Program, Executive Session, March 23, 1942" transcript, pp. 11–14, "National Defense—Rubber Situation" folder, box 117, SV, HST papers, HSTL; Catton, *War Lords*, pp. 212, 267; *New York Times* editorial, November 14, 1942; *Congressional Record* 78:1, pp. 7695–96; *The Nation*, January 24, 1942, pp. 80–81; *Congressional Record* 77:2, pp. A1430, A3804–05; Harry S. Truman, speech to graduating class of Northeast Missouri State Teachers College, Kirksville, Missouri, August 13, 1943, box 2, Speech File, SV, HST papers, HSTL; *Congressional Record* 75:3, appendix pp. 945–46; Harry S. Truman, speech to American Legion, Larchmont, New York, April 20, 1937, box 1, Speech File, SV, HST papers, HSTL; *Kansas City Times*, October 22, 1942; *Kansas City Star*, September 21 and December 23, 1943.

26. "Buchmanism" memorandum, c. April–October 1944, "Moral Rearmament" folder, box 113, SV, HST papers, HSTL.

27. *Congressional Record* 75:3, appendix pp. 864–65; *Kansas City Times*, October 20, 1943; *Congressional Record* 76:2, appendix p. 202; Harry S. Truman to Bess Truman, November 11 and December 5, 1939, box 7, FBP, HST papers, HSTL; Harry S. Truman, undated speech on "The Value of Industrial Safety," "Speeches" folder, box 163, SV, HST papers, HSTL; *U.S. Senate Report 480*, part 5, p. 52, 77 Cong, 2 Sess.

28. *Congressional Record* 76:1, pp. 6826–30; *U.S. Senate Document 82*, 76 Cong, 1 Sess.

29. *Congressional Record* 76:2, appendix pp. 608–12; *Congressional Record* 76:1, appendix p. 3620; Harry S. Truman to Bess Truman, October 25, October 31, and November 11, 1939, box 7, FBP, HST papers, HSTL.

30. Harry S. Truman to Bess Truman, November 11, 1939, box 7, FBP, HST papers, HSTL; Harry S. Truman to Franklin D. Roosevelt, November 8, 1939, Franklin D. Roosevelt to Harry S. Truman, November 15, 1939, FDR papers microfilm, HSTL.

31. "You Can Defend America!" booklet with John Roots to Harry S. Truman, November 7, 1940, "Moral Rearmament" folder, box 113, SV, HST papers, HSTL.

32. Ibid.

33. *Army & Navy Journal*, May 6, 1944, quoted in Peter Howard, *The World Rebuilt* (New York: Duell, Sloan & Pearce, 1951), p. 210; Harry S. Truman to George Seldes, August 15, 1944, Harry S. Truman to Marianna Schaupp, October 3, 1944, "Moral Rearmament" folder, box 113, SV, HST papers, HSTL.

34. Harry S. Truman to Frank N. D. Buchman, November 20, 1940, January 1, 1942, Harry S. Truman to Robert Patterson, June 24, 1942, Harry S. Truman to H. W. Brown, April 6, 1942, Harry S. Truman to H. Birchard Taylor, June 1, 1943, H. Birchard Taylor to Harry S. Truman (with enclosures), May 24, 1943, Harry S. Truman to Carl Hatch, June 3,

1943, news releases April 12, 1943, John Roots to Harry S. Truman, May 21, 1944, "Moral Rearmament" folder, box 113, SV, HST papers, HSTL; Harry S. Truman to Frank Buchman, John Roots, and Ray Purdy, December 31, 1941, "Harry S. Truman—Personal October–December 1941" folder, box 169, SV, HST papers, HSTL; Frank N. D. Buchman to Harry S. Truman, February 3, 1942, "Harry S. Truman—Personal January–October 1942" folder, box 169, SV, HST papers, HSTL; Harry S. Truman to Franklin D. Roosevelt, April 16, 1942, "White House" folder, box 216, SV, HST papers, HSTL; Harry S. Truman to Bess Truman, July 15, and November 27, 1939, box 7, FBP, HST papers, HSTL; Howard, *World Rebuilt*, pp. 182–83.

35. George Seldes to Harry S. Truman, August 8, 1944 (with enclosures of *In Fact*, January 18, 1943, March 6, March 20, and May 29, 1944), Harry S. Truman to George Seldes, August 15, 1944, Harry S. Truman to Marianna Schaupp, October 3, 1944, "Buchmanism" memorandum, c. April–October 1944, "Moral Rearmament" folder, box 113, SV, HST papers, HSTL.

Chapter 15   THE BUSINESS OF WAR

1. Harry S. Truman to Merrill Meigs, January 13, 1943, "Harry S. Truman—Personal November 1942–January 1943" folder, box 169, SV, HST papers, HSTL; Catton, *War Lords*, pp. 118–19; Harry S. Truman, speech at Philadelphia, Pennsylvania, February 23, 1942, printed in *Congressional Record* 77:2, pp. A673–74; "Truman and Nelson," *The New Republic*, June 29, 1942, reprinted in *Congressional Record* 77:2, p. A2479; *Congressional Record* 77:2, pp. 381–82, 5324–28; "List of officials in the O.P.M." folder, box 12, Speech File, SV, HST papers, HSTL; Harry S. Truman to J. A. Tapee, February 3, 1942, "National Defense Committee" folder, box 119, SV, HST papers, HSTL; Helm, *Harry Truman*, p. 183; *Kansas City Star*, January 15, 1942.

2. Helm, *Harry Truman*, pp. 181–83; *Congressional Record* 77:1, p. 7117; Lou Holland to Mason Brittain, March 5, 1941, "National Defense—Lou E. Holland" folder, box 116, SV, HST papers, HSTL; Harry S. Truman to William Southern, Jr., September 9, 1941, "Labor Situation" folder, box 73, SV, HST papers, HSTL; H. Vaughan to E. E. Pershall, November 18, 1941, "Harry S. Truman—Personal October–December 1941" folder, box 169, SV, HST papers, HSTL; "Draft of speech for Senator Truman 2-5-43," "Draft of speech for Senator Truman, February 7, 1943," "Personal Correspondence—Harry S. Truman—Senator" folder, Lou Holland papers, HSTL; *Kansas City Star*, February 8, 1941, September 25, 1942; Harry S. Truman to Bess Truman, June 25, 1942, box 8, FBP, HST papers, HSTL.

3. Catton, *War Lords*, p. 290; Harry S. Truman to Lewis Schwellenbach, November 27, 1941, "(Hon.) Lewis B. Schwellenbach" folder, box 159, SV, HST papers, HSTL; *Congressional Record* 78:1, pp. 842–43, 845, 849–51; *Congressional Record* 77:1, p. 7117; Harry S. Truman to C. Wayland Brooks, September 8, 1941, "National Defense Committee Contract Investigation—June 1941" folder, box 122, SV, HST papers, HSTL; Harry S. Truman to Lou Holland, February 12 and June 20, 1942, "National Defense—Lou E. Holland" folder, box 116, SV, HST papers, HSTL; "Draft of speech for Senator Truman 2-5-43"; "Draft of speech for Senator Truman, February 7, 1943"; *Kansas City Times*, July 22, 1941, January 23, 1942.

4. Editorial, *St. Louis Post-Dispatch*, January 13, 1942, reprinted in *Congressional Record* 77:2, p. A128; Harry S. Truman to Bess Truman, June 19, 1941, June 16 and June 17, 1942, box 8, FBP, HST papers, HSTL; Robert Patterson to Franklin D. Roosevelt, December 13, 1941, anon. to General Watson, c. December 11, 1941, Franklin D. Roosevelt to General Watson, December 16, 1941 with attachment, FDR papers microfilm, HSTL; *Congressional Record* 77:1, December 10, 1941, pp. 9600–01; Harry S. Truman to Walter Mitchell, March 6, 1942, "National Defense Committee" folder, box 119, SV, HST papers, HSTL; Harry S. Truman to David Proctor, July 29, 1942, "National Defense Committee" folder, box 120, SV, HST papers, HSTL; Senator O'Mahoney, *Congressional Record* 77:2, p. 6650; Harry S. Truman to Ethel Noland and Nellie Noland, September 8, 1949, Mary Ethel Noland papers, HSTL; Harry S. Truman to William Marsh, August 26, 1942, Harry S. Truman to William Welling, May 5, 1943, "War Situation" folder, box 216, SV, HST papers, HSTL; Harry S. Truman to Robert Patterson, March 1, 1943, "National Defense Committee—-February 1943" folder, box 121, SV, HST papers, HSTL. In the interim between Pearl Harbor and FDR's approval for continuance of the Truman committee's work, Truman himself considered abandoning the committee in order to command a field artillery unit. The War Department told him that he was two years past the upper age limit. (*Kansas City Star*, December 28, 1941; Harry S. Truman to Lewis Schwellenbach, December 31, 1941, "Harry S. Truman—Personal Telegrams" folder, box 173, SV, HST papers, HSTL; Daniels, *Man of Independence*, p. 228; Harry S. Truman to Harry Vaughan, February 26, 1942, "Harry H. Vaughan—Personal" folder, box 175, SV, HST papers, HSTL; Harry S. Truman to W. E. Hicks, August 26, 1942, June 5, 1944, "W. E. Hicks" folder, box 62, SV, HST papers, HSTL; Harry S. Truman to John Groves, January 2, 1942, Harry S. Truman to H. L. Boggess, December 11, 1941, "Harry S. Truman—Personal October–December 1941" folder, box 169, SV, HST papers, HSTL; Truman, *Autobiography*, pp. 74–75.)

5. Edward Flynn to Harry S. Truman, May 13, 1941, "National Defense Investigating Committee—Items for Report" folder, box 123, SV, HST

papers, HSTL; *Kansas City Times,* June 27 and September 9, 1941; H. Vaughan to James Nugent, July 1, 1941, Harry S. Truman to J. A. Guthrie, July 16, 1941, "National Defense Commission—General" folder, box 119, SV, HST papers, HSTL; *U.S. Senate Report 480,* part 1, 77 Cong, 1 Sess (see also appendixes in part 1 reprint within part 5, 77 Cong, 2 Sess); *Congressional Record* 77:2, pp. 4259–60, 7117; Harold Ickes to Franklin D. Roosevelt, July 14, 1941, "Interior Department" folder, box 67, SV, HST papers, HSTL; *U.S. Senate Report 10,* part 16, pp. 65–68, 78 Cong, 2 Sess.

6. Helm, *Harry Truman,* pp. 183–87; *Congressional Record* 77:1, p. 7117; *Congressional Record* 77:2, p. 383.

7. *Kansas City Star,* January 15, 1942; Fred Canfil to Harry S. Truman, January 23, 1942, "Fred Canfil" folder, box 51, SV, HST papers, HSTL; *Congressional Record* 77:2, p. 384; Brown Harris to Harry S. Truman, May 22, 1942, November 18, 1943, Harry S. Truman to Brown Harris, November 22, 1943, "Brown Harris" folder, SV, HST papers, HSTL; Harry S. Truman to Harry Vaughan, February 1943, "Harry H. Vaughan—Personal" folder, box 175, SV, HST papers, HSTL; Harry S. Truman, speech on Blue Network, October 4, 1943, box 2, Speech File, SV, HST papers, HSTL; *Congressional Record* 77:1, p. 7117; *Congressional Record* 78:2, p. 2425; *U.S. Senate Report 10,* part 10, pp. 16–26, 78 Cong, 1 Sess.

8. Harry S. Truman to Lewis Schwellenbach, July 29, 1942, "(Hon.) Lewis B. Schwellenbach" folder, box 159, SV, HST papers, HSTL; *Kansas City Star,* July 28, July 31, and August 12, 1942.

9. *Congressional Record* 77:1, p. 7857; *Congressional Record* 77:2, pp. 6647–48, 6782; *Time,* April 5, 1943, pp. 92–93; Hugh Fulton to all Truman committee members, May 26, 1944, "National Defense Committee—April 1943" folder, box 121, SV, HST papers, HSTL; Truman, radio speech on Blue Network, October 4, 1943; *Newsweek,* April 5, 1943, p. 67; H. C. Engelbrecht and F. C. Hanighen, *Merchants of Death* (New York: Dodd, Mead, 1934), pp. 53–54; *U.S. Senate Report 10,* part 7, 78 Cong, 1 Sess.

10. Harry S. Truman to Paul Waters, January 21, 1942, "National Defense—Fuel Oil Situation (Jan. 1943–May 1944)" folder, box 114, SV, HST papers, HSTL; *Kansas City Times,* October 22, 1942; *Newsweek,* January 26, 1942, pp. 47–48; Oscar Cox to Harry Hopkins (with enclosure), March 26, 1942, book 7: Rubber, container 327, Harry L. Hopkins papers, FDRL.

11. Subcommittee on Rubber, Truman committee, closed hearing, March 23, 1942, transcript pp. 40–41, "National Defense—Rubber Situation" folder, box 117, SV, HST papers, HSTL.

12. *U.S. Senate Report 480,* part 6, pp. 2, 4, 77 Cong, 2 Sess, part 7, pp. 28–42; *U.S. Senate Report 10,* part 17, pp. 3–10, 78 Cong, 2 Sess; *Congressional Record* 77:1, appendix pp. A439–41. In addition to these reports, the Truman committee hearings and other government investigations yield information

on ties between U.S. corporations and America's military enemies. Some government and private investigators felt less reticent than Truman about publicizing these matters. These include William Stevenson, *A Man Called Intrepid: The Secret War* (New York: Harcourt Brace Jovanovich, 1976), Joseph Borkin and Charles A. Welsh, *Germany's Master Plan* (New York: Duell, Sloan & Pearce, 1943), Joseph Borkin, *The Crime and Punishment of I.G. Farben* (New York: The Free Press, 1978), Howard Watson Ambruster, *Treason's Peace* (New York: Beechhurst Press, 1947), Josiah E. Dubois, Jr., *The Devil's Chemists* (Boston: Beacon Press, 1952), Sylvia F. Porter, *The Nazi Chemical Trust in the United States* (Washington, D.C.: The National Policy Committee, 1942), James Pool and Suzanne Pool, *Who Financed Hitler: The Secret Funding of Hitler's Rise to Power 1919–1933* (New York: Dial Press, 1976), Guenter Reimann, *Patents for Hitler* (New York: Vanguard Press, 1942). Truman endorsed the Reimann book, and owned a copy.

13. Harry S. Truman to Lewis Schwellenbach, July 29, 1942, "(Hon.) Lewis B. Schwellenbach" folder, box 159, SV, HST papers, HSTL; Harry S. Truman to Edward McKim, February 12, 1942, "Edward McKim" folder, box 81, SV, HST papers, HSTL; James Henle to Harry S. Truman, August 28, 1942, Harry S. Truman to James Herle, September 12, 1942, "National Defense Committee—September 1942" folder, box 120, SV, HST papers, HSTL; *Congressional Record* 77:2, pp. 4550, appendix A2327; Harry S. Truman, speech to University of North Carolina Political Union, April 30, 1942, box 1, Speech File, SV, HST papers, HSTL.

14. Ambruster, *Treason's Peace*, p. 68; Borkin and Welsh, *Germany's Master Plan*, pp. xiv–xv; Thurman Arnold, *Fair Fights and Foul* (New York: Harcourt Brace Jovanovich, 1965), pp. 83, 145; George W. Stocking and Myron W. Watkins, *Cartels in Action* (New York: 20th Century Fund, 1946), pp. 423, 423n.–424n.

15. Reimann, *Patents for Hitler*, pp. 7–9, 25, 26, 30, 32, 61, 82–87; Arnold, *Fair Fights and Foul*, p. 83.

16. Reimann, *Patents for Hitler*, pp. 287–88, 306.

17. Catton, *War Lords*, pp. 311–12.

18. Harry S. Truman, speech to American Trucking Association, St. Louis, Missouri, October 20, 1942, box 2, Speech File, SV, HST papers, HSTL.

19. Harry S. Truman, speech to Post-War Planning Forum, Junior Chamber of Commerce, Cleveland, Ohio, June 2, 1944, box 4, Speech File, SV, HST papers, HSTL; *Congressional Record* 78:1, p. 9173; *U.S. Senate Report 10*, part 12, 78 Cong, 1 Sess.

20. *Kansas City Star*, December 12, 1942; Lou Holland to Harry S. Truman, December 15, 1943, "Personal Correspondence—Harry S. Truman—Senator" folder, Lou Holland papers, HSTL; Harry S. Truman to Hugh Fulton, March 22, 1943, "National Defense Committee—February 1943" folder, box 121, SV, HST papers, HSTL.

Chapter 16   PROMOTED TO GLORY

1. Truman, *Memoirs,* p. 121; Harry S. Truman to Bess Truman, June 19, 1941, all August 1942, July 5, 1943, box 8, FBP, HST papers, HSTL.
2. Herb Graffis to Harry S. Truman, February 23, 1943, Harry S. Truman to Herb Graffis, March 2, 1943, "Edward McKim" folder, box 81, SV, HST papers, HSTL; William Duke to Harry S. Truman, March 17, 1943, Harry S. Truman to William Duke, March 27, 1943, "National Defense—Sugar Situation" folder, box 118, SV, HST papers, HSTL; Harry S. Truman to Tom Harris, March 13, 1943, " 'Time' Magazine Article" folder, box 166, SV, HST papers, HSTL; Harry S. Truman to L. A. Pickard, May 11, 1943, "Harry S. Truman—Personal for January–July 1943" folder, box 169, SV, HST papers, HSTL; Harry S. Truman to Bess Truman, July 12, 1943, box 8, FBP, HST papers, HSTL; December 14, 1943 *Boston Herald* clipping with Bryce Smith to Harry S. Truman, December 28, 1943, "Bryce B. Smith" folder, box 162, SV, HST papers, HSTL; Harry S. Truman to Vivian Truman, February 12, 1944, box 173, SV, HST papers, HSTL; *Kansas City Times,* March 30, April 18, and July 14, 1944; *Kansas City Star,* April 12, 1944; Harry S. Truman to Joe Healey, April 18, 1944, "Coast Guard August 1944" folder, box 53, SV, HST papers, HSTL; Harry S. Truman to Frank Schwartz, June 16, 1944, "Truman for Vice President" folder, box 173, SV, HST papers, HSTL; Lou Holland to Harry S. Truman, November 29, 1943, "Personal Correspondence—Harry S. Truman—Senator," Lou Holland papers, HSTL.
3. Harry S. Truman to Bess Truman, September 27, 1942, box 8, FBP, HST papers, HSTL; Harry S. Truman to William Duke, March 27, 1943, "National Defense—Sugar Situation" folder, box 118, SV, HST papers, HSTL; Helm, *Harry Truman,* p. 189; H. L. Stimson to Commanding General, Walter Reed Hospital, April 18, 1941, Miscellaneous Historical Document 454, HSTL; William Boyle to B. M. Asch, December 14, 1943, "Miscellaneous Arm-As" folder, box 83, SV, HST papers, HSTL; John Roots to Harry S. Truman, May 21, 1944, "Moral Rearmament" folder, box 113, SV, HST papers, HSTL; Harry S. Truman to James T. Blair, Jr., April 17, 1941, "National Defense Commission—General" folder, box 119, SV, HST papers, HSTL; Harry S. Truman to Leighton Shields, July 17, 1941, "(Hon.) Leighton Shields" folder, box 161, SV, HST papers, HSTL; Harry S. Truman to Sherman Minton, July 17, 1941, Dwight Mason to Harry S. Truman, April 21, 1941, "Harry S. Truman Personal Correspondence for February–September 1941" folder, box 168, SV, HST papers, HSTL; Harry S. Truman to James McCune, October 9, 1941, "Harry S. Truman—Personal October–December 1941" folder, box 169, SV, HST papers, HSTL; William Boyle to Harry S. Truman, April 20, 1943, "Harry S. Truman—Personal January–July 1943" folder, box 169, SV, HST papers, HSTL; Vivian Truman to Harry S. Truman, February 26, 1942, May 15, 1941,

Harry S. Truman to Vivian Truman, March 2, 1942, April 16 and April 21, 1941, June 25, 1943, May 22, 1941, William Boyle to Vivian Truman, July 20, 1942, "Vivian Truman" folder, box 173, SV, HST papers, HSTL; Harry S. Truman to T. H. Van Sant, July 16, 1941, "T. H. Van Sant" folder, box 174, SV, HST papers, HSTL; Harry S. Truman to Sam Wear, June 22, 1943, "Sam N. Wear" folder, box 217, SV, HST papers, HSTL; Harry Vaughan to T. H. Van Sant, July 7, 1941, T. H. Van Sant papers, HSTL; Harry S. Truman to Bess Truman, June 26, June 28, June 30, July 1, July 5, and July 7, 1941, July 24, 1942, February 19, 1943, June 25, 1944 and October 15, 1943, box 8, FBP, HST papers, HSTL; transcript, "Walt Bodine Show," KCUR-FM, May 17, 1984.

4. Ed Pauley interview with Jonathan Daniels, p. 31, MOI notes, Jonathan Daniels papers, HSTL; Daniels, *Man of Independence*, pp. 236–39.

5. *Kansas City Times*, April 18 and July 27, 1944; James W. Gerard to Franklin D. Roosevelt, July 17, 1944, FDR papers microfilm, HSTL; Harry Vaughan oral history, p. 69, HSTL; Helm, *Harry Truman*, p. 226; Jonathan Daniels MOI notes, part IV, quoting George E. Allen, "My Two Years with Truman," *Saturday Evening Post*, June 21, 1947, Jonathan Daniels papers, HSTL; Truman, *Autobiography*, pp. 92–93; Robert E. Sherwood, *Roosevelt and Hopkins: An Intimate History* (New York: Harper & Row, 1948), pp. 881–82; Daniels, *Man of Independence*, pp. 238–43; Harry Easley oral history, pp. 90–95, HSTL.

6. Franklin D. Roosevelt to Robert Hannegan, July 19, 1944, Miscellaneous Historical Document 415, HSTL; William Leahy interview with Jonathan Daniels, August 31, 1949, p. 13, Harry S. Truman interview with Jonathan Daniels, August 30, 1949, p. 6, November 12, 1949, p. 66, MOI notes, Jonathan Daniels papers, HSTL; Helm, *Harry Truman*, p. 226; Harry Easley oral history, p. 97, HSTL; Jim Bishop, *FDR's Last Year: April 1944–April 1945* (New York: William Morrow & Company, 1974), pp. 99–100; Truman, *Autobiography*, pp. 89–90, 92; Daniels, *Man of Independence*, pp. 236, 248–50; Gosnell, *Truman's Crises*, pp. 185, 187, 189, 193; McNaughton and Hehmeyer, *This Man Truman*, pp. 148, 155; Harry S. Truman to Helen Mardorf, March 21, 1942, Harry S. Truman to S. F. Black, April 2, 1942, "Bob Hannegan" folder, box 61, SV, HST papers, HSTL; Harry Vaughan oral history, pp. 70–71.

7. Lou Holland to Mildred Dryden, July 17, 1944, "Harry S. Truman—Personal, 1944" folder, Lou Holland papers, HSTL; Harry S. Truman to John Snyder, January 6, 1944, "John W. Snyder" folder, box 162, SV, HST papers; Harry S. Truman, autobiographical sketch, pp. 57–59, Biographical File, PSF, HST papers, HSTL; *Kansas City Times*, July 20, 1944; Frederick Bowman oral history, pp. 41–42, 44–45, HSTL; Edward McKim oral history, pp. 96–103, HSTL; Lewis Barringer oral history, pp. 22–23, HSTL; Jack Bell oral history, p. 22, HSTL; Ted Sanders oral history, pp. 29–34, HSTL; Gosnell, *Truman's Crises*, pp. 188–89; Harry Easley oral

history, pp. 98–99, HSTL; Tom Evans oral history, pp. 345, 352, HSTL.

8. Harry S. Truman to Bill, October 31, 1959, Desk File, Post-Presidential File, HST papers, HSTL; Harry S. Truman interview with Jonathan Daniels, November 12, 1949, pp. 65–66, MOI notes, Jonathan Daniels papers, HSTL; Harry S. Truman, autobiographical sketch, pp. 57–59, Biographical File, PSF, HST papers, HSTL; Vic Housholder memorandum of conversation with Harry S. Truman, February 7 and 8, 1947, "Correspondence between Harry S. Truman and Vic Housholder, 1945–1949" folder, Vic Housholder papers, HSTL; Helm, *Harry Truman*, pp. 223–25; Jonathan Daniels MOI notes, part IV, quoting Allen, "My Two Years with Truman," Jonathan Daniels papers, HSTL; Truman, *Autobiography*, pp. 88–89; Daniels, *Man of Independence*, pp. 245, 247; Gosnell, *Truman's Crises*, p. 188; McNaughton and Hehmeyer, *This Man Truman*, pp. 150–52. Somehow Truman had scavenged two badly needed new tires for the trip to Chicago (Harry S. Truman to Fred Canfil, July 8, 1944, "Fred Canfil" folder, box 51, SV, HST papers, HSTL).

9. Edward McKim oral history, pp. 96–103, HSTL.

10. *Kansas City Times*, April 18, 1944; *Kansas City Star*, July 20, 1944; Edward McKim oral history, pp. 96–103, HSTL; Arthur Wilson oral history, p. 16, HSTL; Daniels, *Man of Independence*, p. 235.

11. Truman, autobiographical sketch, pp. 57–59, Biographical File, PSF, HST papers, HSTL; *Kansas City Star*, July 20, 1944; Frederick Bowman oral history, pp. 42–43, HSTL; Edward McKim oral history, pp. 96–103, HSTL; Vic Housholder memorandum of conversation with Harry S. Truman, February 7 and 8, 1947, "Correspondence between Harry S. Truman and Vic Housholder 1945–1949" folder, Vic Housholder papers, HSTL; Helm, *Harry Truman*, pp. 226–28; Truman, *Autobiography*, p. 90; Gosnell, *Truman's Crises*, p. 189; Harry S. Truman interview with Jonathan Daniels, August 30, 1949, p. 6, November 12, 1949, p. 66, MOI notes, Jonathan Daniels papers, HSTL; Tom Evans oral history, pp. 353–56, HSTL; Arthur Eisenhower to Dwight D. Eisenhower, August 25, 1943, Arthur B. Eisenhower folder 1, 1941–1946, box 178 Dwight D. Eisenhower principal files 1916–1952, Dwight D. Eisenhower Library. When Hannegan was under consideration for Democratic National Committee chairman he said he didn't want the job. On Truman's advice Hannegan said he wouldn't take the job unless President Roosevelt personally asked him. When Roosevelt actually did phone Hannegan he accepted. Hannegan may have relished the turnabout in Chicago, with Truman the "victim" of the same ploy that had been used on Hannegan. (Harry Vaughan oral history, pp. 70–71, HSTL.)

12. Harry S. Truman, acceptance speech notes, Miscellaneous Historical Document 7, HSTL; Guard, "From Plowboy to President"; Martin V. Coffey, "Harry Truman As I Know Him" (New York: Veterans Advisory Committee, 1948); Bryce Smith to Harry S. Truman, August 15, 1944,

"Bryce B. Smith" folder, box 162, SV, HST papers, HSTL; *Kansas City Times,* July 22, 1944.

13. Harry S. Truman, radio speech on Blue Network, October 2, 1944, box 4, Speech File, SV, HST papers, HSTL.

14. Harry S. Truman, speech to National Society for Advancement of Management, New York City, December 3, 1943, box 3, Speech File, SV, HST papers, HSTL; Harry S. Truman to Jessica Smith, February 8, 1943, "Invitations" folder, box 67, SV, HST papers, HSTL; Harry S. Truman to Susan Blossom, June 1, 1943, "War Situation" folder, box 216, SV, HST papers, HSTL; Harry S. Truman to Bess Truman, December 30, 1941, box 8, FBP, HST papers, HSTL; Harry S. Truman interview with Jonathan Daniels, August 30, 1949, p. 5, MOI notes, Jonathan Daniels papers, HSTL.

15. Harry S. Truman, speech to Lodge No. 3, BPOE, Toledo, Ohio, June 14, 1944, box 4, Speech File, SV, HST papers, HSTL; William D. Leahy interview with Jonathan Daniels, August 31, 1949, pp. 13–14, Harry S. Truman interview with Jonathan Daniels, November 12, 1949, MOI notes, Jonathan Daniels papers, HSTL; Fred Canfil to Harry S. Truman, December 7, 1943, Harry S. Truman to John Thomas, December 6, 1943, H. G. Robinson to Mildred Dryden, December 3, 1943, "Fred Canfil" folder, box 51, SV, HST papers, HSTL; Lewis Schwellenbach to Harry S. Truman, July 1, 1943, Harry S. Truman to Lewis Schwellenbach, July 15, 1943, "(Hon.) Lewis B. Schwellenbach" folder, box 159, SV, HST papers, HSTL; John Abbott oral history, p. 127, HSTL; Harry S. Truman interview with William Hillman, January 1, 1952, interviews folder, "Mr. President" File, box 269, PSF, HST papers, HSTL; Harry Vaughan oral history, p. 68, HSTL; Harry S. Truman to Tom Van Sant, November 25, 1944, box 1, Tom Van Sant papers, HSTL; Tom Evans oral history, pp. 451–53, HSTL.

16. Harry S. Truman to Carter Harrison, February 29 and March 6, 1936, Miscellaneous Historical Document 403, HSTL; Mary Ethel Noland oral history, pp. 172–73, HSTL.

17. Harry S. Truman to Lillie Knight, February 9, 1943, "Chinese Situation" folder, box 51, SV, HST papers, HSTL; Harry S. Truman interview with William Hillman, November 10 and December 14, 1951, interviews folder, "Mr. President" File, box 269, PSF, HST papers, HSTL; *Congressional Record* 75:3, p. 88.

18. *Congressional Record* 76:1, appendix pp. 2231–32.

19. Robert Wagner to Harry S. Truman, February 5, 1941, Harry S. Truman to Robert Wagner, February 7, 1941, "Harry S. Truman—Personal Correspondence for February–September 1941" folder, box 168, SV, HST papers, HSTL; Harry S. Truman to Rabbi Abba Hillel Silver, December 31, 1941, Harry S. Truman to Andrew Somers, January 28, 1942, Harry S. Truman to Pierre van Passen, c. late May 1942, "Jews" folder, box 71, SV, HST papers, HSTL; *New York Times,* December 7, 1942; Ste-

phen Wise to Harry S. Truman, February 25, 1941, "Zionist Organizations" folder, box 226, SV, HST papers, HSTL.

20. Harry S. Truman, speech to United Rally to Demand Rescue of Doomed Jews, Chicago, Illinois, April 14, 1943, box 2, Speech File, SV, HST papers, HSTL; Ulysses S. Schwartz to Harry S. Truman, April 8, 1943, "Invitations" folder, box 67, SV, HST papers, HSTL; Harry S. Truman to Roy Harper, April 28, 1943, "Roy Harper" folder, box 62, SV, HST papers, HSTL; Harry S. Truman to Harry Vaughan, April 27, 1943, "Harry H. Vaughan—Personal" folder, box 175, SV, HST papers, HSTL.

21. *The New York Times,* May 4, 1943, p. 17; Harry S. Truman to Peter Bergson, May 7, 1943, Scott Lucas to Harry S. Truman, May 11, 1943, Harold Schradzke to Harry S. Truman, May 14, 1943, Harry S. Truman to Stephen Wise, June 1, 1943, "Jews" folder, box 71, SV, HST papers, HSTL.

22. Phineas Smaller to Harry S. Truman, with enclosure, December 2, 1943, Harry S. Truman to Phineas Smaller, December 7, 1943, "Jews" folder, box 71, SV, HST papers, HSTL.

23. Carl Dubinsky to Harry S. Truman, February 4, 1944, Harry S. Truman to Carl Dubinsky, February 8, 1944, "Jews" folder, box 71, SV, HST papers, HSTL.

24. Harry S. Truman, speech at Des Moines, Iowa, July 30, 1943, box 2, Speech File, SV, HST papers, HSTL; Harry S. Truman, speech to United Nations Forum, January 17, 1944, box 3, Speech File, SV, HST papers, HSTL; Harry S. Truman, speech at Lamar, Missouri, August 31, 1944, box 4, Speech File, SV, HST papers, HSTL; *Congressional Record* 78:1, p. 8993; Harry S. Truman to J. Lionberger Davis, May 27, 1941, "Miscellaneous" folder, box 82, SV, HST papers, HSTL; *Kansas City Times,* August 12, 1943.

25. *Kansas City Star,* September 4, 1944; Catton, *War Lords,* pp. 234, 283.

26. *Congressional Record* 78:2, p. 2300.

27. Thomas Sherman to Harry S. Truman, November 10, 1944, Harry S. Truman to Thomas Sherman, December 11, 1944, "Harry S. Truman—Personal December 1944–January 1945" folder, box 170, SV, HST papers, HSTL; Harry Vaughan oral history, pp. 76–77, HSTL; Edward McKim interview with Jonathan Daniels, September 29, 1949, p. 32, MOI notes, Jonathan Daniels papers, HSTL; Schauffler, *Harry Truman,* p. 15; Edgar Hinde oral history, pp. 124–25, HSTL; Harry Easley oral history, pp. 98–99, HSTL; Edward McKim oral history, p. 106, HSTL. Two items about the campaign are worth mention. A separate Truman fund was raised apart from Democratic campaign money. The existence of this fund was kept quiet, but records show that all unexpended monies from it went to the Democratic National Committee. (Lewis Barringer oral history, pp. 28–30, HSTL.) The other item was yet another political boost deriving from war buddies. Col. Elliott's partner in Farm & Home Savings at Kansas

City was Lloyd Pullen. Pullen's daughter was on the *Time* magazine staff during the 1944 campaign, and quietly softened the Luce crowd's efforts to present Truman unfavorably. Truman was grateful for her help. (Mary Pullen to Harry S. Truman, November 3, 1944, Harry S. Truman to Mary Pullen, November 16, 1944, "Harry S. Truman—Personal September–November 1944" folder, box 170, SV, HST papers, HSTL.)

28. Harry Vaughan oral history, pp. 78–81, HSTL; Mildred Dryden oral history, pp. 103–04, HSTL; Harry S. Truman to Lou Holland, February 26, 1945, "Personal Correspondence—Harry S. Truman—Senator" folder, Lou Holland papers, HSTL; Harry Vaughan to Fred Canfil, March 7, 1945, "Fred Canfil" folder, box 51, SV, HST papers, HSTL; Harry S. Truman to Bess Truman, July 25, 1942, box 8, FBP, HSTL.

29. *Congressional Record* 79:1, appendix p. A378; transcript of "America United," January 28, 1945, box 4, Speech File, SV, HST papers, HSTL. Truman's private comments on freedom of the press in wartime were harsh. "The country would be better off if all the column writers were in jail and all the broadcasters were shot." He believed that newspapers should print only government handouts on war news. FDR "told . . . me that's what he intended to do—but you know the Pres" (Harry S. Truman to Bess Truman, July 26, 1942, box 8, FBP, HST papers, HSTL). Yet the Truman committee itself disclosed actual tonnages sunk by Nazi U-boats, and thereby revealed that official U.S. Navy figures were fabrications (*Business Week*, June 26, 1943, pp. 19–22).

30. James Beal to Harry S. Truman, February 7, 1945, Harry Vaughan to James Beal, February 13, 1945, "Negroes" folder, box 131, SV, HST papers, HSTL.

31. *Congressional Record* 79:1, appendix pp. A911–12.

32. Charles F. Curry oral history, pp. 9–22, HSTL; *Kansas City Star*, February 5, 1945; Harry S. Truman interview with Jonathan Daniels, November 12, 1949, pp. 64–65, MOI notes, Jonathan Daniels papers, HSTL; abstract of Grandview farm enclosed with Thomas Madden to Jonathan Daniels, January 25, 1950, box 1, Arthur Mag papers, HSTL; Russell Gabriel to Harry S. Truman, January 27, 1942 (with enclosure), Harry S. Truman to Russell Gabriel, February 3, 1942, "Russell Gabriel" folder, box 60, SV, HST papers, HSTL; Ayers memorandum, July 16, 1951 (two memoranda that date), "Personal—Ayers, E.—trip to Kansas City (June 19–30, 1951)," Eben Ayers papers (23), HSTL; Terence O'Donnell to Vivian Truman, October 2, 1945, Harry S. Truman to Roy Roberts, December 12, 1945, "Roy A. Roberts" folder, Personal File, PSF, HST papers, HSTL.

33. David MacIsaac, *Strategic Bombing in World War II* (New York: Garland Publishing Co., 1976), p. 106.

34. Helm, *Harry Truman*, pp. 230–31.

35. E. L. Clary to Harry S. Truman, March 27, and April 3, 1945, Harry

S. Truman to E. L. Clary, March 30 and April 5, 1945, "Missouri Valley Authority" folder, box 112, SV, HST papers, HSTL.

36. *Kansas City Times*, August 13, 1943; Harry S. Truman, speech to Erie County Democratic Committee, Buffalo, New York, April 7, 1945, box 4, Speech File, SV, HST papers, HSTL.

37. Edward McKim oral history, pp. 120–22, HSTL; McNaughton and Hehmeyer, *This Man Truman*, p. 207; *Congressional Record* 79:1, p. 3320; Truman, *Memoirs*, p. 6.

Index